The Study of Games

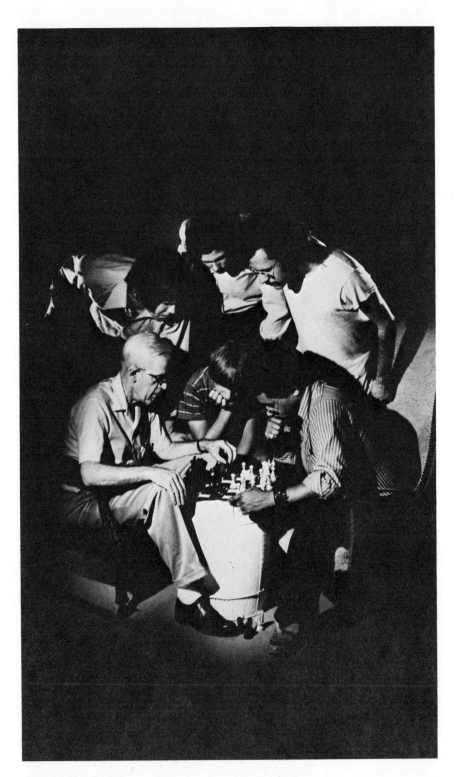

photograph by INGBET

The Study of Games

ELLIOTT M. AVEDON AND
BRIAN SUTTON-SMITH
Teachers College, Columbia University

John Wiley & Sons, Inc., New York · London · Sydney · Toronto

ACKNOWLEDGMENT

We are indebted to many people and organizations for assistance in the development of this volume. Over the years students and colleagues have brought a variety of sources to our attention—sources that have added immeasurably to this inquiry. William Theobald, Fredrick Martin, and Caroline Weiss deserve sincere thanks for tracking down the more obscure references. Ruby Collins is the unique librarian who "discovered" the quotation from St. Augustine, which she thought might interest the authors. Professor Richard G. Kraus merits a large measure of appreciation for his thoughtful criticism of the work while it was in progress, and for his continued enthusiasm and encouragement. We are especially grateful to Ilse Zawadil for typing and correcting the many drafts of the manuscript, and assisting with the production in numerous ways.

We also thank the following individuals and organizations for the use of original material that appears for the first time in this volume or that has appeared initially in another published form.

Professor P, G. Brewster, College of Arts and Sciences, Tennessee Technological University, and the editors of *F.F. Communications,* Helsinki, Finland, and the editors of *The Eastern Anthropologist,* Lucknow, India.

Professor C. J. Erasmus, Department of Anthropology of the University of California at Santa Barbara, and the editors of the *Southwestern Journal of Anthropology.*

Professor K. S. Goldstein, Graduate School of Arts and Sciences, University of Pennsylvania.

Miss D. Howard, and the editors of *Folklore,* London, England.

The editors of *Midwestern Folklore.*

E. W. Paxson, and the Reports Department of the Rand Corporation.

Professor J. S. Coleman, Department of Social Relations, Johns Hopkins University; Professor Ivor Kraft, School of Social Work, Sacramento State College, and the editors of the *National Education Association Journal*.

Elliott Carlson, and the editors of *The Saturday Review*.

Dr. R. A. Ravich, Beth Israel Medical Center, and the editors of the *American Journal of Psychotherapy*.

Professor P. V. Gump, University of Kansas; the editors of *Physical Therapy Review;* the National Association of Social Workers, and Dr. Fritz Redl.

Dr. N. Reider, and the editors of the *International Journal of Psychoanalysis*.

Professor J. M. Roberts, Department of Anthropology, Cornell University, and the editors of *Ethnology*.

ELLIOTT M. AVEDON
BRIAN SUTTON-SMITH

A Note About the Bibliographies Accompanying Each Chapter

At the conclusion of each chapter, the reader will find a list of *selected* references. We have not attempted to provide an exhaustive, comprehensive bibliography for each subject, but instead we have tried to indicate the range of materials available from a variety of sources. The bibliographies have been organized by *subject* rather than by author, and have been subdivided into finer subject categories when feasible. In some instance, a reference may appear on more than one list, for example:

Murray, H.J.R. *A Short History of Chess,* London: Oxford University Press, 1963

would appear on the listing of Historical Studies as well as the listing for Board Games under the sublisting of chess. Finally, because of the many sources, the place of publication is given in most cases for journal articles, as well as books and monographs.

We have made every effort to give the correct citations. If a reader discovers an error, we would appreciate hearing about it. Some of the older citations were found to be consistently incorrect in subsequent publications, and a number of valuable references have not been included because they could not be found as listed in other publications.

E.M.A.

B. S.-S.

CONTENTS

1. INTRODUCTION   1

Reading
  1. P.G. Brewster
    The Importance of the Collecting and Study of Games   9

SECTION 1.   *The History and Origins of Games*   19

2. HISTORICAL SOURCES   21

Reading
  2. P.G. Brewster
    Games and Sports in Shakespeare   27
Bibliography
    The History of Games   48
    Part I   Some General References in the English
            Language   48
    Part II   Selected References Relating to Various
            Historical Periods—Preliterate, Ancient,
            Medieval, and Early Modern Times   50

3. ANTHROPOLOGICAL SOURCES   55

Readings
  3. E.B. Tylor
    The History of Games   63
  4. E.B. Tylor
    *On American Lot-Games, as Evidence of Asiatic
    Intercourse Before the Time of Columbus*   77

ix

5. S. Culin
    Mancala, the National Game of Africa   94
6. S. Culin
    American Indian Games   103
7. C.J. Erasmus
    Patolli, Pachisi, and the Limitation of Possibilities   109
Bibliography
    *Games—Selected References in the English Language
    with Emphasis on Geographic Distribution*   130
    Part   I   Multicultural, Multinational, and
                 Cross-Cultural References   130
    Part   II   Africa   132
    Part   III Europe   135
    Part   IV   Oceania   139
    Part   V   Asia   144
    Part   VI   Central and South America   149
    Part   VII North America   151

4. FOLKLORE SOURCES   159

Readings
8. K.S. Goldstein
    *Strategy in Counting Out:
    An Ethnographic Folklore Field Study*   167
9. D. Howard
    Marble Games of Australian Children   179
10. B. Sutton-Smith
    The Kissing Games of Adolescents in Ohio   194
Bibliography
    Children's Games—Selected References
    Part   I   General References About Children's Games   217
    Part   II   Children's Games in Specific Cultures   219
    Part   III Games with Music   221
    Part   IV   Games with String   222

5. GENERAL SOURCES   225

Bibliography
    *Selected References on Games in Languages
    Other than English (1955–1956)*   230
    Part   I   General   230
    Part   II   Games of Specific Cultures   231
    Part   III Children's Games   233

Part   IV   Sports   235
Part   V   Board Games, Playing Cards, and Dice   236

SECTION 2. *The Usage of Games*   237

6. GAMES USED FOR RECREATIVE PURPOSES   239

Bibliographies
Games for Recreation—Selected References   247
Playing Cards, Dice, and Other Gambling
Games—Selected References   249
Part   I   General   249
Part   II   Dice and Other Gambling Games   250
Part   III   Playing Cards   251
Board and Table Games—Selected References   253
Part   I   General   253
Part   II   Chess   254
Part   III   Count and Capture Games (Mancala
             Variations)   255
Part   IV   Go or Wei: Ch'i   256
Part   V   Mah Jong   256
Part   VI   Backgammon   256
Part VII   Morris Games   257
Part VIII   Miscellaneous Board Games   257
Sports—Selected References   258
Part   I   About Sports   258
Part   II   "How To" References: A Brief Sample   259
Part   III   Sports in Specific Cultures   260
Part   IV   Ball Games   263
Part   V   Target Games: Archery, Darts, and Related
             Sports   266
Part   VI   Foot Racing, Gymnastics, and Track Events   266
Part VII   Boxing and Wrestling   267
Part VIII   Water and Snow Sports   267
Part   IX   Sports Involving Animals   268
Part   X   Sports and Persons with Physical Disability   268
Part   XI   Bibliographies   269

7. MILITARY USAGES   271

Reading
11. E.W. Paxson
     War Gaming   278

Bibliography
    Games in Military Science—Selected References   302

8. BUSINESS AND INDUSTRIAL GAMES   305
Bibliography
    Games in Business and Industry—Selected References   310

9. GAMES IN EDUCATION   315
Readings
  12. J.S. Coleman
    Learning Through Games   322
  13. I. Kraft
    Pedagogical Futility in Fun and Games?   326
  14. E. Carlson
    Games in the Classroom   330

Bibliography
    Games and Education—Selected References   340
    Part   I   "Turn of the Century" References   340
    Part   II   General References Dealing with the
        Concept   341
    Part   III   Games in the Teaching of Language and
        Literature   342
    Part   IV   Games in the Teaching of Arithmetic
        and Mathematics   343
    Part   V   Games in the Teaching of Social Science   344
    Part   VI   Games in the Teaching of Physical Science   344
    Part VII   Games in the Teaching of Art and Music   345
    Part VIII   Games in the Teaching of Business
        Education and Administration   345
    Part   IX   Games in the Elementary School and Early
        Childhood Education   345
    Part   X   Some Bibliographic References   346

10. GAMES IN DIAGNOSTIC AND TREATMENT
PROCEDURES   347
Readings
  15. R.A. Ravich
    *The Use of an Interpersonal Game-Test in
    Conjoint Marital Psychotherapy*   352
  16. P.V. Gump, and Y.-H. Mei
    Active Games for Physically Handicapped Children   365

17. E.M. Avedon
   Using Recreative Games for Therapeutic Purposes   371
Bibliography
   *Games: Their Use in Psychiatry, Physiatry, General
   Medicine, and Related Diagnostic, Treatment and
   Care Programs—Selected References*   376

SECTION 3.   *Structure and Function*   381

11. GAMES IN SOCIAL SCIENCE   383
Readings
18. P.V. Gump, and B. Sutton-Smith
   The "It" Role in Children's Games   390
Bibliography
   *Games in Political Science, Economics, and
   Sociology—Selected References*   398

12. GAMES AS STRUCTURE   401
Readings
19. F. Redl, P. Gump, and B. Sutton-Smith
   The Dimensions of Games   408
20. E.M. Avedon
   The Structural Elements of Games   419
Bibliography
   Mathematical Game Theory—Selected References   427

13. THE FUNCTION OF GAMES   429
Readings
21. N. Reider
   Chess, Oedipus, and the Mater Dolorosa   440
22. J.M. Roberts, and B. Sutton-Smith
   Child Training and Game Involvement   465
23. B. Sutton-Smith, V.J. Crandall, and J.M. Roberts
   Achievement and Strategic Competence   488
Bibliography
   The Function of Games—Selected References   498
Bibliography of Bibliographies   500
Index of Authors & Researchers   503
Index of Historic Personages   514

Cultural Index   516
Subject Index   519
Index of Games   522
References to Games in English Literature
(Tudor-Stuart Period)—Cited in Chapter II   528

CHAPTER 1

INTRODUCTION

The Study of Games represents the collaboration of two game buffs who, much to their mutual surprise, found their range of understanding and their knowledge of this subject matter much extended by interdisciplinary contact. The authors (coming from the fields of recreation and psychology) assume that others from such divergent fields as business, anthropology, education, psychiatry, folklore, military science, might profit also from a similar cross-disciplinary experience. The present work is a general reference manual of representative readings and comprehensive bibliographies developed from excursions into many different disciplines.

As important new research begins in such matters as the cognitive implications of play, the sociology of sport, simulations in education, and interaction behavior, it is vital that researchers and students have easy access to some of the major historical and current information on the study of games, and of play.

The Study of Games is the first of two companion volumes, this one being devoted to games, and the second to play. In the present work, there are chapters dealing with historical studies of game origins, the practical uses of games, and the scientific study of game functions and structures. Each chapter includes an introductory account of a particular field of inquiry, representative readings from the relevant literature, and related bibliographic references.

Although any serious scholarly study should begin with the definition of its subject matter, in the present case such definitions are elusive. The term *game* is used by children and adults with recreative intent; by military strategists and businessmen to apply to logistic and industrial applications; by health personnel to rehabilitative devices; by anthropologists to cultural forms; by psychiatrists to diagnostic procedures; by behavioral scientists to research tools; by educators to curriculum materials; and by recreation personnel to program content.

In some of these cases, the games are being dealt with as authentic cultural phenomena, in other cases games are used as representations of distinct social and psychological behaviors, and finally in some cases games are conceptual models for thinking about human behavior. What then is the definition of a game?

From the material already cited, and those that follow, it would not be impossible to defend the position that a game is what we decide it should be; that our definition will have an arbitrary character depending on our purpose.

For example, if the matter is approached on etymological grounds, the word *game* has both diverse origins and diverse meanings. The Indo-European root from which the word game appears to have evolved is *ghem,* meaning "to leap joyfully, to spring." Some of the linguistic differentiations which are associated with this root in modern English are:

gam-	a leg, especially a woman's leg
gamb-	an animal's leg or shank
gamba-	abbreviation for the musical instrument viola da gamba which has a part that could be considered a "leg"
gambado-	a leap of a horse; or a long legging attached to a saddle
gambit-	an opening move in chess when a piece is sacrificed
gamble-	to participate in a chance venture
gambol-	a jumping or skipping about
gambrel-	the hock of a horse or similar animal
gammon-	the bottom end of a side of bacon; or a victory in backgammon

The three most familiar usages for the word are:

1. A form of play, amusement, recreation, sport, or frolic involving specific rules, sometimes utilizing a set of equipment, sometimes requiring skill, knowledge, and endurance.
2. A condition of a leg when someone is lame or injured and they limp.
3. Wild animals, birds, or fish that are hunted for sport, or for use as food.

The reader may wonder why the same word is used for such diverse thoughts. The reasons are quite complex, but some etymologists offer the following explanation.[1] They say preliterate man used the word *ghem* to describe not only the behavior of humans, but also the behavior of animals. As the original word went through many transformations in a number of languages that have evolved from Indo-European, it became attached through local usage to certain related ideas, that is, in Germanic *ghem* became *gaman*, in Hellenic it became *kampe*, in Italic it became *camba*, in Old French it became *jambe*. Thus we have related words such as camp, campus, jamb, and jamboree. In Old Norse it became *gems* and meant "to come together and congregate as a school of whales do," and eventually came to mean a social visit at sea. Our word *cammock*, the name of the stick used in hockey, was originally a Celtic word from the stem word *cam*, meaning twisted—a variation of *ghem*. *Gambado* was originally a Spanish word from the Latin *camba* meaning hoof or fetlock. In this manner, the word *ghem* with its many linguistic transformations was always associated with the notion of an unrestrained animal (wild, free), and the movement of a leg in a bent or twisted position during a jumping or leaping motion. As a result we still use the word *game* to refer to nondomesticated animals and to an impairment in ambulation. The third meaning may be found in the affective component of the initial idea, for example, joyfully! Indeed, this latter meaning is indicative of the nature and quality of games used for recreative purposes, and presents part of the rationale for calling a specific cultural form a game. It is descriptive of adult intent with reference to game playing, for example, to experience joy. However, today all game playing is not predicated on this intent—yet we continue to classify a number of diffuse activities as games. Consider for example, hide and seek, ring-a-roses, solitaire, chicken, bingo, football, zero-sum, wooden leg, criscom, simuload. No one has yet successfully incorporated these into a single theoretical system, despite the fact that the category label "game" is still applied to all of them!

Another aspect of this problem is the assertion made by anthropologists in the late nineteenth century and more recently by some behavioral scientists that games are universal. This assertion is in opposition to the empirical evidence. Recent cross-cultural studies indicate that there are

[1] In addition to standard dictionaries of the English Language, the following were employed for the etymological analysis: Skeat, W. W. *An Etymological Dictionary of the English Language.* London: Oxford University Press, 1935. Stratmann, F. H. *A Middle-English Dictionary.* London: Oxford University Press, 1891. Sweet, H. *The Student's Dictionary of Anglo-Saxon.* London: Oxford University Press, 1896. Onions, C. T. *Oxford Dictionary of English Etymology.* London: Oxford University Press, 1966.

some cultures that do not have competitive games. These nongame cultures seem to be of two kinds—those that never had games, and those that have lost them through a process of deculturation.[2]

When nongame playing cultures are compared with game playing cultures they tend to be tropical groups with simple subsistence patterns, simple technology, low political organizations, no class stratification, kin-homogeneous communities, and to have low stress in child socialization. Obviously these cultures are relatively noncomplex in a variety of ways, not just in failing to have games.

If competitive games are not universal then they must be cultural inventions and relate to levels of cultural development. Therefore, when we discuss games, we are not discussing certain biologically inevitable occurrences, though they may be ethologically probable. Rather, we are discussing multidimensional phenomena, varied in the cultural purpose to which they are applied and inherently susceptible, for these varied reasons, to many possible systems of conceptual analysis.

A brief review of the recent history of game scholarship serves to show that this is indeed what has happened. The first scholarly approaches to games made by anthropologists, folklorists, and psychologists toward the end of the past century were sustained by an underlying evolutionism. Workers in all branches of scholarship were committed to demonstrating the universality of games in the scheme of things. Classifications tended to be in terms of theoretical notions about the way in which games had been diffused, or in terms of the rituals from which they were supposedly derived. Psychologists, for their part, tended to classify games by certain inevitable and universal stages of growth that they were supposed to represent. Social scientists through probability theory and game theory later conferred permanent and mathematical sanctification on the traditional games of *chance* and *strategy*. Currently, there is a frenzy of Piagetian ingeniousness going into the creation of educational toys and games. Perhaps in the future, we can expect to see shelves in stores labeled as primary circular-reaction toys, secondary circular-reaction toys, object-permanence toys, and so on, right alongside the other current educational enthusiasm "Simulation Games for the Social Studies Classroom."

Transcending these various twentieth century approaches to taxonomy, athletic sports of one sort or another have always received support—sometimes from the State because of their military value (as in archery), and sometimes from the elite classes because of the supposed character training value involved (as in Rugby football). An approach that con-

---

[2] Roberts, J. M. and Sutton-Smith, B. "Cross-cultural Correlates of Games of Chance," *Behavior Science Notes*, 3, 1966, pp. 131–144.

tinues despite the fact that investigations indicate that quite the contrary can be true and often sporting events among adolescents precipitate violent behavior, rather than "build character."[3]

Whether the recent fairly metaphoric use of games by psychiatrists and sociologists such as Berne, Szasz, Jackson, Goffman, and others will also crystallize in our consciousness to the point where, like Berne,[4] we go around seeing the world in terms of games such as "Schlemiel," "The Stocking Game," and "Frigid Woman," is hard to say.

Our point is that in each of these different usages the taxonomy has served the purposes of the categorizer. The system was not inevitable, it was constructed as a certain way of viewing human behavior. Each categorizer created his own "word game" about games, and by so doing, marked off some sections of discourse as his own domain.

Still it could be protested that this attitude overlooks the possibility that the word *game* could not have been used by different scholars unless there was some common meaning, some point of intersection of the varied sets. Even if they were all only *ghem*, that would seem to imply something in common. Nevertheless, at this point in game scholarship, we must admit to a great reluctance and unwillingness to commit ourselves to specifying what this common meaning may be. To define games with a degree of precision when the subject is just beginning to attract exacting research, has the ring of prematurity. Actually it makes more sense to map the subject matter rather than to define it, and that is what this book does in the main. However, a few brief definitions are in order at this stage, to provide the reader with a frame of reference. *Play* must be defined, and *game* must be defined.

Play may be seen as a type of behavior. For example, consider Piaget's account of the two-month-old baby who found that by dropping his head backwards in a certain position he could focus on a ceiling light. He persisted with this discrimination for several weeks, and then ". . . he seemed to repeat this movement with ever-increasing enjoyment and ever-decreasing interest in the external result. He brought his head back to the upright position and then threw it back again time after time, laughing loudly."[5]

In commonsense parlance this type of behavior is engaged in "for fun's sake," "for the pleasure of the action without thought to the consequence," or because "it is non utilitarian." In commonsense also, behavior

[3] Kraus, R. *Public Recreation and the Negro: A Study of Participation and Administrative Practices.* New York: Center for Urban Education, 1968.

[4] Berne, E. *Games People Play.* New York: Grove Press, 1964.

[5] Piaget, J. *Play, Dreams, and Imitation in Childhood.* London: Heinmann, 1951, p. 91.

such as this has been regarded as unimportant or trivial and of no consequence. Unfortunately this "triviality" categorization is a wastebasket category, which includes within play, behaviors that could be regarded as exploration, magical thinking, humor, and so forth.

Biologically the problem with play has been that it has seemed to be unfunctional, if function is defined in terms of service to major psychological, personal, or social needs. On the other hand, its presence is also associated phylogenetically with evolution; the higher the species the greater the amount of play. This presents the paradox that although play does not seem to be of immediate functional value, it appears to have functional implications for the species. For this reason, some have suggested that play is preadaptive; it prepares the player in general, but not in a specific way. It increases combinatorial powers and the range of novel responses, so that under adaptive pressure, the player has more resources at hand.[6] Against this notion it could be objected that the paradox itself is caused by too restrictive a concept of adaptation in the first place. It might be argued, for example, that traditional scientific definitions of adaptation give insufficient emphasis to the development of the voluntary control of behavior in humans. Such voluntary control implies various forms of mastery, such as the anticipation of outcomes, the choice of instrumental behaviors, freedom from immediate sensory controls, a capacity to sustain the direction of behavior over a number of responses, sequential organization, and skill in mobilizing resources. All of these phenomena are often included among traditional definitions of play. From a biological point of view, therefore, it might make some sense to regard play as an exercise of voluntary control systems. Presumably, only the freedom and "as if" quality of play can guarantee the exercise of such controls.

We obtain the same emphasis if psychological definitions of the behavioristic order are presented. In these terms, play has been described as the novel variation of the subject's own responses, more or less irrespective of the variation of the stimulus qualities of the objects with which he is engaged.[7] This complements the biological emphasis on voluntary control. Similarly, the phenomenological type of definition, which emphasizes the player's feelings of mastery and his sense of being the cause, do likewise. We may find then some preliminary consensus across these three approaches if we define play as an *exercise of voluntary control systems*. But what of games?

[6] Sutton-Smith, B. "Novel Responses to Toys," *Merrill-Palmer Quarterly*, **14**(2), 1968, pp. 151–158.

[7] Welker, W. I. An analysis of exploratory and play behaviors in animals. In *Functions of Varied Experience*. D. W. Fiske and S. R. Maddi, Eds. Homewood, Ill.: Dorsey Press, 1961.

We speak of "playing" a game or game "play." For example, a baby of about four months old, sitting in his mother's lap while he is being fed with a bottle, grasps the mother's finger. The mother pulls it away, and the baby grasps it again, sometimes interrupting the feeding process because of the pleasure of these alternations. We say in this instance that the baby is "playing a game" with his mother. In this instance, unlike the play example from Piaget given above, the baby or the mother does not have the same complete freedom to follow impulse or stimulus, and each is relatively more confined both in the range of his own behaviors and by those of his opponent. Each "plays" with a certain goal in mind—in this case to capture or to avoid the capture of the mother's finger by the baby. From a cultural point of view it is usual to emphasize that play is unique and individual, but ephemeral; whereas a game is sufficiently systematic that it may be repeated by others in other places. Thus, in the above examples, the baby throwing his head back required his own particular situation for that play event, but the "finger game" could be repeated and instigated by mothers with babies in almost any culture. Games are repeatable because of their systematic pattern and their predictable outcomes. Play on the other hand is less systematic, and is open-ended with respect to outcomes. In a game, the participant's voluntary control over procedures has been subordinated in anticipation of, but without guarantee for, a given goal.

Again, games imply some opposition or antithesis between players. Even in solitary games (puzzles) it seems that this same sense of opposition is present. That is, the player contends against impersonal obstacles or against fortune, or he mentally pits one aspect of himself against another. In games that do not seem to have opposition, such as the preschooler's "Mulberry Bush," opposition is present in the child's attempt to have his body obey. The stylized rhythmic movements may not be a challenge to the older child or the adult, but it is to the preschooler.

In the finger game cited, we have the opposition of mother and baby (as actor and counteractor). Their performance of holding and withholding fingers are prescribed within a certain range. Even in this game there are implicit procedural and contingency rules. When the baby finally grasps the mother's finger after several attempts and gurgles with laughter, we can speak of a goal being achieved and momentarily at least, there is a winner. Even in the elementary game we have a repeatable pattern, opposition, and outcome. At its most elementary level then we can define a game as *an exercise of voluntary control systems in which there is an opposition between forces, confined by a procedure and rules in order to produce a disequilibrial outcome.*

In subsequent chapters we shall expand the elements of this definition to encompass the more complex games of adult life. In the meantime, however, such a definition perhaps explains why it is possible to use the term *game* for a variety of activities. It stands for voluntary behavior whether on a cultural or a theoretical level, it can apply to what people do with each other, or what they do dyadically within themselves.

We include in this introductory chapter, a paper by Brewster who is neither a psychologist nor in the field of recreation, but yet seems to be very much aware of the potential multidisciplinary interest in the study of games.

1

The Importance of the Collecting and Study of Games

PAUL G. BREWSTER

The definitions and interpretations of the term *game* are many and widely varied. On the theory that "ontogeny recapitulates phylogeny," G. Stanley Hall sees in the games of children the reproduction of activities natural, and even essential, to our early ancestors but having little or no relation to the modern *milieu*. This point of view has been adopted more recently by Reany, who divides the child's play-life into five stages (animal, savage, nomad, pastoral, and tribal), assigning an age span to each.[1] Groos, on the other hand, after having studied and described both the play of human beings and that of animals, concludes that in the child's game we have what is essentially an exercise contributory to the development of the physical organs. The game is motivated by some basic instinct: the urge for physical contact (as in wrestling), the urge to chase, etc. Following the same theory, Car sees in the social games of the child a reminiscence of the collective unconscious and an exercise fixing the newly acquired functions or duties. The functional theory advanced by Claparède was inspired by Groos, but diverges somewhat from the views of the latter. For Claparède the game represents a kind of apprenticeship for the duties and responsibilities of life, under the influence of instinct.

SOURCE. *Eastern Anthropologist,* 10(1), 1956, pp. 5–12.

---

[1] Mabel J. Reany, *The Psychology of the Organized Group Game* (Cambridge University Press, 1916). According to her classification, the animal period covers the years from birth to age 7, the savage period from 7 to 9, the nomad from 9 to 12, and the pastoral and tribal stages from 12 to 17.

This emphasis upon the part played by instinct is, however, not acceptable to modern psychologists, who look upon an explanation giving instinct for the motivating force as equivalent to an admission of ignorance.

Under the influence of Freud and his disciples, the game has been regarded by some students of the subject as a compensation or substitution for instincts suppressed by the normal conscience. Presented in the innocent form of a game, they are accepted by society without question.

Piaget sees in the game:

". . . sous ses deux formes essentielles d'exercices sensori-moteur et de symbolisme, une assimilation du réel à l'activité propre, fournissant à celle-ci son alimentation nécessaire et transformant le réel en fonction des besoins multiples du moi. C'est pourquoi, ajoute-t-il, les méthodes actives d'éducation des petits exigent toutes que l'on fournisse aux enfants un matériel convenable, afin qu'en jouant ils parviennent à s'assimiler les réalités intellectuelles qui, sans cela, demeurent extérieures à l'intelligence infantile."

J. Château denies that there is in the child's game this assimilation of the *réel* to himself, but says that the assimilation comes slowly and as a consequence of serious, rather than play, activities. The child makes of himself the center of the world, and does not seek to explore anything beyond himself. Objects interest him only when he is permitted to exercise his powers (of touch, taste, etc.) upon them. The driving force in the child's play activities, as he begins to try out his muscles and his senses, is the desire to become strong or in some other way superior.

According to Huizinga, all play is a voluntary activity.[2] He goes on to say that it has two basic aspects; it is either a contest for something or a representation of something.[3]

Herbert Spencer has pointed out that play uses up surplus energy in young who have no need to feed or to protect themselves, all such care being the responsibility of the parents. To this idea, early psychoanalysis added the so-called "cathartic" theory, according to which play has a definite function in the growing child in that it furnishes him a means by which he can work off past emotions and find imaginary relief for past frustrations.[4]

Notwithstanding the wide diversity of opinion as to what constitutes play or a game, there is a pretty general feeling among those who have

[2] John Huizinga, *Homo Ludens: A Study of the Play-Element in Culture* (trans. R. F. C. Hull), London, 1949, p. 7.

[3] *Ibid.*, p. 13.

[4] See Erik H. Erikson, *Childhood and Society* (New York, 1950), p. 187.

studied the subject that the game is perhaps a more fruitful and more important field for investigation than has hitherto been realized, and a growing awareness of the need for collecting and studying the traditional games before they are completely replaced by those of more modern origin.

Anthropologists, ethnologists, and others studying native tribes have, on the whole, been strangely indifferent to the pastimes of the peoples among whom they happen to be working. True, such scholars as Haddon, Im Thurn, Roth, Griaule, Itkonen, Costermans, Comhaire-Sylvain, and others have given us a great deal of valuable information, but a far greater number have interested themselves almost exclusively in the economic, political, and/or religious life of the tribe under study.

This apparent indifference has in many instances been remarked upon and deplored by field workers themselves. Dr. Padmanabhachari writes:

Human life and human institutions can be better understood by—and indeed cannot be thoroughly understood at all without—a study of the life of primitive peoples including even their pastimes, the games they played, the sports they engaged in . . . Play patterns are an integral part of all human culture wherever mankind is found and in whatever state of advancement the culture may be. A study of the play of primitive peoples will throw much needed light on the nature of the play tendencies of mankind as a whole. Moreover, a study of games and sports will reveal to us the nature and extent of civilisation of the race.[5]

Professor Bell, writing on the Tanga, comments:

I believe that the play-life of a people is just as efficient a guide to its ethics as its magico-religious life or its economic life. The study of primitive play has been sadly neglected, and probably stands in much the same position as the study of primitive economics stood until quite recently.

One of the essentials of human happiness is indulgence in some form of play. I feel that this is a universal postulate which may be applied to all peoples of all cultures, and I would appeal to all those who are in a position to study primitive peoples to pay a close attention to the subject of primitive play . . . .[6]

In his series of articles on Nigerian games, Professor Newberry writes:

Many educationists and anthropologists have voiced the opinion that

[5] T. R. Padmanabhachari, "Games, Sports and Pastimes in Prehistoric India," *Man in India,* XXI, 2–3 (April-September, 1941), 128.

[6] F. L. S. Bell, "The Play Life of the Tanga, II," *Mankind,* II, 4 (June, 1937), 86.

too often is it the case that the study of a tribe or people is confined almost entirely to adult life from puberty onwards, and that only occasionally is a detailed account of children's games given in what are in other respects comprehensive accounts.[7]

Raum expresses his views on the matter in the following words:

Since modern sociological schools of Social Anthropology are almost exclusively interested in "structural" analyses of social ways and relations, certain areas of "primitive" life—and among them games—have passed out of the focus of attention of anthropologists. This is to be regretted.[8]

Similar statements are to be found in the writings of many other anthropologists and students of native life.

In recent years the situation has changed somewhat for the better, although one still encounters in professed ethnological studies such cavalier treatment of games as the following:

N'dri and Quodie had crossed the road to a group of dark men playing *some game* in the shelter of a great uprooted tree. The game consisted of *tossing pellets very rapidly into the holes of what resembled a wooden muffin tin.* . . . Ruth, who was forever trying to outwit an amazing variety of patently unfounded inferiority complexes, saw a challenge here, for she was very good at games. . . .

"Ah, oui," sighed N'dri as Ruth moved in among a tribe he considered inferior to his own, which was Baole, and Ruth was indeed playing *clack-click, click-clack,* and winning all the marbles. . . .[9]

Although the author's interest here lies in a more serious subject, one might reasonably expect him at least to identify the game in question, particularly since he must have met with it many times in the course of his travels.

The benefits to be derived by the anthropologist or the ethnologist from a study, particularly a comparative study, of games are many. Perhaps one of the greatest of these is the evidence often found in games of direct borrowing or of adaptation of games materials of neighbouring peoples. Sometimes these borrowings or adaptations are of fairly recent

---

[7] R. J. Newberry, "Some Games and Pastimes of Southern Nigeria," *The Nigerian Field,* **VII**, 2 (April, 1938), 85.

[8] O. F. Raum, "The Rolling Target (Hoop-and-Pole) Game in Africa: Egyptian Accession Rite or Multiple Ritual Symbolism," *African Studies,* **XII**, 3 (September, 1953), 105.

[9] Hassoldt Davis, *Sorcerers' Village* (Boston, 1955), pp. 26–27, Italics mine.

date; sometimes the internal evidence points to a much earlier period. In either event, theories regarding culture contacts between certain peoples are often materially strengthened by the discovery of non-indigenous elements in the games played by a particular tribe or nationality. As one Indian scholar has well expressed it:

It seems to me that . . . the importance of the comparative study of such games, from the ethnological standpoint, does not lie so much in the details of their similarities and differences as in the light it throws on so-cial contact between different groups of people. Culture traits may mi-grate in various ways, and these migrations maye be due either to actual movements of people or, as so often happens, to contact. The tracing of the possible routes of migrations of these games, as in all other single traits, furnishes important clues regarding the general contact—meta-morphosis of different people or the displacement of one by the other. Whichever may be the basic reason in a particular locality or particular tribes, it provides important clues and evidence which are of consider-able value to the historical study of their culture.[10]

If the investigator finds it difficult or impossible to gain admittance to a peculiarly sacred ceremony or to learn the substance of a jealously guarded ritual, he can sometimes learn a great deal, though perhaps not all, about these by observing closely the imitations of them by the chil-dren. Since children are extremely clever imitators, possess retentive memories, and, above all, are conservative, their versions of the cere-monies and rituals are by no means to be taken lightly. And no matter how sacred the ceremony or how strong the taboos surrounding it, it is almost sure to have its counterpart in the games of the children. Bell, for example, mentions the imitating by Tanga boys and girls of the *dafal*, a puberty rite,[11] and Schwab has described in detail the imitation of the well-known sasswood ordeals by boys and girls in Liberia.[12] According to Haddon, one of the favourite pranks of boys in British New Guinea is to mask and then to imitate the *fulaari*, a kind of village constabulary whose duty it is to enforce àny *afu* or taboo imposed by the chief.[13] An anony-mous Indian writer tells how he himself, as a child, used to imitate in

[10] Sunder Lal Hora, "Sedentary Games of India," *Journal and Proceedings of the Asiatic Society of Bengal*, N. S. **XXIX** (1933), 5.

[11] F. L. S. Bell, "The Play of the Tanga, I," *Mankind*, **II**, 3 (1937), 57.

[12] George Schwab, *Tribes of the Liberian Hinterland* (Papers of the Peabody Museum of American Archaeology, XXXI), Cambridge (Mass.), 1947, p. 223.

[13] A. C. Haddon, "Notes on Children's Games in British New Guinea," *Journal of the Royal Anthropological Institute*, **XXXVIII** (1908), 294.

play the Muktad, or Dosla, ceremonies. One of his statements is worth repeating here:

> With change of times, the original rituals and ceremonies may possibly pass away, giving place to some new forms, but the children, who are conservative, may retain and continue them till it may be difficult to identify them and to trace their origin.[14]

Ghosts and evil spirits still play their roles in the games of children though the adult members of the society may no longer believe in them, and the dart- and spear-throwing games still popular among many peoples take us back to a time when these were not games but an important part of the training process by which young men were developed into warriors and hunters.

Many of the games played by twentieth-century children, even by those of the most highly civilized societies, contain traces of very ancient and even primitive beliefs and practices: water worship, the foundation sacrifice, the symbolism of colours, the efficiency of spittle as a *fuga daemonum*, the witch, the "Black Man," crossing the fingers to avoid being taken prisoner, and many many others, all of them of interest to the ethnologist and the folklorist.

However, it is not only the anthropologist who can benefit from a study of games. Since in a number of them there are many archaic words, they should be of interest and value also to the philologist. In the case of many, if not most, of the counting-out rhymes used to determine which player is to be "It" in a chasing game, which is to have first turn, etc., the majority of the words appear to be mere gibberish and are so regarded both by adults and by the players themselves. However, a careful study reveals that in many instances these have not been made up by the players but are either archaisms or unintelligible corruptions of words still in current use.[15] Bolton and others working in this field have found in counting-out rhymes fragments of Latin prayers from the Middle Ages, phrases from Masonic ritual, bits of incantations and spoken charms, words from the gypsies' Romany, tinkers' slang, and the professional jargon of strolling mountebanks.[16] Curious admixtures of this kind are occasionally to be found also in songs, rhymes, and dialogue

---

[14] *Journal of the Anthropological Society of Bombay*, **X**, 5, (1915), 374–375.

[15] F. R. Chapman, "*Koruru*, the Maori Game of 'Knuckle-Bone'," *Journal of the Polynesian Society*, **VII**, 2 (June, 1898), 114 ("It appears to be a genuine Maori game, as the people could not give me the meanings of the words, which they say are old Maori ones").

[16] See H. O. Bolton, *The Counting-out Rhymes of Children, Their Antiquity, Origin, and Wide Distribution* (London, 1888).

within the game proper. As is frequently the case in religious or magic rituals,[17] participànts in games may sometimes be found using special vocabularies. This, however, is more likely to be encountered in games engaged in by adults than in those played by children.

Certain games are of particular interest, or should be, to the psychologist, the psychiatrist, and, in a slightly lesser degree perhaps, the physician. One of these, and probably the best example of the type, is the *hantu musang* or *main musang* of Malaysia.[18] In this game, which is played by boys and on occasion by men, one of the participants is hypnotized by the rest. Then follows a chant of invocation in which the spirit of an animal (civet cat, monkey, goat, etc.) is invited to enter the body of the boy.[19] When the transfer has been effected, the hypnotized player performs, with amazing fidelity, the characteristic actions of the animal in question. While in this state he does feats which would be quite impossible for him were he in his normal condition. The game is not without its dangers (injury as a result of falling from a height, for example) for the boy who is possessed, and great care must be exercised in bringing him out of the hypnotic state. Since trances and possession are features of religious groups in many widely separated parts of the world, games of this kind should have some appeal also for the student of comparative religion. In the former, however, the trance seems, ordinarily at least, to be self-induced, aided perhaps by sounds, perfumes, etc., but not requiring any physical contact such as is frequently found in games of the hantu musang type. The priest or shaman or even an humble worshipper may be possessed by a saint, a god, or a god manifesting himself as an animal-spirit. Dr. Verrier Elwin writes me:

I have not come across any game in India which resembles the *hantu musang* but I have witnessed scenes where priests or shamans have been possessed by an animal-spirit and have behaved very like the animal concerned. Thus among the Hinduised Gonds of Madhya Pradesh the spirit of Hanuman sometimes possesses a man during the harvest festival and this man then behaves exactly like a monkey to the great entertainment

[17] For a good example of this, see Frederick Kaigh, *Witchcraft and Magic of Africa* (London, 1947), pp. 31–56, 60.

[18] Other names are *hantu kra* (monkey), *hantu kambing* (goat), *hantu kuching* (cat), *sintren, lais, main peteri,* and *lokang* (*lokan*). Dr. Polunin, of the faculty of Medicine, University of Malaya, has made a film of *main peteri* and *lokang;* and Dr. de Jong, of the Institute of Malay Studies, has a tape recording of the introductory portion of the ceremony. I have for some time been collecting materials on *hantu musang* and hope eventually to publish a study of it and other games of the type.

[19] There is a difference of opinion here. Some writers who have witnessed it regard it as only a clever bit of imitation.

of the spectators. He appears to be in a state of trance when this happens, and this is probably induced by a long period of drumming, chanting, and drinking.[20]

The educator, too, can learn much from the games of children if he is a careful observer. He will note, for example, that although the games are spontaneous and unsupervised,[21] there are certain rigid rules, learned from elders or formulated by the children themselves, to which they conscientiously adhere. And he will note, further, that any infraction, no matter how slight, of these rules will result in the culprit's being severely rebuked if not expelled from the playing group. He will probably be surprised to learn that number games were being played by children of so-called primitive societies long before they were introduced into modern education as a teaching technique, and may well be amazed at the youngsters' skill in mental computation and at their grasp of the principle of counter distribution. It is largely because of their having been encouraged as children to take part of such games that in adulthood they are so proficient in *mancala* and similar board games.[22]

From very early times the agility and grace of playing children have furnished subjects for the artist and the sculptor, as have also, to a lesser extent, games of a sedentary nature. A terra cotta group in the British Museum, representing two girls playing astragals or knucklebones, has been dated as 800 B.C.[23] Erman has copies of wall paintings of board games, jumping games, *kollabismos*, and other games, all dating from the Fifth Dynasty or the Middle Kingdom.[24] Mlle Auboyer's recent fine work contains drawings from wall paintings and sculpture depicting ball games,

---

[20] In a letter from Shillong on March 7, 1956.

[21] There is really, of course, no other kind. As Huizinga (*op. cit.*, p. 7) puts it, "First and foremost, then, all play is a voluntary activity. Play to order is no longer play; it would at best be but a forcible imitation of it."

[22] This game, or some form of it, is played all over the Far East and among most African tribes. It is known also as *Chanka* (Ceylon), *Chongkak* (India), *Chuncajon* (Philippines), *La'b hakimi* or *L'ab akila* (Syria), *Medjiwa* (Bali), *Dakon* (Malaya), *Gabatta* or *Madji* (Abyssinia), *Wari* (West Coast), *Toee* (Bongo), *Bau* (Wadschagga), etc. Some natives become so expert that they play blindfolded and are able to play two or three opponents simultaneously; see Alan P. Merriam, "The Game of *Kubuguza* Among the Abatutsi of North-East Ruanda," *Man*, LIII (November, 1953), 171.

[23] E. Lovett, "The Ancient and Modern Game of Astragals," *Folk-Lore*, X, 3 (September, 1901), 280.

[24] Adolf Erman, *Aegypten und Aegyptisches Leben im Altertum* (ed. Hermann Ranke), pp. 175, 279, 290, 292.

the playing of board games with dice, and the spinning of tops.[25] Some of these paintings and carvings are as old as 200 B.C. A wall painting of a hand-clapping game being played by two young Egyptian girls, which for centuries has adorned the tomb of Ak-hor, has been reproduced in Culin and Falkener.[26] Later artists who have painted the games of children include the elder Pieter Brueghel, whose "Children's Games" is perhaps the best-known example of the genre; B. Dahlerup; N'Guyen Phan Chanh, whose painting of two small Annamite children playing a board game while two others look on has been reproduced in Béart's recent two-volume work on West African games;[27] and Jan Molenaer, whose *La Main Chaude* hangs in the Museum of Fine Arts, Budapest.

Singing-games and dancing-games have much of value for the musicologist and the choreographer. The study of games of this type has been, for example, a very important part of the work of the sisters Danica and Ljubica Yankovic, of Belgrade, whose books and articles on folk-dancing are recognized by all folklorists as models of thorough research and meticulous scholarship.

Workers in the fields both of mental and of physical therapy have in the games of children extremely valuable tools, and particularly so since for almost any condition a suitable game or pastime can be found.

Finally, it should be stressed that one need not be a specialist on games in order to collect them. True, it might be better if he were, but if all he can do is set down carefully and in full detail all that he sees and hears from beginning to end of the game, he is still making a valuable contribution not only to colleagues in his own field but to workers in other fields as well.

---

[25] Jeannine Auboyer, *La vie publique et privée dans l'Inde ancienne* (Paris: Presses Universitaires de France, 1955).

[26] Stewart Culin, *Korean Games, with Notes on the Corresponding Games of China and Japan* (Philadelphia, 1895); Edward Falkener, *Games Ancient and Oriental* (London, 1892).

[27] Ch. Béart, *Jeux et jouets de l'ouest africain*, II (Dakar, 1955), 481.

The History and Origins of Games

Since most of the students of games in the early part of the modern era (after 1880) were concerned primarily with origins, this is a logical place to begin the present inquiry. In effect there are two questions to be asked—one methodological and one theoretical. That is, *how* can the origins of games be studied, and what is the *meaning* of their origin and diffusion. Chapter 2 deals with the types of sources from which scholars have derived their data on games and the scholarly disciplines that have become involved with games, and to that extent answers the first question. Chapters 3, 4, and 5, provide some of the attempts of anthropologists, folklorists, and other scholars to answer the second question.

Besides the historical justice in giving such a large play to origins, however, we have the larger philosophical purpose of raising the question whether this is the most valid way to think about games. Various scholars have sought to trace the origins of games in ritual, history, racial atavism, and personal tensions (to name just a few forms of reductivism). More recently, as we shall indicate, some scholars have questioned these interpretations.

19

CHAPTER 2

HISTORICAL SOURCES

Information about early games and game playing has been provided by archaeology (artifacts, graphics), legislation, manuscripts, and, unintentionally as well as intentionally, in some early written records. Illustrations of each of these types of sources follow, though the reader is referred to the accompanying bibliography for a more complete accounting.

Archaeologists have made information about early games available by recovering game *artifacts* from ancient tombs and temples. A Sumerian game board (c. 2600 B.C.) recovered from the royal cemetery at Ur of Chaldees is an example. Similarly, Egyptologists have recovered dice and game boards from the tomb of Queen Hatasu (c. 1600 B.C.), and game boards of the "Morris" type (complex versions of ticktacktoe!) have been discovered cut into the roofing slabs of the Temple of Kurna, Egypt, dating from 1400 B.C. "Morris" boards have been cut into the cloister seats of the cathedrals of Norwich, Canterbury, Gloucester, Salisbury, and Westminster Abbey, dating from A.D. 1300. Remnants of ceremonial ball courts (c. A.D. 1000) have been discovered in Mexico at Tula. In sum, one source of historical information about games is the equipment employed in the play of the game or the special setting in which the game was played.

Another source is *graphic information.* Archeologists have restored a number of tomb murals and paintings that depict ancient people playing games. One famous mural in an Egyptian tomb illustrates two persons playing the finger game of "odds and evens." A number of vase paintings depict Achilles and Ajax playing a game similar to backgammon, which Homer alludes to in the *Illiad.* Others illustrate Grecian foot races, box-　21 ing, wrestling, and a host of additional games. Sometimes a tomb mural or a vase painting has clarified how a game artifact was to be used. Pieter Breughel's famous painting, "Children's Games" (c. A.D. 1560) has been used as an illustration of over eighty games that were once in the common domain.

Many ancient writers, without intending it, included information about games. For example, Homer discusses the game playing of Achilles and Ajax during the Trojan War (c. 550 B.C.). Similarly, authors such as Plato, Pliny, Plutarch, Seneca, and Xenophon recorded information about games played in ancient times, although this was not their intent. Ovid, writing during the Augustan age offers information about a "Morris" game in *Ars Amatoria*. Tacitus (c. A.D. 55–117) in his ethnographical work *Germania*, discusses dice playing. Information about the ancient Olympic games can be derived from the writings of Aristophanes, Aristotle, Flavius Arrianus, Athenaeus, Herodotus, Pausanias, Philostratus, Plato, Plutarch, Socrates, Publius Papinus Statius, Thucydides, Xenophon, and others.

Another historical source of information about games is *legislation*. Antigambling laws appear to have been first instituted in Rome over 2000 years ago purportedly because of excesses at the gaming tables. People were not only betting next week's salary, but also their homes, wives, children, and anything else they felt they owned. When golf was getting too popular and distracting young men from practising archery, the Scottish Parliament of A.D. 1457 passed legislation prohibiting the playing of golf. Even stricter legislation had to be enacted in 1471 and again in 1491. In the latter enactment, both golfers and promoters of the game were penalized. The town council statutes in Nuremberg in A.D. 1503 limited the play of marble games to a meadow outside of town; and in the village of St. Gall, the town council statutes authorized the Sacristan of St. Laurence to use a cat-o-nine-tails on boys ". . . who played at marbles under the fish-stand and refused to be warned off."[1]

Some very early manuscripts that discussed games by intent were the ancient *Chinese Five Classics*. One of these discusses the free time of agricultural workers and their gambling games. Wilkinson[2] reports that reference books concerning Chinese dice games were available as early as the eight century A.D., and Bell[3] states that ". . . 'Wei-chi' is first mentioned in Chinese writings from Honan about 625 BC."

[1] Portmann, P. *Brueghel: Children's Games*. Berne: Hallwag, Ltd., 1964, p. 18.

[2] Wilkinson, W. H. "Chinese Origin of Playing Cards," *The American Anthropologist*, **VIII**, January, 1895, p. 64.

[3] Bell, R. C. *Board and Table Games From Many Civilizations*. London: Oxford University Press, 1960, p. 109.

In the Middle East, an early volume to deal exclusively with a game was *Kitab Ash-Shtranj* (Book of Chess) written by Abu-Bakr Muhammad Ben Yahya as-Suli about A.D. 920. Although there are early Sanskrit records (as early as c. 800 B.C.) which discuss some of the forerunners of chess (Ashtapada and Shaturanga), *Kitab Ash-Shrtanj* was the first book on the subject. The author was a chess master at the court of the Caliph of Baghdad, who recorded his ideas about the game of chess. During the ensuing years additional documents about games written in Arabic, Latin, and other languages became available.

Probably the first scholarly historical treatise on games was *De Historia Shahiludii* (1689) and its companion volume *De Historia Herdiludii* (1694). These volumes were written by Thomas Hyde, a professor of Arabic at the University of Oxford. The books contain information on such games as backgammon, chess and "wei-ch'i."

Another famous book of the period was *The Complete Gamester* written by Charles Cotton about 1674. Published anonymously because of Cotton's social position, it was not until the fifth edition (published in 1734) that he was acknowledged as the author. Another early book in the English language that is viewed as a companion volume to Cotton's work, is Theophilus Lucas' *Memoirs of the Lives, Intrigues and Comical Adventures of the Most Famous Gamesters*. Both books have been republished recently under the title, *Games and Gamesters of the Restoration*.[4]

Hoyle of "According to Hoyle" published his first game book in 1742. It was titled:

A short treatise on the Game of Whist, containing the Laws of the Game; and also some Rules whereby a Beginner may, with due attention to them, attain to the Playing it well. Calculations for those who will Bet the Odds on any point of the score of the Game then playing and depending. Cases stated, to shew what may be effected by a good player in Critical Parts of the Game. References to cases viz. at the End of the Rule you are directed how to find them. Calculations directing with moral Certainty, how to play well any Hand or Game, by Shewing the Chances of your Partner's having 1 2 or 3 certain cards. With Variety of Cases added in the Appendix. Printed by John Watts for the Author, London, 1742.

During the next twenty years Hoyle published short treatises on backgammon, piquet, brag and many other games that are now rarely played.

---

[4] Cotton, C. *The Compleat Gamester*, 1674, bound with Lucas, T. *Lives of the Gamesters*, 1714, republished as *Games and Gamesters of the Restoration*. London: G. Routledge and Sons, 1930.

During the period 1800 through 1850 a number of articles on chess, playing cards, and athletic games and contests began to appear in a variety of popular and scholarly journals in English, German, French, and other European as well as Oriental languages. For example, in the preface to *Card Essays, Clay's Decisions, and Card-Table Talk*, we read that, ". . . in the present volume the Author has reproduced with corrections and numerous augmentations, some miscellaneous papers on subjects connected with Cards, which have hitherto been buried in back numbers of periodicals."[5]

A famous book of the period first published in 1801 and reissued numerous times was Strutt's *Sports and Pastimes of the English People*. A similar volume published in 1825 was Aspen's *Picture of the Manners, Customs, Sports, and Pastimes of the Inhabitants of England to the Eighteenth Century*. A sample of other titles appearing at the time include: *Backgammon, Its History and Practice* (1844), Henry Ellis' revision of John Brand's *Observations on Popular Antiquities* (1813), *On the Burma Game of Chess Compared with the Indian, Chinese and Persian* (1803), *Researches into the History of Playing Cards* (1816) and William Hone's *Every Day Book and Table Book* (1838). Also during the period, similar publications began to appear in the United States, such as Smith's *Festivals, Games and Amusements: Ancient and Modern* (1831).

While most people were writing about games for recreative purposes, publications concerning games for other purposes also began to appear during this period. The first of these, published in French in 1797, was *Rules of a New War Game for the Use of Military Schools*, by Venturini. The publication was based on an earlier published essay (1780) by Helwig, who discussed the use of games in teaching military tactics to young noblemen, an origin we shall discuss in more detail in the section on military science. These were followed during the next hundred years by a variety of similar publications on the subject in German, French, Italian, Japanese, and English. U.S. publications concerning war games began to appear after the Civil War period.

While these latter examples were probably motivated by the intuitive belief that games were useful pedagogic devices, the increased interest in games in the late eighteenth and early nineteenth centuries is usually said to have been associated with an emerging interest in antiquarianism in the scholarship of that period, with romanticism in literature, and with increasing urbanization in the sociopolitical world. As there has

---

[5] "Cavendish" *Card Essays, Clay's Decisions and Card-Table Talk*. London: Thomas De La Rue & Co., 1879, p. ix.

been little or no scholarship on the history of game scholarship itself, however, these statements must remain, at best, generalized guesses.

In the last fifty years of the nineteenth century and throughout the twentieth century reports and documents about games were no longer to be found in out of the way places—they became part of the mainstream of publishing. Anthropological, folklorist, and psychological interest in games began seriously during the last thirty years of the nineteenth century; a more detailed discussion of these interests will be found in subsequent chapters of this section. A high point in game scholarship was reached in 1913 with the publication of Murray's nine-hundred-page, exhaustive, classic study, A *History of Chess*.[6] This work serves as a major source and prototype for most works of this genre.

It is also during this period that books about games in relation to the education of children began to appear. Although publications about war games in the education of the military had been available for over a century, widespread concern for use of games in elementary education did not appear until after 1900. An early publication was titled: *Education by Plays and Games* (1907). This was followed by such titles as: *Gymnastic Games Classified* (1907) and *Graded Games and Rhythmic Exercises for Primary Grades* (1908). A doctoral dissertation on "The Psychology of the Organized Group Game," which concerned the use of games in schools, appeared in the *British Journal of Psychology* in 1916. In the same year (1916) *Games and Exercises for Mental Defectives* was published, signifying another type of interest in games. In the following decade, a related area of interest, the medical aspects of games, was evidenced by such articles as "Medical and Surgical Aspects of Sports and Games," *Baily's Magazine*, London, 1921.

Other types of focus that appeared at the time included special publications offered by religious groups—*Popular Amusements—Destructive and Constructive*, 1925; *The Playtime Guidebook for Churches*, 1926; the teaching of specific academic subjects in schools, that is, *Games for Spanish Clubs* (1926).

During the "thirties" more of the same types of materials appeared, and in addition to these, the first texts for personnel concerned with organized recreation service became available, such as *Education through Recreation* (1932), and *Leisure and Recreation* (1936).[7] Titles such as: *Emotion and Sport* (1932); *Psychoanalytic Theory of Play*

---

[6] Murray, H. J. R. A *History of Chess*. London: Oxford University Press, 1913.

[7] Jacks, L. P. *Education Through Recreation*. New York: Harper 1932; Neumeyer, M. H. and Neumeyer, E. S. *Leisure and Recreation*. New York: A. S. Barnes and Co., 1936.

(1933) indicated the interest of psychoanalysts. Sociologic concern was evidenced by the publications of George H. Mead (1934) and Johan Huizinga (1938). In 1944, von Neumann and Morgenstein published *The Theory of Games and Economic Behavior,* which had profound implications for the future of social science. Specific developments from this period on are examined in detail in Section II—*The Usage of Games.*

It seems quite clear from the foregoing historical overview, and, in fact, from the publication of this book itself, that games, long regarded as rather "trivial" concerns in a dominantly puritanic culture, have moved nearer to the center of cultural concern, in man's continuing attempt to understand himself and the world in which he lives.

To conclude this chapter we include a paper by Brewster, who demonstrates how written documents can be used as a resource for the historical study of games. The paper also serves as an illustration of the continuity of games themselves in Western culture.

2

Games and Sports in Shakespeare

PAUL G. BREWSTER

The universality of Shakespeare has long been axiomatic; in a sense he has become "all things to all men." Scholars have noted his facile and accurate use of the language of medicine, of law, of philosophy; and so familiar is he with these fields and with their idioms that he has been thought a physician, a lawyer, or a philosopher. As a recent Shakespeare scholar and critic puts it: "One by one all the philosophies have been discovered in Shakespeare's works, and he has been charged—both as virtue and weakness—with having no philosophy. The lawyer believes he must have been a lawyer, the musician a musician, the Catholic a Catholic, the Protestant a Protestant."[1] The fallacy in such reasoning lies, of course, in the unwarranted assumption that an intimate knowledge of the language peculiar to a profession or an occupation can be acquired only through an active participation in it.

The fact that Shakespeare mentions nearly fifty different games and sports in the plays does not mean that he was a folklorist or a specialist in games any more than his familiarity with legal procedure proves him to have been a lawyer. Nor is it necessary to assume that he was a sports enthusiast. No doubt he did participate in some, perhaps all, of the games and sports mentioned. However, even had he not done so, he would certainly not have been unaware of their existence. Here, as in other respects, Shakespeare was very much a man of his time and thoroughly conversant with what was going on in it.

SOURCE. *FF Communications*, **72** (177), 1959, pp. 3–26.

[1] Harold C. Goddard, *The Meaning of Shakespeare* (University of Chicago Press, 1951), p. 1.

As will be noted, the allusions take different forms. In some instances the dramatist gives us what is almost a word picture of the sport in question:

> Or as a bear, encompass'd round with dogs,
> Who having pinched a few and made them cry,
> The rest stand all aloof, and bark at him.

Sometimes the mention of the game appears in the form of a figure of speech, usually a simile or a metaphor:

> As one would set up a top
> I am tied to the stake, and I must stand the course.

In still other cases there appears only the name of the game or sport or some term used in connection with the playing of it:

> Let's to billiards
> Pitch, rub, bias, etc.

The act and scene divisions used here are those of Craig[2]; the abbreviations employed for titles of the plays are those suggested by the *Shakespeare Quarterly*.

ARCHERY[3]

This sport held first place during the reigns of Henry VII and Henry VIII, reaching its zenith under the latter, who was himself a fine archer and who expected his subjects also to become proficient with the bow. To this end, every male below the age of sixty was compelled to shoot with it, and fathers were required by law to instruct their sons in its use as soon as the latter reached the age of seven. Both Henry VII and Henry VIII favored the longbow over the crossbow, restricting the use of the latter by limiting the use of it to those holding property valued at three hundred marks, and by imposing a fine of ten pounds for each shot unlawfully fired.

By the end of the Elizabeth's reign archery had declined into a mere healthful pastime, practised only by those who enjoyed it. However, this decline was not owing to any lack of interest or encouragement on the part of Elizabeth, who was herself a skilled and enthusiastic bowman and who at one time organized a corps of archers from among the ladies of

---

[2] Hardin Craig (ed.), *The Complete Works of Shakespeare* (New York, 1951).

[3] Although it may well have been the Saxons who first developed archery in England, since it is from their words *boga* and *arewa* that our "bow" and "arrow" are derived and since, too, we have in the Bayeux Tapestry what appears to be added confirmation, it was probably not until Norman times that archery became a really important factor in the national defence.

the court. It was simply that the musket had arrived and the bow was no longer a national asset.[4]

The sport is alluded to in *Lear* I.i.145 ("The bow is bent and drawn, make from the shaft"), 160–161 ("See better, Lear, and let me still remain The true blank of thine eye"); *Much* I.i.42 (". . . and challenged him at the bird-bolt"), 259 ("bottle," a basket of wicker to hold the cat used as a target in shooting matches); II.i.254 ("man at a mark")[5]; *Shrew* V.ii.186 ("Twas I won the wager, though you hit the white"); *L.L.L.* IV.i.135–136 ("Wide o' the bow hand! i' faith, your hand is out." "Indeed, a' must shoot nearer, or he'll ne'er hit the clout"); *3 H VI* I.i.29 ("butt"); *Oth.* III.iv.128 ("blank"); *Romeo* II.iv.16 ("pin"); *W.T.* II.iii.5 ("blank"); *2 H. IV* III.ii.48–53 (". . . a' drew a good bow, and dead! a' shot a fine shoot; John a Gaunt loved him well, and betted much money on his head. Dead! a' would have clapped i' the clout at twelve score; and carried you a forehand shaft a fourteen and fourteen and a half, that it would have done a man's heart good to see"); *Ham.* IV.iii.47 ("bent").

BEAR-BAITING[6]

This had been a popular sport in the Middle Ages[7], and retained its popularity well into the reign of Charles II. Under Henry VIII and Elizabeth, special bears were bred for it, and dogs could be commandeered by the Master of Bears. Not only bears but also donkeys, horses, and other animals were baited.[8]

Allusions to bear-baiting appear in the following plays: *Wives* I.i. 297–309 ("Why do your dogs bark so? be there bears i' the town? . . ."); *Twel.* II.v.8 (". . . you know he brought me out o' favour with my lady about a bear-baiting here"); *W. T.* IV.iii.109 (". . . he haunts wakes, fairs, and bear-baitings"); *3 H. VI* II.i.15–17 ("Or as a bear, encompass'd

---

[4] In view of the fact that the bow as a weapon was almost completely obsolete by the time of Charles I (1625–1649), it is somewhat surprising to find Benjamin Franklin, more than a hundred years later, seriously advocating the use of the bow by certain units of the Continental army. He pointed out, among other things, that the bow could be more easily replaced than a firearm, that the procuring of ammunition would be a comparatively simple matter, and that there would be no puff of smoke to reveal the archer's position.

[5] The reference here is to a man who stood near the target to check off the arrows of the contestants.

[6] This was one of the diversions with which Elizabeth entertained foreign diplomats and other distinguished visitors.

[7] L. F. Salzman, *English Life in the Middle Ages* (Oxford University Press, 1926), p. 83.

[8] Norman Wymer, *Sport in England: A History of Two Thousand Years of Games and Pastimes* (London, 1949), p. 77.

round with dogs, Who having pinched a few and made them cry, The rest stand all aloof, and bark at him"); *Caesar* IV.i.48–49 (". . . for we are at the stake, And bay'd about with many enemies"); *Macb.* V.vii.11–12 ("They have tied me to a stake; I cannot fly, But, bear-like, I must fight the course"); *Twel.* III.i.129–130 ("Have you not set mine honour at the stake, And baited it with all the unmuzzled thoughts That tyrannous heart can think?"); I.iii.96 ("I would I had bestowed that time in the tongues that I have in fencing, dancing, and bear-baiting"); *H. V.* III.vii. 152 ("Foolish curs, that run winking into the mouth of a Russian bear and have their heads crushed like rotten apples!"); *2 H. VI* V.i.144 ("Call hither to the stake my two brave bears, That with the very shaking of their chains They may astonish these fell-lurking curs: . . . Oft have I seen a hot o'erweening cur Run back and bite because he was withheld; Whom being suffer'd with the bear's fell paw, Hath clapp'd his tail between his legs and cried . . .").

BILLIARDS[9]

Billiards followed shovel-board as one of the most popular pastimes. It was played on oblong tables having three pockets on each side and being railed around the top with a ledge stuffed with cotton. At one end of the table was a small ivory arch called the "port" and at the other a peg known as the "king." The sticks used were tipped with ivory at one end, and only two balls were used in the game. The object was to drive the ball through the "port" and to touch the "king" without knocking it over. Fines were imposed for breaking either. A variant, known as "trucks," were played on a larger table having ten pockets on either side.[10]

The game is mentioned in *Antony* II.v.4 ("Let's to billiards"). Actually, however, it was not in existence at the time of this play.

BLINDMAN'S BUFF[11]

This very ancient game, still popular, is mentioned in *Ham.* III.iv. 76–77 ("What devil was't that thus hath cozen'd you at hoodman-blind?") and *All's W.* IV.iii.138 ("Hoodman comes!").

---

[9] Since the player of billiards needed steady nerves, the billiardroom was perhaps the only place where the conduct of onlookers (who were merely tolerated, not welcomed) was strictly governed. No "kibitzing" was permitted, and the unlucky bystander who forgot himself and ventured to speak without having been asked for his opinion was requested to leave the room or, if allowed to remain, could do so only on condition of "instantly forfeiting two pence for the good of the company."

[10] Wymer, p. 99.

[11] Other literary works in which this game is mentioned include Massinger, *The*

BOWLING[12]

Bowling, like archery, was under Henry VIII subject to restrictive laws. The first excuse advanced for these was that it interfered with the practice of archery. In 1511 the King termed it "a harmful pastime," and some twenty-five years later, when he himself was a keen exponent of the game, spoke against it even more strongly and took measures to suppress it among the common people. These restrictive laws were not repealed until the time of Victoria, but were overlooked by Elizabeth, in whose reign bowling was a common sport in the innyards.

In the early form of the game, two players, each with a ball, would stand a certain distance apart. After they had placed cones on the ground by their feet, they would take turns rolling a ball along the ground in an attempt to knock over the opponent's cone. Later, the two cones were replaced by a single ball, the "jack," at which the players aimed alternately.[13]

Allusions to the game occur in the following plays: *Cym.* II.i.1 (". . . when I kissed the jack, upon an up-cast to be hit away!"); *L.L.L.* IV.i.139–141 ("She's too hard for you at pricks, sir; challenge her to

Guardian (III.vi); Middleton, *A Mad World, My Masters* (III.iii); Porter, *Two Angry Women of Abington;* Heywood, *The Wise Woman of Hogsden;* Rowland, "Letting of Humors Blood"; *2 The Return from Parnassus,* Prologue, line 40. For descriptions of early forms of the game, see Alice B. Gomme, *The Traditional Games of England, Scotland, and Ireland* (London, 1894–1898), I, 137; Joseph Strutt, *The Sports and Pastimes of the People of England* (2nd ed., London, 1831), p. 392; G. F. Northall, *English Folk-Rhymes* (London, 1892), p. 402.

[12] Allusions to bowling appear in Dekker, *The Honest Whore, II* (V.ii); Middleton, *No Wit, No Help Like a Woman's* (II.iii); Chapman, *All Fooles* (III.i); Massinger, *The City Madam* (I.ii); Beaumont and Fletcher, *The Scornful Lady* (I.i); Webster, *The Weakest Goeth to the Wall* (III.i; IV.iii); Farquhar, *The Beaux' Stratagem* (I.i.168); Field, *A Woman Is a Weathercock* (III.ii); Porter, *The Two Angry Women of Abington;* Chamberlayne, *Angliae Notitia;* Wilson, *The Three Ladies of London;* Webster, *The White Devil* (I.ii); Rollins, *Pepys Ballads,* I, 192 ("A Mad Crew"); Congreve, *The Old Bachelor* (I.i) and *The Double-Dealer* (II.i); and the anonymous *Look About You* (xiii). Strutt (1838 ed.), p. 270, cites *Country Contentments* (". . . your flat bowles being best for allies, your round bayzed bowles for open grounds of advantage, and your round bowles, like a ball, for green swarthes that are plain and level") and on p. 273 *The Merry Milkmaid of Islington* ("I'll cleave you from the skull to the twist, and make nine skittles of thy bones"). In Dekker's *The Bellman of London* (1608) a character is described as one "whose inn is a bowling-alley, whose books are bowls, and whose law-cases are lurches and rubbers."

For descriptions and pictures of twelfth and thirteenth century bowling, see Strutt (1838 ed.), pp. 266–274. Five of these drawings are reproduced in Carl-Herman Tillhagen, "Till kägelspelete historia i Sverige," *Saga och Sed* (1949), pp. 19–20, a study which treats of English, as well as Swedish, forms of the game.

[13] Wymer, pp. 38, 68–69.

bowls." "I fear too much rubbing"); V.ii.587 ("He is a marvellous good neighbour, faith, and a very good bowler"); *Lear* II.ii.160–161 ("Whose disposition, all the world knows, Will not be rubb'd nor stopp'd"); *R. II* III.iv.3–5 ("Madam, we'll play at bowls." "Twill make me think the world is full of rubs, And that my fortune runs against the bias."); *Ham.* III.i.65 ("Ay, there's the rub"): *Shrew* IV.v.24 (". . . thus the bowl should run, And not unluckily against the bias"); *Troi.* III.ii.52 ("So, so; rub on, and kiss the mistress"); *Cor.* V.ii.19 (". . . nay, sometimes, Like to a bowl upon a subtle ground, I have stumbled past the throw"); *H. V.* II.ii.188 ("We doubt not now But every rub is smoothed on our way").

CHERRY-PIT[14]

This is a children's game in which the players pitch cherry stones (seeds, pebbles, etc.) at a small hole in the ground.[15]

It is mentioned in only one of the plays, *Twel.* III.iv.129 ("What man! 'tis not for gravity to play at cherry-pit with Satan").

CHESS[16]

Invented in northwest India, probably about A.D. 570, chess spread to France by 1070 and was being played in England before 1100.[17]

---

[14] Cherry-pit is mentioned also in Ford, *The Lover's Melancholy* (III.i); Dekker, *The Witch of Edmonton;* Herrick, *Hesperides.* Perhaps the earliest allusion to it occurs in the anonymous interlude *The World and the Child* (1522).

[15] Gomme, I, 66.

[16] In the Middle Ages, chess seems to have been the favorite pastime, at least among the upper classes, with tables perhaps occupying the second place in popularity. Mention of it is found in the *Cursor Mundi* ("I ha ne liked . . . til idel games, chess, and tables"), in the Auchinleck MS. of *Guy of Warwick* (line 3175 f.: "Into þe chaumber go we baye, / Among þe maidens for the playe; / At tables to playe & at ches"), in verse 1277 of *Sir Tristram* ("His harp, his croude was rike, / His tables, his chess he bare"), in Robert Manning's *Handlyng Synne* ("Take furþe the chesse or þe tables"), in Chaucer's *Death of Blanche* (line 51: "For me thoughte it better play / Than playe at chesse or tables") and the *Franklin's Tale* ("They dauncen and they playen / At ches and tables"), and in many other writings of the time.

In Tudor days, Elyot included a knowledge of chess among the essentials for a liberal education, expressing his views on the subject in his *Instruction of a Gentleman* ("The games of Chests and Tennisplay, because thone is an ancient pastime, and proffyteth the wyt, the other good for ye exercise of the body, measurably taken are mete to be used").

References to chess appear frequently in Elizabethan and Stuart drama and also in the polemical writings of the time, e.g. *Pap with a Hatchet,* published in 1589 in the course of the Marprelate controversy ("If a Martin can play at Chestes as well

Mention of it occurs in *Temp.* V.i.172 (Stage direction: Here Prospero discovers Ferdinand and Miranda, playing at chess) and *A.Y.L.* V.iv.85 ("counter-check," a metaphor from the game).

COCK-FIGHTING[18]

Henry VIII had his private cock-pit at his palace at Whitehall, and so generally loved was the sport that contests were held even on board ship. Its popularity was even greater in the Restoration and after.[19]

The sport is alluded to in *Antony* II.iii.35 ("His cocks do win the battle still of mine . . .").

DICE[20]

Dicing was widely prevalent in Elizabeth's time, as it has been in every period, and the allusions to it in the literature are many. However,

as the nephewe his Ape, he shall knowe what it is for a Scaddle pawne, to crosse a Bishop in his owne walke. Such dydoppers must be taken up, els theile not stick to check the King"). Probably the most interesting dramatic production associated with the game is Thomas Middleton's *A Game at Chess,* performed at the Globe just eight years after Shakespeare's death and printed a short time later. Written at a time when negotiations were being carried on for Prince Charles's Spanish marriage, the play satirized the Church of Rome and the Spanish ambassador, Gondemar, so bitterly that, at Gondemar's protest, the authorities withdrew it after the ninth performance. The players were ordered to appear before the Privy Council, and, according to one account, Middleton was imprisoned for a time.

[17] H. J. R. Murray, *A History of Board-Games Other than Chess* (Oxford, 1952), p. 84. See also the same author's *A History of Chess* (Oxford, 1913).

[18] Although popular in the Tudor Age, cock-fighting was not to reach its peak until the Restoration. Besides that of Henry VIII, we find only two other enclosed cock-pits mentioned. However, open-air contests were being held in the country and in the inn-yards. The name of London's Cockspur Street bears witness to the influence of the sport.

[19] Wymer, p. 76.

[20] Allusions to dicing are to be found in Jonson's *Bartholomew Fair* (I.i); Shirley's *The Lady of Pleasure* (V.i); and *The Famous Victories of Henry the Fifth.* Dice were used also to determine the moving of counters in such board-games as the sixteenth century Doublets and Catch-dolt and the later Snake; see Strutt (1838 ed.), p. 437.

References abound in the earlier literature: Caxton's *Reynard the Fox* ("A pylgrym of deux aas"); Brant's translation of the *Narrenschiff* ("Thoughe sys or synke them fayle / The dyse oft renneth upon the chaunce of thre"); *The History of Beryn* ("I bare thre dise in myne own purs; / . . . cast them forth all three, / And too fil amys ase"); Chaucer's *Monke's Tale* ("Empoysened of thin ouyne folk thou were; / Thyn sis fortune hath turned into aas") and *Pardoner's Tale* ("Seuene is my chaunce and thyn is cynk and treye"); *The Harrowing of Hell* ("Still be thou, Sathanas! / The ys fallen ambes aas"); etc.

it appears not to have reached its peak until the eighteenth century, when, as Trevelyan writes, "Society . . . was one vast casino. On whatever pretext, and under whatsoever circumstances, half a dozen people of fashion found themselves together . . . the box was sure to be rattling, and the cards were being cut and shuffled."[21]

Allusions appear in *All's W.* II.iii.85 ("I had rather be in this choice than throw ames-ace for my life"); *Wives* I.iii.94 ("fullam," a kind of false dice loaded at the corner); *1 H. IV* IV.i.45–48 (". . . were it good To set the exact wealth of all our states All at one cast? to set so rich a main On the nice hazard of one doubtful hour?"); *Merch.* II.i.32 ("If Hercules and Lichas play at dice . . ."); *W. T.* I.ii.132 (". . . false As dice are to be wished by one that fixes no bourn 'twixt his and mine"); IV.iii.27 ("die"); *Antony* II.iii.35 (". . . the very dice obey him"); *H. V* IV.v.8 ("Be these the wretches that we play'd at dice for?"); IV, prologue, 19 ("Proud of their numbers and secure in soul, The confident and overlusty French Do the low-rated English play at dice"); *Othello* IV.ii.132 ("cogging," cheating with loaded dice); *R. III* V.iv.10 ("Slave, I have set my life upon a cast, And I will stand the hazard of the die"); *L.L.L.* L.ii.48 ("You know how much the grosse summe of deuce-ace amounts to . . . which the base vulgar call three"); .ii. 232 (". . . well run, dice!"); *Cym.* II.iii.2 ("Your lordship is the most patient man in losse, the most coldest that ever turn'd up ace").

DUN'S IN THE MIRE[22]

This is not so much a game as what Strutt calls it, "a mere Christmas gambol with a great log of wood."[23]

Mention of it occurs in only one of the plays, *Romeo* I.iv.41 ("If thou art dun, we'll draw thee from the mire").

FALCONRY[24]

That hawking was one of the favorite Elizabethan sports is amply attested by the frequent references to it in the literature of the period.

---

[21] G. O. Trevelyan, *Early History of Charles James Fox* (New York, 1880), p. 77.

[22] For other allusions to this sport, see Beaumont and Fletcher, *Woman Hater* (IV.iii); Dekker and Webster, *Westward Ho* (II.iii); Gifford's edition of the works of Jonson (VII, 283); Shirley, *St. Patrick for Ireland;* Brand, *Dutchesse of Suffolke;* Chaucer's prologue to the *Manciple's Tale;* Rowland, "Letting of Humors Blood" and "Humors Ordinaire."

[23] *Sports* (1903 ed.), p. 313.

[24] This sport is alluded to also in Chapman, *The Gentleman Usher* (I.i.64); Jonson, *Every Man in His Humour* (I.i); Beaumont and Fletcher, *Philaster* (V.iv); Fletcher, *The Wild Goose Chase* (III.i); Dekker, *The Honest Whore, II* (V.ii); Heywood, *A Woman Killed With Kindness* (I.iii).

Among those in the Shakespeare plays are the following: *Ham.* I.v.115 ("Hillo, ho, ho, boy! Come, bird, come"); II.ii.449 ("We'll e'en to't like French falconers, fly at anything we see"); *Twel.* II.v.124 ("staniel," an inferior kind of hawk); 125 ("checks," leaves quarry for another bird); III.i.71–72 ("And, like the haggard, check at every feather that comes before his eye"); *Temp.* IV.i.206 (". . . shall hoodwink this mischance"); *Romeo* I.iv.21 ("pitch"); III.ii.14 ("hood" . . . "unmann'd"); *Caesar* I.ii.78 ("pitch"); *2 H. VI* II.i.1–12 (". . . for flying at the brook, I saw not better sport these seven years' day; Yet, by your leave, the wind was very high; And, ten to one, old Joan had not gone out . . . "But what a point, my lord, your falcon made, And what a pitch she flew above the rest! . . ."); *H. V* III.vii.121 ("hooded valour"); IV.i.111–112 (". . . and though his affections are higher mounted than ours, yet, when they stoop, they stoop with the like wing"); *Shrew*, Induction, ii.45–46 ("Dost thou love hawking? thou hast hawks will soar Above the morning lark . . ."); *Othello* III.iii.210 ("seel," sewing eyelids of hawk together), 260 ("haggard," an inferior hawk), 261 ("jesses," straps for fastening legs of trained hawk); *Antony* III.xii.112 ("seel"); *1 H. VI* II.iii.55 ("pitch"); *2 H. VI* II.i.5 ("point"); *Romeo* III.ii.14 ("hood") *3 H. VI* I.i.47 ("shake his bells"); *Tit.* I.1.14 ("pitch").

FAST AND LOOSE[25]

This is a gambling game, sometimes known also as Pricking at the Belt (or Girdle). A leather belt was folded intricately so that one fold appeared to be in the middle. A player thrusting a knife or a skewer into this fold would think that he had made the belt fast to the table. Wagers were made as to whether the belt would be fast or loose, hence the name.

The game is mentioned in *L.L.L.* III.i.104 ("To sell a bargain well is as cunning as fast and loose"); *Antony* IV. xii.27–28 (". . . like a right gipsy, hath at fast and loose, Beguiled me to the very heart of loss").

FENCING[26]

There are allusions to this sport in *2 H. IV* III.ii.70 ("backsword mann"); *Romeo* II.iv.20–27 ("He fights as you sing prick-song, keeps

[25] The game is mentioned in Whetstone, *Promos and Cassandra* (II.i); Fletcher, *The Wild Goose Chase* (III.i.72); and Jonson, *The Gipsies Metamorphosed* (part 1, line 120). The trick is explained in Reginald Scot, *Discoverie of Witchcraft* (Ch. 29, p. 336).

An Iranian student of mine informs me that this trick is still being played in the less-frequented streets and courts of Teheran.

[26] See also Jonson, *Every Man in His Humour* (I.v; IV.vii.iv). It appears likely

time, distance, and proportion; rests me his minim rest, one, two, and the third in your bosom: the very butcher of a silk button, a duellist, a duellist; a gentleman of the very first house, of the first and second cause: ah, the immortal passado! the punto reverso! the hai!"); *Ham.* IV.vii.96–103; V.ii.264; *L.L.L.* V.i.62 ("venue," a thrust).

FOOTBALL[27]

As early as the Middle Ages, football had been banned by Edward II and other medieval kings because of the danger to life and limb, and both Henry VIII and Elizabeth did all they could to stamp it out completely, but with only partial success. Sir Thomas Elyot (1531) saw in it "nothing but beastly fury and extreme violence whereof proceedeth hurte," and Stubbe, writing several decades later, speaks of broken backs and necks, of a player's hitting another over the heart with his elbow with the deliberate intention of killing or maiming him.[28] Nevertheless the game continued to be popular (even among women), and rules for playing were eventually drawn up so that the hazards were lessened.

Football is mentioned in two of the plays: *Lear* I.iv.94 (". . . you base foot-ball player") and *Errors* I.ii.83–84 ("Am I so round with you as you with me, That like a football you do spurn me thus?").

HANDY DANDY[29]

This is a very simple guessing-game played by children. One player takes a small object in one hand, closes both, and then, holding them out toward another child, challenges him to guess which of the hands contains the object. If the guess is correct, the two exchange roles; if not, the game continues as before.

The sole allusion appears in *Lear* IV.i.155 ("Hark, in thine ear; change places; and, handy-dandy, which is the justice, which is the thief?").

that Shakespeare knew and drew material from *Vicentio Saviolo his Practice* (1595), written by the famous Italian master of fence. Relations between English professionals and Italian fencing instructors resident in London were, in general, not very cordial; see Wymer, pp. 67–68.

[27] Football is mentioned also in Webster, *The White Devil* (IV.i.135); Massinger, *A New Way to Pay Old Debts* (V.i); and Rowley, *All's Lost by Lust* (III.i.147).

[28] See Wymer, pp. 39, 73.

[29] Mention of this game occurs in *Piers Plowman* (ed. Wright), p. 69; Jonson, *Bartholomew Fair* (III.i); and Browne, *Britannia's Pastorals* (I.v).

HAZARD[30]

This is a gambling game, played with two dice. Any number of players could participate.[31]

There is an allusion to it in *H. V.* III.viii.93 ("Who will go to hazard with me for twenty prisoners").

HIDE AND SEEK[32]

References to this game appear in the following plays: *Ham.* IV.ii.32 ("Hide fox, and all after") and *L.L.L.* IV.iii.78 ("All hid, all hid; an old infant play").

HUNTING

Both Henry VIII and Elizabeth were ardent huntsmen, the former sometimes wearing out as many as ten horses in the course of a day and the latter being noted for her skill in bringing down driven deer with a bow. Both monarchs indulged also in the hunting of otter. Although the hunting of fallow and red deer was the prerogative of royalty and the nobility, those of the lower class were free to hunt the hare and other small animals.[33]

Some critics have cited Shakespeare's vivid descriptions of hunting scenes, and more particularly, his giving of names to the dogs (Echo, Silver, etc.) as evidence of his keen personal interest in the sport.

Allusions are to be found in *A.Y.L.* IV.ii.1; V.iv.111 ("He uses his folly like a stalking-horse and under the presentation of that he shoots his wit"); *Merch.* I.ii.22 (". . . such a hare is madness the youth, to skip o'er the meshes of good counsel the cripple"); *3 H. VI* II.v.129 ("Edward and Richard, like a brace of greyhounds Having the fearful flying hare in sight . . . Are at our backs . . ."); *Dream* IV.i.110; *Tit.* II.iii.25 ("The hunt is up . . ." "I have dogs, my lord, will rouse the proudest panther in the chase, And climb the highest promontory top." "And I have horse will follow where the game Makes way, and run like swallows o'er the plain"); *Temp.* I.ii.81 (". . . trash for over-topping," checking a hound by

---

[30] There are allusions to hazard in Chapman, *Eastward Hoe* (V.i); Dekker, *The Gull's Hornbook* (ed. McKerrow), p. 55; and Webster, *The White Devil* (I.ii).

[31] Hazard was also a technical term in tennis; see Robert Tailor, *The Hog Hath Lost His Pearl* (Dodsley's *Old Plays*, ed Collier), VI, 334.

[32] Hide and Seek (All Hid) is mentioned in Tourneur, *The Revenger's Tragedy* (III.v); Porter, *The Two Angry Women of Abington;* and Dekker, *Satiromastix.*

[33] Wymer, pp. 60–61.

hanging a weight to his neck to prevent his running too far ahead of the rest of the pack); *Much* II.iii.95 (". . . stalk on, stalk on; the fowl sits"); *2 H. IV* I.ii 103 ("You hunt counter . . ."); *Ham.* IV.i.110 ("counter"); *Errors* IV.ii.39 ("runs counter"); *Shrew*, Induction, i.14 ("Huntsman, I charge thee, tender well my hounds: Brach Merriman, the poor cur is emboss'd; and couple Clowder with the deep-mouth'd brach. Saw'st thou not, boy, how Silver made it good At the hedge-corner, in the coldest fault? I would not lose the dog for twenty pound." "Why, Belman is as good as he, my lord; He cried upon it at the merest loss And twice to-day pick'd out the dullest scent; Trust me, I take him for the better dog." "Thou art a fool; if Echo were as fleet, I would esteem him worth a dozen such. But sup them well and look unto them all: To-morrow I intend to hunt again").

LEAPFROG[34]

This old and widespread game is mentioned in only one of the plays, *H. V.* V.ii.140 ("If I could win a lady at leap-frog . . .").

LOGGATS[35]

Loggats, sometimes known also as Kayles (from the French *quilles*), was played much like Ninepins. A number of pins were set up and the player threw a cudgel to knock them down.[36] The game was prohibited by Henry VIII.

This only allusion to it occurs in *Ham.* V.i.100 ("Did these bones cost no more the breeding, but to play at loggats with them?").

MORE SACKS TO THE MILL

This was more of a scramble than a game. A group of boys threw an unfortunate comrade on the ground, piled on top of him, and called out, "Bags to the mill!"[37]

There is a mention of it in *L.L.L.* IV.iii.81.

---

[34] Allusions to this game appear in Jonson, *Bartholomew Fair;* Dekker, *The Honest Whore,* II (V.ii); Rollins, *Pepys Ballads,* II, 122 ("A New Merry Ballad I Have Here"); and Rowland, "Letting of Humors Blood."

[35] Loggats is mentioned in Jonson, *A Tale of a Tub* (IV.v) and Rowland, "Letting of Humors Blood."

[36] Strutt (1838 ed.), pp. 266–274.

[37] Gomme, I, 390.

MORRIS

Allusions to the Morris occur in *All's W.* II.ii.25 ("a morris for May-day"); *H. V* II.iv.24–25 (". . . a Whitsun morris-dance"); *2 H. VI* III.i.365 ("I have seen Him caper upright like a wild Morisco, Shaking the bloody darts as he his bells"); and Fletcher and Shakespeare's *The Two Noble Kinsmen* V.ii.51 ("He'll dance the Morris twenty miles an hour").

MUSS[38]

This appears to have been merely a scramble among boys for some object thrown upon the ground. The single allusion to it is in *Antony* III. xiii.91 ("Like boys unto a muss . . .").

NINE MEN'S MORRIS

This game was played either on the ground or on a board or table. A playing board was about eight inches square, with twenty-four holes in it. Each player was provided with nine wooden pegs (of different shapes or colors), and the object was to get three pegs in a straight line. In early times this was a favorite game with shepherds, who played it on the ground with stones. The name is from the French *merelles* or *mereaux*, which was later corrupted to *morrals* and then to *morris*. The prints reproduced in Strutt indicate that the English game is at least as old as the fourteenth century.[39]

Perhaps the earliest Nine Men's Morris or Nine Holes diagrams known are those incised on roofing slabs of the temple at Kurna in Thebes. The erection of this temple was begun in the reign of Rameses I (1400–1366 B. C.) and completed in that of Seti (1366–1333 B. C.)[40] A form of the game was carried into Spain by the Moors, and thence it has spread over practically the whole world. There were also Three Men's Morris, Five (or Six) Men's Morris, Eleven Men's Morris, and Twelve Men's Morris. A related game is Noughts and Crosses, now played principally by children.

Only one allusion to the game appears in the plays, that in *Dream* II.i.98 ("The nine men's morris is filled up with mud").

[38] The game is mentioned also in Jonson, *Magnetic Lady* (IV.iii); Middleton, *A Mad World, My Masters* (III.iii).

[39] See p. 317.

[40] Murray, *A History of Board-Games*, p. 18.

NODDY[41]

This was a card game somewhat similar to cribbage. It appears to have been most popular with the lower classes.

Mention of it occurs only in *Troi.* I.ii.212 ("Will he give you the nod?").

NOVUM

Novum was a game of dice, played by five or six persons. The correct name is *Novem quinque,* since the two principal throws were nine and five.

It is alluded to in *L.L.L.* V.ii.546 ("Abate throw at novum").

ONE AND THIRTY[42]

This was a game of dice somewhat resembling the French *vingt-et-un.* The only reference to it is in *Shrew* I.ii.32 (". . . two and thirty, a pip out").

PRIMERO[43]

Primero was another card game, very popular in the time of Elizabeth.

There are many allusions to it: *Wives* IV.v.101 ("I never prospered since I forswore myself at primero"); *H. VIII* V.i.7 ("I . . . left him at primero with the Duke of Suffolk"). The expression "to set up one's rest" (i.e. to stake all), which derives from this game, appears frequently: *Lear* I.i.126 ("I loved her most, and thought to set my rest On her kind nursery"); *H. V* II.i.18 ("That is my rest"); *Dream* IV.iii.27 (". . . he that

---

[41] For other allusions to this game, see Heywood, *A Woman Killed With Kindness* (III.ii); Shirley, *Hyde Park* (IV.iii); Middleton, *Blurt, Master Constable* (III.ii); *Poor Robin's Almanac* for 1715; Rowland, "Letting of Humors Blood;" Rollins, *Pepys Ballads,* II, 98 ("The Beggar's Intrusion"); Dekker and Webster, *Westward Ho* (IV.i); *2 The Return from Parnassus,* Prologue, line 22.

[42] There is a reference to this game in Shirley's *Love's Cruelty* (I.ii).

[43] This was apparently one of the most popular card games of the time. It is mentioned in Jonson, *Volpone* (III.v.37–39; III.vii); *The Alchemist* (I.ii; II.iv; V.iv); *Every Man Out of His Humour* (I.i); and *Cynthia's Revels* (III.i); Gascoigne, *Supposes* (III.ii); Chapman, *Eastward Hoe* (IV.i); Field, *A Woman Is a Weathercock* (III.ii); Middleton, *Your Five Gallants* (I.i); Beaumont and Fletcher, *Monsieur Thomas* (IV.ix); Ford, *'Tis Pity She's a Whore* (V.iv); Middleton, *Spanish Gypsy* (IV.ii); Dekker, *The Gull's Hornbook* (ed. McKerrow), pp. 55, 79; *2 The Return from Parnassus,* Prologue, lines 15, 23.

sets up his rest . . ."); *Merch.* II.ii.110 ("I have set up my rest to run away"); *Romeo* IV.V.6 ("The County Paris hath set up his rest . . ."); *All's W.* II.i.138 ("Since you set up your rest 'gainst remedy . . .").

PRISON BASE[44]

It is not always possible to know to what kind of Base an allusion refers. In the true Prison Base the members of one group try to make prisoners of those of the other, and keep them in a special place. They can be released by their comrades if the latter are able to approach near enough to touch them. It is probable that some of the passages mentioning the game refer to other forms of it, of which there are several.

The game is mentioned in the following plays: *T.G.V.* I.ii.97 ("Indeed, I bid the base for Proteus"); *Cym.* V.iii.20 (". . . lads more like to run the country base than to commit such slaughter"); and in *Venus* 1. 303 ("bid the wind a base").

PROVERB-CAPPING[45]

This, one of the few intellectual amusements of the time, is somewhat reminiscent of the flyting of an earlier period and of the riddle-contests and wit-combats which were so popular a little later. The object here is to outlast an opponent in quoting proverbs having some bearing on the topic which elicited the first.

Perhaps the best example in Shakespeare is that in *H. V* III.vii. 123–132.

[44] Base is mentioned also in Marlowe, *Edward the Second* (IV.iii); Jonson, *The Sad Shepherd* (I.ii); Spenser, *Faerie Queene* (Canto V, 8); Drayton, *Polyolbion* (30th song); Chettle, *Hoffman;* Brome, *Antipodes;* and Rowland, "Letting of Humors Blood."

[45] It is interesting to note that Indian children in Bombay and vicinity play a game somewhat resembling this. Rather, it is a combination of proverb-capping and "spelling by the last letter." One child recites a *sloka* (proverb), and the next must then recite another beginning with the last letter of the first. If he is unable to do so, his opponent wins a point. See my "A Collection of Games from India . . . ," *Zeitschrift für Ethnologie,* LXXX, 1 (1955), 99.

This sort of thing is still a living tradition in the Buru ceremonial antiphony known as *Inga fuka,* currently being studied by Professor de Josselin de Jong, of the University of Leyden. Somewhat similar are the poetical contests between Annamite young men and girls; see Nguyen van Huyen, *Les chants alternés des garçons et des filles en Annam* (Paris, 1933).

PUSHPIN[46]

In this game, known also as Blowpoint, the player tries to push (or to blow) his pin so that it will lie across that of his opponent.

The only mention of it occurs in *L.L.L.* IV.iii.169 ("And Nestor play at pushpin with the boys").

QUAIL-FIGHTING

Although never as popular as Cock-fighting, this sport was occasionally indulged in by the nobility. The birds were enclosed in hoops to make them fight.

The only allusion to this pastime is that on *Antony* II.iii.36 (". . . and his quails ever Beat mine, inhoop'd, at odds").

QUINTAIN[47]

The original quintain seems to have been merely the trunk of a tree; later it consisted of a wooden image (usually of a Turk or a Saracen) mounted on a pivot. If the contestant failed to strike it on the nose or in the center of the forehead, it swung around and hit him with a wooden sword or a club. The game was practised both on foot and on horseback. Another form was that in which a mast bearing a shield was set up in the river bed, and the contestant, in a boat carried toward it by the tide, attempted to strike the shield. A failure resulted in his falling from the boat into the river, whence he would be pulled out by watchers stationed nearby for the purpose.[48]

The sport is mentioned in two plays: *A.Y.L.* I.ii.261–263 ("My better parts Are all thrown down, and that which here stands up Is but a quintain, a mere lifeless block") and *Shrew* I.i.145 ("He that runs fastest gets the ring").[49]

---

[46] Pushpin is mentioned in Nash, *Apologie* (1593); Middleton and Rowley, *The Changeling* (I.ii.208); and 2 *The Return from Parnassus* (III.i.39), where it is called "blow-point."

[47] See also Shirley, *The Grateful Servant* (V.i); Field, *A Woman Is a Weathercock* (I.ii); Middleton, *The Family of Love* (V.iii); Webster, *The Duchess of Malfi* (I.ii); Massinger, *A New Way to Pay Old Debts* (IV.iii.95); Marston, *The Malcontent* (I.iii.79); Dekker and Webster, *Northward Ho* (I.iii); *Shirburn Ballads* (ed. Clark), p. 364 ("The Mery Life of the Countriman"); Child, *The English and Scottish Popular Ballads*, 181A ("The Bonny Earl of Murray").

[48] Wymer, pp. 50–51.

[49] This was a later development, in which the mounted contestant tried to thrust

QUOITS[50]

One of the speeches of Falstaff contains an allusion to this game: *2 H. IV.* II.iv.266 (". . . a' plays at quoits well . . ."). The word *quoit* appears also in line 206 but as a verb ("Quoit him down, Bardolph, like a shove-groat shilling").

SHOEING THE WILD MARE[51]

According to Hazlitt's edition of *Brand's Popular Antiquities* (II, 544), "Shoeing the Wild Mare . . . was a diversion among our ancestors, more particularly intended for the young, and that the Wild Mare was simply a youth so called, who was allowed a certain start, and who was pursued by his companions with the object of being shoed [*sic*], if he did not succeed in outstripping them."[52] The Gaelic game of the same title, *Crudhadh an Capuill Bhain,* was played quite differently:

A beam is suspended from the roof by two ropes of about equal length, and high enough from the ground to prevent anyone astride of it touching the floor with his feet. The feat consists in keeping your seat on this white mare without touching the ropes. When it is called "shoeing the mare," the rider is supposed to be the smith, and has a piece of wood in his hand to drive in the nails of the shoes, striking the lower part of the beam four times eight blows. He who could complete the shoeing of the horse without being thrown off was of course a master of smithcraft.[53]

The term Wild Mare is sometimes applied also to the game of Seesaw.[54]

This game is mentioned only once in Shakespeare, in *2 H. IV* II.iv.268 (". . . and rides the wild-mare with the boys . . .").

his lance through a suspended ring. The sport is mentioned in Massinger, *A New Way to Pay Old Debts* (IV.iii).

[50] References to this game are to be found in Massinger, *The Guardian* (I.i); Webster, *The Duchess of Malfi* (II.v); and Ascham's *Toxophilus.*

[51] Shoeing the Wild Mare is mentioned in Beaumont and Fletcher, *The Knight of the Burning Pestle* (I.iv); Jonson, *Love Restored;* Nicholas Breton, *Fantasticks* (1626); and George Wither's "A Christmas Carol."

[52] William Carew Hazlitt (ed), *Brand's Popular Antiquities of Great Britain: Faiths and Folklore, a Dictionary of National Beliefs, Superstitions and Popular Customs,* 2 v. (London, 1905).

[53] Robert Craig Maclagan, *The Games and Diversions of Argyleshire* (London, 1901), p. 197.

[54] Craig so identifies the allusion in *2 H. IV* II.iv.268.

SHOVE-GROAT[55]

In this game a shilling was balanced on the edge of a table and then struck with the palm of the hand into one of the numbered squares into which the top of the table was divided.

Mention of it occurs in a line of *2 H. IV* II.iv.206 ("Quoit him down, Bardolph, like a shove-groat shilling").

SHOVELBOARD[56]

The game of Shovelboard was played on a table about three feet wide and some thirty feet long. The players, usually two, stood at one end. At the opposite end a line was drawn parallel to the edge and three or four inches from it, and another line about four feet back of the first. The counter, a flat metal plate, was *shoved* by the players. If a piece fell off the edge, it did not count, nor did a push count unless the piece passed the first line. If it balanced on the edge of the table, it counted three points; if it stopped between the farther line and the edge, it counted two; if between the two lines, it counted one. Play was for eleven points. This was one of the favorite games of Henry VIII.

The sole allusion to the game in Shakespeare occurs in *Wives* I.i.159 (". . . two Edward shovel-boards").[57]

SNAPDRAGON

This game, played usually during the Christmas season, consisted in "snapping" with the mouth the raisins or plums in a bowl of burning brandy.

There are the following allusions to it: *L.L.L.* V.i.45 (". . . thou art easier swallowed than a flap-dragon"); *W.T.* III.iii.100 (". . . to see how the sea flap-dragoned it"); *2 H. IV* II.iv.268 (". . . and drinks off candles' ends for flap-dragons").

SPAN COUNTER[58]

This is a marble game, usually played by two. The first shoots a marble to any distance he desires. The second then shoots in an attempt

---

[55] This game is mentioned in Jonson, *Every Man in His Humour* (III.v); Middleton, *The Roaring Girl* (V.i); Rowland, "Letting of Humors Blood; "Pepys *Diary* (entry for June 11, 1664); and *Poor Robin's Almanac* for 1715.

[56] There is a reference in Chamberlayne, *Angliae Notitia* (1676).

[57] This term was applied to large shillings coined during the reign of Edward VI.

[58] There are references to the game in Beaumont and Fletcher, *Monsieur Thomas* (IV.ix); Dekker and Webster, *Northward Ho* (I.ii); and Donne (Satire IV).

to hit the first player's marble or to get close enough to it to span the distance between them. If he succeeds in doing so, he wins. If he fails, he must let his marble lie where it stopped, where it becomes a target for the first player. It is known also as Hit or Span, Boss and Span, and Boss Out.[59]

The only mention of the game in Shakespeare is in *2 H. VI* IV.ii.166 (". . . Henry the Fifth, in whose time the boys went to span-counter for French crowns").

TABLES[60]

This is a form of backgammon. Nares (quoting Douce) equates it with the game of Fayles.[61]

An allusion to it appears in *L.L.L.* V.ii.326 ("This is the ape of form, monsieur the nice, That, when he plays at tables, chides the dice In honourable terms").

TENNIS[62]

Tennis, a French importation, was popular in England even before the accession of Henry VII, and its popularity increased during his reign

[59] Gomme, II, 210.

[60] This game is mentioned in Gascoigne, *Supposes* (II.ii); Middleton, *Blurt, Master Constable* (V.ii); Kyd, *Arden of Faversham;* Rollins, *Pepys Ballads,* II. 67 ("Sure My Mother Was a Witch"); and *Poor Robin's Almanac* for 1715.

Contrary to popular opinion, the term *tables* is not the name of a particular game but a generic term applied to all board-games. However, the word does not derive from the table or board on which the game was played but from the pieces (*tabulae*) which were moved upon it. The number and the direction of these moves were determined by the throwing of dice by the players.

The earliest mentions of this game in literature appear to be those in the *Polycraticus* of John of Salisbury, completed sometime before 1159, and Layamon's *Brut* (*c.* 1205).

[61] Robert Nares, *A Glossary; or, Collection of Words, Phrases, Names, and Allusions to Customs, Proverbs, etc. . . . in the Works of English Authors* (London, 1859), p. 298.

[62] Allusions to this game are particularly numerous: Jonson, *The Silent Woman* (I.i); *The Staple of News* (IV.i); and *Cynthia's Revels* (I.i; II.i); Beaumont and Fletcher, *The Scornful Lady* (I.i) and *The Knight of the Burning Pestle* (I.ii.95); Chapman, *Eastward Ho* (II.i) and *All Fooles* (I.i.154); Ford, *The Fancies, Chaste and Noble* (V.i; V.iii) and *The Witch of Edmonton* (II.i); Middleton, *Blurt, Master Constable* (II.i) and *The Phoenix* (II.ii); Webster, *The White Devil* (II.i); Porter, *The Two Angry Women of Abington;* Chamberlayne, *Angliae Notitia;* the anonymous *Look About You* (scene 32); Dekker, *The Gull's Hornbook* (ed. McKerrow), pp. 36, 49, 51; Rollins, *Pepys Ballads,* I, 12 ("The Battle of Agincourt"); Drayton, "The

and that of Henry VIII, who built in 1529 one of the first covered courts. Balls were made by the Ironmongers Company and stuffed with hair; the net was simply a cord with tassels hanging from it. There were in Shakespeare's time no uniform rules, the people of each town or village playing the game as they wished.[63]

Allusions are numerous: *All's W.* II.iii.313 ("Why, these balls bound; there's noise in it"); *H. V* I.ii.261 ("When we have match'd our rackets to these balls, We will, in France, by God's grace, play a set Shall strike his father's crown into the hazard"); II.iv.131–132 (". . . I did present him with the Paris balls"); *Much* III.ii.45 (". . . the old ornament of his cheek hath already stuffed tennis-balls"); *L.L.L.* V.ii.29 ("Well bandied both; a set of wit well play'd"); *A.Y.L.* V.i.61 ("bandy with thee in faction"); *Lear* I.iv.92 ("bandy"); *H. VIII* I.iii.30 (". . . renouncing clean The faith they have in tennis . . ."); *John* V.ii.107 ("And shall I now give o'er the yielded set?"); *2 H. IV* II.ii.19 ("But that the tennis-court-keeper knows better than I; . . ."); *Ham.* II.i.59 ("There's falling out at tennis . . ."); *Per.* II.i.63 ("A man whom both the waters and the wind, In that vast tenniscourt, have made the ball For them to play upon, entreats you pity him").

TICK-TACK

This is a race-game, invented in France about 1500. Games are won by scoring points for the different possibilities of move given by the throws of two dice.[64]

Mention of it occurs in *Meas.* I.ii.196 (". . . foolishly lost at a game of tick-tack").

TOPS[65]

The playing of Tops is referred to in several of the plays: *Wives* V.i.26 ("Since I plucked geese, played truant and whipped top, I knew

Battle of Agincourt", Middleton, *A Trick to Catch the Old One* (IV.iv) and the same author's masque, *The World Tost at Tennis* (1620); Fletcher and Shakespeare, *The Two Noble Kinsmen* (V.i.55); and *The Famous Victories of Henry the Fifth*. There are references to it also in Dekker and Webster, *Northward Ho* (IV.iv) and Lee, *Princess of Cleve* (I.i.67).

[63] Wymer, p. 71.

[64] Murray, *A History of Board-Games*, p. 124.

[65] Other plays containing references to this sport are Jonson, *The New Inn* (III.ii); Beaumont and Fletcher, *The Scornful Lady* (I.i) and *The Night Walker* (I.i); Webster, *The Duchess of Malfi* (III.iv). There is an allusion to it also in Fulke Greville's "Coelica" (1633).

not what 'twas to be beaten till lately"); *Twel.* I.iii.43 (". . . he's a coward and a coystrill that will not drink to my niece till his brains turn o' the toe like a parish-top"); *Cor.* IV.v.161 ("as one would set up a top"); *L.L.L.* IV.iii.167 ("To see great Hercules whipping a gig"); V.i.69 ("go, whip thy gig").

TRAYTRIP[66]

This has been described both as a dice game and as a game resembling Hopscotch. It is more likely the former.[67]

The only allusion to it appears in *Twel.* II.v.208 ("Shall I play my freedom at tray-trip, and become they bond-slave?").

TROLL-MY-DAME[68]

The title of this game is a corruption of the French *Troule-in-madame.* It appears to have consisted in rolling small balls into holes at one end of the game-board.

The only reference to it is in *W. T.* IV.iii.92 ("A fellow, sir, that I have known to go about with troll-my-dames . . .").

WRESTLING

References to this sport are to be found in the following plays: *A.Y.L.* I.i; *Much* V.i.142 (". . . he knows how to turn his girdle")[69]; *Oth.* II.i.314 ("on the hip"); *Merch.* I.iii.47 ("If I can catch him once upon the hip, I will feed fat the ancient grudge I bear him").

[66] A mention of this game appears in Jonson, *The Alchemist* (V.iv).

[67] Gomme, II, 307.

[68] Allusions will be found also in Rowley, *New Wonder* (I.i); Chamberlayne, *Angliae Notitia;* and *Poor Robin's Almanac* for 1715, where it is called "drive knaves out of town."

[69] The probable explanation here is that one preparing to wrestle turned his girdle so as not to be inconvenienced by the dagger, which at this time was carried at the front. In earlier times it was worn at the back; see *Romeo* V.iii.203–205 ("This dagger hath mista'en, for, lo, his house is empty on the back of Montague, And is missheathed in my daughter's bosom!").

The History of Games

(This listing has been prepared to offer the reader an indication of the range of materials which are available, and does not attempt to offer an exhaustive listing of the materials which are available. The researcher who is investigating the history of a particular game is advised to consult the many bibliographies throughout this volume.)

PART I

Some General References in the English Language

Aspen, J. *Pictures of the Manners, Customs, Sports, and Pastimes of the Inhabitants of England to the Eighteenth Century,* London: J. Harris, 1825.

Bell, R. C. *Board and Table Games from Many Civilizations,* London: Oxford University Press, 1960.

Bett, H. *The Games of Children: Their Origin and History,* London: Methuen and Company, 1929.

Bland, E. A. *Fifty Years of Sports,* London: Daily Mail, 1946.

Bowdoin, W. G. "Playing Cards, Their History and Symbolism," *Art and Archaeology,* Washington, D.C., **11,** 1921, pp. 106–112.

Collins, F. D. *Popular Sports: Their Origin and Development,* Chicago: Rand McNally Co., 1935.

Combrie, J. W. "History of the Game of Hop Scotch," *Journal of the Royal Anthropological Institute,* **10,** 1886, pp. 403–408.

David, F. N. *Games, Gods, and Gambling: Origins and History of Probability and Statistical Ideas from the Earliest Times to the Newtonian Era,* New York: Hafner Publishing Co., 1962.

Deschner, R. B. *Evolution of Sports,* St. Louis: Fred Medart Co., 1946.

Durant, J. *Sports of Our Presidents,* New York: Hastings House, 1964.

Dulles, F. R. *History of Recreation,* New York: Appleton Century Crofts, 1965.

Espinosa, R. "Canute: A Game Handed Down From the Indians to Spanish Settlers in New Mexico Still Lives on in Native Homes," *New Mexico,* Santa Fe, **11** (5), 1933, pp. 16–17, 46–48.

Etherton, P. T. "Polo Through the Ages," *Asia,* New York, **31**, 1931, pp. 364–641, 664–666.

Eyler, M. H. "Origins of Contemporary Sports," *Research Quarterly,* Washington, D.C., **32** (4), December 1961, pp. 480–488.

Fiske, W. *Chess in Iceland: With Historical Notes on Other Table Games,* Florence, Italy: Florentine Typographical Society, 1905.

Gomme, A. B. *Traditional Games of England, Scotland, and Ireland,* 2 volumes, London: David Nutt, 1894 & 1898. Reprinted, New York: Dover Publications, Inc., 1964.

Hannemann, E. "Games and Modes of Entertainment in the Past Among the People of the Mandang District," *Mankind,* Sidney, **5**, 1959, pp. 333–344.

Hargrave, C. P. *A History of Playing Cards,* New York: Houghton Mifflin Co., 1930.

Harlan, H. V. *History of Olympic Games,* London: G.B. Foster, & Co., Ltd, 1931.

Hildebrand, J. "The Geography of Games: How the Sports of Nations Form a Gazetteer of the Habits and Histories of Their Peoples," *National Geographic Magazine, Washington, D.C.,* **36**, 1919, pp. 89–144.

Hole, C. *English Sports and Pastimes: With a Bibliography Covering the History of British Recreation,* London: Batsford, 1949.

Hyde, T. *De Ludis Orientalibus libri duo* (includes *De Historia Shahiludii* and *De Historia Nerdiludii*), Oxford, 1694.

Meadows, K. *Backgammon, Its History and Practice,* New York: Barry Vail Corp., 1931.

Monckton, O. P. *Pastimes in Times Past,* London: West Strand Publishing Co., 1913.

Morley, H. T. *Old and Curious Playing Cards, Their History and Types,* London: B.T. Batsford, Ltd., 1931.

Moss, P. *Sports and Pastimes Through the Ages,* New York: Arco Press, 1963.

Murray, H. J. R. *A Short History of Chess,* London: Oxford University Press, 1963.

———. *History of Board Games Other Than Chess,* London: Oxford University Press, 1952.

———. *A History of Chess,* London: Oxford University Press, 1913.

Nally, T. H. *The Aonach Tailteann and the Tailteann Games; Their Origin, History and Ancient Associations,* Dublin: Talbot Press, Ltd., 1928.

Rudolph, R. C. "The Antiquity of T'ou Hu," *Antiquity,* Newbury Berks, **24**, 1950, pp. 175–178.

Salt, L. E. *Recreation: Past and Present*, London: Oxford University Press, Junior Encyclopaedia Series, **9**, 1956.

Smith, H. *Festivals, Games, and Amusements: Ancient and Modern*, New York: J. & J. Harper, 1831.

Szukovathy, I. "Some Notes on the History of Sports Bibliographies," *Research Quarterly*, Washington, D.C., no. 8, 1937, pp. 3–14.

Tylor, E. B. "Lecture: The History of Games," *Proceedings of the Royal Institution*, 9, March 14, 1879, p. 125. Also published in *Popular Science Monthly*, **15**, p. 225.

Young, J. P. *History and Bibliography of War Gaming*, Arlington, Va.: Armed Services Technical Information Agency, Staff Paper ORO-SP-13, April, 1957.

Young, J. P. *Survey of Historical Developments in War Games*, Mclean, Va.: Research Analysis Corp., ORO-Staff Paper no. 98, August 1959.

PART II

Selected References Relating to Various Historical Periods — Preliterate, Ancient, Medieval, and Early Modern Times

Preliterate

Amsden, C. "A Prehistoric Rubber Ball," *The Masterkey*, Los Angeles, **10**, 1936, pp. 7–8.

Im Thurn, E. F. "Primitive Games," *Argosy*, Georgetown, 1890, pp. 270–307.

Im Thurn, E. F. "Primitive Games," *Timehri*, Demerara, 3, pt. 2, Dec. 1889. Reviewed in *The American Anthropologist*, 3 (3), July 1890, p. 293, by John Murdock.

Im Thurn, E. F. "Primitive Games," *Thoughts, Talks, and Tramps*, London, 1934, pp. 32–58.

Mehl, E. "Baseball in the Stone Age," *Western Folklore*, Berkeley, **7**, 1948, pp. 145–161.

Padmanabhackari, T. "Games, Sports, and Pastimes in Prehistoric India," *Man in India*, Ranchi, **21**, 1941, pp. 127–146.

Ancient

"Ancient Mesopotamian Die (c. 2750 B.C.) Goes To Museum," *El Palacio*, **31** (3), p. 41, July 22, 1931.

Austin, R. G. "Greek Board Games," *Antiquity*, Gloucester, England, 14, 1940, pp. 257–271.

Austin, R. G. "Roman Board Games," *Greece and Rome*, London, 4, 1934.

Austin, R. G. "Zeno's Game of Table," *Journal of Hellenic Studies*, 44, 1934, p. 202.

"Backgammon Almost Four Thousand Years Ago," *El Palacio*, Santa Fe, New Mexico, 1931, pp. 84–85.

"Boxing and Wrestling Five Thousand Years Ago near Baghdad," *El Palacio*, 43 (1,2,3), July 7, 14, and 21, 1937, pp. 16–17.

"Egyptian Dice," *Field Museum News*, Chicago, 1 (10), 1930, p. 1.

Erman, A. "Recreation," *Life in Ancient Egypt*, London: Macmillan Company, 1894, pp. 234–258.

Falkener, E. *Games Ancient and Oriental*, New York: Dover Publications, Inc. Reprint of the 1892 edition, 1961.

"Football—An Ancient Game," *Natural History*, New York, 22, 1922, pp. 574–575.

Gadd, C. J. "Babylonian Chess?" *Iraq*, London, 8, 1946, pp. 66–72.

Gadd, C. J. "The Palm Tree Game," *Illustrated London News*, no. 23, Oct. 1936, p. 709.

Gardiner, E. N. *Athletics of the Ancient World*, Oxford: Clarendon Press, 1930.

Gardiner, E. N. *Greek Athletic Sports and Festivals*, London: Macmillan and Company, 1910.

Gusman, P. "Tabula," *Pompeii, The City, Its Life and Art*, London, 1900.

Kerl, H. "Ancient Games and Popular Games," *American Imago*, 15, 1958, pp. 41–89.

Lanciani, R. "Gambling and Cheating in Ancient Rome," *North American Review*, 1892, pp. 97–105.

Martin, R. "Babies Rattles from 2600 B.C. and Other Ancient Toys," *Field Museum News*, Chicago, 8 (8), 1937, p. 5.

Nash, W. I. "Ancient Egyptian Draughtsboards and Draughtsmen," *Proceedings of the Society of Biblical Archaeology*, London, 24, 1902, p. 341.

Parker, H. "Alquerque," *Ancient Ceylon*, London, 1909, pp. 579, 644.

Poole, L. *History of Ancient Olympic Games*, London: Vision Press, 1963.

Ridgeway, W. "The Game of Thirty Squares," *Journal of Hellenic Studies, London*, 16, 1896, p. 288.

Tacitus, C. "Dice," *Germania A.D. 99*, Chapter 26.

Thompson, D. W. "Games and Playthings," *Greece and Rome*, London, Oxford University Press, 2, pp. 71–79.

Towry-White, E. "Types of Ancient Egyptian Draughtsmen," *Proceed-*

ings of the Society of Biblical Archaeology, London, **24**, 1902, p. 261.

Wilson, J. A. "Ceremonial Games of the New Kingdom," *Journal of Egyptian Archaeology*, London, **17**, 1931, pp. 211–220.

Woolley, L. "The Sumerian Game," *Ur, The First Phase*, London: Penguin Books, 1946.

Young, N. D. "Did the Greeks and Romans Play Football?," *Research Quarterly*, Washington, D.C., **15**, 1944, pp. 310–316.

Medieval

Allen, A. B. *Games of the Sixteenth Century*, London: Rockcliffe New Project Pamphlets, 1949.

Anderson, A. J. "Home Diversions of the Aztec Chief," *El Palacio*, **55**, 1948, pp. 125–127.

Armitage, R. J. "The Savon Game Hnefatafl," *Time of St. Dunstan*, London: Oxford University Press, 1923, p. 69.

Bennett, H. "Games of the Old Time Maori," *The New World*, Christchurch, N.Z., 1958, pp. 45–47.

Borhegyi, S. F. "Ball-Game Handstones and Ball-Game Gloves," *Essays in Pre-Columbian Art and Archaeology*, Cambridge, Mass., 1961, pp. 126–151.

Brandes, R. S. "An Early Ball Court Near Globe Arizona," *Kiva*, Tuscon, **23** (1), 1957, pp. 10–11.

Brewster, P. G. "Games and Sports in 16th and 17th Century English Literature," *Western Folklore*, Berkeley, California, **6**, 1947, pp. 143–156.

Caso, A. "Notes on Ancient Games," *Mexican Folkways*, Mexico, **7** (2), 1932, pp. 56–60.

Diego, A. "Ancient Games in Ancient Plazas," *New Mexico*, Albuquerque, **14** (7), 1936, pp. 22–23, 43.

Ekholm, G. F. "Puerto Rican Stone Collars as Ballgame Belts," *Essays in Pre-Columbian Art and Archaeology*, Cambridge, Mass., 1961, pp. 356–371.

Emory, K. P. "Sports, Games, and Amusements," *Ancient Hawaiian Civilization*, 1933, pp. 141–153.

Finney, B. R. "Surfing in Ancient Hawaii," *Polynesian Society Journal*, Wellington, N.Z. **68**, 1959, pp. 327–347.

Goellner, W. A. "The Court Ball Game of the Aboriginal Mayas," *Research Quarterly*, Washington, D.C., **24** (2), May 1953, pp. 147–168.

Hencken, H. O'N. "A Gaming Board of the Viking Age," *Acta Archaeologica*, Copenhagen, 1933, pp. 85–104.

Kenn, C. W. "Ancient Hawaiian Sports and Pastimes," *Mid-Pacific*, Honolulu, **48**, 1935, pp. 308–316.

Kutscher, G. "Ceremonial Badminton in the Ancient Culture of Peru," *Third Proceedings of the International Congress of Americanists*, Copenhagen, 1958, pp. 422–432.

Micklewaith, J. J. *Indoor Games of School Boys in The Middle Ages*, London: 1892.

Parsons, E. W. C. "Some Aztec and Pueblo Parallels," *American Anthropologist*, **35**, (4), Oct.–Dec. 1933, pp. 611–631.

Redstone, V. B. "The Game of Fox and Geese," *England Among The War of The Roses*, Transactions of the Royal Historical Society, **21**, 1902, p. 195.

Sjovold, T. "The Nine Men's Morris Game," *The Viking Ships*, Oslo, 1954, p. 7.

Smith, A. L. "Types of Ball Courts in the Highlands of Guatemala," *Essays in Pre-Columbian Art and Archaeology*, Cambridge, Mass., 1961, pp. 100–125.

Spence, L. *Myth and Ritual in Dance, Game, and Rhyme*, London: Watts and Co., 1947.

Tylor, E. B. "On American Lot Games as Evidence of Asiatic Intercourse Before the Time of Columbus," *International Archives for Ethnography*, Supplement to 9, pp. 55–67, 1896.

Tylor, E. B. "On the Game of Patolli in Ancient Mexico and Its Probably Asiatic Origin," *Journal of the Royal Anthropological Institute*, **8**, April 9, 1878, pp. 116–131.

Wright, T. *History of the Domestic Manners and Sentiments in England During The Middle Ages*, London, 1862.

Early Modern

Backus, E. M. "Ancient Game of Courtship from North Carolina," *Journal of American Folklore*, **13** (48), Jan.–Mar. 1900, p. 104.

Betts, J. R. "The Technological Revolution and the Rise of Sport," 1850–1900," *Mississippi Valley Historical Review*, September 1953.

Cotton, C. *The Compleat Gamester*, 1674, bound with Lucas, T. *Lives of the Gamesters*, 1714, titled, *Games and Gamesters of the Restoration*, London: G. Routeledge and Sons, 1930.

Durant, J. *Pictorial History of American Sports: from Colonial Times to the Present*, New York: A. S. Barnes, 1952.

Ewing, W. C. *The Sports of Colonial Williamsburg*, Richmond, Va.: The Dietz Press, 1937.

Fink, R. W. "Recreation Pursuits in the Old South," *Research Quarterly*, Washington, D.C., 1951, **22**, 298–311.

Henderson, R. W. *Early American Sports: Prior to 1860,* New York: A. S. Barnes Co., 1953.

Heywood, W. *Palio and Ponte; An Account of the Sports of Central Italy from the Age of Dante to the Twentieth Century,* London: Methuen and Co., 1904.

Holliman, J. *American Sport: 1785–1835,* Durham, N.C.: The Sieman Press, 1931.

McKenzie, B. "The Seminoles Were Recognized as the Leading Ball Players Years Ago," *American Indian,* Tulsa, 1 (5), 1927, p. 10.

Manchester, H. *Four Centuries of Sport in America: 1490–1890,* New York: Derrydale Press, 1931.

Mason, B. *Primitive and Pioneer Sports for Recreation,* New York: A. S. Barnes and Co., 1937.

Portmann, P. *Brueghel: Children's Games,* Berne: Hallwag, Ltd., 1964.

Rider, C. "The Sporting Scene: 1864," *American Scholar,* 15, Summer, 1946, pp. 348–352.

Smith, H. W. *A Sporting Family of the Old South,* New York: J. B. Lyon Co., 1936.

Wanchope, R. "The Middle American Ball Game in 1750," *El Palacio,* Santa Fe, 55, 1948, pp. 299–301.

Weaver, R. B. *Amusements and Sports in American Life: During the Past 300 Years,* Chicago: University of Chicago Press, 1939.

Weiss, H. B. *Early Sports and Pastimes in New Jersey,* Trenton: Pastimes Press, 1960.

Whitehouse, F. R. B. *Table Games of Georgian and Victorian Days,* London, 1951.

CHAPTER **3**

ANTHROPOLOGICAL SOURCES

In the last two decades of the nineteenth century games became the subject matter of systematic modern scholarship, particularly in anthropology and folklore. In *anthropology,* Tylor is usually accepted as the first to have pointed out that games might be used to provide clues about cultural contacts. Holding the view that complex aspects of culture could only have arisen at one time and in one place, Tylor pointed to the games as providing evidence that civilization had spread "from South East Asia over the vast Malayo-Polynesian district as far as New Zealand."[1] He also argued that games were brought to the North American Continent from the Asian mainland when a land bridge existed across the Bering Strait.[2]

The most vigorous proponent of game universalism and game diffusion, however, was Stewart Culin. In the field of anthropology he still ranks as the major game scholar of the past 100 years. For this reason we have included here a brief biographical account of his activities, viewpoints, and major publications.

STEWART CULIN

Culin was born in 1858 in Philadelphia and in 1892 was appointed Director of the University of Pennsylvania's Museum of Archaeology and Palaeontology. In 1903 he became curator of Ethnology at the Institute

[1] Tylor, E. B. "Remarks on the Geographical Distribution of Games," *Journal of the Royal Anthropological Institute,* March 11, 1879, p. 23.
[2] Tylor, E. B. "On American Lot Games As Evidence of Asiatic Intercourse Before the Time of Columbus," *International Archives of Ethnography,* Supplement to 9, 1896, pp. 57–67.

of Arts and Sciences of the Brooklyn Museum in New York City. At various times he served as consultant to the United States Bureau of American Ethnology; he was on the Editorial Board of the *American Anthropologist,* and was a contributing member of the American Folklore Society. He had a profound interest in the occult and the mysterious, as evidenced by his articles on the subjects of voodoo, Chinese secret societies, and sorcery. Bell states:

He went on several field expeditions to Japan, China, Korea and India, setting out with his fare, a lead pencil, a set of ideas and a smile. He came back with the same smile, more ideas and many packing cases whose contents were used to reconstruct the very air of the visited country in the exhibition hall of the Brooklyn Museum.[3]

In 1889, the Oriental Club of Philadelphia published Culin's first account on games, a pamphlet, *Chinese Games with Dice.* This was followed in 1891 by a pamphlet, *Gambling Games of the Chinese in America,* published by the University of Pennsylvania, and by an article "Chinese Games with Dice and Dominoes," published by the United States Government in the *Annual Report of the U.S. National Museum,* 1893. Two other papers were published during this period that do not deal with things "Chinese," but concern related topics—*Italian Marionettes in New York City* (1890), and *Street Games of Boys in Brooklyn* (1891).

In 1891 Culin worked on an exhibit of games of the world for the Columbian Exposition in Chicago. In the preface to his book on *Korean Games* published in 1895, Culin said:

The incentive to the preparation and publication of this work was primarily the inspiration drawn from suggestions based upon his studies of the institutions and games of primitive American peoples, made to me by my friend and collaborator, Mr. Frank Hamilton Cushing, of the Bureau of American Ethnology, of Washington. In his suggestions as to the object and origin of American games, I recognized a means of removing the study of games and allied customs from the uncertain domain of so called Folklore into the realm of true scientific investigation. I have left the direct comparison of the games of the two continents to Mr. Cushing, while I have carried forward the investigation of the Asiatic games. . . .[4]

[3] Bell, R. C. *Board and Table Games From Many Civilizations.* London: Oxford University Press, 1960, pp. 192–193.

[4] Culin, S. *Korean Games, With Notes on the Corresponding Games of China and Japan.* University of Pennsylvania Press, 1895. Reprinted as *Games of the Orient.* Rutland, Vermont: Charles Tuttle Co., 1958, p. v.

From the time of the Columbian Exposition, Culin published many reports on games in a variety of cultures. In the 1894 annual report of the Board of Regents of the Smithsonian Institution (published in 1896) we find that,

These researches have also brought to light many significant facts bearing on the usages, beliefs and ethnic relations of early peoples, and the material result of the investigation is an elaborate paper on "Arrow games and their variants in America and the Orient," under the joint authorship of Messrs. Cushing and Culin, now well advanced in preparation.[5]

A detailed search of the literature has not turned up this paper. Cushing died in 1900, and Culin seems to have taken on the task by himself. In his preface to *Games of the North American Indian* (1907) he states:

During the course of the (Columbian) exposition . . . attention was directed by Mr. Frank Hamilton Cushing to the remarkable analogies existing between the oriental and modern European games in the collection and those of American Indians. A joint work in which Mr. Cushing would discuss the American games, and the writer those of the Old World was then projected. Mr. Cushing's ill health delayed and finally prevented his proposed collaboration. Deeply impressed with the importance of the subject, the present author took up the systematic study of American games, constantly aided by Mr. Cushing's advice and suggestion.[6]

Culin's interests changed after publication of the book on Indian games. He became more concerned with costume, fashion, and furniture. Culin's contribution is best summed up by the words of W. H. Holmes, Chief of the Bureau of American Ethnology, in a 1903 report to the Secretary of the Smithsonian Institution:

The popular notion that games . . . are trivial in nature and of no particular significance as a subject of research soon gave way, under the well-conducted studies of Mr. Culin, to an adequate appreciation of their importance as an integral part of human culture. Although engaged in by both men and women, apparently as a pastime, and played persistently. . . . games of all classes are found to be intimately connected with religious beliefs and practices, and to have universally a devotional aspect and in some cases a divinatory significance. Mr. Culin's studies,

---

[5] *Annual Report to July, 1894 of the Board of Regents of the Smithsonian Institution.* Washington, D.C.: United States Government Printing Office, 1896, p. 53.

[6] Culin, S. "Games of the North American Indians," *Twenty-Fourth Annual Report of the Bureau of American Ethnology*, Washington, D.C.: United States Government Printing Office, 1907, p. 29.

therefore, not only afford an understanding of the technology of the games and of their distribution, as well as their bearing on history . . . , but they contribute in a remarkable manner to an appreciation of native modes of thought and of the motives and impulses that underlie the conduct of primitive peoples generally. (Culin) . . . creates the science of games and for the first time gives this branch its proper place in the science of man.[7]

There follows an annotated bibliography of Culin's principal publications on games. Culin published over 65 papers, articles, and books on a variety of subjects, ranging from the practice of Chinese medicine in the United States, to the evolution of fashion as found in works of fine art.

1889 *Chinese Games with Dice* (pamphlet). Philadelphia: Oriental Club, 21 pages. Games described ". . . are chiefly those of Chinese laborers in America. . . ." Although most of these were played in Canton province, reference is made to similar games from India and Japan. Pictures of required equipment are included.

1890 *"Italian Marionettes in New York City"* (article). *Journal of American Folklore*, 3, pp. 155–157. Discussion of a visit to a marionette theater operated by a non-English speaking troupe from Sicily. Theater seats 100 adults, seats are reserved for ladies, plays are the same as those offered in Europe. Theater serves the neighborhood population as it did in Europe.

1891 *Gambling Games of the Chinese in America* (pamphlet). University of Pennsylvania Series in Philology, Literature and Archaeology, Philadelphia: University of Pennsylvania Press, Vol. I, No. 4, 17 pages. Detailed explanation of "Fan T'an," a table game involving coins and special equipment; and "Pak Kop Piu," a type of lottery. Pictures of required equipment are included.

1891 "Street Games of Boys in Brooklyn" (article). *Journal of American Folklore*, 4, pp. 221–237. Describes street games played by both boys and girls before the turn of the century. Discusses modification of games to suit the urban environment. Some diagrams are included.

1893 "Chinese Games with Dice and Dominoes" (paper). *Annual Report of the U.S. National Museum*, Washington, D.C.: United States Government Printing Office, pp. 491–537. In addition to providing detailed information on dice and dominoes, considerable information on backgammon and other games is presented. The narrative and illustrations are not limited to Chinese games.

---

[7] Holmes, W. H. *Twenty-Fourth Annual Report of the Bureau of American Ethnology.* Washington, D.C.: United States Government Printing Office, 1907, pp. 39–40.

Information is presented on Korean, Malayan, Siamese, Japanese, Indian, Philippine, Burmese, Celebes, Eskimo, Egyptian, Syrian, Tibetan, European, and Ancient Roman games.

1893 "Exhibition of Games at the Columbian Exposition." *Journal of American Folklore*, 6, pp. 205–227. Describes types and kinds of games on exhibit at the Columbian Exposition in Chicago. Includes information similar to the type found in subsequent articles, but in less detail.

1894 "Mancala, the National Game of Africa" (paper). *Annual Report of the U.S. National Museum*, Washington, D.C.: United States Government Printing Office, pp. 597–606. Describes many variations of the game as played in Africa, Turkey, Asia Minor, India, Ceylon, and other places. Discusses the spread of the game due to Arab influence. Photographs and diagrams of many types of boards are included.

1895 *Korean Games, with Notes on the Corresponding Games of China and Japan* (book). Philadelphia: University of Pennsylvania Press, 177 pages. Reprinted as *Games of the Orient*, Rutland, Vermont: Charles Tuttle Co., 1958. ". . . intended not only as a survey of the games of Korea, but as a practical introduction to the study of games of the world." Includes hundreds of adults' and children's games from many countries. Games which require special equipment, nonequipment games, and information on toys with numerous illustrations and diagrams are presented. Introduction sets forth Culin's theory of the function of games in society. Includes bibliography.

1896 "Chess and Playing-Cards" (article). *Annual Report of the U.S. National Museum*, Washington, D. C.: United States Government Printing Office, pp. 665–942. Comprehensive exploration of chess, playing cards, and other table and board games as played in Europe, Asia, North America, and South America. Some content deals with similarity of North American Indian games and the games played in Europe and Asia.

1898 "American Indian Games" (article). *Journal of American Folklore*, Oct.–Dec., pp. 245–252. Preliminary exploration of the meaning and distribution of these games (see 1903 and 1907).

1899 "Hawaiian Games" (article). *American Anthropologist*, New Series, 1, (2), pp. 201–247. Describes equipment and nonequipment games as played by children and adults in a number of islands of the Pacific, ranging from the Hawaiian group to New Zealand and other places in Oceania. Includes many diagrams and illustrations, and a special illustrated section on "cat's cradle."

1900 "Philippine Games" (article). *American Anthropologist*, New Series, 2, pp. 643–656. Games of Spanish, Chinese, Malay, and Hindu origin as played in the Philippine Islands are present with illustrations and diagrams.

1903 "American Indian Games" (article). *American Anthropologist, New Series*, 5, pp. 58–64. Revised conclusions about the meaning and distribution of these games. Presents some of the ideas which are expressed more fully in the 1907 monograph.

1907 "Games of North American Indians" (book). *Twenty-Fourth Annual Report of the Bureau of American Ethnology*, Washington, D.C.: United States Government Printing Office, 846 pages. "Monographic study of American Indian games . . . affording an understanding of the technology of the games and their distribution, as well as their bearing on the history of the tribes." Probably the most comprehensive work on the subject. Includes hundreds of pictures and illustrations.

1920 "Japanese Game of Sugoroku" (article). *Brooklyn Museum Quarterly*, 7, October, pp. 213–233. Detailed examination of the place of this game in Japanese society and its significance. Includes illustrations and a bibliography.

1924 "Game of Ma-Jong" (article). *Brooklyn Museum Quarterly*, 11, October, pp. 153–168. Detailed discussion of the origin and significance of the game and its relationships to other games. Photographs and illustrations are included.

1925 "Japanese Swinging Bat Game" (article). "Japanese Game of Battledore and Shuttlecock" (article). *Brooklyn Museum Quarterly*, 12, July, pp. 133–150. Two articles with accompanying illustrations indicating the relationship of these two games to festival holidays in Japan.

It is clear that Culin's interest in games persisted well beyond their demise as serious and theoretically sustained subject matters in anthropology. Early in the twentieth century the generalizations of Culin and others came under attack. It was argued that "diffusionists" like Culin pointed to the similarities of parallel games in different cultures without paying sufficient attention to the differences, which were in as much need of explanation as the similarities. Universal statements about games, it was said, were inconsistent with new information that indicated cultural traits could only be properly understood within their own functional context. In consequence apart from Culin's work and the writings of Elsdon Best (1925)[8] and Alexander Lesser (1933)[9] there has been little

[8] Best, E. "Games and Pastimes of the Maori," *Dominion Museum Bulletin No. 8*, Wellington, 1925.

[9] Lesser, A. "The Pawnee Ghost Dances Hand Game: A Study of Cultural Change,"

important anthropological work on games since the last century, although the new studies of Roberts and others (1959),[10] to which we shall refer later, suggest that the topic is about to be reopened within anthropology.

GAME DIFFUSION

We shall complete this section on anthropology by stating some of the generalizations about game diffusion that were made by anthropologists of this early period. This is done in full cognizance of the fact that there is really no final agreement about these matters. Take for example the "court ball game" which is somewhat of a cross between soccer and basketball, played between the eighth and eighteenth centuries by the Mayas of Yucatan. Goellner (1953)[11] and a number of others have claimed that the Mayas originated the game and taught it to neighboring tribes ranging from as far north as Arizona to the southern tip of Guatemala. On the other hand, some scholars have stated that the game was taught to the Mayas by a tribe in Central Mexico, and yet others indicate that the game made its way north from South America. Mitchell earlier had suggested that all these ideas on diffusion of this game are wrong because it parallels a game played in Ancient Egypt (1935)! Which is to say that there is nothing very final about the following diffusionist propositions although they do carry with them a certain degree of apparent self-evidence.

It was argued by Culin and others that the spread of games was from the:

1. Lower river valleys of the Nile, Euphrates, and Tigris (Sumer, Mesopotamia, and Egypt) with diffusion west to Assyria, and the land of the Hittites and the Greeks, and also south to parts of Africa; Greece west to Sicily, Italy, and north to Anatolia and southern Russia; Rome west to France and Britain, north to Germany and Denmark, east and south to other places where peoples had contact with Roman Legions. Scandinavia west to Britain, Wales and Ireland, and to the North American Continent.
2. North India and the Indus River valley to Nepal, Tibet, and China, later west to Persia, then south throughout India to Ceylon and Indonesia; China east to Korea, Japan, and South to Siam, and the Malay

Columbia University Contributions to Anthropology, 16, New York: Columbia University Press, 1933.

[10] Roberts, J. M., Arth, M. J., and Bush, R. R. "Games in Culture," American Anthropologist, 61 (4), August, 1959, pp. 597–605.

[11] Goellner, W. A. "The Court Ball Game of the Aboriginal Mayas," Research Quarterly, 24 (2), May, 1953, pp. 147–168.

Archipelago and South Pacific Islands; possibly early interchange with North American Continent.

3. Arab world of the Middle East to North Africa and the Iberian Peninsula and parts of Asia.

4. The Crusaders who brought games home to Europe from the Middle East.

5. European colonists who taught native populations in the Americas, and islands in the Pacific, and in Africa.

6. American Indians (north, south, and central) who taught their games to Europeans who in turn took these games back to Europe.

7. Central African and Oceanic peoples who taught their games to missionaries and who in turn taught them to others.[12]

Thus, according to diffusionists, games have crisscrossed many nations and cultures at various periods of history as a result of commerce, warfare, exploration, education, and a host of other reasons.

In this chapter we include a selection of the game studies by Tylor and Culin. Most of these are in relatively inaccessible journals and they contain a colorful record of the interests of this early anthropological period. We enclose also a paper by Erasmus, which is an interesting modern commentary of Tylor's earlier remarks on Patolli, suggesting as it does that diffusionist explanations may not after all be necessary to account for the similarities between games found in very different parts of the world.

[12] See Murray, 1913; Hildebrand, 1919; Stearns, 1890; and Tylor, 1879.

3

The History of Games

E. B. TYLOR

Before examining some groups of the higher orders of games, with the view of tracing their course in the world, it will be well to test by a few examples the principles on which we may reason as to their origin and migrations. An intelligent traveller among the Kalmuks, noticing that they play a kind of chess resembling ours, would not for a moment entertain the idea of such an invention having been made more than once, but would feel satisfied that we and they and all chess-players must have had the game from the original source. In this example lies the gist of the ethnological argument from artificial games, that when any such appears in two districts it must have travelled from one to the other, or to both from a common centre. Of course this argument does not apply to all games. Some are so simple and natural that, for all we can tell, they may often have sprung up of themselves, such as tossing a ball or wrestling; while children everywhere imitate in play the serious work of grownup life, from spearing an enemy down to moulding an earthen pot. The distinctly artificial sports we are concerned with here are marked by some peculiar trick or combination not so likely to have been hit upon twice. Not only complex games like chess and tennis, but even many childish sports, seem well-defined formations, of which the spread may be traced on the map much as the botanist traces his plants from their geographical centres. It may give us confidence in this way of looking at the subject if we put the opposite view to the test of history and geography to see where it fails. Travellers, observing the likeness of children's games in Europe

SOURCE. *The Fortnightly Review, London: Chapman and Hall,* **25**, N.S., Jan. 1–June 1, 1879, pp. 735–747.

and Asia, have sometimes explained it on this wise: that the human mind being alike everywhere, the same games are naturally found in different lands, children taking to hockey, tops, stilts, kites, and so on, each at its proper season. But if so, why is it that in outlying barbarous countries one hardly finds a game without finding also that there is a civilised nation within reach from whom it may have been learnt? And what is more, how is it that European children knew nothing till a few centuries ago of some of their most popular sports? For instance, they had no battledore-and-shuttlecock and never flew kites till these games came across from Asia, when they took root at once and became naturalised over Europe. The origin of kite-flying seems to lie somewhere in South-east Asia, where it is a sport even of grown-up men, who fight their kites by making them cut one another's strings, and fly birds and monsters of the most fantastic shapes and colours, especially in China, where old gentlemen may be seen taking their evening stroll, kite-string in hand, as though they were leading pet dogs. The English boy's kite appears thus an instance, not of spontaneous play-instinct, but of the migration of an artificial game from a distant centre. Nor is this all it proves in the history of civilisation. Within a century, Europeans becoming acquainted with the South Sea Islanders found them down to New Zealand adepts at flying kites, which they made of leaves or bark cloth, and called *mánu*, or "bird," flying them in solemn form with accompaniment of traditional chants. It looks as though the toy reached Polynesia through the Malay region, thus belonging to that drift of Asiatic culture which is evident in many other points of South Sea Island life. The geography of another of our childish diversions may be noticed as matching with this. Mr. Wallace relates that being one wet day in a Dayak house in Borneo, he thought to amuse the lads by taking a piece of string to show them *cat's-cradle*, but to his surprise he found that they knew more about it than he did, going off into figures that quite puzzled him. Other Polynesians are skilled in this nursery art, especially the Maoris of New Zealand, who call it *maui* from the name of their national hero, by whom, according to their tradition, it was invented; its various patterns represent canoes, houses, people, and even episodes in Maui's life, such as his fishing up New Zealand from the bottom of the sea. In fact, they have their pictorial history in cat's-cradle, and whatever their traditions may be worth, they stand good to show that the game was of the time of their forefathers, not lately picked up from the Europeans. In the Sandwich Islands and New Zealand it is on record that the natives were found playing a kind of draughts which was not the European game, and which can hardly be accounted for but as another result of the drift of Asiatic civilisation down into the Pacific.

Once started, a game may last on almost indefinitely. Among the children's sports of the present day are some which may be traced back toward the limits of historical antiquity, and, for all we know, may have been old then. Among the pictures of ancient Egyptian games in the tombs of Beni Hassan, one shows a player with his head down so that he cannot see what the others are doing with their clenched fists above his back. Here is obviously the game called in English *hot-cockles*, in French *main-chande*, and better described by its mediæval name of *qui fery?* or "who struck?"—the blindman having to guess by whom he was hit, or with which hand. It was the Greek *kollabismos*, or buffet-game, and carries with it a tragical association in those passages in the Gospels which show it turned to mockery by the Roman soldiers: "And when they had blindfolded him . . . they buffeted him . . . saying, Prophesy unto us, Christ, Who is he that smote thee?" (Luke xxii. 64; Matt. xxvi. 67; Mark xiv. 65.)

Another of the Egyptian pictures plainly represents the game we know by its Italian name of *morra*, the Latin *micatio*, or flashing of the fingers, which has thus lasted on in the Mediterranean districts over three thousand years, handed down through a hundred successive generations who did not improve it, for from the first it was perfect in its fitting into one little niche in human nature. It is the game of guessing addition, the players both at once throwing out fingers and in the same moment shouting their guesses at the total. Morra is the pastime of the drinking-shop in China as in Italy, and may, perhaps, be reckoned among the items of culture which the Chinese have borrowed from the Western barbarians. Though so ancient, morra has in it no touch of prehistoric rudeness, but must owe its origin to a period when arithmetic had risen quite above the savage level. The same is true of the other old arithmetical game, *odd-and-even*, which the poet couples with riding on a stick as the most childish of diversions, "Ludere *par impar,* equitare in arundine longâ." But the child playing it must be of a civilised nation, not of a low barbaric tribe, where no one would think of classing numbers into the odd-and-even series, so that Europeans have even had to furnish their languages with words for these ideas. I asked myself the question whether the ancient Aryans distinguished odd from even, and curiously enough found that an answer had been preserved by the unbroken tradition not of Greek arithmeticians, but of boys at play. A scholiast on the Ploutos of Aristophanes, where the game is mentioned, happens to remark that it was also known as ζυγὰ ἢ ἄζυγα, "yokes or not-yokes." Now this matches so closely in form and sense with the Sanskrit terms for even and odd numbers, *yuj* and *ayuj,* as to be fair evidence that both Hindus and

Greeks inherited arithmetical ideas and words familiar to their Aryan ancestors.

Following up the clues that join the play-life of the ancient and modern worlds, let us now look at the ball-play, which has always held its place among sports. Beyond mere tossing and catching, the simplest kind of ball-play is where a ring of players send the ball from hand to hand. This gentle pastime has its well-marked place in history. Thus the ancient Greeks, whose secret of life was to do even trivial things with artistic perfection, delighted in the game of Nausikaa, and on their vases is painted many a scene where ball-play, dance, and song unite in one graceful sport. The ball-dance is now scarcely to be found but as an out-of-the-way relic of old custom; yet it has left curious traces in European languages, where the *ball* (Low Latin *balla*) has given its name to the dance it went with (Italian *ballare, ballo,* French *bal,* English *ball*), and even to the song that accompanied the dance (Italian *ballata,* French *ballade,* English *ballad*). The passion of ball-play begins not with this friendly graceful delivery of the ball into the next hand, but when two hostile players or parties are striving each to take or send it away from the other. Thus, on the one hand, there comes into existence the group of games represented by the Greek *harpaston,* or seizing-game, where the two sides struggled to carry off the ball. In Brittany this has been played till modern times with the hay-stuffed *soule* or *sun*-ball, as big as a football, fought for by two communes, each striving to carry it home over their own border. Émile Souvestre, in his *Derniers Bretons,* has told the last story of this fierce game in the Ponthivy district—how the man who had had his father killed and his own eye knocked out by François, surnamed le Souleur, lay in wait for that redoubted champion, and got him down, soule and all, half-way across the boundary stream. The murderous soule-play had to be put down by authority, as it had been years before in Scotland, where it had given rise to the suggestive proverb, "All is fair at the ball of Scone." The other class of hostile ball-games differs from this in the ball having not to be brought to one's own home, but sent to the goal of the other side. In the Greek *epikoinos,* or common-ball, the ball was put on the middle line, and each party tried to seize it and throw it over the adversary's goal-line. This game also lasted on into modern Europe, and our proper English name for it is *hurling,* while *football* also is a variety of it, the great Roman blown leather ball (*follis*) being used instead of the small hand-ball, and kicked instead of thrown. Now as hurling was an ordinary classical game, the ancients need only have taken a stick to drive the ball instead of using hands or feet, and would thus have arrived at *hockey.* But Corydon never seems to have thought of borrowing

Phillis's crook for the purpose it would have so exactly suited. No mention of games like hockey appears in the ancient world, and the course of invention which brought them into the modern world is at once unexpected and instructive.

The game known to us as *polo* has been traced by Sir W. Ouseley, in Persia, far back in the Sassanian dynasty, and was at any rate in vogue there before the eighth century. It was played with the long-handled mallet called *chugán,* which Persian word came to signify also the game played with it. This is the instrument referred to in the *Thousand and One Nights,* and among various earlier passages where it occurs is the legend told by the Persian historian of Darius insulting Alexander by sending him a ball and mallet (*guï ve chugán*) as a hint that he was a boy more fit to play polo than to go to war. When this tale finds its way to Scotland, in the romance of King Alisaunde, these unknown instruments are replaced by a whipping-top, and Shakspere has the story in the English guise of a newer period in the scene in Henry V.: "What treasure, uncle?" —"Tennis-balls, my liege." By the ninth century the game of *chugán* had established itself in the Eastern Empire, where its name appears in the barbarous Greek form τζυκανίζειν. In the Byzantine descriptions, however, we find not the original mallet, but a long staff ending in a broad bend filled in with a network of gutstrings. Thus there appear in the East, as belonging to the great sport of ball-play on horseback, the first shapes of two implements which remodelled the whole play-life of mediæval and modern Europe, the chugán being the ancestor of the mallets used in pallmall and croquet, and of an endless variety of other playing clubs and bats, while the bent staff with its network was the primitive racket. The fine old Persian drawing of a match at chugán, which is copied by Ouseley in his *Travels in the East,* justifies his opinion that the horseback game is the original. We should not talk of polo as being "hockey on horseback," but rather regard hockey as dismounted polo, and class with it pall-mall, golf, and many another bat-and-ball game. Indeed, when one comes to think of it, one sees that no stick being necessary for the old foot game of hurling, none was used, but as soon as the Persian horsemen wanted to play ball on horseback, a proper instrument had to be invented. This came to be used in the foot game also, so that the Orientals are familiar both with the mounted and dismounted kinds. The horseback game seems hardly to have taken hold in Europe till our own day, when the English brought it down from Munniepoor, and it has now under the name of *polo* become a world-wide sport again. But the foot game made its way early into Europe, as appears from a curious passage in Joinville's *Life of St. Louis,* written at the end of the thirteenth century. Having seen the game on his crusade, and read about it in the Byzantine historians, he argues that the Greeks must have borrowed their *tzycanisterium* from the French, for it is, he says, a game played in Languedoc by driving a boxwood ball with a long mallet, and called there *chicane*. The modern reader has to turn this neat and patriotic argument upside down, the French *chicane* being only a corruption of the Persian *chugán;* so that what Joinville actually proves is, that before his time the Eastern game had travelled into France, bringing with it its Eastern name. Already, in his day, from the ball-game with its shifts and dodges, the term *chicane* had come to be applied by metaphor to the shuffles of lawyers to embarrass the other side, and thence to intrigue and trickery in general. English has borrowed *chicane* in the sense of trickery, without knowing it as the name of a game. Metaphors taken from sports may thus outlast their first sense, as when again people say, "Don't *bandy* words with me," without an idea that they are using another metaphor taken from the game of hockey, which was called *bandy* from the curved stick or club it was played with.

In France, the name of *crosse*, meaning a crutch, or bishop's crosier, was used for the mallet, and thence the game of hockey has its ordinary French name, *jen de la crosse*. In Spanish, the game has long been known as *chueca*. The Spaniards taught it to the natives of South America, who took kindly to it, not as mere boys' play, but as a manly sport. It is curious to read accounts by modern European travellers, who seem not to recognise their own playground game when transplanted among the Araucanians of Chile, even though it shows its Spanish origin by the name of *chueca*. Seeing this, one asks whence did the North American Indians get their famous ball-play, known from California right across the Indian country? It is to all intents the European *chueca, crosse,* or *hockey,* the deerskin ball being thrown up in the middle, each of the two contending parties striving to throw or drive it through the adversaries' goal. The Iroquois say that in old times their forefathers played with curved clubs and a wooden ball, before the racket was introduced, with which to strike, carry, or throw the leather ball. Of all the describers of this fine game, Catlin has best depicted its scenes with pen and pencil, from its beginning with the night ball-play dance, where the players crowded round their goals, held up and clashed their rackets, and the women danced in lines between, and the old men smoked to the Great Spirit and led the chant for his favour in the contest. The painter would never miss a ball-play, but sit from morning till sundown on his pony studying the forms of the young athletes in their "almost superhuman" struggles for the ball, till at last one side made the agreed number of goals, and divided with yells of triumph the fur robes and tin-kettles and miscellaneous property staked on the match. Now, as to the introduction of the game into North America, the Jesuit missionaries in New France as early as 1636 mention it by their own French name of *jeu de crosse*, at which Indian villages contended "à qui crossera le mieux." The Spaniards, however, had been above a century in America, and might have brought it in, which is a readier explanation than the other possible alternative that it made its way across from South-east Asia.

When the Middle Ages set in, the European mind at last became awake to the varied pleasure to be got out of hitting a ball with a bat. The games now developed need not be here spoken of at length proportioned to their great place in modern life, as the changes which gave rise to them are so comparatively modern and well known. The Persian apparatus kept close to its original form in the game of *pall-mall*, that is, "ball-mallet," into which game was introduced the arch or ring to drive the ball through, whereby enough incident was given to knocking it about to make the sport fit for a few players, or even a single pair. An account of pall-mall and its modern revival in *croquet* will be found in Dr. Prior's little book. Playing the ball into holes serves much the same purpose as sending it through rings, and thus came in the particular kind of bandy called *golf*, from the clubs used to drive the ball. The *stool-ball*, so popular in mediæval merrymakings, was played with a stool, which one protected by striking away with his hands the ball which another bowled at it; the in-player was out if the stool was hit, or he might be caught out, so that here is evidently part of the origin of cricket, in which the present stumps seem to represent the stool. In *club-ball* a ball was bowled and hit with a club; and a game called *cat-and-dog* was played in Scotland two centuries ago, where players protected not wickets but holes from the wooden cat pitched at them, getting runs when they hit it. We have here the simple elements from which the complex modern cricket was developed. Lastly, among the obscure accounts of ancient ball-play, it is not easy to make out that the ball was ever sent against an opposite wall for the other player to take it at the bound and return it. Such a game, particularly suited to soldiers shut up in castle-yards, became popular about the fourteenth century under the name of *pila palmaria*, or *jeu de paulme*, which name indicates its original mode of striking with the palm of the hand, as in *fives*. It was an improvement to protect the hand with a glove, such as may still be seen in the ball-play of Basque cities, as at Bayonne. Sometimes a battledore faced with parchment was used, as witness the story of the man who declared he had played with a battledore that had on it fragments of the lost decades of Livy. But it was the racket that made possible the "cutting" and "boasting" of the mediæval tennis-court, with its elaborate scoring by "chases." No doubt it was the real courtyard of the château, with its penthouses, galleries, and grated windows, that furnished the tennis-court with the models for its quaintly artificial grilles and lunes so eruditely discussed in Mr. Julian Marshall's *Annals of Tennis*. A few enthusiastic amateurs still delight in the noble and costly game, but the many have reason to be grateful for lawn-tennis out of doors, though it be but a mild version of the great game, to which it stands as hockey to polo or as draughts to chess.

Turning now to the principal groups of sedentary games, I may refer to the evidence I have brought forward elsewhere,[1] that the use of lots or dice for gambling arose out of an earlier serious use of such instruments for magical divination. The two conceptions, indeed, pass into one another. The magician draws lots to learn the future and the gambler to decide the future, so that the difference between them is that between "will" and "shall." But the two-faced lot that can only fall head or tail can only give a simple yes or no, which is often too simple for either the diviner or the gambler. So we find African negroes divining with a number of cowries thrown together to see how many fall up and how many down; and this, too, is the Chinese method of solemn lot-casting in the temple, when the falling of the spoon-like wooden lots, so many up and so many down, furnishes an intricate result which is to be interpreted by means of the book of mystic diagrams. When this combination of a number of two-faced lots is used by gamblers, this, perhaps, represents the earlier stage of gaming, which may have led up to the invention of dice, in which the purpose of variety is so much more neatly and easily attained. The first appearance of dice lies beyond the range of history, for though they have not been traced in the early periods in Egypt, there is in the Rig-Veda the hymn which portrays the ancient Aryan gambler stirred to frenzy by the fall of the dice. It is not clear even which came first of the various objects that have served as dice.

In the classic world, girls used the astragali or knucklebones as playthings, tossing them up and catching them on the back of the hand; and to this day we may see groups of girls in England at this ancient game, reminding us of the picture by Alexander of Athens, in the Naples Museum, of the five goddesses at play. It was also noticed that these bones fall in four ways, with the flat, concave, convex, or sinuous side up, so that they form natural dice, and as such they have been from ancient times gambled with accordingly. In India nature provides certain five-sided nuts that answer the purpose of dice. Of course, when the sides

---

[1] *Primitive Culture,* chap. iii.

are alike, they must be marked or numbered, as with the four-sided stick-dice of India, and that which tends to supersede all others, the six-sided *kubos,* which gave the Greek geometers the name for the *cube.* Since the old Aryan period many a broken gamester has cursed the hazard of the die. We moderns are apt to look down with mere contempt at his folly. But we judge the ancient gamester too harshly if we forget that his passion is mixed with those thoughts of luck or fortune or superhuman intervention, which form the very mental atmosphere of the soothsayer and the oracle-prophet. With devout prayer and sacrifice he would propitiate the deity who should give him winning throws; nor, indeed, in our own day have such hopes and such appeals ceased among the uneducated. To the educated it is the mathematical theory of probabilities that has shown the folly of the gamester's staking his fortune on his powers of divination. But it must be borne in mind that this theory itself was, so to speak, shaken out of the dice-box. When the gambling Chevalier de Méré put the question to Pascal in how many throws he ought to get double-sixes, and Pascal solving the problem, started the mathematical calculation of chances, this laid the foundation of the scientific system of statistics which more and more regulates the arrangements of society. This accurate method was applied to the insurance table, which enables a man to hedge against his ugliest risks, to eliminate his chances of fire and death by betting that he shall have a new roof over his head and a provision for his widow. Of all the wonderful turns of the human mind in the course of culture, scarce any is more striking than this history of lots and dice. Who, in the Middle Ages, could have guessed what would be its next outcome—that magic sunk into sport should rise again as science, and man's failure to divine the future should lead him to success in controlling it?

Already in the ancient world there appear mentions of games where the throws of lots or dice, perhaps at first merely scored with counters on a board, give the excitement of chance to a game which is partly a draught-game, the player being allowed to judge with which pieces he will move his allotted number. In England this group of games is represented by *backgammon.* When Greek writers mention dice-playing, they no doubt often mean some game of this class, for at mere hazard the Persian queen-mother could not have played her game carefully, as Plutarch says she did, nor would there have been any sense in his remark that in life, as in dicing, one must not only get good throws, but know how to use them. The Roman game of the twelve lines (*duodecim scripta*) so nearly corresponded with our trictrac or backgammon, that M. Becq de Fouquières, in his *Jeux des Anciens,* works out on the ordinary backgammon board the problem of the Emperor Zeno that has vexed the soul of many a critic. All these games, however, are played with dice, and as there exist other games of like principle where lots are thrown instead of dice, it may, perhaps, be inferred that such ruder and clumsier lot-backgammon was the earlier, and dice-backgammon a later improvement upon it. Of course things may have happened the opposite way. Lot-backgammon is still played in the East in more than one form. The Arabic-speaking peoples call it *tab*, or game, and play it with an oblong board or rows of holes in the ground, with bits of brick and stone for draughts of the two colours, and for lots four palm-stick slips with a black and white side. In this low variety of lot-backgammon, the object is not to get one's own men home, but to take all the adversary's. The best represensative of this group of games is the Hindu *pachisi*, which belongs to a series ancient in India. It is played on a cross-shaped board or embroidered cloth, up and down the arms of which the pieces move and take, in somewhat the manner of backgammon, till they get back to the central home. The men move by the throws of a number of cowries, of which the better throws not only score high, but entitle the player to a new throw, which corresponds to our rule of doubles giving a double move at backgammon. The game of pachisi has great vogue in Asia, extending into the far East, where it is played with flat tamarind-seeds as lots. It even appears to have found its way still farther eastward into America, forming a link in the chain of evidence of an Asiatic element in the civilisation of the Aztecs.[2] For the early Spanish-American writers describe, as played at the Court of Montezuma, a game called *patolli*, played after the manner of their European tables or backgammon, but on a mat with a diagram like a + or Greek cross, full of squares on which the different-coloured stones or pieces of the players were moved according to the throws of a number of marked beans. Without the board and pieces, the mere throwing hazards with the beans or lots, to bet on the winning throws, furnishes the North American tribes with their favourite means of gambling, the game of plumstones, game of the bowl, etc.

It is a curious inquiry what led people to the by no means obvious idea of finding sport in placing stones or pieces on a diagram and moving them by rule. One hint as to how this may have come about is found in the men at backgammon acting as though they were "counters" counting up the throws. The word *abax*, or *abacus*, is used both for the reckoning-board with its counters and the playboard with its pieces, whence a plausible guess has been made that playing on the ruled board came from a

[2] See the author's paper in the *Journal of the Anthropological Institute,* November, 1878.

sportive use of the serious counting instrument. The other hint is that board-games, from the rudest up to chess, are so generally of the nature of *kriegspiel,* or war-game, the men marching on the field to unite their forces or capture their enemies, that this notion of mimic war may have been the very key to their invention. Still these guesses are far from sufficient, and the origin of board-games is still among the anthropologist's unanswered riddles. The simpler board-games of skill, that is, without lots or dice, and played by successive moves or draws of the pieces, may be classed accordingly as games of *draughts,* this term including a number of different games, ancient and modern.

The ancient Egyptians were eager draught-players; but though we have many pictures, and even the actual boards and men used, it is not clear exactly how any of their games were played. Ingenuity and good heavy erudition have been misspent by scholars in trying to reconstruct ancient games without the necessary data, and I shall not add here another guess as to the rules of the draughts with which Penelope's suitors delighted their souls as they sat at the palace gates on the hides of the oxen they had slaughtered; nor will I discuss the various theories as to what the "sacred line" was in the Greek game of the "five lines," mentioned by Sophocles. It will be more to the purpose to point out that games worth keeping up hardly die out, so that among existing sports are probably represented, with more or less variation, the best games of the ancients. On looking into the mentions of the famous Greek draught-game of *plinthion,* or *polis,* it appears that the numerous pieces, or "dogs," half of them of one colour and half of the other, were moved on the squares of the board, the game being for two of the same colour to get one of the other colour between them, and so take him. The attempt to reason out from this ·the exact rules of the classic game has not answered. But on looking, instead of arguing, I find that a game just fitting the description still actually exists. The donkeyboys of Cairo play it in the dust with "dogs," which are bits of stone and red brick, and the guides have scratched its *siga,* or diagram, on the top of the great pyramid. If it was not there before, it would have come with Alexander to Alexandria, and has seemingly gone on unchanged since. There is an account of it in Lane's *Modern Egyptians,* and any one interested in games will find it worth trying with draughts on a cardboard square. One kind of the Roman game of *latrunculi* was closely related to this, as appears from such passages as Ovid's "cum medius gemino calculus hoste perit," referring to the stone being taken between two enemies. The poet mentions, a few lines farther on, the little table with its three stones, where the game is "continuasse suos," to get your men in a line, which is, of course, our own childish game of *tit-tat-to*. This case of the permanence of an ancient game was long ago recognised by Hyde in his treatise, *De Ludis Orientalibus*. It is the simplest form of the group known to us as *mill, merelles, morris*, played by children all the way across from Shetland to Singapore. Among the varieties of draught-games played in the world, one of the most elaborate is the Chinese *wei-chi*, or game of circumvention, the honoured pastime of the learned classes. Here one object is to take your enemy by surrounding him with four of your own men, so as to make what is called an "eye," which looks as though the game belonged historically to the same group as the simpler classic draughts, where the man is taken between two adversaries. In modern Europe the older games of this class have been superseded by one on a different principle. The history of what we now call *draughts* is disclosed by the French dictionary, which shows how the men used to be called *pions*, or pawns, till they reached the other side of the board, then becoming *dames*, or queens. Thus the modern game of draughts is recognised as being, in fact, a low variety of chess, in which the pieces are all pawns, turned into queens in chess-fashion when they gain the adversary's line. The earliest plain accounts of the game are in Spanish books of the Middle Ages, and the theory of its development through the mediæval chess problems will be found worked out by the best authority on chess, Dr. A. van der Linde, in his *Geschichte des Schachspiels*.

The group of games represented by the Hindu *tiger-and-cows*, our *fox-and-geese*, shows in a simple way the new situations that arise in board-games when the men are no longer all alike, but have different powers, or moves. Isidore of Seville (about A.D. 600) mentions, under the name of *latrunculi*, a game played with pieces of which some were common soldiers (*ordinarii*), marching step by step, while others were wanderers (*ragi*). It seems clear that the notions of a kriegspiel, or war-game, and of pieces with different powers moving on the chequer-board, were familiar in the civilized world at the time when, in the eighth century or earlier, some inventive Hindu may have given them a more perfect organization by setting on the board two whole opposing armies, each complete in the four forces, foot, horse, elephants, and chariots, from which an Indian army is called in Sanskrit *chaturanga*, or "four-bodied." The game thus devised was itself called *chaturanga*, for when it passed into Persia it carried with it its Indian name in the form *shatranj*, still retained there, though lost by other nations who received the game from Persia, and named it from the Persian name of the principal piece, the *shah*, or king, whence *schach, eschees, chess*. According to this simple theory, which seems to have the best evidence, chess is a late and high development arising out of the ancient draught-games. But there is another theory maintained by Professor Duncan Forbes in his *History of Chess,* and prominent in one at least of our chess handbooks, which practically amounts to saying that chess is derived from backgammon. It is argued that the original game was the Indian fourfold-chess, played with four half-sets of men, black, red, green, and yellow, ranged on the four sides of the board, the moves of the pieces being regulated by the throws of dice; that in course of time the dice were given up, and each two allied half-sets of men coalesced into one whole set, one of the two kings sinking to the position of minister, or queen. Now this fourfold Indian dice-chess is undoubtedly a real game, but the mentions of it are modern, whereas history records the spread of chess proper over the East as early as the tenth century. In the most advanced Indian form of *pachisi,* called *chapur,* there are not only the four sets of different-coloured men, but the very same stick-dice that are used in the dice-chess, which looks as though this latter game, far from being the original form of chess, were an absurd modern hybrid resulting from the attempt to play backgammon with chess-men. This is Dr. van der Linde's opinion, readers of whose book will find it supported by more technical points, while they will be amused with the author's zeal in belabouring his adversary Forbes, which reminds one of the legends of mediæval chess-players, where the match naturally concludes by one banging the other about the head with the board. It is needless to describe here the well-known points of difference between the Indo-Persian and the modern European chess. On the whole, the Indian game has substantially held its own, while numberless attempts to develop it into philosophers' chess, military tactics, etc., have been tried and failed, bringing, as they always do, too much instructive detail into the plan which in ancient India was shaped so judiciously between sport and science.

In this survey of games I have confined myself to such as offered subjects for definite remark, the many not touched on including cards, of which the precise history is still obscure. Of the conclusions brought forward, most are no doubt imperfect, and some may be wrong, but it seemed best to bring them forward for the purpose of giving the subject publicity, with a view to inducing travellers and others to draw up minutely accurate accounts of all undescribed games they notice. In Cook's *Third Voyage* it is mentioned that the Sandwich Islanders played a game like draughts with black and white pebbles on a board of 14 by 17 squares. Had the explorers spent an hour in learning it, we should perhaps have known whether it was the Chinese or the Malay game, or what it was; and this might have been the very clue, lost to native memory, to the connection of the Polynesians with a higher Asiatic culture in ages before a European ship had come within their coral reefs.

It remains to call attention to a point which this research into the development of games brings strongly into view. In the study of civilisation, as of so many other branches of natural history, a theory of gradual evolution proves itself a trustworthy guide. But it will not do to assume that culture must always come on by regular unvarying progress. That, on the contrary, the lines of change may be extremely circuitous, the history of games affords instructive proofs. Looking over a playground wall at a game of hockey, one might easily fancy the simple line of improvement to have been that the modern schoolboy took to using a curved stick to drive the ball with, instead of hurling it with his hands as he would have done if he had been a young Athenian of B.C. 500. But now it appears that the line of progress was by no means so simple and straight, if we have to go round by Persia, and bring in the game of polo as an intermediate stage. If, comparing Greek draughts and English draughts, we were to jump to the conclusion that the one was simply a further development of the other, this would be wrong, for the real course appears to have been that some old draught-game rose into chess, and then again a lowered form of chess came down to become a new game of draughts. We may depend upon it that the great world-game of evolution is not played only by pawns moving straight on, one square before another, but that long-stretching moves of pieces in all directions bring on new situations, not readily foreseen by minds that find it hard to see six moves ahead upon a chessboard.

4

On American Lot-Games, as Evidence of Asiatic Intercourse Before the Time of Columbus

E. B. TYLOR

It is now nearly twenty years since I brought forward in the *Journal of the Anthropological Institute* and elsewhere[1] a comparison between two elaborate games of mingled chance and skill, namely *pachisi,* an ancient and still popular sport in Hindustan, and *patolli,* which was an established diversion in Mexico at the time of the Spanish conquest. My argument was that the principle and even the details of these two games bear so close a resemblance, as to make their independent invention improbable, justifying the inference that at some date before 1500 the Asiatic game had passed over to America. Such a theory, if well-founded, supports the opinion long ago enunciated by Alexander von Humboldt, that the old civilization of Mexico bears unmistakable traces of Asiatic influence. Accordingly, the problem of the two games became matter of anthropological controversy, their alleged connexion being claimed by some as convincing, and by others not less positively rejected, while admitted on both sides as bringing to a definite issue the question of American civilization before the European period. New evidence which has

SOURCE. Supplement to *International Archives for Ethnographie* 9, 1896, pp. 56–66.

[1] On the Game of Patolli in Ancient Mexico and its probably Asiatic Origin; *Journal of the Anthropological Institute of Great Britain and Ireland,* 1878. Backgammon among the Aztecs, in *Macmillan's Magazine,* Dec. 1878, etc.

since come in, makes it desirable for me to return to the discussion. Especially not only has the text of Father Diego Duran's *History of the Indies* been published, but the picture-writing on which he commented has been reproduced; his chapter on *patolli* is thus fully available, and with it the authentic representation of two Aztecs playing the game. . . . I have to thank Sir Alfred Lyall for providing the fit pendant to this picture by having a photograph taken in India, of a match at *pachisi* between a Hindu and a Mohammedan. The mere comparison of the two groups seems to me sufficient to set up a primâ facie case, that the gamesters of the Old and New World are engaged at games which, though not quite the same, are closely connected varieties from one original.

The group to which *pachisi* and *patolli* belong is most familiar to Europeans in trictrac or backgammon, though some other forms are in use, such as the "royal game of goose" (jeu de l'oie, jeugo de la oca, etc.) and various race-games and others. In their complete forms, games of this class are played by opponents who move pieces on a diagram or board in opposition to one another, the number of places moved being determined by the players throwing lots or dice. It has to be noticed that just as dice-throwing by itself serves as a means of gambling, so it is with lot-throwing, the appearance of which latter in America has to form part of the present argument. Dice and their use need no special remark here, but this kind of gaming with lots is less familiar, and must be briefly considered. The lots used are two-faced, and their earliest purpose may have been for divination, before they came to serve for sport. The sacred lots consulted in Confucian temples are halves of a bambu root which are solemnly thrown down, both round sides up giving a negative, both flat sides an indifferent, and one round and one flat side an affirmative answer of the oracle. By a larger number of lots gamesters obtain a greater variety of results, in a mode which may be best explained by setting down, according to the elementary rule of probability, the frequency of the combinations of heads and tails when n coins are tossed together

$$\left(1, n, \frac{n(n-1)}{2}, \frac{n(n-1)(n-2)}{2.3}, \text{etc.}\right)$$

and thence the proportionate value of each combination. For example, let five coins be tossed, and let the value of the two best throws, five heads or tails, be taken as 25.

Heads up			5	4	3	2	1	0
or								
Tails up			0	1	2	3	4	5
Frequency			1	5	10	10	5	1
Value of Throw			25	5	2½	2½	5	25

When the calculated values of the throws are compared with the values given to them in the various games to be presently described, it will be seen that the rules of scoring are in general inexact. For instance the game of *pachisi*, played by throwing five cowries, ought to conform in the scoring to the figures just given, but in fact it only shows an imperfect similarity. At the same time, the whole series of lot-games displays a consciousness of the infrequency of throws of all, or nearly all the faces one way, as compared with throws where the faces are nearly equally divided. When these games were invented, the mathematical method of working out the combinations had not been reached, and apparently the only guide was experience, showing which throws were rarest and therefore ought to count most. Thus these games are of interest in the history of mathematics, as showing the early empirical stage of the doctrine of chances, which reached its logical development in the hands of Pascal and Fermat far on in the 17th century. As a means of gambling except in its simplest forms, the casting of two-faced lots is a clumsy process in comparison with the use of numbered dice, which tends to supersede it wherever both are known, so that it may be reasonably thought that the lot-games represent the original form, out of which the dice-games arose.

As a simple Old World type of lot-backgammon, the game called in colloquial Arabic *tâb*, and popular in Moslem countries, may be specified. The lots thrown are slips of split palm-branch about a span long, white on the inside, while the outside is left green, these sides being called white and black respectively. They are thrown against a wall or an upright stick, and the throw counts according to how many white sides come uppermost, thus:

Whites up	. . .	4	3	2	1	0
Score	. . .	4+	3	2	1+	6+

Those marked + give a new throw. Their values agree fairly well with the calculated odds, which are 6, $1\frac{1}{2}$, 1, $1\frac{1}{2}$, 6. The game is played by moving pieces, usually bits of stone on one side and red brick on the other, on a diagram scratched on the ground, or with a more formal board and men. The *tâb*-board (Fig. 1) is divided into four rows of an odd number of squares; each of the two players placing a number of his pieces or "dogs" in the outer row on his own side. The lots are thrown by the players alternately till one player throws one white, which throw is called "*tâb*" and gives him the right to move one of his pieces from its original place; while there it is called a Nazarene, but when moved and able to go out to fight it becomes a Moslem. Throwing four whites or blacks, or one white, gives a new throw. Each player moves his right-hand man first, the course being from left to right in his own row, then right to left in the row in front, then from left to right again; a piece moved into a

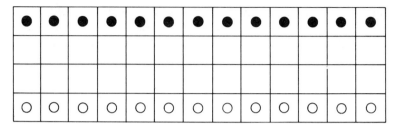

Fig. 1.   Diagram for game of *tab*.

place occupied by one of the adversary's pieces takes it; if a player has
two or more pieces on one square, they move together as one; pieces
which have reached the adversary's row are in safety. The lot-throwing
part of the game may be played by itself, the throwers of 6 and 4 being
called Sultan and Wezir, from whom the unfortunate thrower of 2 receives blows on the soles of his feet with a palmstick. . . .[2]

There is a Chinese variety of the game of four sticks, popular under
the name of *nyut* in Korea, where Mr. Stewart Culin describes it.[3] Four
lots are used, made of bow-wood, plano-convex and with one black and
one white side. The scoring is

Whites up	. . .	4	3	2	1	0
Score	. . . .	4+	3	2	1	5

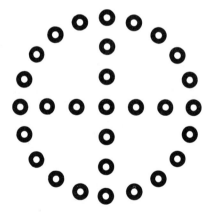

Fig. 2.   Diagram for game of *nyut*.

[2] E. W. Lane, *Manners and Customs of the Modern Egyptians*, **II**, chap. IV. Hyde,
De Ludis Orientalibus, **II**, p. 217.

[3] Culin, *Korean Games* (Philadelphia 1895). I.A.f.E. **IX**. Suppl.

Four blacks give another throw. The calculated values would be 4, 1, $\frac{2}{3}$, 1, 4.

Little sticks or other objects are used as markers or pieces, called horses (*má*) of which each player has from one to four, which move and take along the spots of the diagram.

Sanskrit literature furnishes early mentions of this family of games in India. The game of *ayânaya*, luck and unluck, has been discussed by Prof. Albrecht Weber,[4] and the mention of *panchikâ*, a game played with five cowries, may refer to *pachisi*, with which we are specially concerned, and which will now be briefly described. [A] cloth embroidered with squares which commonly serves as the board [is] often carried by zealous players rolled in their turbans. [There are] pieces (*got*) . . . of four colours, a set of four of one colour being played by each of four players, or by two playing two sets each. . . . The five cowries thrown as lots score as follows:

Mouths up . . .	5	4	3	2	1	0
Score	25+	4	3	2	10+	6+

The calculated value has been already given, 25, 5, $2\frac{1}{2}$, $2\frac{1}{2}$, 5, 25. The name of the game *pachisi* (= 25) or *dás pachisi* (= 10 25) is taken from the two highest throws. The scoring with five cowries is from a good authority,[5] but Dr. Rajendralâla Mitra, who has been good enough to send me a careful account, takes six cowries as the usual number, which requires the addition of 6-up, counting 12+, to the scoring with five cowries. In playing *pachisi,* the object of each of the four players is to move his pieces from the central space down the middle row of his own arm to its end, then along the outer lines of squares from left to right (against the sun) till having made the circuit of the whole board they come back, each reaching the end of its proper arm and returning home as it came, the winning player being he who gets his four pieces round first. The pieces move onward as many squares as the score of the throw, but a piece can only be started from the central space, or return there from the last square, by means of the starting 1 which is given to the thrower of *dás* (10) or *pachisi* (25) in addition to his proper score. The high throws 25+, 10+, 6+, entitle the player to a new throw. A single piece on a square is taken by an enemy's piece moving on to that square, and has to go home and begin afresh. But two or more on one square hold it safely; also in the crossed squares or forts (*chik*) a single piece is in safety, and

[4] A. Weber, *Indische Studien*, **XIII**, p. 471.
[5] *Qanoon-e-Islam*, transl. by Herklots. London 1832, p. LII.

blocks the entrance of an enemy. It will have been noticed that the relation of *pachisi* to *tâb* is close, *pachisi* being reduplicated to admit four players. A further change is to replace the cowries by dice; these are of a peculiar long form with four faces. . . . Thus modified, *pachisi* passes into the game known as *chûpur*.[6]

In this manner a simple lot-game like *tâb* may have given rise to the dice-game which prevails with so great similarity across the world, that ordinary European names may be used for it almost indifferently, such as tables, trictac, backgammon. Its introduction may be assigned to Western Asia, probably to Persia, where it was known at the time of Artaxerxes, and flourishes still under the name of *nard*. It is needless to discuss its later history here, but attention should be drawn to a point which touches the present enquiry. While the dice-game is common to the Eastern and Western worlds, so that an Icelander could easily play backgammon with a Japanese on an ancient Roman board, the lot-game which seems to have preceded it spread east rather than west. At any rate, if any game like *tâb* or *pachisi* played with two-faced lots ever reached Western Europe, it is not commonly known, nor recorded in ordinary books on the history of games. In now examining the American games, it will be seen that this bears forcibly, though not indeed conclusively, on the question whether these correspond more closely with games belonging to Asiatics or to Europeans.

As early as 1519, the Spanish invaders on their way to the city of Mexico noticed cloths worked in chessboard-pattern from which they judged that the dice-boxes of chequers were also in use in the country.[7] The only known Mexican game for which these cloths were likely to have been intended was *patolli*. Of this game the description by Lopez de Gomara was written between 1540–50, as follows: Sometimes Montezuma looked on as they played at *patoliztli*, which much resembles the game of tables, and which is played with beans marked like one-faced dice which they call *patolli*, which they shake between both hands and throw on a mat or on the ground where there are certain lines like a merell-board, on which they mark with stones the point that came up, by taking off or putting on a little stone.[8] Juan de Torquemada partly follows this account

[6] See Hyde, *De Ludis Orientalibus*, II, p. 68. Falkener, *Ancient Games*, London, 1892, p. 257. Another variety is known as *ashta-kashte*.

[7] Petr. Martyr. *De nuper repertis Insulis*, Basileæ 1521 p. 38; *De Orbe novo*, Compluti 1530, p. 86. "Lodices uarias gossampinas, cãdido, nigro et flavo coloribus intextas, duas auro et gemmis dites, tresq: alias pennis et gossampino intextas scacorum ludo; quod argumentum est et scarcorum fritillos habere eos in usu." "Non est alienum a re, licet ludricum, quibus ludis utantur dicere: scacorum fritillos habere notum est, per scacos in lodicibus contextos."

[8] Francesco Lopez de Gomara, *Istoria de las Indias*, Saragossa 1552, fol. 42. "Al-

but gives further details: "there was another game they call *patolli*, which somewhat resembles the game of royal tables, and is played with beans having points made in them after the manner of one-faced dice, and they call it the game of *patolli* because these dice are so called; they throw them with both hands on a thin mat which is called *petate*, with certain lines drawn on it in the form of a St. Andrew's cross and others across them, marking the point which fell upwards (as is done with dice) taking off or putting on stones of different colour, as in the game of tables.[9] Bernardino de Sahagun has other details to contribute, especially as to the marking of the beans. He mentions *patolli* as a pastime of the lords, describing the lots as "four large beans, each having a hole," and again that "they made on the mat a painted cross full of squares . . . they took three great beans with certain dots made in them, and let them fall on the painted cross. By the time of this writer the game, at which gold and jewels used to be staked, had been given up under suspicion of idolatry.[10]

The already mentioned *History of the Indies* bearing the name of Diego Duran appears from the critical examination by Ramirez and Chevero to have been more or less an earlier composition written by a native

gunas vezes mirauia Moteççuma como jugauan al Patoliztli, que parece mucho al juego de las tablas. Y que se juega con hauas, o frisoles raiados como dados de harinillas que dizen Patolli. Los quales menean entre ambas manos. Y los echan sobre una estera, o en el suedo, donde ay ciertas raias, como alquerque, en que señalan con piedras el punto que cayo arriba, quitando, o poniendo china." The harinillas or arenillas were dice used in Spain at the game of rentilla, they had points on only one face, numbering one to six.

[9] Juan de Torquemada, *Monarquia Indiana*, Seville 1615, book XIV, c. 12 "Auia otro juego que llaman *Patolli*, que en algo parece al juego de las tablas reales, y juegase con hauas y frisoles, hechos puntos en ellos, a manera de dados de arenillas, y dizenle juego *Patolli*, porque estos dados se llaman assi; echanlos con ambas manos sobre una estera delgada que se llama *petate*, hechas ciertas rayas a manera de aspa y atrauessando otras señalando el puto que cayò hazia arriba (como se haze en los dados) quitando, o poniendo chinas de diferente color, como en el juego de las tablas."

[10] Bernardino de Sahagun, "Historia Universal de las Cosas de Nueva España," in Kingsborough, *Antiquities of Mexico*, VII, book VIII, c. 10, 17. "Tambien los Señores por su pasatiempo jugaban un juego que se llama *Patolli*, que es como el juego del castro ó alquerque ó casi, ó como el juego de los dados, y son cuator frisoles grandes que cada uno tiene un agujero, y arrojanles con la mano sobre un petate como quen juega a los carnicoles donde está hecha una figura. A este juego solian jugar y ganarse cosas preciosas, como cuentas de oro y piedras preciosas, turquesas muy finas. Este juego y el de la pelota hanlo dejado, por ser sospechosos de algunas superstitiones idolatricas que en ellos hay." "El segunde pasatiempo que tenian era un juego como dados; hacien en un petate una cruz pintada llena de cuardros semejantes al juego del alquerque ó castro, y puestos sobre el petate sentados tomaban tres frisoles grandes hechos ciertos puntos en ellos, y dejabanlos caer sobre la cruz pintada, y de alli tenian su juego."

Mexican, probably in his own language. The picture-writing accompanying it, though so late as to be much Europeanized, is an authentic document. The whole may be taken as a record from, or near, the first generation after the conquest in 1521. Chapter C. treats chiefly of *patolli*, at which and other games the Indians not only would gamble themselves into slavery, but even came to be legally put to death as human sacrifices. So covetous were these gamblers that they took as their particular gods the instruments of their game, if it was dice-playing they held the dice as a god and the lines and figures marked on the mat, as seen in the picture, which gods they worshipped with particular ceremonies not only at this game but at all their other games. They played the game of *merells* or draughts imitating the game of chess played by the Spaniards, taking one from the other the back and white stones or pieces. "There was another game, which was that they made on a plaster floor little hollows after the manner of a game-board, and one took ten stones and the other ten others, and the one placed his stones on the one edge and the other on the other on contrary sides, and taking some reeds split down the middle they threw them on the ground so that they sprang up, and as many reeds as fell with the hollow side upward so many places he moved his stones forward, and thus one followed the other, and all such stones as he overtook, he took one after another till he left his adversary without any." There was also the game of the mat, which was the keenest they played, at which many could play jointly and in company, "the game they played on this mat they called *patolly*, which is the same word we now use for cards." On this mat they had pointed a large St. Andrew's-cross filling the mat from corner to corner, within the hollow of which cross there were some transverse lines serving for squares, which cross and squares were marked and drawn with diluted olin (caoutchouc) . . . . for these squares there were twelve small stones, six red and six blue, which stones they divided between the players so many to each; if two played as was usual, each took six, and although many might play, one always played for all, they following his play . . . . who had the best throws of the dice, which were some black beans, five or ten according as they wished to lose or gain, which had some little white holes in each bean by which were marked the number of squares which were gained on each hand, where five were marked they were ten, and ten twenty, and if one, one, and if two, two, and if three, three, and if four, four, but marking five they were ten, and if ten, twenty, and thus these little white dots were the lots and counting of the lines which were gained, and for moving the stones from some squares to others." So many spectators and gamblers crowded round the mat, some to play and some to bet, that is was wonderful, and if the game was played on a sudden and there was no olin to make the lines of the gamingboard with on the mat, they used plants, as gourds or a herb called *chichicpatly* or bitter medicine, with the soot of pine-wood. The gamblers used to go about with the mat under their arms, and the dice tied in a cloth, and as in our day gamesters go with the cards in their breeches from one gaming-house to another, so these carried the dice and stone pieces of the game in a little basket, doing reverence to them as gods, and talking to them as they played as to intelligent creatures, which as our author says, he does not wonder at, seeing how Christians of our nation who pride themselves on their delicate judgment will with hands crossed beg the cards for good points, and afterwards if they do not gain utter a thousand blasphemies against God and his saints, so these natives talked to the little beans and the mat with a thousand loving words and then would set the little basket in the place of adoration with the instruments of the game and the painted mat beside it and bring fire and throw incense into it, and doing their sacrifice in front with an offering of food, set to play with all the confidence in the world. . . . The name of the god of dice was *Macuilxochitl*, that is to say Five Roses,[11] him the gamblers invoked when they threw the beans from their hand, which was in the manner I shall state, that the beans which serve as dice are five in honour of that god who has the name of Five Roses, and to throw a main they carry them first a while turning them over between the hands, and in throwing them on the mat where is the figure of their gaming-board and score, they called in a loud voice *Macuilxochitl*, and gave a great clap of the hands and turned to see the points they had got, and this *Macuilxochitl* was solely for this game of dice." There was another god who was for games in general, named *Ometochtly* or Two Rabbits, and whenever in this or other games they wished deuce to be thrown they invoked him. He was also the god of pulque and tavern-keepers, and Fray Diego winds up his account by saying that he remembered when the magistrates were putting down the games and apprehending and punishing the gamblers, tearing up the *patolli*-mats and burning the beans, in order at once to put an end to the superstitious practices and the harm and waste caused by gambling.[12]

[11] More correctly Five Flowers.

[12] Diego Duran, *Historia de las Indias*. 2 vols & Atlas. Mexico, 1867–80. II. cap. C. The somewhat abridged translation of this diffuse account may serve to interpret the author's meaning, but some of his statements are obscure. I have to acknowledge help kindly given by Don Fernando de Anteaga, Lecturer in Spanish in the University of Oxford, in dealing with these difficult passages, but he thinks it impossible to make sense of some of them.

Cap. C. "En todas las naciones hubo y hay juego y tahures que los inventasen y jugasen no solo para perder sus haciendas y dineros pero algunos pierden las vidas y lo que peor es que juntamente las almas (lo cual es mucho de doler) de los cuales juegos no careció esta nacion mexicana pues ténían juegos y maneras de perder sus haciendas y á sí mismos despues de perdidas se jugaban y se volvían esclavos perpetuos de los cuales ganaban y perdían juntamente las vidas pues era notorio que vuelto esclavo venían á parar en ser sacrificados á sus dioses. Había en aquel tiempo tantos y tan codiciosos tahures y era tanta la codicia que había entre ellos de ganar que los que eran dados á este vicio tenían por dios particular suyo à los instrumentos del juego cualquiera que fuese por que si era de dados á osos dados tenían por dios y á las rayas y efigies que en la estera estaban señaladas (como en la muestra vimos) á quien con particulares ofrendas y con particulares ceremonias honraban y reverenciaban no solamente á este juego empero á todos los demas de que usaban jugar con interes de perder ó ganar los cuales juegos eran muchos y diversos con diferentes instrumentos y maneras. Jugaban el juego del alquerque ó de las damas imitando el juego que nosotros jugamos del adjedrez prendiéndose las chinas el uno al altro las cuales piedras servían de piedras las unas blancas y las otras negras.

Había otro juego que era que hacían encima de un encalado unos oyos pequeñitos á manera de fortuna y el uno tomaba diez piedras y el otro otras diez y el uno ponía sus piedras por la una acera y el otro por la otra en contrarias partes e con unas cañuelas hendidas por medio daban en el sue lo y saltaban en alto y tantas cuantas cañuelas caían lo güeco hácia arriba tantas casas adelantaba sus piedras y así seguían el uno al otro y todas cuantas chinas le alcanzaba se las iba quitando hasta dejalle sin ninguna y acontecía habelle quitado cinco y seis y con las cuatro que le quedaban decirle tambien las cañuelas que revolvía sobre el otro y ganalle el juego. Había este juego de la estera que era el mas recio que se jugaba casi como entre nosotros la primera ó las presas que son juegos para de presto como dicen á este juego podían jugar muchos juntos y de compañia como querían y así era el juego mas usado que había del cual principalmente pienso tratar y declarallo pues nuestro principal intento es en este capítulo tratar de él y del modo que de jugalle tenían para lo cual es de saber que al juego que sobra esta estera jugaban llamaban *patolly* que es el mesmo bocablo que agora llamamos *naypes*. Sobre esta estera tenían pintada una aspa grande de que tomaba el petate de esquina á esquina dentro del güeco de esta aspa había atravesadas unas rayas que servían de casas la cual aspa y casas estaban señaladas y rayadas con olin derretido . . . . para estas casas había doce piedras pequeñas las seis coloradas y las seis azules las cuales piedrezuelas partian entre los que jugaban á cada cual tantas: si jugaban dos que era lo ordinario tomaba las seis y el otro las otras seis y aunque jugasen muchos siempre jugaba uno por todos atendiéndose á la suerte de aquel como entre los españoles se juegan los albures ateniéndose á la mejor suerte así se atenian acá al que mejor meneaba los dados, los cuales eran unos frijoles negros cinco ó diez como querían perder ó ganar los cuales tenían unos agugerillos blancos en cada frijol por donde pintaban el número de las casas que se aventajaban en cada mano donde se pintauan cinco eran diez y diez veinte y si uno uno y si dos dos y si tres tres y si cuatro cuatro pero pintando cinco eran diez y si diez veinte y así aquellas pintillas blancas eran suertes y cuenta de las rayas que se ganaban y para mudar las piedras de unas casas en otras. Al cual juego cuando se jugaba acudian tantos miradores y tahures que estaban unos sobre otros sobre la estera unos para jugar otros para apostar que era cosa estraña. Cuando las rayas de esta estera (si el juego se inventaba de presto) no había olin para hacellas había particulares yerbas para hacer las rayas de aquella fortuna como eran hojas de cala-

I pass over descriptions of *patolli* by later writers,[13] who had no direct knowledge of the game and in no way improve on the statements of the early chroniclers. The foregoing citations from these may have seemed to the reader of tedious length, yet there is hardly a sentence in them which is not evidence in the case. The accounts of the popularity of the

baza ó la mesma calabacilla pequeñita ó una yerba que ellos llaman *chichicpatly* que quiere decir la medicina amarga ó con tigne de *ocotl*. en lo cual mezclaban supersticion por causa de que había de ser con esta yerba y con esta y no con otra siempre teniendo obgeto á idolatria. Andaban los tahures de este juego siempre con la estera debajo del sobaco y con los dados atados á un pañito como algunos tahures de este tíempo que siempre andan apercibidos con los naypes en las calzas de tablage en tablage aquellos dados juntamente con las piedrezuelas del juego traian en una baserita pequeña á los cuales hacian reverencia como á dioses fingiendo en ellos haber alguna virtud y así les hablaban cuando jugaban como á cosa que tuviese algun sentido ó inteligencia de lo que le pedian y no me espanta ni me maravillo que les hablasen pues era gente de no tan agudo juicio como lo son los de ntra. nacion les hablasen y pidiesen les fuesen favorables y ayudasen en aquel juego pues hay cristianos de nuestra nacion que presumen de muy delicados juicios que puestas las manos piden al naype buen punto y buena suerte y si no le entró despues de haber adorado los naypes si así se puede decir (con las manos puestas) decir mil blasfemias contra Dios y sus santos así estos naturales hablaban á los frijolítos y al petate y decían mil palabras de amor y mil requiebros y mil supersticiones y despues de habelles hablado ponían la petaquilla en el lugar de adoracion con los instrumentos del juego y la estera pintada junto á ella y traia lumbre y echaba en la lumbre incienzo y ofrecía su sacrificio ante aquellos instrumentos ofreciendo comida delante de ellos. Acabada la ofrenda y ceremonias iban á jugar con toda la confianza del mundo . . . El nombre del Dios de los dados era *Macuilxochitl* que quiere decir cinco rosas á este invocaban los jugadores cuando arrojaban los frijoles de le mano lo cual era á la manera que diré que los frijolillos que sirven como de dados son cinco á honra de acquel Dios que tiene nombre de cinco rosas y para echar la suerte tráenlos primero un rato refregándolos entre las manos y al lanzallos sobre la estera donde esta la figura de la fortuna y cuenta suya que es á la manera de dos bastos llamaban á alta voz *Macuilxochitl* y daban una gran palmada y luego acudían á ver los puntos que le habían entrado y este *Macuilxochitl* era solamenta para este juego de los dados había empero otro dios que era general para todos los juegos el cual es el que ves presente y tenía por nombre *Ometochtly* que quiere decir dos conejos y así para el juego dicho como para los demas todas las vezes que querían que les entrase el dos hacían la mesma invocacion al soltar de las arenillas dando aquella palmada *Ometochtly* que quiere decir dos conejos. Tambien es necesario que al vino que beben tuvieron estos por dios antiguamente y llamanbanle *Ometochtly* y todos los taberneros y taberneras le celebraban sus ritos y ceremonias y ofrendas con toda la solemnidad y devocion posible . . .

Acuérdome que antiguamente andaban las justicias seglares á destruir estos juegos y a aprehender y castigar los jugadores poniéndoles graves penas rompiendoles las esteras en que tenían pintadas aquellas fortunas la causa de aqueste rigor era por destruir las supersticiones y malas venturas ete. etc.

[13] Clavigero, *Storia antica del Messico*. Cesena 1780, II, p. 185. Brasseur de Bourbourg, *Histoire des Nations Civilisées du Mexique et de Amérique Centrale*, Paris 1858, III p. 671.

game at the time of the conquest, the mention of its special god and the ceremonies of his worship, preclude the idea of the Europeans having brought it into the country with their own cards and dice which have long since superseded it. The descriptions given by the Spaniards indeed show that the game was new to them, for they noticed its resemblance to the game of tables and in a less degree to draught-games; had they known anything nearer they would have said so. The only difficulty lies in the descriptions of the lots and the scoring, the very confusion of which seems to show that the Spaniards were not familiar with the device of lot-scoring, as a Hindu or Arab would be, or they would have expressly distinguished it from the use of numbered dice or tallies.

Here, however, other evidence is available, in that some variety of the game, more or less simplified or broken-down, appears to have spread northward among the wilder Indian tribes, where it remained in vogue after its disappearance from among the Aztec nation. Father Joseph Ochs, a Jesuit missionary in this part from 1754–68, and who lived among the Tarahumara and Pima Indians, writes thus: "Instead of our cards they have slips of reed or wooden sticks a thumb wide and almost a span long, on which, as on a tally, different strokes are cut in and stained black. These they hold together tight in the hand, raise them as high as they can and let them fall on the ground. He who has the more strokes or pips for him wins the stakes. This game is as bad as the notorious hazard. They call it *patole*. As it is forbidden on pain of blows, they choose a place out in the woods, yet the noise of these bits of wood has discovered for me many sharpers hidden in the bush. To play the more safely they spread a cloak or carpet, so as not to be betrayed by the noise."[14] Thus the Aztec name of *patolli* was still in use among a distant people of alien language to denote gambling with wooden lots. Another account, probably from an old authority, describes a more complete form among the South Californian Indians. "Fifty small pieces of wood, placed upright in a row in the ground at distances of two inches apart, formed the score. The players were provided with a number of pieces of split reed, blackened on one side; these were thrown, points down, on the ground, and the thrower counted one for every face that remained white side up, if he gained eight he was entitled to another throw. If the pieces all fell with the blackened side up they counted also. Small pieces of wood placed against the upright pegs marked the game. They reckoned from opposite ends of the row, and if one of the players threw out so many as to make his score

14 Murr, *Nachrichten von verschiedenen Ländern des Spanischen America*, Halle 1809, part. I. p. 256.

exactly meet that of his opponent, the former had to commence again."[15]
This description may be compared with the particulars noted by Mr. Robert Frazer of Philadelphia as to the Apache game of *tze-tiehl* or "stone
and sticks," which account he kindly sent me with the diagram (Fig. 3)
and a set of the lot-sticks on his return from a visit to the Apache country
in 1884. These lot-sticks are thrown against the centre stone shown in the
diagram and score thus:

Convex up . . .	3	2	1	0
Score	10+	3	1	5

According to calculation the numbers would be 10, $3\frac{1}{3}$, $3\frac{1}{3}$, 10. Three
up gives another throw. Fig. 3 shows the position of 40 small stones
placed in quadrants round the centre, the two players moving their mark-
ing-sticks, which are the pieces in the game, in opposite directions, and
the player whose stick falls on his opponent's taking it up and sending it
back, from which it is evident that the game is won by getting first round.
If now this Apache game be compared with the Chinese-Korean game of
nyut (Fig. 2) the resemblance will be seen to be so close that the Indians
might conceivably have learnt it from the Chinese who for years past have
swarmed in this part of America. But in one form or another the game
prevails among the native tribes. . . . It has been seen that the earlier accounts from the district date from times before the Chinese immigration.
At this point the evidence comes in of the often described "game of the

Fig. 3.   Diagram of stones arranged for Apache lot-game.

[15] Bancroft, *Native Races of the Pacific States of North America*, I. p. 415.

bowl" among the Indian tribes further north in the region of the great lakes. The Jesuit missionaries describe it among the Hurons so early as 1636, close on the first years of intercourse with the whites. Father le Jeune describes this "jeu de plat" as played with six plumstones, white on one side and black on the other, in a dish which was struck hard against the ground so as to turn the stones over. He thought the game was simply to get the faces all black or all white, but perhaps he did not take the trouble to examine thoroughly anything so trivial as a savage sport.[16] His account is implicitly contradicted on this point by Father Lafitau, who remarks that although the plumstones have only two sides, white and black, the Indians have a number of combinations rendering the game long and agreeable. This learned observant missionary-anthropologist noticed that the American game resembled one brought by the negros from Africa to the West India Islands.[17] . . . [A] bowl and peach stones as used half a century ago in the festival games of the Iroquois [is] described by L. H. Morgan. This diversion was believed to have come down from the beginning of the Iroquois League centuries ago, and the Indians hoped to continue its enjoyment in the happy regions of the future life. The tribes, represented by champion players, gambled ceremoniously in the public councilhouse, when the six peachstones, shaped flattish and burnt black on one side, were shaken in the bowl, scoring thus:

Blacks or whites up .	6	5	4	3	2	1	0
Score	5+	1+	0	0	0	1+	5+

All throws counting gave also another throw. The calculated values being, 5, $\frac{5}{6}$, $\frac{1}{3}$, $\frac{1}{4}$, $\frac{1}{3}$, $\frac{5}{6}$, 5, it results that the scoring corresponds to the nearest whole number, which is the only case of such accuracy I have met with and even suggests the possible intervention of some white schoolmaster. Also, the game was played with a bank, consisting usually of 100 beans between the two sides, these beans being given and taken according to the throws, and the match being won by the side gaining all the other's beans. This arrangement, familiar to the white man, I have not met with any other mention of among the native American tribes. The Iroquois game of deer-buttons, whether played as a family sport or pub-

---

[16] *Relations des Jesuites dans la Nouvelle France.* Quebec reprint 1858, I. (1636). p. 113.

[17] Lafitau, *Moeurs des Sauvages Ameriquains*, Paris 1724, **II.** p. 339. Labat, *Nouvelles Voyages aux Isles de l'Amerique*, **IV.** p. 153; this game is described as played with four perforated cowries, throws of four-up four-down or two each way winning; an account rather founded on fact than correct.

licly, did not differ essentially. The eight lots, cut out of elk-horn with one side blackened, were thrown from the hands, and the throws taking a corresponding number of beans from the bank reckoned.

Blacks or whites up	8	7	6	5	4	3	2	1	0
Score	20+	4+	2+	0	0	0	2+	4+	20+

The theoretical computation is $20, 2\frac{1}{2}, \frac{5}{7}, \frac{5}{14}, \frac{2}{7}, \frac{5}{14}, \frac{5}{7}, 2\frac{1}{2}, 20$ which is wanting in the accuracy of the peachstone game.[18] The game of the bowl is not yet forgotten by the Indians, and . . . a dish and bone buttons with a white and a red side . . . were given me by a lady, familiar with Indian life, Miss Abby Alger of Boston. The score is put down as

Whites up	6	5	4	3	2	1	0
Score	20	6	3		3	6	15

Schoolcraft has described among the Dakotas and Ojibways more elaborate bowlgames, in which the lots have on them figures of tortoises, warclubs etc., and his account has had much popularity through being worked by Longfellow into the poem of Hiawatha. These games, though founded on the native Indian games, are Europeanized hybrids of late times.[19]

Examination has now to be briefly made of the results of the preceding evidence. The existence in Mexico before the Spanish period of a game allied to *tâb* and *pachisi* may be maintained as hardly open to question. How the Aztec players moved and captured the coloured pieces along the rows of places on the diagrams according to regulated chance, is known by positive description and even by an authentic picture. The manner of the deciding chances, though sometimes indistinct, is on the whole recognizable. The use of simple two-faced lots, which have lasted on till now among the wilder northern tribes, is unmistakeable; the Aztec split reeds, and the beans with a hole on one side, can have been nothing else. The marking by several lines or dots may very well have been for the same purpose, but it is not impossible that it served for numbering the canes or beans so as to convert them into rudimentary dice somewhat such as the Spanish arenillas. If this were so, it would follow that the Aztecs knew how to play their game either with lots or dice, as the Hindus do at this day; we meet, however, with no trace of dice in early

---

[18] L. H. Morgan, *League of the Iroquois.* Rochester 1851, p. 302.
[19] Schoolcraft, *Indian tribes of the United States.* Part. II. p. 71. I.A.f.E. **IX.** Suppl.

accounts of the Indian tribes to the north. The descriptions of the moves also agree with lots rather than dice. In Duran's first game we read that the number of canes falling with the hollow side up determined the number of places to be moved, which easy method agrees with the play of the Southern Californians. In Duran's second game which was *patolli* proper, we meet with what seems a rule of probability, giving a much higher value to the extreme throws than to the middle or average throws, which as usual show a tendency to follow the mere number of faces turned up, as in the previous more rudimentary game; the reader sufficiently interested in the problem will make the comparison for himself between Duran's numbers and the scoring lists here given.

The idea that the similarity between the American and Asiatic games resulted from independent invention has seemed probable to more than one anthropologist. This suggestion raises the problem, as yet only imperfectly solved, of determining what kind and amount of similarity in the arts or customs or opinions of different districts may justify us in denying the possibility of their independent development and claiming them as results of transmission. Experience has indeed led the educated world to judge positively on this question in extreme cases. If Englishmen landing on a remote island were accosted by natives in their own language, the notion that English had been developed here as well as in England would be treated as a jest. If the natives were seen shooting with guns or playing chess, the suggestion of guns and chess having been twice invented even in approximate forms would hardly fare better. Where, then, is the limit of similarity which proves common derivation? Popular opinion is no doubt led by accumulated experience to consider that highly special or complex phenomena of thought and habit do not so readily recur as the obvious and simple, and probably this judgment is sound. The subject ought however to be brought to altogether more accurate definition. I have found it useful at any rate as a means of clearing ideas, to attempt a definite rule by analyzing such phenomena into constituent elements showing so little connexion with one another that they may be reasonably treated as independent. The more numerous are such elements, the more improbable the recurrence of their combination. In the case of a language recurrence may be treated as impossible. If the invention of the gun be divided into the blowtube, the use of metal, the explosive, the lock, the percussion etc., and classed as an invention say of the 10th order, and the invention of chess with its six kinds of pieces with different moves indicated as of perhaps the 6th order, these figures would correspond to an immense improbability of recurrence. Such a game as *pachisi*, combining the invention of divining by lot, its application to the sportive wager, the combination of several lots with an appreciation of the law of chances, the transfer of the result to a counting-board, the rules of moving and taking, would place it in perhaps the 6th order, the recurrence of which might be less than that of chess, but according to common experience still far outside any probability on which reasonable men could count.

If this argument be admitted, the relation of the *pachisi-patolli* groups of games in the Old and New World must be accounted for by intercourse before the Spanish conquest, other than that of the Northmen, which fails to answer the conditions. If communication across the Atlantic fails, the alternative is communication across the Pacific from Eastern Asia, where the sportive material required could readily be furnished.

5

Mancala, the National Game of Africa

STEWART CULIN

The comparative study of games is one that promises an important contribution to the history of culture. The questions involved in their diffusion over the earth are among the vital ones that confound the ethnologist. Their origins are lost in the unwritten history of the child-hood of man. Mancala is a game that is remarkable for its peculiar distribution, which seems to mark the limits of Arab culture, and which has just penetrated our own continent after having served for ages to divert the inhabitants of nearly half the inhabited area of the globe.

The visitor to the little Syrian colony in Washington Street in New York City will often find two men intent upon this game. They call it Mancala. The implements are a board with two rows of cup-shaped depressions and a handful or so of pebbles or shells, which they transfer from one hole to another with much rapidity. A lad from Damascus described to me the methods of play. There are two principal ways, which depend upon the manner in which the pieces are distributed at the commencement of the game. Two persons always engage, and ninety-eight cowrie shells (wada) or pebbles (hajdar) are used. One game is called La'b madjnuni, or the "Crazy game." The players seat themselves with the board placed lengthwise between them. One distributes the pieces in the fourteen holes, called bute, "houses," not less than two being placed in one hole. This player then takes all the pieces from the hole at the right of his row, fig.1, G, called el ras, "the head,"

SOURCE. *Annual Report of the U.S. National Museum* Washington, D.C.: U.S. Government Printing Office, 1894, pp. 597–606. Read before the Oriental Club of Philadelphia, May 10, 1894.

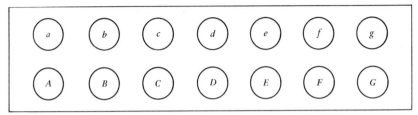

Fig. 1. Mancala.

and drops them one at a time into the holes on the opposite side, commencing with *a,b,c*, and so on. If any remain after he has put one in each of the holes on the opposite side, he continues around on his own row A,B,C. When he has dropped his last piece he takes all the pieces in that hole and continues dropping them around as before. This is done until one of two things happens—his last piece drops into an empty hole, when he stops and his opponent plays, or it drops into a hole containing one or three pieces, completing two or four. In that case he takes the two or four pieces with those in the hole opposite, and if one or more of the holes that follow contains two or four without the intervention of a hole with any other number, he takes their contents with those opposite. The second player takes from the hole *g*, and distributes his pieces around A, B, C. If the head is empty, the player takes from the next nearest hole in his row. When the board is cleared, each player counts the number he has above his opponent as his gains. No skill is necessary or of any avail in this game, the result being a mathematical certainty, according to the manner in which the pieces were distributed in the beginning. La'b hakimi, the "Rational game," or La'b akila, the "Intelligent game," is so called in contrast to the preceding. Success in it depends largely upon the skill of the players. In this game it is customary in Syria to put seven pieces in each hole. The players, instead of first taking from the hole on their right, may select any hole on their side of the board as a starting place. They calculate the hole in which the last piece will fall, and the result depends largely upon this calculation. La'b rosëya is a variety of the first game and is played only by children. Seven cowries are placed in each hole, and the first player invariably wins. My Syrian friend told me that the shells used in the game are brought from the shores of the Red Sea. Mancala is a common game in Syrian cafés. Children frequently play the game in holes made in the ground when they have no board, a devise also resorted to by travelers who meet by the way.

Mancala, the name which the Syrians give to this game, is a common Arabic word and means in this connection the "Game of transferring."

It is not mentioned in the Koran by this name, but must have been known to the Arabs in the Middle Ages, as it is referred to in the commentary to the Kitab al Aghani, the "Book of Songs," which speaks of a "game like Mancala."

Dr. Thomas Hyde gave a very good account of it two hundred years ago in his treatise, "De Ludis Orientalibus," and Lane, in his "Manners and Customs of the Modern Egyptians," describes it very fully as played in Cairo upon a board with twelve holes, quite in the manner I have related. Seventy-two shells or pebbles are there used, and, whether shells or pebbles, are indifferently called hasa. The hemispherical holes in the board are called buyoot, plural of beyt. The score of the game is sixty, and when the successive gains of a player amount to that sum he has won. I soon found that I had learned from my Syrian acquaintance nothing that had not been recorded, but upon visiting the Damascus House in the Turkish village at the Columbian Exposition at Chicago, I was enabled to engage with the Syrians in the game, and was impressed with the peculiar distribution of the game over the world. The Ceylon exhibit contained boards from the Maldives with sixteen holes in two parallel rows, with a large hole at either end. Here the game is called Naranj. Boards in the same exhibit from Ceylon had fourteen holes with two large central cavities, the game being called Chanka. An Indian gentleman informed me that the game was common at Bombay. His Highness the Sultan of Johore exhibited a boat-shaped board with sixteen holes under the name of Chongkak. I learned, too, that the game was common in Java, as well as in the Philippine Islands, where a boat-shaped board with sixteen holes is also used, the game being called Chungeajon. It would thus appear that the game extends along the entire coast of Asia as far as the Philippine Islands. Mancala and a kind of draughts were the favorite amusements of the negroes from the French settlement of Benin on the west coast of Africa in the so-called Dahomey village at the Columbian Fair. They played on a boat-shaped board, with twelve holes in two rows, which they called adjito, with pebbles, adji, the game itself being called Madji. It is with the continent of Africa that the game of Mancala seems most closely identified. It may be regarded, so to speak, as the African national game. In the exhibit of the State of Liberia at Chicago, there were no less than eleven boards, comprising three different forms, said to be from the Deys, Veys, Pesseh, Gedibo, and Queah. They were catalogued under the name of Poo, by which name the game is known to civilized Liberians. The game is, in fact, distributed among the African tribes from the east to the west and from the north to the south. In Nubia, where a board with sixteen holes is used, it is known as Mungala.

In the narrative of the Portuguese embassy of Alvarez to Abyssinia (1520–1527) reference is made to "Mancal" as an unknown game, antiquated in the reign of Don Manuel. Bent has recently described it as still existing in Abyssinia under the name of Gabatta.[1] Dr. George Schweinfurth states that it is played by the Niam-Niam, and is constantly played by all the people of the entire Gazelle district, although perhaps not known to the Monbuttoo. The Niam-Niam call the board, which has sixteen cavities, with two at the end for the reception of the cowrie shells, Abangah, and the Bongo name for the board is Toee. He also says that it is found among the Peulhs, the Foolahs, the Toloofs, and the Mandingos in the Senegal countries, who devote a great portion of their time to this amusement. Rohlfs found it among the Kadje, between the Tsad and the Benue.[2] It also occurs among the Biafren and the Kimbunda. Héli Chatelain, who lived for some time at Augola, described the game to me under the name Mbau, and said that cavities are cut in the rock for this game at the stations where the porters halt. A board collected by him at Elmina, now in the U.S. National Museum, Washington, D.C., has twelve holes in two rows, with large holes at the ends.

Among the Fans of the Gaboon River the game is called Kale,[3] after

[1] Speaking of the peasants of Sallaba, he says: "The primitive people are perfect artists in cow dung. With this material they make big jars in which to keep their grain, drinking goblets, and boards for the universal game, which the better class make of wood. I brought one of these away with me to show how universal this game is among the Abyssinians, from the chief to the peasant, and it reached the British Museum unbroken. This game is called Gabatta, and the wooden boards made by the better class contain eighteen holes, nine for each person. There are three balls, called chachtma, for each hole, and the game is played by a series of passing, which seemed to us very intricate, and which we could not learn; the holes they call their toukouls, or huts, and they get very excited over it. It closely resembles the game we saw played by the negroes in Mashonaland, and is generally found in one form or another in the countries where Arab influence has at one time or another been felt." ("The Sacred City of the Ethiopians," London, 1873, pp. 72–73.)

[2] Richard Andree, "Ethnographische Parallelen," neue folge, Leipzig, 1889, p. 102.

[3] The collector, Rev. A. C. Good, gives the following account of the game: "Two players seat themselves on opposite sides of the board, and four counters are placed in each of the twelve pockets. Then one player takes the counters out of a pocket on his own side and drops one in each pocket around as far as they will go, going to right and back on his opponents side in the opposite direction from that in which the hands of the clock move. They move thus alternately until one manages to make his last counter fall in a pocket on his opponent's side, where there were only one or two counters. When he has done so he has won the counters in that pocket, including his own last counter. These he transfers to the receptacle in the end of the board to his right. A single counter taken from last pocket on player's right can not win from opponent's first pocket opposite, even though it contains only one or two counters. When a pocket has accumulated twelve or more counters, so that

the bean-like seed used in counting. Another board in the U.S. National Museum, collected by that adventurous traveler, Dr. W. L. Abbott, from the Wa Chaga tribe at Mount Kilamanjaro, has tweny-six holes arranged in four rows of six each, with two large holes at the ends. He describes it in his catalogue, published by the Smithsonian Institution, under the name of Ochi, used for playing Ban, a common game throughout Africa, and says that it is played with nicker seeds and pebbles. Bent, in his "Ruined Cities of Mashonaland," gives the following acount of the game: "Huge trees sheltered the entrance to their village, beneath which men were playing Isafuba, the mysterious game of the Makalangas, with sixty holes, in rows, in the ground. Ten men can play at this game, and it consists of removing bits of pottery or stone from one hole to another in an unaccountable manner. We watched it scores of times while in the country, and always gave it up as a bad job, deciding that it must be like draughts or chess learned by them from the former civilized race who dwelt here." He then proceeds to identify Isafuba with the games of Wari played on the west coast of Africa.

Prince Momolu Massaquoi, son of the King of the Vei tribe, described to me the manner of playing the game among the Vei. They call the game Kpo, a word having an explosive sound resembling a note of the xylophone, mimicking the noise made by the seeds or ivory balls with which the game is played when tossed into the holes on the board. The boards, which are made with twelve holes in two rows, with large holes at the ends, are called by the same name. The boards used by the chiefs are often very expensive, being made of ivory and ornamented with gold. He had seen boards which cost 20 slaves. The holes in the boards are called kpo sing or kpo kungo, kungo meaning "cup." The game is usually played with sea beans, which grow on vines like the potato on the west coast, or by the chiefs with the before-mentioned ivory balls. These seeds are called kpo kunje, kunje meaning "seed." He identified a board from the Gaboon River as suitable for the game, although he said that much more elaborate ones, like those in the Liberian exhibit, were

---

a player drops clear around and back to where he began, he must skip the pocket from which he started. When so few counters remain in the pocket on the board that no more can be won, the game is ended and each counts his winnings. The counters that remain in the board at the end of the game are not counted by either player. The game is sometimes varied thus: When a counter wins as above, not only the contents of that pocket is won, but of the pocket or pockets before it on the opponent's side that has contained only one or two counters back until one is reached that has been empty or had three or more counters before the play. This last is rather the better game of the two. The Fans do not play these games skillfully. They seem unable to count ahead to see where the last count will fall. A white man, as soon as he understands the game, will beat them every time.

common. The depression in the middle of the board from the Gaboon
River is intended to catch pieces that do not fall in the hole for which
they are intended. Cheating is practiced, and to guard against it players
must raise their arms and throw the pieces upon the board with some
violence. Two, three, or four play. The game differs somewhat from that
played in Syria and Egypt. A player may commence at any hole in his
side. His play ends when the pieces first taken up are played. He wins
when the number in the last hole is increased to two or to three. He does
not take those in the hole opposite. When two play, four beans are put
in each hole, but when three or four play three beans are put in each
hole. When two play, the pieces are dropped around in the same direction as in the Syrian game, but when three or four play they may be
dropped in either direction. When two play, each player takes one side
of the board; when three play, each takes four holes, two on each side,
dividing the board transversely into three parts, and when four play,
each takes three holes. When two play, a winner takes only what he
"kills" (fá); but when three or four play, when one completes two or
three in a hole by his play, he takes those in the next hole forward. When
a man takes a piece with one next to it, he uses his fingers to squeeze
the pieces into his hand, the operation being called "squeezing" (boti),
but this can only be done when one of the pieces is in one of the player's
own cups and the other one or two in that of an opponent. Players sit
crosslegged upon the ground, and when the chiefs play large numbers
often assemble to watch them. I have given Prince Momolu's account
somewhat at length, as several African travelers have declared the game
incomprehensible to a white man.

Dr. Schweinfurth regards the Mohammedan Nubians as having received Mancala from their original home in Central Africa, and says that
the recurrence of an object even trivial as this is an evidence, in a degree
indirect and collateral, of the essential unity that underlies all African
nations. Mr. Bent justly says that the game is found in some form or
another wherever Arabian influence is felt, but, continuing, states that it
forms for us another link in the chain of evidence connecting the Mashonaland ruins with an Arabian influence. Dr. Richard Andree, in his
well-known work on Ethnological Parallels,[4] in which he has brought
together many accounts of the game, says that he regards its progress
from west to east, from Asia to the coast of the Atlantic. This opinion I
share. Peterman relates that Mancala is played in Damascus with pebbles which pilgrims collect in a certain valley on their way from Mecca.
From the comparatively early mention of the game in Arabic literature,

---

[4] "Ethnographische Parallen," neue folge, Leipzig, 1889, p. 101.

and the retention of its Arabic name in Africa, Arabia would appear to be the source from which it was disseminated. Mohammed proscribed the Meiser game; and games of hazard, although played, are regarded by Mohammedans as prohibited by their religion. Mancala, a game of fate or calculation, appears to be looked upon with toleration, and it is not unreasonable to suppose that its wide diffusion is due to its having been carried by returning pilgrims to the various parts of the Mohammedan world. If we accept this theory of its distribution, we have yet the more difficult question of its origin. This, I fear, is not to be determined directly, and will only be surely known when we attain a greater knowledge of the rules or laws which underlie the development of games, even as they do every other phase of the development of human culture.

I have recently been informed than Mancala is a common amusement of the negroes of San Domingo, who play upon boards scooped with holes. A board in the U.S. National Museum was collected by the Rev. F. Gardiner, jr., in St. Lucia, where the game is played by the negroes under the name of Wa-wee.[5]

It is not unlikely that Mancala may some day take its place among our own fireside amusements, when this account may answer some inquiries that may be made as to its history.

Since the above was written I have learned that the game of Mancala was published in the United States in 1891, under the name of Chuba, by the Milton Bradley Company, of Springfield, Mass., who furnish the following rules and account of the game:

Chuba is an adaptation from a rude game of eastern Africa which is greatly enjoyed by the natives, who squat on the ground and play in holes scooped out of the sand, using shells, young cocoanuts, etc., for counters, which they move from hole to hole. As now presented to the civilized world for its diversion, Chuba is a game of skill for two players. It is made up of a board with 4 parallel rows of holes or pockets, 11 in each row, and 60 small beads used as men or counters.

The board is placed between the players as usual, with the longer

---

[5] Mr. Gardiner writes in a letter to Dr. G. Brown Goode under date of May 2, 1895: "The game of Wa-wee was bought in St. Lucia, but I found it in use also in Barbados and Martinique among the negroes. As far as I could ascertain, they supposed it very old—came from their fathers. I supposed it came from Africa; but no one seemed to know anything about it. It is a regular gambling game." In regard to the method of play, he says: "As near as I can remember, each of the small side holes has a given number of beans put in, each man taking one side and one large hole as a goal. The beans are taken up from one hole in the hand and dropped in a certain order in the other holes, going round the whole circle. If the last one drops in a hole which has a certain number of beans in it (I don't remember the number), he picks that lot up and goes on. The object is to land the most beans of your own and taken from your adversary in the end holes."

sides next to them. Each one confines his playing to the two rows of pockets nearest him. The row close to his edge of the board is his outer row, while the other is his inner row.

Before beginning the game each player places a single counter in each of the pockets of his outer row and two counters in each pocket of his inner row, except that the pocket on his extreme left in the inner row is kept vacant and the one next to it holds but one man. All moves in the inner row are from right to left, and those in the outer row from left to right. As the players face each other the moves in the two inner rows are necessarily in opposite directions.

The privilege of playing first in the first game is left to agreement or chance, not being regarded as of any consequence. In subsequent games the player who was victor in the last contest takes the lead.

The first player chooses any pocket in his inner row which contains more than one man from which to start his first move, and begins the game by picking up all the men in that pocket and dropping one of them in each of the consecutive pockets to his left until all the men in his hand have been distributed. If the last counter drops into a pocket that is occupied, the player continues the move by picking up all the men in that pocket, including the one dropped, and disposing of them as before. His move must continue in this same way until the last counter in his hand falls into an empty pocket, and the move may extend around the course, into the outer row, or even farther, as indicated by the arrows.

If this empty pocket into which the last man falls is in the inner row and has opposite it a pocket in the opponent's inner row containing one or more men, the player captures these men and at once removes them from the board. And if there are one or more men in the corresponding opposite pocket of the opponent's outer row, they must also be taken. Furthermore, he must select another pair of opposite pockets in his opponent's rows from which to remove any men that they contain. In making this choice he is at liberty to pick out any pair of opposites, whether both are occupied or empty, or one is occupied and the other empty.

Suppose the player B had just finished a move by dropping a "last man" in No. 1. He can capture all the men in 2 and 3 by his skill and also in 4 and 5 or from any other two opposite pockets of his opponent's inner and outer rows. Had 2 been vacant, however, he could not have taken any men. Had 3 been vacant, he could have taken the men from 2 and those from 4 and 5. Had his last man fallen in the outer row, in 6 for example, the effect would have been of no avail in capturing anything, because the outer row is always noncombatant.

A man in the outer row can not be moved until he has been played upon by a man from the inner row.

A move can not begin from a pocket holding a single man if the player has a pocket containing more than one man. When a move does begin from a pocket containing a single man, it can not be played into an occupied pocket.

When all the men which a player has become single, those remaining in his outer row which have not been played on are forfeited to the opponent.

The winner is the player who captures all his opponent's men.

It is an advantage to a player to get his counters singled as soon as possible, unless he sees that his opponent is doing the same thing, when a different policy is wise.

If he wishes to cover two or three vacant spaces in order to effect a capture, it can often be done, provided he begins his move far enough back from those vacant pockets.

The loss of counters during the earlier part of the game is not necessarily as great a disadvantage as in most games, because so much depends on the final move, in which there is the chance for a brilliant display of skill.

The native players of the original Chuba say "chee" at the end of each move, which gives notice to the opponent to proceed; and toward the close of the game, when the moves follow in rapid succession, the effect is very amusing.

The natives call the counters in the inner row "man and wife," and those in the outer row "spinsters." But these spinsters are married by passing a counter over them from the inner row, till, in the progress of the game, all the pieces become single, when they are all called "widows." These widows have a double advantage over the married families, and are sure to make havoc among them. The game is appropriately named, as the word chuba means "to extinguish" or "eat up," and the object of each player is to annihilate his opponent by putting the latter's counters in a position from which escape is impossible.

6

American Indian Games

STEWART CULIN

It is with some hesitation that I again present an article on a subject which has engaged my attention for many years. I propose briefly to summarize the results of my investigations of Indian games since 1897, when, in a paper read before the American Folk-lore Society,[1] I announced the conclusions to which I had arrived at that time. Since that period, chiefly through the enthusiastic energy of my friend Dr. George A. Dorsey, a vast amount of new material has been collected which has greatly increased the probabilities of comparative study.

I have now to propose a new classification of Indian games, a classification similar to that used in the arrangement of the collection exhibited by the University of Pennsylvania at the Pan-American Exposition at Buffalo, and one designed to include all our aboriginal games in which implements are employed. Indian children play a great variety of games, chiefly mimetic, without implements, such as tag, etc., corresponding with those of the children of civilization, but their exclusion does not affect the issues which are involved in the present discussion.

The games of the American Indians may be divided into two general classes—games of chance and games of dexterity. Games of pure calculation, such as chess, are entirely absent. The games of chance fall into one of two categories: First, games in which implements, like dice, are thrown at random to determine a number or numbers, the sum of the counts being kept with sticks, pebbles, etc., or upon an abacus or count-

SOURCE. *American Anthropologist,* N.S. **5**, 1903, pp. 58–64.

[1] *Journal of American Folk-lore,* vol. xi, pp. 245–252, Oct.–Dec., 1898.

ing board or circuit; second, games in which one or more of the players guess in which of two or more places an odd or particularly marked lot is concealed, success or failure resulting in the gain or loss of counters.

The games of dexterity may be enumerated as: First, archery in its various modifications; second, a game of shooting at a moving target consisting of a netted wheel or of a ring; third, a game of sliding javelins upon the hard ground or ice; fourth, the game of ball in several highly specialized forms; fifth, the racing games, more or less interrelated to and complicated with the ball games. In addition there is a subclass of the game of shooting at a moving target, of which it is a miniature and solitaire form. Games of all these classes are found among all the Indian tribes of North America, and constitute the games, *par excellence*, of the Indians. Children have a variety of other amusements, but those above described are played only by men and women, youths and maidens, and not by children, and usually at fixed seasons, once as the accompaniment of certain festivals or religious rites.

There is a well-marked affinity and relationship between the manifestations of the same game, even among the most widely separated tribes, the variations being more in the material of the implements, due to environment, than to the object or method of play. Precisely the same games are played by tribes belonging to unrelated linguistic stocks, and in general the variations do not follow the differences in language. At the same time there appears to be a progressive change from what seems to be the oldest form, from a center in southwestern United States along lines north, northeast, and east. Similar changes probably occurred along lines radiating from the same center southward into Mexico. From such accounts of the Aztec games as have come down to us, they appear to be invariably higher developments of the games of the wilder tribes. Under no circumstances could they be regarded as the original forms. In the same way, the old games found in the cliff-dwellings are frequently of more highly developed types than those which exist among living tribes. The games of the Eskimo are all extensions of the same games we find among the Indians, but show always greater simplicity, lack of tradition, and a degradation of form which would preclude their being regarded as the source of the Indian games.

There is no evidence that any of the games above described were imported into America at any time, either before or after the conquest. On the other hand, they appear to be the direct and natural outgrowth of aboriginal institutions in America. They show no modifications due to white influence other than the decay which characterizes all Indian customs under existing conditions. It is possible, however, that the wide distribution of the "hand game" is a matter of comparatively recent date, due to wider and less restricted intercourse through the abolition of tribal wars. Playing cards, and probably the simple board game known to the English as "merrills," are the only games borrowed by the Indians from the whites. On the other hand, we have taken lacrosse in the north and racket in the south; and the Mexicans of the Rio Grande play most of the Indian games under Spanish names.

My first conclusion as to the interrelation and common origin of Indian games was based on a comparative study of the stick-dice game, published in the Report of the U. S. National Museum for 1896. It appeared that the number of the sticks was originally four, and that the dice were originally made of canes, being the shaftments of arrows, painted or burned with marks corresponding with those used to designate the arrows of the four world-quarters. One of the four arrow-canes bore special marks which identified it with the throwing-sticks anciently used in the Southwest to propel an arrow in lieu of a bow. This specially marked cane, which gave an additional count when it fell uppermost, is perpetuated in a similarly marked implement giving an augmented count in a majority of the stick-dice games played throughout the continent. In the same way the marks on the other sticks can be referred very directly to the arrow-cane shaftsments of the world-quarters. Again, in one of the widely distributed types of the guessing games, the number of places of concealment is four, and the implements in which the object was hidden were derived from the four marked arrow-shaftments of the four directions. In general, in all the games we find an arrow, or a derivative of the arrow, the predominant implement, and the conception of the four world-quarters the fundamental idea.

It became apparent that the relation of the Indian games to each other in the same area, and each to its counterpart among all the tribes, is largely dependent on their origin in magical ceremonies. Back of each game we find a ceremony in which the game was a significant part. The ceremony has commonly disappeared, and the game survives as an amusement, but often with traditions and observances that serve to connect it with its original purpose. It follows that a correct understanding of the origin and final significance of our Indian games can be obtained only through a more or less perfect knowledge of the rituals and symbolism of the various tribes. Fortunately there remain certain tribes in which games occupy their original place in the religious life of the people, or a middle stage in which they are practised both as a rite and as an amusement. This is true both in Zuñi and in the Hopi towns of Arizona. The Zuñi war god Ahaiuta is the patron of games, and the offerings deposited at his shrine consist of miniature representations of the gaming implements. On the Hopi altars, which are erected in the kivas at the various annual ceremonies, the gaming implements are the most significant objects. This is especially true of the altars of the Flute fraternities, where we see the miniature ring and dart of the hoop-and-pole game, the kicking billets of the kicked-stick race, and the tubes of the hidden-ball game—the latter often stuck like flowers in two sand mountains, corresponding with the two sand mountains of the Zuñi game.

The altar itself frequently appears to be the place where the divination was performed with the gaming implements. Not a few of the ceremonial offerings that are made at shrines prove to be conventionalized games, and even the images of the gods themselves, round billets, are related in some direct way to the gaming tubes, if, indeed, they are not derived from them. In one instance a sand or dry painting is used as the gaming circuit or diagram.

Turning to the masks and other paraphernalia worn in the dances and ceremonies, we find a constant use of the gaming implements as essential parts of the costume. The ring at the base of the Hopi and Zuñi masks is the gaming ring for the hoop-and-pole game. We discover it again among the Hupa in California, where a feather dart is stuck in either side. It is not unlikely to be the origin of the headbands of the northern coast tribes. Indeed the rings and bands of Indian costume may in general be traced to the game ring. As an illustration in point we find miniature rings surprisingly like game-rings worn as hair-ornaments by the Cheyenne, Arapaho, and Dakota. At last I learn they are prizes for the hoop-and-pole game, awarded to the successful contestant for a year.

Returning to the Hopi masks, we discover that their ring-shaped mouths are also gaming rings. On one the nose consists of a feather dart placed just above it. The masks themselves are derived from the tubes of the hidden ball. Their eyes are the balls that are hidden, and one finds the counting-sticks placed like a visor over certain specimens. Again, the netted hoop of the hoop-and-pole rises as part of the head-dress of other masks. The head-dress of the Flute priest at Oraibi consists of the corn-husk wheel and darts, and the four flower-like cups of the hidden ball.

Nor, as I have already indicated, is this use of gaming implements confined to any particular tribe or tribes. For example, the woven and painted cloth that is worn suspended from the forehead down the back, among the Hupa, is the mat upon which they played their favorite game of sticks, or kiñ.

Turning now from the altars and costumes to the ceremonies themselves, we find the games surviving in their original forms. The idea of the dual principles of nature—the masculine and the feminine—is everywhere conspicuous in their symbolism. The arrow, in general, is regarded as masculine. The common female symbol is the netted wheel or one of its many derivatives. This netted wheel is copied from the spider-web, the attribute of the Spider-woman, the Earth-goddess, the mother of the Twin War-gods. The ceremonies in which it is employed are magical rites to secure fertility, and the games in which it is used are all significant of the same idea. Among the Dakota it is called the elk game. The Pawnee know it as the buffalo game, and play it "to make buffalo." The Wasco of Columbia river play it to insure a good run of salmon. Among the Hopi its employment is bound up with the fertilization and growth of corn. In its miniature and solitaire form, of which I have already spoken, it is played by lovers and is widely known as the "match-making" or "matrimonial" game.

Turning to another of the sacred games for which the implements are sacrificed upon the altar of the War-god, we find the stone ball of the kicking-race ceremonially deposited on the Hopi *Powamu* altar, and the race itself a magical rite to secure fields within its circuit against sandstorms. The ball-race is repeated by many of the adjacent tribes, with some of whom, as with the Mexicans of the Rio Grande, it has lost all ceremonial significance.

In general the ball games have yielded least fruitful results to my comparative study. The two principal games were racket and shinny. The morphology of the racket is not yet clear to me. It appears to have some connection with the web of the Spider-goddess, but I am unable to demonstrate that this was the source of its origin. On the other hand it is a practical throwing contrivance, akin to the throwing-stick. The game of ball with rackets may be a dramatization of war. Mr. Mooney has pointed out that the ball game receives the name of war among the Cherokee. Shinny in general is the woman's game, but among some tribes it is played by men. As to the ball, there are two forms, one bag-shaped, and the other disk-shaped, flat, with a medial seam. The two sides of the latter are frequently painted different colors, and the ball itself has a symbolism, not yet understood, referable to the earth, the moon, or the sun.

Of all the American ball games, the most interesting and peculiar is the widely-distributed woman's game of double ball. I found it among the Hupa, played by men with two billets tied with cords, and was led to refer it to the ceremony in the Hopi Flute "dance" where the Flute-boy and Flute-maid toss an annulet and a billet by means of a slender stick into the meal-traced cloud symbols, as they advance in procession back to the mesa on the ninth day of the ceremony. This theory received unexpected confirmation in a discovery made by the Hyde Exploring Expedition at Pueblo Bonito. Here, in a sacrificial deposit in one of the chambers, were a number of beautful flutes, together with curved billets and sticks for throwing them, easily recognizable as having been used in a game or ceremony akin to the double-ball game.

Time and space do not permit me here to enter into a discussion of the details of the games. To me their direct interest is exceeded by the many side-lights which are thrown by their study on primitive life and thought, by the many practical identifications of things which heretofore have been strange and obscure. A single illustration will suffice: The Zuñi, like many other tribes, play a dice game in a flat basket similar in form to the Oraibi basket-trays. It has been a favorite notion with me that this appliance was in some way a derivative of a shield, and I was led to collect information about the flat Hopi baskets. From a manuscript of the late A. M. Stephen, who spent many years among the Hopi, I learned that their name for shield is *tü-u'-po-o-ta;* but *po'-o-ta* is the name of these flat baskets. With this significant information it became apparent that these baskets, with their figures of eagles, etc., used for offerings on the shrine, were *basket shields*. This identification furnishes a clue to the explanation of many basket patterns. The so-called Navaho marriage basket, with its "life-line," contains a conventionalized bird, made "alive" by the break in the design which thus determines it as a bird. It would seem, too, with this explanation in mind, that the identification of many of the Hopi bowl designs becomes comparatively easy.

7

Patolli, Pachisi, and the Limitation of Possibilities

CHARLES JOHN ERASMUS

Interest in the similarities between the Aztec game of patolli and the Hindu game of pachisi has always had reference to the problem of pre-Columbian contact between the Old and New Worlds. Whether or not there was such contact in pre-Columbian times is not the major concern of this paper. Our primary concern here will be with the historical development of an aspect of ethnological theory which is directly related to the patolli-pachisi question and is well illustrated by it.

According to Culin,

The first writer to discuss the resemblances of the games of the American Indians with those of the Old World, as an argument in favor of the Asiatic origin of the American race, was P. Lafitau in his Moeurs des Sauvages Ameriquains Comparees aux Moeurs des Premiers Temps, Paris, 1724.

The Frenchman, Lafitau, described the North American plum stone and bowl games, which he compared with a similar African negro practice of throwing cowrie shells.[1]

The paper which attracted most attention to the problem of the similarities between New and Old World board games was one by E. B.

SOURCE. *Southwestern Journal of Anthropology*, 6, Winter, 1950, pp. 369–387.

[1] Stewart Culin, *Chess and Playing-Cards* (Report, United States National Museum for 1896, pp. 665–942, 1898), p. 855.

Tylor written in 1879. In comparing the Aztec game of patolli with the Hindu pachisi, he pointed out features which they shared in common. In both cases counters were moved along tracks which were cross-like in shape and drawn upon mats or "boards." In both, the movement of the counters was determined by the throw of lots—six cowrie shells in the Hindu version and five black beans with white dots on one side in the Aztec version. Although the scoring was arbitrary in both cases, there was a tendency in both to give greater weight to more difficult throws. While Tylor knew the rules of moving and taking counters for pachisi, the early chroniclers did not provide complete information for patolli. He relied somewhat on other Middle American and Southwest games which resembled it. To Tylor the similarity between the New and Old World games was so convincing that he concluded that the American lot games, like certain developments in metal work, architecture, astronomy, and political and religious institutions, had come somehow from Asia prior to the time of Columbus.[2]

One interesting aspect of his conclusions pertains to the lot games of what he called the "ruder" northern tribes. In North America, gambling with lots was quite common but without the board and counters found in middle America and the Southwest. Tylor felt that the "lot-casting part" of the game spread northward without the board and counters. We must point out here that the time at which Tylor was writing (1879) was long before the age-area doctrine became fashionable in American ethnology. Had he been writing, say, in the 1920's, he might have considered the simpler form—which was more widely distributed than the complex Mexican one—to be an earlier version. However, in assuming the diffusion of the entire complex from Asia, he implied that the simpler form was a *later* development which disassociated itself from board and counters in its northward spread.

In a second paper in 1896, Tylor attempted to give greater weight to his argument by combining it with the theory of probability. In his words:

I have found it useful at any rate as a means of clearing ideas, to attempt a definite rule by analyzing such phenomena into constituent elements showing so little connection with one another that they may be reasonably treated as independent. The more numerous are such elements, the more improbable the recurrence of their combination. In the case of a language recurrence may be treated as impossible. If the invention of

---

[2] E. B. Tylor, *On the Game of Patolli in Ancient Mexico, and its Probably Asiatic Origin* (Journal Anthropological Institute of Great Britain and Ireland, vol. 8, 1879), p. 128.

the gun be divided into the blow-tube, the use of metal, the explosive, the lock, the percussion, etc., and classed as an invention say of the 10th order, and the invention of chess with its six kinds of pieces with different moves indicated as of perhaps the 6th order, these figures would correspond to an immense improbability of recurrence. Such a game as pachisi, combining the invention of divining by lot, its application to the sportive wager, the combination of several lots with an appreciation of the law of chances, the transfer of the result to a counting board, the rules of moving and taking, would place it in perhaps the 6th order, the recurrence of which might be less than that of chess, but according to common experience still far outside any probability on which reasonable men could count. If this argument be admitted, the relation of the pachisi-patolli groups of games in the Old and New World must be accounted for by intercourse before the Spanish conquest. . . .[3]

Taylor's argument sounds very convincing; it has stalemated the question for over fifty years. As we shall see, Kroeber continues to employ the same probability reasoning in the revised edition of his *Anthropology*.

Two years previous to Tylor's paper of 1896, D. G. Brinton had written of patolli:

This game has lately been made the subject of careful study by Mr. Culin, of the University of Pennsylvania and Mr. Frank Cushing, of the Bureau of Ethnology; and I am authorized to say that both these competent authorities agree that there can be no doubt but that patolli is thoroughly American in origin, no matter how closely it assimilates the East Indian game.[4]

The opinions of which Brinton speaks are revealed in three different publications by Culin between 1898 and 1907. In reviewing these papers, it must be pointed out that the period during which they were written was again prior to that of historical reconstruction from space. It was a time when concern with cultural evolutionism was still very much in the fore. In his first large work on games in 1898, Culin attributes the identity of the games of Asia and America to the identity of universal "mythic" concepts which underlie them—such as the "classification of all things according to the Four Directions."[5] In a short paper in 1903 and

---

[3] E. B. Tylor, *On American Lot-Games as Evidence of Asiatic Intercourse Before the Time of Columbus* (Internationales Archiv für Ethnographie, vol. 9, suppl.: Ethnographische Beitrage, 1896), p. 66.

[4] D. G. Brinton, *On Various Supposed Relations Between the American and Asian Races* (Memoirs, International Congress of Anthropology, Chicago, 1894), pp. 148–149.

[5] Culin, *Chess and Playing-Cards*, pp. 679–680.

again in his huge compilation on *Games of the North American Indians,*
Culin holds to the same underlying explanation, but he makes the following very interesting statement:

There is a well-marked affinity and relationship between the manifestations of the same game, even among the most widely separated tribes, the
variations being more in the material of the implements, due to environments, than to the object or method of play. Precisely the same games
are played by tribes belonging to unrelated linguistic stocks, and in
general the variations do not follow the differences in language. At the
same time there appears to be a progressive change from what seems
to be the oldest form, from a center in southwestern United States along
lines radiating from the same center southward into Mexico. From such
accounts of the Aztec games as have come down to us, they appear to be
invariably higher developments of the games of the wilder tribes. Under
no circumstances could they be regarded as the original forms. There is
no evidence that any of the games described [this includes the lot games]
were imported into America at any time, either before or after the conquest. On the other hand, they appear to be direct and natural outgrowth
of aboriginal institutions in America.[6]

Culin obviously has made deductions which are quite the reverse of
those of Tylor. He sees a progressive development in *space,* and he is
quite definite in his assertion that the higher forms should not be considered the original ones. In brief, he is actually inferring historical reconstruction from space. Why, then, should a man as much interested in
space-time reconstruction as Kroeber have sided with Tylor's explanation
for so many years? Let us skip to a paper written by Kroeber in 1931 in
which he discusses patolli and pachisi with reference to the biological
concepts of analogy and homology.

Kroeber's paper is very pertinent to our subject, for its title is *Historical
Reconstruction of Culture Growths and Organic Evolution.*[7] The author's
purpose is ". . . to discuss certain similarities of aim and method in the
reconstruction respectively of culture growths by anthropologists and or
organic history or 'evolution' by biologists." The main intent appears to
be the justification of the age-area principle first used in biology but
which ". . . seems to have been hit upon independently soon after by

[6] Stewart Culin, *American Indian Games* (1902) (American Anthropologist, vol. 5,
pp. 58–64, 1903), p. 59; *Games of the North American Indians* (24th Annual Report,
Bureau of American Ethnology, 1907), pp. 31–32.

[7] American Anthropologist, vol. 33, pp. 149–156, 1931. The following quotations
are from pp. 149–151.

anthropologists." The chief difference in the application of the principle in the two disciplines seems to lie in the much greater difficulty with which anthropologists distinguish between convergence or independent parallel origin and ". . . relationship by common origin or descent and spread or diffusion." Kroeber wonders why anthropologists do not attempt, like biologists, to determine whether ". . . similarities are specific and structural and not merely superficially conceptual." The distinction, he says, betwen homologous and analogous similarities in the determination of historical relationship has not been clearly made by anthropologists. He refers to patolli and pachisi to illustrate his point:

. . . It is difficult to see only a superficial analogy between the Aztec patolli game and the Hindu pachisi game, long ago analytically compared by Tylor. Their specific structural similarities in two-sided lot throwing, count values dependent on frequency of lot combinations, a cruciform scoring circuit, the killing of opponents' counters that are overtaken, etc., make out a strong case for a true homology and therefore a genetic unity of the two game forms, in spite of their geographical separation. Biologists would almost certainly judge so.

The problem of distinguishing homologies from analogies in culture is an old one and had been discussed in anthropological literature much earlier. The attack on the concept of totemism by Lowie and Goldenweiser during the early part of the second decade of this century brought into prominence the need for care in considering categories of cultural phenomena as identical.[8] In discussing the principle of convergence about this time, Lowie also points out that ". . . the apparent mysticism in the doctrine of convergence disappears at once if the supposed identities are recognized not as ethnological realities, but as *logical abstractions;* not as homologies, but as analogies"[9] [Culin's italics.]

Here, then, is the rub. When do we have assurance that the homologies we observe in culture are not simply the product of what Lowie calls "premature classification"?[10] It is obvious that to compare "structures" in aspects of nonmaterial cultures, for example, we must compare interpretations. This may not be completely different in *kind* from what

[8] A. A. Goldenweiser, *Totemism, an Analytical Study* (Journal of American Folk-Lore, vol. 23, pp. 179–293, 1910); R. H. Lowie, *A New Conception of Totemism* (American Anthropologist, vol. 13, pp. 189–207, 1911).

[9] R. H. Lowie, *The Principle of Convergence in Ethnology* (American Anthropologist, vol. 14, p. 154, 1912).

[10] R. H. Lowie, *On the Principle of Convergence in Ethnology* (Journal of American Folk-Lore, vol. 25, pp. 24–42, 1912), p. 33.

the biologists and paleontologists do, but the degree of difference is enormous.

In distinguishing between homologies and analogies there is another important difference between the cultural anthropologist and the biologist or paleontologist. The latter have developed a fairly comprehensive genetic classification of fossil and living forms which enables them to come to some professional agreement in certain well-defined cases as to what constitutes as homology as compared to an analogy or what constitutes a parallelism as compared to convergence. True, they can point to the fact that the wing of a bird is homologous to that of a bat and analogous to that of a moth, or they can show convergence between such forms as the South American marsupial carnivore and the North American wolf. But there is a middle ground where even paleontologists and biologists have their difficulties. In the case of the tetrapod limb, the monoaxial fin type of the recent and ancient Dipnoi was once considered its prototype. This view was later abandoned as knowledge of the lobed fins of extinct Crossopterygii led to the view that the latter represented a more likely ancestor of the tetrapods.[11] Similarly, Gregory split the classical ungulate grouping by removal of the artiodacyls in the belief that the artiodactyls were derived from carnivores while the other ungulates were derived from some unknown forms of the Cretaceous distinct from carnivores but like early Tertiary condylarths. After 1910, better knowledged of the condylarths demonstrated their close similarity with primitive artiodactyls as well.[12]

Obviously, there have been innumerable occasions in biology and paleontology when the probability of close genetic relationship on the basis of points of structural similarity between two groups of forms has been materially reduced by later evidence and a change of perspective. If, as Kroeber suggests, biologists would consider patolli and pachisi to be homologies on his evidence, this does not mean there is anything immutable in such a judgment.

By 1948 Kroeber felt less definite in his opinion about the patolli-pachisi question. This frame of mind was due to the recognition of what Kroeber considers to be two sets of facts showing contrary probability. First, he says:

There are five or perhaps six specific features in which pachisi and patolli agree: flat dice, scoreboard, cross-shape, several men, killing opponents, penalty or safety stations. The mathematical probability of two games

---

[11] Libbie H. Hyman, *Comparative Vertebrate Anatomy* (Chicago, 1942), p. 131.

[12] George Gaylord Simpson, *The Principles of Classification and a Classification of Mammals* (Bulletin, American Museum of Natural History, vol. 85, 1945), p. 173.

invented separately agreeing by chance in so many quite specific features is very low. On a bet, long odds could be laid against so complex a coincidence, long odds for its not being a coincidence, hence an influence or a connection.[13]

Now, if we go back to Tylor's time, we will recall that he mentioned other similarities between the Old and New Worlds besides pachisi and patolli. On many of these, opinion has since changed, hence Kroeber states:

If pachisi was anciently imported from India to Mexico, as it was later carried from India to England and America, it is extremely unlikely that the people who brought it would have brought that and nothing else; or that only pachisi survived as patolli, but practically everything else brought with it failed to be accepted in Mexico, or died out, or was so altered as to be unrecognizable. To be sure, just this *might* conceivably have happened; but it would admittedly be extraordinary; on the basis of chance, improbable. . . . In short, the context probability is against connection. . . . It will be observed how much weight is put in the argument on probability in terms of the total situation. One identical feature in two games means nothing; half a dozen do mean something. One identical game or trait in two cultures also means nothing; a number do have meaning. . . . When probability is nearly even, the only honest thing is to leave the question open.[14]

Of course, any question is open, and Kroeber is quite right in leaving this one so. We must object, however, to his use of probability mathematics in this case, and we will be concerned here only with the first part of the dilemma, the "independence" of the elements of the two games. For an excellent analysis of the fallacy involved in decisions concerning the probability of trans-Pacific diffusion on the basis of the number of "inventions" common to both hemispheres, the reader is referred to G. D. Gibson's rebuttal to Gilbert Lewis.[15]

To clarify the mathematical principles involved, let us take the case of fifteen pennies thrown randomly into the air. The odds are roughly 30,000 to one against all the pennies falling heads up, since each penny has only one chance in two of coming up heads and fifteen pennies have one chance in two to the fifteenth power. Now, while we know how many sides there are to a penny, we do not know how many alternatives

[13] A. L. Kroeber, *Anthropology* (New York, 1948), p. 551.

[14] *Op. cit.*, pp. 551–552.

[15] Gordon D. Gibson, *The Probability of Numerous Independent Inventions* (American Anthropologist, vol. 50, pp. 362–364, 1948).

there are to each of Tylor's or Kroeber's criteria; therefore our multiples have no size to begin with. Secondly, while the odds are 30,000 to one against fifteen heads being thrown at once by any one individual at any given moment, the combination is quite likely if each of 30,000 individuals were to throw fifteen pennies at once. Moreover, if the major recreation of every person in a town of 30,000 was the throwing of fifteen pennies at once, the combination of fifteen heads might tend to recur at least 10,000 times a week and half a million times a year. Thus, even if we knew the exact number of alternatives to each of Kroeber's or Tylor's elements, we would have to be able to measure their opportunities for combination before we could speak meaningfully of probability. But most important of all is the necessity for the complete independence of the multiples. In the case of the pennies, we could not consider them multiples at all if the occurrence of heads on one penny in any way biased its occurrence among the rest. To consider either Tylor's or Kroeber's elements as mathematically independent and therefore as multiples would be improper if any bias existed between them.

Let us combine both Kroeber's and Tylor's elements in one list and consider each one separately. In doing so, we shall rely for comparative New World evidence mainly on Culin's *Games of the North American Indians.*[16]

We shall begin with the element flat dice. Why the adjective "flat" was important to Kroeber is not clear. According to Tylor's account five black beans were used as dice in the patolli game and six cowrie shells in pachisi.[17] In order to cast lots, the dice must have some quality of discreteness in the form of two or more "sides." A continuous spherical object like a marble could not be used as a die because of the problems that would arise in scoring. The actual flatness of the sides is a relative matter and largely a function of the medium in which they are made. The fruit stone dice popular in northeastern North America were naturally elliptical in cross section. Short lengths of cane or twigs split lengthwise so that one side was flat and the other rounded was a prevalent form of dice in western North America and also in the Gran Chaco.[18] Truly flat dice seem to have been used principally in northeastern North America and to have been always of bone.

---

[16] *Op. cit.*

[17] E. B. Tylor, *On the Game of Patolli in Ancient Mexico,* p. 118.

[18] Erland Nordenskiöld, *Spiele und Spielsachen im Gran Chaco und in Nordamerika* (Zeitschrift für Ethnologie, vol. 42, 1910), p. 428, and *Indianerleben* (Leipzig, 1913), p. 191; Eric von Rosen, *Ethnographical Research Work during the Swedish Chaco-Cordillera-Expedition, 1901–1902* (Stockholm, 1924), p. 153; John M. Cooper, *Games and Gambling* (in *Handbook of South American Indians*, Bulletin, Bureau of American Ethnology, no. 143, 1949), vol. 5, p. 520.

Next, let us consider Tylor's element, "several lots and an appreciation of the law of chances." Tylor considered this important because the scoring of the dice throws in both the New and Old Worlds tended to give greater weight to the more difficult throws. But the scores do not match the computed odds so that we are left with no way to evaluate the meaning of the word "appreciation." Some appreciation of "chance" is inseparable from the use of dice. The study of mathematical probability itself began with the analysis of games of chance and games of chance are still used to explain probability.[19] If Tylor meant that the New World aborigines evinced a knowledge of mathematical probability by their dice scores, he was wrong. Take the Arapaho as just one example. Employing five bone dice equally flat on both their sides, but each with one side marked and the other blank, a score of eight rewarded a throw of five marked sides up and a score of one a throw of five blanks.[20] Apparently the design was appreciated as much as the odds. As Spier once said with reference to certain Southwestern and Mexican counter games, "The entire scoring system is arbitrary and not at all dependent on the probability of occurrence of any score. . . ."[21]

We now come to the next independent multiple called the "counting-board" by Tylor and the "scoreboard" by Kroeber. As we have mentioned, dice occurred widely through North America, and some means of tallying the scores occurred with them. The Eskimo used figure-dice and tallied with the dice themselves by retaining those that landed upright.[22] Tallying with the dice themselves also occurred in the Chaco.[23] Most of North America tallied with beans or small sticks, the latter being reported also for South America by Nordenskiöld.[24] There is no great contrast here between tally sticks and scoreboards. Consider the Nevada Paiute who inserted ten tally sticks in the ground to represent ten fingers and marked their score along them with a movable counter.[25] The California Yokuts employed twenty-five sticks in a row.[26] In the Southwest it was common to tally by moving a stick along a circle of forty stones

[19] Lancelot Hogben, *Mathematics for the Millions* (New York, 1943), pp. 575–576.

[20] Culin, *Games of the North American Indians*, p. 55.

[21] Leslie Spier, *Havasupai Ethnography* (Anthropological Papers, American Museum of Natural History, vol. 29, pt. 3, 1928), p. 351.

[22] Culin, *op. cit.*, pp. 102–103.

[23] Erland Nordenskiöld, *The Changes in the Material Culture of Two Indian Tribes under the Influence of New Surroundings* (Comparative Ethnographical Studies, no. 2, 1920), p. 99.

[24] *Idem, Spiele und Spielsachen im Gran Chaco und in Nordamerika*, p. 428; *Indianerleben*, p. 191.

[25] Culin, *op. cit.*, p. 167.

[26] *Idem*, p. 141.

which had wider openings between every ten.[27] The Zuñi sometimes
traced a rough outline of this broken circle on a pelt and placed corn
kernels instead of stones upon the outline.[28] Within the New World,
then, we find an observable sequence of counting devices in connection
with lot games. While we do not wish to imply that this was necessarily
the actual historical sequence, we do feel it demonstrates a mechanical
continuity. Therefore, without knowledge of the actual historical sequence it would be improper to consider the mat on which the Aztecs
moved their counters according to the score of their dice to be an independent multiple of the dice.

Next we come to what Tylor calls the rules of moving and taking,
which Kroeber breaks into three elements: "killing" opponents, penalty
or safety stations, and the use of several "men" or pieces. Let us consider for a moment the implication in the change to stationary tallies. As
long as tally sticks are employed, the dice will remain the center of attention, the dynamic elements in the game. But as soon as the tallies
become stationary and a counter is moved along them, a new dynamic
element has entered the field of play. Attention can now very easily
switch to the counters, the dice becoming merely the instruments to give
them motion. When this happens, the counting may become secondary
to the race between the counters. Whether the players use one or several
apiece makes no great difference. Actually, it seems to have been customary to put only one counter into play at a time in most of the American
games.[29] Where players had more than one counter apiece, as among the
Kiowa of Oklahoma or the Kekchi of Guatemala, a new counter was introduced upon the loss of a former.[30]

Once the counters have become the center of attention, the dice game
is open to countless variations and modifications of play. But all these
variations are conditional to the two basic conflict situations in dice-and-
counter games: conflict between the counters and conflict between the
counters and the board. If complications are to be added to the game,
they must be one of these two forms. Of these two, the conflict between
counters which happen to land in the same space is the more obvious.
Sending an apponent's counter back to the beginning in this fashion is
common to the counter games of the Southwest and occurs, according

[27] *Idem*, p. 87 (Apache), p. 94 (Navaho), p. 122 (Keres), p. 192 (Tewa); Spier,
op. cit., p. 348–349 (Hopi, Hano, Zuñi).

[28] Culin, *op. cit.*, p. 216.

[29] *Idem*, p. 87 (Apache), p. 121 (Keres), p. 125 (Kiowa), p. 147 (Papago the
exception—used two consecutively), p. 150 (Pima), p. 152 (Tarahumare), p. 160
(Hopi), p. 167 (Paiute), p. 193 (Tewa), p. 208 (Walapai), p. 221 (Zuñi).

[30] Culin, *op. cit.*, pp. 125, 143.

to Nordenskiöld, in the Gran Chaco of South America.[31] Sending a counter back is simply the same as nullifying its score, a practice common enough in any game of quoits where there is a conflict of counters. The Kekchi of Guatemala had a more elaborate system. As soon as a counter landed on that of an opponent, the counter of the latter was taken prisoner, and the former reversed its direction in order to return with its captive before it could be overtaken by another counter and itself made a prisoner.[32] The tribes of the Gran Chaco employed another variation. Opponents sat at each end of a row of twenty holes separated in the middle by a wider space called a "river." The ten holes on each side of the river belonged to the player at that end, who filled the pits with twigs. The point of the game was to move a counter across the river and knock all the opponent's twigs out of the pits by landing on them. Should the two counters conflict, however, the one landed upon had to return to the pit nearest his starting point which still had a twig in it—thereby knocking out one of his own twigs.[33]

Board and counter conflict in the form of a penalty space occurred at least twice in the Southwest as well as in the Gran Chaco game.[34] In all cases it seems to have been a separating space between groups of ten stones or holes. Among the Kiowa of Oklahoma this was a "river." By falling in it, the counter was obliged to return to the beginning, and a point was forfeited.[35] In the Gran Chaco it was also a "river," but if the player threw a score with the dice, he could still get out. A zero score forced him back.[36]

The safety squares of pachisi—formed by two counters of the same player landing in one square or a specially marked square where one counter can block the progress of the opponents' counters—is a refinement of counter-conflict which apparently did not occur in the New World. At Isleta, however, falling in a "river" entitled the player to another throw, and the Tewa considered the "rivers" or "gates" as

---

31 *Idem,* p. 87 (Apache), p. 123 (Keres), p. 126 (Kiowa), p. 147 (Papago), p. 150 (Pima), p. 152 (Tarahumare, p. 194 (Tewa), p. 221 (Zuñi), p. 141 (Yokuts); Erland Nordenskiöld, *Spieltische aus Peru und Ecuador* (Zeitschrift für Ethnologie, vol. 50, 1918), p. 167; *idem, Spiele und Spielsachen im Gran Chaco und in Nordamerika,* p. 428.

32 Culin, *op. cit.,* p. 142.

33 Nordenskiöld, *Spieltische aus Peru und Ecuador,* p. 167; *Spiele und Spielsachen im Gran Chaco und in Nordamerika,* p. 428.

34 Culin, *op. cit.,* p. 123 (Keres), pp. 125, 127 (Kiowa).

35 *Idem,* p. 125.

36 Nordenskiöld, *Spieltische aus Peru und Ecuador,* p. 168.

neutral squares where opposing counters could not "kill" one another.[37] This last is simply another variation on the basic counter-conflict.

The advantage square which allows another throw is interesting. Among many of the northern tribes who used tallies instead of "boards," it was the practice for players to pass the play only on a losing throw, i.e. a throw which made no score.[38] Among the Dakota only five of six possible scoring throws entitled a player to another throw.[39] The Assiniboin, however, retained the lead only for one very exceptional throw.[40] The matter of change of play is thus somewhat arbitrary. Play among the Kekchi of Guatemala, for example, alternated regularly between players, but each player took two throws.[41] In the Southwestern "board" games the lead was usually retained only for a high score of ten.[42] Since every tenth division along the circuit was an opening or "gate," the observer of the Isleta game may have been confused or the Isleta may have transferred the idea of retaining the lead for a high throw of ten to the decimal divisions of the circuit which might often be the same, especially in the case of an initial throw of ten. Under rules of play we might also mention that in the American dice-and-board games, unlike pachisi, counters of opposing players usually proceeded in opposing directions, although in some cases it was optional with the players.[43]

Since there is no complete account of the rules of patolli, it may be that the "penalty or safety stations" to which Kroeber refers pertain to the darkened areas in Duran's illustration of the patolli board.[44] With respect to these I would offer another explanation: they may demonstrate a relationship to the Southwestern games.

As we have seen, the usual playing circuit of stationary tallies in the Southwest was that illustrated in Figure 1a, or a modification of it. It is a simple circle segmented into four decimal divisions. The patolli playing circuit is illustrated in Figure 1b. It will be noticed that the

[37] Culin, *op. cit.*, pp. 191, 193.

[38] *Idem,* p. 50 (Amalecite), p. 54 (Arapaho), p. 56 (Blackfeet), p. 59 (Cheyenne), p. 75 (Micmac), p. 106 (Huron), p. 111 (Onondaga), p. 113, 117 (Seneca), p. 157 (Songish), p. 189 (Haida).

[39] *Idem,* p. 183.

[40] *Idem,* p. 175.

[41] *Idem,* p. 142.

[42] *Idem,* p. 91 (Apache), p. 122 (Keres), p. 124 (Kiowa), p. 221 (Zuñi), p. 160 (Hopi).

[43] *Idem,* p. 91 (Apache), p. 121 (Keres—optional), p. 125 (Kiowa), p. 142 (Kekchi), p. 146 (Papago—optional), p. 150 (Pima), p. 152 (Tarahumare), p. 191 (Isleta—optional), p. 207 (Walapai), p. 221 (Zuñi).

[44] Tylor, *On American Lot-Games as Evidence of Asiatic Intercourse Before the Time of Columbus,* plate 5, fig. 2.

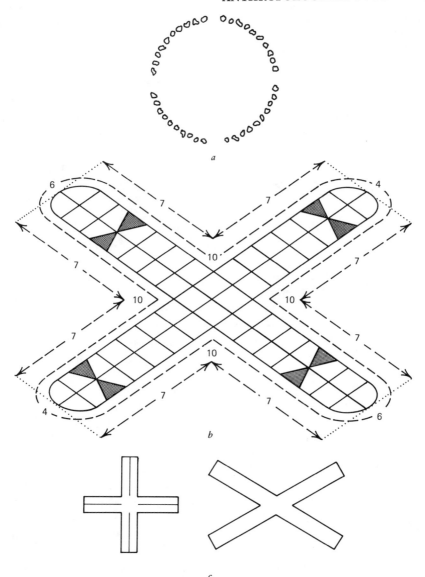

Fig. 1. (*a*) Southwestern playing circuit; (*b*) Patolli playing circuit; (*c*) "Track patterns" of pachisi (left) and patolli (right).

darkened areas segment the circuit into four decimal or two vigesimal divisions except for the ends of each arm. But these terminal divisions also add up to ten on adjacent arms or twenty in all. This irregular division at the ends of the arms may be in part a function of the cruciform arrangement. This is the only way that decimal divisions could be retained without making the arms unequal in length or the squares unequal in size. For example, suppose we wished each arm to end in five squares. We could accomplish this by erasing the line dividing the last two squares on each end of the diagonal ending in six and adding a similar square to each end of the diagonal ending in four. But notice how this would destroy the symmetry of the circuit, for the diagonal formerly ending in four would then have a total length of eighteen squares and the other a total length of sixteen. What is more important is the arbitrary complexity of this entire arrangement as compared to the simplicity of the Southwest form. It seems much more plausible that the patolli arrangement developed from one similar to that of the Southwest than vice versa.

According to the description of patolli quoted by Tylor, there were several "men": two sets of six counters, each set a different color. However, I doubt if one player used more than one at a time. The description says that when more than two played, two played for all the rest.[45] This dual nature is characteristic of dice games all over the Americas. There were usually two players or two teams of players no matter whether the scoring was by tally sticks or counter-boards. The additional counters may have represented additional players, although each team used only one player to throw the dice and move the counters.

Finally we have what Kroeber calls the "cross-shape." Now, in these counter games the moving counter describes a certain figure which we can call the "track pattern." Compare the track patterns of patolli and pachisi in Figure 1c. If the playing area is to be of a convenient size, there is some limitation here to the design made by the track pattern. But even so it would be possible for an enormous range of different patterns to be made, as can be seen in some of our modern games. This is really the best and most non-intrinsic of Kroeber's elements because it does not necessarily have any functional relationship with the rest of the game. But in this case we have to ask whether a cross shape is an unusual design, or, what is more to the point, are these really the same design?

The last two elements are those of Tylor: the invention of divining by lot, and its application to the sportive wager. They boil down to the question of how gambling with dice began in the first place. Here, indeed, we have a difficult problem, but it does not seem unlikely that dice were very old in the New World and may have been introduced at an early date. The fact that the present natives of Siberia did not have

---

[45] Tylor, *On American Lot-Games*, p. 60.

gambling games aboriginally[46] does not destroy this possibility. For those who link age and space, the wide distribution of dice games in the Americas would seem to support their age. Archaeological evidence also looks promising. Dice have been found at pre-pottery Basketmaker,[47] Modified Basketmaker,[48] Developmental Pueblo,[49] Great Pueblo,[50] Mogollon,[51] Mimbres,[52] and transitional Central California[53] sites. Dice have also been reported for the early Lindenmeier site[54] though admittedly they are less convincing. Frankly, the writer sees no reason why patolli and pachisi could not have developed independently from a common wide-spread trait like the use of lots. The features which they share in common are not independent multiples which put their chances for recombination beyond the realm of feasibility. There is an element of bias between the elements which cannot be adequately measured. In short, there is no proof or incontestable evidence for either diffusion or independent development in this case, nor is there likely ever to be. But the

[46] W. Bogoras, *The Chukchee* (Memoirs, American Museum of Natural History, vol. 11, 1904–1909), p. 273; Kroeber, *Anthropology*, p. 552.

[47] A. V. Kidder and S. J. Guernsey, *Archeological Explorations in Northeastern Arizona* (Bulletin, Bureau of American Ethnology, no. 65, 1919), p. 189; J. C. McGregor, *Southwestern Archaeology* (New York, 1941), p. 221; H. M. Wormington, *Prehistoric Indians of the Southwest* (Colorado Museum of Natural History Popular Series no. 7, 1947), pp. 46–47.

[48] P. S. Martin, *Modified Basket Maker Sites: Ackmen-Lowry Area, Southwestern Colorado, 1938* (Anthropological Series, Field Museum of Natural History, vol. 23, no. 3, publication 444, 1939), p. 421; J. O. Brew, *Archaeology of Alkali Ridge; Southwestern Utah* (Papers, Peabody Museum of American Archaeology and Ethnology, vol. 21, 1946), p. 244.

[49] Brew, *loc. cit.*; F. H. H. Roberts, *Early Pueblo Ruins in the Piedra District, Southwestern Colorado* (Bulletin, Bureau of American Ethnology, no. 96, 1930) plate 43; *Idem, Archeological Remains in the Whitewater District, Eastern Arizona: Part 2, Artifacts and Burials* (Bulletin, Bureau of American Ethnology, no. 126, 1940), p. 115.

[50] Brew, *loc. cit.*; S. J. Guernsey, *Explorations in Northeastern Arizona* (Papers, Peabody Museum of American Archaeology and Ethnology, vol. 12, no. 1, 1931), plate 24.

[51] McGregor, *op. cit.*, p. 203; P. S. Martin, *The SU Site Excavations at a Mogollon Village Western New Mexico, 1939* (Anthropological Series, Field Museum of Natural History. vol 32, no. 1, 1940), fig. 31.

[52] H. S. and C. B. Cosgrove, *The Swarts Ruin, a Typical Mimbres Site in Southwestern New Mexico* (Papers, Peabody Museum of American Archaeology and Ethnology, vol. 15, no. 1, 1932), p. 61.

[53] J. B. Lillard, R. F. Heizer, and F. Fenenga, *An Introduction to the Archaeology of Central California* (Bulletin, Sacramento Junior College, Department of Anthropology, no. 2, 1939), plate 20.

[54] F. H. Roberts, *Additional Information on the Folsom Complex* (Smithsonian Miscellaneous Collections, vol. 95, no. 10, 1936), p. 31 and plate 9, fig. e.

latter explanation seems preferable to me. Accepting this explanation, however, still leaves us with the problem of defining in this case the degree of "independence" between the two games. If both pachisi and patolli developed separately from a common element like gambling with lots, we might call this parallelism. But suppose we took Culin's point of view and reduced their origins even further to underlying "mythic" concepts? We might suggest that New World dice may have arisen from such a simple form as that of the Eskimo—tossing figurines in the air and winning those which landed upright. By such reasoning we could always carry parallelism farther back. The decision as to where convergence replaces parallelism in any case of cultural growth, then, might depend entirely on how far back we wish to push our explanations.

In 1891, five years before Tylor expounded his method of analyzing phenonmena into independent elements with respect to the patolli-pachisi games, Boas did very much the same thing with respect to the dissemination of tales. His procedure was to break a tale down into elements which he felt could have developed independently. When a sufficient number of these independent elements occurred in two different places in the same combination, he felt justified in assuming genetic connection. He was careful, however, to point out one serious flaw—that there might, after all, be some logical connection between the elements thus causing one element to lead to another.[55] For some cases therefore, he demanded a further caution: distribution within a continuous area.[56] Boas was not interested in attempts to link up strange practices in widely separated portions of the earth, nor by arranging strata from spatial distributions or get three dimensions out of two. Boas wanted to be sure that the traits he was studying had diffused within his area so that he could study their differential diffusion and integration within the area.[57]

I do not wish to imply that there is anything wrong in making judgments on rough estimates of probability. But it is sometimes dangerous to use the size-language of mathematics for demonstrating relationships between phenomena whose size have not first been determined. It is

[55] Franz Boas, *Dissemination of Tales among the Natives of North America* (Journal of American Folk-Lore, vol. 4, 1891), p. 56.

[56] *Idem*, pp. 14–15; see also Franz Boas, *The Growth of Indian Mythologies* (Journal of American Folklore, vol. 9, 1896), pp. 6–8; *Ethnological Problems in Canada* (Journal, Royal Anthropological Institute, vol. 40, 1910), p. 537, and *Mythology and Folk-Tales of the North American Indians* (Journal of American Folk-Lore, vol. 27, 1914), p. 381.

[57] Boas, *The Growth of Indian Mythologies*, p. 10, and *Ethnological Problems in Canada*, pp. 537–538.

dangerous because it can give the impression that some higher authority is involved than simply the judgment of the observer himself.

A factor that has been too often overlooked in anthropology is the limitation of possibilities that may exist either external to the phenomena being studied or between them. From the time when Goldenweiser first formulated his principle of limited possibilities in 1913 until its revival by Murdock,[58] this concept has been badly neglected. Goldenweiser admitted that both Lowie and Boas, among others, had used the concept previously,[59] but the principle as he stated it was that

. . . limitation in number and character of cultural traits when compared to the multiplicity of possible historical and psychological sources, constitutes a limitation in the possibilities of development, and necessitates convergence.[60]

This principle grew up historically as an alternative to facile explanations based upon an assumption of psychic unity. It calls attention to the fact that limitations can and do exist between phenomena and that it is our business to attempt to determine them. But it is not always clear where the line is to be drawn between this approach and that of psychic unity.

Despite the reaction to cultural evolutionism and psychic unity during the past forty years there have been innumerable references to convergences due to limiting circumstances. We shall mention only a few.

Boas in 1914 mentions "sacred numbers," "revival of the dead," and "power to escape unseen" as ideas whose reoccurrences are not necessarily due to historical transmission. The limitations, however, are defined as "general psychological factors.[61] Lowie, writing in 1917, says, "Rejection of the omnipotence of diffusion has for its inevitable counterpart a partial acceptance of the view that cultural traits may be functionally related."[62]

With reference to language, Boas in 1920 states that similarities may be due to

. . . psychological causes such as the unavoidable necessity of classifica-

---

[58] George P. Murdock, "The Common Denominators of Cultures" (in *Science of Man in the World Crisis*, Ralph Linton, ed., New York, pp. 123–142, 1945); *Idem, Social Structure* (New York, 1949), pp. 115–117, 200.

[59] A. A. Goldenweiser, *The Principle of Limited Possibilities in the Development of Culture* (Journal of American Folk-Lore, vol. 26, 1913), p. 279.

[60] *Idem,* p. 290.

[61] Boas, *Mythology and Folk-Tales of the North American Indians,* pp. 409–410.

[62] R. H. Lowie, *Survivals and the Historical Method* (American Journal of Sociology, vol. 23, 1917–1918), p. 535.

tion of experience in speech, which can lead to a limited number of categories only, or the physiological possibilities of articulations that also limit the range of possible sounds which are sufficiently distinct to the ear for clear understanding.[63]

Malinowski in his essay on *Culture* in 1931 expresses sympathy with Goldenweiser's principle of limited possibilities.[64] Kroeber mentioned the principle in a paper already referred to in which he considered patolli and pachisi to be homologies. He points out that only a few arrow releases or magic numbers are possible, but he finds no exact parallel for this in biology unless it be the limited number of choices between such features as exo-skeletons and endo-skeletons, etc.[65]

Paleontologist Simpson has recently said:

In the most restricted sense virtually all evolution involves parallelism. Homologous genes tend to mutate in the same way. . . . This process is not immediately affected by a discontinuity in the breeding structure of the population. The separate and now discontinuous groups still carry homologous genes, and these still will tend to have the same mutations. Thus such groups may and, in all probability, frequently do develop the same characters, not typical of their ancestry or directly inherited but nevertheless due to inheritance; the inheritance of genes prone to mutate in the same way.[66]

Notice the resemblance of Simpson's statement to the Sapir-Eggan-Herskovits concept of "drift."[67] Both concepts imply certain limiting conditions; both are evolutionary, but neither is in any sense "unilinear." More recently, Simpson states:

There are, of course, certain limitations always present in any existing situation. Evolution fully at random in an unlimited, or even in a very large, number of directions is never possible to a group of organisms. Changes in size of whole organisms or of various of their parts are probably the commonest sort of evolutionary change, and such evolution can be in only one of two directions: toward larger or smaller. There is no conceivable alternative. More subtly, given a metabolic system that

[63] Franz Boas, *The Classification of American Languages* (American Anthropologist, vol. 22, 1920), p. 216.

[64] Bronislaw Malinowski, *Culture* (Encyclopedia of the Social Sciences, vol. 4, New York, 1931), p. 626.

[65] Kroeber, *Historical Reconstruction of Culture Growths and Organic Evolution*, p. 152.

[66] Simpson, *The Principles of Classification and a Classification of Mammals*, p. 9.

[67] Melville J. Herskovits, *Man and His Works* (New York, 1948), pp. 581–588.

requires intake of oxygen, the evolution of a group of animals is limited to environments where oxygen is present and to such structural changes as retain or provide apparatus for extracting oxygen in that environment.[68]

How like this sounds a statement made by Boas in 1932:

If it is possible that analogous anatomical forms develop independently in genetically distinct lines, it is ever so much more probable that analogous cultural forms develop independently. It may be admitted that it is exceedingly difficult to give absolutely indisputable proof of the independent origin of analogous cultural data. Nevertheless, the distribution of isolated customs in regions far apart hardly admits of the argument that they were transmitted from tribe to tribe and lost in intervening territory. It is well known that in our civilization current scientific ideas give rise to independent and synchronous inventions. In an analogous way primitive social life contains elements that lead to somewhat similar forms in many parts of the world. Thus the dependence of the infant upon the mother necessitates at least a temporary difference in the mode of life of the sexes and makes woman less movable than man. The long dependence of children on their elders leaves also an inevitable impress upon social form. . . . The number of individuals in a social unit, the necessity or undesirability of communal action for obtaining the necessary food supply constitute dynamic conditions that are active everywhere and that are germs from which analogous cultural behavior may spring.[69]

In 1937, Cora DuBois wondered if anthropologists had perhaps gone too far in their reaction to social evolution and thus been led to overlook a real problem in psychic unity. She lists what she considers fragmentary evidence for psychic unity, such as universal dream forms.[70] Finally, Murdock in 1945 discusses the ". . . principle of limited possibilities, which is of extreme importance in determining the universal culture patterns." He points out that in some cases the "limitations on potential responses are slight" and in others they are greater. Languages, folktales, and ceremonials permit great variety of detail, but every society can affiliate its children with groups of relatives through only three possible rules of descent: patrilineal, matrilineal, or bilateral. Similarly

[68] George G. Simpson, *The Meaning of Evolution* (New Haven, 1949), p. 141.

[69] Franz Boas, *The Aims of Anthropological Research* (Science, vol. 76, 1932), pp. 609–610.

[70] Cora DuBois, *Some Anthropological Perspectives on Psychoanalysis* (The Psychoanalytic Review, vol. 24, 1937), p. 254.

there are limitations to the number of possible ways of disposing of corpses. "In such cases it is to be expected that different and even historically unconnected peoples will frequently chance upon the identical solution to the same problem."[71]

It would seem that the difference between the "psychic unity" and the "limited possibilities" types of explanation is one of degree rather than kind. As the attempted explanations achieve refinement, the limitations are more readily definable. Our efforts to achieve such refinement will depend upon corresponding refinements in our methodological approach to the study of culture. The cross-cultural perspective illustrated by the work of Murdock is one asset; the careful, comparative functionalism of Boas is another. And, by follow-ups on intensively studied communities in various sectors of the world, we shall come to learn more of the nature and limitations of cultural change. Such changes will not be repetitions of past changes, but they will increase the perspective of our behavioral reference point and better enable us to interpret the limitations in all change.

There are in America today individuals and companies who do nothing but apply their ingenuity to the construction and invention of games with which to amuse the public and thereby derive their sustenance. Yet, despite this concentration of effort, the dice-and-board games of today do not differ in principle from those of the Aztecs and the Hindus. A game as American as *Monopoly* uses the same devices. True, the counter conflict is somewhat more disguised: instead of "killing" one another, *Monopoly* players, by the movement of their counters, establish priority to certain squares along the track which they can later use to tax other players so unfortunate as to have their counters land upon them. The medium of writing also allows the modern game further variations through the use of printed directions upon the board. But the limitations still there are so great that a manufacturer cannot patent such a toy. Even his copyright extends only to certain superficial aspects like the name and the art design.[72] This is a tacit recognition by our society that there are basic limitations in most games with respect to which no one individual or group of individuals has the right to an exclusive prerogative. Were radical innovations common in this medium, their authorship could be recognized and protected.

---

[71] Murdock, "The Common Denominators of Cultures," p. 139.

[72] I am indebted to Mr. John Goins for first calling this point to my attention and to Mr. Edward Montgomery for the following law reference: Whist Club vs. Foster et al., 42 Fed. (2d) 782 (Dist. Ct., S. D. New York, 1929)—"In the conventional laws or rules of a game, as distinguished from the forms or modes of expression in which they may be stated, there can be no literary property susceptible of copyright."

There are, as has been pointed out, differences in degree of limitation. There may be categories of culture like "art," where, within the limitations of the art medium, there might be greater potential range for individual variation of expression. We may, then, get here an allowable "tolerance" or "play" which is greater than that within such a category as economic behavior. Perhaps it is also within categories of such allowable "tolerance" that a society may exercise its more capricious limitations without endangering its livelihood. But within its own arbitrary limitations a society may still allow some variation. Thus, it may be in these cases that we find "involution"[73] or variation within monotony. Here, perhaps, cumulative variations within the arbitrary limitations prescribed by a society may give the appearance of repetitive or cyclic change.

One thing is certain: the concept of the limitation of possibilities, while evolutionary, implies neither unilinearity nor predictability. We might, for example, introduce dice and their use to an experimentally isolated society, but the native elaboration would certainly not develop at the same rate nor in exactly the same manner as patolli or pachisi. We could only say that *if* elaboration took place it would be faced with the same limitations as in those games. We could not even predict with any assurance that any elaboration would ever take place at all.

[73] Alexander A. Goldenweiser, "Loose Ends of a Theory on the Individual, Pattern, and Involution in Primitive Society" (in *Essays in Anthropology Presented to A. L. Kroeber*, R. H. Lowie, ed., Berkeley, pp. 99–104, 1936).

Games—Selected References in the English Language with Emphasis on Geographic Distribution

PART I

Multicultural, Multinational, and Cross-Cultural References

Bell, R. C. *Board and Table Games from Many Civilizations,* London: Oxford University Press, 1960.

Brewster, P. G. "A Worldwide Game and an Indian Legend," *Eastern Anthropologist, Luknow,* **14** (2), 1961, pp. 192–193.

Brewster, P. G. "Forfeit Games from Greece and Czechoslovakia," *Hoosier Folklore,* 8, 1948, pp. 76–83.

Brewster, P. G. "How Many Horns Has the Buck?' Prolegomena to a Comparative Study," *Volkskunde,* 4, 1944–1945, pp. 361–393.

Brewster, P. G. "A Roman Game and Its Survival on Four Continents," *Classical Philology,* 38, 1943, pp. 134–137.

Brewster, P. G. "Priority and Exemption in Children's Games: A Comparative Study," *Volkskunde,* 58 (1), 1957, pp. 21–30.

Brewster, P. G. "Some Games from Other Lands," *Southern Folklore Quarterly,* Gainesville, Florida, 7, 1943, pp. 109–117.

Brewster, P. G. "Some Games from Southern Europe," *Midwest Folklore,* 1, 1951, pp. 109–112.

Brewster, P. G. "Ten Games from Other Lands," *Western Folklore,* Berkeley, California, 8, 1949, pp. 146–151.

Brewster, P. G. "The Egyptian Game Khazza Lawizza and its Burmese Counterpart," *Zeitschrift für Ethnologie,* Braunschweig, 1961, pp. 211–13.

Brewster, P. G. "Three Russian Games and Their Western and Other Parallels," *Southern Folklore Quarterly,* Gainesville, Florida, 23 (2), 1959, pp. 126–131.

Culin, S. "Exhibition of Games at the Columbian Exposition," *Journal of American Folklore,* 6, 1893, pp. 205–227.

Culin, S. "America, the Cradle of Asia," *Harpers Monthly,* 41 (634), 1903, pp. 534–40.

Embree, J. "Kickball and Some Other Parallels Between Siam and Micronesia," *Journal of the Siam Society,* Bangkok, 38 (1), 1948, pp. 33–38.

Frederickson, F. S. "Sports in the Cultures of Man," *Science and Medicine in Exercise and Sports,* (W. R. Johnson, ed.), New York: Harper and Row, 1960, pp. 633–644.

Gadd, C. J. "An Egyptian Game in Assyria," *Iraq,* London, 7–8, 1934, pp. 45–50.

Haddon, A. C. *The Study of Man,* New York: G. P. Putnam's Sons, 1898.

Harbin, E. O. *Games of Many Nations,* Nashville: Abingdon Press, 1954.

Herskovits, M. J. "Wari in the New World," *Journal of the Royal Anthropological Institute,* 42, 1923, pp. 123–137.

Hildebrand, J. "The Geography of Games: How the Sports of Nations Form a Gazetteer of the Habits and Histories of Their Peoples," *National Geographic Magazine,* Washington, D.C., 36, 1919, pp. 89–144.

Hornblower, G. D. "Wrestling: India and Egypt," *Man,* London, 28, 1928, pp. 65–66.

Hunt, S. and Cain, E. *Games the World Around,* New York: A. S. Barnes, 1941.

Hutton, J. H. "A Fijian Game in Assam," *Man, London,* 29, 1929, pp. 156–157.

Leakey, L. S. B. "A Children's Game, West Australia and Kenya," *Man,* London, 38, 1938, pp. 178.

Milojkovic-Djuric, J. "The Jugoslav Children's Game 'Most' and Some Scandinavian Parallels," *Southern Folklore Quarterly,* Gainesville, Florida, 24 (3), 1960, pp. 226–234.

Parsons, E. W. C. "Some Aztec and Pueblo Parallels," *American Anthropologist,* 35 (4), 1933, pp. 611–631.

Roberts, J. M. and Sutton-Smith, B. "Cross-cultural Correlates of Games of Chance," *Behavior Science Notes,* 3, 1966, pp. 131–144.

Schroeder, A. H. "Ball Courts and Ball Games of Middle America and Arizona," *Archaeology,* 8 (3), 1955, pp. 156–161.

Stearns, R. E. C. "On the Nishinam Game of 'Ha' and the Boston Game of 'Props'," *American Anthropologist,* 3 (4), 1890, pp. 353–358.

Stern, T. "The Rubber Ball Games of the Americas," *American Ethnological Society Monograph,* New York: J. J. Augustin, 1950, #17.

Stockum, C. M. *Sport—an Attempt at a Bibliography of Books and Periodicals Published During 1890–1912 in Great Britain, The United States, Germany, France, Austria, Holland, Belgium, Switzerland,* New York: Dodd and Livingston, 1914.

Sutton-Smith, B. "Cross-cultural Study of Children's Games," *American Philosophical Society Yearbook,* 1961, pp. 426–429.

Sutton-Smith, B. "The Fate of English Traditional Games in New Zealand," *Western Folklore,* Berkeley, California, 11, 1953, pp. 250–253.

Sutton-Smith, B. "The Meeting of Maori and European Cultures and Its Effect Upon the Unorganized Games of Maori Children," *Journal of the Polynesian Society,* Wellington, N.Z., 60, 1951, pp. 93–107.

Tylor, E. B. "On American Lot Games as Evidence of Asiatic Intercourse Before The Time of Columbus," *International Archives for Ethnography,* supplement to volume 9, 1896, pp. 55–67. Also in *Source Book in Anthropology,* New York, 1931, pp. 388–397.

Tylor, E. B. "On the Game of 'Patolli' in Ancient Mexico and Its Probable Asiatic Origin," *Journal of the Royal Anthropological Institute,* London, 8, 1878, pp. 116–131.

UNESCO "The Place of Sport in Education—A Comparative Study," *Educational Studies and Documents,* 21 (63), Paris: UNESCO, 1956.

Wohl, A. (ed). *International Review of Sport Sociology,* Warsaw: Polish Scientific Publishers for UNESCO, 1966.

PART II

Africa

General References

Beal, N. *Pygmies are People: Their Folkways, Their Songs, Their Games, Their Dances,* New York: Van Roy Company, 1964.

Brewster, P. G. "Two Games From Africa," *American Anthropologist,* 46 (2), 1944, pp. 268–269.

Brewster, P. G. "Some African Variants of 'Bucca, Bucca,'" *Classical Journal*, 39, 1944, pp. 293–96.

Cúlin, S. "Mancala, The National Game of Africa," *Annual Report of the United States National Museum*, Washington, D.C.: U.S. Government Printing Office, 1894, pp. 597–606.

Powell-Cotton, P. H. E. "A Mancala Board Called Songo," *Man*, London, 31, 1931, p. 133.

Raum, O. F. "The Rolling Target Game in Africa," *African Studies*, Johannesburg, 1953, pp. 104–121; 12 (4), 1953, pp. 1–18.

Wright, R. H. *Fun and Festivals from Africa*, New York: Friendship Press, 1959.

Western Africa

Baker, G. S. "War Games on the Plateau," *West African Review*, Ibadan, 26 (331), 1955, pp. 108–109.

Bennett, G. T. "Wari," *Religion and Art in Ashanti* (R. S. Rattray, ed.), London: Oxford University Press, 1927, pp. 382–398.

Betts, G. "Chess in Borny, Nigeria," *Man*, London, 39, 1939, pp. 31–32.

Brewster, P. G. "Some Nigerian Games with Their Parallels and Analogues," *Societe des Africanistes Journal*, Paris, 24, 1954, pp. 25–48.

Collins, G. N. "Kboo, A Liberian Mancala Game," *National Geographic Magazine*, Washington, D. C., 21, 1910, pp. 944–948.

Fitzgerald, R. T. D. "The Dakarkari People of Sokito Province, Nigeria. Notes on Their Material Culture," *Man, London*, 42, 1942, p. 26.

Howson-Wright, A. E. "Some Pastimes in Nigeria and the British Cameroons," *Nigeria*, Lagos, 20, 1940, pp. 317–320.

Humpidge, K. "An African Game," *Nigeria*, Lagos, 16, 1938, pp. 300–302.

Namme, L. "The Bakweli Wrestling Match," *Nigeria*, Lagos, 15, 1938, pp. 242–243.

Newberry, R. J. "Some Games and Pastimes of Southern Nigeria," *Nigerian Field*, Ibadan, 7 (2), 1938, p. 85.

Parsons, E. W. C. "Three Games of the Cape Verde Islands," *Journal of American Folklore*, Lancaster, Penna., 33, 1920, pp. 80–81.

Perry, R. E. "The Board Game in North-west Africa," *Uganda Journal*, Kampala, 4, 1936, pp. 176–178.

Siegel, M. "A Study of West African Carved Gambling Chips," (The Mackenzie Collection) *Memoirs of the American Anthropological Association*, 55, 1940, pp. 7–77.

Eastern Africa

"A Boat-race in East Africa," *Illustrated London News*, March 27, 1937, pp. 538–539.

Alamayahu, S. "The Game of Ganna," *Addis Ababa University College Ethnological Society Bulletin,* 9, 1959, pp. 9–27.

Anna, M. "The Mweso Game Among the Basoga," *Primitive Man,* Washington, D. C., 11, 1938, pp. 71–74.

Braunholtz, H. J. "The Game of Mweso in Uganda," *Man,* London, 31, 1931, pp. 121–123.

Chaplin, J. H. "A Note on Mancala Games in Northern Rhodesia," *Man,* London, 56, 1956, p. 168.

Courlander, H. "The Ethiopian Game of Gobeta," *Negro History Bulletin,* Washington, D. C., 7, 1943, pp. 21–23.

Harrison, H. S. "A Bolas-and-Hoope Game in East Africa," *Man,* London, 12, 1947.

Hartnoll, M. M. "Some African Pastimes," *Tanganyika Notes and Records,* Dar es Salaam, 5, 1938, pp. 31–38.

Lambert, H. E. "A Note on Children's Pastimes in Kenya," *Swahili,* Arush, 30, 1959, pp. 74–78.

Leakey, L. S. B. "A Children's Game, West Australia and Kenya," *Man,* London, 38, 1938, p. 178.

Martin, G. "Somali Game," *Journal of the Royal Anthropological Institute,* London, 61, pp. 499–511.

Matson, A. T. "The Game of Mweso in Uganda," *Uganda Journal,* Kampala 21 (2), 1957, pp. 221.

Sanderson, M. G. "Native Games of Central Africa," *Journal of the Royal Anthropological Institute,* London, 43, 1913, pp. 726–736.

Shackell, R. "Mweso, The Board Game," *Uganda Journal,* Kampala, 2 1935, pp. 14–20.

Southern Africa

Longmore, L. "A Study of Fah-fee, an African Gambling Institution," *South African Journal of Science,* Johannesburg, 52 (12), 1956, pp. 275–282.

Malan, B. D. "Old and New Rock Engravings in Natal, South Africa; A Zulu Game," *Antiquity,* Cambridge, 31 (123), 1957, pp. 153–154.

Scotch, N. "Magic, Sorcery, and Football Among Urban Zulu," *Journal of Conflict Resolution,* Ann Arbor, Michigan, 5 (1), 1961, pp. 70–74.

Van Zyl, H. J. "Some of the Commonest Games Played by the Sotho People of Northern Transvaal," *Bantu Studies,* 13, 1939, pp. 293–305.

Zengeni, S. "The Game of Matomba," *Nada,* Salisbury, Rhodesia, 17, 1940, p. 7.

Northern Africa

Bolton, H. C. "Seega an Egyptian Game," *Journal of American Folklore,* Boston, 3, 1890, pp. 132–134.

Brewster, P. G. "Egyptian Prototypes of Two Twentieth Century Games," *Zeitschrift für Ethnologie,* Braunschweig, 88 (1), 1963, pp. 98–99.

Brewster, P. G. "Identification of Some Games Depicted on the Tomb of Mereruka," *East and West,* Rome, 13, (1), 1962, pp. 27–31.

Brewster, P. G. "The Egyptian Game of Khazza Lawizza and Its Burmese Counterpart," *Zeitschrift für Ethnologie,* Braunschweig, 1961, 85, pp. 211–213.

Brewster, P. G. "The Game of Sahbi Iddi Zaiat, Moroccan Form: Some Parallels and Analogues," *Hesperis,* 42 (1), 1955, pp. 239–244.

Davis, R. "Some Arab Games and Riddles," *Sudan Notes and Records,* London, 8, 1925, p. 145.

"Egyptian Dice," *Field Museum News,* Chicago, 1 (10), 1930, p. 1.

Gadd, C. J. "An Egyptian Game in Assyria," *Iraq,* London, 1, 1934, pp. 45–50.

Gini, C. "Rural Ritual Games in Lybia," *Rural Sociology,* Lexington, Kentucky, 4, 1939, pp. 283–299.

Petrie, F. "The Game of Seega," *Objects in Daily Use,* British School of Archaeology in Egypt, London, 1927, p. 56.

PART III

Europe

General

Brewster, P. G. "Ten Games from Europe," *Journal of American Folklore,* 55, 1952, pp. 88–90.

Kock, V. de. *The Fun They Had: The Pastimes of Our European Forefathers,* London: Bailey and Swinfen, 1955.

Newell, W. W. "Notes on the Interpretation of European Song Games," *Boas Anniversary Volume,* London, 1906, pp. 404–409.

Orgel, M. "Old European Dice Games," *Graphis,* 16 (89), 1960, pp. 256–261.

British Isles

Altham, H. S. and E. W. Swanton. *History of Cricket,* 2 volumes. London: Allen and Unwin, 1969.

Armitage, R. J. "Saxon Hnefatafl," *Times of St. Dunstan*, London: Oxford University Press, 1923, p. 69.

Aspen, J. *Picture of the Manners, Customs, Sports, and Pastimes of the Inhabitants of England*, London: J. Harris, 1825.

Cotton, C. and Lucas, T. *Games and Gamesters of the Restoration*, London: G. Routeledge and Sons, 1930.

Cruickshank, J. G. "Negro Games," *Manchester*, London, 29, 1929, pp. 179–180.

Douglas, N. *London Street Games*, London, St. Catharine Press, 1916. Revised and enlarged second edition, London: Chatto and Windus, 1931.

Fenton, S. "Lancashire Bowling Game," *Illustrated Archaeologist*, London, **2**, 1894, pp. 48–49.

Frankenberg, R. *Village on the Border: A Social Study of Religion, Politics, and Football in a North Wales Community*, London: Cohen and West, 1957.

Gomme, A. B. *Traditional Games of England, Scotland, and Ireland*, 2 volumes, London: Nutt and Company, 1894 and 1898. Reprinted New York: Dover Publications, Inc., 1964.

Gomme, A. B. *Old English Singing Games*, London: G. Allen, 1898.

Goodman, S. "Good Friday Skipping: Games Played at Burials," *Folklore*, London, **67** (3), 1956, pp. 171–174.

Holdbrook, E. *Children's Games*, Bedford, England: Gordon Fraser, 1957.

Hole, C. *English Sports and Pastimes*, London: Bastsford, 1949.

Maclagan, R. C. *Games and Diversions of Argyllshire*, London: Knutt, 1901.

Miles, E. "Games Which the Nation Needs," *Humane Review*, London, 1901, pp. 211–220.

Nally, T. H. *The Aonach Tailteann and the Tailteann Games; Their Origin, History, and Ancient Associations*, Dublin: Talbot Press, Ltd., 1928.

Opie, Peter & Iona, *Children's Games in Street & Playground*, Oxford: Clarendon Press, 1969.

Osuilleabhain, Sean, *Irish Wake Amusements*, Cork: The Mercier Press, 1967.

Proudfoot, B. F. "An Edinburgh Street Game," *Ulster Folklife*, 3 (1), 1957, pp. 74–75.

Read, D. H. "Games, Sports, and Pastimes," *Handbook of British Folklore* (C. S. Barune, ed.), London, 1914, p. 257.

Redstone, V. B. "Fox and Geese," *England Among The Wars of the Roses*, London: Transactions of the Royal Historical Society, **21**, 1902, p. 195.

Strutt, J. *Sports and Pastimes of the English People*, London: Methune and Company, 1801.

Watson, W. "The Street Games and Rhymes of Scottish Children," *Folklore*, London, **64** (3), 1953.

Webster, D. *Scottish Highland Games*, Glasgow and London: Wm. Collins and Sons, Ltd., 1959.

Whitaker, I. "Traditional Horse-races in Scotland," *Ariv*, **14**, 1958, pp. 83–94.

Whitehouse, F. R. B. *Table Games of Georgian and Victorian Days*, London, 1951.

Williams, M. O. "Great Britain on Parade: Clans Gather for Scottish Games," *National Geographic Magazine*, Washington, D.C., **68**, 1935, p. 153–160.

Czechoslovakia

Brewster, P. G. "Forfeit Games from Greece and Czechoslovakia," *Hoosier Folklore*, 8, 1948, pp. 76–83.

Brewster, P. G. "Some Notes on the Slovenian Game *Volka*," *Bilten Instituta Za Proučavanje Folklora*, 3, 1955, pp. 143–149.

Brewster, P. G. "Some Games from Czechoslovakia," *Southern Folklore Quarterly*, Gainesville, Florida, **21** (3), 1957, pp. 165–174.

Hrabalova, O. and Brewster, P. G. "A Czechoslovak Cat's Cradle Series," *Czechoslovakian Ethnography*, Praha, **5**, 1957, pp. 176–183.

Germany

Geithmann, H. "Stobeck, Home of Chess," *National Geographic Magazine*, Washington, D. C., **59**, 1951, pp. 637–562.

Greece

Austin, R. G. "Greek Board Games," *Antiquity*, Gloucester, England, **14**, 1940, pp. 257–271.

Brewster, P. G. "A String Figure Series from Greece," *Laographia*, 1951, pp. 101–125.

Brewster, P. G. "Forfeit Games from Greece and Czechoslovakia," *Hoosier Folklore*, 8, 1948, pp. 76–83.

Sparkes, B. A. "Kottabos: An Athenian After-dinner Game," *Archaeology*, **13** (3), 1960, pp. 202–207.

Tod, M. N. "Teams of Ball-Players at Sparta," *British School at Athens*, London, 10, 1903–1904, pp. 63–77.

Hungary

Brewster, P. G. "Malomjalik and Related Three-in-a-Row Games," *Acta Ethnographica*, Budapest, 6, 1957, pp. 225–231.

Brewster, P. G. "Some Hungarian Games," *Southern Folklore Quarterly*, Gainesville, Florida, 13, 1949, pp. 175–79.

Italy

Austin, R. G. "Roman Board Games," *Greece and Rome*, London, 4, 1934, p. 30.

Brewster, P. G. "A Roman Game and Its Survival on Four Continents," *Classical Philology*, 38, 1943, pp. 134–137.

Heywood, W. *Palio and Ponte: An Account of the Sports of Central Italy, from the Age of Dante to the Twentieth Century*, London: Methuen and Company, 1904.

The Low Countries

Portmann, P. *Brueghel's Children's Games*, Berne: Hallwag, Ltd., 1964.

Roeder, A. E. *Folksongs and Games of Holland*, New York: G. Schirmer, 1956.

Poland

Brewster, P. G. "Burski and Other Polish Games of Chance and Skill," *Zeitschrift für Ethnologie*, Braunschweig, 83, 1958, pp. 83–85.

Roumania

Brewster, P. G. "Some Traditional Games from Roumania," *Journal of American Folklore*, April–June, 1949, pp. 114–124.

Scandinavia

Fiske, W. *Chess in Iceland: With Historical Notes on Other Table Games*, Florence, Italy: Florentine Typographical Society, 1905.

Hencken, H. O'N. "A Gaming Board of the Viking Age," *Acta Archaeoloica*, Copenhagen, 4, 1933, pp. 85–104.

Sjovold, T. "Nine Men's Morris," *The Viking Ships*, Oslo, 1954, p. 7.

Spain

Gallop, R. "Pelote: Game of the Basques," *Geographical Magazine*, London, 21, 1948, pp. 81–88.

U.S.S.R.

Brewster, P. G. "The Cheremis Game *Sĕlčekteny-Mudone* and the Russian *Sčelčki*," *Zeitschrift für Ethnologie*, Braunschweig, **90** (2), 1965, pp. 265–267.

Brewster, P. G. "Three Russian Games and Their Western and Other Parallels," *Southern Folklore Quarterly*, Gainesville, Florida, **23** (2), 1959, pp. 126–131.

Mehl, E. "A Batting Game on the Island of Runo (Latvia)," *Western Folklore*, Berkeley, California, 8, 1949, pp. 266–269.

Morton, H. W. *Soviet Sport*, New York: Collier Books, 1963.

Seboek, T. A. and Brewster, P. G. *Studies in Cheremis: Games*, Bloomington, Indiana: Indiana University Press, 1958.

Yugoslavia

Brewster, P. G. "A Note on the Distribution of the Slovenian Game: Skarjice brusiti," *Slavic Ethnogrophie*, 8, 1955, pp. 255–258.

Brewster, P. G. and Milojkovic-Djuric, J. "A Group of Jugoslav Games," *Southern Folklore Quarterly*, Gainesville, Florida, **20** (3), 1956, pp. 183–191.

Milojkovic-Djuric, J. "The Jugoslav Children's Game 'Most' and Some Scandinavian Parallels," *Southern Folklore Quarterly*, Gainesville, Florida, **24** (3), 1960, pp. 226–234.

PART IV

Oceania

General

Davidson, D. S. "The Pacific and Circum-Pacific Appearance of the Dart Game," *Journal of the Polynesian Society*, Plymouth, N. Z., **45**, 1936, pp. 99–114, 119–126; **46**, 1937, pp. 1–23.

Hye-Kerkdal, K. "Tika, an Old Mystery Game in the Pacific," *Journal of the Polynesian Society*, Wellington, N. Z., **64** (2), 1955, pp. 197–226.

Jones, K. G. *Games and Physical Activities of the Ancient Polynesians and their Relationship to Culture*, Edmonton: University of Alberta Printing Department, 1967.

Pollock, H. J. "The Polynesian Game of Pua," *Chambers Journal*, London, 9th series, **2**, September, 1948, pp. 487–488.

Melanesia

New Guinea

Aufenanger, H. "A Children's Arrow-thrower in the Central Highlands of New Guinea," *Anthropos*, Freiburg, **56**, 1961, p. 633.

Aufenanger, H. "Children's Games and Entertainments Among the Kumngo Tribe in Central New Guinea," *Anthropos*, Freiburg, **53**, 1958, pp. 575–584.

Barton, F. R. "Children's Games in British New Guinea," *Journal of the Royal Anthropological Institute*, London, **38**, 1908, pp. 259–279.

Bell, F. L. S. "The Play Life of the Tanga," *Mankind*, Sidney, **2**, 1937, pp. 56–61; 3, 1938, pp. 83–86.

Burridge, K. O. L. "A Tangu Game: New Guinea," *Man*, London, **57**, 1957, pp. 88–89.

Carter, D. S. "Dayak Cockfight," *Corona* **11** (2), 1959, pp. 51–52.

Haddon, A. C. "Games and Toys," *Cambridge Anthropological Expedition to Torres Straits Report*, Cambridge, England, **4**, 1901–1912, pp. 312–314.

Haddon, A. C. "Notes on Children's Games in British New Guinea," *Journal of the Royal Anthropological Institute*, London, **38**, 1908, p. 294.

Hannemann, E. "Games and Modes of Entertainment in the Past Among the People of the Madang District (Papua, N. G.)," *Mankind*, Sidney, **5** (8), 1959, pp. 333–344.

Roheim, G. "Children's Games and Rhymes in Duau (Normandy Island, N. G.)," *American Anthropologist*, **45**, 1943, pp. 99–119.

Sandin, B. "Cock-Fighting, The Dayak National Game," *Sarawak Museum Journal*, Kuching, **9** (13–14), 1959, pp. 25–32.

Fiji

Hocart, A. M. "Two Fijian Games," *Man*, London, **9**, 1909, pp. 184–185.

Hornell, J. "String Figures from Fiji and Western Polynesia," *B. P. Bishop Museum Bulletin*, **39**, 1927, pp. 3–88.

Hutton, J. H. "A Fijian Game in Assam," *Man*, London, **29**, 1929, pp. 156–157.

Sharp, F. "Fiji Sports," *Mid-Pacific Magazine*, Honolulu, **45**, 1933, pp. 132–134.

Stumpf, F. and Cozens, F. W. "Some Aspects of the Role of Games, Sports, and Recreation Activities in the Culture of Modern Primitive Peoples: The Fijians," *Research Quarterly*, Washington, D.C., **20** (1), 1949, pp. 2–20.

New Hebrides

Watt, W. "Some Children's Games from Tanna, New Hebrides," *Mankind*, Sidney, **3**, 1946, pp. 261–264.

Micronesia

Embree, J. "Kickball and Some Other Parallels Between Siam and Micronesia," *Journal of the Siam Society*, **37** (1), 1948, pp. 33–38.

Maude, H. C. "String-figures from the Gilbert Islands," *Polynesian Society Memoirs*, Wellington, **13**, 1958, pp. 1–161.

Youd, J. 'Notes on Kickball in Micronesia," *Journal of American Folklore*, Montpelier, Vermont, **74**, (291), 1961, pp. 62–64.

Polynesia

Samoa

Churchill, L. P. "Sport of the Samoans," *Outing*, **33** (6), March, 1899, pp. 562–568.

Dunlap, H. L. "Games, Sports, Dancing, and other Vigorous Recreational Activities and Their Function in Samoan Culture," *Research Quarterly*, Washington, D.C., **22** (3), 1951, pp. 298–311.

Turner, F. M. "Sport in Samoan Craft," *Outing*, **25** (2), October, 1894, pp. 17–21.

Hawaii

Blake, T. *Hawaiian Surfboard*, Honolulu: Paradise of the Pacific Press, 1935.

Bolton, H. C. "Some Hawaiian Pastimes," *Journal of American Folklore*, Boston, **4**, 1891, pp. 21–26.

Culin, S. "Hawaiian Games," *American Anthropologist*, New Series, **1** (2), 1899, pp. 201–247.

Emerson, J. S. "Hawaiian String Games," *Folk-lore*, Poughkeepsie, N.Y., **5**, 1924, pp. 1–18.

Emory, K. P. "Sports, Games, and Amusements," *Ancient Hawaiian Civilization*, 1933, pp. 141–153.

Finney, B. R. "Surfing in Ancient Hawaii," *Polynesian Society Journal*, Wellington, N. Z., **68**, 1959, pp. 327–347.

Finney, B. R. "The Development and Diffusion of Modern Hawaiian Surfing," *Polynesian Society Journal*, Wellington, N. Z., **69** (4), 1960, pp. 315–331.

King, C. W. "Ancient Hawaiian Sports and Pastimes," *Mid-Pacific Magazine*, Honolulu, **48**, 1935, pp. 308–316.

Pukui, M. K. "Games From My Hawaiian Childhood," *California Folklore Quarterly*, Berkeley, California, **2**, 1943, pp. 205–220.

Westervelt, W. D. "Old Hawaiian Games in Honolulu," *Mid-Pacific Magazine*, Honolulu, **12** (4), October, 1916, pp. 345–347.

Philippine Islands

Cruz, E. C. "Diaka and Putlan-Bolo Game," *Philippine Magazine*, Manila, **31**, 1934, p. 472. Also in *Journal of East Asiatic Studies*, **4** (2), 1955, pp. 255–256.

Culin, S. "Philippine Games," *American Anthropologist*, New Series, **2** (4), 1900, pp. 643–656.

Jenks, A. E. "Tang-ga, A Philippine Pa-Ma-Ta Game," *American Anthropologist*, **8** (1), 1906, pp. 82–87.

La Cruz, B. A. de "Aklan Superstitions About Toys," *Philippine Magazine*, Manila, **30**, 1933, p. 30.

Serrano, C. "Gambling Among the Negritos of Panay," *Primitive Man*, Washington, D.C., **14**, 1941, pp. 31–32.

Simms, S. S. "Bontoc Igorot Games," *American Anthropologist*, **10** (4), 1908, pp. 563–567.

Worchester, D. C. "Field Sports Among the Wild Men of Northern Luzon," *National Geographic Magazine*, Washington, D.C., **22**, 1911, pp. 215–267.

Australia

Berndt, R. M. "Card Games Among Aborigines of the Northern Territory," *Oceania*, Sydney, **17**, 1947, pp. 248–269.

Berndt, R. M. "Some Aboriginal Children's Games," *Mankind*, Sydney, **2**, 1940, pp. 289–293.

Clark, J. H. *Field Sports of the Native Inhabitants of New South Wales*, London: E. Orme, 1813.

Haddon, A. C. "Australian Children's Games", *Nature*, **66**, 1914, pp. 380–381.

Harney, W. "Sport and Play Amidst the Aborigines of the Northern Territory," *Mankind*, Sydney, **4**, 1952, pp. 377–379.

Hobbs, J. F. "Australian Aboriginal Sports and Wood Craft," *Outing*, **31**, 1898, pp. 445–452.

Howard, D. "Australian Hopscotch," *Western Folklore*, Berkeley, California, **17** (3), 1958, pp. 163–175.

Howard, D. "Ball Bouncing Customs and Rhymes in Australia," *Midwest, Folklore*, **9** (2), 1959, pp. 77–87.

Howard, D. "The Game of Knucklebone in Australia," *Western Folklore*, Berkeley, California, **17** (1), 1958, pp. 34–44.

Howard, D. "The Toodlembuck-Australian Children's Gambling Device and Game," *Journal of American Folklore*, **73** (287), 1960, pp. 53–63.

Kennedy, K. "An Aboriginal Implement of Sport," *North Queensland Naturalist*, **90**, 1949, p. 21.

Leakey, L. S. B. "A Children's Game, West Australia and Kenya," *Man*, *London*, **38**, 1938, p. 178.

McCarthy, F. D. "The String Figures of Yirrkalla," *Records of the American-Australian Expedition to Arnhem Land*, (C. P. Mountford, ed.), **2**, 1960, pp. 415–512.

Meggitt, M. J. "Two Australian Aboriginal Games and a Problem of Diffusion," *Mankind*, Sydney, **5** (5), 1958, pp. 191–194.

Roth, W. E. "Games, Sports, and Amusements," *North Queensland Ethnography: Bulletin No. 3*, Brisbane, Northern Protector of Aboriginals, Queensland, March 1902.

Salter, M. A. *Games and Pastimes of the Australian Aboriginal*, Edmonton: University of Alberta Printing Department, 1967.

Tinsdale, N. B. "A Game from the Great Desert of Australia," *Man*, London, **38**, 1938, pp. 128–129.

New Zealand

Anderson, J. C. "An Article on Supposed Maori Bowls," *Polynesian Society Journal*, New Plymouth, N. Z., **42**, 1933, pp. 222–225.

Anderson, J. C. "Maori String Games," *New Zealand Journal of Science and Technology*, Wellington, N. Z., **3**, 1920, pp. 81–208; Second Series, **4**, 1921, pp. 145–154; Third Series, **6** (5–6), 1924, pp. 289–309; Fourth Series, **8** (3), 1926, pp. 173–188; Fifth Series, **8** (4), 1926, pp. 53–57.

Armstrong, A. *Maori Games and Hakas*, Wellington: A.H.&A.W. Reed, 1964.

Bennett, H. "Games of the Old Time Maori," *Te Ao Hou—The New World*, Christchurch, N. Z., **6** (2), 1958, pp. 45–47.

Best, E. "Games and Pastimes of the Maori," *Dominion Museum Bulletin*, Wellington, **8**, 1925.

Best, E. "Maori Games and Pastimes: Stilt-walking," *New Zealand Journal of Science and Technology*, Wellington, **5**(5), 1922, p. 255.

Best, E. "Pastimes of Maori Children," *New Zealand Journal of Science and Technology*, Wellington, **5** (5), 1922, p. 254.

Best, E. "The Maori Game of Mu-Torere," *New Zealand Journal of Science and Technology*, Wellington, 8 (3), 1926, pp. 189–191.

Chapman, F. R. "Koruru, the Maori Game of Knuckle-bone," *Journal of the Polynesian Society*, Wellington, 7 (2), 1898, p. 114.

Reed, A. W. *Games the Maoris Played*, London: Bailey and Swinfern, 1958.

Skinner, H. D. "Bowling Discs from New Zealand and Other Parts of Polynesia," *Journal of the Polynesian Society*, Wellington, 55, December, 1946, pp. 243–262.

Stumpf, F. and Cozens, F. W. "Some Aspects of the Role of Games, Sports, and Recreation Activities in the Culture of Modern Primitive Peoples: The New Zealand Maoris," *Research Quarterly*, Washington, D.C., 18 (3), 1947, pp. 198–210.

Sutton-Smith, B. "New Zealand Variants of the Game Buck-Buck," *Folklore*, London, 63, 1952, pp. 329–333.

Sutton-Smith, B. *The Games of New Zealand Children*, Los Angeles: University of California Press, Folklore Studies #12, 1959.

Sutton-Smith, B. "The Traditional Games of New Zealand Children," *Folklore*, London, 12, 1953, pp. 411–423.

Sutton-Smith, B. "The Game Rhymes of New Zealand Children," *Western Folklore Quarterly*, Berkeley, Calif.: 12, 1953, pp. 411–423.

Sutton-Smith, B. "The Fate of English Traditional Games in New Zealand," *Western Folklore Quarterly*, 11, 1953, pp. 250–253.

Sutton-Smith, B. "The Meeting of Maori and European Cultures and Its Effects upon the Unorganized Games of Maori Children," *Journal of the Polynesian Society*, Wellington, 60, 1951, pp. 93–107.

PART V

Asia

General

Brewster, P. G. "The Earliest Known List of Games: Some Comments." (From the Dialogues of the Buddah.) *Acta Orientalia*, Copenhagen, 23 (1–2), 1958, pp. 33–42.

Brewster, P. G. "Some Kindred Games of the Far East," *Geografica Helvetica*, Berne, 15 (1), 1960, pp. 33–38.

Culin, S. *Games of the Orient*, Rutland, Vermont, C. E. Tuttle, 1958. (Reprint of *Korean Games with Corresponding Games of China and Japan*, Philadelphia: University of Pennsylvania Press, 1895.)

Newell, W. H. "A Few Asiatic Board Games Other Than Chess," *Man*, London, **59**, 1959, pp. 29–30.

"Playing Cards of Asia," *Asia*, New York, **31**, 1931, pp. 152–55.

India

Auboyer, J. "Archery: a Royal Sport and Sacred Game in Ancient India," *Arts and Letters*, London, **301** (1), 1956, pp. 3–12.

Brewster, P. G. "A Collection of Games from India, with some Notes on Similar Games in Other Parts of the World," *Zeitschrift für Ethnologie*, Braunschweig, **80**, 1955, pp. 88–102.

Brewster, P. G. "A Worldwide Game and an Indian Legend," *Eastern Anthropologist*, Luknow, **14**, (2), 1961, 192–193.

Brewster, P. G. "Four Games of Tag from India," *Midwest Folklore*, **1** (4), 1951, pp. 239–241.

Brewster, P. G. "The *Kitte ande ból* Game of India," *Southern Folklore Quarterly*, Gainesville, Florida, **7**, 1943, pp. 149–52.

Bromick, P. K. "Recreation Life of the West Bengal Lodhas," *India Folklore*, **2** (1), 1959, pp. 65–84.

Brown, W. N. "The Indian Games of Parchisi, Chaupar, and Chausar," *Expedition*, Philadelphia, **6** (3), 1964, pp. 32–35.

Carey, M. A. "A Beadwork Gaming Board from North-West India," *British Museum Quarterly*, London, **24** (1–2), 1961, pp. 59–60.

Chakravarti, T. N. "Some Information About Sports, Indoor Games, and Pastimes, in the Ancient Literature and Early Inscription of Bengal and Assam," *East and West*, **7**, 1956, pp. 56–60.

Gupta, H. C. D. "A Few Types of Sedentary Games Prevalent in the Punjab," *Man in India*, Ranchi, India, **6**, 1926, p. 76.

Gupta, H. C. D. "Notes on a Type of Sedentary Game Prevalent in Many Parts of India," *Man in India*, Ranchi, India, **5**, 1925, pp. 244–349.

Gupta, H. C. D. "Two Types of Sedentary Games Prevalent in British Garhwal," *Man in India*, Ranchi, India, **8**, 1928, p. 91.

Hornblower, G. D. "Wrestling: India and Egypt," *Man*, London, **28**, 1928, pp. 65–66.

In Thurn, E. F. "Indian Children's Games," *Timehri*, Demerara, 3, 1884, pp. 147–148.

La Hora, S. "Sedentary Games of India," *Journal and Proceedings of the Asiatic Society of Bengal*, **29**, 1933.

Mishra, D. "Recreation of Baiga Children," *Vanyajati*, Delhi, **6** (2), 1958, pp. 70–73.

Mistry, D. K. "The Indian Child and His Play," *Sociology Bulletin*, Bombay, **8** (1), 1959, pp. 86–96; **9** (2), 1960, pp. 48–55.

Padmanabhachari, T. "Games, Sports, and Pastimes in Prehistoric India," *Man in India,* Ranchi, India, **21** (2–3), 1941, pp. 127–146.

Patel, J. S. and Brewster, P. G. "The Indian Game of Sagarote (Kooka, Bombay)," *Zeitschrift für Ethnologie,* Braunschweig, **82** (2), 1957, pp. 186–190.

Ceylon

Deraniyagela, P. "Some Blood Games of the Sinhalese," *Man,* London, **38**, 1938, pp. 46–47.

Gunasekara, W. M. "The Sinhalese New Year: Games and Festivals," *Ceylon Today,* **6** (4), 1957, pp. 13–18.

Parker, H. "Alquerque," *Ancient Ceylon,* London, 1909, pp. 579, 644.

Raghamen, M. "Ethnological Survey of Ceylon," *Spolia Zeylanica,* Ceylon, **27**, 1953, pp. 171–178.

Indo-China, Malay Peninsula, and Malay Archipelago

Bazell, C. "The Rules for Some Common Malay Games," *Journal of the Royal Asiatic Society,* Malayan Branch, Singapore, **6** (4), 1928, pp. 46–48.

Blomberg, R. "Cricket-Fighting in Bali," *Ethnos,* Stockholm, **11**, 1946, pp. 126–132.

Brewster, P. G. "The Egyptian Game Khazza Lawizza and Its Burmese Counterpart," *Zeitschrift für Ethnologie,* Braunschweig, **85**, 1961, pp. 211–213.

Brewster, P. G. "The Malayan *Hantu Musang* and Other Possession Games of Indonesia and Indochina," *Oriens,* Wiesbaden, **2** (1–2), 1958, pp. 162–176.

Brown, O. O. Kelantan Bullfighting," *Journal of the Royal Asiatic Society,* Malayan Branch, Singapore, **6** (1), 1928, pp. 74–83.

Chakravarti, T. N. "Some Information About Sports, Indoor Games, and Ancient Pastimes, in the Ancient Literature and Early Inscriptions of Bengal and Assam," *East and West,* Rome, **7**, 1956, pp. 56–60.

Dussek, O. T. "Notes on Malay Games," *Journal of the Royal Asiatic Society,* London, **80**, 1919, pp. 69–71.

Embree, J. "Kickball and Some Other Parallels Between Siam and Micronesia," *Journal of the Siam Society,* **37** (1), 1948, pp. 33–38.

Haas, M. R. "Thai Word-Games," *Journal of American Folklore,* Richmond, Virginia, **70** (276), 1957, pp. 173–175.

Hill, A. H. "Some Kelantan Games and Entertainments," *Journal of the Royal Asiatic Society,* Singapore, **25**, 1952, pp. 20–34.

Hutton, J. H. "A Fijian Game in Assam," *Man,* London, **29**, 1929, pp. 156–157.

"Malay Card Games," *Journal of the Royal Anthropological Institute,* London, **17**, 1897, pp. 136–139.

Wilkinson, R. J. "Malay Amusements," *Papers on Malay Subjects, Life and Customs,* London **3**, 1910, p. 25.

Tibet

Hummel, S. and Brewster, P. G. *Games of Tibetans,* Helsinki: Suomalainer Tiedeakatenia, Academia Scientiarum Fennica, 1963.

Mongolia

Montell, G. "Mongolian Chess and Chessmen," *Ethnos,* Stockholm, **4**, 1939, pp. 81–104.

Korea

Culin, S. *Korean Games, With Notes on the Corresponding Games of China and Japan,* Philadelphia: University of Pennsylvania Press, 1895. Reprinted: C. E. Tuttle, Rutland, Vermont, 1958.

Starr, F. "Korean Games," *The Dial,* May, 1896, pp. 302–304.

Japan

Culin, S. "Burro-Burri Citcho Game," *Brooklyn Museum Quarterly,* Brooklyn, New York, **12** (3), 1925, pp. 133–138.

Culin, S. "Japanese Swinging Bat Game; Japanese Game of Battledore and Shuttlecock," *Brooklyn Museum Quarterly,* **12** (3), 1925, pp. 139–150.

Culin, S. "Japanese Game of Sugoroku," *Brooklyn Museum Quarterly,* **7** (3), 1920, pp. 213–233.

Culin, S. *Korean Games, With Notes on the Corresponding Games of China and Japan,* Philadelphia: University of Pennsylvania Press, 1895. Reprinted: C. E. Tuttle, Rutland, Vermont, 1958.

Ichikawa, S. "Kyu-do, The Way of Archery in Japan," *Natural History,* New York, **33**, 1933, pp. 139–152.

Kanai, S. and Farrell, M. *Mah Jong for Beginners,* Rutland, Vermont: C. E. Tuttle Company, 1952.

Lasker, E. *Go and Go-Muku: Oriental Board Games,* New York, Dover Publications, Inc., 1934; Revised 1960.

Morse, E. S. "Indoor Games of the Japanese," *Science,* London, 1952, **2** (32), 1883, pp. 366–367.

Ohara, E. *Japanese Chess: The Game of Shogi,* London: Patterson, 1958.

Opler, M. K. "A Sumo Tournament at Tule Lake Center," *American Anthropologist,* **47** (1), 1945, pp. 134–139.

Plath, D. *The After Hours: Modern Japan and The Search for Enjoyment,* Berkeley, California: University of California Press, 1964.

Smith, A. *The Game of Go. The National Game of Japan,* Rutland Vermont: C. E. Tuttle Company, 1956.

Van Rensselear, J. K. "Playing Cards from Japan," *Proceedings of the United States National Museum,* Washington, D.C., **13**, 1890, pp. 381–382.

Yoshino, N. *Gimmi 88: The Popular Japanese Card Game,* New York: Katagri Brothers, 1929.

China

Culin, S. *Chinese Games with Dice,* Philadelphia: Oriental Club, 1889.

Culin, S. "Chinese Games with Dice and Dominoes," *Annaul Report of the United States National Museum,* Washington, D.C., 1893, pp. 491–537.

Culin, S. "Game of Mah-Jong," *Brooklyn Museum Quarterly,* Brooklyn, N.Y., **11** (3), 1924, pp. 153–158.

Culin, S. *Korean Games With Notes on the Corresponding Games of China and Japan,* Philadelphia: University of Pennsylvania Press, 1895; Reprinted: C. E. Tuttle, Rutland, Vermont, 1958.

Headland, I. T. *Chinese Children's Games,* London: Revell, 1906.

Long Sang Ti. *Mah-Jong: The Ancient Game of China,* New York: A. Langstater, Inc., 1923.

Montagu, I. "Sports and Pastimes in China," *United Asia,* Bombay, **8**, 1956, pp. 150–152.

"Paraphernalia of China's Cricket Cult," *Field Museum News,* Chicago, **14**, (618), 1943, pp. 7–8.

Rudolph, R. "Notes on the Riddle in China," *California Folklore Quarterly,* Berkeley, California, **1**, 1942, pp. 65–68.

Strauser, K. and Evans, L. *Mah Jong Anyone?,* London: Prentice Hall, Inc., 1964.

Volpicelli, Z. "Wei-Chi," *Journal of the China Branch, Royal Asiatic Society,* London, **26**, 1894, p. 80.

Wilkinson, W. H. "Chinese Origin of Playing Cards," *American Anthropologist,* **8** (1), 1895, pp. 61–78.

Middle East

Brewster, P. G. "A sampling of Games from Turkey," *East and West,* Rome, **11** (1), 1960, pp. 15–20.

Brewster, P. G. "Treatise on Iranian Games," *Acta Orientalia,* Copenhagen, **25** (1–2), 1960, pp. 15–28.

Gadd, C. J. "An Egyptian Game in Assyria," *Iraq,* London, **1**, 1934, pp. 45–50.

Hasluck, M. "Traditional Games of the Turks," *Jubilee Congress of the Folklore Society*, London, 1930.

PART VI

Central and South America

General

Borhegyi, S. "American Ballgame (Mesoamerica)," *Natural History*, New York, **69** (1), 1960, pp. 48–58.

Borhegyi, S. "Ballgame Handstones and Ballgame Gloves," *Essays in Pre-Columbian Art and Archaeology*, Cambridge, Mass., 1961, pp. 126–151.

Schroeder, A. H. "Ball Courts and Ballgames of Middle America and Arizona," *Archaeology*, Cincinnati, 8 (3), 1955, pp. 156–161.

Stern, T. "The Rubber Ball Games of the Americas," *Monography #17; American Ethnological Society*, New York: J.J. Augustin, 1950.

Tylor, E. B. "On American Lot Games as Evidence of Asiatic Intercourse Before the Time of Columbus," *International Archives for Ethnographie*, Supplement to Volume 9, 1896, pp. 55–67; Also reprinted in *Source Book In Anthropology*, New York, 1931, pp. 388–397.

Wanchope, R. "The Middle American Ballgame in 1750," *El Palacio*, Santa Fe, New Mexico, **55**, 1948, pp. 299–301.

Mexico

Anderson, A. J. "Home Diversions of the Aztec Chief," *El Palacio*, Santa Fe, New Mexico, **55**, 1948, pp. 125–127.

Beals, R. L. "Games of the Mountain Tarascans," *American Anthropologist*, **46**, 1944, pp. 516–522.

Beals, R. L. "Unilateral Organizations in Mexico (pre-Aztec ballgames and races)," *American Anthropologist*, **34** (3), 1932, pp. 467–475.

Blom, F. F. "The Maya Ball-Game Pokta-pok (called tlachtle by the Aztec)," *Tulane University of Louisiana Middle Amercan Research Series*, New Orleans, 1932, pp. 431–456, 485–530.

Caso, A. "Notes on Ancient Games," *Mexican Folkways*, Mexico City, **7** (2), 1932, pp. 56–60.

Enriquez, Celso, *Sports in Pre-Hispanic America*, Mexico: Litografica Machado, 1968.

Goellner, W. A. "The Court Ball Game of the Aboriginal Mayas," *Research Quarterly*, Washington, D.C., **24** (2), 1956, pp. 147–168.

Islos, G. L. "Children's Games," *Mexican Folkways*, Mexico City, **7** (2), 1932, pp. 63–74.

MacCoby, M. et al. "Games and Social Character in a Mexican Village," *Psychiatry*, 27, 1964, pp. 150–162.

Parsons, F. W. C. "Some Aztec and Pueblo Parallels," *American Anthropologist*, 4 (4), 1933, pp. 611–631.

Toor, F. "Games," *Mexican Folkways*, Mexico City, 7 (2), 1932, pp. 60–63.

Tylor, E. B. "Backgammon Among the Aztecs," *Macmillan's Magazine*, London, 39, 1878, pp. 142–150.

Tylor, E. B. "On the Game of Patolli in Ancient Mexico, and Its Probably Asiatic Origin," *Journal of the Royal Anthropological Institute*, 8 (4), 1878, pp. 116–131.

Caribbean Area

Alegria, R. E. "The Ballgame Played by the Aborigines of the Antilles," *American Antiquity*, Salt Lake City, Utah, 16, 1951, pp. 348–352.

Bechwith, M. W. "Folkgames of Jamaica," *American Folklore Society*, New York, 21, 1928.

Davenport, W. "Jamaican Fishing: A Game Theory Analysis," *Yale University Papers in Anthropology*, 59, New Haven, 1960, pp. 3–11.

Ekholm, G. F. "Puerto Rican Stone Collars as Ballgame Belts," *Essays in Pre-Columbian Art and Archaeology*, Cambridge, Mass., 1961, pp. 356–371.

Goggin, J. M. "A Ballgame at Santo Domingo," *American Anthropologist*, 42 (2), 1940, pp. 364–366.

Central and South America

Brewster, P. G. "Juegos Infantiles (Children's Games)," *Folklore Americas*, Lima, 13 (1), 1953, pp. 3–15.

Cooper, J. M. "A Cross-Cultural Survey of South American Indian Tribes: Games and Gambling," *Bureau of American Ethnology Bulletin*, Washington, D.C., 5 (143), 1949, pp. 503–524.

Jackson, E. "Native Toys of the Guarayu Indians (Venezuela)," *American Anthropologist*, 66 (5), 1964, pp. 1153–1155.

Karsten, R. "Ceremonial Games of the South American Indians," *Comentationes Humanarum Litterarum*, 13 (2), 1930, pp. 3–38.

Kutscher, G. "Ceremonial Badminton in The Ancient Culture of Peru," *Proceedings of the International Congress of Americanists*, Copenhagen, 3, 1958, pp. 422–432.

Reynolds, M. G. "Glimpses of Latin America At Play," *Pan American Union Bulletin*, Washington, D.C., 82, 1954, pp. 41–45.

Smith, A. L. "Types of Ball Courts in the Highlands of Guatemala," *Essays in Pre-Columbian Art and Archaeology*, Cambridge, Mass., 1961, pp. 100–125.

Willems, E. "Acculturation and the Horse Complex Among German-Brazilians," *American Anthropologist*, 46 (2), 1944, pp. 153–161.

PART VII

North America

General

Beauchamp, W. M. "The Snow Snake," *Young Mineralogist And Antiquarian*, Wheaton, Ill., 1, 1884, p. 85.

Betts, J. R. "The Technological Revolution and The Rise of Sport, 1850–1900," *Mississippi Valley Historical Review*, September, 1953.

Blasig, R. "The Practice of Sports Among the Indians of America," *Mind and Body*, 40, 1933–1934, pp. 216–219.

Boroff, D. "A View of Skiers and a Subculture," *Sports Illustrated*, New York, 21, Nov. 23, 1964, pp. 9–14.

Boyle, R. H. *Sport-Mirror of American Life*, Boston: Little, Brown and Company, 1963.

Brewster, P. G. "Long Breath and Taking Fire: Cultural Survivals in Games of Chase," *Eastern Anthropologist*, Lucknow, 12 (1), 1958, pp. 41–46.

Brewster, P. G. "Some String Tricks From the U.S., *Rivista di Etnogrofia*, Naples, 7 (7), 1953, pp. 1–2.

Brewster, P. G. "Two Unusual String Figures From the U.S.," *Der Forschungsdienst*, 6 (1), 1953.

"Brueghel's Games Today," *Recreation*, 45 (9), 1951, pp. 212–213.

Buchner, M. J. "Shinny and Snakes on Rosebuds," *Indians at Work*, Washington, D.C., 2 (24), 1935, pp. 30–31.

Cozens, F. W. and Stumpf, F. S. *Sports in American Life*, Chicago: University of Chicago Press, 1953.

Culin, S. "American Indian Games," *American Anthropologist*, 5 (1), 1903, pp. 58–64.

Culin, S. "American Indian Games," *Journal of American Folklore*, Oct. and Dec. 1899, pp. 245–252.

Culin, S. "Gambling Games of the Chinese in America," *University of Pennsylvania Series in Philology, Literature, and Archaeology*, Philadelphia: University of Penn. Press, 1 (4), 1891, pp. 1–17.

Culin, S. *Games of North American Indians* (Twenty-fourth Annual Report of the Bureau of American Ethnology, pp. 1–846). Washington, D.C.: United States Government Printing Office, 1907.

Cushing, F. H. "Observations Relative to the Origin of the Fylfot or Swastika," *American Anthropologist*, 9 (2), 1907, pp. 334–337.

Durant, J. and Bettman, O. *Pictorial History of American Sports: From Colonial Times to the Present*, New York: A.S. Barnes, 1952.

Fletcher, A. C. *Indian Games and Dances*, Boston: C.C. Birchard and Company, 1915.

Gilmore, M. R. "The Game of Double Ball or Twin Ball," *Indian Notes*, New York, 3, 1926, pp. 293–295.

Gordon, D. "La Crosse: An Indian Contribution to American Recreation," *Masterkey*, Los Angeles, 3, 1962, pp. 97–99.

Haddon, A. C. "A Few American String Figures and Tricks," *American Anthropologist*, 5 (2), 1903, pp. 213–223.

Hallett, L. F. "Indian Games," *Massachusetts Archaeological Society*, Attleboro, 16, 1955, pp. 25–28.

Henderson, R. W. *Early American Sports: Prior to 1860*, New York: A.S. Barnes Company, 1953.

Hofsinde, R. *Indian Games and Crafts*, New York: Morrow, 1957.

Holliman, J. *American Sport: 1785–1835*, Durham, N.C.: The Sieman Press, 1931.

Howell, N. *Sports and Games in Canadian Life: 1700 to the Present*, Toronto: MacMillan, 1969.

McCaskill, J. C. "Indian Sports," *Indians at Work*, Washington, D.C., 3 (2), 1936, pp. 29–30.

Macfarlan, A. A. *Book of American Indian Games*, New York: Association Press, 1958.

Manchester, H. *Four Centuries of Sport in America: 1490–1890*, New York: Derrydale Press, 1931.

Mason, B. *Primitive and Pioneer Sports for Recreation*, New York: A.S. Barnes and Company, 1937.

Mead, M. "The Pattern of Leisure in Contemporary American Culture," *Annals of the American Academy of Political and Social Science*, 313, 1957, pp. 11–15.

Newell, W. W. *Games and Songs of American Children*, New York: Harper Brothers, 1883. Reprinted, New York: Dover Publications, 1963.

Rainwater, C. E. *The Play Movement in the United States*, Chicago: University of Chicago Press, 1922.

Rider, C. "The Sporting Scene: 1864," *The American Scholar*, 15 (2), 1946, pp. 348–352.

Rinaldo, J. B. "American Love of Ball Games Dates Back to Indians," *Chicago Natural History Museum Bulletin*, Chicago, 26 (1), 1955, pp. 3–4.

Sando, J. S. "Indian Olympics," *New Mexico*, Albuquerque, 30 (4), 1952, pp. 22, 43, 45, 47.

Stone, G. "Some Meanings of American Sport," *Sixtieth Annual Proceedings of the Canadian Physical Education Association*, 1957, pp. 6–29.

Sutton-Smith, B. and Rosenberg, B. G. "Sixty Years of Historical Change in the Game Preferences of American Children," *Journal of American Folklore*, **74**, 1961, pp. 17–46.

Watkins, F. E. "Indians at Play," *Masterkey*, Los Angeles, **18**, 1944, pp. 139–141; **19**, 1944, pp. 20–21; **20**, 1945, pp. 81–87.

Weaver, R. B. *Amusements and Sports in American Life*, Chicago: Chicago University Press, 1939.

Woods, C. "Indian Track Meet," *New Mexico*, Albuquerque, N.M., **24** (3), 1946, pp. 16–17, 43, 45, 47.

North Eastern

Beauchamp, W. M. "Iroquois Games," *Journal of American Folklore*, **9**, 1898, pp. 269–277.

Brewster, P. G. "Johnny On The Pony, A New York State Game," *New York Folklore Quarterly*, **1**, 1945, pp. 239–240.

Brown, N. W. "Some Outdoor Games of the Wabanaki Indians," *Transactions of the Royal Society of Canada*, Montreal, **6** (2), 1889, p. 45.

Chase, J. H. "Street Games of New York," *Pedagogical Seminary*, **12**, 1905, pp. 503–504.

Culin, S. "Street Games of Boys of Brooklyn," *Journal of American Folklore*, **4** (3), 1891, pp. 221–237.

Hewitt, J. N. B. "Iroquois Game of La Crosse," *American Anthropologist*, **5** (2), 1892, pp. 189–191.

Holton, G. R. "Playtime Along the Genesee," *Museum Service*, Rochester, N.Y., **30**, 1957, pp. 73, 82.

Hough, W. "Games of the Seneca Indians," *American Anthropologist*, **1** (2), 1888, p. 134.

Parker, A. C. "Snow Snake As Played By The Seneca-Iroquois," *American Anthropologist*, **11** (2), 1909, pp. 250–256.

Paterson, T. "Greenland Eskimos Produce the Most Remarkable String Figures in the World," *Geographical Journal*, London, **92**, 1938, pp. 419–421.

Rochford, D. "New England Ski Trains and Ice Sports," *National Geographic Magazine*, Washington, D.C., **70** (11), 1936, pp. 645–664.

Speck, F. G. "Game Totems Among the Northeast Algonkians," *American Anthropologist*, **19** (1), 1917, pp. 9–18.

Stearns, R. E. C. "On the Nishinam Game of 'Ha' and the Boston Game of 'Props'," *American Anthropologist*, **3** (4), 1890, pp. 353–358.

Weiss, H. B. *Early Sports and Pastimes in New Jersey*, Trenton: Past Times Press, 1960.

South Eastern

Babcock, W. H. "Games of Washington, D.C. Children," *American Anthropologist*, **1** (2), 1888, pp. 243–284.

Backus, E. M. "Ancient Game of Courtship From North Carolina," *Journal Of American Folklore*, **13** (48), 1900, p. 104.

Brewster, P. G. "Children's Games and Rhymes," *The Frank C. Brown Collection of North Carolina Folklore*, **1** (4), Durham, N.C.: University Press, 1953.

Browne, B. W. "The Buzzard in the Folklore of Western Kentucky; Negro Folklore—sayings, games, and dances," *Kentucky Folklore Record*, **4**, 1958, pp. 11–12.

"Cherokee Indian Fair Throws Spotlight on LaCrosse, Archery and Blowgun Contests," *Indians at Work*, Washington, D.C., **7** (4), 1939, pp. 12–14.

Ewing, W. C. *The Sports of Colonial Williamsburg*, Richmond, Va.: The Dietz Press, 1937.

Fink, R. W. "Recreational Pursuits in the Old South," *Research Quarterly*, Washington, D.C., **22**, 1951, pp. 298–311.

Hall, J. "Some Party Games of the Great Smokey Mountains," *Journal of American Folklore*, **54**, 1941, pp. 68–71.

Johnson, G. B. *Folk Culture on St. Helena Island*, Chapel Hill, N.C.: University of North Carolina Press, 1930.

McKenzie, B. "The Seminoles Were Recognized as the Leading Ball Players Years Ago," *American Indian*, Tulsa, Okla., **1** (5), 1927, p. 10.

Mead, M. "A Choktaw Ball Game," *Primitive Heritage*, New York, 1953, pp. 289–295.

Mooney, J. "The Cherokee Ball Play," *American Anthropologist*, **3** (2), 1890, pp. 105–132.

Moses, A. L. "Chocktaw Sports," *Indians at Work*, Washington, D.C., **3** (14), 1936, pp. 15–16.

Myounge, O. "Creeks, Choctaws, and Cherokees Lone Games," *Indians at Work*, Washington, D.C., **2** (24), 1935.

Randolph, V. "The Ozark Play Party," *Journal of American Folklore*, **43**, 1929, pp. 201–232.

Rowell, M. K. "Pamunky Indian Games and Amusements," *Journal of American Folklore*, **56**, 1943, pp. 203–207.

Smith, H. W. *A Sporting Family of the Old South*, Albany, N.Y.: J.B. Lyon Company, 1936.

Speck, F. G. "Catawba Games and Amusements," *Primitive Man*, Washington, D.C., **17**, 1944, pp. 19–28.

Wolfe, K. E. "A Cherokee Indian Ball Game," *Red Man*, Carlisle, Pennsylvania, **3**, 1910, pp. 76–77.

North Central

Brewster, P. G. "Game-songs From Southern Indiana," *Journal of American Folklore*, **49**, 1939, pp. 243–262.

Dorsey, J. O. "Games of Teton Dakota Children," *American Anthropologist*, **4** (4), 1891, pp. 329–345.

Flackard, G. A. "The Chippewa or Ojibway Moccasin Game," *Minnesota Archaeologist*, Minneapolis, **23** (4), 1961, pp. 87–94.

Flannery, R. "Some Aspects of James Bay Recreation Culture," *Primitive Man*, Washington, D.C., **9**, 1938, pp. 49–56.

Gilmore, M. R. "Some Games of Arikara Children," *Indian Notes*, New York, **3**, 1925, pp. 9–12.

Hoffman, W. J. "Remarks on Ojibwa Ball Play," *American Anthropologist*, **3** (2), 1890, pp. 133–135.

Reagan, A. B. "Some Games of the Bois Fort Ojibwa," *American Anthropologist*, **21** (3), 1919, pp. 264–278.

Southworth, P. D. "Recreation on Lac Du Flambeau," *Indians At Work*, Washington, D.C., **2** (24), 1935, p. 41.

Speck, F. G. "Back Again to Indian River: Its People and Their Games," *Archaeological Society of Delaware Bulletin*, Wilmington, **3** (5), 1942, pp. 17–24.

Sutton-Smith, B. "The Kissing Game of Adolescents in Ohio," *Midwestern Folklore*, **9**, 1959, pp. 189–211.

Wolford, L. J. "The Play-party in Indiana," *Historical Society Publications*, Indianapolis, **20** (2), 1959, pp. 103–326.

South Central

Daniel, Z. T. "Kansu: A Sioux Game," *American Anthropologist*, **5** (3), 1892, pp. 215–216.

Lambert, M. F. "Six Game Pieces From Otowi," *El Palacio*, Santa Fe, **48**, 1941, pp. 1–6.

Lesser, A. "The Pawnee Ghost Dance Hand Game: A Study in Cultural Change," *Columbia Contributions to Anthropology*, New York: Columbia University Press, **16**, 1933, pp. 1–337.

Payne, L. W. "Finding List for Texas Play-party Songs," *Folklore Society of Texas*, Austin, **1**, 1916, pp. 35–38.

Pope, C. H. "Texas Rope-Jumping Rhymes Accompanying Children's Games," *Western Folklore Quarterly*, Berkeley, California, **15** (1), 1956, pp. 46–48.

Walker, J. R. "Sioux Games," *Journal of American Folklore*, **18**, 1906, pp. 277–290; **19**, 1907, pp. 29–36.

North Western

Desmond, G. R. *Gambling Among the Yakima*, Washington, D.C.: American Anthropological Association Series Number 14, 1952, pp. 1–58.

Dorsey, G. A. "Certain Gambling Games of the Klamath Indians," *American Anthropologist*, **3** (1), 1901, pp. 14–27.

Ewers, J. C. "Some Winter Sports of the Blackfoot Indian Children," *Masterkey*, Los Angeles, **18**, 1953, pp. 177–183.

Flannery, R. "Social Mechanisms in Gros Ventre Gambling," *Southwestern Journal of Anthropology*, Albuquerque, N.M., **2**, 1946, pp. 391–419.

Merriam, A. P. "The Hand Game of the Flathead Indians," *Journal of American Folklore*, **68** (269), 1955, pp. 313–324.

Moore, R. D. "Social Life of the Eskimo of St. Laurence Island," *American Anthropologist*, **25** (3), 1923, pp. 339–375.

Ramson, J. E. "Children's Games Among the Aluet," *Journal of American Folklore*, **59**, 1946, pp. 196–198.

Randle, M. C. "A Shoshone Hand Game Gambling Song," *Journal of American Folklore*, **66**, 1953, pp. 155–159.

Slaugh, S. F. "The Shoshone Lone Fun," *Indians At Work*, Washington, D.C., **2** (24), 1935, p. 28.

Willett, F. "A Set of Gambling Pegs From the North-west Coast of America," *Man*, London, **61**, 1961, pp. 8–10.

South Western

Aberle, D. F. "Mythology of the Navaho Game Stick Dance," *Journal of American Folklore*, **55**, 1942, pp. 144–154.

Bailey, F. L. "Navaho Motor Habits," *American Anthropologist*, **44** (2), 1942, pp. 210–234.

Brandes, R. S. "An Early Ball Court Near Globe, Arizona," *Kiva*, Tuscon, **23** (1), 1957, pp. 10–11.

Browne, R. B. "Southern California Jump-rope Rhymes: A Study in Variants," *Western Folklore*, Berkeley, California, **14**, 1955, pp. 3–22.

Espinosa, R. "Canute: A Game Handed Down From the Indians to Spanish Settlers in New Mexico Still Lives in Native Homes," *New Mexico*, Santa Fe, **11** (5), 1933, pp. 16–17, 46–48.

Eubank, L. "Legend of Three Navaho Games," *El Palacio*, Santa Fe, **52**, 1945, pp. 138–140.

Fox, J. "Pueblo Baseball: A New Use For Old Witchcraft," *Journal of American Folklore*, **74** (291), 1961, pp. 9–16.

Haile, B. "Navaho Games of Chance and Taboo," *Primitive Man*, Washington, D.C., **6**, 1933, pp. 35–40.

Harrington, J. P. "The Tewa Indian Game of Canute," *American Anthropologist*, **14** (2), 1912, pp. 243–286.

Hodge, F. W. "A Zuni Foot-Race," *American Anthropologist*, **3** (3), 1890, pp. 227–231.

Kolly, I. "Notes on a West Coast Survival of The Ancient Ball Game," *Carnegie Institute of Washington, Division of Historical Research*, Cambridge, Mass., **1**, 1943, pp. 163–175.

Kroeber, A. L. "Games of the California Indians," *American Anthropologist*, **22** (3), 1920, pp. 272–277.

Matthews, D. W. "Navajo Gambling Songs," *American Anthropologist*, **2** (1), 1889, pp. 1–19.

Mook, M. A. "Walapai Ethnography: Games," *Memoirs of the American Anthropological Association*, **42**, 1935, pp. 167–173.

Nelson, F. E. "The Sports of the Zuni," *Indians At Work*, Washington, D.C., **2**, 1936, pp. 35–38.

Opler, M. E. "The Jicarilla Apache Ceremonial Relay Race," *American Anthropologist*, **46** (1), 1944, pp. 75–97.

Parsons, E. W. C. "Hidden Ball on First Mesa, Arizona," *Man*, London, **22**, 1922, pp. 82–90.

Parsons, E. C. "Some Aztec and Pueblo Parallels," *American Anthropologist*, **35** (4), 1933, pp. 611–631.

Reagan, A. B. "Navajo Sports," *Primitive Man*, Washington, D.C., **5**, 1932, pp. 68–71.

Schroeder, A. H. "Ball Courts and Ball Games of Middle America and Arizona," *Archaeology*, Cincinnati, **8** (3), 1955, pp. 156–161.

Stevenson, M. C. "Zuni Games," *American Anthropologist*, **5** (3), 1903, pp. 468–497.

Wayland, V. "Apache Playing Cards," *Masterkey*, Los Angeles, **35** (3), 1961, pp. 84–98.

CHAPTER 4

FOLKLORE SOURCES

While diffusionist thinking is also strong in folklore there is considerable evidence of an earlier linkage with antiquarianism. Folklorists have always been primarily motivated, it seems, by the feeling that the oral traditions were fading and must be written down before they perished from the language. This theme was evident in the first folklore classic on games, *The Games and Songs of American Children* (1883) by William W. Newell. In addition to recording and saving games from decay, however, it was a major motif of Newell and other folklorists that the material of folklore was replete with the survivals of earlier historical times, and that these survivals in games could be used to reconstruct those earlier times. The study of games was a way to reconstruct history. (It was assumed of course, that there was a universal history and a universal diffusion of games). Thus counting-out rhymes were said to be survivals of ancient practices of choosing victims by lot; the singing game of Nuts and May was a relic of marriage by capture; London Bridge was said to be a stylized vestige of the ancient custom of burying a child alive in the foundation of a new structure, or the offering of a human sacrifice to the gods of the water. Tug-of-War was thought to be a "degraded miracle play" exemplifying the battle between good and evil. Similarly anthropologists and ethnologists reported that a variety of games were survivals of religious rites and ceremonies of primitive peoples. Sir James Frazer offered many examples of games in the religious rites of primitive societies.[1] When it later became clear that, as ephemeral imaginative activities, games could hardly be used to recon-

[1] Frazer, J. G. *The Golden Bough.* New York: Macmillan Co., 1951.

struct history, most folklorists continued to offer accounts of game origins as if they were an *explanation* of games. The habit of discussing games in terms of their probable origins became a method of explanation.

Perhaps the clearest account of the historical survival theory is provided by Lady Alice B. Gomme in her two-volume work *The Traditional Games of England, Scotland and Ireland*.[2] She believed that children's games originated in adult customs; that children imitated the games from the adults; and then maintained them intact over the centuries by virtue of their "dramatic faculty." Such historical and ethnological records as we possess, however, suggest that children's games had many points of origin. Caillois has written most explicitly on these matters. In contradiction to the thesis that ". . . in play all is lost . . . ," Caillois writes:

> . . . we are not at all certain that prehistoric children might not have been playing with bows, slingshots, and peashooters 'for fun' at the same time that father used them 'for real,' to use a very revealing expression from children's slang. . . . The game of Monopoly does not follow, but reproduces the function of Capitalism. . . . There are grounds for suspecting that children's games are not a degradation of serious activities, but rather that two different levels are simultaneously involved. In India, the child is playing on the swing at the very moment that the officiant is piously swinging Kama or Krishna in the liturgical swing sumptuously ornamented with precious stones and garlands. Today children play soldiers without armies having disappeared. And is it conceivable that doll play can ever disappear? . . . The structures of play and reality are often identical, but the respective activities that they subsume are not reducible to each other in time or place. They always take place in domains that are incompatible.[3]

Sometimes games played by children today are those formerly played by adults, sometimes they are games formerly played by children, and sometimes they may be games which used to run parallel to the former serious activities of adults (archery), and which have persisted into modern times. Their origins, therefore, are complex, but the explanation for their persistence must lie in the current psychology of the players, as well as in the customs with which they were formerly associated.

---

[2] Gomme, A. B. *Traditional Games of England, Scotland, and Ireland*. Two volumes. London: Nutt and Company, 1894 and 1898. Reprinted with an introduction by Dorothy Howard, New York: Dover Publications Inc., 1964.

[3] Caillois, R. *Man, Play, and Games*. New York: The Free Press of Glencoe Inc., 1961, pp. 61–64.

Recently, Opie has suggested a way in which the earlier emphasis of folklorists and the more recent theories (such as that of Caillois) can be reconciled. In an article titled, "The Tentacles of Tradition" he argues:

It would be wrong, I think, to give the impression that the rise and fall of customs is altogether haphazard, subject to no observable laws. Man himself, as the study of folklore shows, alters little, certainly less than do his surroundings; and I sometimes wonder if the total quality of traditional lore does not remain fairly constant. . . . It is even possible that the extent of man's supernatural and superstitious credulities remain constant, and that the beliefs merely take on more sophisticated forms.[4]

By way of example, Opie indicates that while many rhymes and games have changed their content through modernization, their forms are basically the same as the earliest types.[5] From this point of view, the study of game origins remains important, not for the purpose of reconstructing history, but for the purpose of illustrating the continuity of human nature.

The readings by Tylor and Erasmus in the previous chapter deal with the same problem. Tylor conceptualized the continuity in terms of diffusion and Erasmus in terms of the limitation of possibilities. Whatever the explanation, there is apparently sufficient empirical continuity in games over long periods of time to make historical studies a systematic and scholarly concern.

Still, in dealing with the traditional materials of folklore it would be false to overemphasize such theoretical matters. The main spirit has been "antiquarian"; to collect before the games faded away—a dominantly descriptive enterprise.

PAUL G. BREWSTER

The most prolific folklorist of games has been Paul G. Brewster. He has written over fifty articles and monographs on games during the last thirty years. His publications have appeared in a variety of journals throughout the world and offer much information that is not available elsewhere. In particular, his *Children's Games and Rhymes* from North Carolina is the best single collection of published American children's games. The two articles by Brewster appearing in Chapters 1 and 2

[4] Opie, P. and Opie, I. "The Tentacles of Tradition," *The Advancement of Science*, **XX**, 1963–1964, p. 10.

[5] Opie, P. and Opie, I. *The Languages and Lore of Schoolchildren*. London: Oxford University Press, 1959.

respectively, offer some insight into Brewster's "modus operandi" and his rationale for the study of games.

The following is a bibliography of articles and monographs written by Brewster from 1939 until the present.

1939   "Game-Songs From Southern Indiana," *Journal of American Folklore*, **49**, 243–262.

1943   "A Roman Game and Its Survival on Four Continents," *Classical Philology*, **38**, 134–137.
"Some Games From Other Lands," *Southern Folklore Quarterly* (Gainesville), **7**, 109–117.
"Some Notes on The Guessing-Game, 'How Many Horns Has The Buck?'" *Bealoideas*, **13**, 40–79.
"The *Kitte ande bol* Game of India," *Southern Folklore Quarterly* (Gainesville), **7**, 149–152.

1944   "How Many Horns Has The Buck? Prolegomena to a Comparative Study," *Volkskunde*, **4**, 361–393.
"Some African Variants of Bucca, Bucca," *Classical Journal*, **39**, 293–296.
"Two Games From Africa," *American Anthropologist*, **2**, 268–269.

1945   "'Johnny On The Pony', A New York State Game," *New York Folklore Quarterly*, **1**, 239–240.
"Some Unusual Forms of Hopscotch," *Southern Folklore Quarterly* (Gainesville), **9**, 229–231.

1947   "Games and Sports in Sixteenth and Seventeenth Century English Literature," *Western Folklore*, **6**, 143–156.

1948   "Forfeit Games From Greece and Czechoslovakia," *Hoosier Folklore*, **8**, 76–83.

1949   "Some Hungarian Games," *Southern Folklore Quarterly* (Gainesville), **13**, 175–179.
"Some Traditional Games From Roumania," *Journal of American Folklore*, **62**, 114–124.
"Ten Games From Other Lands," Western Folklore (Berkeley), **8**, 146–151.

1950   "An Attempt At Identification of the Games Mentioned in Basile's *Il Pentamerone*," *Folklore* (London), 5–23.

1951   "A String Figure Series From Greece," *Laographia*, 101–125.
"Four Games of Tag From India," *Midwest Folklore*, **1**, 239–241.
"Some Games From Southern Europe," *Midwest Folklore*, **1**, 109–112.

1952   "Ten Games From Europe," *Journal of American Folklore*, **55**, 88–90.

1953   *American Non-Singing Games*, Norman, Oklahoma: University of Oklahoma Press.

Children's Games and Rhymes, (Frank C. Brown Collection of North Carolina Folklore, 1, no. 4), Durham: University Press.

"Juegos Infantiles," *Folklore Americas* (Lima), **13**(1), 3–15.

"Some String Tricks From the U.S.," *Rivista de Entnogrofia* (Naples), **7**, 1–12.

"Two Unusual String Figures from the U.S.," *Der Forschungsdienst*, Folge 6, Band I.

1954   "String Figures from the Midwestern U.S.," *Oesterreichische Zeitschrift für Volkskunde*, **8** (1–2), 23–32.

"Some Nigerian Games with Their Parallels and Analogues," *Societe des Africanstes* (Paris), **24**, 25–48.

1955   "A Collection of Games From India, with Some Notes on Similar Games in Other Parts of the World," *Zeitschrift für Ethnologie* (Braunschweig), **80**, 88–102.

"A Note On The Distribution of the Slovenian Game: Skarjice Brusiti," *Slavic Ethnogrophie*, **8**, 255–258.

"Some Notes on the Slovenian Game: Volka," *Bilten Instituta Za Proucavanje Folklora*, **3**, 143–149.

"The Game of sahbi iddi zaiat, Moroccan form; Some Parallels and Analogues," *Hesperis*, **42** (1–2), 239–244.

1956   With J. Milojkovic-Djuric, "A Group of Jugoslav Games," *Southern Folklore Quarterly*, **20** (3), 183–191.

"The Importance of the Collecting and Study of Games," *Eastern Anthropologist* (Lucknow), **10** (1), 5–12.

1957   With O. Hrabalova, "A Czechoslovak Cat's Cradle Series," *Checkoslovakian Ethnography* (Praha), **5**, 176–183.

"Malomjalik and Related Three-in-a-row Games," *Acta Ethnogrophica* (Budapest), **6**, 225–231.

"Priority and Exemption in Children's Games: A Comparative Study," *Volkskunde*, **58**, 21–30.

"Some Games From Czechoslovakia," *Southern Folklore Quarterly* (Gainesville), **21** (3), 165–174.

With J. S. Patel, "The Indian Game of Sagargote (Kooka) (Bombay)," *Zeitschrift für Ethnologie* (Braunschweig), **82** (2), 186–190.

1958   "Burski and Other Polish Games of Chance and Skill," *Zeitschrift für Ethnologie* (Braunschweig), **83**, 83–85.

"The Earliest Known List of Games: Some Comments," *Acta Orientalia* (Copenhagen), **23** (1–2), 33–42.

"Long Breath and Talking Fire: Cultural Survivals in the Games of Chase," *Eastern Anthropologist* (Lucknow), **12** (1), 41–46.

With T. A. Seboek, *Studies in Cheremis: Games,* Bloomington, Indiana: Indiana University Press.

"The Malayan *Hantu Musang* and Other Possession Games of Indonesia and Indochina," *Oriens* (Wiesbaden), 11 (1–2), 162–176.

1959 *Games and Sports in Shakespeare,* Helsinki: Suomalainen Tiedeakatemia Academia Scientiarum Fennica.

"Symbolism and Allegory in Card and Board Games," *Southern Folklore Quarterly* (Gainesville), 23 (3), 196–203.

"Three Russian Games and Their Western and Other Parallels," *Southern Folklore Quarterly* (*Gainesville*), 23 (2), 126–131.

1960 "A Sampling of Games From Turkey," *East and West* (Rome), 11 (1), 15–20.

"Some Kindred Games of the Far East," *Geografica Helvetica* (Bern), 15 (1), 33–38.

"Treatise on Iranian Games," Acta Orientalia (Copenhagen), 25 (1–2), 15–28.

1961 "A Worldwide Game and an Indian Legend," *Eastern Anthropologist* (Lucknow), 14 (2), 192–193.

"The Egyptian Game Khazza Lawizza And Its Burmese Counterpart," *Zeitschrift für Ethnologie* (Braunschweig), 85, 211–213.

1962 "Identification of Some Games Depicted on The Tomb of Mereuka," *East and West* (Rome), 13 (1), 27–31.

1963 "Egyptian Prototypes of Two Twentieth Century Games," *Zeitschrift für Ethnologie* (Braunschweig), 88 (1), 98–99.

"Games and Toys," *Encyclopedia of World Art,* 6, 2–11.

With S. Hummel, *Games of Tibetans,* Helsinki: Suomalainen Tiedeakatemia Academia Scientiarum Fennica.

1965 "The Cheremis Game *Selcekteny-Mudone* and the Russian Game *Scelcki,*" *Zeitschrift für Ethnologie* (Braunschweig), 90 (2), 265–267.

Brewster's work on games is somewhat atypical within folklore. The customary approach has been to work with children's, rather than adult games, and to work directly with children as informants, rather than to derive material from secondary sources. The major figures in this respect in the English speaking world are Peter and Iona Opie whose books are *The Language and Lore of Schoolchildren.*[6] Their writing can be viewed as a sequel to the work of Lady Gomme's "Traditional Games" of the 1890s. In the United States, others of note known for occasional work with children's games include Herbert Halpert, Carl Withers, Roger Abrahams, Alan Dundes and Kenneth Goldstein; however, the major

[6] Opie, and Opie, op. cit., 1959.

figure during the past thirty years would seem to have been Dorothy Howard.

DOROTHY HOWARD

The reader particularly interested in the scholarly study of folk games is referred to her introduction to the recent editions of Gomme's 1894 study *The Traditional Games of England, Scotland and Ireland*,[7] where she presents a most interesting defense of the circumscribed nature of the collections of Alice B. Gomme. The stimulus for this defense was *London Street Games*[8] by Norman Douglas, in which Douglas suggested that more scurrilous things were going on in the streets of London than was implied in the rather refined Victorian Collections of Lady Gomme. Another useful scholarly source is Carl Withers' introduction to the new edition of William Wells Newell's *Games and Songs of American Children*.[9] Howard, (in personal correspondence to the authors) explaining her own interest in children's games, writes:

My father was a tradition-bearer and my maternal grandmother was a tradition-bearer (she lived with us). As a child I loved to sit and listen to my father tell tales, and sing songs, and to my grandmother tell of her childhood days and teach me the games she played. Today my children and grandchildren, nieces and nephews, and grandnieces and nephews still like to sit and listen to me tell the family stories I heard from the past and teach them "William William Tremble Toe" and "Club Fist," as my grandmother taught to me. . . . My first recording of childlore took place one spring day in the early 1930's when my own two children were just beginning their schooldays. I remember the day very clearly. I was teaching in a consolidated rural school in Valhalla, New York; it was a warm spring day, the schoolroom windows were open; I stood at noontime at an open window listening and watching the children at unsupervised play in the school ground. Ropes were turning. Marbles were rolling. Tag games were going. My ear told me that I was hearing rhymes and jingles, some old, some new to me. I jotted down the ones I heard. . . I assumed in my ignorance that most of them had a book origin. But Halliwell, Northall, Chambers and Gomme soon exploded that

---

[7] Gomme, A. B., op. cit., 1964.

[8] Douglas, N. *London Street Games*. London: The St. Catherine Press, 1916. 2nd Edition, London: Chatto and Windus, 1931.

[9] Newell, W. W. *Games and Songs of American Children*. New York: Harper Brothers, 1883. Republished with an introduction by Carl Withers, New York: Dover Publications Inc., 1963.

monstrous fallacy. Thus I was off on a quest which has lead me to far places and into devious paths. . . .[10]

Howard's first publication was a lighthearted article in *The New Yorker Magazine*, *"Songs of Innocence"* (Nov. 13, 1937 pp. 32-36) Much of her later work stems from her Fulbright sponsored mission at the age of 70 to collect the games of Australian children.

While Howard's work was done first in the United States, then in Australia, Sutton-Smith reversed the process beginning with New Zealand,[11] and then studied the games of American children. As references throughout this book indicate his work is not easily catalogued, some of it being consistent with the folklorist tradition, other articles reflecting his activities as a social scientist, focusing on the use of recent historical changes in game playing as a way of interpreting historical changes in child nature, and on chronological age changes in children's play as a way of interpreting child development.

One of the most promising developments in recent folklore has been a somewhat greater concern for the actual conditions of the game playing. Games as described in the abstract and games as played do not always turn out to be the same reality as is indicated by Goldstein's original article on game strategies, which follows.

We also include an example of Howard's work concerning marble games of children, and an example of Sutton-Smith's documentation of adolescent kissing games. Since much folklore activity concerning games deals with children's games, we include a list of selected references on this topic. For a more extensive bibliography on the folklore of games, the reader is directed to the published indices of the *American Journal of Folklore,* and the number of regional folklore journals published in the United States, for example, *Hoosier Folklore, Midwest Folklore, Western Folklore, Southern Folklore Quarterly.* In addition, folklore journals are published in a number of other nations, for instance, *Volkskunde, Folklore (Britain), India Folklore.*

[10] Howard, Dorothy. Personal correspondence, September 1, 1963.

[11] Sutton-Smith, B. *The Games of New Zealand Children.* University of California Press, 1959.

8

Strategy in Counting Out:
An Ethnographic Folklore Field Study

KENNETH S. GOLDSTEIN

Though considerable attention has been paid to game activities by travellers, historians, antiquarians, and numerous others for almost two centuries, much of the scholarship of such pastimes, until well into the twentieth century, consisted of little more than gathering and publishing descriptions and the related texts.[1] A few scholars attempted interpretation and analysis,[2] but the majority were content to present their texts and descriptions in regional and national collections with occasional comparative references to analagous items among other peoples.[3]

SOURCE. Previously unpublished.

---

[1] See, for example, Joseph Strutt, *The Sports and Pastimes of the People of England*, London, 1801, and numerous later editions; the many editions of John Brand's *Observations on Popular Antiquities*, Newcastle, 1777, London, 1810, itself based on Henry Bourne's *Antiquitates Vulgares*, Newcastle, 1725, and later revised and edited by Henry Ellis, London, 1813, two volumes, culminating in a completely new edition in dictionary form by W. Carew Hazlitt under the title *Faiths and Folklore*, London, 1905, two volumes.

[2] A prime example is William W. Newell in his *Games and Songs of American Children*, New York, 1883, new edition 1903. Many of Newell's speculations and theories, especially those concerning games as "survivals" of earlier times and places, were popular with other collector-scholars for many years before being challenged and discarded.

[3] For example, James O. Halliwell, *The Nursery Rhymes of England*, London, 1841, with later editions; Robert Chambers, *Popular Rhymes of Scotland*, Edinburgh, 1925, though the important edition for our purpose is the third edition of

It is no wonder, then, that so little attention of any serious nature was paid to this folklore genre until after World War II. When this new interest finally manifested itself, it was more through the work of social and behavioral scientists than of folklorists that this previously "minor" genre was raised to the status of an area of prime interest and importance. The work of Huizinga and Caillois in defining the nature of play,[4] the social-psychological insights into children's play activities of Piaget and Erikson,[5] and, more recently, the work of Roberts, Arth, Bush, and Sutton-Smith in relating games to other aspects of culture[6] have written new chapters in game scholarship. Among folklorists the recent work of Robert Georges with his interest in the relevance of behavioral models for the analyses of traditional play activities, of Alan Dundes and his interest in the structural analysis of games, and of Roger D. Abrahams and his application of rhetorical models to the performance of folklore, show promise of removing game scholarship from the arid and sterile domain of description and comparativist annotation along historical and geographical lines.[7]

Folklorists, moreover, have the means to make a still larger contribution to the study of games by the application in their field work of the concept which has come to be known as the "ethnography of speaking folklore," or the study of folklore "texts in their contexts" for the purpose

1842 and its later reprintings; Alice Bertha Gomme, *The Traditional Games of England, Scotland and Ireland*, London, 1894, 1898, two volumes; G. F. Northall, *English Folk Rhymes*, London, 1892; continental works of the same order were Eugène Rolland, *Rimes et jeux de l'enfance*, Paris, 1883, and F. M. Böhme, *Deutsches Kinderlied und Kinderspiel*, Leipzig, 1897.

[4] J. Huizinga, *Homo Ludens: A Study of the Play Element in Culture*, English translation, London, 1949, New York 1950; Roger Caillois, *Man, Play, and Games*, Glencoe, Ill., 1961.

[5] Jean Piaget, *The Moral Judgement of the Child*, New York, 1965, and *Play, Dreams and Imitation in Childhood*, London, 1951; Erik H. Erikson, *Childhood and Society*, 2nd revised and enlarged edition, New York, 1963.

[6] John M. Roberts, Malcolm J. Arth, and Robert R. Bush, "Games in Culture," *American Anthropologist* 61 (1959), 597–605; Brian Sutton-Smith, "Cross Cultural Study of Children's Games," *American Philosophical Society Yearbook*, 1961, 426–429; John M. Roberts and Brian Sutton-Smith, "Child Training and Game Involvement," *Ethnology* I (1962), 166–185, and "Cross Cultural Correlates of Games of Chance," *Behavior Science Notes* 3 (1966), 131–144.

[7] Robert A. Georges, "The Relevance of Models for Analyses of Traditional Play Activities," *Southern Folklore Quarterly* 33 (1969), 1–23; Alan Dundes, "On Game Morphology: A Study of the Structure of Non-Verbal Folklore," *New York Folklore Quarterly* XX (1964), 276–288; Roger D. Abrahams' work on rhetorical models in folklore is a continuing project, and its application to games is in preparation at the time of this writing.

of determining the rules which govern any specific folklore event.[8] Since much of the recent research and scholarship on games involves correlations of game types to other aspects of culture (e.g., social systems, religion, child training, etc.),[9] the classification of games can be crucial to the findings. And the accurate classification of games by types calls for better understanding of play events and the rules which govern those events. Folklorists whose field research is directed at developing ethnographies of games may find the work rewarding not only to their own better understanding of the mechanics by which folklore is expressed, performed, transmitted, circulated, and used, but to the development of closer interdisciplinary ties between folklore and the behavioral sciences.

The prospect of doing such ethnographic studies of games is especially intriguing because of all the genres of folklore the games genre is one of the few for which rules of performance are consciously recognized by the participants and are sometimes overtly expressed. The opportunity thus presents itself to study the manner in which the stated rules relate to the actual rules which operate in playing the games. Any attempt at doing an ethnography of a game could serve not only as a model for the collecting of data concerning game events, but also as a base for evaluating the reliability of earlier descriptions of games and thus of effecting criticism of research in any way involving game classification based on such descriptions.

This paper is an attempt at an ethnographic study of the game activity known as "counting-out." The game was selected because all previous studies of this game type had consisted of descriptions of the manner in which certain rhymes were used, of their poetics, music, rhyme, and rhythm patterns, or attempts at devising a classification system for its many texts.[10] Nowhere, however, was there any description of the rules actually at work in "counting-out."

My field work was carried out in a six block area in the East Mount Airy section of northwest Philadelphia between January 1966 and June

---

[8] Alan Dundes and E. Ojo Arewa, "Proverbs and the Ethnography of Speaking Folklore," *American Anthropologist* 66 (1964), No. 6, part 2, 70–85.

[9] See note 6.

[10] For some of the more important works on "counting-out" see Henry C. Bolton, *The Counting-Out Rhymes of Children,* London, 1888; Emil Bodmer, Empros oder Anzählreime der französischen *Schweiz,* Halle, 1923; Jean Baucomont, Frank Guibat, Tante Lucile, Roger Pinon and Philippe Soupault, *Les Comptines de langue française,* Paris, 1961, containing an extensive international bibliography on "counting-out." I am grateful to Roger Pinon for making the latter two works available to me.

1967. The area, a racially integrated middle class neighborhood, contains young whitecollar workers, professionals, and businessmen, mainly homeowners with larger than average size families. Their children use the mostly tree-shaded, exclusively residential streets as their playgrounds.

My informants consisted of 67 children between the ages of four and fourteen, who comprise eight separate, independent, and essentially non-overlapping play groups. As might be expected these groups were peer-oriented according to age. The eight groups consisted of four pairs of age groups, the first containing larger pre-school and kindergarten children whose ages ranged from four to seven, the second pair of school children from six through eight, the third of children from eight through twelve, and the fourth from eleven through fourteen. The first two pairs, containing the youngest children, had both boys and girls, though one group in each age category was predominantly male and the other mainly female. The members of each of the oldest groups were exclusively male or female. The groups were selected from among the many to be found in the neighborhood because of their age and sex composition after an initial survey indicated these were the major factors contributing to their own sense of group identity and awareness.

Collecting methods employed in obtaining data for this paper consisted of observations made both in natural and induced natural[11] contexts, followed first by non-directed and then by directed interviewing, the latter including hypothetical situation questioning.[12] Interview data was then checked by additional observations, reinterviewing of the same informants over time, and interviewing informants from one group on information obtained from other groups.

GENERAL DATA

"Counting-Out" is used for selecting personnel for two other kinds of game activities: for games for which an "it" figure must be chosen, and for games for which sides must be chosen. "Counting-out" is introduced to younger children in the first age group (four through seven years) by

---

[11] For a description of the induced natural context technique, see Kenneth S. Goldstein, *A Guide for Field Workers in Folklore*, Hatboro, Penna., 1964, 87–90, and "The Induced Natural Context: An Ethnographic Folklore Field Technique," *Essays on the Verbal and Visual Arts: Proceedings of the 1966 Annual Spring Meeting of the American Ethnological Society*, Seattle, 1967, 1–6.

[12] The hypothetical situation is described in Melville J. Herskovits, "The Hypothetical Situation: A Technique of Field Research," *Southwestern Journal of Anthropology* 6 (1950), 32–40.

older members of the group who report learning it from siblings and from contacts with members of the second age group (six through eight years) on the street and in school play. The rhymes are learned first (as early as two years of age) and the activity later (at four or five). It is less frequently used by both sexes in the final age group (eleven through fourteen), with other selection methods employed in its place (e.g., coin tossing, bat holding, drawing lots, and spinning bottles). Girls employ "counting out" more frequently for choosing sides than for determining who shall be "it," with boys reversing this pattern. Though size of the play group employing "counting out" may theoretically vary from two to quite large numbers, in actual play conditions it was never used when the group numbered more than ten. At such times (and such cases were only among boys), selection was made by "odds or even" coin tossing or finger matching, though there were no "rules" against the use of "counting-out" in such instances.

STEPS INVOLVED IN "COUNTING-OUT"

1. One member of a group suggests playing a specific "it" game or one for which sides must be chosen.
2. A number of others verbally agree (sometimes a majority of the group, at other times only one or two with the others silently acquiescing).
3. The method of selection is determined by the first suggestion made.
4. If "counting-out" is suggested the counter is appointed by one of the following methods:

   a. The person who suggests the game announces himself as counter.
   b. A recognized leader of the group assumes the role without asking or being asked.
   c. A suggestion is made by one member of the group that some other member should do the counting, with the others agreeing verbally or silently.

5. The other members of the group gather in a circle around the counter or are lined up by him in a specific order.
6. The counter begins, sometimes with himself and at other times with the nearest person on his left. The direction of counting is clockwise.
7. Counting continues until the counter indicates who is "it," or until sides have been chosen.

The steps outlined above follow in the order given. After the counter has been selected (step 4), the alternative forms of succeeding steps are left completely to his choice.

REASONS FOR USING "COUNTING-OUT" AS THE METHOD OF SELECTION

When queried as to why "counting-out" rather than some other method was employed in the task of choosing "it" or in determining the composition of sides, the answers given were as follows:

equal chance .... 90% (Typical answers: "Everybody has the same chance." "It's more democratic.")

removal of friction ... 18% Typical answers: "We don't fight about it." "Less trouble.")

supernatural decision .. 8% (Typical answers: "Fate decides." "God does the choosing.")

(The percentages add to more than 100 because some children gave more than one answer.)

The answers given would appear to clearly indicate that the great majority of the children queried considered "counting-out" to be a game of chance. It should be noted that this is also the opinion of those scholars who have tried their hand at classifying games; Roger Caillois and Brian Sutton-Smith, among others, refer to "counting-out" as a game of chance.[13] It is, however, precisely on this matter that my field work resulted in my finding that for a large number of the children involved "counting-out" is far from being a game of chance. It is, rather, a game of strategy in which the rhymes and movements of the players are manipulated to limit or remove chance as a factor in selection.

THE STRATEGY OF COUNTING-OUT

What we find here is that children—like their parents—do *not* in fact do or believe what they *say* they do or believe. As stated earlier, more than for any other folklore genre, rules are an essential part of games at an overt and sometimes verbalized level. But the rules which are verbalized by informants and which are then presented by collectors in their papers and books for our analysis and study are an idealized set of rules—they are the rules by which people *should* play rather than the ones by which they *do* play. The field results presented in the remainder of this paper indicate that for games we may have to know *two* sets of

[13] Roger Caillois, *Man, Play, and Games*, Glencoe, Ill., 1961, 36; Brian Sutton-Smith, *The Games of New Zealand Children*, Berkeley and Los Angeles, 1959, 89–90.

rules: the ideal ones *and* those by which the ideal rules are applied, misapplied, or subverted.

Only a few of the children were at first willing to admit that "counting-out" rhymes, player movements, or both were manipulated by certain of their peers. By using the hypothetical situation interview technique, I was able to discover how, by whom, and when manipulative strategies were applied, and through later observations and reinterviews I confirmed earlier collected data as well as adding several strategy devices to my list. The following is a description of the strategies employed by the children in the groups I studied:

Extension of Rhyme

If the counter finds that the rhyme ends on a child whom he does *not* wish to be "it," he may add one or more phrases or lines to the rhyme until it ends on the one whom he wishes to be "it." In the example given below, when the "Eenie, meenie, meinie, mo" rhyme was used in a group of six children, the final word ended on player 4. The counter wanted someone else to be "it" and extended the rhyme so it ended on player 5. He could similarly extend it still further to have it end on 6, or carry it out to end on any one in the group including himself.

Position of Players

1	2	3	4	5	6
Eenie	meenie	meinie	mo,	Catch	a feller
by the	toe;	If he	hollers	let him	go,
Eenie	meenie	meinie	mo. #	(My	mother
says	that	you	are	it.) #	(But
I	say	that	you	are	out.) #

(John J., age 10)

Controlling selection of "it" by extending the rhyme is the most common "counting-out" strategy, with better than fifty per cent of both boys and girls in the two oldest age groups employing it.

Specific Rhyme Repertory

In order to insure the selection of himself when he wishes to be "it," the counter may employ one of a special set of rhymes, the specific rhyme to be used depending upon the number of players involved. Each of the rhymes has a different number of stresses, and the counter knows which of the rhymes to apply in any specific group numbering up to eight players so that the final stress will end on himself. In the example given below, the informant had a fixed repertory of four rhymes, including ones of seven stresses, eight stresses, nine stresses, and sixteen stresses. If there are three players in the group she may employ either the seven or sixteen stress rhyme; for four players she would use the nine stress rhyme; for five players the sixteen stress rhyme; for six players the seven stress rhyme; for seven players the eight stress rhyme; and for eight players the nine stress rhyme. Conversely, if the counter wanted to be sure she was *not* "it," she would select a rhyme—again according to the number of players—in which the final stress would fall on someone other than herself.

Seven stresses: Andy / Mandy / Sugar / Candy //
              Out / Goes / He. #
              Counter is "it" when there are 3 or 6 players; not "it" when there are 4, 5, 7, or 8 players.

Eight stresses: Inka / Bink / A Bottle / Of Ink //
              I / Say / You / Stink. #
              Counter is "it" when there are 7 players; not "it" when there are 3, 4, 5, 6, or 8 players.

Nine stresses: Apples / Oranges //
              Cherries / Pears / And A Plum //
              I / Think / You're / Dumb. #
              Counter is "it" when there are 4 or 8 players; not "it" when there are 3, 5, 6, or 7 players.

Sixteen stresses: Eena / Meena / Mina / Mo //
              Catch /A Tiger / By The / Toe //
              If He / Hollers / Let Him / Go //
              Eena / Meena / Mina / Mo. #
              Counter is "it" when there are 3 or 5 players; not "it" when there are 4, 6, 7, or 8 players.
(Sarah M., age 11)

Use of specific rhyme repertory to control "counting-out" was employed by three children, all girls in the eight through twelve age group. Each of the girls employed a different set of rhymes, and each was aware that the others employed a similar strategy.

Skipping Regular Counts

To insure against his being "it," the counter will skip over himself on the second and successive times around. In the example given below, in which five players were involved, the counter simply passed by himself each of the last three times. Normally the rhyme would have ended on the counter, but by omitting himself he arranged for it to fall on someone else.

> Back / Side / Front / Side //
>   1   2   3   4
>
> Looking / For A / Little / Ride; //
>   5   2   3   4
>
> In / And Out / And Up / And Down //
> 5   2   3   4
>
> Goes In / Red / And Comes Out / Brown. #
> 5   2   3   4

(Jerry B, age 9)

> The numbers below the text indicate the positions of the players on whom each of the words fall.

The children employing this strategy have no idea whether any particular rhyme will end on them and, when they don't wish to be "it," will use this strategy with any "counting-out" rhymes they perform. Skipping regular counts is the second most popular form of strategically manipulating "counting-out;" one-third of all informants have done it at one time or another. It should be noted that while other strategies were considered "clever," this one was frowned upon as being "dishonest" and "against the rules!"

Stopping or Continuing

The first person "counted-out" may be designated "it" or the counter may continue by repeating the rhyme until all but one player has been "counted-out" and that player is "it." In the case of the "one potato, two potato" rhyme, the "potatoes" are the fists which the players extend for counting. The fist which the counter points to on the word "more" is withdrawn. The counter repeats the rhyme until both fists of one player have been withdrawn and that person may be designated "it" or, if the counter wishes someone else to be "it," he may continue repeating the rhyme until there is one player left who has not been "counted-out" and that player is "it." If, for example, there were five players, the first to be counted out would be number three; if the counter continued the rhyme he himself would be the last remaining person counted. The informants who used this strategy (with the one exception of the case cited in 5, below) did so without knowing on which players the first or last "out" would fall. They were merely shifting the chance factor from first to last but not to any specific player. The choice of stopping or continuing was employed by twenty children, evenly distributed between sexes in the six through eight and eight through twelve age groups.

Changing Positions

The counter, using the "One Potato, Two Potato" rhyme mentioned above, had memorized the "first out" position for any number of players from two through ten. After each player was counted out, he would start the rhyme again from his own position after first moving to a new position either himself or the next player he wanted to count out, according to the memorized list of "first out" positions for the specific number of players remaining. In the example given below, involving ten players, the counter wanted a specific player to be counted-out first. He therefore placed that player in the second position. The next player whom he wished to count-out was originally in the fourth position; he therefore shifted his own position so that player would be in the eighth position and would be counted-out next.

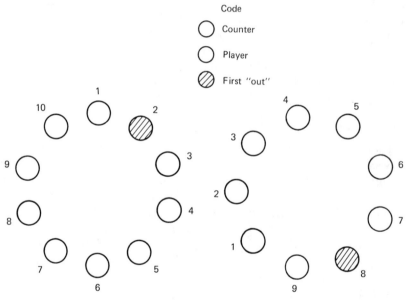

Fig. 1.

In addition to employing this strategy for choosing sides, the informant also employed a variation of it together with the "stopping or continuing" strategy for selecting "it." By memorizing both the "first out" and the "last remaining" position for any number of players through ten, he could always place himself relative to any other player so as to be able to completely control the selection according to his whim.

In the table given below, for use with the "One Potato, Two Potato" rhyme, the positions of the players are those in relation to the counter who is in position number 1. The first column indicates the number of players. The second column refers to the position of the first player to be counted "out" and the third column refers to the position of the "last remaining" position for any number of players through ten.

Number of Players	Position of Player	
	First Out	Last Remaining
10	2	1
9	8	3
8	8	4
7	7	4
6	6	3
5	3	1
4	3	2
3	1	3
2	1	2

(Samuel G., age 9)

The "changing position" strategy was used by one extremely precocious nine year old boy who was considered somewhat of a mathematical genius at school. One member of his play group, who was aware that some kind of manipulation was going on without knowing exactly what it was, would frequently thwart the change of position of the counter by changing his own position in the remaining group. Eventually, the precocious boy who had worked out the strategy began to count out the other youngster first so he would be free to make his further manipulations without interference.

Respite by Calling Out

When a child wished to remove himself from the possibility of becoming "it" or to thwart any of the strategies indicated above, he could do so by calling out "safe" (in one group), "free" (in another group), or "in-or-out" (in a third group). This could be done only after counting began, and only one child in any instance of "counting-out" would be permitted to do so. What is surprising is that despite the fact that all eight groups had respite or truce terms for other game activities only three had specific terms for removing oneself from a "counting-out" situation.

From the data given in this paper it is readily apparent that at least for some children "counting-out" is a game of strategy rather than of chance. If games serve as mechanisms through which children are prepared for adult roles in life, as some social psychologists maintain, then identifying a game as one of chance when it, in fact, is one of strategy may complicate any attempt at relating the end result of a socialization process with prior childhood activities. Similarly, if one sees in the play activities of children a mirror of the real adult world and its values, concepts, tendencies, and ways of thought, then incorrect classification of a society's games may result in a wholly reversed or otherwise inappropriate or false picture of that world.

If we are to fully utilize the great store of information imparted to us in the cross cultural game studies of Roberts, Arth, Bush, and Sutton-Smith[14] in which game types have been correlated with other facets of culture and from which various generalizations have been made as to the involvements of individuals and groups in games, the cultural and social functions of games, and the cultural evolution of games, then a clear and precise classification and identification of games must be made before such correlations may be entirely trusted.

Though carefully selected, my sample was a small one and may be viewed by some as inadequate for making any generalization other than that some children in Northwest Philadelphia play "counting-out" as a game of strategy.[15] If, however, the reclassification of *one* game results from an intensive ethnographic study of the manner in which it is played, then it should certainly prove profitable to reexamine other games employing the same methods.

[14] See note 6.

[15] After the presentation of this paper at the American Folklore Society Meeting in Toronto, November, 1967, several members of the audience informed me they knew of similar and, in some cases, other strategies employed in "counting-out" in other parts of the United States, Canada, Europe, and Africa. To my knowledge none of these has been reported in print.

9

Marble Games of Australian Children[1]

DOROTHY HOWARD

Although American imports into Australia during and since World War II, including ideas as well as manufactured goods of both excellent

SOURCE. *Folklore*, **71**, September 1960, pp. 165–179.

[1] In 1954–5, the author spent ten months in Australia as an American Fulbright Research Scholar sponsored by the University of Melbourne, collecting and studying Australian white children's traditional play customs. Information was obtained: by visiting playgrounds and classrooms of both government and non-government schools; visiting public playgrounds; visiting in homes; loitering on streets and public beaches where children were playing; from written compositions of school children and letters from older people; by talking with school masters and mistresses, fathers, mothers, educationists, physical educationalists, ministers, priests, anthropologists, psychologists, people on buses, trams, trains, and planes; by studying school syllabi; searching libraries; visiting toy shops; and through publicity in newspapers and magazines throughout Australia and radio addresses in Canberra and in Perth.

Search of Australian libraries revealed: no collections of Australian children's traditional games; no copy of the Brian Sutton-Smith manuscript collection of New Zealand children's games—see *Folklore* Vol. 64, September 1953. Ethnograph monographs on aborigine games around 1900 were found in the library of the University of Queensland and in the South Australian Library, Adelaide. Also the South Australian Library, *Early Memories* (a manuscript) written by Sir Joseph Verco, described his childhood games from 1860–70. In the Mitchel Library in Sydney, a file of old newspapers purportedly carried some information on children's games before the turn of the century but library rules, red tape and protocol forbade use of the material during the author's brief stay there.

Australian adults said repeatedly and regularly that their children had no traditional games, yet a ten-month search produced enough factual material to demonstrate that traditional games and customs were alive in the process of adaptation and evidence of more material ready to be collected.

179

and shoddy quality, may have influenced the so-called Australian-way-of-life, as some Australians believe, no evidence was found in 1954–5 of the importation of marble tournaments now rampant in the United States. In the U.S.A. national marble tournaments sponsored by schools, city recreation departments and other adult-supervised organizations have established a standardized marble game with printed rule-book in use from the Atlantic to the Pacific (I do not yet know about Alaska and Hawaii); with standardized marble gauge, national marble championship cups; and a standardized motto: "All championship marble shooters play for fair" enforced by an official referee.[2]

Although Australian educationalists (like Americans) have been tampering with children's traditional play customs for some time thinking to improve folkways, they had, apparently in 1954–5, overlooked marble games. To my delight, I found considerable variety in game names, terms and game ways (characteristics of folk customs everywhere).

This happy omission on the part of scheming adults did not mean that a changing adult-imposed environment had had no effect on Australian children's marble games. According to the memoirs of Sir Joseph Verco: "In those days (1860–70) . . . the footpaths belonged to the small boys as much as to the city council, and they had no compunction in digging their 'nuck' holes wherever they wanted to play and neither the citizens nor the police ever interfered with their mining operations nor with their play." Even as late as twenty-five years ago, I was told, children played on open paddocks, earthy playgrounds and sandy footpaths; and could dig their marble holes anywhere they chose. In the nineteen-fifties, with the population concentrated more and more in city areas with more hard-surfaced playgrounds and footpaths, the old hole

No attempt was made to study aboriginal Australian children's play nor to assess the interaction, if any, that may have taken place between the English-speaking children and the aborigines. A visit was made to one government school in New South Wales (The LaPerouse School) where the children were aborigine or part aborigine. Mr C. P. Mountford, South Australian anthropologist, who had spent many years living with tribes in the Northern Territory held the opinion that there had been little, if any, play exchange between the two groups of children; that any possible exchange would have been the imposition of white children's play upon the aborigines, most of whom live in the "outback" away from city influences, charges of the Commonwealth Government. No evidence of marble games or similar games was found among aborigine children.

[2] Peter and Iona Opie (*The Lore and Language of Schoolchildren*, Ox. Un. Press, 1959, p. 249) reporting on Good Friday celebrations say: "At Tinsley Green, just north of Three Bridges, a marble championship (now, with American participation, assuming an international character) continues year after year. . . ."

marble games seemed to be diminishing in favor of surface games played on diagrams of various shapes. With urban areas becoming more congested, leaving less play-space for children, adult supervision of school playgrounds had increased. The amount of adult supervision varied from state to state and community to community. On some, though not all, city school playgrounds, all play was supervised in groups segregated by age, sex and social class (a social class system existed as the result of "state" and "non-state" school systems); and the play programmes were set down in state syllabi. I saw no marble games in progress and found no evidence of them on the supervised city playgrounds. I also found no marble games, as such, included in sports syllabi; in some cases, however, syllabi were not made available to me. During World War II, I was told, marbles (which have always been imported) were unavailable in Australian shops; therefore one whole generation of children went without marbles except for those inherited from parents and uncles and aunties. In consequence, the game languished for a time. Surviving a fast-changing environment by the process of adaptation, Australian marble games in 1954–5 had thus far eluded scheming adults. What the situation now is in 1961 I do not know.

This report on Australian marble games is selected data from a larger collection of sometimes fragmentary facts which may one day be useful to scholars with more time, opportunity and skill to collect information and delve into the whys and wherefores thereof. The selected facts include: names of games, kinds of games, ways of playing, kinds of marbles used, game terms, and beliefs of Australian adults about marble games. Very little analysis has been attempted and no moral judgments pronounced. A tourist-collector, such as I, may profitably report a few careful observations. That is all. Wise conclusions demand many years of field work and study.

Chasing games were the simplest of Australian children's marble games. The first one I saw in progress was played by two boys about nine and eleven years old on the carpeted floor of three adjoining lounges in a Canberra hotel. One boy tossed his marble on to the floor at some distance. The second boy tossed his after, trying to hit the first. If he hit, he picked up the first player's marble, put it in his pocket and the first player then tossed out a second marble; if not, the first player took a turn tossing his marble at the second one. The game continued in silence, the rules apparently understood and accepted by the two. I tried unsuccessfully to engage the players in conversation but they picked up their marbles and disappeared from sight, perhaps seeking another playing field secure from a meddling foreign-sounding adult.

Subsequently, I found that the most common name throughout Australia for this marble-chasing game was "Follow-Me-Taw" (pronounced "Tor").[3]

Eventually I decided that the marble games could be categorized as *hole games* and *surface games* (chasing games being the simplest of the latter type); with a third category lazily designated as *miscellaneous* to label games employing special devices such as: a board with carved arches (similar to "Nine Holes" as described by Gomme, Strutt and Sutton-Smith[4]); a cardboard pyramid ("Prince Henry"); "Wall"; and non-marble games in which marbles functioned only as gambling currency ("Toodlembuck" or "Stick on Scone").

Other *surface games,* more complicated than the simple chase games, were played on diagrams on the ground or hard-surfaced play yard, marked with chalk, stick, slate, stone, or by hand, foot or penknife. The diagrams were: circles (of various sizes), half circles, ovals, squares, triangles and lines. Nine circle games were observed or reported.[5] Sir Joseph Verco described "In the Ring" as he played the game in 1860–70:

On the hard smooth surface of the original red loamy soil of our untilled and undisturbed land, as in the school playground a circle was marked out with a pen knife or a piece of wood or a stone. The size of the circle would vary with the skill and the age of the players. The smaller and less skilful would have a ring of two or three feet in diameter, the older and more capable would draw one of a couple of yards across. In the centre a short straight line would be drawn and on this the two opposing players would arrange an equal number of marbles of equal value, whether commonies, stoneys or glassies. They would then toss up for "first fire" or more commonly (as money, even pence, was then rather

[3] Other marble-chasing games were called: "Follow"—Brisbane; "Black Track"—Melbourne; "Track Taws"—Perth (Mt Lawley Government School); "Tractor Kelly" —Perth (Carlisle Government School); "Tractor Taw"—Perth (Collier Government School); "Kiss and Span"—Perth (Geraldton Government School). In Scottsdale, Tasmania, a small country community, a Mrs Chugg told of her "Follow-Me-Taw" game as she played it in 1900 and of the day she won one hundred marbles on her way to school and on her way home in the afternoon.

[4] A. B. Gomme, *The Traditional Games of England, Scotland and Ireland,* Vol. I, London, 1894, pp. 413–14. J. Strutt, *The Sports and Pastimes of the People of England,* 1801 (new edition, J. C. Cox, London, 1903), p. 222 and p. 304. B. Sutton-Smith, "*The Games of New Zealand Children,*" *Folklore Studies,* 12, Berkeley and Los Angeles, Un. of Cal. Press, 1959, p. 89.

[5] Circle games: "The Ring," "Circle," "Big Ring," "Little Ring," "Big Circle," and "Little Circle" were current names throughout Australia; "Poison Ring," "Jumbo," and "Eye Drop" were reported from Brisbane; and "Pyramids" (with marbles dubbed up in a circle) from St Helens, Tasmania.

scarce), one boy would put his hands behind his back, and then bring his closed fists to the front, in one of which was a marble. His opponent would guess which fist enclosed the marble. If on opening both hands it was found that he had fortunately guessed correctly he had the advantage of first "shot," if wrongly, the other lad led the attack. Down on his knees, he would take his "taw" between the knuckle of his thumb and his forefinger, and from the line of circumference of the ring fire his taw at the marbles in its centre, with the object of knocking some of them out of the ring. All he knocked out belonged to him. If one of them stopped absolutely on the line of the ring it was put back to the centre. If his taw came out of the ring whether he had knocked out any of the marbles or not he ceased firing and his playfellow had his opportunity. If he had knocked one or more marbles out of the ring, and his taw remained in the ring, he had the privilege of firing his taw at any marble still anywhere in the ring and if he knocked it out of the ring it became his; and if his taw was still in the ring he could repeat the process time after time. A skilful player might thus knock out one marble after another until every one originally on the central line had been accounted for and he had "skun the ring." If however the first player had hit the marbles on the line in the centre of the ring and scattered them about but had knocked none of them out of the ring, or had in any other way "finished his shot" the marbles were not put back on the central line for the next player, but were left where they had been scattered, wherever they might be. Some would be close to it and fired at with a side stroke at close quarters might easily be knocked out of the ring and be secured as his. He would also try, while he knocked out this marble to so strike it as to keep his taw in the ring, and if skilful enough would at the same time strike the marble in such a way as to rebound so as to "fetch up" near another marble in the ring and so secure as many of them as possible. In this way a great amount of skill could be acquired and displayed in the game, which in some respects resembled the more patrician game of billiards.

Some boys instead of keeping their knuckles on the line when firing their taw would jerk their hand forward into the ring so as to get nearer their mark before releasing their taw for the impact. This was denominated "funnicking" and directly it was noticed it raised the cry of "fen funnicks" or "none of your funnicking," and the practice had to cease as unfair.

Three current circle games—"Poison Ring," "Jumbo" and "Eye Drop" were described in writing by a school mistress in Queensland. Of "Poison Ring" she wrote:

To make a ring, place the heel firmly on the ground and twist the foot around in a circle. The marbles dubbed up are placed in the imprint of the heel. The ring is called "Poison." Then players pink to see who has first go. Any player who pinks into the ring is out. If a player's taw stays in the ring when he hits a marble out, he must put his winnings back in the ring and he is out of the game. If a player hits a marble out of the ring and his marble (taw) does not stay in the ring, his taw then becomes "Poison." When a poison taw hits another taw, that man is out. To "dub up" means to place marbles in the ring before pinking. This is a boys' seasonal game.

Another circle game—"Pyramids"—was described by a twelve-year-old boy, St Helens, Tasmania:

One player builds a pyramid with his own marbles and draws a little circle around the pyramid. Then another player, by paying the pyramid-owner a marble, is allowed to shoot at the pyramid one shot. If his aim is successful, any marble that rolls out of the circle belongs to him. Then the pyramid is built up again for the next player. The owner makes his profit out of those who aim without hitting. A marble must be paid for every shot. The game continues until all marbles are knocked out of the ring. No taw can be taken but the owner of the taw must hand over another marble.

Most surface game names were delightful metaphors.[6] "Football" played on an oval diagram, was described by an eleven-year-old girl in Scottsdale, Tasmania:

A football is drawn and a line is drawn down the middle long ways. Each player places one marble on the line crossing the football. Then each player stands back at the shooting line and throws a marble trying to come as near the football as possible to see who will have first go. If a player goes into the ring, then all must throw again. The one who has first go shoots to knock the marbles out of the ring. If all agree he may keep the marbles he shoots from the ring. He shoots until he misses. The game is over when there are no more marbles in the ring. Boys and girls play this.

---

[6] Half-circle games: "Half Moon" and "Townsey"—Brisbane; and "Mooney Ted First"—Perth. Oval diagrams: "Football"—Scottsdale, Tasmania; "Fats"—Perth (Doubleview Government School); "Eye Drop" (similar to the circle, "Eye Drop" in Brisbane)—Perth (Collier Government School). Triangle diagrams: "Killy"—Adelaide, South Australia, and "Three Corner Killy"—Perth (Geraldton Government School). Square diagrams: "Square Ring"—Perth (Collier Government School). Line diagram: "Liney"—Perth (Geraldton Government School).

A twelve-year-old boy in Perth wrote a description of his game of "Fats":

This game is played by two people. You can play it on sand or clay; or you can play it on asphalt. But if you play it on sand or grass, your marble will not bounce or roll or go into the "Kill" or "Fats."

And he ended his composition by commenting:
This game is exciting when you win all the other boy's marbles but it isn't when you lose all yours.

Of the *hole games*, five one-hole games (current or obsolete) were observed or recorded.[7] No evidence was found of two-hole games either current or obsolete; and no current three-hole games were found though Sir Joseph described a three-hole game of his childhood called "Nucks" or "Nux." Five four-hole games were observed or reported.[8] One eleven-hole game called "Poison Hole," played in Canberra by eleven-year-old boys, was reported by two schoolmasters and two schoolmistresses in the A.C.T. government schools.

Sir Joseph described "In the Hole" (one-hole game):

A hole about as big as a breakfast cup was dug in the ground. Each player put down an equal number of marbles, and lots were drawn as to who should have first throw. The fortunate lad stood toeing a line drawn at a measured distance from the hole; it might be ten or twenty feet according to mutual agreement. With all the marbles in his hand he bowled them toward the hole, and as many as rolled into it and remained there were his. The remainder were now thrown in the same manner by the other player, and the game proceeded until the last marble had been holed, when the players could count up their losses or gains and start again.

"Goot" a current one-hole game was described by a twelve-year-old girl, Melbourne (East Camberwell Girls' Secondary School) who gave a demonstration, then wrote the following description accompanied by a diagram:

[7] One-hole games: "Basins"—Mallee Country, Victoria ("played in years gone by"); "In the Hole" played by Sir Joseph Verco in 1860–70; "Bunny Hole"—Melbourne (Errol Street Government School); "Holey"—Fremantle Government School; "Goot"—Melbourne (East Camberwell Girls' Secondary School).

[8] Four-hole games: "Castles" played about 1890 in Sea View, South Austrailia and about 1945 in Horsham, Victoria; "Pot Holes"—Perth (Mt Lawley Government School); "Holes"—Brisbane; "Poison"—Brisbane; and "Basins"—Swansea, Tasmania.

The first thing to do in this game is to dig a small, shallow hole in the ground. This is called the "Goot." Next a line at an agreed distance from the hole—one yard is about right. Now with everything ready for the game to start the two or more players each get their marble and fire it to stop as close as possible to the goot. The person whose marble is nearest it is the first to start playing. The others follow in order of their marbles. The leader fires again from the line towards the hole and tries to place his marble in it. If he fails the marble is left where it is and the others have their turn. But if he succeeds in getting into the goot he may fire out of it a little way and wait for another person to fire from behind the line.

When they have done this, the next turn he has, he can chase them and try to "kill" them. To kill, you have to hit another person's marble three times in succession and then he is out of the game.

Once he kills one person he has to get back into the goot once more, before chasing another. All the other marbles do the same of course, and when everyone except one person is killed, he is the winner.

In Goot it is a rule that you can only have one shot when it is your turn except when you have hit another person, or when you have got into the goot. In each of these cases, another shot may be had at a marble, but if it misses you may not have another shot until your next turn. By then probably the other marble will have moved away or shot at you and the chase begins again.

"Nucks" or "Nux" (three-hole game described by Sir Joseph):

One of their games they called "Nucks" or "Nux." How it was to be spelt is unknown, never having been seen in print. Three holes about the size of small saucers had to be dug in the ground with a pen knife they were about a yard apart, and in a line with one another from a "starting" line about half a yard from the first hole the player had to make his first shot. He had a marble which he called his "taw," and of which he was very careful; because as he became used to it in his many games he was more able to do what he wished with it. This "taw" he fired with his right thumb and two fingers, so as to locate it in the nearest of the three holes. If it was lodged in this, he went up to this hole, and took from it his "taw" and with his thumb as a centre at the further margin of his first hole he spread out his fingers and described a semi-circle, and from this in advance of the first hole he "fired" his "taw" to try and lodge it in the second hole. If he succeeded he continued the same progress into the third hole, and if successful he proceeded to carry out the same manoeuvres on the reverse journey, and this play was continued up and down until such time as he failed to lodge his taw in a hole. Then he had to leave his "taw" wherever it might have stopped. Now it was his opponent's turn to try his hand in the same way. If at any point he found his taw anywhere near the first player's marble, he had the privilege of firing carefully at this, and if he struck it very gently, or "kissed" it as the touching was called, he had the privilege of firing as hard as he pleased at the enemy marble and knocking it as far away as he could, and then continuing at his own progress from hole to hole. As soon as he missed fire in any way or play No. 1 player took his turn again and tried to get into the hole which he had previously failed to enter; and he may have been knocked so far away that it would need two or more attempts before he managed to gain it. The boy who first went up and down the series of three holes three times had won the game. It had to be played necessarily kneeling down, and no otherwise and, so tended to produce a definite bagging of the trousers at the knees, and the wearing of holes there, as well as an accumulation of dirt and even of abrasion at the knuckles of the hands.

"Poison," a four-hole game was reported by a teachers' college student in Brisbane and described as her nine-year-old brother and his friends played it:

Four holes are made—three in a line and one about five feet to one side of the last three. This last is called "Poison." The player pinches into the first hole, then into the second, the third; and then back to first, second and third again. Then he goes on to "Poison." After "Poison," he can go into any hole; if in doing so, he hits a marble, he can claim the marble.

"Basins" as described by a twelve-year-old boy, Swansea, Tasmania, illustrates varying terminology from state to state:

Boys and girls, mainly boys ten years old, play this game at home. Four or five holes are dug in the ground. Two people stand back about two yards from the first hole. The players in turn flick marbles at the holes in order. The first player who gets in all the holes is "Poison." If "Poison" can hit the other player's marble, he wins the game. When you get in a basin (hole), you take a span before flicking for the next hole.

In the miscellaneous category of marble games are four: "Prince Henry," current in 1955; "Toodlembuck," or "Stick on Scone," current about 1910; Sir Joseph's un-named game (similar to "Nine Holes") 1860–70; and "Wall."

"Prince Henry" as demonstrated by an eleven-year-old girl, Coromandel Valley Government School, South Australia, employed a cardboard pyramid with a hole at the apex of the cone into which each player, in turn, tried to shoot his taw from a position on the ground some three feet away from the foot of the pyramid, meanwhile chanting:

> Prince Henry had a thousand men
> And a thousand men had he
> He marched them to the top of the hill
> And he marched them down to the sea
> And when they were up they were up
> And when they were down they were down
> And when they were half way up
> They were neither up nor down.

The first player to place his marble in the hole collected a marble from each of the losers (if playing for keeps; and this rule was decided before the game started).

"Toodlembuck" as played in Ballarat, Victoria about 1910 was described by Dr T. H. Coates, University of Melbourne. The same game, called "Stick on Scone" was current in Melbourne around 1900, according to Professor G. S. Browne, University of Melbourne.[9] For apparatus the game required two four-inch lengths of one-inch-diameter broomstick and one trousers button, in addition to a pocket full of marbles for currency. According to Dr Coates:

A circle was drawn on the ground, usually by putting the thumb down as a centre and using the little finger to describe the circumference. In the centre of this circle one stick was placed upright with the button sitting on top. Three yards from the circle a line was drawn and from this line the player had to bowl the second stick, trying to knock the first stick over in such a way as to make the button fall into the ring (or outside the ring—I forget which). Marbles, which we always called "alleys" were staked on the result. The entrepreneur would sing or rather chant:

> "Try your luck on the toodlembuck
> An alley a shot and two if you win."

Dr Coates also related stories of the difficulties boys had at home over missing trousers' buttons donated to toodlembuck games.

---

[9] "Notes and Queries," *Journal of American Folklore*, Vol. 73, No. 287, pp. 53–4, gives a description of an entirely different Australian game called "Toodlembuck."

Sir Joseph's old game employed a board with seven arches of different sizes into which marbles were bowled (Joseph Strutt's similar game employed a board with nine holes); no similar current game was found in 1955, unless by a stretch of analysis, the game can be linked to the Australian adult-gambling-game, "Two-up," which employs a board, minus arches, with money for currency where the skill is on one side "the plausibility on the other."

Some boys played a game, if game it could be called [wrote Sir Joseph] when the skill was all on the one side, and the plausibility on the other. The latter provided himself with a board of some length in which holes were cut of different heights and widths gradually increasing from one end of the board to the other, and over each hole was a number, the lowest No. 1 over the widest hole and the highest No. 7 over the smallest hole. [The holes in Sir Joseph's diagram were semi-circular arches.] This board was held upright on the flat ground by its owner and at a certain distance off a firing line was marked. From this a boy fired his taw, and sought to send it through one of the holes. If he shot it through No. 1, he was given one marble as his prize, if he failed to get his taw through any hole, he had to forfeit a marble. If he were an expert shot he might win quite a number of marbles, but unless he were an expert marksman, he forfeited more than he won and the owner of the board profited to the extent of the difference.

Another game defying classification was "Wall," reported current in Deloraine, Tasmania, about 1938. The object in the game was to toss a marble against a wall and hit an opponent's marble on the bounce or ricochet, then take it.

With the trend toward surface games, Australian marble games of the mid-twentieth century were less leisurely than those of the mid-nineteenth and early twentieth centuries. Old games surviving were simplified, required less skill, and had lost much accompanying verbal ritual. It appeared that there were fewer kinds of marbles, and fewer marble names and terms.

Two kinds of marbles seen were: agate and glass; of two sizes—one, about three-fourths inches in diameter and the other, about five-eighths.

The only marble names I heard from children were "Taw" and "Agate Taw" (pronounced "Tor"). The first was in general use throughout Australia; the second, I heard from one twelve-year-old boy in Adelaide, South Australia. When I asked what they called other marbles—not taws —, the answer was 'marbles'. Photographs of Melbourne and Perth games show that all the marbles in each game are the same size. The "Taw" means the favourite marble for "firing" or "drizzying"—the playing marble.[10]

Adults told me that the words "Commonies" and "Steelies" were current among children in 1954–5 as in past years but I did not hear them. "Alley" as a general word for marble was reported in use in Ballarat, Victoria, about 1910. "Stanker" for "taw" was a favourite term in Balwyn, Victoria, in "years gone by."

Sir Joseph Verco, reporting on marble names of 1860–7 wrote:

There were no fewer than five different genera,—"agates," "glass allies," "stoneys" and "commonies." "Agates" were the most costly and of course the most prized, and one agate was equal to several glass allies, more stoneys and still more commonies. They were ground out of special kind of stone whence their name or manufacture and burned and coloured with some opaque polish. It was an achievement to win an agate in a game.

The name "glass alley" indicates its structure. It varied in size from a small cherry to a walnut and was made of clear glass, and had a very wide range of ornament inside it, both as regards the colouring and pattern and figuring.

The "stoneys" were mostly about the size of small cherries, were white and opaque and without any colour pattern.

The "Commonies" were of the same size, but of a mud colour, opaque.

Marble language of 1954–5 included various words to indicate rules for use of the taw. Rules were rigid in each play-group and included stance in kneeling, squatting or standing; and manner of holding the taw for "firing," "flicking," "pinching," "shooting," "dribbling," dribbying," "drizzying," "pinking," "throwing," or "bowling."

Photographs taken in Melbourne and in Perth demonstrate two peer-group rules for holding the taw: Perth boys held the taw between thumb and tip of forefinger of the unsupported right hand while squatting to fire; Melbourne boys held the taw between thumb and crook of forefinger of the right hand supported by the left fist—forefinger pointed—resting on the ground, with right knee kneeling. Sir Joseph described two methods of holding the taw for firing: "The 'taw' he 'fired' with his right thumb and two fingers. . . ." Later he said, "with thumb and finger."

Terms used when a player shot at a hole or at another marble were:

[10] J. Strutt reported (page 304) "Taw" as the name of a game where players each placed a marble or marbles in a ring and then shot at them to knock them out. A. B. Gomme, Vol. 1, page 350, lists "Long Tawl" as the name of a marble game.

"Fire" (in general use throughout Austrialia); "flick" (in Tasmania and in Perth); "pinch" (in Brisbane); and "shoot" (in St Helens, Tasmania).

When players stood and bowled or tossed their taws either toward a line, leaf or some designated object to determine who would fire first in the game, or on to the field simply to start a game such as "Follow-Me-Taw," the following terms were in use: "dribbling" (in Canberra); "dibbying" and "drizzying" (in Perth); and "pinking" (in Brisbane).

Other marbles-game-language included: "kill," widely used when a player hit another player's taw and thus put him out of the game. "Kiss," heard in Perth, meant the same thing. "Span" (Perth) meant coming within a hand-span of another player's taw or of a hole or of a line; or taking a hand-span after hitting a marble or going into a hole before firing again. "Dub" or "dubbed up" (Brisbane) meant stacking the marbles in a pile in the middle of a ring, square or other geometric figure. "Poison" which named a game in Brisbane, also meant a place (Brisbane) "where you go when you fire and get caught in the ring" as well as a marble in Swansea, Tasmania, where "first the player who gets his taw in all the holes is 'poison' and if 'poison' hits another player he wins the game." "Draw" (Perth) "is when two boys drizzy and their marbles are even they call it a draw and they drizzy again."

Two charms called "moz" were reportedly used in marble games in Victoria from 1910–20. To bring good luck, a player chanted:

"Under the Kaiser's hoof."

To bring bad luck to an opponent he chanted:

"The poor old Kaiser's dead
He died for want of bread
They put him in a coffin
He fell through the bottom
The poor old Kaiser's dead."

A widely held belief among Australian adults was that marbles is a seasonal game. Adults who were questioned always answered emphatically either "spring" or "autumn." I actually saw marble games in progress in different parts of Australia in early spring, late spring, early summer and in autumn but I could find no seasonal pattern in what I saw.

Dr. Brian Sutton-Smith, in his "Observations on the 'Seasonal' Nature of Children's Games in New Zealand"[11] wrote:

The supposedly mysterious way in which children's games come and go, wax and wane . . . has been remarked upon at great length by the

[11] *Western Folklore*, Vol. XII, No. 3, p. 186.

romanticists of children's games. It is a favourite theme, and the complexity of the factors involved lends itself easily to mysticism . . . . It can be shown that children's play seasons result from the interaction of children's groups with a variety of influences in their environment.

And he continued to say later that "climatic seasons represent one factor among many." Among mid-twentieth-century Australian children, hard-surfaced playing fields make an environmental factor affecting marble games—as well as other games—the year round.

Australian adults considered marbles a boys' game. The degree of accuracy in that belief is problematic. Many Australian girls were playing marbles. That boys and girls played their games in separate groups at school was the result of separate playgrounds. Outside of school I saw boys and girls playing together and reports indicated that home and neighbourhood marble games were often mixed groups. Perhaps the male proprietary attitude was more fancy (aided by controlled environment) than fact.

Australian children's play environment is changing as the nation changes from a "98 per cent British people" to include other ethnic groups; from a pastoral to an industrial arrangement of the population. In addition, modern modes of mass entertainment and recreation are not condusive to self-motivating activities like marble games which require skill developed through patient practice. With increasing adult-supervised, adult-motivated and adult-rewarded play (badges and championship cups), incentive for peer-approval decreases. Hence, marble games —old gambling games of individual skill—change or disappear; a pocket full of marbles is not sufficient reward; the gambler prefers the adult's golden cup.

Scholars differ in their points of view about adult supervision and standardization of children's play life. They differ about how much adult-imposed change has taken place in traditional play and they differ about the moral and psychological aspects of those changes. Paul Brewster and Norman Douglas lament the modern adult-supervised playground.[12] Brian Sutton-Smith, psychologist and former physical educationalist, defends it. He says: ". . . society of today does not require that children be craftsmen of play; it requires, rather that they be competent social mixers in play, or to use a term of some current vogue, it requires that they be 'gamesmen'."[13] The Opie's newest book (*The Lore and Language of Schoolchildren*), encyclopedic in size and nature, indicates that chil-

12 P. Brewster, *American Nonsinging Games*, Norman, Oklahoma, 1953, p. xx. N. Douglas, *London Street Games*, London, 1931, p. xi.

13 B. Sutton-Smith, *The Games of New Zealand Children*, pp. 160–4.

dren—English, Scottish and Welsh children, at any rate—are making tradition as fast as designing adults can annihilate it.

Whatever the moral and psychological implications of adult-imposed changes in children's play may be, the study of no other traditional play custom illustrates the extreme adult intervention found in marble tournaments.

It is yet to be seen whether or not Australians will import marble tournaments along with American comic books. If they do, the old games of "Goot," "Three Corner Killy" and "Rabbit Hole" will disappear. The time may come when children, the world over, will play one standardized marble game. Perhaps the time may come when an Australian child, an American child and an English child will compete in a world marble championship tournament on a space platform anchored somewhere in the wild blue yonder. In this event, this world will surely be left a dull, brave new world."

10

The Kissing Games of Adolescents in Ohio

BRIAN SUTTON-SMITH

There do not appear to be any English language folklore collections which include kissing games within one special category. In general, these games are to be found under the titles of "Courtship" "Marriage" "Forfeits" and "Play-Party" games. In this century, however, the explicit and formalized elements of courtship, marriage, forfeiture and play-party dancing have been practically discarded in adolescent play, while kissing has continued and increased in importance as a formal element in many games. The primary aim of the present study, therefore, is to record a collection of the contemporary kissing games of adolescent children. Subsidiary aims are to note the origins of these games and the reasons for the changes that have come about in the way in which they are played.

METHOD

Games, game descriptions and accounts of the circumstances of play were collected by questionnaire from 246 children (135 boys and 111 girls) in a northwestern Ohio rural high school (Sandusky County), and from 100 college students (50 men and 50 women) in a state university also in northwestern Ohio (Wood County). The high school children were in the fifth to twelfth grade classes with approximately thirty children in each class. The college students were mainly sophomores of eighteen and nineteen years of age. The items in the questionnaire are those listed in the table. These items were derived from previous lists made out by the college students. High school and college students were requested to check only those games that they had played themselves, indicating whether or not they liked or disliked the game. The great majority of these students came from towns in Ohio.

The games appeared in the questionnaire list as follows:

Kiss in the Ring   L   D
Post Office   L   D

The percentage of each group, high school and college students checking the games and the rank order of preference is indicated in the table. This table includes only the twenty-two games listed on the original questionnaire. It does not include the thirty-two other game names dis-

TABLE 1

Name of Game	Rank Order in High School Gp. (N = 246)	Percentage of High School Gp. check. item	Rank Order in College Group (N = 100)	Percentage of Coll. Gp. Checking Item
Spin the bottle	1	57	1	91
Post office	2	38	5	70
Winks	3	32	12	23
Mistletoe kissing	4	26	3	83
Chew string	5	25	10	34
Necking	6	22	2	89
Biting the apple	7.5	21	11	25
Truth and consequences	7.5	21	13	22
Endurance kissing	9.5	20	9	39
Flashlight	9.5	20	7	49
Hayride kissing	11	18	6	69
Passing the orange	12	17	8	45
Musical circle	13	14	15.5	9
Kissing tag	14.5	13	15.5	9
Chase and kiss	14.5	13	17.5	8
Perdiddle	16	12	4	72
Numbers	17.5	10	17.5	8
Kiss in the ring	17.5	10	19	6
Sardines	19	7	20	5
Clap in, clap out	20	6	21.5	0
This or that	21	5	14	10
Minx	22	4	21.5	0

covered in the course of the investigation. These are mentioned in the alphabetical collection below. All of these games have been played at sometime during the 1950's. A smaller group of students in another rural high school also contributed descriptions of some of their games.

THE COLLECTION

The games collected are listed alphabetically below. Where there is more than one name for the game, the description of the game is given under that name most commonly used. Some of the following games are played more often without kissing but are included here because kissing is occasionally a part of the game. Games of this nature are "Chew the String" and "Pass the Orange." There are other games which do not contain kissing, but for which much of the fun consists in the close contact of the partners, and the near kissing they experience, for example "Biting the Apple" and "Pass the Lifesaver."

When the information was derived from the major high school sample this is indicated by the reference in parentheses to "Thompson." Descriptions derived from the minor high school sample are indicated by the reference "Woodville." References to other places in Ohio or elsewhere indicate that the information was derived from the college sample. Where the game was reported by only one person and is probably an ephemeral pastime, this is indicated. It will be noticed that while the majority of the games have not appeared before in earlier collections, some elements of most of them are traceable to earlier games.

Base Kiss

The boy stands on the pitcher's base. He covers his eyes. The girls run from the home base around the diamond. When he shouts out "base" they must stop. If any girl is on a base he kisses her. This also is called "Baseball Kissing" (Thompson). This appears to be a unique adaptation of baseball to more romantic ends.

Biting the Apple

This is a relay race in which couples compete against couples. The apples hang from the roof on a piece of string and the couples, hands behind their backs, endeavor to be the first to get the apple eaten. It is played throughout the year although some still report it as played only at Halloween which is the traditional time for it (Toledo).[1] "Kissing

[1] Alice B. Gomme, *The Traditional Games of England, Scotland and Ireland*, I (London, 1894–98), 42 ("Bob Cherry").

occurs only by accident and is something to avoid" (Swanton). The game may be played also with doughnuts (Rossford) or candy bars (Southington).

Boys Catch Girls

There are two sides. The ones who are caught are kissed. The boys may catch the girls or the girls may catch the boys (Thompson). Informal activity of this type appears to be practically universal throughout the Western World. I have observed it most often in eight and nine-year-old children, but it is certainly not restricted to that age level. Children often engage in activities of this sort without giving a name to them.

Bridge

This is played the same way as Perdiddle, but bridges are used instead of motor car headlights. Naturally, this has the effect of increasing the number of occasions on which the game may be played (Thompson).

Candy, Cigarettes

Girls and boys in two teams take the names of say, cigarettes (boys) candy (girls). Each group then takes turns at calling out any example of the category of nomenclature chosen by the opposite sex ("Lucky Strike"). If this happens to be someone's name, that person is kissed (Industry, Penn.) This is one of a group of games which emphasize the chance element in the selection of partners. Other games of this sort which follow are: "Draw and Kiss," "Dynamite," "Five Minute Date," "Heavy Heavy Hang Over the Head," "Musical Circle," "Numbers," "Post Office," "Professor," "Spin the Bottle" and "This or That." There is precedent for this chance selection of partners in traditional games.[2]

The Card Game

This game is known also as Hearts (Cleveland). The players go round in a circle, and take turns to pick a card from a pack. Having picked a card they then pick a person of the opposite sex. If they pick a spade they slap the person they have chosen on the back. If a club, they shake hands. If a diamond it is a public kiss. If a heart, a private kiss (Woodville). There are variations in the interpretation of these suits. From the same locality, for example, another version was: club=slap; spade=shake hands; heart=kiss in public; diamond=kiss in private. Yet another interpretation from Cleveland had it that a club=a kiss on the hand; a

---

[2] Gomme, II, 255 ("Three Flowers").

diamond=a kiss on the forehead; a spade=a kiss on the cheek; and a heart=a kiss on the lips. Here again we have a game which emphasizes the fortuitous choice of partners although the "chance" element is here provided by a pack of cards, rather than some traditional game performance. The game of "Hearts," and "Kings and Queens" are of the same sort.

Chase

The girls snatch the boys' hats and in order to get them back the boys have to kiss the girls (Ohio).

Chase and Kiss

One person sits on a chair, all the rest take the numbers (odd for boys, even for girls). The person on the chair calls out two numbers (an odd and an even). If it is a girl on the chair, then the boy called out tries to kiss her before he is kised by the girl whose number was also called. If he succeeds he takes the player's place on the chair. If he fails and is kissed first, then the chair player calls out again (Monclova). There are traditional games which are similar to this, all involving couples who chase each other for kisses.[3]

Chew the String

This is a relay race in which couples compete against each other. There is a long piece of string. The partners chew from each end until they meet in the middle. In most cases this is simply a race to see which couple can get all the strings out of sight first. But it may be played to see who can be first to eat a lifesaver (Summit, N. J.) or marshmallow (Thompson) in the middle. Or it may be a race to see which partner can eat the most (Whittier, Cal.). In some cases the partners are reported as finishing the ordeal with a rather clumsy kiss (Celina, Cincinnati, Chicago, Dayton, Portage).

Choo Choo

This is a variant of "Pony Express." A couple go into another room. They ask a third person to join them. These three then run all around the house like a train. When they stop in the secluded room, the first kisses the second, who kisses the third. A fourth person is asked to join them and the game proceeds as before and so it goes on with chain kissing at

---

[3] Edwin F. Piper, "Some Play Party Games of the Middle West," JAF, XXVIII (July, 1915), 266 ("Chase That Squirrel").

the end of each episode. The train alternates boys and girls. When the last person is chosen, the kissing commences, the second to the last person instead of kissing the final player, gives him a slap (Ohio). This victimization of a player also occurs in "Pony Express" and is a familiar element in children's games.[5] Players holding on behind each other is of course familiar in "Fox and Goose."[6]

Clap in, Clap out

No description reported in this research but it is a traditional game frequently mentioned in the literature.[4]

Draw and Kiss

All the player's names are placed in a dish. All the players place their hands in together and draw a name. They must kiss the name drawn out as well as be kissed by the person who has drawn their name. As soon as they have kissed and been kissed they may run to take their place in a line of chairs. There is one chair short, and the person who is left over must kiss everyone (Thompson). This game, which appears to be a new one, combines elements of "Musical Chairs" and "Forfeits."[7]

Dynamite

All the boys leave the room. Each girl selects a magazine and lays it on the floor. There are several magazines placed on the floor but belonging to no one. These are known as "dynamite." The boys come in one at a time and step on a magazine. If they step on one belonging to someone, they must kiss that person. If they step on one belonging to no one, then dynamite—they must kiss everyone in the room. Sometimes a small magazine is placed inside a large magazine. If someone steps on these, they have a double dynamite, kissing everyone twice (Ohio).

Like the traditional game of "Clap In, Clap Out" and the game of "Winks" this is a game so contrived to make the boys play out their choices in front of the girls.

[4] Gomme, I, 215 ("Kiss and Clap"); *The Frank C. Brown Collection of North Carolina Folklore*, I (Durham, 1952) 123; Paul G. Brewster, *American Nonsinging Games* (Oklahoma, 1953), 154.

[5] B. Sutton-Smith, The Historical and Psychological Significance of the Unorganized Games of New Zealand Primary School Children." (Ph.D. Thesis: Univ. of New Zealand, 1954), p. 718 (Microfilm copy of typescript, 2 reels, positive, Ball State Teacher's College, Muncie, Indiana).

[6] Gomme, I, 139.

[7] Gomme, I, 137 and 148.

Endurance Kissing

This has been reported as a game played by a few couples together, or by a group of couples at a party. It is essentially a comical endurance test, in which a couple sees how long they can hold a kiss without breathing. A watch is used. The bystanders laugh at the competitors. It is done usually only with one's steady date. On a double date the losers might be expected to buy a coke for the winners. The endurance kissing may also occur with breathing allowed, in which case it is a contest to see which couple can keep their mouths together for the longest period of time. Under the name "Football" it is described as follows: "About three or four couples would start kissing at the same time and the couple who held out the longest would score a touchdown. They would then go for the extra point, gaining this by again out-enduring their competitors. If a game was played for long a score would be kept. Sometimes a couple could hold out for 45 minutes" (Burgoon).

Fiddle Diddle

This is another name for the game of "Perdiddle" (Woodville).

Five Minute Date

One player sits on a chair blindfolded. On each side of him sits a member of the opposite sex. He takes their hands in his, and drops the one he doesn't want. He takes off his blindfold and goes on a five minute date with the one he has chosen (Woodville). The blindfolding of the players who must then exercise a guess is a familiar element in games.[8]

Flashlight

This is known also under the names of "Willpower" and "Spotlight." The game is played in a number of different ways. In the most common, couples sit around the edge of a dark room. One person sits in the center with a flashlight. If he flashes it onto a couple that is *not* kissing, then he joins the opposite sex member of that couple, and the other member takes his place in the center with the flashlight. In only one or two reports did the It character in the center escape his position because he found a peripheral couple that *was* kissing. In short it was normal in this game to be kissing, not normal to be caught unembraced. In another type of flashlight game the central character is blindfolded. He is then spun around. When his light falls on someone, if it is a person of the opposite sex, she kisses him. If a person of the same sex, he is spun again.

[8] Sutton-Smith, p. 507.

If he can guess who it is that has kissed him, he may leave the center. If not the game continues as before.

This is clearly a new game, but even so contains several elements that are quite traditional. It is very normal in the It games of adolescence for the central person to be left-over character or scapegoat.[9] He is like the "Jolly Miller" who can't get himself a wife.[10] It is traditional too for a torch to be a dangerous possession.[11]

Football

Another name for "Endurance Kissing."

Freeze Tag

When the It kisses you, you stay frozen to the spot and cannot move until some other player comes and unfreezes you with a kiss (Thompson). This is a variant of the well known chasing game of the same name.

Hayride Kissing

In most cases hayrides are occasions which may or may not include kissing, not strictly speaking a game in themselves. For example, there are reports of playing "Flashlight" and "Endurance Kissing" while out on hayrides. However, there is at least one report of kissing proceeding sequentially around the conveyance in the order of sitting (Rockford).

Hearts

All players have cards and take turns at turning them up. If hearts are matched the two players involved kiss while the light is turned out momentarily (Erie, Penn.).

Heavy, Heavy, Hang over the Head

An object is taken from each player as a means of identification. These objects are put in an ash tray and held over the head of a person called the teacher. The holder lifts out an object and indicates whether it belongs to a boy or girl.

Holder: "Heavy Heavy hang over the head. What should this boy do to get back his ring"
Teacher: "He must sit on the couch with .... and kiss her everytime I tell him to do so" (Rossford).

---

[9] Sutton-Smith, p. 718.
[10] Brown collection, p. 111.
[11] Gomme, I, 256 ("Jack's Alive"); Henry Betts, *The Games of Children* (London, 1929), p. 75.

In a briefer version, everyone simply puts object in a hat, takes out an object and kisses the owner (Cleveland). This is a classic element in "Forfeits."[12]

Kings and Queens

Children stand in a circle around a deck of cards. One by one they turn up the cards. If a girl turns up a king she may choose a boy and go off into another room with him. If a boy turns up a queen he goes into another room with his choice (Willoughby).

Kissing Tag

This game is also called "Kissing Tab" (Woodville).

The person who is It catches and kisses someone who is then It and must also pass it on by kissing (Lorain). In another game with the same name a person in the center is blindfolded. The others circle around him. When he calls "Kissing Tag" he chases the others, and the person he catches he kisses for five minutes (Thompson). These are again variations on the traditional games of "Chase" and "Blindman's Buff."

Kiss under Water

Players try to kiss each other while swimming under water. One report only (Woodville).

Minx

One player is It and tries to catch the other players without their fingers, arms or legs crossed. If the It so catches anyone he "minxes" that person which means simply he kisses them, and that person takes his place in the center (Ohio). This crossing of fingers, limbs, etc. is a common way in which children symbolize being "safe" in game terms.[13] Safety tag games are numerous.

Mistletoe Kissing

A Christmas and New Year custom, not usually regarded as a game, but made into one in some cases. For example, the mistletoe is hung in the doorway under which the couples march. The couple under the mistletoe when the whistle blows must kiss (Fostoria). There are reports in which boys struggled to drag girls under the mistletoe in order to kiss

---

[12] William Wells Newell, *Games and Songs of American Children* (New York, 1883), p. 143.

[13] Sutton-Smith, p. 501.

them, or took the mistletoe to the girls and held it over their heads as a pretext for kissing them (Lorain, Anna).

Murderer and Detective

Two versions are mentioned. One person is appointed the detective and he leaves the room. Another is appointed the murderer, but the detective does not know who this child is. The lights are turned out and the murderer kisses someone. The detective is called in and he must guess the name of the murderer (Woodville). This is a kissing version of another game of the same name.[14] In another variety, the game has a "Spin the Bottle" pattern. Someone spins the bottle. The person it points to becomes the detective. The detective spins the bottle. If it points to a person of the opposite sex, that person is a murderer. The detective then chases the murderer and attempts to kiss her (Woodville).

Musical Circle

The boys are in a circle and the girls form a circle around them. The music is played and the boys walk around; when it stops, they kiss the girl facing them (Ohio). Circle forms of courting games were common in earlier days, though not this particular form.[15]

Necking

This is not normally considered a game, but in some reports elements of ritual show up that approximate it to play. "This was done in a car at some spot well frequented by teenagers. One of our favourite spots was the Pumping Station overlook, Presque Isle Bay on Lake Erie. Our favorite expression at that time was that we were going to watch the 'submarine races'." Or, "We usually went to the park that closed at 11 p. m. But soon the park police found out and would quietly pull up along side the car and shine their spotlight on you. Then it became a fad to be caught necking like this. Many times a bunch of us would park the car and just wait for the police. When they pulled up and shone their flashlights we would just sit there laughing" (Cleveland).

Numbers

A boy or girl goes into another room which is in the dark. This is preferably a bedroom. The members of the opposite sex are assigned numbers. The first person calls out a number and the chosen one enters the room and "necks" for a period of one minute. The same number can-

14 E. O. Harbin, *The Fun Encyclopedia* (New York, 1940), p. 145.
15 Brown collection, pp. 89–133.

not be called for more than three times. When all numbers have been called, a member of the opposite sex goes into the room (Dayton).

Pass the Kiss

Players stand in a circle and pass around a kiss (Thompson). A traditional form though usually it is a whisper or a button that is passed round the periphery.[16]

Pass the Lifesaver

A relay or couple game in which each player holds a toothpick in the mouth, and then players endeavor to pass the lifesaver from one toothpick to another without dropping it. A game which brings faces into proximity though it does not necessarily result in kissing (Elmore).

Pass the Orange

This is usually played as a relay. The orange is placed under the chin and then the next player, a member of the opposite sex endeavors to get it under his chin without use of hands (Berea). Or it may be played with the members of each sex alternating around in a circle (Lorain). In another version the partners stand with faces close together with the orange supported between their foreheads. The competition is to see which couple can keep it there the longest (Warren). In a number of reports the couple must kiss if they drop the orange while passing it from one chin to the next (Poland, Cleveland, Westlake). In one, they kiss if they pass it on successfully (Green Bay, Wis.).

Perdiddle

This game is known also as "Fiddle Diddle," "Popeye" and "Rinky Dink." A boy and girl are riding in an automobile. If a car with one light goes by, then if the boy says "perdiddle" first he can claim a kiss from the girl. "It used to give us the nerve to take a kiss," says one report (Middletown). But if the girl sees the light first and says "perdiddle" she can slap the boy. It is played in other ways also. Sometimes the couples save up their "perdiddles" throughout the evening and have a reckoning before departure. "In this way we didn't get all messed up on our way to the function" (Findlay). Other versions ignore the slapping and either partner may take a kiss when the one light provocation appears (Toledo, Elmore). According to some, a truck light is good for an extra long kiss (Berea).

---

[16] Newell, p. 151.

Photography

"The lights are turned out to see what develops" (Findlay). This is just a pretext for kissing between couples in the group setting. However, as such it is a more obvious example of a characteristic of so many of these games.

Pony Express

This is similar to the game of "Choo Choo." A boy leads a girl out, with her hands on his waist, into a secluded and darkened room and kisses her. They return and a second boy couples on behind the girl. They depart once more, and once again the first boy kisses the first girl, and she turns and slaps the second boy. They return to the group and a second girl couples on behind the second boy. A kisses B, B kisses C and C slaps D. And on the game goes until all are kissed. The pairs are usually made up of couples going steady with each other. There is much laughter, astonishment and some annoyance (Bascom). It is reported also as being the same game as "Post Office" but played much faster (Woodville). In addition there is an expression relating to this game, which is not actually a game in itself, but rather game-like in that it has become a conventional smart saying. The question is asked:

"Do you want to play 'Pony Express'?"
"What is that?"
"The same as 'Post Office,' but a little more horsing around" (Thompson).

Popeye

Another name for "Perdiddle" (Painesville).

Post Office

There are several versions. One is similar to those found in the collections of traditional games.[17] In this version there is a player in another room (the postman) who sends a message via the intermediary that he has a letter for such and such a person. He may nominate the value of the letter, that it has a three-cent stamp or a six-cent stamp etc., and this is meant to indicate the number of kisses he intends to give that person. The elected person goes to the postmaster, kisses, and then replaces him as postmaster (Newton Falls). In another version, more frequently reported, the boys choose odd numbers and the girls choose even numbers, or vice versa. The postman then calls out any number without knowing

---

[17] Gomme, p. 404 ("American Post"); Brewster, p. 154.

who has that number. They kiss, and the number called becomes the new postmaster (Toledo, Oregon, Poland, Industry, Penn.). In yet other versions, the postman writes a number (one to five) on a piece of paper. The girl who guesses his number kisses him that many times (Toledo). Or the postman is out of sight and the opposite sex persons do not know who it is. They come one at a time and ask for a given number of stamps. They get that many kisses (Cleveland). Or the couples simply line up and have turns at going into another room to kiss for one minute (Vienna). In a number of reports there was indication that the rules were not well known and the many variations in the game seems to confirm that position. It is of interest that the main change from the traditional to the modern form is from an explicit selection of partners to kiss, to a chance selection. Most versions, however, retain the private kissing, and the giving of the couple a limited time to go ahead with it, say, one or two minutes. If they take longer there will be much banter and laughter when they finally appear. "Usually after the first kiss the couple sat on the edge of the bed and made the springs squeak. This was always a big hit with those in the other room when it could be heard" (Ohio).

The expression "Dog Sled" is used in connection with this game.

"Do you want to play 'Dog Sled?'"

"What is that?"

"The same as 'Post Office,' only a little more mush" (Thompson).

Pretty Please

This is more of a ritual than a game. Every time the boy says, "Pretty Please" to his girl she must kiss him. One report only (Thompson).

Professor

Numbers are written on pieces of paper, then cut in two. The boys receive one half, the girls the other half. Players see if they can match their pieces. Those whose papers match go to some private place to kiss. After they have kissed, the boy says to the girl, "Do I pass?" If she liked the kissing she says, "No," and he continues to kiss her until she says he passes (Thompson).

Rinky Dink

Another name for "Perdiddle" (Ginn).

Sardines

One couple goes and hides, then another couple finds them and hides in the same place; in the end everyone is hiding together. This game can be played with or without kissing, though usually it is played without kissing.[18]

Serve it in the Dark

"The boy should raise her chin to the right level, then bake her in the young man's arms for fifteen minutes, and finally beat it before her old man gets home." One report only (Thompson).

Show Kiss

A boy and a girl go to a movie which is according to this report a "Love Show." Every time the screen characters kiss, the boy and girl kiss too. Only one report (Thompson).

Spin the Bottle

All versions have the traditional circle of players with one player in the center spinning the bottle, though in two reports it was a flashlight in the center with the room in darkness[19] (Toledo, Poland). Generally, the center player must kiss the peripheral player pointed out by the bottle. Usually the kissing is done in public, but the couple may go off and do it in private (Payne, Lancaster). If it points to a player of the same sex that player may go into the center, or it may be spun again, or the person to the right may be kissed, or this situation may be avoided by having two sexually segregated circles with an opposite-sex person spinning the bottle. Usually, however, the sexes alternate around the circle. Sometimes when the bottle points between two of them, those two have to kiss (Chicago). There is much report of pretending to avoid the bottle, and of cheating so that it ended up pointing toward the pretty or the handsome, and not towards the unattractive. This is an interesting application of the sociometric determination of game behaviors first described by Whyte.[20]

Spotlight

Another name for "Flashlight" (Thompson). But used also for the practice of shining a spotlight on a group of dancing couples. The couple on whom the spot alights must stop dancing and kiss.

This or That

One child goes out of the room. Two other children of the opposite sex are named "This" and "That." The outside child returns and

---

[18] Jessie H. Bancroft, *Games for the Playground, Home, School, and Gymnasium* (New York, 1909), p. 172.

[19] Gomme, II, 312 ("Turn the Trencher"); Brewster, p. 32 ("Spin the Plate").

[20] W. H. Whyte, *Street Corner Society* (Chicago, 1943).

nominates "This" or "That," without knowing who they are, and kisses the one he thus ignorantly chooses. The other child ("This" or "That"), then goes out and the game carries on (Upper Sandusky). In another similar version a girl goes into another dark room; a person who has been out before names two boys "This" and "That." The girl outside calls back, "This" (or "That") and the person named goes into the room with her. She can kiss him if she likes or she can shake hands with him if she doesn't want to kiss him. She comes back and he remains behind. The process is repeated. However, if the boy tries to shake hands with a girl, she can either shake hands with him or slap his face (Upper Sandusky).

Games of fortuitous choice like this have forerunners in traditional game collections.[21]

Truth or Consequences

An It persons asks embarrassing questions of group members in turn. If the member will not tell the truth, then he must take the consequences. Questions asked are of the nature of: "Do you like Johnny?" Whether he or she is telling the truth depends upon group decision. Consequences vary. They may involve kissing, singing a song, proposing, running around the block etc. (Rossford).[22]

Turtle Climb

One member of the couple starts telling the story of how the poor little turtle tried to climb the hill. He uses his arms to demonstrate the turtle climbing. When the turtle finally reaches the top, the two arms are clear around the partners neck. The person narrating says: "What are we talking about turtles for?" and gives the other a kiss. One report only (Findlay).

Willpower

Another name for "Flashlight." But used also for a pursuit type of "Flashlight." There are several versions. In one, the person with the flashlight comes into a dark room, turns on his flashlight and kisses the person upon whom it alights, if of the opposite sex (Newton Falls). In another version, the boys as a group have flashlights and they pursue the girls who hide. They kiss the girl whom they catch in their light beam (Toledo, Dayton), or they stay with the girl they catch in the light beam (Willoughby).

---

[21] Gomme, II, 255 ("Three Flowers").
[22] Brewster, p. 37 (forfeits but no kiss).

Windshield Wiper

Two couples stand with the same sexes opposite each other, and arms about each others shoulders or waists. They turn heads from side to side like windshield wipers, kissing as they do so. One report only (Cleveland).

Winks

This game is known also as "Popeye" (Chicago). Members of one sex, more usually the boys, stand in a circle behind chairs, all of which contains girls, except one. The boy with the empty chair tries to entice the girls in the other chairs to come over to his chair. They may come only if he winks at them. When he winks they try to rush over to his chair, but the boy behind them tries to prevent them from doing this by taking hold of their shoulders and arms, or perhaps simply by tagging them. There may be no kissing. More usually they are kissed by the boy who has winked at them when they succeed in getting to his chair. Occasionally they are also kissed by the boy behind them when he succeeds in holding them (Upper Sandusky). This is a traditional game.[23]

CIRCUMSTANCES OF PLAY

For the purposes of this discussion the games are grouped into three sections:

I. *Chasing Kiss Games; which includes, "Base Kiss," "Boys Catch Girls," "Chase," "Chase and Kiss," "Freeze Tag," and "Kiss in the Ring."*

The first group of games are most typical of the preadolescent age group of thirteen years. This investigation did not provide much information about these games except that they are mostly played out of doors or in school grounds, and are limited to small numbers of children. That is, many children do not mention them. The games are mentioned mainly by the high school sample and there is some evidence that rural children are sometimes precocious in these respects.[24] Kinsey-type data would lead to the hypothesis that this sort of precocious aggressive osculatory play would be more marked amongst lower class children.[25] However, this thesis requires further investigation.

II. *Mixing Kiss Games: which include: (a) "Candy-Cigarettes," "Card Game," "Clap In Clap Out," "Draw and Kiss," "Dynamite," "Five Minute*

---

[23] Brown collection, I, 154; Brewster, p. 153.
[24] Sutton-Smith, p. 664.
[25] H. J. Eysenck, *Uses and Abuses of Psychology* (Middlesex, 1953), pp. 184ff.

Date," "Hearts," "Kings and Queens," "Heavy Heavy Hang Over the Head," "Minx," "Murder & Detective," "Numbers," "Post Office," "Spin the Bottle," "This or That," "Truth or Consequences," "Winks." (b) "Bite the Apple," "Chew String," "Musical Circle," "Pass the Lifesaver," and "Pass the Orange."

The mixer games of group II (a) are the kissing games of the junior high school period. The games of group (b) are played at the junior high school age level, at the senior high school age level and by older persons. They are frequently reported as games played on fraternity-sorority visits. Their main appeal is their ludicrous nature. In all the games of group II the couples are not paired off before the game begins; pairing occurs in the games but it is characteristically of a momentary sort.

III. *Couple Kiss Games: which include* (a) "Choo Choo," "Flashlight," "Hayride Kissing," "Mistletoe Kissing," "Pass the Kiss," "Photography," "Pony Express," "Sardines," "Spotlight," "Willpower," (b) "Bridge," "Endurance Kissing," "Necking," "Perdiddle," "Pretty Please," "Serve it in the Dark," "Show Kiss," "Turtle Climb," "Windshield Wipers."

The couple games of group III are most characteristic of the senior high school years. Here the couples are usually matched off beforehand and the games permit them to continue their interest in each other. Type (a) are games played at group events such as parties. Type (b) usually take place amongst a few couples or between one couple in a motor car or other suitable place.

A child's experience of these games may be extensive or limited. There are varying degrees of acquaintance and varying types of occasions on which the games are played. Some of the varieties of experience are as follows: (1) There are those who have never played these games. In the high school group 42% of the children did not check any games in grade 5, 6, and 7. From the 8th grade on, however, only 8% failed to check any items. In short while most children have some experience of these games during childhood, a small minority records no experience of them. One informant explained that he had attended a boys' boarding school and was unacquainted with these games. (2) A few explained that they had never played games like "Spin the Bottle" and "Post Office" on formal occasions, but had played them clandestinely in the daytime out of doors, or inside only when their parents were absent from home. (3) A considerable group indicated having played the games only occasionally at birthday or New Years parties, or, for example, in a recreation hall when a school picnic had been abandoned because of wet weather. On these occasions adults were usually supervising the games. (4) For another considerable group these games constituted an important part of their social life throughout the high school years. These are the children who report playing these games at all their regular parties, which might be held every few weeks, on birthday parties, class parties, or following special occasions such as football games, music recitals, shows, plays, or as a precursor to slumber parties. The games generally took place in a recreation room or basement; but only occasionally out of doors in a backyard. Parents were generally in the house but not directly supervising activities. A game like "Spin the Bottle" might go on for over an hour, before another of a similar nature such as "This or That" was taken up. One report mentions a father who took motion films of the activities then showed them at the next meeting of the group. Although the evidence is not clear cut, it seems probable that more frequent participation in these activities is a part of an upper-middle socioeconomic course of events.[26]

ORIGINS

The basic collections of Gomme and Newell demonstrate that in the nineteenth century, kissing occurred mostly in the games of marriage, courtship and lovemaking, or in their play-party equivalents. "Forty years ago half the play-party amusements were built about some ceremony for kisses."[27] The above alphabetical list contains no games of that sort with the exception perhaps of "Kiss in the Ring." Examination of the present collection shows that it is composed largely of what Gomme termed "Forfeits and Amusements." Yet kissing was not as typical of the forfeits and amusements cited by Gomme as it is of these games as played today. Gomme classifies sixteen games as forfeits, and kissing occurs in only two of them. Furthermore, the kissing in Gomme's games was more often a penalty than it is today. "I command yee to kiss the crook . . . his naked lips must kiss the sooty implement."[28] For the greater part the forfeit games of today do not contain very unpleasant consequences; at the worst a slap ("Perdiddle" and "Pony Express"). Newell supplies stronger precedent for the present position when he says, under the heading "Redeeming Forfeits":

[26] Harold R. Phelps and John E. Horrocks, "Factors Influencing Informal Groups of Adolescents," *Child Development*, XXIX, 78.

[27] Edwin F. Piper, "Some Play Party Games of the Midwest," *JAF*, XXVIII (July, 1915), p. 262.

[28] Gomme, II, 325 ("Wadds and Wears").

The following are examples of old penalties, which usually involved kissing, with infinite variety of method: *To go to Rome.* To kiss every girl in the room. *Flat-irons.* The lad and lass lay their hands on the wall and kiss. *Measuring yards of tape, and cutting it off.* To kiss with arms extended. *"I'm in the well." "How Many Fathoms Deep?"* (Any number is answered.) *"Whom will you have to take you out?"* (Someone in the company is named.)[29]

Each fathom represents a kiss. The basic inventiveness in these expressions is very near in kind to that in our alphabetical list above. The rather surprising way in which so many games have been turned to kissing purposes in the above collection was clearly forecast in this record published by Newell in 1883.

Analysis of the formal pattern of the marriage games of yesterday in one of the most comprehensive collections[30] shows that the commonest procedure was for the central player to choose the partner that he would kiss. That is, at the end of an appropriate verse, the player in the center of the dancing circle, chose a player from the periphery, kissed him and was then replaced by that person in the center. Yet in the largest number of forfeit games of today, and those played most frequently [the mixer group II (*a*)] the choice of kissing partner is made fortuitously.

In short, two major changes have occurred in kissing games. First kissing takes place in forfeit type games rather than in marriage games. Secondly, it takes place less often by the explicit choice of one person for another and more often by chance. Some of the reasons that can be advanced to explain these changes are as follows. The first change is due to the fact that modern parents and the church are no longer averse to the fiddle and no longer restrict their children to the play-party game; it is due to the rise of the modern dance; to the fact that forfeit and amusement games are still as suitable to the indoor parlor and party setting as they were in the last century; to the large amount of freedom given modern children to develop these games in accordance with their own interests. The second change from choice of kissing partner to chance allotment of kissing partner, is probably due to the fact that the play-party games of yesterday were designed to suit late adolescence (although they were played by younger children also). An older age group is certainly implied in Dulles' statement. "The violin (fiddle) was taboo, but we sang songs and danced to them and hugged the girls until they would often grunt as we swung them clean off the

[29] Newell, p. 143 (No. 88).
[30] Brown collection, pp. 89–133.

floor or the ground, in the barn or house or on the green."[31] The equivalent of these games today are the couple games of Group III above.
The forfeit games of the mixer group today are played mainly by children
of early teen age who are most of the time not yet mature enough to risk
such explicit choices. As far as can be judged, the emergence of these
kissing games from forfeits and amusements is a spontaneous "folk"
occurrence. An examination of a number of "Party" and "Indoor" game
books dating from early in the century does not give any indication of
adult encouragement for the type of games being discussed here. In fact,
the reverse is the case. Great lengths are traversed in order to avoid the
introduction of kissing, even in an event such as St. Valentine's Day.
There are games with the titles of "Proposals," "Famous Lovers,"
"Flowery Romance," "Cupid's Carnival of Hearts," "Heart's Desire,"
"Heart's Fate," but no kissing. There are games of "Chew the String,"
"Bite the Apple," "Spin the Platter," "Postman," "Forfeits" and "Heavy
Heavy Hang Over Your Head," but no kissing. The only mention of kiss-
ing in all the books cited below is kissing a stone. "Kissing the Blarney
Stone!" Clearly these party books continue the puritan tradition of the
play-party.[32]

DISCUSSION

The picture of developmental change represented by these games
must be taken into consideration briefly in order to explain why these
games have persisted and increased in the modern world, a world not
generally propitious to the persistence of ancient pastimes. Although,
the role of games in development cannot be dealt with fully here, the
general position taken is that a game performs something of a bridge
function in development. It allows for the expression of given impulses
but at the same time safeguards the players by putting limits on the way

[31] Foster Rhea Dulles, *America Learns to Play* (New York, 1940), p. 275.

[32] J. H. Bancroft, op. cit., pp. 80, 254, and 257. Mary J. Breen, *The Party Book*
(New York, 1939), pp. 23-24. Arthur M. Depew, *The Cokesbury Party Book* (New
York, 1932), pp. 82 and 178. George Draper, *School, Church, Home and Gym Games*
(New York, 1927), pp. 180 and 203. Helen and Larry Eisenberg, *The Omnibus of
Fun* (New York, 1956), pp. 375 and 336. Edna Geister, *Geister Games* (New York,
1930). E. O. Harbin, *The Fun Encyclopedia* (New York, 1940), pp. 245, 254, 820
and 821. William Ralph La Porte, *A Handbook of Games and Programs* (New York,
1922), p. 54. Sidney Lear and M. B. Mishler, *The World's Best Book of Games and
Parties* (Phil. 1926), p. 106. Snyder Madelin, *My Book of Parties* (New York, 1928).
Bernard S. Mason and E. D. Mitchell, *Social Games for Recreation* (New York,
1935), pp. 71, 85 and 216. Theresa Hunt Wolcott, *The Book of Games and Parties*
(Boston, 1911).

in which those impulses can be expressed.[33] That is, the game allows the player to grow along the lines that he desires, but it safeguards him against the danger of risking too much. The game is essentially an adventure of a nonhazardous kind.

In group I, for example, the players are at the preadolescent age level which is characterized by indifference and hostility between the sexes. When boys and girls of this age level begin to show an interest in each other, they often do so in a rough, clothes-pulling, and arm-twisting manner. Their embryonic heterosexuality is aggressively displayed. They move into adolescent relationships in terms of the feelings they have learned in their preadolescence. The games of group I, boisterous though they are, place limits on these appetites at the same time as gratifying them. In "Freeze Tag," for example, you are permitted to kiss, and to chase, but only according to the rules. Although kissing in Western Culture is a symbol of the mature intimate relationship, in these games it is but a frenetic approximation to the form, with little of its spirit.

In the games of group II, thirteen, fourteen and fifteen-year-old children show less hurly-burly in their play but not much more expertise in handling their relationships with each other. These games provide a socially structured means by which they can be brought into relationship with each other, even to the extent of taking partners and kissing, but without responsibility for the partner choices that are made. The forfuitous elements in these games provide the youngsters with a form of trial-and-error partnership, but without the danger of being taken too seriously. They are able to indulge their own general interest in the opposite sex, but are defended against its outcome ("Could I help it if the bottle pointed my way!"). We need to remember that this is the age of tongue-tied and incompetent early dating. By playing these games the children can be with the other sex and by following the rules they can act fairly competently. At the same time they are *protected from a commitment to another person* for which they may not yet be ready. Not unnaturally, most of the kissing is described by the participants as a "peck" rather than a kiss. During the games the manner of the play will vary with the maturity of the players. Some will be eager for the kissing. Some will be reluctant. The virtue of the games is that they allow some to reach quickly towards their heterosexual goals and others to drag their feet, and yet by participating still to remain members of their social group. In general, girls show an earlier interest in promoting these games than do boys. The greater physiological maturity of the girls and the

[33] B. Sutton-Smith, "A Formal Analysis of Game Meaning," *Western Folklore,* XVIII (Jan., 1959), 13–24.

greater cultural interest of women in romance is probably sufficient explanation for this. This earlier interest is demonstrated in the figures from the high school sample. The average number of games checked per child for the 5th, 6th and 7th grades was; boys: 2.9 and girls: 2.7. For the 8th and 9th grades; boys: 2.7 and girls: 6.6. For the 10th, 11th and 12th grades; boys: 7.1 and girls: 6.6. In sum, girls showed a marked increase in checking these games at the age of 13. Boys did not show an equivalent increase until the age of 15. These ages parallel closely the average ages for the onset of puberty. Total figures for likes and dislikes by boys and girls show that while girls check an average of five games, boys check only four. However, there is no significant tendency for girls to like these games more than boys do. Both sexes show approximately the same ratio of likes to dislikes (2:1).

In the group III stage there are girl informants who talk of getting together after the party to discuss which of the boys were the best kissers. But also reports in which boys were said to favor the more advanced games of Group III while the girls were trying to stay with the more guarded Group II games and thought of games such as "Flashlight" and "Endurance Kissing" as "quite disgusting." These differences are, however, simply further evidences of the varying levels of maturity and perhaps varieties of moral attitude involved. The important question to be asked of the games of the Group III stage, is why, if the couples are chosen, should there be any need for games? And in some reports indeed it was mentioned that parties would break up early so that each couple could go off on its own way for sometime before the required hour of arrival at home. However, when couples of sixteen, seventeen and eighteen years are not able to go off on their own, or have a social reason for staying together such as a birthday party, it is not unnatural that they develop these group games of unabashed indulgence. Once again, of course, there will be less-mature children present who are happier holding the flashlight than cuddling in the corners of the room. Or, perhaps more important, there will still be children who prefer the relatively public nature of these games to the face-to-face intimacy of being alone with their date. Paradoxically as it may seem the public and funful nature of "Flashlight" and "Endurance Kissing" may be less anxiety provoking for some than the total and serious intimacy of necking in private. Just as "Spin the Bottle" provides a defense against the responsibility of choice, so "Flashlight" provides a *defense against the possibility of intimacy* which is, according to dynamic theory, quite a hurdle for the maturing child.[34] This is to say again that these games, like the

[34] E. H. Erikson, *Childhood and Society* (New York, 1950), p. 229.

others serve a bridge function. They provide a guarantee of certain gratifications, in this case relationship with the opposite sex, but they place limitations upon excess. One may enjoy a kissing relationship, but be protected from a more total and intimate commitment. The uncertainty of what "might " happen is removed by the structure of the game. It may, for example, be safer to "perdiddle" all the way home than to venture into the other unknown possibilities of an immature relationship.

Here then are a number of psychological reasons why the kissing games have not decreased as have so many other games but have prospered in the freer society of the young and immature.

SUMMARY[35]

This article describes approximately fifty kissing games collected from between three and four hundred persons. The games are categorized into the three classes of chasing-kiss, mixing-kiss and couple-kiss games. Various modes of play are described. It is shown that the kissing games of today are related historically to forfeit and amusement games, and that they have taken the place of the older marriage and courting games. It is suggested that they have prospered and developed in the modern world because they are appropriate to the parlor settings in middle and upper-middle-class homes, and because they satisfy the desire of adolescents for increasing heterosexual experience, but at the same time safeguard them against too open a commitment to, or too much intimacy with, the other sex. Thus these historically derived forms are changed and sustained by particular sociological and psychological circumstances of the present day.

[35] I wish to acknowledge the assistance of David W. Smith in collecting the high school sample and Judy Trumbell in preparing the manuscript.

Children's Games — Selected References

PART I

General References About Children's Games

Baggally, W. "A Note on a Child's Game," *International Journal of Psychoanalysis*, **28**, 1947, pp. 198–201.

Bett, H. *The Games of Children: Their Origin and History*, London: Methuen and Co., 1929.

Bolton, H. O. *The Counting-Out Rhymes of Children; Their Antiquity, Origin, and Wide Distribution*, London, 1888.

Brewster, P. G. "Some Unusual Forms of Hopscotch," *Southern Folklore Quarterly*, Gainesville, Florida, **9**, 1945, pp. 229–231.

Brewster, P. G. "Priority and Exemption in Children's Games," *Volksunde*, **58** (1), 1957, pp. 21–30.

Conn, J. H. "Children's Awareness of Sex Differences: Play Attitudes and Game Preferences," *Journal of Child Psychiatry*, **2**, 1951, pp. 82–99.

Cramer, M. W. "Leisure Activities of Privileged Children," *Sociology and Social Research*, **34**, 1950, pp. 440–450.

Crombie, J. W. "History of the Game of Hop Scotch," *Journal of the Royal Anthropological Institute*, London, **10**, 1886, pp. 403–408.

Daiken, L *Children's Games Throughout The Year*, London: B. T. Batsford, 1949.

Evans, P. H. *Rimbles: A Book of Children's Classic Games*, New York: Doubleday and Company, 1961.

Fletcher, H. *Study of Children's Games*, Buffalo, N.Y.: School of Pedagogy, 1896.

Ford, R. *Children's Rhymes, Games, and Songs*, Paisley: Alex Gardner, 1904.

Gomme, A. B. and Scarp, C. J. *Children's Singing Games*, London: Novello and Co., Ltd., 1909.

Gullen, F. D. *Traditional Number Rhymes and Games*, London: University of London Press, 1950.

Gump, P. V. and Sutton-Smith, B. "The 'It' Role in Children's Games," *The Group*, **17**, 1955, pp. 3–8.

Hofer, M. R. "Singing Games and Their Sources," *Kindergarten Magazine*, New York, **12** (9–10), 1901, pp. 449–471.

Holdbrook, E. *Children's Games*, Bedford, England: Gordon Frazer, 1957.

La Porte, W. P. *Handbook of Games and Programs For Children*, New York: Abingdon Press, 1920.

Martin, R. A. "Babies Rattles from 2600 B.C., and other Toys," *Field Museum News*, Chicago, **8** (8), 1937, p. 5.

Monroe, W. S. "Counting Out Rhymes of Children," *American Anthropologist*, **6** (1), 1904, pp. 46–50.

Piaget, J. *Play, Dreams and Imitations in Childhood*, New York: Norton and Company, 1952.

Phillips, R. H. "The Nature and Function of Children's Formal Games," *Psychoanalytic Quarterly*, **29**, 1960, pp. 200–207.

Portmann, P. *Brueghel's Children's Games*, Berne: Hallwag, Ltd., 1964.

Powell, R. B. *Scouting Games*, London: C. A. Pearson, 1910.

Redl, F. "The Impact of Game Ingredients on Children's Play Behavior," *Transactions of the Fourth Conference on Group Processes*, New York: Josiah Macy, Jr. Foundation, 1959, pp. 33–81.

Roberts, J. M., and Sutton-Smith, B. "Child Training and Game Involvement," *Ethnology*, **1** (2), 1962, pp. 166–185; Reprinted in the *Bobbs-Merrill Series in Social Science*, 1966.

Smith, L. R. *Sixty Musical Games and Recreations For Little Musicians*, New York: C. H. Ditson, and Comp., 1914.

Sutton-Smith, B. "Cross-Cultural Study of Children's Games," *American Philosophical Society Yearbook*, 1961, pp. 426–429.

Sutton-Smith, B. "Some Comments on the Class Diffusion of Children's Lore," *Midwest Folklore*, **9**, 1959, pp. 225–228.

Wells, H. G. *Floor Games*, Boston: Small, Maynard and Company, 1912.

PART II

Children's Games in Specific Cultures

Aufenanger, H. "A Children's Arrow-thrower in the Central Highlands of New Guinea," *Anthropos*, Freiburg, 56, 1961, p. 633.

Aufenanger, H. "Children's Games and Entertainments among The Kumngo Tribe in Central New Guinea," *Anthropos*, Freiburg, 53, 1958, pp. 575–584.

Babcock, W. H. "Games of Washington, D.C. Children," *American Anthropologist*, 1 (2), 1888, pp. 243–284.

Barton, F. R. "Children's Games in British New Guinea," *Journal of the Royal Anthropological Institute*, London, 38, 1908, pp. 259–279.

Berndt, R. "Some Aboriginal Children's Games," *Mankind*, Sidney, 2, 1940, pp. 289–293.

Best, E. "Pastimes of Maori Children," *New Zealand Journal of Science and Technology*, Wellington, 5 (5), 1922, p. 254.

Brewster, P. G. *Children's Games and Rhymes: Frank C. Brown Collection of North Carolina Folklore*, 1 (4), Durham: University Press, 1953.

Brewster, P. G. "Johnny On The Pony: A New York State Game," *New York Folklore Quarterly*, 1, 1945, pp. 239–240.

Browne, R. B. "Southern California Jump-rope Rhymes: A Study in Variants," *Western Folklore*, Berkeley, California, 14, 1955, pp. 3–22.

Chase, J. H. "Street Games of New York," *Pedagogical Seminary*, 12, 1905, pp. 503–504.

Culin, S. "Street Games of Boys of Brooklyn," *Journal of American Folklore*, 4, 1891, pp. 221–237.

Dorsey, J. O. "Games of Teton Dakota Children," *American Anthropoligist*, 4 (4), 1891, pp. 329–345.

Douglas, N. *London Street Games*, London: The St. Catherine Press, 1916; 2nd Edition, London: Chatto and Windus, 1931.

Dunne, R. *Games of City Street Boys*, London: 1904.

Gilmore, M. R. "Some Games of Arikara Children," *Indian Notes*, New York, 3, 1925, pp. 9–12.

Gomme, A. B. *Traditional Games of England, Scotland and Ireland*, 2 Volumes, London: Nutt, 1894 and 1898; Reprinted, New York: Dover Publications, Inc., 1964.

Goodman, S. "Good Friday Skipping: Games Played at Burials," *Folklore*, London, 67 (3), 1956, pp. 171–174.

Haddon, A. C. "Notes on Children's Games in British New Guinea," *Journal of the Royal Anthropological Institute,* **38**, 1908, p. 294.

Headland, I. T. *Chinese Children's Games,* London: Revell, 1906.

Howard, D. "Australian Hopscotch," *Western Folklore,* Berkeley, California, **17** (3), 1958, pp. 163–175.

Howard, D. "Marble Games of Australian Children," *Folklore,* London, **71**, 1960, pp. 165–179.

Howard, D. "Ball Bouncing Customs and Rhymes in Australia," *Midwest Folklore,* **9** (2), 1959, pp. 77–87.

Howard, D. "The Toodlembuck-Australian Children's Gambling Device and Game," *Journal of American Folklore,* **73** (287), 1960, pp. 53–63.

Im Thurn, E. F. "Indian Children's Games," *Timehri,* Demerara, **3**, 1884, pp. 147–148.

Islos, G. L. "Children's Games," *Mexican Folkways,* Mexico City, **7** (2), 1932, pp. 63–74.

Jackson, E. "Native Toys of the Guarayur Indians (Eastern Venezuela)," *American Anthropologist,* **66** (5), 1964, pp. 1153–1155.

La Cruz, B. A. "Aklan Superstitions About Toys," *Philippine Magazine,* Manila, **30**, 1933, p. 30.

Lambert, H. E. "A Note on Children's Pastimes in Kenya," *Swahili,* Arush, **30**, 1959, pp. 74–78.

Leakey, L. S. B. "A Children's Game, West Australia and Kenya," *Man,* London, **38**, 1938, p. 178.

Milojkovic-Djuric, J. "The Jugoslav Children's Game 'Most', and Some Scandinavian Parallels," *Southern Folklore Quarterly,* Gainesville, Florida, **24** (3), 1960, pp. 226–234.

Mishra, D. "Recreation of Baiga Children," *Vanyajati,* Delhi, **6** (2), 1958, pp. 70–73.

Mistry, D. "The Indian Child and His Play," Parts I & II, *Sociology Bulletin,* Bombay, **8** (1), 1959, pp. 86–96; **9** (2), 1960, pp. 48–55.

Newell, W. W. *Games and Songs of American Children,* New York: Harper Brothers, 1883; Reprinted, New York: Dover Publications, Inc., 1963.

Proudfoot, B. F. "An Edinburgh Street Game," *Ulster Folklife,* **3** (1), 1957, pp. 74–75.

Pukui, M. K. "Games of My Hawaiian Childhood," *Western Folklore Quarterly,* Berkeley, California, **2**, 1943, pp. 205–220.

Ramson, J. E. "Children's Games Among the Aluet," *Journal of American Folklore,* **59**, 1946, pp. 196–198.

Roheim, G. "Children's Games and Rhymes in Duau (Normandy Island, N.G.)," *American Anthropologist.* **45**, 1943, pp. 99–119.

Stearns, R. E. "On The Nishinam Game of 'Ha' and the Boston Game of 'Props'," *American Anthropologist*, **3** (4), 1890, pp. 353–358.

Sutton-Smith, B. "The Fate of English Traditional Games in New Zealand," *Western Folklore*, Berkeley, California, **11**, 1953, pp. 250–253.

Sutton-Smith, B. *The Games of New Zealand Children*, Folklore Studies #12, Los Angeles: University of California Press, 1959.

Sutton-Smith, B. "The Game Rhymes of New Zealand Children," *Western Folklore*, Berkeley, **12**, 1953, pp. 411–423.

Sutton-Smith, B. "The Kissing Game of Adolescents in Ohio," *Midwest Folklore*, **9**, 1959, pp. 189–211.

Sutton-Smith, B. "The Meeting of Maori and European Cultures and Its Effect upon the Unorganized Game of Maori Children," *Journal of the Polynesian Society*, Wellington, **60**, 1953, pp. 93–107.

Sutton-Smith, B. "Sixty Years of Historical Change in The Game Preferences of American Children," *Journal of American Folklore*, **74**, 1961, pp. 17–46.

Sutton-Smith, B. "The Traditional Games of New Zealand Children," *Folklore*, London, **12**, 1953, pp. 411–423.

Watson, W. "The Street Games and Rhymes of Scottish Children," *Folklore*, London, 1953.

Watt, W. "Some Children's Games from Tanna, New Hebrides," *Mankind*, Sidney, **3**, 1946, pp. 261–264.

PART III

Games with Music

Aberle, D. F. "Mythology of the Navaho Game Stick-Dance," *Journal of American Folklore*, **55**, 1942, pp. 144–154.

Beal, N. *Pygmies are People: Their Folkways, Their Songs, Their Games, Their Dances*, New York: Van Roy Company, 1964.

Brewster, P. G. "Game-songs from Southern Indiana," *Journal of American Folklore*, **49**, 1939, pp. 243–262.

Browne, B. W. "The Buzzard in the Folklore of Western Kentucky (Negro Folklore: Sayings, Games, Dances)," *Kentucky Folklore Record*, **4**, 1958, pp. 11–12.

Fletcher, A. C. *Indian Games and Dances*, Boston: C. C. Birchard & Co., 1915.

Gomme, A. B. *Old English Singing Games*, London: G. Allen, 1898.

Hall, J. "Some Party Games of the Great Smoky Mountains," *Journal of American Folklore*, 54, 1941, pp. 68–71.

Hofer, M. R. "Singing Games and Their Sources," *Kindergarten Magazine*, New York, 12, 1901, pp. 449–471.

Lesser, A. *The Pawnee Ghost Dance Hand Game*, Columbia University Contributions to Anthropology, New York: Columbia University Press, 16, 1933.

Newell, W. W. *Games and Songs of American Children*, New York: Harper and Brothers, 1883; Reprinted: New York, Dover Publications, 1963.

Newell, W. W. "Notes on the Interpretation of European Song-games," *Boas Anniversary Volume*, 1906, pp. 404–409.

Payne, L. W. "Finding List for Texas Play-party Songs," *Folklore Society of Texas*, Austin, 1, 1916, pp. 35–38.

Randolph, V. "The Ozark Play Party," *Journal of American Folklore*, 43, 1929, pp. 201–232.

Roeder, A. E. *Folksongs and Games of Holland*, New York: G. Schirmer, 1956.

Wolford, L. J. *The Play Party in Indiania*, Indianapolis: Historical Society Publications, 20 (2), 1959, pp. 103–326.

PART IV

Games with String

Anderson, J. C. "Maori String Game," *New Zealand Journal of Science and Technology*, Wellington, N.Z., 3, 1920, pp. 81–208; 4, 1921, pp. 145–154; 6, 1924, pp. 289–309; 8 (3), 1926, pp. 173–188; 8 (4), 1926, pp. 53–57.

Boas, F. "The Game of Cat's Cradle," *International Archiv für Ethnographie*, Leiden, 1, 1888, pp. 538–539.

Brewster, P. G. "Some String Tricks from the United States," *Rivista de Ethnografia*, Naples, 7 (4), 1953, pp. 1–12.

Brewster, P. G. "Two Unusual String Figures from the United States," *Der Forschungsdienst*, Folge 6, Band I, 1953.

Davidson, D. S. "Some String Figures of the Virginia Islands," *Indian Notes*, New York, 4, 1927, pp. 384–395.

Emerson, J. S. "Hawaiian String Games," *Folklore*, Poughkeepsie, N.Y. (Vassar College), 5, 1924, p. 18.

Haddon, A. C. "A Few American String Figures and Tricks," *American Anthropologist*, 5 (2), 1903, pp. 213–223.

Haddon, K. "Some Australian String Figures," *Proceedings of Royal Society of Victoria*, 30, 1917–1918 pp. 121–136.

Hrabalova, O. and Brewster, P. G. "A Czechoslovak Cat's Cradle Series," *Checkoslovakian Ethnography*, Praha, 5, 1957, pp. 176–183.

Leeming, J. *Fun With String: A Collection of String Games*, New York: Frederick Stokes and Company, 1940.

McCarthy, F. D. "The String Figures of Yirrkalla," *Records of the American-Australian Expedition to Arnhem Land*, (C.P. Mountford, ed.), 2, 1960, pp. 415–512.

Maude, H. C. "String Figures from the Gilbert Islands," *Polynesian Society Memoirs*, Wellington, N.Z., 13, 1958, pp. 1–161.

Mountford, C. P. "String Figures of the Adnyamatana Tribe," *Mankind*, 5 (4), 1950, pp. 183–189.

Patterson, T. "Greenland Eskimos Produce the Most Remarkable String Figures in the World," *Geographical Journal*, London, 92, 1938, pp. 419–421.

Sayne, C. F. *String Figures and How To Make Them*, New York: Dover Publishers, 1962.

CHAPTER 5

GENERAL SOURCES

Not all those interested in the theoretical origins of games worked within the confines of late nineteenth century anthropological or folklorist thinking—even though many of their assumptions were often of a similar character.

We can present here only a scattering of the scholars within the historical, literary, and recreation fields who have presented their views on the origins of games. Some, for example, have been of the opinion that games evolved from activities that originally had a variety of purposes related to human physical survival. Erman, a German historian, explained it in this manner:

As a nation advances toward the higher stages of civilization, there are many pursuits which, though no longer necessary . . . for maintenance of life, do not . . . fall into oblivion. Though exercised more rarely, they appear to give purer pleasure than before, and with the absence of constraint, the hard work of former ages becomes a delight and a sport. . . . Similar instances are to be found in the history of all people and all ages. It stands to reason however, that these old crafts could only be exercised later by those who cared little what they gained by them.[1]

A dart game would be a contemporary example, as would a horse race, some table games, drag-strip and surfboard racing.

Eyler, after a study of the origins of 95 contemporary sports, contends that about half evolved into recreative activities from activities that were

[1] Erman, A. *Life in Ancient Egypt* Chapter 2, "Recreation." London: Macmillan, 1894, p. 234.

used to earn a living, used for communication, used for transportation, or used in warfare. Of the balance, he reports only ten percent have evolved from religious ceremonies, in contrast to fifteen percent invented for recreative purposes. He indicates that additional research will be needed to determine the origins of the remaining twenty-five percent. There is the suggestion here that games that are sports were more likely to have a nonreligious origin than other types of games, for example, children's games and table games.

Others have attempted to delve into the question of origins by looking at interrelationships *within* the different types of games themselves. Most of this writing, though quite speculative, is not without interest because of the issues it raises. Wykes, for example writing on gambling games says:

Most games are contests of one sort or another, and almost certainly the first kind of game to be played was a contest of strength, in which one man could prove his physical superiority over his opponent. Contests of skill—such as games in which targets are involved—presumably came later. . . . Unskilled players probably developed games that simulated games of skill, but in which luck rather than ability decided the winner. Instead of aiming a stone or spear at a target, the early gamesters might have flung the stone—or shell or bone— into the air, so that chance could decide its position on reaching the ground. Dice would be a logical development from stones, shells, or bones. . . . Contests of speed, or races, probably appeared at the same time as contests of strength; and the simulation of racing brought about such games as *backgammon*. Backgammon is the oldest known game of chance simulating racing; variations of it crop up in every known civilization.[2]

Murray, the British historian of board games, writes in a similar vein. In 1913 he published his monumental *A History of Chess*. In 1952 he published the sequel, *History of Board-Games Other Than Chess*. In this latter publication, drawing on numerous sources and years of research, he presented this theory of the origin of games:

If we want to find out how . . . games originated, we must go back at least to the beginnings of a civilization . . . all that primitive man needs for play is the opportunity . . . The opportunity can only occur when he has time to spare in his waking hours . . . when the daily needs of his family are met, man's initiate urge to be doing something still impels him to action, if only to the handling of objects at hand, whether natural

[2] Wykes, A. *Gambling*. London: Aldus Books Ltd., 1964, p. 30.

like pebbles, or some of his household goods of his own making, at first aimlessly, but as soon as his attention is held, to explore their capabilities for new uses. I suggest that it was in this way that the habit of using objects at hand as playthings, and so as materials for games. . . .

Man is naturally gregarious, and learnt early to combine with his fellows for attack and defense against enemies, for the hunt for food, and for the cultivation of the soil. So much of his life must have been spent in common action with his neighbors, that it must have been a natural consequence for him to share his leisure hours with his fellows and to find both recreation and amusement in playing with them. In this way, I believe that . . . games originated.[3]

In contrast to these views and those presented in the previous chapters, J. Huizinga, writing in *Homo Ludens: A study of the play element in culture*, presents the thesis that play did not originate in various other aspects of culture or by accident, but was itself a mainspring of many cultural forms:

When speaking of the play element in culture we do not mean that among the various activities of civilized life an important place is reserved for play, nor do we mean that civilization has arisen out of play by some evolutionary process, in the sense that something which was originally play passed into something which was no longer play and could henceforth be called culture. The view we take in the following pages is that culture arises in the form of play, that it is played from the beginning.[4]

This is a crucial statement because it implies that most of the previous statements on the origins of games are based on the typical premise of our civilization that work and play are quite distinct, whereas Huizinga is saying on the contrary that they are not. It is not that games are the relics of earlier culture, or the residues of other activities, but rather that play's formal qualities interpenetrate all our activities. Huizinga says

Play is a voluntary activity or occupation executed within certain fixed limits of time and place, according to rules freely accepted, absolutely binding, having its aim in itself and accompanied by a feeling of tension, joy and the consciousness that it is different from ordinary life.[5]

[3] Murray, H. J. R. *History of Board Games Other than Chess*. London: Oxford University Press, 1952, pp. 235–238.

[4] Huizinga, J. *Homo Ludens: A Study of the Play Element in Culture*. London: Routledge, 1949, p. 46.

[5] *Ibid.*, p. 28.

And yet, as he also shows, these same formal ludic qualities are to be found in our language habits, our law, war, philosophy, poetry, and art —in fact throughout all civilization. In short, work and play are not as easily separated as the traditional images of the hard worker in the fields, and the dilettante at the tennis court might lead us to suppose. As Darwin destroyed the dualism of man and animal, and Freud destroyed the dualism of rational and irrational, Huizinga destroys yet another reductive dualism that has also been a part of the origins of modern science and modern philosophy in Western Civilization; a dualism that, in the case of games, has led to the notion that play was somehow a trivial expression of more consequential antecedents such as work, rituals, religion, or important historical events. The best current, if essayistic, documentation of this interpenetration of play and work is to be found in the writings of Erving Goffman such as *Encounters: Two Studies in the Sociology of Interaction*,[6] which includes a section entitled "Fun in Games," and *Interaction Ritual: Essays on Face to Face Behavior*,[7] which has a chapter entitled "Where the Action Is," illustrative of the difficulties in maintaining the traditional dualism of play and work. From this work it follows that games have no origins that are not immediately apparent in the forms of our contemporary life. If games appear to have been more involved with ritual, religion, or other cultural phenomena in earlier societies, this is in part a matter of our selective reading of history, and in part due to the fact that in most preliterate cultures there is more interpenetration of cultural forms.

Thus it appears that the interpenetration of cultural forms in preliterate societies was originally used by anthropologists and folklorists to reduce game forms (as historical residues) to the "serious" customs with which they were originally associated. Huizinga, Goffman, and others indicate that the same interpenetration and association still exists, but the "serious" customs can be reduced to the forms of play. Caillois sums up the alternative in the following adroit way:

To explain games as derived from laws, customs, and liturgies, or in reverse to explain jurisprudence, liturgy and the rules for strategy, syllogisms or esthetics as a derivation of play, are complementary, equally fruitful operations provided they are not regarded as mutually exclusive. The structures of play and reality are often identical but the respective

[6] Goffman, E. *Encounters: Two Studies in the Sociology of Interaction*. Indiana: Bobbs-Merrill, 1961.

[7] Goffman, E. *Interaction Ritual: Essays on Face to Face Behavior*. New York: Anchor, 1967.

activities that they subsume are not reducible to each other in time or place. They always take place in domains that are incompatible.[8]

We complete this section on "origins" therefore, with the notion that work and play are separate cultural domains (though each can be viewed in terms of the other), and add as a final subtlety, that the "separation" may not be as naively given as Caillois suggests, but like the thinking of Tylor or Huizinga, is equally a product of the conceptual systems with which we approach our study in the first place.

In this chapter we include a bibliography of selected references in languages other than English to offer the reader some notion of the types of approaches used throughout the world in search of game origins.

[8] Caillois, R. *Man, Play, and Games.* New York: The Free Press of Glencoe Inc., 1961, p. 64.

Selected References On Games In Languages Other Than English 1955-1965

PART I

General

Caillois, R. "For a Broader Theory of Games" (Para una Teoria Ampliada de los Juegos), *Revista de la Universidad de Buenos Aires*, Buenos Aires, **2** (3), July–Sept. 1957, pp. 350–357.

Caillois, R. "Games and Civilizations" (Jogos e Civilizações), *Anhembi*, São Paulo, **28** (83), Oct. 1957, pp. 229–243; **28** (84), Nov. 1957, pp. 451–461.

Caillois, R. "Structure and Classification of Games" (Estructura e Classificação dos Jogos), *Anhembi*, São Paulo, **24** (72), Nov. 1956, pp. 446–459.

Dorrer, A. "Cult and Games in Flood and Tide" (Kult und Spiele in Fluss und Slauung), *Zeitschrift für Volkskunde*, Stuttgart, **53**, 1956–1957, pp. 91–117.

López Ibor, J. J. "Anthropological Significance of Game" (Significación Antropológica del Juego), *Cuadernos Hispanoamericanos*, Madrid, **30** (94), Oct. 1957, pp. 13–25.

Picaud, A. "Ethnology of Popular Games" (Ethnologie des Jeux Populaires), *Bulliten Societé Dauphinoise d'Ethnologie et d'Anthropologie*, **8**, 1953, pp. 331–352.

PART II

Games of Specific Cultures

Annaev, K., G. Balakaev and K. Mommyev. *Turkmenian National Games* (Turkmenskie Nacional'nye Igry). *Sojuz Sportivnyh Obščestv i Organizacij Tuŕkmenskoj SSR*, Ashabad, 1962, 124 pp.

Breda, E. A. *Games and Amusements among the Indians of the Rio de la Plata* (Juegos y Deportes entre los Indios del Rio de la Plata). Ed. Theoria, Buenos Aires, 1962, 34 pp.

Griffith, W. J. "Jillawol and Dare—Fulani Game", *Nigerian Field*, Lagos, **21** (3), 1956, pp. 122–124.

Hummel, S. "The Tibetan 'Kungser' Game" (Das Tibetische Kungser-spiel), *Acta Ethnographica*, Budapest, **7** (1–2), 1958, pp. 219–221.

Ittmann, J. "Games of the Kosi in the Cameroons" (Spiele der Kosi in Kamerun), *Afrika und Übersee*, Berlin, **45** (1–2), 1961, pp. 123–158.

Ittmann, J. "Games of the Tribes Around Ambas Bay" (Spiele der Stämme Rings um die Ambasbucht), *Afrika und Übersee*, Berlin, **43** (1), 1959, pp. 37–68.

Kähler-Meyer, E. "Games of the Bali in the Cameroons" (Spiele bei den Bali in Kamerun), *Afrika und Übersee*, Berlin, **39** (4), 1955, pp. 179–190.

Kauffmann, H. E. and L. G. Löffler. "Games of the Marma. Chittagong Hill Tracts, East Pakistan" (Spiele der Marma. Chittagong Hill Tracts, Ost-Pakistan), *Zeitschrift für Ethnologie*, Braunschweig, **84** (2), 1959, pp. 238–253.

Kolpakova, N. P. "Russian Popular Game-Song" (Russkaja Narodnaja Igrovaja Pesnja), *Russkij Fol'klor*, Moscow **3**, 1958, pp. 69–91.

Kuret, N. "The Game Skarjice Brusiti in the Slovenian Territory" (Igra Škarjice Brusiti' na Slovenskem Ozemlju), *Slovenski Ethnograf*, Ljublana, **8**, 1955, pp. 259–260.

Lebédinskij, L. N. *Bashkir Folk Songs and Games* (Baškirskie Narodnye Pesni i Naigryši), Moscow, Muzyka, 1965, 245 pp.

Leont'ev, V. "National Games of the Chukchi" (Nacional'nye Igry Čukčej), *Na Severe Dal'nem SSSR*, 1, 1960, pp. 127–137.

Masüger, J. B. "Common Features in Ancient Movement Games of Northern Europe and Switzerland" (Über Gemeinsames in Alten Bewegungsspielen Nordeuropas und der Schweiz), *Schweizerisches Archiv für Volkskunde*, Basel, **55** (4), 1959, pp. 258–278.

Melo, V. de. *Popular Games in Brazil* (Jogos Populares do Brasil), Porto, Douro Litoral, 1956, 66 pp.

Melo, V. de. "Popular Games in Brazil" (Jogos Populares do Brasil), *Revista do Arquivo Municipal*, São Paulo, **162**, 1959, pp. 335–382.

Molnár, I. "Aubade with a Flag—a Popular Easter Sprinkling Game at Tordatfalva" (Zászlos Hajnalozo' öntözö Husvéti Népi Játék Tordátfalván), *Néprajzi Közlemények*, Budapest, **7** (1), 1962, pp. 3–17.

Németh, J. "Turkish Balassa Texts in Karagöz Games" (Türkische Balassa-Texte in Karagöz-Spielen), *Acta Orientalia*, Budapest, **5** (3), 1955, pp. 175–180.

Obradović, M. "Folk Games of the Region of Srebrenica, Vlasenica, and Zenica" (Društvene Igre iz Okoline Srebrenice, Vlasenice, i Zenice), *Glasnik Zemaljskog Muzeja u Sarajevu Etnologià*, **13**, 1958, pp. 183–191.

Petraschk, M. "Shepherds Houses and Shadow-Games from Sebnitz" (Sebnitzer Hirtenhäuser und Schattenspiele), *Sächsische Heimatblätter*, Dresden, **9** (6), 1963, pp. 528–533.

Poliscuk, N. S. "On Some New Aspects of Collective Leisure Time Activities of the Miner and Metallurgists of Nižnij Tagil" (O Nekotoryh Novyh Čertah Kellektivnogo Otdyha Gornjakov i Metallurgov Nižnego Tagila), *Sovetskaja Etnografija*, Moscow, (4), July–Aug. 1963, pp. 35–45.

Ragimov, E. T. "Azerbaijan Folk Games and Leisure Time Activities" (Narodnye Azerbajdžanskie Igry i Razvlečenija), *Sbornik Naučno—Teoreticeskih Metodiceskih Trudov. Azerbajdzanskij Institut Fiziceskoj Kul'tury*, Baku, **2**, 1959, pp. 74–77.

Sabbatucci, D. "Ritual Hazard Game" (Gioco d'Azzardo Rituale), *Studi e Materiali di Storia delle Religioni*, Rome, **35** (1–2), 1964, pp. 23–86.

Seeberger, M. "Adult Games in Lötschen" (Erwachsenenspiele in Lötschen), *Schweirerisches Arch. für Verkehrswissenschaft und Verkehrspolitik*, Zürich, **52** (1), 1956, pp. 35–48.

Sieber, S. "Christmas Games of Miners of the Erzgebirge" (Weihnachtsspiele Erzgebirgischer Bergleüte), *Anschnitt*, Essen, **13** (6), 1961, pp. 9–13.

Slawik, A. "The Snail and the Spiral in Japanese Children's Games" (Schnecke und Spirale in Japanischen Kinderspielen), *Beiträge zur Namenforschung*, Vienna, **1** (2), 1955, pp. 113–116.

Tugutov, I. E. "Social Games of the Buryat" (Obščestvennye Igry Burjat), *Etnografičeskij Sbornik Burjatskij Komleksnyi Naučno—Issledovatel' nyj Institut, SSSR*, (2), 1961, pp. 43–65.

Veiga De Oliveira, E. "Toupiolegame in Portugal" (O Jeu de Toupiole em Portugal), *Trabalhos de Antropologica e Etnologia*, Porto, **15** (1–2), 1954, pp. 110–115.

Zazoff, P. "Ephersmos. An Ancient Greek Game" (Ephersmos. Ein Altgriechisches Spiel), *Antike und Abendland,* Hamburg, **11**, 1962, pp. 35–42.

PART III

Children's Games

Arbat, Ju. "Kargopolsky Toys" (Kargopolskie Igruški), *Dekorativnoe Iskusstvo SSSR,* Moscow, **6**, 1959, pp. 31–33.

Barlen-Ebert, S. "May Song Proclamation and Youth Games in a Locality in the Aachen Region" (Mailiedausrufen und Jungenspiel in einem Ort des Aachener Raumes), *Hessische Blätter für Volkskunde,* Giessen, **51–52** (1), 1960, pp. 5–28.

Böhmer, E. "With Tiny Stones and Tiny Bones. A Children's Game and its Culture-Historical Signification" (Mit Steinerlein und Beinerlein'. Ein Kinderspiel und seine Kultur-Geschichtliche Bedeutung), *Beiträge zur Heimatkunde der Stadt Schwelm und ihrer Umgebung,* Schwelm, **14**, 1964, pp. 46–49.

Castro, P. R. de A. *Catalonian Customs—Children's Games* (Costumes da Catalhuna Jogos Infantis). Porto, Sep. Douro Litoral, 1965, 5 pp.

Casullo, F. H. "Children's Folklore. Bull-Fighting in Children's Games" (El Folklore de los Niños. Los Sorteos en los Juegos Infantiles), *Revista de Educación,* Huancayo, **1** (4), Apr. 1965, pp. 256–261.

Červenák, J. "Children's Games of Lisov" (Detské Hry z Lišova), *Slovenský Národopis,* Bratislava, **5** (1), 1957, pp. 87–96.

Corrain, C. "The Ethnographic Importance of Boy's Games. Data from Observations in the Venetian Plain" (L'Interesse Etnografico di Alcuni Giochi dei Fanciulli. Dati Desunti da Osservazioni Nella Pianura Veneta), *Archivio per L'Antropologia e la Etnologia,* Firenze, **87**, 1957, pp. 133–158.

Endrei, W. "The Origin of Two Toys" (Kétgyermekjáték Eredetéröl), *Ethnográfia,* Budapest, **68** (3), 1957, pp. 521–525.

Fritzsch, K. E. "Books Containing Patterns of Toys from the Erzgebirge" (Erzgebirgische Spielzeugmusterbücher), *Deutsches Jahrbuch für Volkskunde,* Deutschland, **4** (1), 1958, pp. 91–128.

Gómez, A. "Children's Games in the State of Lara" (Los Juegos Infantiles en el Estado Lara), Archivos Venezolanos de Folklore, Caracas, **3** (4), 1955–1956, pp. 89–136.

Guevara, Castillo L. "The Children's Games in the Community of Cota" (Los Juegos Infantiles en el Municipio de Cota), *Thesaurus,* Bogotà, **12**, 1957, pp. 228–233.

Haiding, K. "Essay on Similarity Between Simple Javanese and European

Children's Games" (Proeve van Overeenkomst Tussen Enkele Javaanse en Europese Kinderspelen), *Volkskunde*, Bruxelles, **55** (2), 1954, pp. 60–71.

Hohlova, E. N. "The Ceramic Toy" (Keramičeskaja Igruška), *Sbornik Trudy*, Moscow, (1), 1962, pp. 125–148.

Il'ina, T. "Artistic Forms of Toys" (Hudožestvenny Obraz v Igruške), *Dekorativnoe Iskusstvo SSSR*, Moscow, **10**, 1958, pp. 8–11.

Krieger, K. "The Hausa Games for Boys" (Knabenspiele der Hausa), *Baessler-Archiv*, Berlin, **23** (3), 1955, pp. 225–232.

Löffller, L. G. "A Children's Game Rhyme of the Marma and its Parallels Among the Mru" (Ein Kinderspielvers der Marma und seine Parallelen Bei Mru), *Zeitschrift für Ethnologie*, Braunschweig, **84** (2), 1959, pp. 254–256.

Melchert, S. "Popular Children's Games and Competitive Exercises in Germany about 1800" (Volkstümliche Kinderspiele und Wettübungen in Deutschland um 1800), *Wissenschafliche Zeitschrift der Friedrich Schiller-Universität Jena. Gesellschafts- und Sprachwissenschaftliche Reihe*, Jena, **14** (1), 1965, pp. 119–124.

Meszáros, I. "King Ladislaus the Pale in Our Popular Children's Games" (Népi Gyermekjátékaink 'Lengyel' László Királya), *Ethnographia*, Budapest, **74**, 1963, pp. 272–278.

Pérez de Castro, J. L. "Game Precedents in the Imaginative Folklore of Children" (Los Precedentes de Juego en el Folklore Infantil Figuerense), *Revista de Dialectologiá y Tradiciones Populares*, Madrid, **12** (4), 1956, pp. 457–488.

Peščereva, E. M. "Toys and Children's Games Among the Tadzhiks and Uzbeks. According to Materials of 1924–1935" (Igruški i Detskie Igry u Tadžikov i Uzbekov. Po Materiálám 1924–1935 g), *Sbornik Muzeja Antropologii i Etnografii. Institut Etnografii Imeni N.N. Mikluho-Maklaja, Moskva,* Leningrad, **17**, 1957, pp. 22–94.

Riedl, A. and R. M. Klier. *Children's Songs, Rhymes and Games in Burgenland* (Lieder, Reime und Spiele der Kinder im Burgenland), Eisenstadt: Burgenländisches Landesmuseum, 1957, 320 pp.

Romero, E. "Traditional Children's Games in Peru" (Juegos Infantiles Tradicionales en el Perú), *Folklore Studies*, Lima, **3** (3), 1955, pp. 94–120.

Sovet Promyslovoj Kooperach RSFSR. *Artistic Crafts and Toys* (Hudožestvennye Promysly i Igruški). Moscow, KOIZ, 1959, 60 pp.

Svobodova-Goldmannová, F. *Sayings and Games of Slovak Children* (Řikadla a Hry Slováckych Děti). Gottawaldow: Krajské Muzeum, 1958, 182 pp.

Uspenskaja, S. "The Russian Popular Toy" (0 Russkoj Narodnoj Igruške), *Dekorativnoe Iskusstvo SSSR*, Moscow, **10**, 1958, pp. 12–16.

Valnickaja, S. "Popular Toys from Iavorov" (Javorovskaja Narodnaja Igruška), *Dekorativnoe Iskusstvo SSSR*, Moscow, 8, 1959, pp. 27–28.

Vysotskaja, O. "A Visit to Toys: on the Materials of the Exhibition of Popular Toys" (V Gostjah u Igruški: Po Materialam Vystavki Narodnoj Igruški), *Iskusstvo Zodčih Uzbekistana*, Taškent, 11, 1959, pp. 28–33.

Watson, W. "Children's Games in a Community of the Eastern Coast of England" (El Juego entre los Niños en una Comunidad de la Costa Oriental de Inglaterra), *Folklore Americano*, Lima, 5 (5), 1957, pp. 169–183.

Zwinge, H. "Children's Games of the Gunantuna in New Britain" (Kinderspiele der Cunantuna auf New Britain), *Anthropos*, Freiburg, 51 (1–2), 1956, pp. 112–128.

PART IV

Sports

Gomes de Freitas, L. G. "Old Time Rural Sportive Games" (Antigos Jogos Děsportivos da Campanha), *Revista do Museo Júlio de Castilhos e Arquivo Histórico de Rio Grande do Sul*, Póto Alegre, 6 (7), 1957, pp. 12–19.

Karasek-Langer, A. "German Heroic Sword Fighting Games on the Northern Slope of the Carpathian Mountains" (Deutsche Herodesund Schwertfechterspiele am Nordrand der Karpaten), *Jahrbuch für Volkskunde der Heimatvertriebenen*, Salzburg, 5, 1959, pp. 190–239.

Körbs, W. "The Origin of Cult and the Early Development of Sports" (Kultische Wurzel und Frühe Entwicklung des Sportes), *Studium Generale*, Berlin, 13 (1), 1960, pp. 11–20.

Kretzenbacher, L. "Knight's Games and Ring Riding in the Southeast of Europe" (Ritterspiele und Ringreiten im Europäischen Südosten), *Festschrift für Balduin Saria zum 70. Geburtstag*, Munich, Oldenburg, 1964, pp. 460–478. Also published in *Südost-Forschung*, 22, 1963, pp. 437–455.

Löffler, L. G. "Ceremonial Ball-Game in the South-East Asian Area" (Das Zeremonielle Ballspiel im Raum Hinterindiens), *Paideuma*, Wiesbaden, 6 (2), Aug. 1955, pp. 86–91.

Lommatzsch, H. "The Fencing Game Combats of Clausthal-Zellerfeld. An Example of the Penetration of North German Urban Customs in the Mining Districts of the Oberharz" (Das Schwertfechterspiel von Clausthal-Zellerfeld. Ein Beispiel für das Eindringen Niederdeutsch-

Städtischen Brauchtums in dem Bergbaugebiete des Oberharzes),
Braunschweigische Heimat, Braunschweig, 48 (2), 1962, pp. 38–45.

Mendner, S. *Ball Games in the Life of the Peoples* (Das Ballspiel im
Leben der Völker). Münster, Aschendorff, 1956, 170 pp.

Načkebija, K. G. *Georgian Folk Games with Horses* (Gruzinskie
Narodnye Konnye Igry). Sabčota Sakartvelo, Tbilisi, 1964, 50 pp.

Ortiz, S. E. "Three Modes of Ball Playing in Colombia" (Tres Modos de
Jugar a la Pelota en Colombia), *Revista Colombiana de Folclor,*
Bogotá, 3 (8), 1963, pp. 79–88.

PART V

Board Games, Playing Cards, and Dice

Israel, H. "Alaskan Board Games from Walrus Teeth" (Alaskische Spiel-
bretter aus Walrosszähnen), *Abhandlungen und Berichte aus dem
Staatüchen Museum für Völkerkunde,* Dresden, 22, 1963, p. 15–24.

"New Contributions to the Age of the Playing Cards" (Neue Beiträge
zum Alter der Spielkarten), *Archiv für Geschichte des Buchwesens,*
Frankfurt am Main, 3 (4–6), 1961, pp. 555–566.

Pahaev, E. Ja. "The Shatra. An Ancient Altaic Table Game" (Šatra.
Starinnaja Altajskij Nastol'naja Igra), Učenye Zapiski (Gorno-Al-
tajskogo Naučno-Issledovatelskogo Instituta) *Istorii, Jazyka i Litera-
tury,* Corno-Altaj, 3, 1960, pp. 145–156.

Riemschneider, M. "Playing Board and Playing-Bag during Antiquity
and the Middle Ages" (Spielbrett und Spielbeuted in Antlike und
Mittlelalter), *Acta Ethnographica,* Budapest, 8 (3–4), 1959, pp. 309–
326.

Rohlfs, G. *An Ancient Game of Knuckle-Bone from the Greek Empire*
(Antikes Knöchelspiel im Einstigen Grossriechenland). Tübingen:
Max Niemeyer Verlag, 1963, 28 pp.

Rohlfs, G. "The Ancient Game of Knuckle-Bones" (L'Antico Giuoco
Degli Astragali), *Lares,* Florence, 30 (1–2), Jan.–June 1964, pp.
1–13.

Rosenfeld, H. "The Age of Playing Cards in Europe and in the East"
(Das Alter der Spielkarten in Europa und im Orient). *Archiv für
Geschichte des Buchwesens,* Frankfort am Main, 2 (7–10), 1960,
pp. 778–786.

Rosenfeld, H. "The Relationship between European Playing Cards and
the Orient and Ancient Chess" (Die Beziehung der Europäischen
Spielkarten zum Orient und zum Ur-schach), *Archiv für Kul-
turgeschichte,* Marburg, 42 (1), 1960, pp. 1–36.

The Usage of Games

T he various usages given games are persuasive evidence both for their lability and for the assumption that they have functional value. Practitioners apparently have long been committed to the usefulness of games, even if scholars and researchers could provide them with no good reason for their confidence. Our survey includes some statements about game usage in recreation, military science, business, education, diagnosis and treatment, social and behavior science.

The evidence suggests that games for recreative purposes are the fountainhead for all other game usage. Games in military science were first based on table games such as chess and playing cards. Games used in business and industry were derived from games used in military science. Both of these approaches were primarily educational and are closely related to games used in educational institutions. Games used in education although rooted in recreative games, have undergone considerable refinement and, like military science and business games, the roots are sometimes difficult to identify. Games used in health-related programs on the other hand have not altered to any extent game structure and content, but utilize recreative games for non-recreative purposes. Finally, games used in the social and behavioral sciences apparently straddle both approaches, sometimes using preexisting games and sometimes using newly invented gamelike structures, game simulations, and so forth.

237

The following chapters offer a brief overview of the history of game usage in each field, a description of current usage with examples of each, some readings when suitable and available for republication, and selected references for the reader who wishes to examine the area in more depth.

CHAPTER **6**

GAMES USED FOR
RECREATIVE PURPOSES

Four major examples may be cited of the use of games for recreative purposes: the body politic and its use of games, professional personnel in the field of recreation and their use of games in organized programs of service to the public, gamblers and athletes who uses games as a source of employment, and entrepreneurs who use games as a marketable product in society.

Phenomenologically, recreation may be considered as a psychic phenomenon that occurs while an individual, of his own volition, engages in *any* activity—that is, when he is both agent and object of his actions, the affirmer and the affirmed of his behavior. Certain activities retained by civilization apparently have no obvious practical value in relation to the maintenance of society, except that there is mutual acknowledgement of the potential of these activities for recreative experience. It is this popular conception that determines when a given activity shall be called a "recreation activity." Traditionally, participation in these activities occurs during "leisure," a period of time when one is not obligated to engage in other acts that are necessary for physical survival. The possession of this period of time presupposes a quality of existence which is unhurried, noncompulsive, and conducive to a recreative experience. In this context, society long ago acknowledged *games* to possess the potential for recreative experience, and thus the body politic primarily equates games with recreation.

It is, of course, impossible to do justice to the subject of games used for recreative purposes in a limited chapter, and therefore we offer some 239 scattered illustrations of the many different ways in which games are used for this purpose—that is, the games the adult plays at home or in a variety of nonprofit and commercial settings; the games children play at home, in school, on the playground, and in community agencies; and the games professional gamblers and athletes play. Furthermore, it is impossible to summarize the fascinating history of even a few very popular games; for example, Murray's *History of Chess* is over 900 pages. Selected references concerning the history of games can be found in Chapter 2, and at the conclusion of this chapter. However, to illustrate the nature of what one is about, when inquiring into the history of an individual game used for recreative purposes, we offer the deck of common playing cards used in games of bridge, poker, or rummy, and limit the illustration to a brief sketch of the history of the picture cards.

Decks of cards were probably introduced into Europe at about the tenth century, but really began to be popular in the fourteenth and fifteenth centuries. The four suits represent the four classes of medieval European society, that is, spades, the nobility; hearts, the clergy; diamonds, the merchants; and clubs, the peasants. Bridge and poker players will recognize this same hierarchical progression in the games they play today. The pictures on the honor cards were taken from stylized portraits of that time. Early decks were not standardized until the late nineteenth century. Often, the early cards were painted by hand and therefore various existing portraits were used as models. The standard king of spades is thought to be King David of biblical fame. He used to be pictured holding a harp, but as standard printing techniques developed, his portrait became even more stylized. For a time Napoleon's portrait was used for the king of spades, as was the Duke of Wellington's. The king of hearts has had a varied career, starting out as Charlemagne, then Constantine the Great, Charles the First of Britain; even a portrait of Victor Hugo was used for a while. However, the universally adopted king of hearts is Charlemagne. The king of diamonds has always been Julius Caesar, and the club king is Alexander the Great.

Queens have had a varied career too. The queen of spades was first a portrait of Pallas Athena. Many people insisted that a pagan goddess was not a suitable consort for King David, and so a likeness of Bathsheba was used at one time, and then Joan of Arc. The Scandinavians preferred one or the other of the Teutonic goddesses. The queen of hearts started out as Helen of Troy, but was switched to St. Helena, (the mother of Constantine the Great). At another time the heart queen was Dido, Juno, Joan of Arc, Elizabeth the First of Britain, Roxane, Rachel of biblical fame, Fausta, and finally the biblical Judith. The queen of diamonds was at first not a real person. A portrait of Penthisilea, the

Queen of the Amazons in Greek mythology was used. The modern queen of diamonds is the biblical Rachel. The queen of clubs was the infamous Lucretia, and then Hecuba, Queen of Troy was used. Eventually card manufacturers settled on an artificial personage whom they called Argine—an anagram of the word Regina.

Jacks have led a less checkered career. The jack of spades has always been Ogier the Dane, or Holger Danske, or Hogier La Danois. He was a legendary character who slew dragons and was constantly restored to youth by his wife, Morgan le Fay, the sister of King Arthur. The jack of hearts was Etienne de Vignoles, a sort of Robin Hood who soldiered under Charles VII of France. An early jack of diamonds was Roland, Charlemagne's nephew, and later the portrait of Hector de Maris, a knight of the round table was used. The jack of clubs was another knight of the round table—none other than Sir Lancelot. To illustrate that card history is still being written, when South Africa broke with the Commonwealth in March, 1961, one of the things they did was to change the symbols used on playing cards—that is, spades became wagon wheels, hearts became powder horns, diamonds became tent pegs, and clubs became shoes.[1]

Dice and other gambling games offer examples that can be traced from very early ancient civilizations. In many societies, because of rigid antigambling laws, people who wished to gamble did so in secret. Today, gambling is legalized in many locales, and governments use lotteries as a source of public income.

Today in affluent societies (and not-so-affluent societies as well), games for recreative purposes continue to receive the same human energies and daily concern that they always have. Children engage in some of the same games Breughel painted a few hundred years ago, in addition to some newer ones, but the pattern does not change much. For example: a terra-cotta figurine from c. 300 B.C. shows two young Greek girls playing a game called "pollax," which involves tossing an object in the air and grasping other small objects from the ground before the tossed object hits the ground. Young children still play this game today, only we call it "Jacks." Adults are attracted to many of the same games of chance and strategy that have been played for over a thousand years. These games in some instances have been modified in relation to current tastes and cultural mores. Many of the sports (games of skill) are modified with regard to mass taste and today's semiprofessional and professional abilities.

With the advent of mass production methods it is no longer necessary

---

[1] Wykes, A. *Gambling*. London: Aldus Books Ltd., 1964, Chapter vii.

for participants to fabricate their own equipment for games; these are now generally available for purchase. Furthermore, the introduction of plastics, metal alloys, and a variety of production and marketing techniques have brought many games within the range of most people's pocketbooks. Increased free time for the housewife at all levels of society has made it possible for more women to engage in the playing of games. It has been observed in the United States, for example, that women from lower socioeconomic classes show a preference for playing a game such as bingo and upper-middle-class women prefer bridge. In a survey of game data in several nationwide polls Sutton-Smith, Roberts, and Kozelka concluded that "In the present study, games of strategy have been shown to be associated with women and higher status, games of chance with women and lower status, and games of physical skill with men and higher status."[2]

A recent study concerning U.S. participation in outdoor games and sports in relation to formal education indicated that:

For the population 25 years or over, playing outdoor games and sports is directly related to number of years of formal schooling, the rate increasing from 0.11 for those with less than 4 years of formal schooling to 4.31 for those who have had 4 years or more of college . . . Golf, tennis, and baseball are the games . . . represented by high participation among the better educated adult population. . . .

Considered by occupation, farm workers have quite low rates . . . while professional, technical, and kindred workers have the highest rate. . . .[3]

Game play in the commercial sphere is big business. For example, personal expenditure for attendance at commercial baseball, football, basketball, and other such events rose from 98 million dollars in 1940 to approximately 301 million dollars in 1963—a threefold increase. There are even larger increases in expenditure for golfing equipment and green fees, and in other commercial games such as bowling and billiards.[4]

Games are of public interest as indicated by daily newspaper columns concerning bridge, chess, baseball, racing, and the like, as well as nightly radio and television reports of game results either from play earlier in the day, or on the spot reporting of, for example, golf games and tennis

[2] Sutton-Smith, B., Roberts, J. M., and Kozelka, R. M. "Game Involvement in Adults," *Journal of Social Psychology*, **60** (1), 1963, p. 21.

[3] Ferris, A. L., et al. "National Recreation Survey," *ORRRC Study Report 19*. Washington, D.C.: United States Government Printing Office, 1962, p. 10.

[4] Goldfield, E. D. *Statistical Abstract of the U. S.* Washington, D.C.: United States Government Printing Office, 1965, pp. 208–209.

matches. Although it is commonplace to see someone reading a periodical concerned with a game, such as golf, chess, and bridge, the "afficinado" can now subscribe to a bimonthly publication that is concerned with table games;

It keeps you up to date on rule changes and new game releases. . . . you get names and addresses of other players and you are entitled to place 'opponents wanted' ads at no charge. . . . Every issue contains contests, tips on strategy, questions and answers columns. . . . Now in its third year. . . .[5]

Another recent innovation is "Games and Public Relations" as evidenced by the presentation of a new game, "Future," to a select list of governmental and industrial leaders in the United States, to commemorate the twentieth anniversary of the Kaiser Aluminum and Chemical Corporation. The game was designed by two Rand Corporation scientists. During the course of play one learns of probable events that might occur in the next twenty years—hence the name of the game. This game was not for sale, but a limited supply was manufactured and sent as a gift to some of the nation's "opinion leaders."[6] In contrast, colleagues report that on recent trips to Africa and Asia one can still find adults crouching in the dust and playing the game of "Mancala" (count and capture) on a makeshift board scratched in the ground. One colleague writes in a letter from Taiwan:

Games are hard to come by here . . . because . . . in the usual tourist stores they are selling books, lacquerware, pottery, etc., *but no games.* I bought two . . . where the residents shop. . . . The best of the two games is one that looks like checkers. There are red on black discs and white on black. I see the men playing this game during their lunch hour on the street corners. . . . I tried to get the board too, but it didn't work. They didn't have any and looked surprised that I wanted one. They explained to me that in the box is a paper, on which the squares are drawn. From the look of the boards the men use, I think they are home made. . . . Also, I've seen some men squatting on the ground playing the game with little stones on a "board" marked out in the dust of the street.[7]

Similar findings were reported fifty years ago by Culin and others, and indicate that culture and habit seem only to influence the form a game

[5] From a brochure issued by the Avalon Hill Games Corporation, 4517 Harford Road, Baltimore, Maryland, 1966, p. 4.

[6] Wright, R. A. "Future at Kaiser—It's A Game," *New York Times,* October 22, 1966, p. 37; and correspondence with the Kaiser Aluminum Corporation.

[7] Personal correspondence with Professor Catherine Nelson, March 13, 1967.

takes. Affluent Lebanese and Iranian businessmen play the same game today as the men in Taiwan do, but their "boards" are carved ivory, and the "counters" are precious stones or coins. During periods of free time in Vietnam, U.S. servicemen bored with poker or dice, are finding some satisfaction in a Vietnamese game called "O-lan," which is a wooden version of this same game. Games that were originally developed for educational purposes, such as "WFF'N PROFF" and "Equations" have also begun to find their way into the lucrative recreation market.

Apart from the use by the public at large, games have been offered for many years under the auspices of a variety of community agencies. The Olympics in modern times is sustained by numerous local community recreation programs throughout the world. There are even "paraolympics" for persons who have physical disability. The aim of these games is:

. . . to unite paralyzed men and women from all parts of the world in an international sports movement, and your spirit of true sportsmanship today will give hope and inspiration to thousands of paralyzed people. No greater contribution can be made to society by the paralyzed than to help, through the medium of sport, to further friendship and understanding amongst nations.[8]

These games are modeled after the Olympics and include modified versions of many of the same olympic games.

Some local agencies provide organized games as a service to persons with other types of disability. Such groups as the U.S. National Association For Retarded Children and Adults offer through their local affiliates in many communities, modified games in programs of recreation; similarly, this is done by the United Cerebral Palsy Association, National Multiple Sclerosis Society, Associations for the Blind and Partial Sighted, National Society for Crippled Children and Adults, and others. Various community mental health associations, both public and private, offer recreation programs utilizing games modified for convalescent mental hospital patients. A variety of correctional programs for youthful offenders offer these same services. A number of these agencies work in cooperation with local municipal and county recreation departments who offer year-round sports programs and a large variety of lounge programs that feature table and board games for the public. Public recreation departments offer resources for such games as bowling, golf, hand-

[8] *The 1964 International Stoke Mandeville Games, Tokyo, 8th-12th November.* Aylesbury, Bucks, England: Hunt Barnard and Company Ltd., no Publication date, p. 1.

ball, soccer, table tennis, scrabble, bingo, checkers, chess, and many others. Numerous school-related recreation programs provide these and other games to preschoolers and school-age children.

A look at a typical schedule from a community recreation center offers a listing of times when the following types of games are available—party games, progressive games, singing games, active games, circle games, relay games, tag games, quiet games, billiards and pool, ping pong.

Within the United States there are a number of national organizations that offer assistance and information to agencies providing programs of recreation to the public. Some of these are:

> The National Recreation and Park Association
> 1700 Pennsylvania Avenue, Washington, D.C. 20003
>
> The International Recreation Association
> 345 East 46 Street, New York, New York
>
> American Bowling Congress
> 3925 W. 103rd Street, Chicago, Ill. 60655
>
> Association of Playing Card Manufacturers
> 420 Lexington Avenue, New York, N.Y. 10017
>
> National Golf Foundation
> 408 Merchandise Mart, Chicago, Ill. 60640
>
> The Athletic Institute
> 805 Merchandise Mart, Chicago, Ill. 60640

In other countries similar organizations exist; for example, the British counterpart of the National Recreation and Park Association is the National Playing Fields Association, in Japan it is the National Recreation Association of Japan.

In addition to public and private agencies that offer recreation service, many industries employ professional recreation personnel to organize and structure the "company bowling league" and the like. Many firms offer golf, as well as other game tournaments. The Association of Playing Card Manufacturers recently issued a publication for Industrial Recreation Personnel, which outlines procedures for establishing employee canasta, pinochle, and cribbage tournaments.

Organized game playing has found its way into other types of "industries" as well, for there is an American Medical Golf Association, American Medical Tennis Association, and a number of others. Whether this portends the future for other professions is difficult to say at this time; however, it is interesting to note that the Olympic model relied on geographic identification for participation, and many "amateur" tournaments today (in the United States at least) are sponsored by industrial or professional groups.

Finally, it is fitting to mention other types of institutions that offer organized game playing, for example, Las Vegas, San Juan, Baden Baden, Estoril, and of course Monte Carlo. Some of these institutions have a long and detailed history, while others have evolved their reputations in the past decade. For the not-so-affluent, there is always the neighborhood service station, which has provided a variety of gambling games over the past few years, and the neighborhood supermarket, which also does this. For others, there is bingo and gambling games at their church or senior center. There are legal and illegal betting facilities at race tracks, and for others, commercial sports. For some there is the "Numbers Game"—generally illegal, and generally available to the adult public. Finally there is the biggest game of all, carefully controlled by the federal government—the stock market.

Thus, games for recreative purposes are played by the public in their own homes, in local community recreation agencies, private clubs, churches, commercial casinos, and a variety of other institutions. Games are offered as part of personnel benefits in business and industry, and are a source of employment for gamblers and athletes. Games for recreative purposes, whether offered on an organized basis by professional personnel, commercial interests, or employers, whether legal or illegal, whether free or costly, apparently have been a part of man's living situation since the dawn of recorded history, and probably before. Some of the same games and patterns of play in vogue today, will probably continue until the end of recorded history.

Perhaps one of the most interesting aspects of all of this is the fact that games fascinate man to such a degree that he is not satisfied with limiting the use of them to recreative endeavors as the chapters in the balance of this section indicate.

We have not included a reading with this chapter. However, the list of selected references that follows offers a variety of the types of sources available. The list is divided into four major sections—that is, general compendiums of games that are played today; references on playing cards, dice, and other gambling games; references on popular table and board games such as chess, checkers, backgammon, and the like; and, finally, references on sports and athletic contests.

Games for Recreation — Selected References

Anderson, D. *Encyclopedia of Games*, Grand Rapids, Michigan: Zondervan Publishers House, 1954.

Brooke, M. *Fun For The Money*, New York: Scribner's Sons, 1963.

Buranelli, R. "They Started The Crossword Puzzle Craze," *Collier's Magazine*, New York, 75, 1925, p. 12.

Carlson, B. W. *Fun For One Or Two*, New York: Abingdon Press, 1954.

Chapman, E. C. *Murder In Your Home—A Crime Drama Game*, New York: Cong and R. R. Smith, Inc., 1932.

Donnelly, R., et al. *Active Games and Contests*, New York: Ronald Press, 1958.

Fox, T. *How to Make Money With Carnival Games*, San Jose, California, 1956.

Frankel, L., and Frankel, G. *101 Best Games for Girls and 101 Best Action Games For Boys*, New York: Sterling, 1953.

Harbin, E. O. *The Fun Encyclopaedia*, Nashville, Tenn.: Abingdon Press, 1940.

Hedges, S. G. *Games For the Not So Young*, New York: Philosophical Library, 1957.

Hindman, D. *Handbook of Active Games*, Englewood Cliffs, New Jersey: Prentice-Hall, Inc., 1955.

Hunt, S., and Cain, E. *Games The World Around*, New York: A.S. Barnes, 1941.

Kraus, R. G. *The Family Book of Games*, New York: McGraw-Hill, 1960.

Kraus, R. G. "Games For Every Occasion," *Recreation Today*, New York: Appleton-Century-Crofts, 1966, pp. 63–93.

Mason, B., and Mitchell, E. *Social Games For Recreation*, New York: Ronald Press, 1955.

Pick, J. B. *180 Games For One Player*, New York: Philosophical Library, 1954.

Powell, R. B. *Scouting Games*, London: C. A. Pearson, 1910.

Shea, J. J. *Its All In The Game*, New York: Putnam Press, 1960.

Sparkman, C. F. *Games For Spanish Clubs*, New York: Instituto De Ias Espanas Enlos, 1926.

Wells, H. G. *Floor Games*, Boston: Small, Maynard, and Comp., 1912.

BIBLIOGRAPHY

Playing Cards, Dice, and Other Gambling Games— Selected References

---

PART I

General

Bergler, E. *The Psychology of Gambling*, New York: Hill and Wang, 1957.

Bloch, H. A. "The Sociology of Gambling," *American Journal of Sociology*, **57**, 1951, pp. 215–221.

Cooper, J. M. "Games and Gambling: A Cross-Cultural Survey of South American Indian Tribes," *Bureau of American Ethnology Bulletin*, **5** (143), 1949, pp. 503–524.

Culin, S. *Gambling Games of the Chinese American*, (*University of Pennsylvania Series in Philology, Literature, and Archaeology*, Volume I, Number 4), Philadelphia: University Press, 1891.

Desmond, G. R. *Gambling Among the Yakima*, (*American Anthropological Association Anthropological Series*, Number 14), Washington, D.C. The Association, 1952.

Devereux, G. "Psychodynamics of Mohave Gambling," *American Imago*, **7**, 1950, pp. 55–65.

Dorsey, G. A. "Certain Gambling Games of the Kalamath Indians," *American Anthropologist*, **3** (1), 1901, pp. 14–27.

Fenstermaker, G. B. "Archaeological Findings Show That Tribes Had Gambling Games," *Pennsylvania Archaeologist*, Milton, Pennsylvania, **8**, 1936, pp. 85–86.

Flannery, R. "Social Mechanisms in Gros Ventre Gambling," *Southwestern Journal of Anthropology*, Albuquerque, New Mexico, **2**, 1946, pp. 391–419.

Galdston, I. "The Psychodynamics of the Triad Alchoholism, Gambling, and Superstition," *Mental Hygiene*, **35**, 1951, pp. 589–598.

Games and Gamesters of the Restoration, London: G. Routeledge and Sons, 1930. (Includes: The Complete Gamester by Charles Cotton, 1674; and Lives of the Gamesters by Theophilus Lucas, 1714).

Greenson, R. P. "On Gambling," *American Imago*, 4, 1947, pp. 61–77.

Haile, B. "Navaho Games of Chance and Taboo," *Primitive Man*, Washington, D.C., **6**, 1933, pp. 35–40.

Lanciani, R. "Gambling and Cheating in Ancient Rome," *North American Review*, 1892, pp. 97–105.

Lidner, R. M. "The Psychodynamics of Gambling," *Annals of The American Academy of Political and Social Science*, **269**, 1950, pp. 93–107.

Longmore, L. "A Study of Fah-fee: An African Gambling Institution," *South African Journal of Science*, **52** (12), 1956, pp. 275–282.

Matthews, D. W. "Navajo Gambling Songs," *American Anthropologist*, **2** (1), 1889, pp. 1–19.

Morris, R. P. "An Exploratory Study of Some Personality Characteristics of Gamblers," *Journal of Clinical Psychology*, **13**, 1957, pp. 191–193.

Olmstead, C. *Heads I Win, Tails You Lose: The Psychology and Symbolisms of Gambling Games*, New York: Macmillan Co., 1962.

Randle, M. C. "A Shoshone Hand Game Gambling Song," *Journal of American Folklore*, **66**, 1953, pp. 155–159.

Roberts, J. M. and Sutton-Smith, B. "Cross-Cultural Correlates of Games of Chance," *Behavioral Science Notes*, **3**, 1966, pp. 131–144.

Sellin, T., (editor). *Gambling, Annals of the American Academy of Political and Social Science*, **269**, May, 1950.

Serrano, C. "Gambling Among the Negritos of Panay," *Primitive Man*, Washington, D.C., **14**, 1941, pp. 31–32.

Wykes, A. *Gambling*, London: Aldus Books, Ltd., 1964.

PART II

Dice and Other Gambling Games

"Ancient Mesopotamian (c. 2750 B.C.) Die Goes To Museum," *El Palacio*, Santa Fe, New Mexico, **31** (3), 1931, p. 41.

Brewster, P. G. "Burski and Other Polish Games of Chance and Skill," *Zeitschrift für Ethnologie*, Braunschweig, **83**, 1958, pp. 83–85.

Brooke, M. *Fun For The Money*, New York: Scribner's Sons, 1963.

Butler, B. R. "The Prehistory of the Dice Game in the Southern Plateau," *Tebiwa*, **2**, (1), 1958, pp. 65–71.

Culin, S. *Chinese Games with Dice*, Philadelphia: Oriental Club, 1889.

Culin, S. "Chinese Games with Dice and Dominoes," *Annual Report of The United States National Museum*, Washington, D.C., 1893, pp. 491–537.

Culin, S. "Japanese Game of Sugoroku," *Brooklyn Museum Quarterly*, Brooklyn, New York, **7** (3), 1920, pp. 213–233.

Chapman, F. R. "Koruru: The Maori Game of Knuckle-Bone," *Journal of the Polynesian Society*, Wellington, N.Z., **7** (2), 1898, p. 114.

"Egyptian Dice," *Field Museum News*, Chicago, **1** (10), 1930, p. 1.

Howard, D. "The Game of Knucklebone in Australia," *Western Folklore*, Berkeley, California, **17** (1), 1958, pp. 34–44.

Lovett, E. "The Ancient and Modern Game of Astragals," *Folklore*, London, **12** (3), 1901, pp. 280–293.

Orgel, M. "Old European Dice Games," *Graphis*, **16** (89), 1960, pp. 256–261.

Siegel, M. "A Study of West African Carved Gambling Chips: The Mackenzie Collection," *Memoirs of the American Anthropological Association*, **55**, 1940, pp. 7–77.

Sparkes, B. A. "Kottabos: An Athenian After-Dinner Game," *Archaeology*, Cincinnati, **13** (3), 1960, pp. 202–207.

Tylor, E. B. "On American Lot Games As Evidence of Asiatic Intercourse Before the Time of Columbus," *International Archives For Ethnography*, Supplement to Volume 9, 1896, pp. 55–67. Also in *Sourcebook in Anthropology*, New York, 1931, pp. 388–397.

Willett, F. "A Set of Gambling Pegs from the North-West Coast of America (Alaska)," *Man*, London, **61**, 1961, pp. 8–10.

PART III

Playing Cards

Berndt, R. M. "Card Games among the Aborigines of the Northern Territory," *Oceania*, Sidney, **17**, 1947, pp. 248–269.

Bowdoen, W. G. "Playing Cards: Their History and Symbolism," *Art and Archaeology*, Washington, D.C., **11**, 1921, pp. 106–112.

Brewster, P. G. "Symbolism and Allegory in Card and Board Games," *Southern Folklore Quarterly,* Gainesville, Florida, **23** (3), 1959, pp. 196–203.

Cavendish, (pseudonym). *Card Essays, Clay's Decisions, and Card-Table Talk,* London: De La Rue & Company, 1879.

Crespi, I. "Social Significance of Card Playing As A Leisure Activity," *American Sociological Review,* **21**, 1956, pp. 717–721. Corrections: **23**, 1958, p. 85.

Goren, C. H. *Goren's Hoyle Encyclopedia of Games,* New York: Graystone Press, 1961.

Hargrave, C. P. *A History of Playing Cards,* New York, Houghton Mifflin, Company, 1930.

Hoyle, E. *Games of Whist, Quadrille, Piquet, Chess, and Backgammon,* London, 1742. (Subsequently there have been over 300 editions).

McDonald, J. D. *Strategy in Poker, Business, and War,* New York: Norton, 1950.

McGlothlin, W. H. "A Psychometric Study of Poker Playing," *Journal of Consulting Psychology,* **18**, 1954, pp. 145–149.

"Malay Card Games," *Journal of the Royal Anthropological Institute,* London, **17**, 1897, pp. 136–139.

Mann, S. *Collecting Playing Cards,* New York: Crown Publishers, Inc., 1966.

Morley, H. T. *Old and Curious Playing Cards, Their History and Types,* London: B.T. Batsford, Ltd., 1931.

"Playing Cards of Asia," *Asia,* New York, **31**, 1931, pp. 152–155.

Van Rensselear, J. K. "Playing Cards From Japan," *Proceedings of The United States National Museum,* Washington, D.C., **13**, 1890, pp. 381–382.

Wayland, V. "Apache Playing Cards," *Masterkey,* Los Angeles, **35** (3), 1961, pp. 84–98.

Wilkinson, W. H. "Chinese Origin of Playing Cards," *American Anthropologist,* **8** (1), 1895, pp. 61–78.

Yoshino, N. *Gimmi 88: The Popular Japanese Card Game,* New York: Katagri Brothers, 1929.

Board and Table Games—
Selected References

PART I

General

Austin, R. G. "Greek Board Games," *Antiquity*, Gloucester, England, **14**, 1940, pp. 257–271.

Austin, R. G. "Roman Board Games," *Greece and Rome*, London, **4**, 1934, p. 30.

Bell, R. C. *Board and Table Games from Many Civilizations*, London: Oxford University Press, 1960.

Brewster, P. G. "Symbolism and Allegory in Card and Board Games," *Southern Folklore Quarterly*, Gainesville, Florida, **23** (3), 1959, pp. 196–203.

Murray, H. J. R. *History of Board Games Other Than Chess*, London: Oxford University Press, 1952.

Newell, W. H. "A Few Asiatic Board Games Other Than Chess," *Man*, London, **59**, 1959, pp. 29–30.

Perry, R. E. "The Board Games in North-West Africa," *Uganda Journal*, Kampala, **4**, 1936, pp. 176–178.

Van der Smissen, B. and Knierim, H. *Recreational Sports and Games: A Manual of Game Procedures and Construction Plans for Sports, Board Games, Puzzles, etc.*, Minneapolis: Burgess Publishing Company, 1964.

Whitehouse, F. R. B. *Table Games of Georgian and Victorian Days*, London: Reter Garnett, 1951.

PART II

Chess

Betts, G. "Chess in Borny, Nigeria," *Man*, London, **39**, 1939, pp. 31–32.

Bunt, C. E. "The Lion and The Unicorn: History of Chess," *Antiquity*, Gloucester, England, **4** (16), 1930, pp. 425–437.

Colby, K. M. "Gentlemen, The Queen," *Psychoanalytic Review*, **40**, 1953, pp. 144–148.

Culin, S. "Chess and Playing Cards," *Annual Report of the Board of Regents of the Smithsonian Institution: Report of the U.S. National Museum*, 1896, Washington, D.C., 1898, pp. 655–942.

Elo, A. E. "Chess: A Cultural Phenomenon," *Lore*, Milwaukee, **2**, 1952, pp. 36–42.

Fine, R. *Psychoanalytic Observations on Chess and Chess Masters*, New York: National Psychological Association for Psychoanalysis, Inc., 1956.

Fiske, W. *Chess in Iceland: With Historical Notes on Other Table Games*, Florence: Florentine Typographical Society, 1905.

Gadd, C. "Babylonian Chess?" *Iraq*, London, **8**, 1946, pp. 66–72.

Geithmann, H. "Stobeck, Home of Chess," *National Geographic Magazine*, Washington, D.C., **59**, May 1931, pp. 637–652.

Harsha, "The Origin of Chess," *March of India*, Delhi, **11** (2), 1959, pp. 38–39.

Kerr, B. A. "The Aboriginal Chess-Player," *Sydney Bulletin*, **3**, 1958, p. 16.

Montell, G. "Mongolian Chess and Chess Men," *Ethnos*, Stockholm, **4**, 1939, pp. 81–104.

Murray, H. J. R., and Brown, B. G. *A Short History of Chess*, London: Oxford University Press, 1963.

Murray, H. J. R. *A History of Chess*, London: Oxford University Press, 1913.

Ohara, E. *Japanese Chess: The Game of Shogi*, London: Patterson, 1958.

Raverty, H. "The Invention of Chess and Backgammon," *American Antiquarian*, **25**, 1903, pp. 255–258.

Reider, N. "Chess, Oedipus, and the Mater Dolorosa," *International Journal of Psychoanalysis*, **40**, 1959, pp. 320–333.

Sullivan, M. W. *A Programmed Introduction to the Game of Chess*, New York: McGraw-Hill Book Company, Inc., 1963.

Wichmann, H. & Wichmann, S. *The Story of Chesspieces from Antiquity to Modern Times*, New York: Crown Publishers, 1960.

PART III

Count and Capture Games
(Mancala variations)

Alamayahu, S. "The Game of Ganna," *Ethnological Society Bulletin*, Addis Ababa, **9**, 1959, pp. 9–27.

Anna, M. "The Mueso Game Among the Basoga," *Primitive Man*, Washington, D.C., **11**, 1930, pp. 71–74.

Bennett, G. T. "Wari," *Religion and Art in Ashanti*, (R.S. Rattay, ed.), Oxford: Oxford University Press, 1927, pp. 382–98.

Braunholtz, H. J. "The Game of Mueso in Uganda," *Man*, London, **31**, 1931, pp. 121–123.

Bolton, H. C. "Seega, an Egyptian Game," *Journal of American Folklore*, **3**, 1890, pp. 132–134.

Chaplan, J. H. "A Note on Mancala Games in Northern Rhodesia," *Man*, London, **56**, 1956, p. 168.

Collins, G. N. "Kboo, A Liberian Game," *National Geographic Magazine*, **21**, 1910, pp. 944–948.

Courlander, H. "The Ethiopian Game of Gobeta," *Negro History Bulletin*, Washington, D.C., **7**, 1941, pp. 21–23.

Culin, S. "Mancala, The National Game of Africa," *Annual Report of The United States National Museum*, Washington, D.C., 1894, pp. 597–606.

Herskovits, M. J. "Wari in the New World," *Journal of the Royal Anthropological Institute*, London, **42**, 1923, pp. 23–37.

Jobson, R. "Wari," *The Golden Trade* (1623), London, 1904, p. 48.

Martin G. "Somali Game," *Journal of the Royal Anthropological Institute*, London, **61**, 1931, pp. 499–511.

Matson, A. T. "The Game of Mueso," *Uganda Journal*, Kampala, **21** (2), 1957, p. 221.

Petrie, F. "Seega," *Objects in Daily Use*, London: British School of Archaeology in Egypt, 1927, p. 56.

Powell-Cotton, P. H. "A Mancala Board Called Songo," *Man*, London, **31**, 1931, p. 133.

Rohrbough, R. *Count and Capture, The World's Oldest Game*, Delaware, Ohio: Cooperative Recreation Service, 1955.

Shackell, R. "Mueso, The Board Game," *Uganda Journal*, Kampala, **2**, 1935, pp. 14–20.

PART IV

Go or Wei Ch'i

Cheshire, F. *Go or Wei Ch'i*, London: Hastings, 1911.

Lasker, E. *Go and Go-Moku: Oriental Board Games*, New York: Dover Publications, Inc., 1934. Revised, 1960.

Pecorini, D., and Tong Shu. *The Game of Wei-Ch'i*, London: Longmans, 1929.

Smith, A. *The Game of Go, The National Game of Japan*, Rutland, Vermont: Charles E. Tuttle Co., 1956.

Volpicelli, Z. "Wei-Chi," *Journal of the China Branch of the Royal Asiatic Society*, London, **26**, 1894, p. 80.

PART V

Mah Jong

Culin, S. "Game of Ma-Jong," *Brooklyn Museum Quarterly*, Brooklyn, New York, **11** (3), 1924, pp. 153–168.

Kanai, S., and Farrell, M. *Mah Jong For Beginners*, Rutland, Vermont: Charles E. Tuttle, Co., 1952.

Long Sang Ti. *Mah-Jong: The Ancient Game of China*, New York: A. Langstater, Inc., 1923.

Strauser, K., and Evans, L. *Mah Jong Anyone?* London: Prentice Hall International, Inc., 1964.

PART VI

Backgammon

"Backgammon Almost Four Thousand Years Ago," *El Palacio*, Santa Fe, New Mexico, **30**, 1931, pp. 84–85.

Meadows, K. *Backgammon, Its History and Practice*, New York: Barry Vail Corp., 1931.

Raverty, H. "The Invention of Chess and Backgammon," *American Antiquarian*, **25**, 1903, pp. 255–258.

Richard, W. L. *Complete Backgammon*, London: G. Bell and Sons, 1938.

Tylor, E. B. "Backgammon Among The Aztecs," *Macmillan's Magazine*, London, **30**, December 1878, pp. 142–150.

PART VII

Morris Games

Brewster, P. G. "Malomjalik and Related Three-in-a-row Games," *Acta Ethnographica*, Budapest, **6**, 1957, pp. 225–231.

Redstone, V. B. "Fox and Geese," *Transactions of the Royal Historical Society*, London, **21**, 1902, p. 195.

Roberts, J. M., et al. "Pattern and Competence: A Consideration of Tick Tack Toe," *El Palacio*, Santa Fe, New Mexico, **72** (3), 1956, pp. 17–30.

Sjovold, T. "Nine Men Morris," *The Viking Ships*, Oslo: 1954, p. 7.

PART VIII

Miscellaneous Board Games

Brown, W. N. "The Indian Games of Parchisi, Chaupar, and Chausar," *Expedition*, Philadelphia, **6** (3), 1964, pp. 32–35.

Carey, M. A. "A Beadword Gaming Board From North West India," *British Museum Quarterly*, London, **24** (1–2), 1961, pp. 59–60.

Erasmus, C. J. "Patolli, Parchisi, and The Limitations of Possibilities," *Southwestern Journal of Anthropology*, Albuquerque, New Mexico, **6**, 1950, pp. 369–387.

Hencken, H. "A Gaming Board of the Viking Age," *Acta Archaeologica*, Copenhagen, **4**, 1933, pp. 85–104.

La Roux, M. *The Complete Draughts Player*, London: Arco Publishers, 1955.

Malan, B. D. "Old and New Rock Engravings in Natal: A Zulu Game," *Antiquity*, **31** (123), 1957, pp. 153–154.

Nash, W. I. "Ancient Egyptian Draughtsboards and Draughtsmen," *Proceedings of the Society of Biblical Archaeology*, London, **24**, 1902, p. 341.

Ridgeway, W. "The Game of Thirty Squares," *Journal of Hellenic Studies*, London, **16**, 1896, p. 288.

Towry-White, E. "Types of Egyptian Draughtsmen," *Proceedings of The Society of Biblical Archaeology*, London, **24**, 1902, p. 261.

Tylor, E. B. "On The Game of Patolli in Ancient Mexico and Its Probably Asiatic Origin," *Journal of the Royal Anthropological Institute*, London, **8**, April 9, 1878, pp. 116–131.

Sports—Selected References

PART I

About Sports

Beisser, A. *The Madness in Sports,* New York: Appleton-Century-Crofts, 1967.

Brewster, P. G. *Games and Sports in Shakespeare,* Helsinki: Suomalainen Tiedeakatemia, Academia Scientiarum Fennica, 1959.

Collins, F. D. *Popular Sports: Their Origin and Development,* Chicago: Rand McNally, Co., 1935.

Dawson, L. *Sport in War,* New York: Charles Scribner and Sons, 1937.

Deschner, R. B. *Evolution of Sports,* St. Louis: Fred Medart Co., 1946.

Eyler, M. H. "Origins of Contemporary Sports," *Research Quarterly,* Washington, D.C., **32** (4), 1961, pp. 480–488.

Gerwig, G. *Emotion and Sport,* Pittsburgh: Frick Educational Commission, 1932.

Hanna, W. A. "The Politics of Sport," *American Universities Field Staff: South East Asian Series,* **10**, 1966, pp. 13–19.

Hildebrand, J. "The Geography of Games: How the Sports of Nations Form a Gazetteer of Their Habits and Histories of Their Peoples," *National Geographic Magazine,* Washington, D.C., **36**, 1919, pp. 89–144.

Howard, G. E. "Social Psychology of the Spectator," *American Journal of Sociology,* **18**, 1912, pp. 33–50.

Johnson, W. R. "A Study of Emotion Revealed in Two Types of Sport," *Research Quarterly,* Washington, D.C., **20**, 1949, pp. 72–79.

Johnson, W. R. *Science and Medicine in Exercise and Sports,* New York: Harper and Row, 1960.

Jokl, E. *Heart and Sport*, Springfield, Ill.: Charles C Thomas, Inc., 1964.

Jokl, E. (ed.) *Medical Sociology and Cultural Anthropology of Sport*, Springfield, Ill.: Charles C Thomas, Inc., 1964.

Jokl, E., et al. *Sports in the Cultural Pattern of the World*. Helsinki: Institute of Occupational Health, 1956.

McIntosh, P. C. *Sports in Society*, London: C. A. Watts and Co., 1963.

Moore, R. M. *Sports and Mental Health*, Springfield, Ill.: Charles C Thomas, 1966.

Morris, S. W. "Sports Heal War Neuroses," *Recreation*, 39 (10), 1945, 343–344.

Moss, P. *Sports and Pastimes Through the Ages*, New York: Arco Press, 1963.

Scott, M. G. "Analysis of Selected Sports Activities," *Analysis of Human Motion*, New York: Appleton-Century-Crofts, 1963, pp. 252–320.

Slovenko, R., and Knight, J. A. *Motivations in Play, Games, and Sports*, Springfield, Ill.: Charles C Thomas, 1967.

Slusher, Howard S., *Man, Sport, and Existence*, Philadelphia: Lea & Febiger, 1967.

Staley, S. C. *The World of Sport*, Champaign, Ill.: Stipes Publishing Co., 1955.

Tunis, J. R. *Sports, Heroes, and Hysterics*, New York: John Day Co., 1928.

UNESCO. "The Place of Sport in Education: A Comparative Study," *Educational Studies and Documents*, Paris, 21 (63), 1956.

Wenkart, S. "The Meaning of Sports For Contemporary Man," *Journal of Existential Psychiatry*, 3, Spring, 1963, pp. 397–404.

Wilson, P. "Organized Sports For Leisure Time," *Societies Around The World*, New York, 2, 1953, pp. 556–558.

Wohl, A. *International Review of Sport Sociology*, Warsaw: Polish Scientific Publishers for UNESCO, 1966.

PART II

"How to" References: A Brief Sample

Ainsworth, D. S. *Individual Sports For Women*, Philadelphia: W.B. Saunders, Co., 1955.

Danford, H. G. "Sports and Games," *Creative Leadership in Recreation*, Boston: Allyn and Bacon, 1964, pp. 186–231.

Kraus, R. G. "Sports in Recreation," *Recreation Today, Program Planning and Leadership,* New York: Appleton-Century-Crofts, 1966, pp. 94–128.

Menke, F. G. *The Encyclopedia of Sports,* New York: A.S. Barnes, Inc., 1960.

Mitchell, E. D. *Sports For Recreation,* New York: Ronald Press, 1952.

Sapora, A. V., and Mitchell, E. D. "School and Community Sports and Athletics," *The Theory of Play and Recreation,* New York: Ronald Press, 1961, pp. 461–488.

Scott, H. A. *Competitive Sports in Schools and Colleges,* New York: Harper and Brothers, 1951.

Werner, G. I. *After School Games and Sports,* Washington, D.C.: National Education Association, 1964.

PART III

Sports in Specific Cultures

Aspen, J. *Picture of the Manners, Customs, Sports, and Pastimes of the Inhabitants of England to the 18th Century,* London: J. Harris, 1825.

Bailey, F. L. "Navaho Motor Habits (Sport)," *American Anthropologist,* 44 (2), 1942, pp. 210–234.

Baker, G. S. "War Games on the Plateau," *West African Review,* Ibadan, 26 (331), pp. 108–109.

Best, E. "Maori Games and Pastimes: Stilt-Walking," *New Zealand Journal of Science and Technology,* 5 (5), Wellington, 1922, p. 255.

Betts, J. R. "The Technological Revolution and the Rise of Sport, 1850–1900," *Mississippi Valley Historical Review,* September, 1953.

Bland, E. A. *Fifty Years of Sport in England,* London: Daily Mail, 1946.

Blasig, R. "The Practice of Sports Among the Indians of America," *Mind and Body,* 40, 1933–1934, pp. 216–219.

Boyle, R. H. *Sport-Mirror of American Life,* Boston: Little, Brown and Co., 1963.

Carlson, R. E., et al. "Sports and Games," *Recreation in American Life,* Belmont, California: Wadsworth Publishing Company, Inc., 1963, pp. 455–464.

Chakravarti, T. M. "Some Information about Sports, Indoor Games, and Pastimes in the Ancient Literature and Early Inscriptions of Bengal and Assam," *East and West,* Rome, 7, 1956, pp. 56–60.

Cozens, F. W., and Stumpf, F. S. *Sport in American Life*, Chicago: University of Chicago Press, 1953.

Dulles, F. R. *A History of Recreation: America Learns to Play*, (Four chapters on Sports), New York: Appleton-Century-Crofts, 1965.

Dunlap, H. L. "Games, Sports, and other Vigorous Recreational Activities and Their Function in Samoan Culture," *Research Quarterly*, Washington, D.C., **22** (3), 1951, pp. 298–311.

Durant, J., and Bettman, O. *Pictorical History of American Sports; From Colonial Times to the Present*, New York: A.S. Barnes, 1952.

Durant, J. *Sports of Our (U.S.) Presidents*, New York: Hastings House, 1964.

Emory, K. P. "Sports, Games, and Amusements," *Ancient Hawaiin Civilization*, 1933, pp. 141–153.

Ewing, W. C. *Sports of Colonial Williamsburgh*, Richmond, Virginia: The Dietz Press, 1937.

Gardiner, E. N. *Athletics of the Ancient World*, Oxford: Clarendon Press, 1930.

Gardiner, E. N. *Greek Athletic Sports and Festivals*, London: Macmillan and Co., 1910.

Govett, L. A. *The King's Book of Sports*, London: Elliot Stock, 1890.

Harlan, H. V. *History of the Olympic Games*, London: G.B. Foster, and Co., Ltd., 1931.

Harney, W. "Sport and Play Amidst the Aborigines of The Northern Territory," *Mankind*, Sidney, 1952, pp. 377–379.

Heywood, W. *Palio and Ponte; An Account of the Sports of Central Italy From The Age of Dante to the 20th Century*, London: Methuen and Co., 1904.

Henderson, R. W. *Early American Sports*, New York: A.S. Barnes Co., 1953.

Hole, C. *English Sports and Pastimes*, London: Batsford, 1949.

Holliman, J. *American Sport: 1785–1835*, Durham: The Sieman Press, 1931.

Kenn, C. V. "Ancient Hawaiian Sports and Pastimes," *Mid-Pacific*, Honolulu, 48, 1935, pp. 308–316.

Krout, J. A. *Annals of American Sport*, New Haven: Yale University Press, 1929.

McCaskill, Joseph C. "Indian Sports," *Indians At Work*, Washington, D.C., **3** (22), 1936, pp. 29–30.

Manchester, H. *Four Centuries of Sport in America*, New York: Derrydale Press, 1931.

Mason, B. *Primitive and Pioneer Sports for Recreation*, New York: A.S. Barnes and Co., 1937.

Montagu, I. "Sports and Pastimes in China," *United Asia,* 8, Bombay, 1956, pp. 150–152.

Morton, H. W. *Soviet Sport,* New York: Collier Books, 1963.

Moses, A. L. "Choctow Sports," *Indians at Work,* Washington, D.C., 3 (14), 1936, pp. 15–16.

Nally, T. H. *The Aonach Tailteann and The Tailteann Games; Their Origin, History, and Ancient Associations,* Dublin: Talbot Press, Ltd., 1928.

Nelson, F. E. "The Sports of the Zuniz," *Indians at Work,* Washington, D.C., 3 (2), 1936, pp. 35–38.

Padmanabhachari, T. "Games, Sports, and Pastimes in Prehistoric India," *Man In India, Ranchi,* 21 (2–3), 1941, pp. 127–146.

Pool, L., and Pool, G. *History of Ancient Olympic Games,* London: Vision Press, 1963.

Read, D. H. "Games, Sports, and Pastimes," *Handbook of British Folklore,* (C.S. Barune, ed.), London, 1914, p. 257.

Reagan, A. B. "Navajo Sports," *Primitive Man,* Washington, D.C., 5, 1932, pp. 68–71.

Rider, C. "The Sporting Scene: 1864," *American Scholar,* 15, Summer, 1946, pp. 348–352.

Roth, W. E. "Games, Sports, and Amusements," *North Queensland Ethnography Bulletin,* Brisbane, 4, March, 1902.

Sando, J. S. "Indian Olympics," *New Mexico,* Albuquerque, 30 (4), 1952, pp. 22, 43, 45, 47.

Sharp, F. "Fiji Sports," *Mid-Pacific Magazine,* Honolulu, 45, 1933, pp. 132–134.

Smith, H. W. *A Sporting Family of The Old South,* Albany, N.Y.: J. B. Lyon Company, 1936.

Stone, G. "American Sports: Play and Display," *Mass Leisure,* (E. Larrabee et al., eds.), New York: Free Press of Glencoe, 1958, pp. 253–264.

Strutt, J. *Sports and Pastimes of the English People,* London: Methuen and Co., 1801.

Stumpf, F., and Cozens, F. W. "Some Aspects of the Role of Games, Sports, and Recreational Activities in the Culture of Modern Primitive Peoples: Part I, The New Zealand Maoris," *Research Quarterly,* Washington, D.C., 18 (3), 1947, pp.198–218; "Part II, The Fijians," 20 (1), 1949, pp. 2–20.

Weaver, R. B. *Amusements and Sports in American Life,* Chicago: Chicago University Press, 1939.

Webster, D. *Scottish Highland Games,* Glasgow and London: Wm. Collins and Sons, Ltd., 1959.

Weiss, H. B. *Early Sports and Pastimes in New Jersey*, Trenton: Past Times Press, 1960.

Williams, M. O. "Great Britain on Parade: The Clans Gather for Games," *National Geographic Magazine*, Washington, D.C., **68**, 1935, pp. 137–184.

Worchester, D. C. "Field Sports Among the Wild Men of Northern Luzon," *National Geographic Magazine*, Washington, D.C., **22**, 1911, pp. 215–267.

PART IV

Ball Games

General

Alegria, R. E. "The Ball Game Played by the Aborigines of The Antilles," *American Antiquity*, Salt Lake City, **16**, 1951, pp. 348–352.

Amsden, C. "A Prehistoric Rubber Ball," *The Masterkey*, Los Angeles, **10**, 1936, pp. 7–8.

Beals, R. L. "Unilateral Organizations in Mexico (Ball Games)," *American Anthropologist*, **34** (3), 1932, pp. 467–475.

Blom, F. F. "The Maya Ball Game Poktapok," *Tulane University Middle American Research Series*, New Orleans, **4**, 1932, pp. 431–456.

Borhegyi, S. "American Ball Game in Mesoamerica," *Natural History*, New York, **69** (1), 1960, pp. 48–58.

Gilmore, M. R. "The Game of Double Ball or Twin Ball," *Indian Notes*, New York, **3**, 1926, pp. 293–295.

Goellner, W. A. "The Court Ball Game of the Aboriginal Mayas," *Research Quarterly*, **24** (2), 1956, pp. 147–168.

Goggin, J. M. "A Ball Game At Santo Domingo," *American Anthropologist*, **42** (2), 1940, pp. 364–366.

Hoffman, W. J. "Remarks on Ojibwa Ball Play," *American Anthropologist*, **3** (2), 1890, pp. 133–135.

Kolly, I. "Notes on a West Coast Survival of the Ancient Ball Game," *Carnegie Institute of Washington Division of Historical Research*, Cambridge, Mass., **1**, 1943, pp. 163–175.

McKenzie, B. "The Seminoles Were Recognized As The Leading Ball Players Years Ago," *American Indians*, Tulsa, **1** (5), 1927, p. 10.

Mead, M. "A Choctaw Ball Game," *Primitive Heritage*, New York, 1953, pp. 289–295.

Mooney, J. "The Cherokee Ball Play," *American Anthropologist*, **3** (2), 1890, pp. 105–132.

Parsons, E. W. "Hidden Ball on First Mesa, Arizona," *Man*, London, **22**, 1922, pp. 82–90.

"Rally Around the Ball Pole," *Mental Hospital*, **10** (1), 1953, p. 23.

Roderman, C. R. "Let's Play Ball," *American Journal of Nursing*, **49** (9), 1949, pp. 566–567.

Rinaldo, J. B. "American Love of Ball Games Dates Back to Indians," *Natural History Museum Bulletin*, Chicago, **26** (1), 1955, pp. 3–4.

Stern, T. *The Rubber Ball Games of The Americas* (Monograph #17 of the American Ethnological Society), New York: J.J. Augustin, 1950.

Tod, M. N. "Teams of Ball Players at Sparta," *Annual of The British School of Athens*, London, **10**, 1903–1904, pp. 63–77.

Wanchope, R. "The Middle American Ball Game in 1750," *El Palacio*, Santa Fe, **55**, 1948, pp. 299–301.

Wolfe, K. E. "A Cherokee Indian Ball Game," *Red Man*, Carlisle, Pennsylvania, **3**, 1910, pp. 76–77.

Striking, Hitting, Throwing, and Catching Implements

Addatto, C. "On Play, and The Psychopathology of Golf," *Journal of The American Psychoanalytic Association*, **12** (4), 1964, pp. 826–841.

Altham, H. D., and Swanton, E. W. *History of Cricket* (2 vols.), London: Allen and Unwin, 1960.

Borhegyi, S. F. "Ball Game Handstones and Ball Game Gloves," *Essays in Pre-Columbian Art and Archaeology*, Cambridge, Mass., 1961, pp. 126–151.

Cherokee Indian Fair Throws Sportlight on Lacrosse, Archery, and Blowgun Contests," *Indians at Work*, Washington, D.C., **7** (4), 1939, pp. 12–14.

Culin, S. "Japanese Swinging Bat Game;" "Japanese Game of Battledore and Shuttlecock," *Brooklyn Museum Quarterly*, Brooklyn, New York, **12** (3), 1925, pp. 139–150.

Elkholm, G. F. "Puerto Rican Stone Collars As Ball Game Belts," *Essays in Pre-Columbian Art and Archaeology*, Cambridge, Mass., 1961, pp. 356–371.

Etherton, P. T. "Polo Through The Ages," *Asia*, New York, **31**, 1931, pp. 634–641, 664–666.

Fleming, D. *The Tee Games and How To Play Them*, Melbourne, Australia, 1916.

Gallop, R. "Pelote: Racket Game of the Basques," *Geographical Magazine*, London, **21**, pp. 81–88.

Gordon, D. "Lacrosse: An Indian Contribution to American Recreation," *Masterkey*, Los Angeles, **3**, 1962, pp. 97–99.

Henderson, R. W. *Bat, Ball, and Bishop,* New York: Rockport Press, 1947.

Hewitt, J. N. "Iroquois Game of Lacrosse," *American Anthropologist,* **5** (2), 1892, pp. 189–191.

Kutscher, G. "Ceremonial Badminton in The Ancient Culture of Peru," *Proceedings of the International Congress of Americanists,* Copenhagen, **3**, 1958, pp. 422–432.

Laufer, B. "The Game of Polo," *Field Museum News,* Chicago, **2** (13), 1931, p. 4.

Maigaard, P. "Batting Ball Games," *Genus,* **5**, 1942, pp. 57–72.

Mehl, E. "A Batting Game on the Island of Runo," *Western Folklore,* Berkeley, California, **8**, 1949, pp. 266–269.

McKindree, O. J. "Bowling as a Psychiatric Adjunct," *Psychiatric Quarterly,* **24**, 1950, pp. 303–307.

Stokes, A. "Psychoanalytic Reflections on the Development of Ball Games, Particularly Cricket," *International Journal of Psychoanalysis,* May–June, 1956.

Ball Courts

Brandes, R. S. "An Early Ball Court Near Globe, Arizona," *Kiva,* Tuscon, **23** (1), 1957, pp. 10–11.

Cotton, H. S. "Ball Court Notes," *Plateau,* Flagstaff, Arizona, **13**, 1947, pp. 5–22.

Schroeder, A. H. "Ball Courts and Ball Games of Middle America and Arizona, *Archaeology,* Cincinnati, **8** (3), 1955, pp. 156–161.

Smith, A. L. "Types of Ball Courts in the Highlands of Guatemala," *Essays in Pre-Columbian Art and Archaeology,* Cambridge, Mass., 1961, pp. 100–125.

Baseball, Football, Kickball, and Bowling

Anderson, J. C. "An Article on Supposed Maori Bowls," *Polynesian Society Journal,* New Plymouth, N.Z., **42**, 1933, pp. 222–225.

Embree, J. "Kickball and Some Other Parallels Between Siam and Micronesia," *Journal of the Siam Society,* **37** (1), 1948, pp. 33–38.

Fenton, S. "Lancashire Bowling Game," *Illustrated Archaeologist,* London, 1894, pp. 48–49.

"Football, an Ancient Game," *Natural History,* New York, **22**, 1922, pp. 574–575.

Fox, J. "Pueblo Baseball: A New Use For Old Witchcraft," *Journal of American Folklore,* **74** (291), 1961, pp. 9–16.

Frankenberg, R. *Village on the Border: A Social Study of Religion, Politics, and Football in A North Wales Community,* London: Cohen and West, 1957.

Mehl, E. "Baseball In The Stone Age," *Western Folklore*, Berkeley, Calif., 7, 1948, pp. 145–161.

Scotch, N. "Magic, Sorcery, and Football Among Urban Zulu," *Journal of Conflict Resolution*, Ann Arbor, Michigan, 5 (1), 1961, pp. 70–74.

Tunis, J. R. "The Great God Football," *Harpers Magazine*, 157, 1928.

Youd, J. "Notes on Kickball in Micronesia," *Journal of American Folklore*, 74 (291), 1961, pp. 62–64.

Young, N. D. "Did The Greeks and The Romans Play Football?" *Research Quarterly*, Washington, D.C., 15, 1944, pp. 310–316.

PART V

Target Games: Archery, Darts, and Related Sports

Auboyer, J. "Archery: A Royal Sport and Sacred Game in Ancient India," *Arts and Letters*, 301 (1), 1956, pp. 3–12.

Aufenanger, H. "A Children's Arrow-thrower in the Central Highlands of New Guinea," *Anthropos*, Freiburg, 56, 1961, p. 633.

"Cherokee Indian Fair Throws Spotlight on Lacross, Archery, and Blow-gun Contests," *Indians at Work*, Washington, D.C., 7 (4), 1939, pp. 12–14.

Cruz, E. C. "Biaka and Putlon-Bolo Game," *Philippine Magazine*, Manila, 31, 1934, p. 472; also in *Journal of East Asiatic Studies*, 4 (2), April, 1955, pp. 255–256.

Davidson, D. S. "The Pacific and Circum-Pacific Appearance of the Dart Game," *Journal of the Polynesian Society*, Plymouth, N.Z., 45, 1936, pp. 99–114; 46, 1937, pp. 1–23.

Ichikawa, S. "Kyudo—The Way of Archery in Japan," *Natural History*, New York, 33, 1933, pp. 139–152.

Raum, O. F. "The Rolling Target Game in Africa," *African Studies*, 12 (3), September, 1953, p. 105.

PART VI

Foot Racing, Gymnastics, and Track Events

Arnold, E. *Gymnastic Games Classified*, New Haven: The Author, 1907.

Brewster, P. G. "Four Games of Tag From India," *Midwest Folklore*, 1 (4), 1951, pp. 239–241.

Hodge, F. W. "A Zuni Foot Race," *American Anthropologist*, **3** (3), 1890, pp. 227–231.

Opler, M. E. "The Jicarilla Apache Ceremonial Relay Race," *American Anthropologist*, **46** (1), 1944, pp. 75–97.

Woods, C. "Indian Track Meet," *New Mexico*, Albuquerque, **24** (3), 1946, pp. 16–17, 43, 45, 47.

PART VII

Boxing and Wrestling

"Boxing and Wrestling 5000 Years Ago," *El Palacio*, Santa Fe, **43** (1,2,3), 1937, pp. 16–17.

Gordon, H. M. "Wrestling," *Man*, London, **28**, 1928, p. 199.

Hornblower, G. D. "Wrestling: India and Egypt," *Man*, London, **28**, 1928,

Namme, L. "The Bakweli Wrestling Match," *Nigeria*, Lagos, **15**, 1938, pp. 242–243.

Opler, M. K. "A Sumo Tournament at Tule Lake Center," *American Anthropologist*, **47** (1), 1945, pp. 134–139.

Weinberg, S. K., and Arond, H. "The Occupational Culture of the Boxer," *American Journal of Sociology*, **57** (5), 1952.

PART VIII

Water and Snow Sports

"A Boat Race in East Africa," *Illustrated London News*, London, March, 1937, pp. 538–539.

Boroff, D. "A View of Skiers and A Subculture," *Sports Illustrated*, New York, **21**, November, 1964, pp. 9–14.

Ewers, J. C. "Some Winter Sports of Blackfoot Indian Children," *Masterkey*, Los Angeles, **18**, 1953, pp. 177–183.

Finney, B. R. "Surfing in Ancient Hawaii," *Journal of the Polynesian Society*, Wellington, N.Z., **68**, 1959, pp. 327–347.

Finney, B. R. "The Development and Diffusion of Modern Hawaiian Surfing," *Journal of the Polynesian Society*, Wellington, N.Z., **69** (4), 1960, pp. 315–331.

Rochford, D. "New England Ski Trails and Ice Sports," *National Geographic Magazine*, Washington, D.C., **70**, 1936, pp. 645–664.

Smith, H. *Water Games*, New York: Ronald Press, 1962.

PART IX

Sports Involving Animals

Blomberg, R. "Cricket Fighting in Bali," *Ethnos, Stockholm,* 11, 1946, pp. 126–132.

Brown, O. O. "Kelantan Bull Fighting," *Journal of the Royal Asiatic Society, Singapore,* 6 (1), 1928, pp. 74–83.

Carter, D. S. "Dayak Cockfight," *Corona,* 11 (2), 1959, pp. 51–52.

Carter, W. H. "The Story of the Horse and Equestrian Sports," *National Geographic Magazine,* Washington, D.C., 44, 1923, pp. 455–566.

Davenport, Wm. Jamaican Fishing: A Game Theory Analysis," *Yale University Papers in Anthropology,* New Haven, 59, 1960, pp. 3–11.

Deraniyagela, P. "Some Blood Games of the Sinhalese," *Man,* London, 38, 1936, pp. 46–47.

Laufer, B. "Cockfights," *Field Museum News,* Chicago, 1 (10), 1930, p. 1.

Hunt, W. "On Bull Fighting," *American Imago,* 12 (4), 1955, pp. 343–353.

"Paraphernalia of China's Cricket Cult," *Field Museum News,* Chicago, 14 (6), 1943, pp. 7–8.

Sander, B. "Cock Fighting: The Daynak National Game," *Sarawak Museum Journal,* Kuching, 9 (13), 1959, pp. 25–32.

Scott, G. R. *History of Cock Fighting,* London: Skilton, 1957.

Williams, E. "Acculturation and the Horse Complex Among German-Brazilians," *American Anthropologist,* 46 (2), 1944, pp. 153–161.

Witaker, I. "Traditional Horse Races in Scotland," *Ariv,* 14, 1958, pp. 83–94.

PART X

Sports and Persons with Physical Disability

Bauer, D. "Big-Ten Football—Wheelchair Style," *Recreation,* 52 (11), 1959, pp. 386–387.

Brachman, D. S. "Observations on the Cardiac Unit of a Fresh Air Camp: Recommendations on the Use or Avoidance of Sports," *Journal of Aviation Medicine,* 3 (6), 1932, pp. 109–115.

Buell, C. D. *Sports For The Blind*, Ann Arbor: Edwards Brothers, 1947.

Chapman, F. M. "Sports and Games," *Recreation Activities For the Handicapped*, New York: Ronald Press, 1960, pp. 235–276.

Pomeroy, J. "Active Games and Sports," *Recreation for the Physically Handicapped*, New York: Macmillan Company, 1964, pp. 303–324.

Sapora, A. V. "Values of Sports and Games," *Recreation For The Ill and Handicapped*, **1** (4), 1957, p. 10.

Shaw, C. "Medical and Surgical Aspects of Sports and Games," *Baily's Magazine of Sports and Pastimes*, London, 1921, **116**, pp. 250–256, **117**, pp. 7–10.

Stafford, G. T. *Sports For The Handicapped*, New York: Prentice Hall, 1947.

Wolf, G. *Adapted Sports, Games, and Square Dances—Recreation for the Handicapped*, Hartford, Conn.: Connecticut Society for Crippled Children and Adults, 1962.

PART XI

Bibliographies

Stockum, C. M. *Sport—Attempt At A Bibliography of Books and Periodicals Published During 1890–12 in Great Britain, United States, France, Germany, Austria, Holland, Belgium, and Switzerland*, New York: Dodd and Livingston, 1914.

Szukovathy, I. "Some Notes on the History of Sports Bibliographies," *Research Quarterly*, Washington, D.C., **8**, 1937, pp. 3–14.

CHAPTER 7

MILITARY USAGES

While there is no exact record of the first usage of games as military exercises there are accounts in the ethnological literature of war games among tribal groups. We can assume, therefore, that the practice is an old one. As far as we can judge, war games were exercises in physical skill and strategy. In their earliest formalizations in Western culture they seem to have been mixtures of geometry and chess. During the eighteenth century:

The tactical and strategical writings of that epoch had, for the greater part, an outlandish resemblance to a course in geometry; a true strategist of that epoch did not know how to lead a corporal's guard across a ditch without a table of logarithms.[1]

The idea of using a recreative game to teach military tactics is said by military historians to have been put forth in 1780 by Helwig, a master of pages at the Court of the Duke of Brunswick. Brunswick, who later became the head of the Prussian armies, was looked on with favor by the Emperor Frederick the Great. Because of this, many young nobles from various German provinces were sent to the Duke's court to learn military tactics. Like any school teacher, Helwig faced a rather impossible task, and looked around for a better "mousetrap" to make the task easier. His "mousetrap" turned out to be a modification of a game that was over a thousand years old by Helwig's time. He put it this way:

[1] Heistand, H. D. S. "Foreign War Games," *Selected Papers Translated From European Military Publications.* (Translated from Revue De L'Etranger) Washington, D.C.: United States Government Printing Office, Publication No. XVIII, Document No. 57, 1898, p. 237.

The idea came to me . . . of rendering sensible, not to say palpable, a few principles and rules of the military art . . . to pages of the Duke . . . those young noblemen destined some day for military service. Independently of this chief objective my secondary one was to offer . . . an agreeable recreation by laying before them a game which, at first sight, presented different objects and operations, and which depended upon nothing but the rules and combinations made by the players. The first thought which presented itself to my mind was that the learning of my game ought not to be burdened with too many details if it was to fulfill its mission. . . . I should achieve my objective in the quickest way if I took for its basis the game of chess. . . . my idea was to adapt the game of chess to my own game. . . .[2]

This was not such a radical idea, since chess is a game of war and had long been used for lessons in strategy. Murray is of the opinion that chess, or its ancient forebear called *Chaturanga*, was the "conscious and deliberate invention of an inhabitant of North-west India."[3] *Chaturanga* is a Sanskrit word meaning "the army game." The unknown inventer of the game used the Indian armies of the fifth century as his model, that is, the king, the minister, the elephant (which later became the bishop in Europe), the horse (knight), the chariot (rook) and the footsoldier (pawn). The movement of the pieces were symbolic of the movement of the Indian army of the time, for example: "the war chariot which rolled forward, wheel ever to the ground, which stopped dead at choice, and which retreated at choice, is symbolized by the Rook's move in chess." Other examples would be that of the horse (knight) who is able to leap and jump, cannot stop at will, but must complete the move, or the slow steady march of the foot soldier (pawn), and the stately movements of the king. The chess board used initially was the board for a much older game, but suggested a battle fought on level terrain. As the playing of chess spread from country to country modifications were made to the pieces in relation to the strength of the elements of the army. Modifications were also made to the board. Cultural factors entered into the modifications, as evidenced by the substitution of the bishop for the elephant, and the introduction of the queen.

Another reason why the use of chess was not a radical idea was that chess had been popular among the upper classes in Germany for centuries before Helwig's time. It was a common belief among the upper

[2] Heistand, op. cit., 1898, p. 238.
[3] Murray, H. J. R. *Short History of Chess*. London: Oxford University Press, 1963, p. 1.

classes that chess, in addition to being recreative, offered training in mental and moral discipline.[4] Earlier, during the reign of Louis XV, two card games with military symbols were also invented and utilized to help teach military students military information. We do not know whether Helwig knew about these card games, but he settled on chess and that is how the concept of "war games" was initiated in modern times.

Helwig made a board of 1666 squares, each square being a little over an inch long and tinted various colors to represent different terrains. He represented varied terrains by putting certain colors together. Black and white meant level ground, red indicated mountains inaccessible to troops, green represented marshes that permitted troops to fire over the surface even though they could not cross them. Another shade of green indicated forests, while blue represented bodies of water such as lakes and ponds. There were colors for cities and towns, and lines were drawn to indicate frontiers and fortifications. Although he used pieces similar to chess pieces, they received values in relation to the army of the time, that is, battalions of infantry; squadrons of cavalry; battalions of fusileers or grenadiers; squadrons of dragoons, hussars, and light cavalry; batteries of seige guns and field pieces; and platoon boats. "I was not deceived in my expectations," Helwig wrote, "and experience confirmed the wisdom of my judgement, for chess players were the first to welcome my invention; they found it a great source of amusement, and set to work to make it better known."[5]

Many men during this period tried to improve on Helwig's game. Venturini, a tactician, published a sixty-page monograph, *Rules of a New War Game for the Use of Military Schools*. The Prussian, General Van der Goltz had said of this:

The whole resembles very closely the game of *poste et de voyage* in vogue a few years ago, where upon making an unlucky throw of the dice, one tumbles into a swamp, or breaks an axletree, or experiences some other such mishap. . . . Venturini hopes thus to render clear his confused and perplexed ideas. . . . This war game is a bad product of the refined military education of the period, which had piled up so many difficulties that it was incapable of taking a step in advance.[6]

In 1824, a young lieutenant, von Reisswitz, from Breslau published a

---

[4] Murray, H. J. R. *A History of Chess*. London: Oxford University Press, 1913, p. 852.

[5] Heistand, op. cit., 1898, p. 238.

[6] Heistand, op. cit., 1898, p. 238.

new type of war game, which served as a prototype until 1875. His game differed from Helwig's in a number of ways. He used maps and sand tables. The scale for the playing surface was approximately four miles, and troops were represented by lead pieces colored red and blue for opposing sides. They were painted with symbols to depict the various branches of the service. Another difference was that instead of playing by a fixed procedure as in chess, original situations based on actual battles were given in writing to the players by a director or umpire with the kind of information about the terrain and the enemy that each side normally would have. Orders, reports, and information were put in writing as the game progressed and were transmitted through the umpire. Time intervals for certain movements were taken into account, and the outcome of a battle was determined by the throw of the dice.

In 1876, du Vernois, a prominent officer in the Prussian Army, separated war games into two major types, *free Kriegspiel* and *rigid Kriegspiel*. *Rigid Kriegspiel* was Helwig's game and the many variations that others had made through the years. Games were systematized, rules and information were standardized and were based on such battles as were fought during the Franco-Prussian War.

Free Kriegspiel on the other hand drew its inspiration from the work of a Lieutenant Meckel, a professor at the Hanover War School who established games that allowed for free play, divorced from cumbersome rules and procedures, and that required umpires to use military experience to decide who won. During this period *rigid Kriegspiel* was played in England, Austria, Italy, France, Russia, Turkey, and the United States. The British and the Russians also had developed some naval war games, but these were similar to the army games. On the other hand because it was Meckel who introduced war games in Japan, the Japanese war college only used *free Kriegspiel* from the outset, and military historians are inclined to attribute Japan's success in the Russo-Japanese war to this fact.

War games in the United States during most of the nineteenth century were of the *rigid Kriegspiel* type, and varied from European games only insofar as they used U.S. Civil War battles as models. Their games were essentially updated versions of Reisswitz's game. Shortly after the turn of the century they were also using a naval war game, and a coast artillery war game. The U.S. military began to incorporate some of du Vernois' ideas into these games, and made some modifications using blackboards, charts illustrating coast lines, harbors, and miniature boats to represent ships. Other technical modifications made it possible to do away with more of the chesslike equipment.

The Germans continued to improve on war games and many of their battles in World War I were rehearsed by these means. Because of the restrictions placed on the German military after World War I, they were forced to continue the development and use of war games in all military training since they could not hold real maneuvers. Battles of World War II, such as the invasion of Czechoslovakia, are said to have been "gamed" ahead of time. In one instance, it is reported that the allied attack on the German forces in the Ardennes in November 1944 was repulsed by German troops who were following orders that were being issued by Field Marshal Model and his staff playing out the battle in the game room while the battle was raging. The Germans also "rehearsed" the invasion of the Ukraine and the invasion of England.[7] Similarly, the Japanese were involved in very detailed war game play in the late 1930s and early 1940s.

Staffs of the various Japanese Fleets held frequent games. . . . Late in August 1941 Cinc Combined Fleet ordered all Fleet Commanders and their key staff members to Tokyo for further war games. . . . On September 2 the final and most important games started. . . . In these early days of September the teams studied two general problems: the details of a surprise raid on Pearl Harbor, and second, a carefully worked-out schedule for occupying Malaya, Burma, the Dutch East Indies, the Philippines, the Solomons, and the Central Pacific Islands, including Hawaii.[8]

During the time between the World Wars, little development and use of war gaming could be found in the United States, except perhaps to teach military tactics. For this purpose two types of games were used: sand-table games (a chess variation) and field maneuvers that simulated battles. Since World War II, the United States appears to have taken a lead in the development and use of war-game techniques. Many kinds of war games are in use for a variety of military purposes. The basic pattern is still the same, *free Kriegspiel* and *rigid Kriegspiel*, but with a number of variations. Helmer points out that "if a game is concerned with overall planning, it is a *strategic* game. If it deals with the immediate actions and reactions of an individual, it is a *tactical* game."[9] Strategic and tactical games have always been a basic interest of the military, but as

[7] Young, J. P. *History and Bibliography of War Gaming.* Arlington, Virginia: Armed Services Technical Information Agency, Staff Paper ORO-SP-13, April, 1957, p. 21.

[8] Specht, R. D. *War Games.* Santa Monica, California: The Rand Corporation, 1957, pp. 3–4.

[9] Helmer, O. *Strategic Gaming.* Santa Monica, California: The Rand Corporation, February, 1960, p. 15.

of late, *logistics* gaming has become as important because of the introduction of technology into warfare, and the growing dependence of the military on industrial organization and production in every country.

Recognizing that it is impossible for a human being to remember and process all the information needed in a complex rigid game, the military at present have developed five levels of war games, which require a variety of computer assistance:

1. Unaided human play.
2. Human play aided by a machine for routine computations.
3. Human player determines the moves, a machine computes outcome.
4. Human planner selects overall strategy, a machine plays the game in accordance with the strategy.
5. Human designer describes the strategy space and sets up rules for selecting strategies from it, complete machine play of game including choice of strategy.

There are over sixty organizations in the United States today that are interested in or engaged in war gaming. They use games for testing plans, for training, and for research and development. In addition, the United States Army Strategy and Tactics Analysis Group (STAG) estimates that of the more than 200 organizations engaged in analysis in support of military decision making about one-quarter of approximately 3000 projects per year in which these organizations are engaged utilize some war-gaming techniques.

War games today have enough variability and difference to warrant individual names. Some take their names from the first initial of the words that indicate what the game is intended to do, for example, PARM, program analysis for resource management; PERT, program evaluation and review technique. Some follow a similar pattern, but appear to suggest that their developers have a sense of humor, that is, SWAP, strategic war planning; FASTVAL, forward air strike evaluation. Other names have a more macabre flavor—SURVIVAL, RISK II, DYNAMO, CRISIS-COM!

War games have changed considerably in the past 200 years; perhaps most of all in the general acceptance of "gaming" as a military procedure. One of the very few familiar things that would help von Reisswitz recognize that today's games are based on his original idea, is that players still refer to the opposing sides as the red and the blue. We include in this chapter a recent article by Paxson of the Rand Corporation, as an example of the types of current published information that is available. Paxson reviews the types of war games used in the decision-making process by the military today. While information on war games is often restricted, the list of selected references that follows the Paxson article indicates a number of sources from which details regarding other types of war games may be obtained.

11

War Gaming

E. W. PAXSON

INTRODUCTION

Like medieval churchmen, operations research practitioners are prone to debate the meanings of the terms in their mystique. War gaming is a first-rate example. Presumably, confusion as to the relative ascendancy of the terms *operational gaming, simulation,* and *Monte Carlo* is common. This chapter will not contribute to this particular debate, which has been reviewed and critiqued by Thomas and Deemer [1]. It seems more to the point to give examples of these three techniques and to discuss their values and deficits on the grounds that the reader is more interested in the craft of the playwright than in the craftiness of the critic. For editorial convenience, all three terms are here subsumed under "war gaming" with the preliminary observations that not all operational gaming is properly two-sided, and that simulation and Monte Carlo methods are also generally used for ends other than war gaming.

A war game is a model of military reality set up by a judicious process of selection and aggregation, yielding the results of *the interactions of opponents with conflicting objectives* as these results are developed under more or less definite rules enforced by a control or umpire group. A war game should have a clear objective in mind, such as determining tactics to achieve desired results at least cost in matériel, or

SOURCE. Memorandum RM-3489-PR, February 1963. This research is sponsored by the United States Air Force under Project RAND—Contract No. AF 49(638) 700 —monitored by the Directorate of Development Planning, Deputy Chief of Staff, Research and Technology, Hq USAF. Views or conclusions contained in this Memorandum should not be interpreted as representing the official opinion or policy of the United States Air Force.

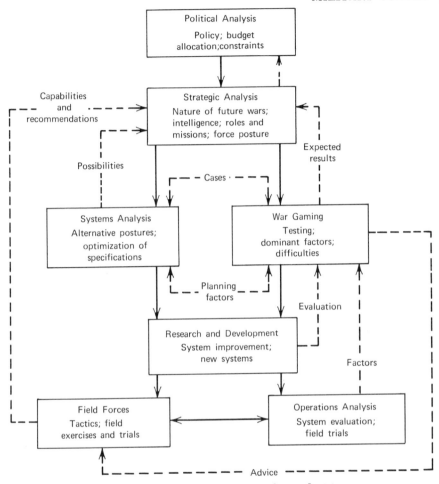

Fig. 1. Analysis in support of military decisions.

an hypothesis in view, such as establishing the operational and logistical feasibility of highly dispersed attack aircraft.

War gaming is used for training, exposition, examination of tactics and strategy, testing of present and future postures and the war plans based on them, and to provide a context for the analysis of proposed weapons systems. The position and role of war gaming as part of analysis in support of military decision is shown in Figure 1. The various inner feedback loops in this figure are not included for pictorial effect. They exist, with varying weights, in the real world.

Prior to the last decade, war games were largely played for purposes of training military personnel and examining tactics and strategies.

Historical details need not be rehearsed here because a rather complete review has been provided by Young [2].

Young's survey quite properly devotes appreciable space to Livermore's *American Kriegspiel* [3]. His game has three significant technical features: (1) systematic numerical factors to evaluate engagements based, insofar as possible, on past military events; (2) an allowance for psychological factors, such as the diminution in effective strength of troops who have been under fire or who are fatigued, or the inability to direct the fire of troops to a distant target when a dense enemy first line is inflicting serious damage upon those firing; and (3) the use of elementary Monte Carlo methods, such as the throw of dice, to assess the effect of fire, assuming an underlying probability distribution. Much modern operational gaming would profit if greater attention were paid to the first two of these points. However, Livermore is not concerned with such current fripperies as value of the game, replications, sensitivity, branchings, or player learnings, some of which will be discussed later. He proposes rigid and free versions, also discussed at length below.

Livermore provides advice of obvious value to the novice game director in regard to the period of war time a "move" may represent:[1]

The length of the move in every case should be determined by the time that would elapse before the conduct of one side would be so modified by that of the other that a truthful representation of warfare would make it necessary for the troop-leaders to know what has transpired before making further indications.[2]

Since the publication of Young's review, the United States Army Strategy and Tactics Analysis Group[3] (STAG) has prepared a directory of organizations and activities engaged or interested in war gaming. STAG's survey gives information on the purpose for which gaming is undertaken (testing plans, research and development, training) and continues with a rather detailed description of the work underway in each organization. This directory now covers 60 organizations of which less than one-half are civilian, indicating the current importance of war gaming in military operations research.

However, STAG's review has not yet exhausted the field since it is estimated[4] that in the United States alone there are approximately 200 organizations engaged in analysis in support of military decision, that these organizations produce close to 3000 reports per year, and that

[1] See [3], p. 17.
[2] See Livermore Reference No. 3.
[3] 4815 Rugby Avenue, Bethesda 14, Maryland
[4] Author's estimate

operational gaming and simulation techniques or results are used to some degree in about one-quarter of all projects undertaken.

This chapter covers the following topics:

1. Monte Carlo methods as used in war games.
2. Man-machine games in which massive computer programs are required.
3. Rigid manual games, with detailed rules, which are largely concerned with the planning of a military posture and an assessment of the worth of the planning by an associated campaign game.
4. Semi-rigid or free games in which the control group's judgment takes precedence over a detailed book of rules and which deal largely with military campaigns. Each move in these games demands a host of separate military decisions and evaluations.
5. An over-all summary and critique of war gaming.

Much of the above material has been covered recently in a symposium conducted by the Washington Operations Research Council [4]. The examples in this chapter will differ from those sketched in that symposium and will, in some respects, be examined in greater depth. These examples, while typical of the game type they illustrate, are far from being the sole members of their classes. They are chosen because of the author's personal relations with them.

The chapter will not discuss the important types of war games which use real military staffs, troops, and hardware—the field exercise, the command post exercise, the combat development experiment. These deserve far more attention from the military operations research community than they now receive.

MONTE CARLO

Military events are frequently, if not always, concatenations of chance subevents. A fighter aircraft attempting to intercept and shoot down a bomber is a classic example. The chance that this event is successful can be modelled as a product of the probabilities that (1) ground radar detects, tracks, and correctly identifies the bomber in time for feasible intercept, (2) the interceptor is combat ready, (3) it does not abort after launch (i.e., suffer some malfunction after taking off), (4) it is vectored (i.e., directed to the vicinity of the target), (5) a tallyho (i.e., a sighting by sensors in the interceptor) occurs, (6) the target is acquired (i.e., the fire control system locks on and tracks the target), (7) the armament system does not itself abort, and (8) the ordnance released splashes (i.e., kills or disables) the bomber.

Field trials, usually supplemented by separate theoretical studies for new systems, assist in assessing these component probabilities. The subevents should properly be described by probability distributions, e.g., probability of radar detection at a given range or circular error of the ordnance, and most are conditional distributions, e.g., the chance of sighting given that the vectoring places the interceptor at a given bearing and distance with respect to the bomber.

The simplest-minded approach is to push aside these refinements and assign a probability to each subevent and multiply them under appeal to the theorem of compound probability. This would result in some such statement as "In 10 per cent of the cases, an incoming bomber will be shot down by a given interceptor."

This procedure, in fact, is very common in practical work, partly because the parameters of the many subordinate compound distributions are themselves subject to a distribution which is not precisely definable and partly because excessive technical fastidiousness is incompatible with project deadlines. Nonetheless, in war-gaming applications it can and should be rejected for various reasons.

First, there may be hundreds of aircraft (and missiles) involved on both sides. The simple multiplicative formulation to include recycling of aircraft and multiple attacks soon becomes unmanageable. Because digital computers are needed to keep track of the elaborate events in space-time, it is easy to resort to the Monte Carlo method: *the use of sampling to estimate the answer to a mathematical problem.* That is, at each chance stage of each engagement, a random number should be generated in the computer, compared with the appropriate distribution, and a specific outcome selected for that particular stage. Thus the entire air battle has a particular history, with a statement, if desired, of exactly which interceptors succeed against which bombers.

Second, the simple mean-value procedure does not show the spread of results. It is useful to be able to make such statements as "There is a 90 per cent chance that at least 30 bombers will be splashed." The digital Monte Carlo simulation of the air battle can be repeated many times with no change in tactics—i.e., in flight plans for the bombers or commitment policy for the interceptors—leading to statistical statements of interest.[5] In practice, one is frequently content with about ten such runs, since the pay of computing machines is not trivial.

Third, even in those cases in which a complete analytic formulation

---

[5] Cases, perhaps pathological, leading to bimodal distributions have arisen to discomfit the mean value approach.

of interlocking distributions can, in principle, be written out, the computer program is more complicated and the computing time much greater than would be the case with a Monte Carlo approach.

Those interested in the details of formulating air battle models will find the accounts of Thomas [5], Taylor [6], Leibowitz and Lieberman [7], Brotman and Seid [8], and Adams and Jenkins [9] helpful.

Monte Carlo is an exercise in statistical sampling. Hence the question of increasing its efficiency by proper experimental design should be raised. The experimenter would like to decrease the standard deviation of the estimate to his problem's solution by means other than increasing the sample size. This is done not only for reasons of elegance but, as noted earlier, because of the cost of computer time. Such an approach is commonly used by those applying Monte Carlo methods to problems in, for example, nuclear physics, but these methods do not seem to have widely permeated operations research applications, or war gaming in particular.

Seven methods have been discussed by Kahn and Mann [10]. They are

1. Importance sampling—which increases the probability that the sample comes from an "interesting region";
2. Russian roulette and splitting—which kill off uninteresting samples and break interesting ones into branches;
3. Expected values—in which some part of a problem can be calculated;
4. Correlation and regression—by which a single experiment can yield a comparison of two methods;
5. Systematic sampling—which calculates the first part of a multi-stage problem;
6. Stratified sampling—which is a combination of methods 1 and 5;
7. Specialized techniques—such as using all combinations of each choice of a set of random numbers.

The savings resulting from these methods can be dramatic, but discussion beyond the above cryptic remarks would be inappropriate in this chapter. Kahn [11] has also indicated how correlation and weighting can be used in comparing different bombing strategies.

The Monte Carlo method is a highly useful tool in maximizing the information potentially available in what is usually a submodel in a large war game. The larger assertion, sometimes heard in the land, that gaming in general is an example of the Monte Carlo approach does not appeal to the journeyman war gamer.

MAN-MACHINE GAMES

A characteristic feature of war is the day-by-day or even moment-by-moment allocation of limited resources by opposing commanders to various competing missions or tasks. Feedbacks from the results of the interactions condition the two sequences of decisions. The determination of optimum allocations, though of clear importance in its own right, may also contribute to the planning of a military posture (the numbers and specifications of the component weapons systems), as well as to logistics and intelligence problems. Man-machine games are designed to explore such allocations.

The game model drawn up for the analysis requires human decisions which, like moves in chess, are few in number and simple to describe but the consequences of which require the repeated routine solution of mathematically defined systems. A symbiosis between man and machine is indicated. The human cortex is used as a steepest ascent calculator to seek a way up to an optimum in the vast space of combinations of decision patterns, while the computer's registers provide the results of each step in that journey.

Many plays of the game are possible because each partner, in his fashion, is quick. After experience, it may happen that the machine can take over and explore, unattended, a subspace of decision possibilities. Or the man may produce an analytic solution, with all its advantages. A particular symbiosis has sometimes been broken in these ways by man or machine. New ones always form.

One must distinguish between simultaneous and consecutive man-machine games. In the simultaneous game, men and machines work in parallel, or rather men are almost continuously changing machine inputs and the machine is faithfully showing outcomes. In consecutive games, access to the machine is restricted, so that changes in input can be made only occasionally, with rather long periods of computing intervening. Either type may be appropriate, and examples of each will be discussed. Historically, simultaneous games have usually been played on analogue computers and consecutive games on digital equipment. Even when it is desirable to play a simultaneous game on a digital computer, this is rarely possible under modern computing service management because only the computermen can be the gods of the machine.

TAGS[6] [12], [13] is a good example of a simultaneous man-machine game played on a general analogue computer. This game emphasizes

---

[6] Tactical Air Ground Study. For an example of a ground combat machine game, see Hebron in [4], p. 39ff.

the allocation problems of tactical air commanders in a major theater who must assign daily, in some proportion, their residual stocks of combat-ready fighters, fighter bombers, and light bombers to the primary missions of counter-air (against airfields), interdiction, and close support of ground forces.[7] In addition, only fighters can be used for air defense and escort of attack aircraft. Atomic bombs can be allocated to the three primary missions. All of these allocations are simulated by adjusting potentiometers on command panels serving as inputs of the desired percentages to the machine.

The daily (in war time) test of these tactical choices is the to-and-fro movement on the ground of what may be called, in view of the date of TAGS (1954), the Main Line of Resistance between two ground armies. This movement depends on relative remaining strengths, rates of supply, and air effort. It is given by a formula derived largely from World War II and comparable experience. Hence the machine, and not the airman, plays ground forces. The position of this phase line and *one's own* current stocks of aircraft, divisions, supplies, and bombs appear on meter faces on a status panel. Intelligence play can be supplied by an umpire or controller.

Additional potentiometers permit adjustment of initial conditions and parameter values in the model to test for sensitivity or to introduce degradation factors. Stop-start switches provide machine dead-time to permit players to digest information and make decisions. A "campaign" of several months' duration can be conducted in a few minutes.

The model requires about 100 equations, divided symmetrically between the two sides. These are simple first-order differential equations,[8] algebraic equations of balance, and functions to be evaluated. Because no hereditary effects or lags are included, ordinary general purpose analogue equipment is suitable. The preparatory labor in establishing these equations, fitting them to combat data, and deducing values for parameters should not be underestimated.

Subsequently, Dresher and Berkowitz [14] were able to formulate analytically and solve by game theory a not oversimplified version of TAGS. The solution of the extensive game shows how richly allocation strategies vary during a campaign, depending on initial force ratios and on the duration of the campaign.

Among other dangers in game theory, there is one which should be

[7] In military operations, the nightly conference of air and ground commanders to "discuss" this allocation also has certain game features.

[8] For air attrition, Lanchester's square law seems appropriate; but for movement of a phase line on the ground, the logarithmic law in which casualty rate per unit is constant appears more faithful to historical fact.

mentioned here. The optimum solution to a game may involve extreme strategies, i.e., the principle of concentration pushed inevitably by the mathematics to the point where a mission may have no resources applied to it. The reason is that this is the correct solution for a *model* which cannot reflect all the smoothing-out factors in the real world. If the interpretation is judicious, the value of the model or the game results based on it is not necessarily lost.

There is an additional subtlety of importance in this connection. Manual or man-machine games may use mixed strategies intuitively but they do not calculate them. Game theory does. In the analytic form of TAGS, the weaker side is instructed to randomize and concentrate his efforts in a particular way on different missions, i.e., he must take a chance on an early payoff. This may well run counter to all (peacetime) military doctrine [15]. Yet calculation, in the Dresher-Berkowitz analysis, shows that the expected payoff of the randomized strategy may be perhaps 40 per cent more than that yielded by military doctrine.[9] The matter deserves further airing.

Turn now to an example of a consecutive man-machine game. The problem is to analyze force requirements for a major atomic attack with gravity bombs on a large enemy air complex. As in most operational gaming, there is no clearly defined payoff or criterion. One does have in mind some such notion as determining campaign tactics which will leave the enemy with a prescribed residual offensive capability, accomplishing this at the least cost in bombers lost. But this is specious. By concentrating aircraft in successive waves, it is conceivable that a longer campaign may achieve the same results at lower cost in lost aircraft. But then the enemy has more time to hit back during the campaign. Again, what level of residual capability should be set?—the marginal cost of killing the last few enemy bombers may be very great indeed. These difficulties are characteristic of realistic operational gaming. Hence a sequence of games is designed which will contribute numerically to these and other questions by examining various tactics and determining their results. Command decisions must always be made using contextual factors not included in any particular war game.

As in experiments in physics, the time to get the apparatus ready very greatly exceeds the time spent on the experiment itself. First, a major compilation of intelligence data on enemy order of battle is required,

---

[9] There is a theme here for the military historian. Captains in battle (and in war games) frequently violate principles and doctrines spectacularly. Are their appraisals based on special circumstances or is this an intuitive use of randomized strategies?

giving his airbase and support structure, his communications and tracking nets, and his defense alignment. Second, operational assessments of his capabilities are needed to provide planning factors for such matters as in-commission rates, detection probabilities, lags in hand-over of control from one sector to another, and the like. This is a job for an A-2.5 section, midway between conventional Air Intelligence and Air Operations. Third, corresponding planning factors must be refurbished for one's own forces. Fourth, computer programs must be produced and debugged for (1) the air battles during the campaign; (2) the damage done to elements of the air complex, depending on weapon used, circular probable error of the bomb drop, and the vulnerable subcomponents of the aircomplex elements; (3) the residual and recuperative sortie potential of aircraft on a damaged base; and (4) the fallout effects over a wide area. If lucky, the agency designing the game can use or adapt programs or flowcharts existing in the organization or available to it, because new programs of these types may take six or more months to produce.

Procedure is now routine. Control establishes overall restrictions such as (1) bases available to the attacker for staging (both strike and post-strike), (2) size of force available, (3) rate of commitment (campaign tempo), and (4) weapons available.

The attack commander plans (1) the deployment schedule to reach his launch bases, (2) what targets will be taken on and in what order (e.g., sweeping to take out radar and fighters on the way to bomber bases), (3) the balance between strike and reconnaissance effort, (4) tracks and profiles, including coordination and timing, and (5) weapon selection.

The defense commander decides on his rules of engagement (rate and direction of defense force commitment).

The campaign is now fought by waves (successive air battles), each evaluated by the first computer program. Control then supplies appropriate combat intelligence on results to the two sides (as determined by the first two programs). The defense commander redeploys his residual forces (determined by the third program), the attack commander plans a new wave based on his reconnaissance information, and the campaign continues.

In man-machine games of this nature, as in war games in general, perhaps a hundred or more separate numerical planning factors must be estimated and compounded in the models. A systematic and complete evaluation of the sensitivity of the over-all results to changes in these values is not feasible. Reflection will usually isolate key factors (e.g., the number of hours before a base, evacuated under warning or attack, returns to operational status). After experience with several games, relatively simple hand computation usually shows the effect of perturbations in such factors.

War gamers are invariably serendipitists. In a particular example of a game of this type, it was found that rudimentary intelligence would establish a good feel for the attacker's deployment schedule, permitting an estimate of high occupation densities at strike-staging bases and so a determination of periods of their greatest vulnerability.

SIMULATION

The temptation is strong to discuss large-scale experiments simulating organizations under the heading of "man-machine games." Applications to military logistics and to air defense centers and nets have proved highly profitable. Yet, these simulations are not rigorously in the spirit of war gaming, because the opposition is a laboratory staff whose play of enemy action and nature is "canned," serving to supply suitably timed inputs to the organization being modelled.

It is also essential in these experiments that there be roughly a one-to-one relationship between the echelons or functions of the real world organization and its laboratory representation, and a precise relation between real time and laboratory time, which may be one to one for operational organizations or many to one for administrative structures. In war games designed for analytic ends these relationships are quite flexible.

These techniques deserve a full exposition which will not be attempted here. But they should not be dismissed without a précis of certain of their principles.

In operational organizations such as an air defense center, the standard operating procedures of the experimental group can be pushed to error or complete breakdown by overload of input to be processed. It is psychologically of first importance to conduct an immediate debriefing and indicate to the group exactly what mistakes were made. It is precisely because the input is canned and is known in all detail that this is possible [16], [17]. Next, the experimental group can be asked to revise its procedures to deal with what was previously considered an overload. In war gaming a similar type of learning and revision occurs. In a measure, this presents the director of the game with a problem. Does he have a "faithful" representation of future warfare? Is the effect of the players' learning an invalidation of his game? Or should he view this learning as one of the values of his synthetic war experience? The latter position seems best, provided the project involves a sequence of games.

An essential feature of organizational simulation of administrative structures [18] is their telescoping of real time, so that the life history of a weapons system under different supply policies, which in the real world might cover many years, consumes only a few weeks of laboratory time. War games are not normally so fortunate. In gaming a complicated engagement, it is not at all unusual for game time to be a healthy multiple of real time. Hence, if an entire campaign is being gamed, the project leader can only hope for relatively quiet war periods—which must and do occur—so that he can get through a relatively long period in one tactical bound without violating Livermore's precept.[10] Project leaders like to claim that they have gamed complete campaigns.

RIGID MANUAL GAMES

Manual war games require the players to make a very large number of major and minor decisions per move. To assess the consequences of these decisions, relatively little and hand calculation is normally needed. Many games of this genus have the additional feature that the moves, relatively few in number, can be evaluated by the application of a complete set of rigidly prescribed and applied rules, available to the players in all detail. Because of their associated apparatus, rigid manual games are sometimes called board or bookkeeping games. These qualifiers seem irrelevant.

SAFE (Strategy and Force Evaluation) [19], a current, game, is a good example of the rigid manual family. It is concerned with strategic air war planning and is rigorously two sided. It examines alternatives in procurement strategies, research and development planning, strategic intelligence, force composition, and operational strategies (to test the preceding planning) for a possible central strategic air war toward the end of the 1960's.

SAFE provides a conceptual framework within which to generate and examine new ideas. It helps to systematize issues and supply gross evaluation of alternative strategies. It keeps the outlines of all components in two interacting "big pictures" in balance and in focus. In an instruction version, it is currently (1962) part of the curriculum for the first class at the U.S. Air Force Academy.

One complete play of SAFE takes four days, starting with orientation and grand-strategy planning sessions and terminating with a systematic postmortem. Successful play can involve as few as two players on each team, plus a game director and two assistants, one assigned to each team room.

---

[10] See p. 4.

The procurement phase has three moves, each concerned with procurement and R & D planning for a three-year period. Decisions involve budget allocation, the phasing in and out of weapon systems, and construction. Players must make about 40 such decisions for each period. The success of R & D and intelligence programs, as well as the budget available, is partly determined by chance.

It is not known to the players whether the operational phase will occur at the beginning or at the end of the third procurement period. This tempers extreme strategies. During this phase, decisions on a gross war plan and on the details of missile and aircraft strikes must be made. The outcome is assessed in terms of military losses, urban destruction, and mortalities.

Who wins or loses a war game is not clear. In fact, it is unwise to set a criterion because play is apt to be distorted toward this special end. SAFE illustrates the flexibility of ideas which arise when a criterion is not prescribed.

A player must, however, have some underlying strategic principle in mind to guide him through the game. For example, he may decide to minimize his urban casualties by a massive shelter or dispersal program. Or he may draw fire from his cities by locating the bases for his weapons in remote parts of his country. Or he may try to have the largest possible residual stack of missiles when the war is declared "ended." This flexibility justifies SAFE's research orientation.

It is curiously difficult to devise a "stable" set of rules for a game such as SAFE, i.e., rules without soft spots which the gamester in every game can exploit. Each postmortem of a SAFE game serves to refine the stock, indicating what may be oversensitivity of outcome to certain rules or assumptions, or which rules seem to dominate. Of course, a game is to be treasured if it can turn up "rules" which are, with likelihood, dominant or representative of soft spots in the real world.

The latter point has a technical aspect. Games are frequently censured on the grounds that they involve useless detail, serving only to cloud the true issues, and also on the opposite grounds that in some major respect they are overaggregated. In fact, after his first quick survey of the rules of SAFE, the analytically minded novitiate persuades himself that he can structure the game quite simply in order to block out an over-all strategy and assess its consequences before he initiates play. Try it. Each such attempt fails to include a key feature and so requires successive expansion of the structure. This is a measure of the skill in the constructor's choice of game detail and perhaps the complexity of the phenomena it purports to mirror. In any event, no abstract theory of war game aggregation seems to have been proposed in the literature or even thoughtfully discussed.

FREE GAMES

It sometimes seems that as many people are currently studying limited wars as are fighting them. A popular study method is the semirigid or free game, replete with planning factors, but the events of which are generally adjudicated rather than evaluated by completely prescribed rules. The SIERRA[11] series of limited war studies is a full-blown example whose research motivation and methodology will illustrate the category. Weiner [20] has given a rather complete discussion of the techniques developed, which will consequently only be briefed here.

The research objectives are to uncover possible deficiencies in military capabilities, in doctrine, and in weapons systems for the prosecution of limited wars which might confront us, and to suggest for consideration feasible improvement in capabilities, changes in doctrine, and more appropriate weapons systems, particularly as these apply to the U.S. Air Force.

This is a broad canvas, necessarily broad if limited war is to be examined. The role of no one service can be looked at independently of the operations of the others. Characteristically, limited wars are strongly conditioned by the interaction of military, economic, and political considerations. Political considerations determine the war objective, the vigor with which it is pursued, and hence constrain military operations in regard to sanctuary areas, base availability, weapons that can be employed, and target systems that can be selected. The analysis will also have to examine campaigns of appreciable duration, will necessarily deal with many different geographical areas, and above all must consider the implications of each of a set of possible policy decisions for each type of event. Finally, if new weapons systems are to be studied, a major time dimension is introduced. Administratively, these games are not cheap. A continuing investment in time and men is required.

Preceding any game of a series is a sequence of preparatory actions. These are (1) deciding on game objectives and hypotheses to be tested, (2) data collecting, (3) writing a scenario for events leading up to the war, and (4) preparing the game context.

Obviously, background information is needed on all the characteristics

---

[11] Name chosen solely to popularize what was at the time of the project's initiation a relatively new phonetic alphabet.

of the area of operations that affect military operations. The public library is no substitute for experienced people with access to the appropriate documents. Planning factors must be collected and codified. These may deal with the operational characteristics of weapons systems, with the weather, with attrition rates, and with logistics capabilities. To generate these factors may call for substudies. The planning manuals of the military services do not seem to discuss the in-commission rate of elephants or combat between armed sampans and junks. Not all planning factors needed can be anticipated. In fact some are generated during the course of play of many games in which evaluation of many like events ultimately leads to a new planning factor.

The SIERRA pregame scenario requires RED to prepare a build-up plan giving time and place of attack, objectives, and forces required and where deployed. Appropriate strategic intelligence is given to BLUE. War game planning emphasizes equally estimates of capabilities *and* intentions. The game context is the set of over-all ground rules under which that particular game will be played. The components of the context, primarily policy constraints, are defined on the basis of "relevance" (will they help achieve the purpose of the particular game?), "credibility" (are they plausible though not necessarily probable?), and "materiality" (are they absolutely essential?).

A synthetic campaign is fought by RED and BLUE teams, occupying separate rooms, and interacting only through a CONTROL team. Interactions are systematized and simplified through the exchange of various forms and map overlays. Coordination of the interactions is achieved by three war clocks whose jumps (rather than continuous operation) are under CONTROL's hand.

The primary function of each team is Operations. They prepare phased campaign plans, detail move plans, and readjust actions interior to a move. They have access to political, technological, and logistics advice. Each military service should have an experienced representative whose changes of insignia of rank will be rapid as he plays many different command roles during the game.

CONTROL has the function of (1) highest echelon political control of each team (and so of the game); (2) adjudication of the credibility, relevance, and materiality of the plans submitted by the teams; (3) evaluation of operational and logistics feasibility of plans and moves; (4) evaluation of move outcomes; (5) supply of the finished end-product of combat intelligence to the teams, based partly on team collection activities, at the appropriate suspense times; (6) maintenance of the "pacing" (realistic time, space, and decision scaling) of the game; and (7)

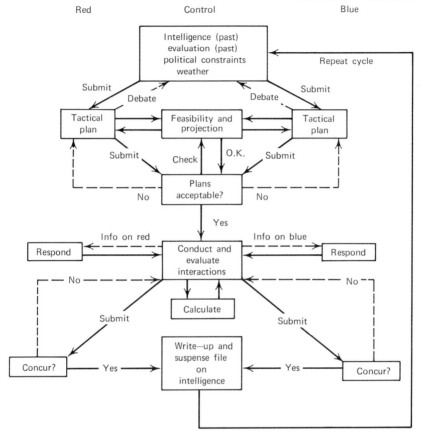

Fig. 2. Move cycle.

maintenance of the "integrity" of the game (e.g., so that destroyed bridges are not crossed immediately).

Players have the right of *reclama*[12] during the evaluation of plan or move outcomes, not for reasons of morale, but to produce as many partisan pros and cons as possible to assist CONTROL in balanced rulings.

The general course of events during a move cycle is given in Figure 2. Not much more will be said here in regard to move technique, since war gaming, like other emotion-charged activities of man, can only be learned through participation.

There are certain over-all aspects of the play which should be brought out. Decision or branch points frequently arise representing choices

[12] A Filipino word meaning *anguished protest*.

among truly major courses of action for a team, such as escalating (e.g., committing strategic forces) or pressing for a peace conference. Here, CONTROL quite deliberately proceeds on the basis of relevancy rather than credibility. That branch is selected which is most relevant to the purpose of the game, e.g., full implications of a policy decision [21] or full examination of the capability of a weapon system. An alternative method of choice is to select that branch leading to the most complex situation. This provides more material for analysis and may even permit estimating the outcome of a less complicated branch as a lesser included event. Branches involving catastrophic "unique" events, such as the death of a political leader, are excluded.

The method of free gaming sketched above, which sometimes bears the ponderous name of a closed-information predetermined form game, involves directly about 20 people and may require a game duration equal to that of the war it tries to model. After appreciable experience, a group inevitably finds ways to telescope the effort and essentially to maximize the number of plays for a given project period. These procedures illustrate the dominance of integrated team planning over the strict planning factor and computing approach. These methods are

1. *Projection.* The subsequent course of events is spelled out without detailed gaming.
2. *Meshing.* A subsequent game return to a major decision point and explore that branch, thus meshing with the original game.
3. *Series.* A sequence of games may change only some initial assumptions, such as weapon type that can be used.
4. *Joint Adjudication.* Opposing teams plan their tactical moves separately but assess the results and resolve interplays jointly with CONTROL. Detail, particularly in regard to intelligence play, is sacrificed, but speed is unquestionably gained.
5. *Seminar.* RED, BLUE, and CONTROL work together around a war map[13] for the entire duration of the "game." Operations are proposed, feasibility determined, and results assessed, all in the open.
6. *Building Blocks.* When numerous game histories are accumulated for a given area under series play, it may be possible to take various blocks of results from some games and use these to compose variations. For example, wings of tactical and strategic bombers, separated in two games, may be combined to assess a third.

With suitable record-keeping discipline, these games accumulate de-

---

[13] This is the Napoleonic method, which required only map boards, map pins, a carriage, and ability.

tailed histories of air, ground, and sea operations and logistics, and other events. These can be viewed as synthetic war histories and examined for lessons (and mistakes). At this stage of analysis of the game output, however, one is much more concerned with gross conclusions, which seem to stand out clearly and which must make sense in their own right. The whole game sequence is then viewed as an impartial structure which has turned up deficiencies and dominating factors, perhaps largely unexpected, whose acceptance does not depend critically on the fine grain of the games. This is not to say that the fine structure is then discarded. It can be mined for planning factors and can be used as a test bed for concepts not in the original experimental happenstances. For example, such games can supply a check list with which to confront, say, proposals for weapons systems calling for highly dispersed operations, which may be logistically self-defeating in detail.

Some philosophical points on over-all game management may perhaps be briefed. A major problem in the art of running a free war game is how to cause events to happen at a realistic rate. Working on paper, with aggregated representations, one may soon find that actions are occurring much too fast and with a high precision which would not occur in the real world. In war both sides intermittently set objectives and deploy their resources to achieve them. During the deployment time the enemy is achieving his objectives in part through his deployment. This causes a further time-consuming change in decision and deployment.

The timing problem within the game mechanism is partly met by paying proper attention to logistics movements, to the effect of losses, to delays and lags in intelligence, and to allowances for command lag time. The latter lag may exercise overriding control. For example, a military formation which may deploy or recycle at relative leisure when events appear to be ominous has quite a different character from one which must await a last-minute decision to leap globally.

There is a more subtle aspect to the war game pacing problem which has received insufficient attention from the theoreticians. In any military world there are many command and control levels and decision echelons. To each echelon is attached a span of control and a scale of time of interest to it, proportioned to its level in the hierarchy. Each echelon also has its own intelligence level in regard to detail and staleness. There is no such thing as complete knowledge of the war at any one place, such as CONTROL has in war games. The interaction of these spans and scales generate unknown lags and nonbenevolent feedbacks. A man-machine game using free game scenarios as fodder may be an appropriate analytic tool with which to investigate this question. In fact, its

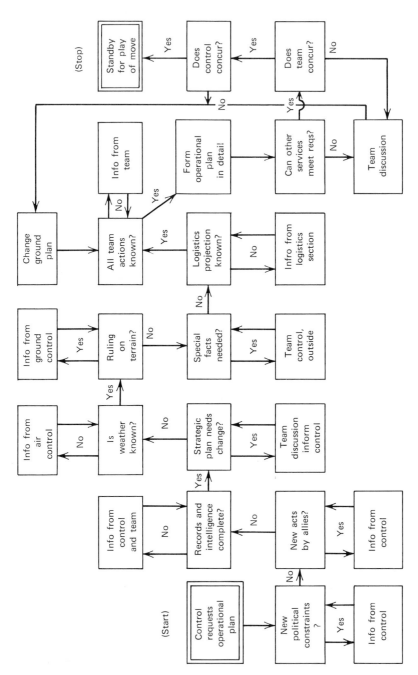

Fig. 3. Red or blue ground-planning cycle.

program may contribute to solution of the real world's command and control problems.

In a curious way, sometimes painful to the game's director, exactly the same problem arises when he tries to organize the interlocking tasks of his people. Figure 3 schematizes the work required of the ground player on either team during the planning portion of one move. Each team member, each member of CONTROL, and each member of the supporting cast has a similar pattern of activities. The actions are partly in parallel and partly staggered. Information inputs are needed to keep various chains of work alive. It can easily happen that A is waiting for B who is waiting for C who is waiting for A to complete a task. Is the organization properly designed when the director does not spend all of his time on the override button? This is a grand arena for the group-minded psychologist.

CRITIQUE

So that the conventions may be observed, something must be said about the strengths and weaknesses of war gaming. We are, of course, concerned only with gaming as a research tool. Consider first the advantages.

Gaming gives full scope to the enemy's actions and reactions, to his capability and his persistence. No staff planner writes a paper showing how his plan will fail and no engineer points out how the weapon system he has designed can be circumvented.[14] These one-sided analyses, replete with detailed calculations, assume a somewhat chuckleheaded and rather friendly enemy whose course of action is transparently clear and rigid and who seems quite vague about what he will do later on as the plan or weapon system moves smoothly to success. Gaming, on the contrary, supplies the most hostile of reviews.

Gaming provides a framework within which experts in the relevant fields can systematically apply and pool their ideas and techniques. This framework requires *all* relevant fields to be represented so that the logistician can tether the weapon designer, and the political scientist frustrate the operational planner. Each expert is forced to see a context which may modify his dogmatism and in fact stimulate his ingenuity.

By definition, *a* play of a war game is a sequence of moves each involving a concrete situation. Generalities and pontifications must show

---

[14] In all fairness, in preparing his Estimate of the Situation the wise Commander may foster interaction between his intelligence and operations sections to beget opposing points of view.

their applicability. Doctrine and belief are explicitly tested. The sequence of events forces a "thinking through" of an operation or campaign to the end.

Like Chinese medicine, the military profession is most successful if the client does not become a patient. War gaming can assist in designing a balanced deterrent posture, because we make our mistakes on paper and we can check plans and force structures for feasibility and balance. Since there is little secret about our military posture, one can hope that the enemy will conduct his own war games based on the inherent capabilities of that posture—not on its intentions—and detect no soft spots.[15]

But now it is the critics' turn. There are many of these people. Polemics, as well as semantics, is a characteristic of operations research. A discussion of their strictures may bring out aspects of war gaming other than those reviewed above.

Critic: Because of the enthusiasm and conviction war games engender in the participants, they lose all sense of logic, they confuse their model with reality.

Protagonist: Gaming is hard work. The gamers I know were either cynical when they started or lost their glow in a few weeks and never found it again.[16] They are well aware that the game is only a model; albeit sufficiently close to operations in the real world so that some guidance and insight are provided. If they are Players, they argue with Control about the validity of the assumptions and the assessments. They continually find branches that should be explored. If they are Controllers, they may beg the Players to put on their old uniforms in order to reproduce lags arising from interservice "considerations."

Crit: Your players are completely persuaded by the elaborate detail and work put into one play.

Pro: You are repeating yourself. Some of the players are not persuaded after ten plays. War gaming is not an exercise in mass self-hypnosis. But the Players do become convinced that a war game is an experiment, undoubtedly imperfect. They know that intuition and judgment intervene. This is equally true in any scientific endeavor. Any conclusions from the game or games must be subject to critical review, independent of the details of the game. The important point is that the game produces new ideas or phrases alternative concepts sharply and sketches explicitly possible consequences.

Crit: Even so, your people are assuming roles they never approximated

---

[15] Unlike Admiral Yamamoto's war gaming of Pearl Harbor.

[16] (Sotto voce) Some *are* hard losers.

in the real world. Hence they will "learn" in unpredictable ways during the game sequence.

Pro: What kind of people do you hire to do responsible gaming? As for "learning," this is precisely the feature desired in gaming, although it should be called generating new research ideas and finding out what mistakes could be made. Out-and-out strategic or tactical errors must of course be located and the game re-assessed. Although a game may be finished, the gamers are not finished with the game.

Crit: You simply cannot produce a set of realistic rules. Your people will exploit them, they will "play the game" against itself.

Pro: Negative. You are dealing with a group which is not only research minded but which has (or should have) an appreciable continuity. When one side does not point out flagrant unrealities, the other certainly will. In the course of time, refinement of rules and procedures is inevitable.

Crit: Your games are larded with deceptive detail. Each detail is a parameter and each must have a value. You don't know these values and even worse, in the ensemble, you have a hopelessly uncontrolled situation in the statistical sense, because you can't possibly have enough plays. You should stick to analytic methods. Or if you insist on games, strip away all your ornaments and find a simpler formulation which will give you a precise statement of problems and results, and which will let you understand what is going on.

Pro: You are talking as emotionally as a war gamer. But your points are all worth attention. In fact, you have arrived at the right conclusion by the wrong course of argument.

First, there *is* a lot of detail in war games. The reason is that the designer does not know in advance what factors may prove critical. He strives instead to cover what must be the range of contextual factors more or less clearly relevant to the game's objective. Reasoning by imperfect analogy *is* one of the thirty-four dishonest ways to win an argument, but here, comparing this phase of war gaming with dimensional analysis in physics is not grossly unfair. Dimensional analysis fails utterly if one essential physical quantity is omitted. Systems analysis may produce a completely worked-out and "optimum" system which may also be completely wide of the mark because of operational factors not considered.

Second, each parameter must be assigned a value, or even better, a range of values. Choosing this value is a matter of workmanship, and exactly the same problem arises in the study of any problem in military operations research by any method whatsoever.

Third, the conscientious war gamer must always be conscious of his tolerances. He must calculate or assess, if only by seminaring, the sensitivity of his *over-all* conclusions to variation in parameter values. Of course, he is never satisfied that he has completed this job.

Fourth, the number of plays of any one game that *should* be made is usually grossly overexaggerated by appeal to superficial combinatorial arguments. Once the main assumptions for a given branch of a game are set out, the flexibility in strategy and tactics is not nearly so rich as is presupposed, if only the main lines of the over-all course of events are to be made out. Perturbations of the main line can usually be assessed satisfactorily by those experienced in the game. A war game is no more chess than chess is a war game—in regard to the criticality of the fine structure.

Fifth, you are completely correct in saying that the real problem is to understand what is going on. Analysis of a sequence of war games is performed to deduce those few dominant key factors, assumptions, and general results whose relative weights and interactions are actually pertinent to the conclusions drawn. Most of the detail of the game now seems irrelevant.

Finally, war gaming is only one tool of military operations research. But there are many problems which must be tackled for which no other tool is yet available. Above all, gaming is a preresearch technique, generating ideas and sketching their outlines. Military operations research of necessity must be conducted with suspense dates in view. Gaming can make a major contribution to pressing questions which cannot await refinements in methodology.

Crit: Yes, but look at the cost and inefficiency—

Pro: Enough! You will like the next chapter.

REFERENCES

1.   Thomas, C. J., and W. L. Deemer, "The Role of Operational Gaming in Operations Research," *Operations Research*, Vol. 5, February, 1957, pp. 1–27.

2.   Young, John P., "A Survey of Historical Developments in War Games," Operations Research Office Staff Paper 98, August 1959, 116 pp. (Now Research Analysis Corporation.)

3.   Livermore, William R., *The American Kriegsspiel*, rev. ed., W. B. Clarke Co., Boston, Mass., 1898.

4.   Washington Operations Research Council, *First War Gaming Symposium Proceedings*, ed. by J. Overholt, November 30, 1961.

5.   Thomas, C. J., *The Estimation of Bombers Surviving an Air Battle*, Operations Analysis Technical Memorandum 49, August 1956.

6.   Taylor, James L., "Development and Application of a Terminal Air Battle Model," *Operations Research*, 7, November-December 1959, pp. 783–796.

7. Leibowitz, Martin L., and Gerald J. Lieberman, "Optimal Composition and Deployment of a Heterogeneous Local Air-Defense System," *Operations Research*, 8, May–June 1960, pp. 324–337.

8. Brotman, Lewis, and Barry Seid, "Digital Simulation of a Massed-Bomber, Manned-Interceptor Encounter," *Operations Research*, 8, May–June 1960, pp. 421–423.

9. Adams, R. H., and J. L. Jenkins, "Simulation of Air Operations with the Air-Battle Model," *Operations Research*, 8, September–October 1960, pp. 600–615.

10. Kahn, Herman, and Irwin Mann, *Monte Carlo*, The RAND Corporation, P-1165, July 30, 1957.

11. Kahn, Herman, "Use of Different Monte Carlo Sampling Techniques" in *Symposium on Monte Carlo Methods*, John Wiley & Sons, 1956.

12. Siska, C. P., L. A. Giamboni, and J. R. Lind, *Analytic Formulation of a Theater Air-Ground Warfare System*, The RAND Corporation, RM-1338 (ASTIA No. AD 86022), September 13, 1954.

13. Brom, J. R., *Narrative Description of an Analytic Theater Air-Ground Warfare System*, The RAND Corporation, RM-1428 (ASTIA No. AD 86709), February 10, 1955.

14. Dresher, Melvin, *Games of Strategy: Theory and Applications*, The RAND Corporation, R-360, May 1961. (Also published by Prentice-Hall, Inc., Englewood Cliffs, N. J., 1961.)

15. Haywood, O. G., "Military Decision and the Mathematical Theory of Games," *Air University Quarterly Review*, 4, 1950.

16. Kennedy, J. L., *The Systems Research Laboratory and Its Program*, The RAND Corporation, P-657, October 17, 1955.

17. Kennedy, J. L., and R. L. Chapman, *The Background and Implications of the System Research Laboratory Studies*, The RAND Corporation, P-740, September 21, 1955.

18. Geisler, M. A., W. W. Haythorn, and W. A. Steger, *Simulation and the Logistics Systems Laboratory*, The RAND Corporation, RM-3281-PR, September 1962.

19. Helmer, O., and R. E. Bickner, *How to Play SAFE: Book of Rules of the Strategy and Force Evaluation Game*, The RAND Corporation, RM-2865-PR (ASTIA No. AD 266900), November 1961.

20. Weiner, M. G., *War Gaming Methodolgy*, The RAND Corporation, RM-2413, July 10, 1959.

21. Ellis, J. W., Jr., and T. E. Greene, "The Contextual Study: A Structured Approach to the Study of Political and Military Aspects of Limited War," *Operations Research*, 8, September–October 1960, pp. 639–651.

BIBLIOGRAPHY
Games in Military Science— Selected References

Andrus, A. F. "Bringing War Game Simulations into the Classroom," *Proceedings of Fourth War Gaming Symposium*, McLean, Virginia: East Coast War Games Council, Research Analysis Corporation, 1965, pp. 195–203.

Bibliography on War Gaming, Chevy Chase, Maryland: Johns Hopkins University Operations Research Office, 1957.

Cushen, W. E. *Generalized Battle Games on a Digital Computer*, Chevy Chase, Maryland: Johns Hopkins University Operations Research Office, Technical Memorandum #ORO-T263, 1954.

Directory of Organizations and Activities Engaged or Interested in War Gaming, Bethesda, Maryland: United States Army Strategy and Tactics Analysis Group, 1962.

"Fabulous War Game, 'Ready'," *Naval Aviation News*, January, 1959, pp. 16–17.

Heistand, H. O. S. "Foreign War Games," *Selected Papers Translated From European Military Publications* (Translated from *Revue Militaire De L'Etranger*), Washington, D.C.: U.S. Government Printing Office, 1898, Publication #18, Document #57.

Helmer, O. *Strategic Gaming*, Santa Monica, California: The Rand Corporation, 1960.

Kahn, H. and Mann, I. *War Gaming*, Santa Monica, California: The Rand Corporation, 1957.

McDonald, T. J. "JCS Politico-Military Desk Games," *Proceedings of the Second War Gaming Symposium*, Washington, D.C.: Operations Research Council, 1964, pp. 63–74.

Mahler, G. H. *The Practical Application of War Gaming Techniques to Naval Planning*, Newport, Rhode Island: U.S. Naval War College Research Paper, 1960.

Navy War Games Manual, Washington, D.C.: U.S. Office of Naval Operations, 1965.

Nolan, J. E. "Tactics and the Theory of Games; The Theory of Games Applied to the Battle of Guadalcanal," *Army,* August, 1960, pp. 77–81.

Pennington, A. W. *War Game Techniques,* Silver Springs, Maryland: Johns Hopkins University Planning Analysis Group, 1960.

Specht, R. D. *War Games,* Santa Monica, California: The Rand Corporation, 1957.

"The War Game and How It Is Played," *Scientific American,* December 5, 1914, pp. 470–471.

Thomas, C. J. "Military Gaming," *Progress in Operations Research,* Vol. I, New York: John Wiley and Sons, 1961.

Thrall, R. M. "An Air War Game," *Research Review,* December, 1953, pp. 9–14.

"War Games: Key To Doctrine?", *Marine Corps Gazette,* November, 1960, pp. 9–10.

Young, J. P. *History and Bibliography of War Gaming,* Arlington, Virginia: Armed Services Technical Information Agency, Staff Paper ORO-SP-13, April, 1957.

Young, J. P. *Survey of Historical Developments in War Games,* McLean, Virginia: Research Analysis Corporation ORO Staff Paper #98, August, 1959.

Zimmerman, R. E. "A Monte Carlo Model for Military Analysis," *Operations Research For Management,* Vol. II, Baltimore: Johns Hopkins Press, 1956.

CHAPTER 8

BUSINESS AND INDUSTRIAL GAMES

It is generally thought that the first logistic game (the forerunner of games used in business and industry) was *Monopologs*, developed by the Rand Corporation in the mid-1950s. *Monopologs* concern the Air Force system of supply, bases being consumers, the depot being the distributor, and the player functioning as inventory manager. The player plays the game by making various decisions related to his role.

In 1957, the American Management Association, wanting to "provide a learning experience in which participants could increase their understanding of the decision-making process," introduced the first practical business game—*The Top Management Decision Simulation*.[1] Although the rationale for calling this game a "simulation" is not available, one can conjecture that there was a heated discussion regarding the desirability of hard-headed businessmen playing games! The phrase "business simulations" has become, in consequence, a euphemism for games. This first game required each participant to

. . . play the role of a member of top management of one of several company teams which compete with each other in a hypothetical market involving a single product. Each company begins the simulation in an identical position (cash available, beginning inventory and plant capacity), and decisions for each period of play represent those for a simulated quarter of a year's operations . . . . the companies are given

[1] Greenlaw, P. S., Herron, L. W., and Rawdon, R. H. *Business Simulation*. Englewood Cliffs, New Jersey: Prentice-Hall Inc., 1962.

the option of purchasing different kinds of market research information which may be of value to them in their decision-making . . . . each company receives a statement from the game administrators as to its sales income for the quarter . . . . At the end of each year of decision-making, each team is given . . . an annual report . . . for all companies . . . . game administrators make it a practice to furnish . . . other information as simulation play progresses . . . . several games are normally played . . . and in no way attempts to provide a closely detailed representation of the real world.[2]

The success of this game opened the door for the development of additional games for a variety of business purposes. As in war games, the past decade has seen the introduction of the man-machine game as well as exclusively human play.

But business games have developed differently from war games, often having an educational as well as a strictly business significance. For example, AT&T developed a game called *Tinker-Toy Objects Game* for five to seven participants; it is used in a training course aimed at the problems of newly appointed first level personnel in making the transition to management. The General Electric Company used a game called *Simuload,* which is a master scheduling and loading game used at the opening session of GE's educational programs in Production Control. The Pillsbury Company used a game called *Sales Management Simulation Exercise* for five or more participants; it is designed for use in training sales managers. Additional games for purposes of preservice-business education have been developed by several major universities.

There are a great many business games in use today. Some games are multipurpose, that is, they can be used for planning, education, or research; whereas others are single-purpose games. Some are concerned with either the subject matter for a given industry or the decision-making process involved. Many business games, regardless of the industry, are concerned with marketing, development, finance, and production. A few games are concerned with procurement, employee relations, and other similar matters. Business games are usually designed with specific business purposes in mind, as well as with specific participants in mind, for example, middle management, top level, salesman.[3]

Although business games are only a decade old their growth has been rapid. One of the newer games developed at the University of Chicago perhaps portends the future. The game is called *INTOP* (International

[2] Greenlaw et al., op. cit., 1962, p. 15.
[3] Vance, S. *Management Decision Simulation: A Non-Computer Business Game.* New York: McGraw-Hill Book Company Inc., 1960.

Operations Simulation). The increasing problems of international trade and overseas operations have stimulated the University to develop a game with a "rather high degree of realism . . . (that) brings out the fact that effective solution of international business problems . . . requires diagnostic ability and conceptual thinking. . . ."[4]

Although there is little scientific evidence of the worth of these games, like the military games that have been played for centuries, their pursuit is apparently convincing to their advocates. Whether this conviction is based on a certain intoxication that goes with game playing or has the substance of their claims, cannot yet be known. Though as a precaution we should remember that for about a century athletic coaches have been discussing the character training value of sports, with much enthusiasm and practically no evidence. Their enthusiasm has not abated, but the evidence is still practically nonexistent.

With these precautions in mind, we record the following digest of the "values" of business games to be found in that literature. Business games are said to offer the player a conflict situation that is an abstraction of the competitive reality of the business world. Games are designed to provide a prototype of real-life business situations that require the player to use practical business judgement and skills. We are told that the games offer the players an opportunity to gain experience not only from the play of the game, but also from the feedback of the results. Games foster the making of decisions that the player must live with during the game, and thus, because of this high degree of involvement, behavioral modification is said to be immediate. Games are thought to be more effective than traditional business training methods because they offer the opportunity to "learn by doing," to enhance the practice of technique, and to provide lengthy experience in a relatively short period of time. In the area of management principles, games require participants to "live" with the consequence of their decisions, to be specific because generalizations are not enough, and to exercise their judgment in relation to problem solving. In addition, it is said that business as well as military games help the player avoid a historical outlook—"the tendency to fight the last war instead of the next." They give the player a healthy respect for the unforeseen in dynamic and constantly changing situations, in which decisions must be made under pressure.

We conclude this account with a sample game from the IBM Laboratory in Yorktown Heights, New York. The game is designed to teach basic economics through man-machine play.

[4] Thorelli, H. B., and Graves, R. L. *International Operations Simulation*. Glencoe, Ill.: The Free Press, 1964, p. 32.

THE SUMERIAN GAME[5]

A student assumes the role of a priest-king of a Sumerian City-State of the late fourth millennium. Factors in the environment are represented by information typed out on a typewriter terminal controlled by a computer program. The general situation is presented by a narrative with pictorials. An agricultural cycle of planting and harvesting is introduced. The initial problem of how much grain to set aside for the next planting is posed. The priest-king must arrive at a satisfactory figure. The population will tend to grow, limited technology prevents grain from being stored for long periods of time, rotting and destruction by rodents will take place, natural and man-made catastrophes must be considered, floods, storms, fires, etc.

The student will use a trial and error method to determine the proper planting figure. Each time he enters a figure, the computer will give him a food-supply position at the end of harvest. Other problems are introduced. The decreasing number of mature plants due to the proximity of the seeds, thus more land must be tilled. Irrigation ditches must be built, etc. This gives the student an opportunity to order public work projects. Large scale starvation is the result of late decision to increase acreage. Periods of starvation may so lower the vitality of the civilization that it can no longer survive. If the city-state survives, it can begin to build a small surplus. If the level of nutrition is maintained over a number of years, technological innovations will come about, arts and crafts will flourish, inventions will be reported at various times (in keeping with the historical period), and the student will use these as he sees fit to capitalize on currently available energy.

As time goes on the game gets more complicated with the introduction of household attendants, soldiers, businessmen, traders, neighboring city-states, and the like.

In summary, the object of the game is to make decisions in such a way that the city-state survives a series of natural political crises, that the population grows, and that a high rate of technological innovation is maintained. These goals are numerous, diffuse, and possibly conflicting, compared with typical parlor games.

The goals of this game are clearly much broader than a typical business game in that the intent here is to offer the player not only an opportunity

---

[5] Abstracted from "The Sumerian Game: Teaching Economics With A Computerized P. I. Program," by Bruce Moncreiff, *Programmed Instruction*, 4 (5), February, 1965, pp. 10–11.

to make decisions of an economic nature, but to give the player an understanding of the processes at work in the economic development of civilization. However, the example illustrates how far game playing has come in the world of business and industry.

Whatever one may think of these games, the generality of the view that individuals learn to be better businessmen by playing games is impressive. The state of the art is such at the present time that the reader will note that our list of selected references that follows, includes a number of text books on the subject used in college and university schools of business administration.

Games in Business and Industry—Selected References

Acer, J. W. *Business Games: A Simulation Technique,* Iowa City, Iowa: State University of Iowa, 1960.

"Amstan's Business Game: The Industry's Top Training Tool," *Plumbing, Heating & Air Conditioning Wholesaler,* August 1960.

Andlinger, G. R. "Business Games—Play One!" *Harvard Business Review,* **36** (2), March–April 1958.

Basil, D. *Executive Decision-Making Through Simulation,* Columbus, Ohio: Chas. E. Merrill Books, Inc., 1965.

Bellman, R., et al. "On the Construction of a Multi-Stage, Multi-person Business Game," *Operations Research,* **5** (4), August 1957.

Buchan, J. *A Management Decision Game,* New York City: Division of Management Sciences, Touche, Ross, Bailey & Smart, April 1960.

"Business Games for Marketing Decision," *Journal of Marketing,* July 1960.

Cohen, K. J. and E. Rhenman. *The Role of Management Games in Education and Research,* Pittburgh, Pennsylvania: Carnegie Institute of Technology Graduate School of Industrial Administration, Working Paper No. 22, September 1960.

Cohen, K. J., et al. "The Carnegie Tech Management Game," *Journal of Business,* **33** (4), October 1960.

Corbin, A. and G. Blagowidow. *Decision Exercises in Marketing,* New York: McGraw-Hill Book Company, Inc., 1964.

Craft, C. J. "Management Games Using Electronic Computers," *Management Controls,* October 1960.

Craft, C. J. "Management Games Using Punched Cards and Computers: Realism Without Ruin," *Punched-Card Data Processing,* September–October 1959.

Craft, C. J., J. M. Kibbee, and B. Nanus. *Management Games,* New York City: Reinhold Publishing Corporation, 1961 (2nd edition forthcoming).

Cushen, W. E. "Operational Gaming in Industry," *Operations Research for Management,* (J. F. McCloskey, and Coppinger, J. M. ed.), Baltimore: Johns Hopkins Press, 2, 1956.

Dale, A. G., and C. R. Klasson. *Business Gaming,* Austin, Texas: Bureau of Business Research, The University of Texas, 1964.

Deacon, A. R. L., Jr. and A. M. Lang. *Descriptions of American Management Association Games: General Management Simulation Model No. 4; Decision Making Simulation Model No. 6; Materials Management Simulation Model No. 2; Physical-Distribution Simulation Model No. 1,* Saranac Lake, New York: AMA Academy.

Dill, W. R. "The Research Potential of Management Games," *Proceedings of the National Symposium of Management Games,* Lawrence, Kansas: University of Kansas, 1959.

Dill, W. R., *et al. Proceedings of the Conference of Business Games,* New Orleans: Tulane University School of Business Administration, 1961.

Greene, J. R. and R. L. Sisson. *Dynamic Management Decision Games,* New York City: John Wiley & Sons, Inc., 1959.

Greenlaw, P. S., *et al. Business Simulation,* Englewood Cliffs, N. J.: Prentice-Hall, Inc., 1962.

Herder, J. H. "Do-It-Yourself Business Games (Non-Computer Simulation)," *Journal of the American Society of Training Directors,* September 1960.

Huggens, S. G. *Business Management Games and Simulations: A Special Report,* New York: American Management Association, August 1966.

"In Business Education, the Game's the Thing," *Business Week,* July 25, 1959.

"Intercollegiate Business Games," *Business Week,* November 28, 1959.

Jackson, J. R. "Learning from Experience in Business Decision Games," *California Management Review,* Winter 1959.

Jackson, J. R. *UCLA Executive Game No. 2: A Preliminary Report,* Los Angeles, California: Management Sciences Research Project, University of California, Discussion Paper No. 66, April 2, 1958.

Jackson, J. R. and K. R. Wright. *UCLA Executive Game No. 2: Mathematical Model and Computer Code,* Los Angeles, California: Management Sciences Research Project, University of California, Discussion Paper No. 70.

Kay, I. M. "An Executive's Primer on Simulation," *Data Processing Magazine,* October 1966.

Kibbee, J. M. "Design Aspects of Management Games," paper presented at the Institute of Management Sciences Conference, New York City, October 21, 1960.

Kibbee, J. M., et al. Management Games: A New Technique For Executive Development, New York: Reinhold, 1961.

Kotler, P. "The Competitive Marketing Simulator—A New Management Tool," California Management Review, Spring 1965.

Malcolm, D. G. Bibliography on the Use of Simulation in Management Analysis, Santa Monica, California: Systems Development Corporation, 1959.

Malcolm, D. G. "Bibliography on the Use of Simulation in Management Analysis," Operations Research, March–April 1960, pp. 169–177.

"Management Games: Toy or Trend?" Office Management and American Business, September 1960.

Martin, E. Top Management Decision Simulation, New York: American Management Association, 1957.

McDonald, J. D. Strategy in Poker, Business, and War, New York: Norton, 1950.

McDonald, J. and F. M. Ricciardi. "The Business Decision Game," Fortune, March 1958.

Nanus, B. "The Varieties of Management Game Experience," paper presented at The Institute of Management Sciences Conference, New York City, October 21, 1960.

Pessemier, E. A. "Forecasting Brand Preference Through Simulation Experiments," Journal of Marketing, April 1964.

Rowe, A. J. and R. R. Smith. "Now Training for Production is a Play-to-Win Game," Factory Management and Maintenance, 116 (3), March 1958.

Schrieber, A. N. "Gaming—A New Way to Teach Business Decision-Making," University of Washington Business Review, 17 (7), April 1958.

Shubik, M. "Games Decisions and Industrial Organization," Management Science, 6 (4), July 1960.

"Simulation and Gaming," American Management Association Management Reports, American Management Association, No. 55, 1961.

Simuload: A Master Scheduling and Loading Game, New York City: General Electric Co., 1958.

Steele, J. D. "Simulated Management Experience: Some Comments on Business Games," Kansas Business Review, Section 2, October 1958.

"The Serious Business of Business Games," Management Record, February 1960.

Vance, S. *Management Decision Simulation: A Non-Computer Business Game,* New York: McGraw-Hill Book Company, Inc., 1960.

Watkins, H. R. "Business Games in Business," *Operational Research Quarterly,* **10** (4), December 1959.

CHAPTER 9

GAMES IN EDUCATION

In this chapter as in the previous one, we note an unbounded enthusiasm for games. The usual justification is again given that the students learn by playing games. A closer reading suggests, however, that the most important feature of the games may be that the students enjoy themselves more while they are playing than when they are not. So that whatever they learn (whether it be as much as usual, or less), is learned with enjoyment. This in turn perhaps contributes to the ease with which teachers can manage their students. Games may be so acceptable because they solve motivational problems for the students and management problems for the teachers not unimportant considerations in an age of "drop outs." We shall examine some of the usages on grade school and college levels, as well as survey some of the "values" confidently attributed to such game playing.

We do not know when some enterprising school teacher arrived at the conclusion that students would learn more effectively if the subject matter under consideration were offered in the form of a game. The example of the "spelling bee" is well known—although the spelling bee is said not to be a "good" game because it does not help the poor speller learn how to spell. "Good" games, according to those who develop curriculum for the elementary and secondary school, are those that help the learner to learn. For example, at the start of a school term it is important for everyone to learn the name of everyone else in the class. A game that is often played for this purpose in the elementary school is called *Namo*, a variation of *Bingo* in which children enjoy playing a game and at the same time they become familiar with the other children's names.

Critics argue that many of these "educational" games do not do what **315** they are supposed to do, particularly in the elementary school. They say that children lose sight of the objectives, see games in a fun context, and do not really learn anything by playing them. On the other hand, those in favor of games suggest a Mary Poppins type of argument—"A spoonful of sugar makes the medicine go down!" Regardless of the reasons, the use of games in the teaching of academic subjects is so embedded in instructional technique that the only issue most school teachers are really concerned with is whether they can find a suitable game for their purposes.

There are a number of publishing companies ready to oblige with such titles as: *Games Make Spelling Fun, A Teaching Aid to Better Spelling, Arithmetic Games: for Kindergarten through Sixth Grade, 100 Learning Games for Boys and Girls from Five to Eight, Games for Learning Mathematics, Reading Games, Listening Games, Language Games, Social Studies Games*, and a host of others. A number of professional journals for school teachers feature articles on the subject, and offer a considerable amount of "how-to-do-it" information. Some publishing houses supply game equipment designed for the elementary classroom, for example, *Language Lotto*. . . . "A Series of Programmed Games teaching children to understand and to speak standard English better."[1]

Texts for the elementary teacher indicate a variety of ways in which games can be used in the elementary classroom. In addition to the usual methods for teaching *reading*, the teacher today has at her command games that are said to help children learn the alphabet, or games that enhance word recognition. Other games are used to teach vowel sounds, initial consonants, consonant blends, syllabification, to increase vocabulary, to stimulate interest in reading, or to help "build general cultural background." When it comes to teaching *writing*, there are games such as acrostics, anagrams, and crossword puzzles. There are others that assist in teaching to write sentences, to use action words, or to become familiar with the parts of speech. There are games to expand oral word usage, auditory discrimination, and articulation.

The use of games in the teaching of reading and writing, although not a new idea, is not as old as the use of games in the teaching of *arithmetic*. Charles Dodgson, the noted British mathematician (better known as Lewis Carroll the author of *Alice in Wonderland*) published a number of books on "mathematical recreations" during the 1890s. Subsequently, many other books and articles on the subject have been made available to teachers of arithmetic. Gardner, in his introduction to volume I of the

---

[1] Gotkin, L. G. *Language Lotto.* New York: Appleton-Century-Crofts, no date, page 2 in a brochure describing the game.

Scientific American Book of Mathematical Puzzles and Diversions says:

The pedagogic value of recreational mathematics is now widely recognized. One finds an increasing emphasis on it in magazines published for mathematics teachers, and in the newer textbooks, especially those written from the "modern" point of view.[2]

Such games are said to help the beginning student recognize numerals or number sequences.[3] Other games help the student to learn arithmetic processes. In addition to special games designed for these purposes, familiar games such as ticktacktoe are utilized as an introduction to several branches of modern mathematics. Since mathematics is a graded affair with respect to the school curriculum, so too are games used for this purpose. The teacher has available games that are graded for each of the elementary and secondary levels—both "noncommercial games," and those games that are manufactured for sale to the general public. In addition to well-known commercial game manufacturers, a number of corporations specialize in the manufacture of games for use in the teaching of mathematics in the classroom.

Beyond the "3 R's," games are used in the teaching of *social studies,* These studies run the gamut from teaching children to develop responsibility for helping at home, to becoming aware of the problems of modern civilization. Kindergarten children play a game like "Mulberry Bush" in order to learn ideas about the way "we" do things—for example, wash our face, comb our hair, pick up our toys. Older students who study history in elementary or secondary school may be exposed to games to learn about famous dates, places, or people. Occasionally sand-table games like the early "Kriepspiel" are used. Students of geography may learn about latitude and longitude in a game, or how to use a compass, and a host of other things. Crossword puzzles dealing with current events are popular games for older students.

The Teachers Publishing Corporation in a recent publication, *Social Studies Games and Activities,*[4] presented over one hundred games that have been developed for social studies. They also indicated that many commercial games can be used for these purposes as well, such as *Across the Continent, Around the World, Game of the States, Monopoly, Politics, Wide World, Guadalcanal, Gettysburg,* and many others.

---

[2] Gardner, M. *Scientific American Book of Mathematical Puzzles and Diversions.* New York: Simon and Schuster, 1, 1959, p. x.

[3] Turner, E. M. "Aids and Ideas in Teaching Mathematics," *Service Bulletin,* New York: Holt, Rinehart, and Winston Inc., 1965, p. 1.

[4] Wagner, G. et al. *Social Studies Games and Activities.* Darien, Conn.: Teachers Publishing Corporation, 1964, p. 5.

Other uses of games in the elementary and secondary curriculum are for teaching science, music, foreign languages, and other specific subjects. Just as Helwig tried to find a better "mousetrap" to teach young noblemen military strategy, or the American Management Association sought more effective ways to teach management decision-making techniques, the average school teacher seeks more effective ways to teach her pupils a variety of things. Games are thought to provide the answer. As we have mentioned there is little objective evidence to indicate that games are a more effective method of teaching.

In general, the authors of books and articles concerning games in education focus on describing procedures and rules of games. In a few instances, an author precedes his descriptions of games with a value judgment, for example, "Games are attention-getters which stimulate the student to think about the subject at times when they are about to go on vacation or when they have just returned from vacation."[5] In some instances authors present a general introductory statement about teaching games and suggest criteria for their selection. Occasionally, authors include a discussion of principles of teaching, a set of "how to" directives, and may specify which games to use with children at various grade levels of ability. In a few instances, an author reports that the games have been "tried out" by teachers in various settings, for example, faculty and students of a graduate school; faculty, students, and some elementary school children. The intended effect of games is given some attention, but relationships of teaching objectives to learning experiences are rarely made explicit. In one instance, the authors state that "experience has shown" that the arithmetic games in their book help children "see patterns, note relationships, develop insight, enlarge concepts, discover facts, improve computational skills."[6] None claim to have engaged in research studies prior to writing their books or articles, with the exception of a reading series described as:

. . . the direct result of almost fifty years of experimentation and research in the field of education . . . , experienced, creative teachers furnished the supportive teaching material. Concepts grew out of interactive thinking by faculty on problems of teaching reading in big city schools. Testing of materials in New York City and Norwalk, Connecticut Public Schools (followed) use of early materials in the college laboratory school

[5] Smith, S. L. "Adding Interest Via Shorthand Games," *Journal of Business Education*, 41, April, 1966, p. 279.

[6] Wagner, G. et al. *Arithmetic Games and Activities: Strengthening Arithmetic Skills with Instructional Aids*. Darien, Conn.: Teachers Publishing Corporation, 2nd printing, 1966.

. . . evaluations from in-servive teachers, supervisors and administrators.[7]

When we leave the elementary and secondary classroom for the university, we find that the playing of games is once again referred to as "simulations." After business and industry started using games for in-service education, the more formal preservice university programs followed suit. At first, similarly related areas such as economics became involved. More recently political science curricula have used games as an outgrowth of some of the newer aspects of war gaming. Thus a student in political science may become involved in a game called "Inter-Nation Simulation."[8] A business major may play "the Carnegie Tech Management Game" in a course in business administration to develop experience in complex management situation.[9] Social-psychology majors may study interpersonal conflict and bargaining, and play the "Acme-Bolt" game.[10]

Some educators say that the "simulations" used in higher education are not really "games"—but are simulations of actual life situations. Sociologists at Johns Hopkins University have developed games that simulate a variety of social situations, and are said to be useful in the teaching of social relations. Some of these are: *The Life Career Game, The Family Game, The Representative Democracy Game, The Community Response Game, The High School Game,* and *The Consumer Game.*[11]

Currently, research and development of games with simulated environments is being carried out by sociologists in collaboration with anthropologists, curriculum specialists, economists, historians, political scientists, psychologists, systems analysts, and teachers in six major research centers.

1. Abt Associates, Inc., Cambridge, Massachusetts.
2. BOCES (Board of Cooperative Educational Services), Northern Westchester, New York.
3. Carnegie Tech Management Game, Carnegie Institute of Technology, Pittsburgh, Pennsylvania.

---

[7] *Bank Street Reading Series.* New York: The Macmillan Company, 1966, introduction.

[8] Guetzkow, H. et al. *Simulation in International Relations.* Englewood Cliffs, New Jersey: Prentice-Hall, 1963.

[9] Dill, W. R., and Doppelt, N. "The Acquisition of Experience in A Complex Management Game," *Simulation Models for Education,* N. A. Fattu and S. Elam (Eds.) Bloomington, Ind.: Phi Delta Kappa Inc., 1965.

[10] Deutsch, M. and Krauss, D. "Studies of Interpersonal Bargaining," *Journal of Conflict Resolution,* March, 1962, pp. 52–76.

[11] Coleman, J. S. "Learning Through Games," *NEA Journal,* January, 1967, pp. 69–70; and Boocock, S. S. *Simulation Games in Learning,* Beverly Hills, California: Sage Publications, 1968.

4. Department of Social Relations, Johns Hopkins University, Baltimore, Maryland.
5. Northwestern University International Relations Program, Department of Political Science, Evanston, Illinois.
6. Project SIMILE, Western Behavioral Sciences Institute, La Jolla, California.

The games created are used to teach problem solving and decision-making techniques within the context of such diverse subjects as banking, business management, careers, community response to disaster, credit buying, cultures of other lands, democratic and other governmental processes (including legislation), economics, evolution, free market competition, geography, history, international relations, parent-child relationships, and political science. Other games are in various stages of design, development, and production. Some are available for general use, others can be used for research by special arrangement.

The values that various practitioners attribute to their games are endless. We can list only a sampling here. They are all conjectural, though not necessarily false.

Those who have created the recent simulations, for example, argue that people learn by experiencing the consequences of their actions, and that traditional teaching methods are not geared to provide opportunities to learn how to make decisions and solve problems in a complex society. It is said that simulation games present approximations of various facets of modern society; so that a person can gain some insight in a controlled situation rather than get it "the hard way—from uncontrolled experiments in the real world, with irreversible effects."[12]

In general, the rationale for using games is that they help create an "atmosphere" in the classroom in which students at various levels of ability can work together to acquire communications skills, develop desirable attitudes, and instill correct practices. Although "few critics deny that games spur enthusiasm," as Carlson points out in the reading that follows this chapter, the few studies that have been made fail to confirm that students learn anything from them that they could not have learned from conventional methods.[13]

Research and development of educational games and simulations has been characterized by two phases. The first phase involved simulations of international relations in which computerized methods played a large

[12] Holland, E. P. "Principles of Simulation," *American Behavioral Scientist*, **9**, September, 1965, p. 10.
[13] Carlson, E. "Games in the Classroom," *Saturday Review*, April, 1967, pp. 62–64, 82–83.

part. Reports of these experiments began to appear in the late 1950s and have been considered "largely impressionistic and subjective." The second phase began around 1962. New kinds of games were developed and tested in regular classroom situations, and researchers attempted to be more objective in reporting their findings. These studies centered on testing the following hypotheses:

1. Games with simulated environments engender more student *interest* than the more conventional classroom activities.
2. By participating in games students will *learn* more facts and principles than by studying in the conventional manner.
3. Students will *retain* information learned in games longer than information presented through conventional methods.
4. Students will acquire more *critical thinking* and *decision-making* skills by participating in games with simulated environments.
5. Student's *attitudes* will be significantly altered by taking part in games.

The only hypothesis that has been completely accepted so far is the first one—students *are* more interested in simulation activities than in conventional classroom exercises. Therefore, it may be said that what is now *known* about games and simulations as instructional media is this: *they are useful devices for getting and holding student interest and attention.*[14]

This chapter is followed by several readings illustrative of approaches to games with an educational purpose.

[14] Cherryholmes, C. H. "Some Current Research on Effectiveness of Educational Simulations," *American Behavioral Scientist,* **10,** October, 1966, pp. 4–7.

2

Learning Through Games

JAMES S. COLEMAN

Playing games is a very old and widespread form of learning. The child first comes to understand the meaning of a rule—that a rule must be obeyed by all—in a game with others where, if the rules are broken, the game does not function.

Recently, educators have begun devising games for high school and pre-high school students that simulate complex activities in a society. One of the ways that simulation and games were first combined was in war games. Many of the oldest parlor games (chess and checkers, for example) were developed as war simulations long ago, and today armies use war games to develop logistic and strategic skills.

From war games developed the idea of management games, a simulation of management decision-making which is used in many business schools and firms to train future executives by putting them in situations they will confront in their jobs.

The games that I and my associates at Johns Hopkins have developed simulate some aspect of society. There is a Life Career Game, a Family Game, a Representative Democracy Game, a Community Response Game (in which a community responds to some kind of disaster) a High School Game which is really for pre-high school students), and a Consumer Game (in which the players are consumers and department store credit managers).

Other sets of academic games on topics ranging from international relations to mathematics have been developed and tested by other persons or institutions—Clark Abt, Cambridge, Massachusetts; Harold Guetzkow,

Northwestern University; Layman Allen, Yale; and Western Behavioral Sciences Institute, La Jolla, California.

A description of one of the games developed at Johns Hopkins, a legislative game designed to teach the basic structure of representative government, gives some idea of what and how the games are designed to teach. Six to eleven players sit around a table or circle of desks. The chairman deals a set of fifty-two cards, each representing a segment of a constituency and giving the positions of constituents on one of eight issues. The cards a player holds represent the positions of his constituents on some or all of the eight issues: civil rights, aid to education, medical care, defense appropriation, national seashore park in Constituency A, offshore oil, federal dam in Constituency B, and retaining a military base in Constituency C.

The player, as legislator, is attempting to gain reelection, and he can do so only through satisfying the wishes, as indicated on his cards, of a majority of his constituents. For example, if he has 80 constituents in favor of an aid to education bill and 20 against it, he has a net gain of 60 votes toward reelection if the bill passes or a net loss of 60 if it fails.

After a player brings an issue to the floor, a two-minute negotiation session ensues. The negotiation consists largely of an exchange of support among the players. A legislator will offer his support for or against issues his constituents have no interest in, in return for support on legislation in which they are interested. A vote of legislators, with each player-legislator having one vote, is then taken and the session proceeds to an issue raised by the next player. When all bills have been acted on, each legislator calculates his reelection or defeat by adding up votes of satisfied and dissatisfied constituents. The overall winner is the legislator who is reelected by the largest majority. This is the first "level" of the game, which altogether consists of eight levels, each introducing more of the complexity of legislative functioning.

I developed an interest in simulation games several years ago while I was making a study of high school adolescents in Illinois. The study suggested that high schools either did not reward academic activity or rewarded it in wrong ways. In my opinion, the organization of academic work in school acts to keep down the amount of effort and attention a student gives to academic pursuits as compared to extracurricular activities.

The structuring of athletic activity, for example, is very different from the structuring of academic activity. A student making a touchdown for the football team or winning the half-mile at track achieves for both the school and himself, something he can seldom do academically.

It seemed, for this and other reasons, that making use of the simulation techniques of war and management games might be particularly appropriate for schools. First of all, it would make possible a reward structure which would focus on achievement for the school as well as on individual academic achievement. Last spring in Fort Lauderdale, Florida, for example, a number of schools from eight states participated in the "Nova Academic Olympics," playing an equations game, a logic game, and a legislative game in the kind of interscholastic tournament often reserved for athletics.

A more important asset of simulation games is that they constitute an approach to learning that starts from fundamentally different premises than does the usual approach to learning schools. The first premise is that persons do not learn by being taught; they learn by experiencing the consequences of their actions. Games which simulate some aspects of reality are one way a young person can begin to see such consequences before he faces the real actions and the real consequences as an adult.

A second premise underlying the development of these games is that schools find it difficult to teach about the complexity that characterizes modern society, with the result that students have had little or no experience to prepare them for facing a multitude of decisions and problems in adult life. The games we and others have created present the student with an approximation of certain facets of modern society that he will have to face later.

Learning through games has a number of intrinsic virtues. One of these is its attention-focusing quality. Games tend to focus attention more effectively than most other teaching devices, partly because they involve the student actively rather than passively. The depth of involvement in a game, whether it is basketball, Life Carreer, or bridge, is often so great that the players are totally absorbed in this artificial world.

Another virtue of academic games as a learning device is that using them diminishes the teacher's role as judge and jury. Such a role often elicits students' fear, resentment, or anger and gives rise to discipline problems. It may also generate equally unpleasant servility and apple-polishing. Games enable the student to see the consequences of his actions in his winning or losing. He cannot blame the teacher for his grades; instead he is able to understand the way in which his own activity is related to the outcome. The teacher's role reverts to a more natural one of helper and coach.

In developing an appropriate sense of consequences contingent upon action, the amount of chance in a game is quite important. If a game has the appropriate mixture of chance and skill, persons of somewhat different abilities can play together, and success will depend in part, but not entirely, upon their relative skill.

A special value of academic simulation games appears to be the capacity to develop in the player a sense that he can affect his own future. A massive study conducted by the U.S. Office of Education shows that one attribute strongly related to performance on standard achievement tests is a child's belief that his future depends on his own efforts rather than on a capricious environment. Many disadvantaged pupils appear to lack this belief.

Seeing the consequences of one's actions in a game develops the sense of predictable and controllable environment. When a game simulates aspects of a student's present or future life, the student begins to see how his future depends very directly upon present actions, and thus gives meaning to these actions.

Still another virtue of academic games is the range of skills a game can encompass. A teacher's class presentation has a fairly narrow range: Some students fail to understand unless it is very simple; others are bored when it is that simple. Games, however, can encompass a much larger range of skills. One example indicating the wide range of simulation games is the successful use of the Representative Democracy Game with high school classes of slow learners and, in identical form, with a group of faculty and graduate students in political science and sociology.

Games of this sort hold the attention of bright students in part because they continue to think of new variations in strategy and in the rules. When the rules are not merely accepted but examined and perhaps modified, possibilities for creativity are opened up that the classroom situation often inhibits. The same game may be played successfully— usually at a less sophisticated level, but not always—by children who perform poorly in school. Several groups in a classroom may be playing the same game at different levels of skill.

When a game is designed to illustrate a general principle, some students understand the principle, while others will not do so without guided discussion after play. Thus games are clearly not a self-sufficient panacea for education, although they are more than simply another educational device.

They can be used in many ways ranging from merely inserting them into an existing curriculum to transforming the curriculum by using games and tournaments to replace quizzes and tests.

In the broadest sense, the development of academic simulation games is a response to two challenges: that posed by a complex, difficult-to-understand society and that posed by children uninterested in or unprepared for abstract intellectual learning. These challenges may be blessings in disguise if they force the development of approaches to learning in school that more nearly approximate the natural processes through which learning occurs outside school.

13

Pedagogical Futility in Fun and Games?

IVOR KRAFT

Who can be against games? No one, for the world would be a much poorer place without tag and checkers, charades and even ticktacktoe. I have nothing against games in general.

Also, one can hardly object to games and simulation methods in certain fields—military tactics, mathematics, business management—which the author of the preceding article mentions. These are fields in which what is simulated is very close indeed to the reality under study.

Before stating my objections to Dr. Coleman's approach, I would like to affirm my agreement with his views on the "Nova Academic Olympics" and the advantages of stressing group rather than individual achievement in many school contexts. These are established and honored principles of pedagogy, though there is no necessary connection between them and Professor Coleman's game approach to the social studies.

In the high school which I attended in the Midwest in the 1930's, we had intramural orating and debating meets, and in recent years we have seen the proliferation (not always commendable) of science fairs. I agree with Coleman that these are basically sound ideas that deserve to be improved and extended.

Finally, I am in sympathy with the view that learning should be a pleasant experience, affording joy, fun, and humor where possible, and that games help it to be this. Courses in astronomy would doubtless be much more fun if students were to invent constellation recognition games and to read exclusively the pages of the *Flying Saucer Review*. I don't deny that you can make a game out of anything if you try hard enough.

Briefly, my quarrel with Dr. Coleman is that he has applied a modestly useful teaching device to inappropriate subject matter—the social studies. I am convinced that few if any students will acquire a deeper understanding of social processes by playing games of the kind developed at Johns Hopkins.

The legislative game which Dr. Coleman cites by way of illustration exhibits the weaknesses of his approach. He believes that his game teaches the "basic structure of representative government," but it does nothing of the sort. Instead, it indoctrinates the player into a number of naive misconceptions about the nature of the American Congress and American politics.

The game compels the player to assume (it makes no provision for questioning the assumption) that a legislator can gain reelection only by satisfying the wishes of a majority of constituents. Since when? There are many ways of gaining reelection in American politics by running roughshod over the interests of large majorities. A far more common way of winning an election is to align oneself with small interest groups that command the chief instruments of political power—money, newspapers, TV time, and control of local political machines. In the history of the American legislature we have more frequently had representatives of lobbies—cotton, sugar, railroads, oil, banking, even "China"—than representatives of "the people."

And what about those rare but brave souls who occasionally defy the wishes of powerful interest groups and even broad majorities of voters by voting their consciences? Sometimes they survive and do the nation a great service by championing just but unpopular causes that later win the day. Dr. Coleman's game makes no provision for them, thus leading the players to assume their nonexistence or insignificance.

Whoever heard of a two-minute negotiation session consisting largely of an "exchange of votes"? What can a player possibly learn from this that will offset the impact of being compelled to decide on the merits of civil rights in a two-minute "negotiation"? What earthly connection is there between this kind of gamesmanship and the actual complexities that resulted in the passage of recent civil rights legislation?

The winner of Coleman's game is the one elected with the largest majority. Even this is a distortion. We know about gerrymandering and are aware that a president can be elected without actually receiving a majority of the popular vote.

Instead of achieving the announced aim—"to teach about the complexity that characterizes modern society," the Johns Hopkins group has succeeded in inventing a game that not only distorts and falsifies the reality of American politics, but also takes the difficult and controversial issues of American democracy, and reduces them to a species of play dough suitable for the nursery.

Any high school student will learn more about representative government by two weeks' participation in an unrigged and typical student council than he will by a year's playing of "Legislature."

I believe that Dr. Coleman has allowed his fascination with games to confuse his views on human psychology. For example, I question his notion that a child first comes to understand the meaning of a rule by taking part in a game situation (". . . if the rules are broken, the game does not function").

Typically, the child first grasps the meaning of the abstraction, *rule*, in simple life situations which have nothing to do with games. He is punished, rewarded, deprived, or offered some pleasure in connection with what seem to him to be arbitrary aspects of life: He gets his bottle if he cries lustily; the cat scratches him if he pulls its tail. The child later applies this concept to games, although he also quickly grasps the idea that sometimes one can get away with breaking the rules (cheating) in such a way as to enable the game to go on functioning. Cheating happens to be a widespread phenomenon wherever games are played and grades are awarded. (This important point seems to have been overlooked by Dr. Coleman.)

Aside from the merits or demerits of a single game such as "legislature," or the psychological misconceptions which underlie game playing as a pedagogical strategy, I fear an emphasis on gamesmanship because it betrays a number of inaccurate views of the role of the teacher and of schooling in modern life.

Games such as Dr. Coleman describes do little to prepare students for intelligent participation in a free, open, and rich society. Playing games in which values are set in advance and are not open to discussion will not help young people understand why human beings and societies cherish the values that they do cherish, and how one goes about deciding, in a world of conflicting values, what is indeed worth striving for and getting. The point of schooling, it seems to me, is to encourage students to examine values and confront reality, not to play with indoctrinated values while mechanizing or computerizing reality.

Dr. Coleman wants to diminish the teacher's role as judge and jury. Good. (Sensitive and skilled teachers have long since discarded this role.) Teachers should not, however, be urged to the opposite extreme—to become passive scorekeepers and teaching machine attendants.

The inventor of "Legislature" seems to be advocating a mechanization, actually a "decontroversialization" of the teacher's role, as if the chief aim is to prevent the teacher from ever getting on the hook. But what great teacher has ever made it his motto to keep permanently off the hook? From time to time his proper place is definitely on the hook.

As for resentments, rivalries, and unhealthy tensions evoked by the constant grading and testing of students, most progressive school people would agree that the point is not to make it easier or more "objective" for the teacher to record the grade—we have carried that particular art to a ridiculous extreme—but simply to reduce drastically the whole rigmarole of grading and testing which oppresses students and demoralizes so many aspects of the teaching relationship.

Dr. Coleman makes an important and wise point in suggesting that we must foster in adolescents a sense of self-determination, a capacity for influencing the future. This is indeed a chief purpose of education. But I believe that an overindulgence in games blunts and stifles this sense as often as it develops it. There are many poker players, bridge fans, pool addicts, and even chess players who are so interested in playing and winning the game that they let many other parts of life pass them by. As individuals, they are less, not more, self-determining in life style; as gamesters, I doubt that they possess a deeper than normal sense of affecting their own future.

The essence of chess, basketball, or bridge is not that they simulate reality or that they encourage people to confront reality—instead these games comprise a reality of their own. They are their own excuse for being. Boys do not play basketball because they are simulating "team spirit" and "clean living," and housewives do not play bridge because it develops the mathematical centers of the brain. Regardless of the remote origins of chess, you will not find many contemporary chess masters who are generals or field marshals.

I believe that in the high school social studies field, Dr. Coleman's approach has very little to offer. It obscures more than it reveals. It is a step backward from the necessary and difficult task of revising the social studies curriculum so as to bring students as close as possible to the great and controversial social questions of our era. My advice to teachers, therefore, is to be dubious of this approach and to remember that when it comes to high school social studies the rule ought to be: prevarication, never; games, seldom; the search for the unvarnished truth, always.

14

Games in the Classroom

ELLIOT CARLSON

More than 200 high school students from twenty states will descend
on Nova High School in Ft. Lauderdale, Florida, this month for the
school's second annual Olympic games. But the activities at Nova's sump-
tuous spread—part of the 545-acre South Florida Education Center—will
have little to do with the usual athletic exertions conjured by the word
Olympics. Instead, Olympic participants will shun the rigors of the track
for the comforts of the classroom: They will play Equations, a mathematics game devised by a Yale law professor, in an experiment to determine
whether a spate of newly developed strategy games can have an influence
on the adolescent as pervasive as that of athletic programs.

Recognizing that high school athletes generally are accorded recognition and prestige by their peers while scholars are less "acceptable,"
Robert W. Allen, director of Nova's two-year-old Academic Games Project, declares that the Nova Olympics are aimed at restructuring this
"value perspective." In time, through competitive use of a panoply of
games, Mr. Allen hopes the school achievement of adolescents will be
improved by "altering the structure of values and rewards evidenced in
many schools."

Although Nova is the only school to make such games the focus of a
national championship, it is by no means alone in discovering their educational possibilities. A growing number of schools—universities as well as
secondary and elementary schools—are finding that various problem-
solving games can be helpful in teaching everything from mathematics
and business administration to international relations.

 SOURCE. *Saturday Review*, April 15, 1967, pp. 62–64, 82–83.

Hastening entry of the sometimes controversial games into secondary and elementary schools is mounting teacher dissatisfaction with old-fashioned textbook approaches to course material. Some Baltimore and San Diego high schools have found that games can help motivate slow learners. And grade schools in northern Westchester County, New York, working under a U.S. Office of Education grant, have designed games to teach sixth graders the economic problems of an emerging nation and the operation of a retail toy store.

On the university level, the same spirit of innovation is infecting a growing number of graduate schools of business, where some educators contend games may remedy a deficiency in those curriculums overlooking that decision-making occurs in a context of conflict. Four years ago, the University of Chicago's Graduate School of Business introduced a game reflecting the workings of the international trade system. About the same time the Harvard Business School introduced a game for first-year graduate students simulating a consumer goods industry. Last year the University of Pennsylvania's Wharton School of Finance and Commerce introduced a similar game. In all, some fifty university business schools make use of management games, about double the number in 1963, according to one estimate. Business schools by no means monopolize games, however. At Northwestern University, the University of Michigan, and a sprinkling of other colleges, political science students play a game called Inter-Nation Simulation, which supplements courses in international relations.

While it is all the rage in some schools, there is, to be sure, nothing new about gaming itself. War games are as old as gladiators and jousting knights, who used them to develop alternative tactics and strategies. Since the mid-seventeenth century, when a group of Prussian generals adapted chess for an exercise called the King's Game, games played on table tops have provided a respectable means for the study of war and maneuver. But it wasn't until 1956 that a nonmilitary strategy game was devised. Spurred by the growing availability of computers, the American Management Association put together the first widely known management-training game. Soon afterward, games found their way into the university and business communities. Despite their modern complexity, which would have dazzled the Prussian generals, researchers concede that the value of educational games has yet to be established. Nevertheless, the exercises are being used for a bewildering array of purposes by firms, hospitals, labor unions, and even the State Department, which uses them to study counterinsurgency problems. It is in the schools, however, where the games are most varied and where their use may prove most rewarding.

Why are games considered effective learning aids? For one thing, "they spur motivation," claims Kalman J. Cohen, professor of economics and industrial administration at the Carnegie Institute of Technology, which began pioneering in games as early as 1958. "Students get very absorbed in the competitive aspects of the game. They try harder at games than in some courses." More important, he adds, the exercises "give students an opportunity to practice decision-making techniques or approaches studied in the classroom. They force students to live with the consequences of their decisions, an experience hard to get in the classroom."

Typical of business games is Carnegie Tech's, developed to realistically mirror the problems of running a company. The purpose of the game, which involves about eighteen graduate student "executives" representing three competing firms in a fictional detergent industry, is almost breathtakingly ambitious. Dr. Cohen says it is aimed at providing guided experience in managerial decision-making under conditions of competition and uncertainty. At the same time, he says, the game seeks to advance student skills of analysis, advocacy, and negotiation in contacts with outside groups, such as boards of directors, bankers, and union representatives.

As the game gets underway, players huddle over charts and sheets containing background data on their fictional concerns. Then the team makes a decision, usually expressed in dollar terms, on the amount of money to be spent on production, marketing, research, or some other area of the concern's business. The impact of these decisions on a mythical market and, consequently, on the other "companies" in the market, is calculated by an umpire, usually a computer programed with certain cause-and-effect formulas. The umpire changes the situation in accordance with the players' decisions. Reports are issued and then the students, armed with new information, make a new set of decisions, a process that goes on for a predetermined set of "quarters."

Nor is this all. Spicing the game is the requirement that each student-businessman, when he sees that his firm could use a bank loan, travel into nearby Pittsburgh and actually try to talk a local bank out of some cash, fictional though it may be. There, in the plush chambers of bankers such as Francis S. McMichael, vice president of the Mellon National Bank and Trust Company, the young applicant haggles, bargains, and negotiates for the desired amount. Later the student is graded in part on how convincingly he made his case.

How complicated games can get, and how wrapped up students can get in them is illustrated by Inter-Nation Simulation, devised in 1958 by a research team headed by Harold Guetzkow, a professor of political science at Northwestern. Developed originally under the auspices of the

Carnegie Corporation and the Air Force, the game places participants in the roles of decision-makers for make-believe nations. At the same time that the game is supplementing courses in about a dozen universities, Dr. Guetzkow is using it for research, on a $90,000 Defense Department grant.

Dr. Guetzhow explains that players, while working within the limitations of the countries they represent, must attempt to improve their strategic positions in the simulated world arena. Realism is built into the game by requiring the three to five decision-makers representing each "country" to concern themselves variously with foreign affairs, domestic economic matters, defense and military problems. One policy-maker is vested with overall authority, although all of the players can be deposed from power if they fail to improve the country's standard of living or military strength. This is determined by a set of observers, called "validators," who decide the possible consequences for each nation of decisions made by participants.

Still, decision-makers remain free to opt for reduction of political pressures by resorting to international adventures. How the game works in practice was illustrated recently when a group of some thirty Northwestern students in the social sciences participated in sixteen three-hour sessions. Unlike students at the Air Force Academy and some other schools that simulate actual nations, the Northwestern participants divided themselves into five mythical lands with varying "histories" and "capabilities." They were Omme and Utro—two relatively strong nations with high productivity rates—and Algo, Erga, and Engo—three weak nations with limited economic potential.

Professor Guetzhow recalls that the make-believed nations were soon snared in a maelstrom of international tensions. For one thing, both Omne and Utro, through various machinations, grew richer while the economies of the other countries faltered and sputtered. Fueling the uneasiness was the growing military strength of Omne, which alarmed even Utro. Erga called an international conference, ostensibly to discuss economic problems, but in fact to deal with the threat posed by Omne. The poorer countries did glean from the two giants bilateral commitments of economic aid, but they were unable to agree on a strategy to check Omne.

Then Utro rapidly armed, which polarized the "world" system between Omne and Ingo on one side, and Utro and Erga on the other. The only nation without an alliance was Algo, the most impoverished of the five countries. Fearing attack and anxious to carve out a role for itself in the world arena, Algo's policymakers let slip into Ingo's hands a fabricated note, allegedly intercepted from an Erga-Utro courier, revealing plans for an attack on Ingo by the two countries. Ingo immediately called a peace conference, during which Algo offered to act as a mediator between the two blocs. But when tempers flared and tension mounted Algo was forced to admit its authorship of the note. Despite this brinkmanship, peace was maintained; the nations set up a security system that included even Algo. Not all games end so happily. A few, the professor ruefully adds, have ended in nuclear conflagration.

What do students learn from such exercises? Conceding that their value has yet to be proved, Dr. Guetzhow nevertheless insists they are an effective teaching tool. "We put individuals into decision-making posts so they can experience what its like to operate in an international system," he says. "In a simulated situation students get a sense of the reality of decision-making. They learn that it's not as simple as it seems in textbooks."

The students are enthusiastic. After the session, some said they had increased empathy for the plight of small nations in the world arena, while others felt they better understood the phenomenon of nationalism. "I feel like an Omnian," one student confided to an instructor. "In other words, I have developed a nationalist patriotism, pride in Omne's achievements and distress over its failures, which in many ways is just as strong as my American patriotism."

Said another student: "The awareness of the vast number and the complexity of the factors which must be considered by a nation could never have been as vivid from reading a book."

Despite these high marks by students, not all educators are sanguine about games. Indeed, some are downright critical. Discussing the simulation games used by some political scientists, Charles O. Lerche, dean of the school of international services at American University, observes they have "certain advantages in terms of conveying to the student an approximation of reality." But he cautions that the games have "certain built-in limitations. The essence of gaming is that you artificially simplify the universe to single out a few variables. The trouble is that there are few situations in real life where there are only a few variables at work. Life situations are far more complex than these games can make them."

Even on the secondary level not all teachers are enthusiastic about games, which resemble, at least in principle, those played in universities. On both levels games may, but do not always, involve a computer. And even when requiring a computer some games used in high schools seem to border on the frivolous. At least one such game, for example, involves a child's spinning wheel, a pair of dice, and a game board familiar to Monopoly players. Thus the impression persists that games are simply toys, a view that led one Midwest high school last year to turn down a proposal to use in its history classes a seven-year-old politico-military

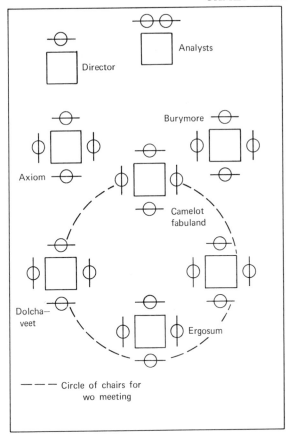

Fig. 1. Diagram of a classroom setup for the international conflict game of "Crisis," developed by Western Behavioral Sciences Institute.

game, called Diplomacy, on grounds that it was "simply entertainment."

Despite such misgivings, use of games on the secondary level is increasing even more rapidly than in the universities. At Johns Hopkins University, James S. Coleman and Sarane S. Boocock, working under a $200,000 Carnegie Corporation grant, are engaged in the development of games with simulated environments. To these academicians the value of games arises in their ability to "bring the future into the present, allowing the child to play roles in a large, differentiated society of which he otherwise gets hardly a glimpse." Also, they claim, games are peculiarly "self-disciplining" and, finally, "self-judging," meaning "a player knows that he has won or lost by his own actions."

Among the eight exercises so far devised at the school are the Game of Democracy, involving bargaining sessions in which players try to get passed or defeated those measures favored by a make-believe constituency; the Disaster Game, in which the winning player is the one who is most efficient in committing his own energies and most visibly cooperative in helping his neighbors overcome a simulated disaster; and the Consumer Game, involving allocation of income in the face of credit financing and other pressures, in which the player "must learn both economics and mathematics, as well as the necessity to defer gratifications."

One of Johns Hopkins's most widely distributed games is Life Career, in which student teams "play" a hypothetical individual as he moves through life and makes decisions about education, jobs, marriage, and other matters. The team that makes the most realistic decisions, given the qualities of the "individual" whose life they are managing, wins the game. This game proved particularly successful recently when used by some Baltimore high schools to motivate slow-learning students.

Slow-learners, in fact, are among the chief beneficiaries of games, say researchers. One game specifically aimed at students considered to be potential dropouts is BMG, developed two years ago by the Western Behavioral Sciences Institute for use in four San Diego schools. Noting that such students are often fond of cars, a WBSI spokesman explains that the young people, for the purpose of the game, play auto manufacturers required both to increase profits and carve out a larger share of the market for their respective "companies."

Like some Baltimore and San Diego schools, Nova High School in Ft. Lauderdale also uses games "to meet the educational needs of the student classified as nonmotivated, under-achiever, or less capable," says Robert Allen. At the same time, he notes that Nova's games are aimed at "the gifted or advanced student; or the student who has formed negative attitudes about a given subject."

Perhaps more deeply involved in gaming than any other school, Nova now uses about fifteen games in its science, mathematics, and social studies classes. Among them are a smattering of games developed at Johns Hopkins, such as Life Career and the Game of Democracy, and two logic games—Wff'n Proof and Equations—developed by Layman Allen, associate professor of law at Yale University and brother of Nova's Robert Allen.

Such games are by no means used simply as teacher aids, however. During 1965, the first year games were used at Nova, the school divided its mathematics classes into two five-week phases of intramural competition using Wff'n Proof and Equations. Now in its second year, Nova's intramural competition consists of ten leagues, each with anywhere from six to twelve teams. Student gamers push the parallel with athletics about as far as it will go. Each week complete statistics are compiled giving individual and team won-lost records, total points scored, and league standings. Further, teams carry names like The Mods, Rat Finks, Brain Kids, and Clear Thinkers; each week Nova names "a player of the week." Winning teams of the intramural leagues eventually compete in a play-off to determine Nova's representative in the emotion-laden Academic Olympics.

Not surprisingly, some Nova educators worry that such competition may lead to an excessive emphasis on winning rather than learning. But whatever the inherent dangers from such contests, the idea has spread to other school systems. This year Allegheny County School District near Pittsburgh organized a ten-team interscholastic league around the game Life Career. The contests proved so popular that at one point last Fall the young people at one school voted to increase their homework in order to allow more time during the day for playing the game.

Few critics deny that games spur enthusiasm. But they point out that the few studies that have been made fail to confirm that students learn anything from them that could not have been learned from conventional methods. After evaluating the results of six different studies on the educational impact of such exercises as Life Career, Disaster Game, Inter-Nation Simulation, and others, Cleo H. Cherryholmes, a political scientist at Michigan State University, said his findings were disappointing. While agreeing that simulations do create more student motivation and interest, he found that they produce no consistent or significant difference in learning, retention, critical thinking, or attitude change. Students do not learn significantly more facts or principles by participating in a simulation than in a more conventional classroom activity, he reported recently in the *American Behavioral Scientist*.

Even so, Dr. Cherryholmes allows that it is "plausible to assume that simulations produce effects that have not been specified and measured" in the studies analyzed. He suggests that more attention-should be given the "social-psychological impact" of games, and it is precisely in this area that Johns Hopkins's Dr. Boocock insists games can have a profound effect. To prove it she tested the impact of Life Career and the Game of Democracy on some 1,200 4-H Club delegates attending a national conference. Half the young people were placed in an experimental group that played the games while the other half were part of a control group that did not.

She found that participants tended to gain from the legislative game a more realistic view of the pressures on legislators that prevent their acting solely on "principle." Perhaps more important, the "data revealed a trend toward greater feelings of political efficacy" on the part of the players after the exercise. Thus, she believes her findings have significance in light of several sociological studies of political behavior, which have shown that the people most likely to take an active part in politics are those with strong feelings of "potency" or efficacy. "In other words, the unique contribution of the simulation experience to feelings of efficacy may be in giving young people the confidence needed to *act* upon the intellectual information they have acquired about a political or other social situation," says Dr. Boocock, writing in the *American Behavioral Scientist*.

There is no question that games, when properly used, can have value. When used in conjunction with other materials, they can provide useful points of departure for discussion. At best, then, games can supplement other educational programs, making real and vivid material that often seems abstract in a textbook. If nothing else, they can convey to the player a feeling for the complexity and multiplicity of factors that must be considered in decision-making. And conceivably they may increase the confidence of young people to deal with real world problems that seem impossibly remote from their own lives.

But the nature of games makes them vulnerable to abuse, particularly in the hands of inexperienced or lazy teachers. Used in isolation from books or discussion groups, the danger arises that games—most of which mirror political and economic institutions as they are—may encourage quiescent and conformist attitudes. In the course of playing, students may hone techniques that enable them to master the game. One may question whether this spurs critical thinking, since success is premised on accepting the "simulated reality" as it is rather than on examining what is wrong with it.

Equally worrisome is the heavy emphasis often placed on winning, which may mislead the player as to the real objectives of learning. That is, the short-term pressures generated for popular success may lead the player to conclude that the ultimate virtue is simply a workable and, at the same time, rather manipulative strategy. So while gaming may produce an academic hero, doubts remain whether the values underpinning his emergence will be any less superficial than those that have glorified the athlete.

It is, of course, too early to resolve such reservations and, for that matter, too early to be pessimistic about the new-fangled exercises. Whatever the uncertainties that now surround games, some things can be said for certain. The burgeoning market for games reflects further movement away from two longtime staples of the classroom: unrealistic and idealized textbook views of American life, and the old teacher-pupil relationship in which the former hands down pronouncements to be regurgitated by the latter. Increasingly the focus is on realism, and increasingly students are expected to learn by themselves. Or at least without the intervention of Grad-grind teachers drilling home facts by slamming rulers on desk tops.

Games and Education— Selected References

PART I

"Turn of the Century" References

Curtis, H. S. *Education Through Play*, New York: Macmillan, 1915.

Fletcher, H. *Study of Children's Games*, Buffalo: School of Pedagogy, 1896.

Gulick, L. H. "Psychological, Pedagogical, and Religious Aspects of Games," *Pedagogical Seminary*, 6, 1899, pp. 135–150.

Johnson, G. E. *Education By Plays and Games*, Boston: Ginn and Company, 1907.

Lee, J. *Play in Education*, New York: Macmillan, 1915.

Micklewaith, J. J. *Indoor Games of School Boys in the Middle Ages*, London, 1892.

Newton, M. B. *Graded Games and Rhythmic Exercises for Primary Grades*, New York: A. S. Barnes, 1908.

Reaney, M. J. "The Psychology of the Organized Group Game: With Special Reference to Its Place in the Play System and Its Educational Value," *The British Journal of Psychology*, Volume I, Monograph Supplement, Cambridge: The University Press, pp. 1–76, 1916.

PART II

General References Dealing with the Concept

Abt, C. C. *Games For Learning*, Cambridge, Mass.: Educational Services, Inc., Occasional Paper Number Seven, 1966.

Abt, C. C. *Heuristic Games for Secondary Schools*, Cambridge, Mass.: Abt Associates, 1965.

Andrus, A. F. "Bringing War Game Simulations Into the Classroom," *Proceedings of the Fourth War Gaming Symposium*, McLean, Virginia: East Coast War Games Council, Research Analysis Corporation, 1965, pp. 195–203.

Boocock, S. S. *Simulation Games in Learning*, Beverly Hills, California: Sage Publishers, 1968.

Boocock, S. S. and Coleman, J. S. "Games With Simulated Environments in Learning," *Sociology of Education*, 39, 1960, pp. 215–236.

Carlson, E. "Games in the Classroom," *Saturday Review*, April 15, 1967, pp. 62–64, 82–83.

Cherryholmes, C. H. "Some Current Research on Effectiveness of Educational Simulations: Implications for Alternative Strategies," *American Behavioral Scientist*, 10, October, 1966, pp. 4–7.

Coleman, J. S. "In Defense of Games," *American Behavioral Scientist*, 10, October, 1966, pp. 3–4.

Coleman, J. S. "Learning Through Games," *National Education Association Journal*, January, 1967, pp. 69–70.

Coleman, J. S., Boocock, S. S. and Schild, E. O. "Simulation Games and Learning Behavior," *American Behavioral Scientist*, 10, October, 1966, pp. 1–32; November, 1966, pp. 3–36.

Farran, D. C. "Games Work with Underachievers," *Scholastic Teacher*, November 9, 1967, pp. 10–11.

Kraft, I. "Pedagogical Futility in Fun and Games," *National Education Association Journal*, January, 1967, pp. 71–72.

Phi Delta Kappa. *Simulation Models for Education*, Bloomington, Indiana: Phi Delta Kappa Symposium on Educational Research, Volume 4, 1962.

Rose, A. W. "Toward Understanding the Concept and Function of Play," *Education Theory*, 31 (778), 1956, pp. 20–25.

Ross, H. "The Teacher Game," *Psychoanalytic Study of The Child* (Eissler, R. S., ed.), New York: International Universities Press, 1965, pp. 228–297.

Sprague, H. T. and Shirts, R. G. *Exploring Classroom Uses of Simulations*, La Jolla, California: Western Behavioral Science Institute, 1966.

PART III

Games in the Teaching of Language and Literature

Bloomer, R. H. *Skill Games to Teach Reading*, Dansville, N.Y.: E. A. Owen Publishing Co., 1961.

Brewster, P. G. "An Attempt at Identification of Games Mentioned in Basile's 'Il Pentamerone'," *Folklore*, London, 1950, pp. 5–23.

Brewster, P. G. *Games and Sports in Shakespeare*, Helsinki: Suomalainen Tiedeakatemia, Academia Scientiarum Fennica, 1959.

Brewster, P. G. "Games and Sports in Sixteenth and Seventeenth Century English Literature," *Western Folklore*, Berkeley, California, 6, 1947, pp. 143–156.

Chicago Public Schools. *Communication Skills: Games for Kindergarten, and Grades 1, 2, and 3*. Chicago: Public School System, 1964.

Dean, J. F. *Games Make Spelling Fun*, Palo Alto, California: Fearon Publishers, 1956.

Humphrey, J. H. "Comparison of the Use of Active Games and Language Workbook Exercises as Learning Media for the Development of Language Understanding with 3rd Grade Children," *Perceptual and Motor Skills*, 21 (1), 1965, pp. 23–26.

McClure, S. "Vowel Tic-Tac-Toe," *The Instructor*, January, 1967, p. 122.

Morris, W. *The Word Game Book*, New York: Harper Brothers, 1959.

Platts, M. E., et al. *Spice: Suggested Activities, and Games to Motivate the Teaching of the Language Arts in the Elementary School*, Benton Harbor, Michigan: Educational Service, Inc., 1960.

Shipley, J. T. *Playing With Words*, Englewood Cliffs, N.J.: Prentice-Hall, Inc., 1960.

Spolin, V. *Improvisation For the Theater Through Theater Games*, Evanston, Ill.: Northwestern University Press, 1963.

Taylor, L. E. *Pantomime and Pantomime Games*, Minneapolis: Burgess Publishing Co., 1965.

Wagner, G., et al. *Language Games: Strengthening Language Skills With Instructional Games*, Darien, Conn.: Teachers Publishing Corporation, 1963.

Wagner, G., et al. *Listening Games: Building Skills with Instructional Games*, Darien, Conn.: Teachers Publishing Corporation, 1966.

Wagner, G., and Hosier, M. *Reading Games: Strengthening Reading Skills With Instructional Games*, Darien, Conn.: Teachers Publishing Corporation, 1966.

PART IV

Games in the Teaching of Arithmetic and Mathematics

Beilen, A. H. *Recreations in the Theory of Numbers*, New York: Dover Publishers, Inc., 1964.

Carroll, L. (Charles Dodson). *The Game of Logic: Mathematical Recreations* (Bound with: *Symbolic Logic*), New York: Dover Publishers, Inc., 1958.

Deans, E. "Games for the Early Grades," *The Arithmetic Teacher*, 13, Feb.–Mar., 1966, pp. 140–141, 238–240.

Dumas, E. *Arithmetic Games*, San Francisco: Fearnon Publishers, Inc., 1960.

Gamow, G. *Puzzle Math*, New York: Viking Press, 1958.

Gardner, M. *The Scientific American Book of Mathematical Puzzles and Diversions*, New York: Simon and Schuster, Volume I, 1959; Volume II, 1961. (See also monthly column, "Mathematical Games," *Scientific American*.)

Golomb, S. W. *Polymonoes*, New York: Charles Scribner's Co., 1965.

Humphrey, J. H. "An Exploratory Study of Active Games in Learning of Number Concepts by First Grade Boys and Girls," *Perceptual and Motor Skills*, 23 (2), 1966, pp. 341–342.

May, L. J. *Mathematics Games for All Grades*, Darien, Conn.: Teachers Publishing Corporation, 1967.

Platts, M. E. *Plus: A Handbook of Experiments, Games, and Activities to Motivate the Teaching of Elementary Arithmetic*, Benton Harbor, Michigan: Educational Service, Inc., 1964.

Schaaf, W. L. *Recreational Mathematics*, Washington, D.C.: National Council of Teachers of Mathematics, 1958.

Seymour, R. "Math Card Game," *The Instructor*, February, 1967, p. 123.

Wagner, G., et al. *Arithmetic Games and Activities: Strengthening Arithmetic Skills with Instructional Aids*, Darien, Conn.: Teachers Publishing Corporation, 1965.

PART V

Games in the Teaching of Social Science

Cohen, B. C. "Political Gaming in the Classroom," *Journal of Politics,* 24, 1962, pp. 367–381.

Gearon, J. D. "Labor vs. Management: A Simulation Game," *Social Education,* 10, 1966, pp. 421–422.

Gearon, J. D. "War or Peace: A Simulation Game," *Social Education,* 11, 1966, pp. 521–522.

Griffin, S. F. *The Crisis Game: Simulating Internation Conflict,* New York: Doubleday, 1965.

Guetzkow, H. S. *Simulation in Social Science: Readings,* Englewood Cliffs, N.J.: Prentice-Hall, Inc., 1962.

Moncreiff, B. "The Sumerian Game: Teaching Economics With a Computerized P.I. Program," *Program Instruction,* 4 (5), February, 1965, pp. 10–11.

Nesbitt, W. A. *Simulation Games for the Social Studies Classroom,* New York: Foreign Policy Association, 1968.

Roy, M. M. *Spark: A Handbook of Games and Activities to Motivate The Teaching of Elementary Social Studies,* Benton Harbor, Michigan: Educational Services, Inc., 1965.

Sprague, H. T. *Using Simulations To Teach International Relations,* La Jolla, California: Western Behavioral Sciences Institute, 1966.

Wagner, G., et al. *Social Studies Games and Activities: Strengthening Social Studies Skills with Instructional Aids,* Darien, Conn.: Teachers Publishing Corporation, 1964.

Wolff, P. *The Game of Empire,* Cambridge, Mass.: Educational Services, Inc., Social Studies Curriculum Program, Occasional Paper No. 9, 1966.

PART VI

Games in the Teaching of Physical Science

Roy, M. M. *Probe: A Handbook of Games, Activities, and Experiments to Motivate the Teaching of Elementary Science,* Benton Harbor, Michigan: Educational Services, Inc., 1962.

Vivian, C. *Science Games for Children,* New York: Sterling Publishing Company, 1963.

Wagner, G. *Science Games and Activities,* Darien, Conn.: Teachers Publishing Corporation, 1967.

PART VII

Games in the Teaching of Art and Music

Carabo-cone, A. *The Playground as Music Teacher; An Introduction to Music Through Games*, New York: Harper, 1959.

Platts, M. E. *Create: A Handbook of Games, Activities, and Ideas to Motivate the Teaching of Elementary Art*, Benton Harbor, Michigan: Educational Services, Inc., 1966.

PART VIII

Games in the Teaching of Business Education and Administration

Godwin, N. (ed.) "Computer Game Teaches College Administrators," *T.C. Week*, New York: Teachers College, Columbia University, **33** (18), 1968, pp. 1, 4.

McKenny, J. C. "An Evaluation of a Business Game in an MBA Curriculum," *Journal of Business*, **35**, pp. 278–286.

Nelson, J. "Typewriter Mystery Games," *The Instructor*, **41**, April, 1966, p. 280.

Smith, S. L. "Adding Interest via Shorthand Games," *Journal of Business Education*, **41**, April, 1966, pp. 279–280.

PART IX

Games in the Elementary School and Early Childhood Education

Association for Childhood Education International. *Play—Children's Business: Guide to Selection of Toys and Games*, Washington, D.C.: The Association, 1963.

Cornelius, R. "Games Minus Competition," *Childhood Education*, **26**, 1949, pp. 77–79.

Landin, L. *One Hundred Blackboard Games*, Palo Alto, California: Fearon Publishers, 1956.

Mulac, M. E., and Holmes, M. S. *The School Game Book,* New York: Harper and Row, Publishers, 1950.

Kautz, J. "Games and Activities for All Grades," *The Instructor,* **76** (6), February, 1967, p. 18.

Kautz, J. "*Games* to Improve Skills," *The Instructor,* **75**, October, 1965.

Reaney, M. J. "The Correlation Between General Intelligence and Play Ability as Shown in Organized Group Games," *British Journal of Psychology,* **7** (2), 1916, pp. 226–250.

Schwander, N. *Game Preferences of 10,000 Fourth Grade Children,* New York: Columbia University, 1932.

Tiedt, S. W., and Tiedt, I. M. *Elementary Teachers Complete Ideas Handbook,* Englewood Cliffs, N.J.: Prentice-Hall, Inc., 1966.

Wagner, G., et al. *Educational Games and Activities,* Darien, Conn.: Teachers Publishing Corporation, 1967.

Wagner, G., et al. *Games and Activities for Early Childhood Education,* Darien, Conn.: Teachers Publishing Corporation, 1967.

Werner, G. L. *After School Games and Sports: Grades 4, 5, 6,* Washington, D.C.: National Education Association, 1964.

PART X

Some Bibliographic References

"Major Centers Involved in Research and Development of Games with Simulated Environments," *American Behavioral Scientist,* **10**, November 1966, pp. 35–36.

Occasional Newsletter About the Use of Simulations and Games for Education. La Jolla, California: Western Behavioral Sciences Institute, Project Simile; **1**, September, 1965; **2**, January, 1966; **3**, April, 1966; **4**, January 1967; **5**, July, 1967; **6**, December, 1967.

"Selective Bibliography on Simulation Games as Learning Devices," *American Behavioral Scientist,* **10**, November, 1966, pp. 34–35.

CHAPTER 10

GAMES IN DIAGNOSTIC AND TREATMENT PROCEDURES

Games used by personnel in health-related services for diagnostic and therapeutic purposes are usually adaptations of games used for recreative purposes. While personnel use games for a variety of health-related purposes, the rationale for therapeutic use is that games provide the patient with a recreative experience that contributes to well-being.[1] Diagnostic approaches in psychiatry vary as do the way games are used in the diagnostic process. In one instance, personnel (a psychiatrist or psychologist) may feel that the game that is played is not important. The game could be chess, shuffleboard, or poker; the important thing is *how* the patient relates to the other players (whether they be staff, other patients, or volunteers). In another instance the personnel may use the game to determine to what degree the patient is "in touch" with reality. Some psychiatrists, clinical psychologists, or psychiatric social workers, use games as a neutral vehicle to create a relationship with a patient, and dispense with the game as a "go-between" when the patient is comfortable enough to talk directly about his problems. In contrast, the classically analytic psychiatrist is interested in which game the patient chooses to play because the symbolism in the game, and the procedures in the game are believed to reveal information about the patient's unconscious conflicts.[2]

Another approach is the employment of games to determine potential

[1] Haun, P. *Recreation: A Medical Viewpoint.* F. B. Arje and E. M. Avedon (Eds.), New York: Teachers College Press, 1965.

[2] Fine, R. *Psychoanalytic Observations on Chess and Chess Masters.* New York: National Psychological Association for Psychoanalysis Inc., 1956.

behavior of a patient. Jenson developed a "psychological test" that incorporates five games ranging from a jigsaw puzzle to a three-legged race to determine the possible adjustment of patients toward wardlife.[3] Similarly a modification of the "Acme-Bolt" game (see chapter 11) has been used to indicate some areas of discord in married couples in conjoint therapy. A reading illustrating this approach is included at the conclusion of this chapter.

Just as diagnostic approaches vary, so too do therapeutic approaches. In some psychiatric treatment programs, psychiatrists feel that what a patient does with his "nonpsychotherapeutic" time (when he is not talking to his psychotherapist) is the patient's own business. On the other hand, some psychiatrists require an even more direct approach in treatment, and write orders to involve patients for specific purposes in a variety of games, for example, playing out of aggression, learning to get along with peers, discharging anger, challenging an authority figure. Although there is little evidence in the psychiatric and related literature that specific games can be used for these purposes, they are so used, and considerable controversy has raged over this point.[4] Most of the material concerning the choice of games for specific therapeutic purposes with regard to psychotherapy is purely subjective. For example, Redl and Gump (whose theoretical approach to games is described later) began by assembling a host of anecdotal reports such as the following. (Most of these reports still remain to be systematically investigated.)

Psychiatric social workers had reported that disturbed children who could normally not play any rule games whatsoever because of their social immaturity and hence their inability to keep the rules, gained their first successes playing at cheating games. These are a series of games in which the major challenge is that of surreptitiously fooling the opponent and getting away with an act that he is supposed to guard against. The players were in a situation of either pretending that something is not so, or in the complementary position of trying to detect one's opponent in such a pretense. Games of this sort are: *redlight, I doubt it, doggie doggie, mother may I,* and in some respects *poker.*

I doubt it, for example, is a card game in which different players "declare" what cards they have without showing their hands. If they are unchallenged in this, they are allowed to record what they have declared as their score. However, if a player is challenged he must show his hand.

---

[3] Morris, W. E., and Jenson, M. B. "Recreation Preferences as Predictors of Participation in Mental Hospital Activities," *Mental Hygiene,* **45** (1), 1966, pp. 77–83.

[4] Meyer, M. W. "Rationale of Recreation as Therapy," *Recreation in Treatment Centers.* 1, September, 1962, pp. 23–26; and Rosen, E. "Selection of Activities for Therapeutic Use," pp. 29–32.

If he has declared truthfully the player who doubts him loses points. If he has lied about his hand, he loses points. Here, then, is a game in which suspicion and cheating have moved into the very center of the game structure and are its main points. To such a challenge, disturbed children were reported to respond with enthusiasm and suffer less frustration than they did in other types of games. In almost any other game, in various degrees depending on the game, suspicion of one's opponent's honesty and attempts on one's own part to beat the rules led to disorganization of the game and mutual hostility among the players. In this game, however, these very things that are liabilities in most games, became assets and sources of considerable gratification.

Among disturbed children who were beginning to gain a greater degree of self-control than those just mentioned, games of steadfastness were said to be very popular. These are a whole series of games and commands that children employ in order to frustrate the very behavior that they indulge in with such enthusiasm and often lack of control. Most teachers will be familiar with the practice in the following form. For example, in the middle of a hilarious time during a lunch hour one child will shout, "The first one to speak is a monkey." Then all the other children must sit mute themselves but also engage in various antics and expressions to encourage somebody else to break down. These might be called games that demand that one does not do what comes naturally. One must not giggle, cry, talk, hit, smile, laugh, and so on. The game will nearly always involve such a restriction and at the same time activity on the part of the players to induce someone else to lose self-control.

Some of the hunches that practitioners reported were about anxious or timid children. For example, it was commented that young inept and sensitive children did not like to be the "it" in *hide and seek*. This was thought to be because the "it" role is a task that requires some responsibility. "It" makes the child question his success in dealing with all the others who are against him. "It" makes him feel that they make him look foolish by sneaking in behind his back or beating him to a goal. The same may be said of the timid child in a game like *circle keep away*. This child may be unduly teased and put under physical pressure in his incompetent attempts to get the ball from children on the outside of the circle who are passing it around. Some recreationists felt that the most suitable games for anxious children to begin with were pencil and paper games in which the amount of interpersonal interaction was greatly diminished. Writing games, such as *dun heep, tick tack toe,* or *twenty-five squares,* provide opportunities for several youngsters to play together without focusing too much on one another, but rather on the material that is between them. Furthermore, a writing game tends to keep the excitement fairly low and is quite distant from the direct physically competitive or attacking situation.

Regardless of the authenticity of these examples, such instances of particular types of games being related to particular types of players could be multiplied. This notion perhaps overemphasizes the importance of the players' anxieties and conflicts. Their abilities and needs may also play an important role.

It may be noted that games have been used in the treatment of mental illness since ancient times. The famous legendary Greek physician Melampus is supposed to have treated the daughters of Proteus of the delusion that they were cows, by having them play a game involved with running.[5]

Akin to the use of games for treatment of mentally ill persons, is the approach employed in the "treatment" of the mentally retarded child. A variety of personnel advocate the use of games as a way of "teaching" mentally retarded children about acceptable modes of social behavior, for example, take your turn, follow the rules, and the like.[6] Though, again, the critics of this approach use the same arguments found in criticism of games used in education; they feel that "treatment" of mentally retarded persons is primarily a remedial educational approach.

The use of games in physical restoration of illness or disability is not a controversial issue. The issue is clear. Either a game has kinetic aspects that are indicated or contraindicated in relation to a specific condition. For example, if a person has a condition in which the physician wishes to have bilateral exercise of upper extremities giving assistance to one limb, or wants to increase shoulder and elbow mobilization, he could prescribe a series of exercises or games that include these types of movements. In the first instance, bilateral exercise of upper extremities is found in the game of Ping-Pong, and a game of darts affords the kinetic movement needed for the second example. Often, game equipment is modified to enhance the kinetic values, for instance, a game of checkers modified for use on the floor, requires foot and leg movement rather than hand-arm involvement for treatments of such conditions as tabes dorsalis and cerebellar ataxia.[7]

---

[5] Gordon, B. L. *Medicine Through Antiquity.* Philadelphia: F. A. Davis Company, 1949, pp. 433–435.

[6] Carlson, B. W., and Ginglend, D. R. *Play Activities for the Retarded Child.* New York: Abingdon Press, 1961.

[7] Blau, L. "Appliances and Remedial Games," *Occupational Therapy,* Springfield, Ill.: Charles C Thomas, 1957, pp. 85–99. See also: Lipkind, E. H. "Recreation and Physical Therapy: A Blueprint for an Integrated Service," *Recreation in Treatment Centers,* 2, 1963, pp. 57–61; and Boeshart, L. K. "Remedial Games in Treatment of

In addition to the use of games in the restoration of persons who are physically disabled, games are also used in general medical settings for a variety of purposes, for example, to alleviate the boredom of hospital routine, to divert attention from pain, to drain anxiety and promote digestion and sleep. Most modern hospitals today employ recreation specialists who are in a position to utilize games for treatment purposes in a variety of situations. Considerable material on the subject is available in the literature. In addition, modified game equipment in relation to specific conditions has been made available for general purchase, for instance, scrabble with braille markings for the blind person; card holders and shufflers for the person whose arm has been amputated, or who because of arthritis or palsy cannot hold the cards; indoor modified bowling equipment for the person who is wheelchair bound.

Thus games for a long time have been part of the armamentarium of physicians, and probably will be for a long time to come. We include three exemplary articles, one using a game approach in psychodiagnostics, one using games in treatment of children with physical disability, and one original article indicating practical methods in the application of games for therapeutic purposes. The readings are followed by a list of selected references that indicates a range of material related to diagnostic and treatment use of games.

Physical Disability," *American Journal of Occupational Therapy*, **5**, March, 1951, pp. 47–48.

15

The Use of an Interpersonal Game-Test in Conjoint Marital Psychotherapy

ROBERT A. RAVICH

INTRODUCTION

In carrying out conjoint psychotherapy with married couples, one becomes acutely aware that the dyadic unit is more than the sum of the characteristics of its male and female members. It is the interaction within the marital dyad *between* the husband-wife pair that conjoint therapy seeks to change. However, the dyad is highly resistant to change and the therapist is likely to find himself baffled and frustrated by two people ostensibly seeking help who seem to be attempting to engage him in a game that might best be labeled "Dump the Doctor."

It is almost impossible to avoid game concepts and game terminology in thinking and writing about marital and family interaction. This led me to explore the literature in the field known as game theory that has developed since the publication in 1944 of the basic theoretical work, *Theory of Games and Economic Behavior,* by J. von Neuman and O. Morgenstern (1). While the many studies in this field throw light on important aspects of human behavior, a unified theory encompassing two-person and *n*-person (three or more person) games has not been developed (1, 2). This theoretical difficulty is constantly confirmed in the course of clinical experience. It is not surprising, therefore, that one of the basic problems in family therapy is whether the dyad or triad is the elementary unit within the family system.

352 SOURCE. *American Journal of Psychotherapy,* **23** (2), April 1969, pp. 217–229.

Several social psychologists, influenced strongly by Kurt Lewin as well as by game theory, have developed experimental games for the purpose of studying decision-making, conflict, and conflict-resolution under controlled laboratory conditions. The "two-person bargaining game" developed by Morton Deutsch and Robert M. Krauss (3, 4) was initially used (5, 6) and then specifically adapted for the clinical studies described in the present article.

METHODOLOGY

In the Deutsch-Krauss paradigm for the "two-person bargaining game," the important features to be noted are that each person operates a vehicle that must travel from separate starting points to separate destinations. Each has a direct route and an alternate route leading to his destination. The vehicles travel at a fixed speed, and there is a profit or loss on each trip that is determined by the length of time required for each vehicle to complete its trip.

A portion of the direct route of each player is a commonly shared, one-lane road, where the vehicles cannot pass each other. Traveling toward each other from opposite directions they will collide head-on if they meet at any point on this common section. Two gates are located near either end of the common section. The gate closest to Player A's destination is controlled by Player B (and vice versa) and can be closed by him to delay or prevent A's vehicle from reaching its destination via the direct route. Traveling on the alternate route, a vehicle cannot collide nor be delayed by closing of the gate. However, the alternate route is three times longer than the direct one.

The Ravich Interpersonal Game/Test (RIG/T) that was developed for clinical use is a concrete version of the Deutsch-Krauss paradigm (Fig. 1). The vehicles are two small (N-gauge) electric trains. The track layouts on either side of a table, which is three by three feet when opened, are separated from each other by a panel. This panel is 14 inches high, so that the two seated players can see each other but cannot see the other person's side of the table. The common section of track has been split, but the collision feature is maintained by means of electrical sensors located on the tracks. When the two vehicles come to the same part of the common section of their respective direct routes, the power cuts off and both trains stop moving.

The player's control panel consists of two route selection buttons by means of which the player chooses the route that he wants his train to take. There is a switch that is used to move the train forward, to put it in reverse or to stop it. Two additional buttons open or close a barrier or

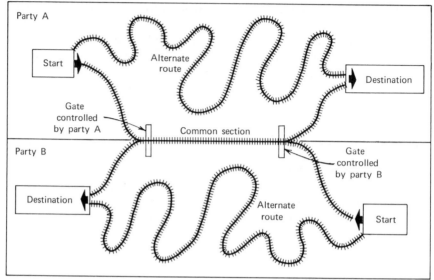

Fig. 1

gate located on the other person's direct route.[1] A green light signals the start of each trip and a flashing red light informs each person whenever a collision occurs. Unidirectional microphones mounted on each player's control panel permit the verbal interaction to be recorded on tape.

The tester's panel is a data-collecting computer that automatically records all of the table moves made by each player. Counters record the time required by each player's train to reach its destination, the time spent in collision, how often each player backs up from collisions or reverses his train and changes routes, how many times and for how long each player closes the barrier. The tester tells the players at the end of each trip how long each vehicle took to complete the trip and how much imaginary money was thereby gained or lost. These announcements of the "score" on each trip allow the recorded data to be readily correlated with the taped conversation so that the behavioral and verbal components of the process of decision-making can be fully integrated.

The instructions read to the couple before they take the RIG/T are

[1] Imaginary gates were a part of the apparatus used in the early experimental studies reported by Ravich, Deutsch and Brown (5). In the subsequent extensive clinical case studies that form the basis for this report, the prototype RIG/T had gates which mechanically stopped the engines. The gates have now been replaced by a traffic signal and an electronically controlled cut-off. The term "barrier" as used here applies to either the gates or the traffic lights, with the recognition that these may lend themselves to slightly different symbolic interpretations which do not appear to be critical.

shown in the Appendix. There are approximately 50 bits of information incorporated in these instructions. It will be noted that they are worded so as to maintain ambiguity in order to avoid giving the couple any indication of what they should try to do. This provides the widest latitude for them to establish their own "set" of how they are going to play and for what purpose. While they are told that they can talk to each other as much as they want, it is not necessary to communicate in order to play the game.

A complete test consists of 20 trips and takes approximately 45 minutes.

OBSERVATIONS

From the very earliest exploratory period of these studies, the response of marital couples to the game-test experience was striking. There was an intense absorption in the task, usually followed by a period of reflection or often extensive discussion on the significance of what had occurred. These ideas and feelings were explored during the interview session regularly held two or three days after the RIG/T was taken. During these "post-game sessions" a high proportion of the couples would then spontaneously draw analogies between what had happened during the course of the game-test and many of their real-life conflict and decision-making situations. In a surprisingly large number of couples the pattern of interaction demonstrated objectively within the context of the game situation was markedly at variance with what each had previously believed about themselves in relationship to one another. Since married couples share certain important concepts about themselves and their relationship, and have long experience in acting out what are very often myths, the data obtained from their game-test behavior and verbal interaction together with the associations during the post-game session were frequently far more revealing than anything that they had previously related to me about their relationship, or even than the interaction that I had observed in the course of earlier clinical interviews.

This article focuses primarily on the behavioral patterns of interaction. The communication patterns are of considerable importance, as are the correlations between what is said and what is done. A systematic approach to this verbal aspect of the game-test data remains to be developed.

PATTERNS OF INTERACTION

During the four-year period that followed the initial utilization of this method, over 350 marital pairs as well as other family dyads have been studied. Four major patterns of interaction, each having several varia-

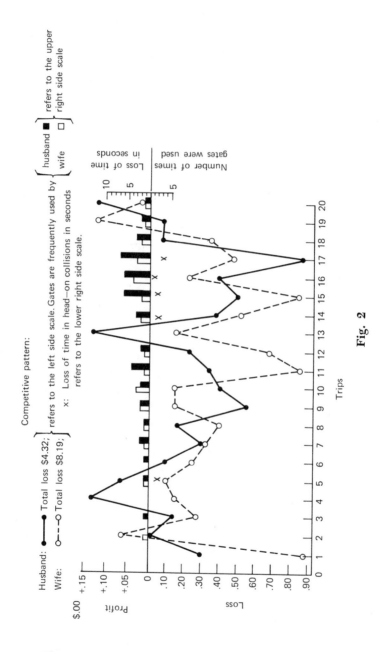

Fig. 2

tions, have emerged. These have been designated as: (1) competitive, (2) alternating, (3) dominant-submissive, and (4) mixed. They are best depicted graphically. In the following figures the horizontal axis represents the 20 trips. The horizontal line (at 0) represents the break-even point. Profits are shown above the 0 line, losses below. The solid line shows the pay-off achieved by the husband and the interrupted line shows the wife's pay-off. The small bars above the break-even line show the number of times the barriers were closed by the man and woman during a particular trip. The total time (in seconds) spent in collisions is indicated by the distance of the X below the 0 line.

The *competitive* pattern of interaction is illustrated in Figure 2. It can be seen that both players lose on most of the trips, that they have repeated collisions, and close the gates frequently. These couples share a competitive orientation, working against each other. Couples showing this pattern communicate with each other either not at all, or do not discuss their plans, since each person is attempting to sustain less of a loss than the other, or to cause the other person to lose more. Having structured the situation as one in which they seek to outdo each other, they show little or no concern for the tester. Because each is reluctant to have the other reach the destination by the direct route, they are often forced to take the alternate route.

The *alternating* pattern of interaction is illustrated in Figure 3. There are but few collisions of brief duration, the gates are rarely used, and both partners win on each trip, sharing equally in the rewards. This is accomplished by the two persons agreeing to allow each other through on the direct route in an alternating "after you Alphonse, after you Gaston" manner. An essential requirement of this pattern is some mutually agreed upon coordinated signaling process. The players are out to "beat

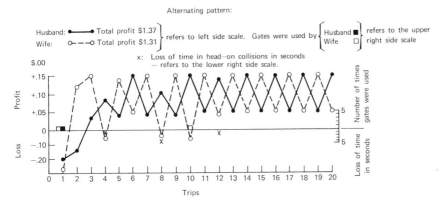

Fig. 3

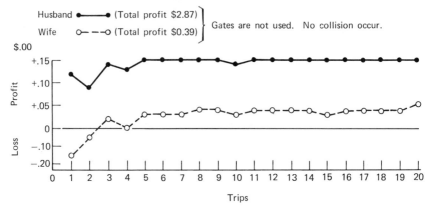

Fig. 4

the game" or the tester by maximizing their profits and sharing the rewards equally. These couples often show an excessive degree of concern about colliding and closing the gates that is expressed in their verbal exchanges but not in their actions. While this appears to be a cooperative pattern, the post-game interview frequently reveals that the pattern has been imposed by one partner and reluctantly accepted by the other.

The *dominant-submissive* pattern is illustrated in Figure 4. Here there are no collisions, and no use of the gates. Both players use the direct route all the time; however one of the partners—in this case the husband —always goes through first and thereby achieves a profit that is approximately three times as great as the wife's. They earn as much as the couple in Figure 3 but share unequally in the rewards.

Mixed patterns of interaction are made up of elements of any two or all three of the patterns previously described. Figure 5 illustrates a couple that on different sequences of trips made use of alternating, competitive, and dominant-submissive interaction patterns. This shift from pattern to pattern takes place in an aimless, desultory, unplanned way.

The charts of cases used for illustration of these interactional patterns provide clear examples of the four major types that have been encountered. A high proportion of the dyads tested can be readily identified as corresponding to one of these four types. However, there are interesting variations within each of the categories that appear to be clinically significant. For example, there is a competitive pattern in which one person repeatedly backs down and takes the alternate route, but the other remains standing at the closed gate; there is a variation of the alternating pattern in which the two people never take the direct route

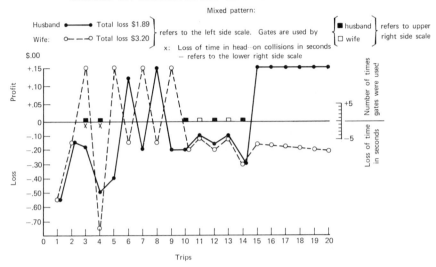

Fig. 5

at the same time, but rather shift back and forth from the direct to the alternate route on successive trips; there is a dominant-submissive pattern in which collisions occur on every trip, but one person backs down each time; also, there is a dominant-submissive pattern in which one person always takes the direct and the other person always takes the alternate route.

In many cases an initial period of confusion involving perceptual and cognitive difficulties is overcome gradually during the early trips so that a clear-cut pattern emerges with learning. Among the upper and middle class couples encountered in private practice we have observed that a repeated pattern will often begin to show up by the ninth or tenth trip, while with lower class couples in a hospital clinic, the pattern may not emerge until the thirteenth to fifteenth trip. We therefore consider 24 trips to be a more suitable test for lower class patients, thus allowing for the slightly longer learning time. There is no definite relationship between the typology of the patterns and intelligence levels, at least for people within the normal range of intelligence. Perceptual capacity not directly related either to intelligence, education, or age is a significant factor, as is cognitive capacity. Sociocultural factors appear to play a significant role in determining the distribution of couples and family dyads within the different categories. Individual psychopathology may influence, but does not determine the pattern of interaction.

The post-game interviews have repeatedly demonstrated that the pattern of interaction employed by a couple in the game-test situation is highly relevant, since it derives from the characteristics of the relationship, particularly its conflict-resolving and decision-making aspects. The most striking finding has been the rigidity of adherence by married couples to their particular type of interactional pattern.

Toward a Strategy of Conjoint Therapy

Psychotherapists generally, and family therapists especially, conceive of their role as being that of an agent of change. However, change is a very broad and too often an ill-defined concept. Change can mean modification or elimination of symptoms, as well as a shift to a more successful adaptational defense mechanism. In conjoint marital psychotherapy, the question of change is often conceived of as improvement in communication that can lead to a more harmonious marital and family existence. When the therapist utilizes the typology of interactional patterns described here, the concept of change becomes more specific. The use of a single stereotyped pattern for resolving most or all conflict situations needs to be sufficiently modified by learning at least one other pattern of interaction that is apprehended adequately so as to be readily available to the couple for use under a variety of stress situations. Obviously, learning a new pattern of interaction is not the same as having it truly available as a coping device. Hence therapy is both a learning experience—learning what the stereotyped pattern is and learning at least one other pattern—as well as training and retraining in the utilization of the new pattern until the couple feels truly secure and confident with it.

Marital pairs who show a competitive pattern of interaction need to learn and to be able to use either an alternating or dominant-submissive pattern, or both. It is surprising how easy it is for many such couples to make this change and to maintain it. The couple's internal competitiveness can be readily turned against the environment. Couples who show an alternating pattern need to learn how to compete with each other openly without the usual overwhelming fear that predominates in these relationships. Inequalities of rewards need to be made acceptable. This is a much longer and harder therapeutic task often involving much deeper analytically oriented conjoint therapy.

The dominant-submissive pattern has proven to be the most resistive to change. A quasi-change may be brought about in which the person who was dominant becomes submissive, and the other person who was submissive becomes dominant. However, while the roles have shifted, the basic pattern is maintained. The resistance of these couples to change is characteristically manifested by a flight from therapy, and it is necessary for the therapist to be prepared for these flights and to exert every effort to have the couple continue in treatment when they occur. This may mean that the therapist must be willing upon occasion to reach out, even to the point of going to the home of the couple in order to carry them through this difficult time. Hospitalization may be temporarily required, usually for the submissive member who is often depressed.

The mixed pattern couples, especially those who aimlessly use all three elements or a combined competitive and dominant-submissive pattern frequently express feelings of life being empty, meaningless, and absurd. Such aimless couples often require a degree of directiveness that therapists may at first be reluctant to undertake. In order to be an agent for change, it is necessary for the therapist to take command in an authoritative manner for a period long enough to permit the couple to perceive the advantages to be gained in establishing some clearly defined pattern of interaction.

DISCUSSION

The RIG/T is significantly different from other "psychologic" tests in a number of respects. It is an instrument for evaluating the dyad as a unit, and for illustrating the decision-making and conflict-resolving characteristics of that unit which are important dynamic aspects of its capacity to adapt to internal differences and environmental situations. The RIG/T is not a method that can be utilized to ascertain psychologic traits or personality characteristics of the individuals per se (7, 8). It gives objective data only about the individual in relation to another individual. The same person may interact very differently in one dyadic relationship than in another. And the same individual may respond differently as a member of the same dyad at different times, under various intrapsychic conditions, or when confronted with new environmental situations.

Another feature of the RIG/T that distinguishes it from other methods is that it elicits both behavioral and verbal interactions within the framework of a mixed-motive situation in which the most significant variable is the past interaction of the dyad (9, 10). The RIG/T, as compared to other test situations, is not anxiety-provoking. Because it is a new, playful, and apparently trivial task it tends to diminish anxiety both within the individual members of the dyad and between them. This has certain advantages in the clinical evaluation of marital couples and families with emotional problems where heightened anxiety often obscures the underlying interactional patterns.

Finally, the RIG/T does not depend upon deception as a means of developing dyadic discord (11). It does not, therefore, run the risk of interfering with the therapeutic process by alienating the subjects. For many couples degrees of mystery exist even within the test situation of the RIG/T, but these are created by their individual and dyadic cognitive, perceptual, and conceptual capacities and limitations.

The degree of influence of the tester upon the results of the test still needs to be established. Theoretically it may be desirable to eliminate the tester as a physically present person. In a few instances, couples and family dyads tested by different testers have not demonstrated significant differences in their patterns of interaction.

Clinical experience with the RIG/T has strongly indicated that specific dyadic units tend to function in a predictable manner under a wide range of circumstances irrespective of changes within the individual members of the dyads. We have repeatedly noted that a movement away from the established pattern by one party will be met by a countermove aimed at maintaining that pattern by the other person. Generally it can be said that the greater the discord between the two members of a dyad, the more rigid, fixed, and stereotyped is the interactional pattern, and thus the more dependable is the RIG/T as a procedure for diagnosing the dynamics of the interactional pattern.

Thus the four patterns of interaction, while they may be applicable in all dyads having an ongoing existence over time, are of maximal significance in discordant dyads. It should be noted, however, that this basic rigidity is frequently disguised by overt disorganization. This discrepancy between the manifest behavior and the latent fixed pattern of interaction makes the clinical tasks of evaluation and diagnosis extremely difficult. The RIG/T for this reason is potentially an important clinical adjunct in the field of conjoint marital and family psychotherapy.

SUMMARY

A procedure developed by social psychologists for the experimental study of conflict and its resolution has been adapted for clinical evaluation of marital and other family dyads. The method involves an interpersonal game-test using N-gauge electric trains. No specific directions are given regarding the purpose or goal of the game, and this causes each couple to establish its own structure of the game. The pattern of behavioral and verbal interaction shown by couples seems to reflect important dynamic aspects of their interaction in many decision-making and conflict situations in their lives.

Four typical patterns of interaction have been identified: (1) competitive, (2) alternating, (3) dominant-submissive, and (4) mixed—that is, with elements of all three or any two of these. Variations on these four patterns and the data obtained in the course of a post-game interview structured on the basis of how couples behaved and communicated in the course of the test are of considerable value in helping the therapist to develop a strategy of conjoint therapy, and a technique for helping couples to gain insight into their past patterns of interpersonal relations and to develop alternative patterns.

APPENDIX

Instructions for the Ravich Interpersonal Game/Test

These are the instructions. Please listen carefully, since I cannot answer any questions.

Each person operates a model train engine which must travel from its start position to its destination at the other end of the table. You each win or lose an imaginary penny for every second under or over 30 seconds that it takes your train to get to its destination. On each trip it is possible for both of you to win, or for both to lose, or for one to win and the other to lose.

The layout of the tracks is exactly the same for both of you, except that your two engines start at opposite ends of the table. The speed of the engines is always the same. A short distance from the start, there is a switch track that leads to a direct route and an alternate route. The short direct route goes along the upright panel in the center of the table. The longer alternate route winds around the side of the table near you.

On the direct route there is a common section of track. Your two trains traveling toward each other on their direct routes will collide if you try to pass each other on this common section. You can't actually see the collision because of the panel that divides the table but when a collision occurs the engines stop moving and the red light on top of the control panel in front of you flashes on and off. Then one or both can back up, or both can stand still head-on.

At the end of the common section of the direct route nearest to your destination there is a barrier. That barrier is controlled by the other person, and you control a similar barrier on the other person's track. If the other person closes the barrier on your direct route, a red light goes on and your engine will stop when it reaches the barrier. By closing the barrier, you can delay or stop each other's engine from passing that point on the direct route. The barriers are open at the start of each trip. They can be closed or opened at any time.

If one or both of you take the alternate route you will not collide. Also, when your train is on the alternate route, it can't be delayed by the barrier.

In order to start your train, you first select the route you intend to use by pressing either the direct or alternate button on your control panel. During a trip, if you want to change routes, you must bring your engine back to the start position. Then you press the button for the other route.

The black lever operates your engine, moving the engine forward or back or stopping it according to the position you place it in.

The other two buttons open and close the barrier on the other person's direct route.

At the beginning of each trip, a green light on the control panel goes on which tells you to start. The red light next to it tells you to press one of the route buttons. Then you move the black lever to the forward position to move your train onto the route that you have selected.

You can talk to each other as much as you want to.

You will be making a number of trips. At the end of each trip, the engines will automatically be returned to the start position. After each trip, you will be told how long it has taken each of you to complete the trip and how much you have won or lost.

This is the end of the directions.

REFERENCES

1. Von Neuman, J. and Morgenstern, O.   *Theory of Games and Economic Behavior.* Princeton University Press, Princeton, N.J., 1944.
2. Luce, R. D. and Raiffa, H.   *Games and Decisions.* John Wiley, New York, 1957.
3. Deutsch, M. and Krauss, R. M.   Studies of Interpersonal Bargaining.   In *Game Theory and Related Approaches to Social Behavior,* Shubik, M., Ed.   John Wiley, New York, 1964, pp. 324–337.
4. ———.   The Effect of Threat upon Interpersonal Bargaining.   *J. Abn. Soc. Psychol.,* **61**:181, 1960.
5. Ravich, R. A., Deutsch, M., and Brown, B.   An Experimental Study of Marital Discord and Decision-Making.   In *Family Structure, Dynamics and Therapy,* Cohen, I. M., Ed.   Psychiatric Research Report No. 20, American Psychiatric Ass., Washington, D.C., 1966, pp. 91–94.
6. Ravich, R. A.   Short-Term Intensive Treatment of Marital Discord.   *Voices,* **2**:42, 1966.
7. Loveland, N. T., Wynne, L. C., and Singer, M. T.   The Family Rorschach: A New Method for Studying Family Interaction.   *Family Process,* **2**:187, 1963.
8. Harrower, M.   The Measurement of Psychological Factors in Marital Maladjustment.   In *Neurotic Interaction in Marriage,* Eisenstein, V., Ed.   Basic Books, New York, 1956, pp. 169–191.
9. Ferreira, A. J.   Decision-Making in Normal and Pathologic Families.   *Arch. Gen. Psychiat.,* **8**:68, 1963.
10. ——— and Winter, W. D.   Family Interaction and Decision-Making.   *Arch. Gen. Psychiat.,* **13**:214, 1965.
11. Goodrich, W. and Boomer, D. S.   Experimental Assessment of Modes of Conflict Resolution.   *Family Process,* **2**:15, 1963.

16

Active Games for
Physically Handicapped Children

PAUL V. GUMP and YUEN-HUNG MEI

Persons familiar with the play of normal children know how much time and energy they devote to running, jumping, throwing, and similar motor activities. Although there are differences in the psychological explanations for this interest there are no serious differences of opinion regarding its existence. Normally energetic children take persistent and intense delight in vigorous bodily movement and in the projection of their own bodies and objects through space. Furthermore, the average life environment of children provides opportunity for the expression of this interest. In gyms, playgrounds, streets, and alleys, games involving much running, kicking, throwing, and batting are provided for normal children and, if the provision is inadequate, children themselves will establish such activities often in the face of considerable opposition from adults whose privacy and property may be affected. So common and so insistent is this interest in mobility that one must conclude that it reflects a fairly universal need (or complex of needs) in children. It is probably a safe assumption also, that if the motor needs exist to such an extent in normal children, they are at least as strong—if not stronger—in the severely handicapped child. Most of the handicapped children however, suffer certain restriction in the expression of this need. They have fundamental physical limitations which may prevent them from running, leaping, or throwing. Furthermore, even if they have capacity in some phases of the motor activities, they remain less competent than normal children

SOURCE. *The Physical Therapy Review,* 34 (4) 1954, pp. 171–174.

and by virtue of this are excluded from any of the active games which children play.

There are several common solutions to the problem of play experience for severely handicapped children. Non-active games are sometimes provided, such as singing and guessing games, and in these the motor handicap is irrelevant. Active games are sometimes offered with special arrangements whereby some adult or other unhandicapped person helps out in the game. Of course, the first "solution" is no solution for the motor need since it is not given expression. The second solution usually has the disadvantage that the child actually participates in only *part* of the game. He is not in command of the entire game; he is merely *helped* to enjoy selected portions of it. We would like to emphasize that establishment of "normal outlets" for the handicapped must include opportunity for normal social interaction. Normal children often play active games without depending upon an adult for instruction, arbitration, and physical assistance and handicapped children also should have the opportunity to experience this independence from adult help and responsibility. The best solution for meeting motor needs would be one in which no help with the game is needed. Participants should be enabled to manage the entire game themselves, and to manage it without undue delays and failures. The authors, therefore, have attempted to select and adapt active games which would achieve this "best solution," games which many physically handicapped children could handle comfortably and which, at the same time offer extensive opportunities for the expression of mobility needs.

In approaching such a problem one must become sensitive to (1) the kinds of physical behaviors required in active games and (2) the common physical disabilities of handicapped children and the way these disabilities affect the game-required behaviors. Once these two questions are answered, the way is open for a rational development of games in which the disabilities are not important.

A review of the active games of children reveals that they involve one or several of the following sub-activities: (1) rapid locomotion of the body (running), (2) vigorous and/or skillful movements of the limbs— especially the arms (hitting), and (3) projection of some object through space (throwing). In the group of children under study the major disabilities were the inabilities to (1) stand without support, (2) walk and/ or run easily and (3) coordinate hand motions.

It is fortunate that the first two of these, while eliminating locomotion of body, did not seriously interefere with movements of arms and the projection of objects through space. This means that throwing and batting activities were still possible for many. But a problem arises in that most active games are played with a free-projectile (ball, disk, or ring). While it requires little effort for a normal child to chase after free projectiles, this task may be almost insurmountable for a crippled child. Obviously, games must be devised which eliminate or drastically reduce the problem of retrieving. (Solution of the inability to make skillful hand motions involves either making the "game task" less difficult or the creation of more easily handled game equipment).

Since the retrieving problem is so central to selection and adaptation of active games for handicapped children one should be aware of the principles by which this problem can be solved. Once these principles are recognized, persons interested in developing active games for the handicapped can easily invent devices and arrangements which far exceed the few examples offered here.

Retrieving problems can be solved on varying levels of completeness and each level represents a principle:

1. *Projectiles may be automatically returned to players.*
   Playing surfaces may be so tilted that the ball rolls "downhill" to the player after its play, or a string or rubber thread may be attached to the projectile so it swings or springs back to the player. (See figure 3)
2. *Projectiles may be caused to remain in a circumscribed area.*
   Use of bean bags and rings (instead of balls) insures that the projectile remains at or near the point of fall. (See figure 2) Back stops and enclosures may be added to further restrict the travel of projectiles. (See figure 1)
3. *Projectiles may be returned to players by other players.*
   This solution is especially feasible when projectiles are used in accordance with solution 2. Players may be placed in opposing positions and alternately throw to targets near one another. (Thus in shuffleboard (Figure 1) players can stand at each end and shove disks back and forth. Shuffleboard is an example of principles 2 and 3 combined.)

With the retrieving solution in mind the authors planned eleven different games some of which involved vigorous motor activity and all of which provided for the projection of objects through space. Seven games were actually built and tried out.[1] A short description of three of these games should serve to illustrate our contention that games can be selected and adapted so as to reduce the interference effect of the most common

[1] Seven constructed games were: Shuffleboard (table); Skee-Ball (table); Ring Toss; Skill Roll; Marble Maze; Tether Ball; and Tether Ping-Pong. Four planned games were: Enclosed Ping-Pong; Bedside Bowling; Bedside Target Shooting; and adapted Kikit. (For photographs of equipment, see original source.)

physical disabilities and still provide for considerable action of hands and arms and for the motion of projectiles through space.

SHUFFLEBOARD—Materials: Plywood,   commercial   bar—shuffleboard metal disks. Gross Measurements: (Approximately) Length—81″, width —24″; banking-board height—4½″. Procedure: 1. Players stand or sit at opposite ends and take turns sliding eight discs or 2. ambulatory players stand side by side and either alternate turns or take four turns each. (Alternation of turns leads to hitting opponents' disc and heightened excitement or frustration.)

The reader will note that the shuffleboard solves a retrieving problem by causing all the discs to drop in or near the end recesses. Furthermore, the shoving action required makes comparatively little demand upon hand coordination. Even children suffering severe athetosis or partial paralysis in both arms were successfully coached and then could carry on the game without help. The extended gliding motion of the disk provides a good example of one kind of projection of objects through space which we assume to be an aspect of the mobility need gratification. Furthermore, the hitting of one object (disk) by another provided obvious satisfaction. The fact that the shuffleboard play was not significantly curtailed by handicaps and that such body and object motion is needed and enjoyed was amply demonstrated in our tryouts. Children who had never played with one another before played together with this game. Shuffleboard was requested time and again. Participants who were initially unsure of their motor skill became avid shuffleboard players. In terms of amount of sheer fun, the game was well worth the $25.00 which went into the cost of its materials.

RING-TOSS—Materials: Target box of hard wood; holes for the dowel-pegs on the surface and indentions on the inside of the back piece to keep a firm hold. Various sets of colored pegs. Eight rope rings. Gross Measurements: Target face—24″ x 27″, thickness—4″ dowel stick lengths—11″ and 7½″. Procedure: Board placed on floor, table or hung on wall, depending upon whether players can stoop. Number and placement of pegs dependent upon skill level of participants.

The ring toss game is included as an illustration of the principle of decreasing the difficulty of the game task. Ordinary ring toss or "horseshoe" games provide only one opportunity for a "ringer." In the above game this opportunity can be multiplied nine times. The most obvious way to simplify such games is to move the target closer to the player; however, this sharply reduces the impressiveness of the projection of an object. With the present arrangement it was possible for poorly skilled players to stand some distance from the board, enjoy the flight of the rings through the air, and yet gain moderate success in terms of "ringers." In the ring toss game, the retrieving problem is handled by the use of a back stop (large target board) and projectiles which tend to lie where they fall. Even less retrieving would be involved if participants threw from opposite positions to opposite target boards. The response to the ring toss game was enthusiastic. (Play unexpectedly revealed interests which we had not anticipated. Among the younger children there was much gratification in setting up the board, inserting the pins and so forth. Also the collection of rings which had scored was a real gratification for the younger children.)

TETHER BALL and Tether Ping-Pong—Materials: Ping-pong ball secured to strand of nylon parachute string by unraveling end and making three sub-strands go around the ball. Glue with Dunco cement. Paddles larger and lighter than ping-pong paddles. Procedure: Free end of nylon string attached to metal pole or to high horizontal wire. Players attempt to hit the ball as it swings around (pole) or down (wire). Bank-board can be used with highwire arrangement and a "hand ball-like" game played. (Similar arrangements for Tether Ball)

Tether ping-pong represents a retrieving solution which actually returns the projectile to the participant. Even players who could stand only with support, and players whose hand coordination was very poor enjoyed the game. Tether ping-pong, as actually played, was quite informal. Players simply batted the ball back and forth and a miss simply meant that the ball would have to be hit on the next swing. This game, more than any other, demonstrated to us the fascination of these children in watching objects in movement through space. Not only were participants highly involved but children came to watch the swiftly moving ball in much the same manner as adults intently follow the to-and-fro motion of the ball in a fast tennis match.

From these games, and others not included in this report, we became impressed with the urgent need of these children to engage in motor activity which combines some skillful or vigorous body motion and the projection of an object through space. Although we had no games well suited to *hard* throwing, the use (and abuse) of these games illustrated this particular activity need. Some children could not resist throwing projectiles that should be tossed or pitched. The average child of ten and over throws in basketball, baseball, and football, but the seriously crippled child has little of such opportunity. It may be that the projection of objects by shoving, throwing, or batting, serves an important *compensation* to these handicapped children. Since they are limited in physical projection of their own bodies (as in leaping and running) the projection of an object becomes a highly valued substitute.

It is a safe assumption that the crippled child's motor needs are as great as those of his normal peers; therefore, it would seem important that ingenuity and effort be directed toward providing expression for these needs in active games.

Two of the three motion ingredients of active games are: (1) The vigorous and/or skillful movement of limbs—especially arms and (2) the projection of objects through space. With the solution of retrieving problems and of difficulties created by inadequate hand skill, these two ingredients become relatively available to most crippled children.

REFERENCES

1. Mei, Yuen-Hung: A Study of the Adaptation of Games for Physically Handicapped Children, unpublished master's thesis, Wayne University, Detroit, 1953. 51 pp.
2. Rogers, Gladys and Thomas, Leah: Toys, Games and Apparatus for Children with Cerebral Palsy, Physical Therapy Review, 29:5–11, Jan., 1949.
3. Schleichkorn, J. S.: Adapting Games for Handicapped Children, Physical Therapy Review, 33:245–247, May, 1953.

17

Using Recreative Games for Therapeutic Purposes

E. M. AVEDON

Personnel in the field of recreation service usually use games to offer participants opportunities for a variety of satisfactions, paramount among these is a chance to have "fun." Lately, a number of behavioral scientists have indicated that a game can be viewed as an "encapsulated social system"—a system that has many of the elements of a reality situation. Thus, when a person has a problem with "living," it offers opportunities to "practice" living. Similarly, a game may be chosen which will help a participant become aware of limitations he must face as a result of impairment or disability, or a game may offer opportunities in which a participant can explore ways to overcome disability and utilize residual abilities. In fact, due to the infinite variety of games, it seems possible to select games in relation to specific therapeutic goals.

PHYSICAL DISORDERS

In order to program for specific therapeutic goals, therapeutic recreation specialists must be able to classify games in relation to sensory-motor demands, cognitive demands, and affective demands. Efforts in this direction have been made by persons in allied health fields, principally in the area of sensory-motor aspects of games. The literature abounds with information regarding essential physical capacities required for performance in a number of games, parts of the body and their positions and movements in performance, and a number of other factors. Published kinesiological analysis of many games are available, and a great many 371 reports on using games for treatment of physical disorders are in the literature. The rationale for using games in treatment of physical disorders is that a game has integral elements which stimulate participation, while often monotonous exercise stifles participation. Thus when sensory-motor aspects of a game offer the same opportunities as an exercise, frequently the game is chosen as the "treatment of choice." Here are some examples:

The Game—Skittles
The Disorder—Partial Quadriplegia
With only slight power of left shoulder and elbow extensors, the patient was given a functional movement pattern for exercising the left arm. The game was utilized to teach her how to pull her body forward and reach out with the left hand.

The Game—Table Cricket
The Disorder—Post Wrist and Elbow Fracture
After removal of the cast, the patient was assigned playing positions which induced mobility of the wrist and lent practice in rapid wrist movements. The game offered opportunities for wrist supination, wrist pronation, wrist hyperextension, and wrist flexion.

The Game—Count and Capture (Mancala)
The Disorder—Cerebral Vascular Accident
In order to improve dexterity, grasp, and other movements of the left hand this game was chosen. In addition, it offered stimulation to the thought process since mild arteriosclerotic changes had taken place in the brain, and the game fostered concentration and counting.

These approaches in the use of games for specific treatment are usually undertaken by a physical therapist in cooperation with recreation personnel. They are often worked out in a rehabilitation setting under the supervision of a physiatrist. At times game equipment must be modified for this purpose. For example, when the problem of grasp was the issue, a colleague modified a checker board, using a peg board instead of squares, and spring clothes-pins instead of checkers. Through these types of collaboration, continuing application of games are made for treatment purposes related to physical disorder.

COGNITIVE DISORDERS

In considering disorders of a cognitive nature, it is important to note that interest since the turn of the century has been manifested in the cognitive aspect of games, particularly in care and treatment programs for persons who are mentally retarded. Some work has been done on analysis of essential cognitive capacities required for playing certain games, as well as study of cognitive skills and their utilization in game playing. Games are often used with young mentally retarded children to prevent further disability and strengthen non-impaired functioning. Rhythmic games for young children are often utilized in this instance to develop a sense of rhythmic movement. Some games are used for other preventative purposes, *i.e.*, to stimulate communication and verbal ability, to stimulate inquisitiveness and initiative. Some games are utilized to teach self-care and grooming habits. With older retarded children and adolescents, a variety of games are used to build strength and stamina and to offer possible pre-vocational skill development. Within the past few years a wealth of published material on this area of concern has become available. However, a considerable amount of material from learning psychology and developmental psychology has yet to be adapted in relation to the cognitive aspects of games. Collaboration between special educators and recreation personnel in a number of settings has produced considerable effort in this direction, and will continue to do so in the future.

AFFECTIVE DISORDERS

The area that has received the least attention is that of the affective aspects of games. Recent interest in psychology in semiosis—signs and symbols as communication—has awakened new interest in games. What semiotic factors in a given game attract a participant and repel another participant? Are there semiotic elements in games which have a direct bearing on psychopathology? These and other similar questions are being asked in a number of psychiatric settings today. Some current theoretical answers suggest that games are a construct of a variety of cultural symbols—symbols which have the potential for conveying ideas, attitudes, and feelings. Some of these symbols are limited and convey only single pieces of information, while others are expansive and convey many pieces of information. The symbols may be the entire method of play in a game, or only one aspect of a game, such as the equipment utilized or the number of persons. Some of the symbols are set, that is they are always the same, such as a board in a given game, while others may change, dependent upon the situation. An example of this latter idea would be in a checker game; two patients (peers) may be in opposition or a patient and a staff member might be in opposition. This situation is thought to offer some opportunity to "play-out" conflict in a variety of relationships. Subsequent to the playing of the game, psychotherapeutic interpretation might be necessary. Here are some examples of other semiotic factors which offer potential in the treatment process regarding mental disorders:

1. Destroying things by throwing a heavy object to knock down other objects—as in bowling.
2. Destroying a possession or the extension of another person—as in shuffleboard, where one is encouraged to knock the opponent's disc from the court, or in horseshoes when one attempts to "top" the opponent's shoe.
3. Striking out at another person—as in table tennis, tennis, badminton, volleyball, etc.
4. Hitting another person—as in dodge ball or swat tag. A non-symbolic activity carrying out the same theme would be a boxing match in which the intent is to actually hit another person, or in fencing in which the intent is to draw blood.

There are many table and board games that incorporate similar ideas, but instead of this taking place in the "play" of the game, it is expressed through the object of the game. For example, in chess the object is to wipe your opponent's army from the board; in *Monopoly* the object is to monopolize as much property as possible, "financially" crush your opponent, and choke him off the board; in *Mr. Ree*, the object is to murder one or more of your opponents.

In addition to providing for the expression of various emotions, certain games generate and enhance specific feelings, or create situations which generate specific emotions. The play in these games may generate the expression of an emotion in a participant, or the conscious awareness in the player of the existence of an emotion. For example, certain games provide a situation in which one of the players is attacked and the rules forbid him to fight back, *i.e.*, in the Korean table game *Nyoot* if your opponent's token lands on the same space which you occupy with your token, you are required to return your token to the starting space, relinquishing your space to your opponent, no matter how close you are to winning; similarly, in *Wide-World*, if your opponent's token lands on your space, he has the option to send you five spaces in any direction— usually the direction which is opposite to the one in which you wish to go. Another example is in the Japanese game of *Go*. In *Go*, when a certain condition exists on the board and your opponent has taken one of your counters, and you appear to be in a position to retaliate, you may not, due to the "rule of Ko."

In contrast, some games require the generation of positive feelings or the player precludes success. Most of these latter games involve partnerships or team involvement. In Bridge, for example, you must cooperate with your partner, and express this cooperation in symbolic language during bidding, or you cannot win.

Thus, if a therapeutic goal is to stimulate release of hostility or rage, you might program an activity which includes symbols that permit these feelings to be expressed in ways that will not make the participant feel guilty or frightened by his "explosive" behavior. If the therapeutic goal is to permit the patient to challenge authority figures, you might choose any number of two-person board games for this purpose and participate yourself as the authority figure. Interaction of psychiatrists and psychologists with recreation personnel in psychiatric settings today is fostering a more pragmatic approach in these uses of games for therapeutic purposes rather than for the former notion of custodial care. Recreation personnel in these instances are able to contribute directly to the therapeutic process.

In the foregoing, I have briefly indicated some of the various ways in which games are being used for therapeutic purposes in clinical settings. Much of the approach is experimental and on a highly individual basis. There is little direct research available which makes it possible to standardize techniques. Much of the success of these approaches is due to the knowledge and expertise of individual Therapeutic Recreation Specialists and their colleagues who collaborate in these endeavors. The trend appears to be for further refinement of technique, and future development in the use of games for therapeutic purposes.

Games: Their Use in Psychiatry, Physiatry, General Medicine, and Related Diagnostic, Treatment and Care Programs—Selected References

Adatto, C. "On Play and the Psychopathology of Golf," *Journal of The American Psychoanalytic Association,* **12** (4), 1964, pp. 826–841.

Archer, J. "Basketball Comes To Hospital Patients," *Recreation,* **47** (4), 1954, p. 227.

Barclay, D. "Emotional Stakes in Playing Games," *New York Times Magazine,* August 7, 1955, p. 43.

Bauer, D. "Big-ten Football, Wheelchair Style," *Recreation,* **52** (11), 1959, pp. 386–387.

Beisser, A. *The Madness in Sports,* New York: Appleton-Century-Crofts, 1967.

Beresford, A. "Team Games and Recreation in Mental Hospitals," *Nursing Mirror,* **180**, November 27, 1959, pp. 5–7.

Bergler, E. *The Psychology of Gambling,* New York: Hill and Wang, 1957.

Berne, E. *Games People Play: The Psychology of Human Relationships,* New York: Grove Press, Inc., 1962.

Blau, L. "Appliances and Remedial Games," *American Journal of Physical Medicine,* **34** (8), 1955, pp. 498–510.

Boeshart, L. K. "Remedial Games in Treatment of Physical Disability," *American Journal of Occupational Therapy,* **5** (3), 1951, pp. 47–48.

Boyd, N. *Hospital and Bedside Games*, Chicago: H.T. Fitzsimons, Comp., Inc., 1919; revised, 1945.

Brachman, D. S. "Observation on the Cardiac Unit of a Fresh Air Camp: On the Use or Avoidance of Sports," *Journal of Aviation Medicine*, 3 (6), 1932, pp. 109–115.

Brown, M. E. "Ten Motion Games For Fun and Therapy," *American Journal of Nursing*, 56 (1), 1956, pp. 44–48.

Brown, M. E. "Therapy for the Orthopedically Exceptional: An Analysis of Twenty-five Games," *American Journal of Occupational Therapy*, 24 (8), 1945, pp. 171–178.

Buell, C. E. *Active Games For The Blind*, Ann Arbor, Michigan: Edwards Brothers, 1947.

Buell, C. E. *Sports For The Blind*, Ann Arbor, Michigan: Edwards Brothers, 1947.

Carlson, G., and Gingland, D. "Table Work and Games," *Play Activities for The Mentally Retarded Child*, New York: Abingdon Press, 1961, pp. 64–93.

Chapman, F. M. "Sports and Games," *Recreation Activities For The Handicapped*, New York: Ronald Press, 1960, pp. 235–276.

Colby, K. M. "Gentlemen, The Queen!," *Psychoanalytic Review*, 40, 1953, pp. 144–148.

Conn, J. H. "Children's Awareness of Sex Differences, Part II: Play Attitudes and Game Preferences," *Journal of Child Psychiatry*, 2, 1951, pp. 82–99.

Danning, E. "The Value of Chess to the Quadriplegic Patient," *Recreation For The Ill and Handicapped*, I(3) 1957.

Delany, E. "Assignment: Games For The Patient," *Recreation*, 54 (1), 1961, pp. 26–29.

Fine, R. *Psychoanalytic Observations on Chess and Chess Masters*, New York: National Psychological Association for Psychoanalysis, Inc., 1956.

Fox, S. S. "Games for Handicapped Children," *Recreation*, 44 (5), 1950, pp. 93–94.

Frankel, L., and Frankel, G. *Muscle Building Games*, New York: Sterling Publishing Corp., 1964.

Galdston, I. "The Psychodynamics of the Triad Alcoholism, Gambling and Superstition," *Mental Hygiene*, 35, 1951, pp. 589–598.

Gerwig, G. W. *Emotion and Sport*, Pittsburgh: Frick Education Commission, 1932.

Goffman, E. "Fun in Games: Studies in the Sociology of Interaction," *Encounters*, Indianapolis: Bobbs-Merrill Comp., Inc., 1961, pp. 17–81.

Greenson, R. P. "On Gambling," *American Imago,* 4, 1947, pp. 61–77.

Gump, P. V., and Sutton-Smith, B. "The It Role in Children's Games," *The Group,* 17, 1955, pp. 3–8.

Gump, P. V., and Yueng-Hung, M. "Active Games for Physically Handicapped Children," *Physical Therapy Review,* 34 (4) 1954, pp. 171–172.

Hastorf, A. H., and Cantril, H. "They Saw a Game: A Case Study," *Journal of Abnormal and Social Psychology,* 49, 1954, pp. 129–134.

Howard, G. E. "Social Psychology of the Spectator," *American Journal of Sociology,* 18, 1912, pp. 33–50.

Hyde, R. W., et al. "Effectiveness of Games in Mental Hospitals," *American Journal of Occupational Therapy,* 27 (8), 1948, pp. 304–308.

Ickis, M. "Games and Puzzles," *Pastimes For The Patient,* New York: A.S. Barnes and Co., Revised Edition, 1966, pp. 251–263.

Johnson, W. R. "A Study of Emotion Revealed in Two Types of Sport," *Research Quarterly,* 20, 1949, pp. 72–79.

Johnson, W. R. *Science and Medicine of Exercise and Sports,* New York: Harper and Brothers, 1960.

Jokl, E. *Heart and Sport,* Springfield, Ill.: Charles C Thomas, 1964.

Linder, R. M. "The Psychodynamics of Gambling," *Annals of The American Academy of Political and Social Science,* 269, 1950, pp. 93–107.

McGlothlin, W. H. "A Psychometric Study of Gambling," *Journal of Consulting Psychology,* 18, 1954, pp. 145–149.

McKindree, O. J. "Bowling as a Psychiatric Adjunct," *Psychiatric Quarterly,* 24, 1950, pp. 303–307.

Marshall, H. "Children's Plays, Games, and Amusements," *Handbook of Child Psychology,* (C. Murchinson, ed.), Clark University Press, 1931, pp. 515–526.

Mignoga, M. *The Selection of Games for Use in Cases of Cardiac Insufficiency,* New York: New York University, 1932.

Moore, R. M. *Sports and Mental Health,* Springfield, Ill.: Charles C Thomas, 1966.

Morris, R. P. "An Exploratory Study of Some Personality Characteristics of Gamblers," *Journal of Clinical Psychology,* 13, 1957, pp. 191–193.

Morris, S. W. "Sports Heal War Neuroses," *Recreation,* 39 (10), 1945, pp. 343–344.

Phillips, R. H. "The Nature and Function of Children's Formal Games," *Psychoanalytic Quarterly,* 35 (6160), 1960, pp. 200–207.

Pomeroy, J. "Active Games and Sports," *Recreation for the Physically Handicapped,* New York: MacMillan Company, 1964, pp. 303–324.

"Rally Around The Ball Pole," *Mental Hospitals,* 10 (1), 1959, p. 23.

Raymond, B. B. "Bridge Anyone?," *Mental Hospitals,* 14 (4), 1963, p. 226.

Redl, F. "The Impact of Game Ingredients on Children's Play Behavior," *Proceedings of the Fourth Conference on Group Processes*, New York: Josiah Macy Foundation, 1959, pp. 33–82.

Reider, N. "Chess, Oedipus, and the Mater Dolorosa," *International Journal of Psychoanalysis*, 40, 1959, pp. 320–333.

Rice, G. E., and White, K. R. "Effect of Education on Prejudice as Revealed in A Game Situation," *Psychological Record*, 14, 1964, pp. 341–348.

Richardson, U. *Games For The Handicapped*, London: C. Arthur Pearson, Ltd., 1956.

Roberts, J. M., and Sutton-Smith, B. *Child Training and Game Involvement*, Indianapolis: Bobbs-Merrill Series in Social Science, Reprinted, 1966.

Roderman, C. R. "Let's Play Ball," *American Journal of Nursing*, 49 (9), 1949, pp. 566–567.

Roger, G., and Thomas, L. "Toys, Games, and Apparatus for Children With Cerebral Palsy," *Physical Therapy Review*, 29 (1), 1949, p. 5.

Sapora, A. W. "Values of Sports and Games for the Ill and Handicapped," *Recreation for the Ill and Handicapped*, 1 (4), 1957, p. 10.

Scott, M. G. "Analysis of Selected Sports Activities," *Analysis of Human Motion*, New York: Appleton Century Crofts, 1963, pp. 252–320.

Shaw, C. "Medical and Surgical Aspects of Sports and Games," *Baily's Magazine of Sports and Pastimes*, London, 1921, 116, pp. 250–256, 117, pp. 7–10.

Slovenko, R., and Knight, J. A. *Motivations in Play, Games, and Sports*, Springfield, Ill.: Charles C Thomas, 1967.

Stafford, G. T. *Sports For The Handicapped*, New York: Prentice Hall, Inc., 1947.

Stokes, A. "Psycho-Analytic Reflections on the Development of Ball Games, Particularly Cricket," *International Journal of Psychoanalysis*, May–June, 1956.

Sutton-Smith, B. "The Psychology of Games," *National Education: Journal of the New Zealand Educational Institute*, 37, 1955, Part I, pp. 228–229; Part II, pp. 261–263.

Sutton-Smith, B., and Gump, P. V. "Games and Status Experience," *Recreation*, 48 (4), 1955, pp. 172–174.

Sutton-Smith, B., and Roberts, J. M. "Game Involvement in Adults," *Journal of Social Psychology*, 60, 1963, pp. 15–30.

Sutton-Smith, B., and Roberts, J. M. "Rubrics of Competitive Behavior in Games," *Journal of Genetic Psychology*, 105, 1964, pp. 13–37.

Sutton-Smith, B., and Rosenberg, B. G. "Manifest Anxiety and Game Preferences in Children," *Child Development*, 31, 1960, pp. 307–311.

Szasz, T. S. "Game Model Analysis of Behavior," *The Myth of Mental Illness: Foundations of A Theory of Personal Conduct,* New York: Hoeber Medical Division, Harper and Row Publishers, Inc., 1964, pp. 223–293.

Verghese, M. "Psychological Values of Games," *Youth Leaders Digest,* **15** (8), 1953, pp. 300–303.

Wenkart, S. "The Meaning of Sports for Contemporary Man," *The Journal of Existential Psychology,* 3, Spring, 1963, pp. 397–404.

Wolf, G. *Adapted Sports, Games, and Square Dances—Recreation for The Handicapped,* Hartford: Connecticut Society for Crippled Children and Adults, Inc., 1962.

Wood, A. *Sound Games: Speech Correction for The Very Young,* New York: E. P. Dutton and Comp., Inc., 1948.

Wrightson, H. A. *Games and Exercises for Mental Defectives,* Cambridge, Mass.: Caustic-Claflin, Comp., 1916.

Structure and Function

W e have dealt with the origins and usages of games in the previous two sections, but have found in neither sufficient explanation. Therefore, with the evidence before us, we return to the questions raised in the introduction —questions that have to do with definition and explanation. In Chapter 11, current uses of "games" as an analytic device in social science are discussed. In Chapter 12, the earlier definition of games is expanded in terms of the structural characteristics that are part of the established game literature. In Chapter 13, games are examined in terms of the traditional ways in which they have been explained.

CHAPTER **11**

GAMES IN SOCIAL SCIENCE

The two most sophisticated mathematical models for human behavior have been derived from games—namely probability theory derived from games of chance, and decision theory derived from games of strategy. Both have had a widespread effect throughout the social sciences. Where events can be assumed to occur at random, then what individuals do in games of chance is a relevant model; and where subjects can be assumed to be rational, what players do in games of strategy is a relevant model. But events are not always random, nor subjects always rational (in the same way).

Different subjects find various utilities in the very same processes. Still, in making the point that probability theory and decision theory were derived from games, it is the theories rather than the games that have been the focal point in social science.

Some of the historical background for the development of these two theories are as follows. Concerning probability theory, a French nobleman, the Chevalier de Méré, (who in contemporary society might be considered a professional gambler,) brought a problem to his friend Blaise Pascal, the mathematician. De Méré wanted to know a logical way in which to divide the stakes in a dice game when the game must be terminated before it is completed. In working out the solution to this problem, Pascal developed a new branch of mathematics, the *theory of probability*. De Méré's problem amounted to determining the probability that each player had of winning the game, at a given stage in the game.[1]

Concerning decision theory, about forty years ago, John von Neumann

[1] Bell, E. T. *Men of Mathematics.* New York: Simon and Schuster, 1937; and Levenson, H. C. *The Science of Chance.* New York: Rinehart and Co., 1950.

383

(a mathematician and poker player), was struck with the fact that a poker player could not increase his winnings or financial gain in the same way as a piece worker in a factory. He hypothesized that no one poker player was in complete control of the game, and no matter what decision a player made, he did not control the decisions of the other players. Nevertheless, these decisions (or strategies) of each player influenced each other player and the eventual course of the game. Although the game depended on chance, there were influential human elements introduced into the game, such as bluffing. Von Neumann theorized that if a player thought of all the other players in the game as one opponent, rather than as several opponents, he could then develop a more meaningful strategy. It could be assumed that each player is trying to win as much as possible, and when he must lose, to lose as little as possible. From this origin came the branch of mathematics known as *game theory*. Like *probability theory* it became applicable to much more than the original game that stimulated its invention.

Rapoport explains games from the mathematician's point of view in this way:

A parlor game represents a limited portion of "life" in which it is possible (in principle) to list all the things that can happen. The acual number of possible events is usually vast beyond comprehension, even in simple games, but only a fraction of these events is normally of interest. So it is not too much of an exaggeration to say that in a parlor game all eventualities can (in principle) be taken into account. The idealized player of such a game can be supposed to be "omniscient". . . . The limits of what can happen are set by the rules of the game. Typically, the course of the game is a sequence of "moves" made by the players in some prescribed order, which may or may not depend on the outcomes of the preceding moves.[2]

Von Neumann, and other mathematicians after him, delimited the elements that they considered necessary and invariant in describing game outcomes, the number of players, rules of the game, strategies that could be employed, results or "pay-off." Primary concern was with strategies employed in a game to minimize losses and maximize winnings (the "minimax concept"). It is evident that this minimax concept has application in many "real" situations—in a war, business, marriage, politics.

Game Theory is a method for the study of decision making in situations of conflict. It deals with human processes in which the individual deci-

---

[2] Rapoport, A. *Fights, Games, and Debates.* Ann Arbor: University of Michigan Press, 1960, pp. 109–110.

sion-unit is not in complete control of other decision units entering into the environment. It is addressed to problems involving conflict, cooperation, or both, at many levels. . . . Diplomats involved in international negotiations, generals engaged in fighting an enemy, labor unions striking against the firms in an industry, members of a family arguing over who should have the car, the missionary trying to talk his way out of the stew pot, a player in a poker game, politicians striving for a nomination, children trying to condition the experimental psychologist, duelists, bandits, and bridge players are all engaged in activities which may be usefully viewed in the context of game situations.

The essence of a "game" in this context is that it involves decision makers with different goals or objectives whose fates are intertwined. The individuals are in a situation in which there may be many possible outcomes with different values to them. Although they may have some control which will influence the outcome, they do not have complete control over others.[3]

An example of one approach which is based on application of game theory is the Acme-Bolt game developed by Deutsch and Krauss. This is a special experimental device, which includes a playing board and a number of electric controls. The two players are asked to imagine that they are in charge of a trucking company that freights merchandise over roads on the playing board. The players are told that the faster they get the freight to the destination, the more profits the company makes. The object of the game varies, it might be to see if one player, The Acme Company—can make more money than the other player, The Bolt Company—or vice versa, or to ignore the other fellow and make as much money as you can. On the playing board is a road map. Each player starts from a warehouse, and each player has a separate destination, and a separate route to take. However, in order to go the shortest distance, they have to take the same one lane road, even though they are going in opposite directions. Of course they can take alternate routes, but that takes longer, and they would lose money. At each end of the one lane road there is a gate. Each player controls one of these gates. By closing the gate, one player can prevent the other player from using the one lane section of the route. Deutsch varies the game by sometimes giving one player control of both gates, or letting one player have one gate, and the other player no gate. Each player sits at a control panel, behind a screen, and cannot see what the other is doing. The only time they know each

[3] Shubik, M. "Game Theory and the Study of Social Behavior: An Introductory Exposition," *Game Theory and Related Approaches to Social Behavior.* M. Shubik (Ed.) New York: John Wiley & Sons, Inc., 1964, p. 8.

other's position on the board is when they meet head-on, on the single lane road; then a traffic light glows on the control panel. The panel also has lights to show if the gates are open or closed. When the traffic light is on, neither player can move unless one moves back and lets the other through. By changing the rules of the game, a number of typical interpersonal situations are possible. By adding channels of communication, many more situations are possible. We include one of the studies from this project, in order to illustrate the way in which the game is used to make inferences about interpersonal bargaining. (See Ravich, reading is in the previous chapter.)

Another game that has been developed for use as an experimental technique is "The Reality Game." In this game a pair of players sit in separate booths divided by a large screen that prevents them from seeing one another. In front of each of the players are three boxes on a table. The boxes are labeled *offer*, *notice*, and *stock sale*, and contain printed message slips that the players will pass through a slit in the screen to each other during the play of the game. Each player also has profit tables, tables indicating profits after stock sales, pencils, envelopes, and other necessary equipment for playing the game. After players are seated, they are given the following instructions:

For the rest of the time that you are here you are asked not to speak. Suppose, now, that you are a realtor who is trying to come to some agreement with another realtor; and what you are trying to agree upon is the number of acres and the cost per acre to be used in the sale of a piece of land. Your objective in arranging this sale is to accumulate as much profit as possible for yourself. If you are both able to arrive at some agreement you will receive a certain profit. The actual amount of profit you receive will depend upon the particular combination of number of acres and cost per acre that you agree upon. If you reach no agreement you will not receive any profit at all. In trying to arrive at the terms of the agreement with the other realtor you will communicate through the use of three types of messages.[4]

There follows a description of the three types of message slips and how they are to be used. The game is used in a series of experiments to determine the effect of threats on interpersonal bargaining, and other factors dealing with bargaining behavior.

Probability theory and decision theory have not been the only source

---

[4] Hornstein, H. A. *The Effects of Different Magnitudes of Threat Upon Interpersonal Bargaining*. Unpublished Doctoral Dissertation, Columbia University, 1964, p. 26.

of game usage in social science. Like business and military investigators, social scientists have also been involved in various types of gaming with computers under such titles as: man-machine simulation, Monte Carlo techniques, digital computer simulation, analog computer simulation, machine simulation, real-time simulation.[5] Each term, although somewhat expressive of a different technique, nevertheless refers to the same general approach. For example: "The Simulamatics Project" is a "computer simulation of likely voter behavior . . . to estimate . . . the probable impact . . . of different issues . . . which might be used by the candidates."[6] One of the more interesting examples is the "Dartmouth Baseball Game." Baseball is a matter of consequence to some people, and a major issue (for the "fans") is the way a manager arranges his batting order. Does he use a scientific approach or does he make judgments from the "seat of his pants?" In order to determine if there was any basis for what an experienced manager does, this situation was simulated:

The machine was given a team of nine men, each player's batting average, frequency of walks, extra base hits and home runs, how likely he was to hit into a double play, etc. The machine was instructed to arrange the batters in a certain order and, following the rules of baseball, play through the 154 games of the entire season, computing how many runs the team scored in a typical season. Then it was told to try other batting orders and play until it found the best batting order.

Results showed that batting order was important. The difference between the best and the poorest batting order averaged about one run per five games, or enough over the season to win the pennant. The best batting order was found to be the one that was actually used in the World Series.

This may not surprise an experienced manager. But these conclusions were reached by a medium-capacity machine in less than a day's work. It takes a manager years to acquire this skill. The machine even predicted streaks and slumps.[7]

Scholars of baseball with limited knowledge of simulation may wonder how the machine determines whether on a given time at bat, a player gets a hit. The machine is simply told that the player has a .180 batting

[5] Dawson, R. E. "Simulation in the Social Sciences," *Simulation in the Social Sciences: Readings.* H. Guetzkow (Ed.) Englewood Cliffs, New Jersey: Prentice-Hall Inc., 1962, p. 6.

[6] De Sola Pool, I., and Abelson, R. "The Simulamatics Project," Guetzkow, op. cit., p. 70.

[7] Fattu, N. A. "Introduction to Simulation," in *Simulation Models for Education.* Bloomington, Ind.: Phi Delta Kappa Inc., 1965, pp. 8–9.

average, and "samples from an array of random numbers among which 18% have been designated as hits."[8]

If the use of games in social science is contrasted with its use in the military, business and education, in the latter it is a training device whose virtues are assumed, whereas in the former it is an analytic device. As an analytic device the game has had a varied history within social science. It is clear in the above examples, from game theory, that there is an awareness of the effect that certain game constituents (number of players, pay off, and so forth) have on the players. This has not always been the case. There is another tradition within social science within which the games are treated as "projective" phenomena, to be used as neutral devices for making assessment of player motives or behavior of a nongame sort. Earlier uses of games as indicators of player intelligence, masculinity, femininity, and so on were of this order. Again, in the studies about the level of aspiration in the psychological literature of the 1940s, games were frequently used to assess the subject's level of aspiration. If the child was asked to throw ten rings over a projecting stick (in ring toss), how many would he estimate he could get over; how would his estimate change after his first efforts? Of if he was asked to choose whether he would throw from a point nearby, from an intermediate point, or from far away, which would he choose? The results showed that children chose various points; that children of high achievement in schoolwork tended to choose an intermediate point from which to throw their rings, while children who did less well, either took a ridiculously easy stance, or threw rings from a long way off, apparently trusting to some miraculous throw to prove their skill. While these studies had a certain value as an application of level of aspiration theory to these game situations, they gave rise to questions that have not yet been answered but are hinted at in some of the readings in Chapter 12. Namely, do children play the same risk strategy in physical skill games that they play in games of strategy or in games of chance. The tendency of social scientists to regard games as neutral and similar has, in the past, precluded answers being given to this type of question. Only the study by social scientists of the character of game structures as independent events can yield knowledge of this sort and can help decide what basis there is for the enthusiasm espoused by those who use games in war, business, and education.

We may sum up these various remarks by suggesting that games have had at least three usages in social science. First, there has been the study of games as a cultural phenomena, which is a type of approach we consider in the next two chapters. Second, games have been used as a

---

[8] Fattu, op. cit., p. 8.

"projection" or mirror of other processes (achievement, anxiety, aggression) with which the investigator has been more fundamentally concerned. Finally, the games have been used as a model for looking at other life processes, as in game theory and probability theory. This last usage has been widespread in recent years, particularly in sociology and psychiatry, where game models of interaction processes (Berne) and small group processes (Goffman) has become a byword.[9] The lack of a genuinely interactional language apparently makes the terminology of games a providential substitute. Beyond that some investigators have suggested that the whole enterprise of social science itself is more like a game, than it is like seeking the scientific solution to a puzzle (Moore & Anderson).[10] The investigators' results affect those who are their subjects. The subjects react to these results, and their responses are no longer the same. So over a period of time by studying culture, social scientists are, in fact, changing it, thus "vitiating" the objective persistence of their own data.

But Berne's, Goffman's, and Moore and Anderson's usage of games does not have the exactness implied by probability and game theory. These writers are, it seems, marking time with metaphors until some more appropriate interactional terminology can be constructed. Perhaps, indeed, the whole current enthusiasm for games of which this book is a manifestation, is itself a part of a general cultural movement toward new forms of group behavior and group analysis. In which case the most important current usage of games in social science is as metaphor. The following article by Gump and Sutton-Smith illustrates the use of games as an experimental technique in the behavioral sciences. The list of selected references that concludes this chapter offers illustrations from the fields of political science, economics, and sociology.

[9] Berne, E. *Games People Play.* New York: Grove Press Inc., 1964; and Goffman, E. *Encounters: Studies in the Sociology of Interaction.* Indianapolis: Bobbs-Merrill Company Inc., 1961.
[10] Moore, O. K., and Anderson, A. R. "Some Puzzling Aspects of Interaction," *Review of Metaphysics,* **15** (3), March, 1962, pp. 409–433.

18

The "It" Role in Children's Games

PAUL V. GUMP AND
BRIAN SUTTON-SMITH

The present experiment was part of a larger research effort on the problem of how the ingredients of different children's activities and programs affect participant's individual and group behavior and experience. The aim of the research is to develop concepts and findings which will assist the practitioner in selecting, inventing, and managing activities so that children's experiences in these activities will be beneficial.

Among the most prominent activities used in group work with children are games. Also, games are relatively coercive activities since they specify the roles persons shall take, the goals they shall seek, and other areas of behavior which many non-game activities leave to the choice of participants. Because games are coercive, they may be expected to determine behavior in a relatively predictable fashion. The prominence and the coerciveness of games suggested that they be given special study.

The ingredients of games differ widely and these differences may be expected to generate parallel variations in the experience and behavior of their participants. Such variations go beyond differences in game-required acts to differences in response to these acts. For example, the games of Tag and Beater-Goes-Around obviously differ in that one requires tag-

SOURCE. *American Association of Group Workers* **17**, 3. (*February*, 1955), *pp.* 3–8. This investigation was supported by research grant M-550 from the National Institute of Mental Health, of the National Institutes of Health, Public Health Service. Its original title is "The Relationship of the Power of the *It* Role to Experience in the *It* Role."

ging and the other beating; however, the response to tagging (and being tagged) may be expected to be different from the response to beating (and being beaten).

Since a large proportion of all active games for children are *It* games, these games were selected for study. *It* games contain a central person who acts in opposition to the rest of the playing group or the "pack." One aspect of these games which seemed important in determining the experience of the *It*—and the reaction of the group or pack to him—was the *game-determined power* of the *It* role. This power is shaped by a number of game provisions: *It's* prerogatives in determining which pack member he will engage in competitive encounter and when this encounter will begin; his "trappings," for example, his game name *or* his power symbols; his protection against the combined efforts of pack members against him; and so forth. Power of this type resides entirely in the *It* role and is separate from the skill of the player occupying the *It* role.

The study investigated how behavior and experience of players in the *It* role were affected by the amount of power of the *It* role. One supposition was that a high-power *It* role would expose its occupants to *fewer* competitive failures in the game than would a low-power *It* role. A second related supposition was that relatively unskilled players could be protected from too frequent failure by enabling them to occupy a high-power, rather than a low power, *It* role. The problem of helping the unskilled participant in situations in which he can become the focal person is a real and a practical one. Readers are doubtless aware of the difficulties which arise when unskilled players are put into certain *It* positions. Their failure to find, catch, or tag skilled members of the pack leads to discouragement for themselves and boredom for the pack. The pack's derision of *It* for his failure intensifies his frustrations. Since a group worker can do nothing immediately to change skill, selecting or managing games so that lack of skill becomes less crucial is a potential solution. The study tested the supposition that lack of skill in *It* games can be partially compensated for by opportunity to occupy a high-power *It* role.

The experiment reported below, then, checked two basic suppositions which are closely related:

1. High-power *It* roles result in fewer game failures for *It* players in general than do low-power *It* roles.
2. High-power *It* roles result in fewer game failures for unskilled *It* players than do low-power *It* roles.

Since number of game failures might be expected to affect *It's* feeling about himself and the pack's feeling toward *It*, data relevant to these issues were also collected.

EXPERIMENT

Games Played

Two games were employed which met the following criteria: the games significantly differed only with respect to the power of the *It;* they required the same basic skill—running speed; they permitted reliable measurement of amount of failure; and they were representative of a popular kind of children's game.

The games were Black Tom, and Dodge the Skunk; both are similar to Pom-Pom-Pullaway.[1] A field was lined with boundaries and with safe or "home" areas at either end. *It* was required to tag pack members as they ran from one home area to the other. Any player tagged was out; when *It* had tagged two of the three pack members, that game session was over and another *It* took over. Each *It* was given a handkerchief tail to wear as a symbol of *It.*

Black Tom, involving a high-power *It* role, differed from Dodge the Skunk, involving a low-power *It* role, in the following ways: The Black Tom *It* called a series of names the last one of which (Black Tom) was the signal that required the pack members to run to the opposite home. In actual play, Black Tom could come fairly close to players at home and then call the running signal when he thought he could tag a particular player. The Dodge the Skunk *It* called no signal and chased players as they ran, at will, from one home to the other. In actual play, *It* ranged about from the middle of the field in order to be able to choose runners from either home. In Black Tom, *It* had the opportunity to choose the time, place, and opponent for a competitive encounter; in Dodge the Skunk, *It* had no such choice; the pack members decided if and when they would attempt the dash across the unsafe field to the opposite home area.

Population Employed

Forty boy campers,[2] seven to ten years old, were divided into ten four-person playing groups. Boys of similar age but who differed in running speed[3] were put into each group. One skilled boy, i.e., a fast runner, two semi-skilled boys, and one unskilled boy were placed in each group. Data were collected on *It* role behavior for only the fast or skilled and

[1] Bancroft, J. H., *Games*, New York, Macmillan, 1952, p. 184.

[2] We wish to thank Mr. Bob Luby, Director the Fresh Air Camp, Brighton, Michigan, for his help in the research. Counselors Al Camiener, Sherman Hesselman, Leonard Rachmiel and Jerry Wolberg contributed time, effort, and ideas to our research.

[3] A series of foot races were held several days before the experiment in order to identify fast, medium and slow runners.

the slow or unskilled boys. Boys of medium skill were included to enlarge the playing group and to screen the fact that the observers were focussing only on skilled and unskilled boys. These semi-skilled boys were *It* in games which observers considered practice sessions but which, to the playing groups, looked like the "real thing."

Administration

One experimenter taught the games using demonstrations and practice sessions so that the limitations and privileges of the *It* and pack roles were clarified. Ordinarily, each game session was over when *It* made two successful tags. However, in eight of the twenty game sessions, unskilled *It* experienced such obvious and complete failure that further play would have been painfully discouraging. When both experimenters agreed that further play would not result in tagging success for the *It*, the game session was terminated and a new *It* assigned.

A total of forty game sessions were included in the experiment: ten skilled boys were *It* once in Black Tom and the same ten were *It* once in Dodge the Skunk; the ten unskilled boys went through this same regime.

Data Collection

The following data were collected: (1) the number of unsuccessful tag attempts made by each skilled or unskilled *It* before he tagged out two pack members, (2) the number and quality of verbal expressions made by *It* players, and (3) the general behavior of the pack toward the *Its*.

RESULTS

Tagging Success

It players were eventually successful in tagging two other members in 32 of the 40 game sessions. The average numbers of tag attempt failures for these 32 games were as follows:

All players in high-power *It* roles: 1.7 tag failures;
All players in low-power *It* roles: 3.7 tag failures.

In general, then, boys endured markedly fewer tagging failures in high-power *It* roles than in low-power *It* roles. When these gross results were broken down to show differences for skilled and unskilled players, the following averages were obtained:

Skilled players in high-power *It* roles: 0.6 tag failures;
Skilled players in low-power *It* roles: 2.2 tag failures;

Unskilled players in high-power *It* roles: 4.4 tag failures;
Unskilled players in low-power *It* roles: 6.7 tag failures.

The above numbers show two results: skilled players had fewer failures than unskilled ones, regardless of the power of the *It* role occupied; and both skilled and unskilled players had fewer failures when in the high-power role. The tendency of the high-power role to help unskilled boys is indicated by one further fact. In 8 of the 40 game sessions, unskilled *Its* completely failed to make the required two tags. However, only three unskilled *Its* so failed in high-power *It* role, while these same three plus *two more* unskilled players failed completely in the low-power *It* role.

Game Actions and Attitudes

The number of tag failures yields an objective picture of the intensity of the *Its* success-failure situation. The response of *It* to his role and the responses of others to him gives a psychological picture of this situation. Observations recorded of taunting and other expressive "side play" justified the following conclusions:

1. *The pack combined against "It" most frequently when he was in a low-power role.* In six of the twenty game sessions, pack members intrigued together against *It;* for example, "Same plan! When you put your hand down, all three of us run." These alliances occurred *only* in the game sessions of Dodge the Skunk (low-power *It*).

2. *The pack disparaged "It" most frequently when he was in the low-power "It" role.* Disparaging remarks were made before the game began to six unskilled *Its;* this happened equally frequently in Black Tom and in Dodge the Skunk. For example, before Dodge the Skunk, it was said of one unskilled boy about to be *It,* "Oh, Peter's easy to beat." Before Black Tom, one unskilled *It* was called "Spaghetti Balls." No skilled *It* received such pre-game disparagement.

   Once the game began, however, it was the *game,* as well as the players' more abiding attitudes toward each other, which dictated the targets of taunts. There were nine occasions of marked taunting of the low-power *It* in Dodge the Skunk—seven times to unskilled and twice to skilled *Its.* "C'mon you chicken. Lay an egg." "This skunk really smells" were typical disparagements of low-power *Its.* Unskilled boys in this low-power *It* role of Dodge the Skunk suffered other humiliations. Pack members began to *walk* past them, to run circles around them, to jeer in their faces, and to pull off their tails.

   No comparable taunting was directed to either skilled or unskilled players in the high-power "It" role. Although it is the unskilled boy who suffers the most disparagement, this occurs mainly in the game role which offers him the least power.

3. *With unskilled players, a sense of failure occurred more often in the low-power "It" role than in the high-power "It" role.* In Dodge the Skunk, three of the ten unskilled boys expressed their sense of failure and powerlessness by sighs and by complaints directed towards the experimenters; they wanted "out." The same boys did not make similar appeals in Black Tom. As it happened they were only slightly more successful in Black Tom, but, apparently they *felt* less failure as a Black Tom *It*.

The tendency for *felt* power to be greater in a Black Tom *It* role was demonstrated also by results from post-game interviews. All of the unskilled boys (and all but one of the skilled boys) preferred to be *It* in Black Tom. Their reasons were that *It* has an easier job and that *It* has more power over players in Black Tom. Sample remarks were: "In Black Tom you can fool people," or "It's like a mystery. They don't know when you're going to say it."

DISCUSSION

Relation of *It* Power to Experience in the *It* Role

The above results demonstrate that the game-given power of a role is an important determiner of game experience. Power affects the amount of objective failure endured by the occupant of a game role, it affects the way this occupant is treated by the rest of the playing group, and it affects how he feels about himself and his situation.

The results also reveal that unskilled players are particularly likely to endure failure and derision in *It* roles. For most of the unskilled boys, failure and derision were less frequently encountered when they played a high-power, rather than a low-power, *It* role.

Relation of Personality to Experience in an *It* Role

Although skill of participants and power of the role were two important factors determining success or failure in the *It* role, it appeared that a personality factor which might loosely be described as "drive" was also important to success. Unskilled boys who gained some success in a high-power *It* role differed from unskilled boys who failed in the following respects:

1. *Successful boys focussed on a target pack member and they used strategy.* In contrast, the unsuccessful unskilled boys *let* things happen

instead of *causing* things to happen. They would stand timidly in the middle of the field and call "Black Tom" and then chase one, then another fleeing player. Concentration of effort and exploitation of the high-power of the *It* role were not employed by unsuccessful unskilled boys.

2. *Successful but unskilled boys sustained effort at climax points.* In contrast, there were those instances in which both observers were sure that an unskilled *It* was about to tag—only to watch a failure. The *It* would hesitate slightly at the crucial moment; he would slow down, or he would *drop,* instead of raise his tagging hand. Whether these "climax failures" were due to simple fear of falling while extending oneself or to an emotional "tagging inhibition" could not be determined. It seemed possible that the aggression or assertion symbolized by the tagging act was sufficiently feared to create a momentary inhibition resulting in tagging failure.

The following game record is an example of a successful, yet unskilled boy using strategy, establishing focus, and maintaining effort at climax points.

Harry, a fat, awkward boy is *It* in Black Tom. At first he has little success as he proceeds up and down the field after his fleet playmates. Then he begins to call "Black Tom" just as soon as the runners are safely home and so forces them to come out again immediately. A half-dozen such rapid calls fatigues the runners and they are now more in Harry's speed class. (Harry doesn't have to run as far as they do since they must go all the way home to be safe.) Harry then centers his efforts on one skilled boy: he chases him home calling, "Black Tom!" as he rushes up to the home line. The call forces the tired runner to leave home and Harry lunges and tags him as he comes out.[4]

Relation of *It* Rotation Procedures to Experience in the *It* Role

Another factor significantly affects the intensity of negative experience in the *It* role. The factor is *time* spent in the role. Amount of time spent in *It* roles is determined partly by the game prescribed arrangement for rotation of *It* players. For example, in the game I Got It, the *It* is chased and when he fails—when he is tagged—he becomes a member of the chasing pack. Although the *It* role in I Got It is one of relatively low-power, prolonged failure in the role is impossible. On the other hand, in

---

[4] The possibilities inherent in *It* games for diagnoses of personality qualities—as opposed to qualities of sheer skill—seem worthy of systematic research. For example, observers also noticed that boys differed widely in terms of their desire to taunt the *It* and in their zest for the fleeing and annoymous pack role as contrasted to the more responsible and limelighted *It* role.

Dodge the Skunk, the failure of *It* to tag leaves him in the *It* role and subject to an extended failure experience. Thus, although low-power *It* roles are likely to result in failure for the *It*, the *extent* of failure in the *It* role is significantly determined by the game-prescribed arrangements for rotation of occupants in the *It* role.

SUMMARY

The ingredients of children's programs and activities were assumed to have important effects upon the behavior and experience of participants. One type of activity—*It* games—was selected for experimentation. One supposition tested was that high-power *It* roles—as contrasted to low-power *It* roles—lead to less failure for *Its*, to fewer negative reactions of the playing groups toward *It*, and to more positive feeling of *It* about himself and his situation. Results showed this supposition to be generally correct. A second and related supposition was that unskilled players could be helped to more frequent success and to a less negative experience if they were placed in high-power, rather than in low-power, *It* roles. Results generally favored this supposition; however, it was found that unskilled boys who also lacked the ability or the personal drive to exploit game advantage were not materially helped by such game role manipulation. The importance of game-prescribed *It rotation procedures* in determining the intensity of failure of unskilled players in the lower-power *It* role was also pointed out.

The present study investigated specifically the effect of the power of an *It* role upon the experience of game participants. However, this factor of *It* power is just one of many game factors which shape the experience of players. For example, the extent to which game arrangements sharpen and centralize competition may be expected to affect the intensity of hostile and other "combative" impulses felt and expressed by participants. The factor of chance, as opposed to skill, is also important in game structure. It is *probable* that the gratifications and frustrations accompanying appeals to chance differ from those accompanying appeals to skill; it is *certain* that the generally unskilled player will have more success in games of chance than in games of skill. Factors inherent in games—such as power of game roles, sharpness of competition, and chance determination of success—are deserving of serious attention from both the practitioner and the researcher. Once these factors are identified and their effects upon various types of participants are known, the way is open for the strategic use of games in work with children. Games then may be employed in a conscious and deliberate fashion so that participants enjoy the maximum of beneficial experience in game play.

Games in Political Science, Economics, and Sociology— Selected References

Bernard, J. "The Theory of Games of Strategy as a Modern Sociology of Conflict," *American Journal of Sociology,* **59**, 1954, pp. 411–424.

Bloch, H. A. "The Sociology of Gambling," *American Journal of Sociology,* **57**, 1951, pp. 215–221.

Bloomfield, L. P. and Padelford, N. J. "Three Experiments in Political Gaming," *The American Political Science Review,* **53**, 1959, pp. 1105–1115.

Braithwaite, R. B. *Theory of Games as a Tool For The Moral Philosopher,* Cambridge, England: Cambridge University Press, 1955.

Brody, R. A. *Political Games For Model Construction in International Relations,* Northwestern University Department of Political Science, June, 1961.

Coplin, W. D. "Inter-Nation Simulation and Contemporary Theories of International Relations," *The American Political Science Review,* **9**, 1966, p. 562.

Creamer, M. W. "Leisure Activities of Privileged Children," *Sociology and Social Research,* **24**, 1950, pp. 440–450.

Crespi, I. "The Social Significance of Card Playing as a Leisure Activity," *American Sociological Review,* **21** (6), 1956, pp. 717–721.

Davidson, W. P. "A Public Opinion Game," *Public Opinion Quarterly,* **25**, 1961, pp. 210–220.

Debevec, R. M. *Laws Governing Amusements; Law of Places and Pleasures,* New York: Oceana Publications, 1960.

Duke, R. D. *Operational Gaming and Simulation in Urban Research: An Annotated Bibliography,* Michigan State University, 1965.

Frankenberg, R. *Village on the Border: A Social Study of Religion, Politics, and Football in a North Wales Community,* London: Cohen and West, 1957.

Gini, C. "Rural Ritual Games in Lybia," *Rural Sociology,* 4, 1939, pp. 283–299.

Goffman, E. "Fun in Games," *Encounters: Studies in the Sociology of Interaction,* Indianapolis: Bobbs-Merrill Company, Inc., 1961, pp. 17–81.

Guetzkow, H. S. *Simulation in International Relations,* Englewood Cliffs, New Jersey: Prentice-Hall, Inc., 1963.

Gump, P. V. and Sutton-Smith, B. "The 'It' Role of Children's Games," *The Group,* 17, 1955, pp. 3–8.

Hanna, W. A. "The Politics of Sport," *Southeast Asia Series,* American Universities Field Staff, 10, 1966, pp. 13–19.

Holland, E. P. "Principles of Simulation," *American Behavioral Scientist,* 9, September, 1965, pp. 6–10.

Howard, G. E. "Social Psychology of the Spectator," *American Journal of Sociology,* 18, 1912, pp. 33–50.

Kahn, A. E. *The Game of Death: Effects of the Cold War On Our Children,* New York: Cameron and Kahn, 1953.

Leites, N. *On the Game of Politics in France,* Stanford, California: Stanford University Press, 1953.

Long, N. "The Local Community as an Ecology of Games," *American Journal of Sociology,* 64, 1958, pp. 251–256.

Mead, M. "The Pattern of Leisure in Contemporary American Culture," *Annals of The American Academy of Political and Social Science,* 313, 1957, pp. 11–15.

Robins, F. G. *Sociology of Play, Recreation and Leisure,* Dubuque, Iowa: Wm. C. Brown, Company, 1955.

Schelling, T. G. *The Strategy of Conflict,* Cambridge, Mass.: Harvard University Press, 1960.

Sellin, T. "Gambling," *Annals of The American Academy of Political and Social Science,* 269, May, 1950.

Shubik, M. *Game Theory and Related Approaches to Social Behavior,* New York: John Wiley and Sons, Inc., 1964.

Shubik, M. *Readings in Game Theory and Political Behavior,* New York: Doubleday, 1954.

Sutton-Smith, B. and Gump, P. V. "Games and Status Experience," *Recreation,* 48, 1955, pp. 142–174.

CHAPTER 12

GAMES AS STRUCTURE

In the introductory chapter a game was defined as an exercise of voluntary control systems in which there is an opposition between forces, controlled by rules in order to produce a disequilibrial outcome. The question arises to what extent do the various perspectives of others conform to our definition? Is there any consensus across investigators, so that some common classification and common definition becomes possible? This chapter and its readings are devoted to that question; at the same time the chapter sets forth a host of details on game structure that are both statements of the classificatory problem and resources for future research. We begin with an outline of some of the historical attempts that have been made to classify the essential structures of games.

For example, Culin, who along with Tylor was the first authority of the modern era, offered the following:

The games of the American Indians may be divided into two general classes: I games of chance; II games of dexterity. Games of pure skill and calculation, such as chess, are entirely absent. . . . Games of chance fall into two categories; 1) games in which implements of the nature of dice are thrown at random to determine a number or numbers, and the sum of the counts is kept by means of sticks, pebbles, etc. or upon an abacus, or counting board, or circuit; 2) games in which one or more of the players guess in which of two or more places an odd or particularly marked lot is concealed. . . . The games of dexterity may be enumerated as: 1) archery in various modifications, 2) a game of sliding javelins or dart, 3) a game of shooting at a moving target . . . , 4) the game of ball in several highly specialized forms; 5) the racing games. . . . In addition there is a subclass related to games of shooting . . . corresponding to the

European game of cup and ball. . . . Children have a variety of other amusements, such as top spinning, mimic fights. . . .[1]

So if we add the games of strategy absent in the study of Indian games from which this statement is drawn we derive from Culin the three classes of chance, dexterity, and calculation.

The noted British historian H.J.R. Murray disagreed with Culin's notion that games were based on certain universal concepts and should therefore be classified in that way. Murray suggested that games symbolize human activities and should be classified with respect to these activities. In 1913, he proposed a taxonomy for table and board games, for example, race games, hunt or siege games, and war games.[2] About forty years later, after considerable data gathering, he expanded this taxonomy into (1) games of alinement and configuration, (2) wargames, (3) hunt-games, (4) racegames, and (5) mancala games.[3] Later in 1960 R. C. Bell,[4] another authority on board games, proposed a taxonomy based on the work of Murray, which included the following examples:

Race games	1. Cross and circle race games.
	2. Spiral race games.
	3. Square board race games.
	4. Peg scoring boards.
	5. The Backgammon group.
War games	1. The Alquerque group.
	2. The chess group.
	3. The draughts group.
	4. The tafl group.
	5. The latrunculorum group.
	6. The running-fight games.
Positional games	1. Morris games.
	2. Three-in a row games.
	3. Five-in a row games.
	4. Replacement games.
	5. Territorial possession.
	6. Patience games.

[1] Culin, S. "Games of the North American Indians," *Twenty-Fourth Annual Report of the Bureau of American Ethnology.* Washington, D.C.: United States Government Printing Office, 1907, p. 31.

[2] Murray, H. J. R. A *History of Chess.* London: Oxford University Press, 1913, p. 31.

[3] Murray, H. J. R. A *History of Board Games Other Than Chess.* London: Oxford University Press, 1952, pp. 4–5.

[4] Bell, R. C. *Board and Table Games From Many Civilizations.* London: Oxford University Press, 1960.

Mancala games	1. Two-rank mancala.
	2. Four-rank mancala.
Dice games	1. Games with two-sided dice.
	2. Games with six-sided dice.
	3. Games with special dice.
Domino games	

Bell's approach to taxonomy is an extension of the type used by the early ethnologists whose focus was on the artifacts employed in the play of games. This approach omits nonequipment games. It is, in effect, a taxonomy for board games alone, namely, games of chance and strategy.

The game theorists mentioned in the chapter on social science have perhaps contributed the greatest experimental evidence of game playing, and although their discussions apply mainly to games of strategy or their derivatives, they are worthy of mention here. We are, after all, in pursuit of those intrinsic considerations that any definition of games must take into account. Game theorists classify games or "conflict situations" by using two factors. The first factor or element is the *number of human players*. Chance is not considered a player, and thus solitaire or a puzzle is not a game in game theory terms, nor is any mechanical game in which the players have no control over events, as in a game with a "one-armed. bandit." The second factor is the results or *"pay-off."* When the losses of one player are equal to the winnings of the other player in a two-person game, this is envisioned as a "zero-sum game," and such games as Ticktactoe, chess, and checkers are called "two-person zero-sum games." A game such as bridge, although involving four people is still in essence a "two-person zero-sum game," as is a war between two armies, or a "price war" between two supermarket chains, or the "rating game" between two major television networks.

Mathematicians have developed formulas or equations for "nonzerosum games," "three-person games," and others. A problem facing game theorists is the development of formulas for "*n*-person games." Game theorists indicate that their work at the present time is incomplete, and when "pursued to completion, perforce leads us to consider other than strategic modes of thought."[5]

Although game theorists consider only four elements in games, games would not be games without additional elements. It is important to recognize that of the four elements that game theorists identify, only three are really part of a game per se, that is, *number of players, rules govern-*

---

[5] Rapoport, A. *Two Person Game Theory.* Ann Arbor: University of Michigan Press, 1966, p. 214.

ing action, and *results.* The fourth identified element—*strategies*—is in reality not part of a game, but something players bring to a game.

Roberts, Arth, and Bush,[6] whose approach was derived from game theory, suggest that there are three basic types of games and combinations. Their triad is surprisingly similar to that of Culin, since it comprises games of physical skill, strategy, and chance. The classes are contained in the article by Roberts and Sutton-Smith in the next chapter. They define games as characterized by organized play, competition, two or more sides, criteria for determining the winner, and agreed-on rules.

Just as we can indicate that Murray and Bell seem limited to classifying board games, and game theory to dealing with games of strategy, so it has to be suggested that Roberts et al. omit a large group of young children's games termed *central person games.*[7] These are games of the sort discussed in the Gump and Sutton-Smith article on *it* games in the last chapter. They are chasing games, girls' games with leaders (for example, Mother May I, Giant Steps). In all of them a central player has an arbitrarily game-granted status that allows her to dictate the course of action, while the other players attempt to escape, or dispossess the central person of her power. In these games, unlike the competitive games of skill, strategy, and chance, the outcomes and the sides are often transitory. They do not fulfill the Roberts et al. game definitions provided above. Still, in their focus on *arbitrary power,* rather than power achieved by skill, strategy, or luck, these games appear to bear some continuity with the other triad of games. They are games of ascribed power, whereas the others might be thought of as games of achieved power.

These central person games have commonly been called games and preoccupy the play of children between the ages of six and nine years. It seems probable that if one adds central person games, (or games of arbitrary power as they may be termed) to games of chance, strategy, and physical skill, then one has included most basic types. The problem is that the classification of a game as a central person game (or as games of ascribed power, or arbitrary power) is a classification in terms of role relationships, whereas the classification in terms of physical, strategic, and chance is a classification in terms of achievement or outcome determinants. And although it does not make taxonomic sense to change classificatory emphasis in mid-course, it is possible to argue that the way in which games change during child development requires this change. Young children are mainly concerned with representing relationships to

[6] Roberts, J. M., Arth, M. J., and Bush, R. R. "Games in Culture," *American Anthropologist,* 61 (4), August, 1959, pp. 597–605.

[7] Sutton-Smith, B. *Children's Games.* Doctoral Dissertation, University of New Zealand, 1954.

arbitrary power figures (therefore, central person games), whereas older children are interested in competitive tests of skill (therefore, physical strength and skill, strategy, and chance).

In both classes, however, we have a contest between powers with the interaction pattern structured in hierarchical terms in the central person games and in egalitarian terms in the usual competitive games.

A common definition for all four groups might center on the *contest of powers*—this could be regarded as their "purpose," or "motif," or "challenge," which are terms considered central to games by several investigators. It is noticeable that both Gump, Redl, and Sutton-Smith (actors and counteractors) and Dundes (two simultaneous action sequences) stress that the purpose of a game lies in the special character of its dual interaction sequences. A contest for power—to seize or avoid arbitrary power, to gain power by skill, luck, or strategy—could be taken as the central purpose or logic of the inverse patterns of interaction of actors and counteractors in all these four types of games.

If we look at the consensus across Culin, Murray, Bell, game theory, and Roberts and Sutton-Smith we have four basic types of game: games of arbitrary power, skill, strategy, and luck. However, in order to do full justice to games we need also to take into account the innumerable dimensions that we have listed in the Redl, et al. and Avedon readings included in this Chapter. These writers not only give a definition of the types of power involved in games, they also include some controlling functions for rules, roles, interaction patterns, prescribed performances, procedures for action, and spatiotemporal contexts. If all of these various facets be epitomized by the term *rules*, then it is possible to restate the definition with which we began this chapter with specific application to the formalized games we have been discussing.

> A game is *an exercise of voluntary control systems, in which there is a contest between powers, confined by rules in order to produce a disequilibrial outcome.*

This definition will hold for games of arbitrary, physical, chance, or strategic contests—which means that it will be true for most formal games. Unfortunately, it will not do for all the phenomena usually included under this heading. For example, there is yet another group often called either pastimes or games such as *ring-a-roses, nuts-in-May,* which have similarities with dance, drama, and song. These are games in the sense that they are organized (rules) and have a fixed sequence of actions (plot) and a resolution (outcome). However, they are not usually competitive, they do not usually have winners, and in fact they are often so cooperative that they are organized by ritual (fixed sequence) rather than rules (contingent sequence). Whether we call them games within the present definition, depends it seems, on whether we decide that there is, in fact, an opposition between the power of the players and an alternative chaos. It is certainly quite a victory for a group of little children to proceed triumphantly to the last "tishoo" in *ring-a-roses*. We could view this as a game of players against their own inchoate social nature. Developmentally speaking, this would be a fair verdict on most of the singing and ritual games of young children. In most of them also, there is an implicit victory for those who are chosen by the player in the center, as in *farmer in the dell*. Never to be chosen is, in a mild sense, to lose. So there are disequilibrial outcomes. Perhaps what we have here is a form of activity that in later childhood differentiates, on the one hand, into songs, drama, and dance, and on the other, into games—hence the difficulty in classification.

Other problems are posed by Caillois in his recent work, *Man, Play, and Games*. On the problem of classification he writes:

Games also possess so many different characteristics that many approaches are possible. Current usage sufficiently demonstrates the degree of hesitance and uncertainty: indeed, several classifications are employed concurrently. To oppose card games to games of skill, or to oppose parlor games to those played in a stadium is meaningless. In effect the implement used in the games is chosen as a classificatory instrument in the one case; in the other qualifications required; in a third number of players and the atmosphere of the game, and lastly the place in which the contest is waged.[8]

Caillois' taxonomy has two dimensions. The first indicates whether a game is dominated by impulse or by control. The second dimension indicates types of opportunities for specific human experience.

Using Huizinga's terms for describing play elements, Caillois classifies all games along the first dimension as *ludus* (subordination to rules) or *paidia* (tumultuous, spontaneous activity), and along the second dimension as *agon* (competition), *alea* (chance), *mimicry* (simulation), or *ilinx* (vertigo). As examples, Caillois classifies chess as agon-ludus (competition dominated by rules), pitching pennies as alea-paidia (chance dominated by tumultuous, spontaneous activity). He feels that the use of this taxonomy enables one to see the dominant interests of a culture, and the preferences of its population.

Being concerned with expression in general, he offers as game examples

---

[8] Caillois, R. *Man, Play, and Games*. New York: The Free Press of Glencoe Inc., 1961, p. 11.

a large number of activities that are not usually thought of as games, for example, waltzing, traveling carnivals, theater, playing pirate. This indicates that his taxonomy is not a game classification system as such, but rather a way of classifying a variety of expressive forms. The agon (competition) and alea (chance) categories remind one of a host of other taxonomies based on "games of skill" versus "games of chance;" while the mimicry (simulation) and ilinx (vertigo) categories appear to describe play behaviors associated with a large variety of free-time experiences. Moreover, the other dimension ludus (rules), paidia (spontaneity) seem to suggest the structured games of adults as opposed to the informal games of children.

Although agon and alea fit our game definition above as a contest of powers, it is uncertain whether mimicry and vertigo can be so easily handled. If episodic, then they would be examples of play. However, mimicry, if developed, might well become drama. Vertigo (as in rollercoaster) seems a lending of oneself to involuntary experience, although again it could be regarded as gamelike, if the subject pitted himself against this involuntary experience and tried to become the master. Here we would be talking of an opposition of forces as in the earlier definition. We reserve the contest of powers for opposition involving actors and counteractors, although it is clearly a subset of the other. The uncertainty of outcome, whether conquering or overwhelmed by the vertigo, would be a disequilibrial outcome. Our definition of games, then, applies to some of these borderline types (*ring-a-roses*, vertigo) only if the way they are played lends themselves to game like voluntarism, opposition, and disequilibrial outcome.

The following two readings approach the subject of the structure of games by delineating aspects that are intrinsic to all games. The list of selected references concluding the chapter concerns the work of mathematical game theorists—as a field of inquiry, the field primarily devoted to structural analysis of games.

19

The Dimensions of Games

FRITZ REDL, PAUL GUMP, AND BRIAN SUTTON - SMITH

The following are dimensions which are thought relevant to the behavior that games may provoke. "Behavior" includes the impulses which are stirred up and gratified, the controls which are supported or weakened. The presence or absence of these dimensions presumably should be a factor in determining which games are suitable for the needs and capacities of different groups of children.

A discussion of some of the dimensions is to be found in F. Redl, "The Impact of Game Ingredients on Children's Play Behavior", in B. Schffner (ed.), *Group Processes, Transactions of the Fourth Conference*, New York: Josiah Macy, 1959, pp. 33–80.

I. Body Contact.
- A. Directness vs. Via Props.
  In *football* there is much direct body contact; in *beetle*— a swatting game—the contact is through a prop (i.e., the swat).
- B. Competitive vs. Non-Competitive.
  Again, in *football* game structure demands competitive, aggressive body contact, but the huddle is a non-competitive body contact element in *football*. In games in which the contact is "joining hands" the contact is non-competitive.

II. Bodily Activity.
- A. Body Mobility and Locomotion.
  1. Static vs. mobile. *Relay games* require periods of just "standing around." *Card games* restrict locomotion even

further. *Tag games*, on the other hand, encourage much locomotion.

    2. Rigid vs. fluid. Rigidity is sometimes added to the requirement of remaining in one spot. Some games ask the player to "freeze"—to be a "statue"—others simply restrict locomotion but complete suppression of postural adjustments, etc. is not required.

  B. Manipulative Opportunities. This probably becomes particularly important when the game restricts body mobility. In parchesi or monopoly a player has props to "fool with" —dice, houses, money, markers, etc.

  C. Vocal Expression. Some games, like Grab, demand shouting and talking. Other games like baseball permit it but do not demand it. Still other games require suppression of vocalization—one must be quiet if the game is to proceed (e.g., parts of Hide-n-Seek).

    Games which do employ vocalization differ in respect to its function. In some games, vocalization is merely a signal function (e.g., calling the warning in Hide-n-Seek) in other games, it is more a part of the progress means in game (e.g., in Grab, one shouts for trading purposes).

III. Skill Requirements. Consideration of these variables helps one decide the capacity required to play a particular game. In-so-far as the exercise of a skill is a functional pleasure in itself, the skill requirements are also possible game gratifications.

  A. Thinking. *Chess* requires concentrated thought, some card games like *Snap* (one must yell "snap" when two similar cards appear) require little thought.

  B. Creative Imagination. *Charades* demand much creative imagination; *Checkers* relatively little.

  C. Manipulating as in Arts & Crafts. *Drawing Charades* (player must represent the idea in symbols other than letters and words).

  D. Manipulation as in Athletics and Body Skills. Playing *Pool* demands hand and eye skills; such skills are not too important in tag games.

  E. Language. Some games demand that participants be reasonably "good talkers." *Contrived Stories* combines creative imagination and language demands.

F.   "Reaction Time." In some games sheer speed of reaction in the major skill reaction (e.g., Card game *Snap*).

IV.   Chance Determination of Success. Skill is not always the determiner of game success. Luck games probably have an important place in game repertoire since they are likely to change the usual distribution of winning gratifications and losing frustrations.

Games involving dice, spinners, and some card games are guided by chance. The chance element is minimal in Checkers, baseball, etc.

V.   Competition Factors. Competition is an ingredient in most games; the question here is how intense is the competition and what creates this intensity.

A.   Centrality of Winning and Losing. A game like *Beetle* has a series of little competitive episodes but no one wins or loses. In *Poison Pin*, (players join hands and circle a bowling pin; each tries to putt the other so that he touches the pin and is out), winning is central to the purpose of game play.

B.   Goal directed vs. Opponent Directed. In a *race* the major purpose is to reach the goal first; in *dodgeball* the major purpose is to do something to an opponent.

C.   Self Enhancement vs. Defeat of the "other." Sometimes the emphasis placed upon winning in an opponent directed game is a determined factor by the players' whims; but there are games like Old Maid where the idea is to defect or humiliate the "other."

D.   Team vs. Individual Competition. Losing as a member of the team might ordinarily be less deeply threatening than losing all by oneself. However, team competition brings on much more approval or disapproval from peers since their fates are tied to the participants success or failure.

E.   Interference with Participants by Participants. In *Football* the obstacles are created by opponents; in relay race, the "obstacle" is space itself—progress cannot be impeded by opponents.

VI.   Use of Space.

A.   Amount available.

B. Freedom in Use of Space. Space useage which demands zoning and taboo areas complicate the game play and add richness at the same time.

VII. Time Considerations.

    A. Amount of time before fun rewards start. In games like baseball, there is a period of organization and placement of players which slow down the fun rewards. For younger children especially, the game is hard to take partly because "nothing happens" for some time.

    B. Presence or Absence of Natural Termination Points. *Beetle* has no natural termination; *Poison Pin* does.

    C. Presence at Absence of Well Closured Steps. *Baseball* is a good example of phases (innings) well marked. *Soccer* tends to go on and on.

VIII. Prop Useage. The impulses stirred up by a game may be partly a function of the props employed. There are three kinds of props: progress making or playing props (the tennis rackets and balls) obstacles props (the hurdles in a race) and boundary and goal props (the basket in basketball).

The kind of playing prop may determine side-play by participants. A good example is the ping-pong paddle which impulsive children invariably beat on the table while playing. Some of these progress props "ask for" a certain non-game use.

Playing Props include:

    A. Clubbing Props (Swat in *Swat Tag*).

    B. Power Projection and Extension Props. These props make the person more capable or give him a dramatic way of asserting power. Baseball bat, dueling sticks, etc.

IX. Role Taking Factors. Some games demand different actions for different players; this brings in problems of status, of comprehension, of chances to be unique, etc.

    A. Amount of Function Differentiation. In Tug-of-War everybody enjoys the same functions (i.e., tugging). But in *Football* some players are always chased, other players always chasing, etc.

Function Differentiation may also include creation of limelight positions and game-guaranteed control positions.

        1. Limelight. In *King of the Hill* one player is before all others, in *baseball* the batter is limelighted. The game

may not have built-in arrangements for even distribution of the limelight.

    2. Control Positions. In Mother May I?, "mother" determines the play that each player may make. A control position makes it possible for one player to "call the turn." Among those game which have a control position there are differences in the permanence with which this control rests on one player.

    3. On-the-spot Positions. Often limelight and/or control positions also have an on-the-spot aspect. *It* is required to be against many other players; invitation to scapegoating is fairly open.

  B. Imagination Roles. Some roles are not only differentiated functionally but by fantasy content. The *pussy* in *Pet the Pussy* has one fantasy role to play; the participant who pets him another.

X. Rule Complexity. Rule complexity can be about two aspects of the game-basic rules about progress making (e.g., chess)—and special rules about "what happens if" (e.g., basically, football rules are simple, but there are many special rules about special things; some table games like *Parchesi* and *Sorry* have many "deflection point" rules.) Rule complexity will have the following effects:

  A. Increase demands on the comprehension of participants.

  B. Enrich game experience (monopoly).

  C. Cause Unexpected advances and reversals. (Deflection Richness: in some table games one suddenly gets extra moves ahead or may be sent back to the start, to jail, home, etc.)

XI. Interdependence of Players. All games imply some interdependence competitive or cooperative—question is whether the poor play or uncooperative play of one participant can significantly affect the continuance of satisfactory play of the rest. In *tag*, play is predominately parallel but in *bridge* one player's disinterest or inability greatly affects others.

Interdependence also often leads to the focalization or limelighting of play of one participant at a time and the concommittant gratifications and frustrations. It will ordinarily increase demands upon comprehension and of impulse expression.

XII. Volume and Distributions of Participation. There are perhaps four levels of participation possible.

    1. Active participation—actually throwing the ball, running, etc.

    2. In-game passive participations—watching play until it comes into one's own area of responsibility (e.g., the second baseman in baseball).

    3. In game waiting—waiting one's turn. Participant does not have to be involved in game but he is still a member of it (e.g., waiting one's turn in *drop out basket shooting*).

    4. Out-of-game waiting. (Elimination games in which one participant after another is out and must wait until game is over before they can play again.)

    To evaluate a game's suitability for given groups one would need to know the following:

    a. *Amount* of Guaranteed Active Participation.

    b. *Rapidity of Shift* from less Active Types of Participation to Active Participation.

    c. Continuity of Active Participation.

The structure of games often determines whether participation can be monopolized by few players. In *baseball*, the total structure is obviously a force against any one player keeping a hit ball. In *basketball*, however, there is no obvious structure that forces a dribbling player to toss the ball to another player.

XIII. Leeway for Marginal Impulse Expression. Question is: "Will the game successfully tolerate 'horse play' "?

XIV. Respite Possibilities. In games where action is fact and perhaps threatening, the presence or absence of respite possibilities may be crucial.

    A. Safety Zones or Positions. *Regular tag* often has none— *Squattag* has a safety position; *wood tag* has safety zones.

    B. Built in rest periods. Play in *Soccer* is relatively continuous but in *football* is frequently interrupted by huddles.

XV. Suspense Emphasis. Some games continue for some time and then a *break* occurs. The period before the break may be full of build up. In *Old Mother Witch* the children tease and harry the witch with a jingle; she continually asks "Whose children are you?" They repeat the jingle and give wrong names—suddenly one of them says "Yours!" and the witch chases the children.

XVI. Switches Between Opposites.

    A. Theme Switch. The participant is asked to take an opposite role—as in Hide-n-seek, he is the hunter, then the hunted.

    B. Action Switch. The participant is asked to reverse his functioning. In Statue Tag, he runs wildly and than must freeze.

XVII. Pleasure-Pain Content of Winning or Losing. (The items just consider the losing end—winning is usually the opposite.)

    A. Loss of "Possessions" (Pauperization) Loser in Monopoly goes "broke."

    B. Implications that one is inadequate skillwise. Loser of Ping-pong game.

    C. Implication that Destiny is against one. Loser in dice game or chance-loaded card game.

    D. Loss of Dignity. Some games have built in humiliation positions or penalties at end for loser (e.g., in Barrel-tilting or Canoe tilting, the loser is tumbled off his perch).

XVIII. Spread of Winnership. (Is winner all by himself or does he have company?)
Possibilities are:

    A. One winner—everybody else loses—elimination games.

    B. One-winner and seconds and thirds (dart game where score is kept for certain period of shooting).

    C. Several winners (high-low poker—team games).

    D. All win but the loser. These games have built-in arrangements for the selection of a scapegoat (Old Maid, Card game of Pig, etc.).

XIX. Penetration of Game by Rewards and Penalties. This is a consideration of the *extent* to which the reward and punishment idea gets into the game as opposed to the *kinds* of pleasure-pain content. A game with much of this penetration gives ample opportunity for safety-guaranteed punitiveness.

    A. Game Play (e.g., because you guessed wrong you must stand on your head).

B. Game End (e.g. Winner gets prize—loser gets three swats).

XX. Institutionalized "Cheating." Some games deliberately sanction and put at game center, acts which are usually considered dishonorable or unfair.

    A. "Lying" and Bluffing. Card Game *I Doubt it*, the player is encouraged to misstate the contents of his hand. The bluffing in poker is well known.

    B. Deliberate Misleading. Certain guessing games permit the holder of the secret to mislead although he may not misstate fact.

    C. Stealing. Steal the Bacon.

    D. Sneaking. *Mother May I?* has opportunity for sneaking in extra steps when "mother's" attention is diverted.

XXI. Nature of the Obstacles in Game. Many games have important obstacles; some kinds of obstacles may be more acceptable or challenging to certain children than others.

    A. Beyond the participant obstacles (Non-Handicaps).

        1. Opponent produced and/or manipulated obstacles (e.g., the actions of a guard in various games like basketball, soccer, hockey).

        2. Impersonal obstacles. The obstacles in an obstacle race.

    B. "Tied-to-Person" Obstacles (Restriction of Function—Handicaps). Blindfold games, sack races, etc.—challenge to adequacy.

XXII. Trust Dependence. For certain groups, some games are full of conflict because they have some participant's action occurring beyond the immediate check of the other players. The participant must be trusted to "do right." (The "It" in Hide-n-seek may peek, the banker in Monopoly may steal, the player in Battleship may deny that one of his ships is hit when it really was.)

XXIII. Permanence of Alliances. For "clique" groups the game required shift to an opposing side is often resisted. Children let themselves be caught in order to be with their pals and the game tends to lose its challenge (e.g., game Rover). These same games, however, encourage the game induced (rather than leader induced) shift of allegiance which is sometimes desirable.

XXIV. Direct Mirroring of Life Themes. Some games directly and obviously take over themes of non-game life. Props, language, and challenges represent open copies of these themes.

A. Contemporary Events and Culture (e.g., Monopoly reflecting the real-estate business of "real life." Games involving spy hunts, G-Man, etc., belong here).

B. Institutionalized Fantasy. This classification is reserved for games about people and problems which do not exist now but about which there is much historical and/or fantasy "data." Players can become involved in a "romantic" *role* and *theme* (e.g., Cowboys and Indians, Space Cadets, etc.).

XXV. Personalization of Game Props. The *ball* in *basketball* is an impersonal prop all can play with, but men in *checkers* belong to players. Props sometimes openly represent one's self or one's power delegates. For some children, the loss of their personalized props may be especially dramatic; the taking of another's props especially significant.

XXVI. Introduction of Ritual to Game. Ritual serves to define and elaborate the basic game challenge. It serves to fill in waiting or suspense—building periods. It probably increases the communality of the group situation. Security factor is often created because ritual makes clear what is going on and what may come next. (e.g., question and answer chants as in the game, Old Mother Witch).

XXVII. Potential Sexualization Range of Games. Games can elicit sexual interests and grant sexually tinged impulses in several ways.

A. Incidental Body Pleasure. (Tagging game, catching game, games in which bodies packed close together at certain game points may be sexual in nature only for certain ages or groups—the game itself is not an appeal to sexual impulsivity.)

B. Eliciting and Tieing Sexual Energies on Certain Given Sublimational Level. (Sexual symbolism obvious but sexual play not involved, e.g., in Balloon and Pin Dance the boy of a couple is furnished with a pin, the girl with a balloon; the couples dance around with the boys attempting to puncture other girls' balloons and at the same time protect their own girls' balloons).

C. Safety-Guaranteed Sexual Gratifications (e.g., Post Office, Spin the Bottle, Wink, Dancing).

XXVIII. Potential Humor-Producing Range of Games. Some games are quite likely to produce humor by putting players in buffoon roles or into "funny relationships" to each other (e.g., games in which boys must roll up trousers, where two players are likely to sit on the same chair, etc. These games relieve embarrassment by provoking and sanctioning "embarrassing" acts).

XXIX. Outcome Clarity. In *Tug-of-war*, the winning and losing is clear to all; in *baseball* there is often real doubt as to whether the player was "safe" or "out." Category is relevant to position an adult game leader may have to assume. Games with many points of unclear outcome may require more frequent adult interference (i.e., umpiring, judging, etc.,) and consequent resentment against leader by one side or another.

XXX. Challenges. These are the themes of the game which put participants in various sorts of relationships to each other. Although these relationships can be considered active-passive; dominant-subservient; etc., the psychological flavor is missed by such labels. These challenges usually do present two roles, however, which roles we might call actor and counter-actor.

Purpose of Actor	Purpose of Counter-Actor
The Race	
To overtake (both are attempts to reach a goal first)	To stay ahead
The Chase	
To try to catch, tackle, tag.	To outdistance, dodge, elude.
The Attack	
To overcome barrier, enter a guarded area, overpower a defense, to injure—psychologically or otherwise. (Attacks may be obvious and frontal or "undercover.")	To defend an area, a person, to ward off assault by maneuver and force, to be on guard (meet force with force—or alert watchfulness).
The Capture	
To take (to take a person, a symbol; includes swiping as well as open grabbing).	To avoid being taken; to avoid loss of symbols or one's allies.

Purpose of Actor	Purpose of Counter-Actor
The Harrassment	
To tease, taunt, lure to mistake or to unsuccessful attack.	To see through the trick, to move suddenly and punish attackers, to "bide one's time" until one can really be successful.
The Hunt	
To find—by chance, by following clue (the object of search may be person, thing, or idea).	To hide—by simple cover, by misleading clues (feigning) (to hide oneself, an object, an idea).
The Rescue	
To "spring" the prisoner. To be the "savior."	To be a jailer—to guard against the escape.
The Seduction	
To tempt another to the "forbidden act" (to talk, laugh, make wrong move).	To resist temptation; to be controlled and not influenced.

20

The Structural Elements of Games

E. M. AVEDON

What are games? Are they things in the sense of artifacts? Are they behavioral models, or simulations of social situations? Are they vestiges of ancient rituals, or magical rites? It is difficult and even curious when one tries to answer the question "what are games," since it is assumed that games are many things and at the same time specific games are different from one another—but are they?

. . . but we enjoyed playing games and were punished for them by men who played games themselves. However, grown-up games are known as 'business' and even though boys' games are much the same, they are punished for them by their elders. No one pities either the boys or the men, though surely we deserved pity, for I cannot believe that a good judge would approve of the beatings I received as a boy on the ground that my games delayed my progress in studying subjects which would enable me to play a less creditable game later in life. . . .[1]

Personnel in the field of recreation have avoided answering the question and have subsequently avoided the adoption of a universal taxonomy for games, since to do so would demand a theory. Thus, many are content with the taxonomies that have appeared in the literature for the past fifty years, i.e., indoor games, outdoor games; games of low organization, games of high organization; equipment games, non-equipment games; paper and pencil games, board and table games; games for girls and women, games for boys and men; children's games, adult games. All of these classifications refer to an element of a game and thus different

---

[1] Saint Augustine (A.D. 354–430), Confessions, Book I:10.

games are grouped together because they have one element in common. This leads one to ask: Are there certain structural elements that are common to all games, regardless of the differences in games or the purposes for which the games are used, or the culture in which they are used? Are there elements that are invariant under certain transformations? If the answer is in the affirmative, then these invariant elements would not only lend themselves to scrutiny, but would enable personnel to standardize game utilization for therapeutic purposes, as well as modify professional program planning practices.

The notion of invariant structural elements in games has been an interest of mathematicians for a number of years. Von Neumann and others have delimited a number of elements which they believe are present in all games, elements that are necessary and invariant, *i.e.*, number of players, rules of the game, results or "pay-off," and strategies that could be employed in play of the game. However, from the point of view of recreation, these elements are not sufficient to make a game. In addition, strategy is something that a player brings to the game; it is not an intrinsic part of a game. It is something that the player develops, based on his past experience, knowledge of the game, and the personality of the other players.

In addition to mathematicians, others have also been interested in the structural elements of games. A contemporary of Von Neumann's, George H. Mead, was primarily interested in the influences of various aspects of society on human growth and development. Mead taught that games were primarily a pattern or set of specific social situations which affect personality. As a by-product of his concerns, he delimited a number of structural elements of games, which he felt influenced behavior.

The game has a logic, so that there is a definite end to be obtained; the actions of the different individuals are all related to each other with reference to that end . . . so that they further the purpose of the game itself. They are interrelated in a unitary, organic fashion. . . .[2]

Thus, one element—the logic of the game, the definite end—may be thought of as the *purpose* or raison d'etre. A second element would be the actions in reference to the purpose, or the *procedures for action*. A third element would be the interrelated actions. Mead indicates that games include social processes which influence or regulate interaction of the players, and thus this third element might be termed *interaction patterns*.

---

[2] George H. Mead, "Play, the Game, and the Generalized Other" *Mind, Self, and Society*, Chicago: University of Chicago Press, 1934, pp. 158–159.

A fourth element Mead specifies is that of the *roles* which games require players to take. The fifth element he identified is the only one which Von Neumann also identified, *i.e., rules governing action.*

Szasz[3] built directly upon Mead's theories. Although applied within a psychiatric frame of reference, he too indicates that games may be viewed as objects affecting personality. He strengthens Mead's delimination of game elements and stresses the factor of interaction patterns. In analyzing the structure of games, he delimits such elements as rules, roles, procedures, etc.

Goffman,[4] contemporary of Szasz, in studying the sociology of interaction also strengthens Mead's delimitation of game elements. Goffman reports on different types of "focused interactions" and stresses the same game elements as others before him. However, Goffman introduces a new element, which he refers to as *fun* or euphoria. He indicates that this element must be present to ensure participation, and that players modify and manipulate various other elements in order to find *fun* in a game. Fun, like strategies, is subjective and is therefore not an intrinsic element in games. As Goffman rightly points out, often the other elements must be manipulated for a participant to have fun.

In addition to the elements Mead identifies, Goffman emphasizes some of the elements Von Neumann and his colleagues have identified. Unlike Szasz, Goffman's concerns are not with the game as a mode of behavior, but the game as a milieu for behavior.

Recently another psychiatrist, Eric Berne, published an exposition on behavior and games.[5] Berne concerned with interaction, uses the term "transaction," while Goffman uses the term "encounters." They both discuss a variety of interaction patterns subsumed under these labels, and indicate that games are only one type of interaction. Berne emphasizes the same elements as Mead, Szasz, and Goffman; however, he uses different labels. A striking aspect of Berne's approach is his identification of seemingly non-game interactions as games. He points out that games are differentiated from other types of interaction because of their intrinsic elements, and many social situations, although appearing not to be games, possess these elements, and are in reality, games, a notion similar to the one expressed by Saint Augustine. He also indicates that some playing is with conscious intent, and some is the result of unconscious

[3] Thomas S. Szasz, "Game Model Analysis of Behavior," Part V. *The Myth of Mental Illness,* New York: 889-7500 Medical Division, Harper and Row Publishers, 1961, pp. 223–293.

[4] Erving Goffman, "Fun in Games," *Encounters,* Indianapolis: Bobbs-Merrill Company, Inc., 1961, pp. 17–81.

[5] Eric Berne, *Games People Play,* New York: Grove Press, 1964.

conflict. Szasz and Berne identify certain qualities in games which have pathological significance.

By combining the work of the mathematicians and the behaviorists, we are able to identify seven elements in games. These are:

1. Purpose or raison d'être.
2. Procedures for action.
3. Rules governing action.
4. Number of required players.
5. Roles of participant.
6. Participant interaction patterns.
7. Results or pay-off.

In addition to these, personnel in the field of recreation have called attention to additional game elements which must be considered. A major element which recreation personnel have long been concerned with are the *abilities and skills required for participation*. Other elements which recreation personnel consider to be of importance are the *environmental requirements* and necessary *physical setting*, and the required *equipment* needed for participation in a game.

From a syntactical point of view then, games are composed of ten elements; possibly, additional elements will be identified at some future date. Presently, the ten elements to consider are as follows:

Element	Example
1. *Purpose of the game;* aim or goal, intent, the raison d'etre.	Checkmate one's opponent (chess). Bid and make a contract (bridge). Complete the course in as few strokes as possible (golf).
2. *Procedure for action;* specific operations, required courses of action, method of play.	Roll dice, move counter in clockwise direction around board, the number of spaces indicated on dice. Act in manner indicated by last space on which counter lands, *i.e.*, take a chance, pay rent, go to jail, etc. (Monopoly). Stand in box, toss two successive shoes at far stake, travel to that stake with opponent, tally score, pitch back to first stake (horseshoes).
3. *Rules governing action;* fixed principles that determine conduct and standards for behavior.	Go back where you were, you didn't say, "May I?" (Giant Steps)

Element	Example
N.B. Some games have very few rules, others have such elaborate sets of rules as to require a non-participant to keep track of infringement of the rules or to enforce the rules.	Regulations regarding weight and types of blows which may be employed. Panel of judges and referee determine infringement of rules, and have responsibility for enforcing rules (boxing).
4. *Number of required participants;* stated minimum or maximum number of persons needed for action to take place.	Minimum of two required, no stated maximum (hide-and-go-seek).
	Eleven men required for each team, minimum and maximum of twenty-two (football).
N.B. Sometimes minimum and maximum are identical.	
5. *Roles of participants;* indicated functions and status.	Goalkeeper, center, others. Each player has a different role (hockey).
N.B. Role and power function may differ for each participant or may be the same.	Each player has no more or less power than the others, and each functions in the same way (backgammon).
6. *Results or pay-off;* values assigned to the outcome of the action.	Money (black-jack). A kiss (spin-the-bottle). A gold medal (relay race).
7. *Abilities and skills required for action;* aspects of the three behavioral domains utilized in a given activity.	
(a) Cognitive domain includes—figural, symbolic, semantic, and behavioral informational content; and operational processes, such as cognition, memory, divergent and convergent production, and evaluation.	Remembering which cards have been played and from which suits, in order to play the best card (hearts).
(b) Sensory-motor domain includes—bodily movement, manipulative motor skills, coordination, sequences and patterns of movement, endurance factors, sight, hearing, etc.	Grasping the ball, walking to the foul line, releasing the ball, etc (bowling).

Element	Example
(c) Affective domain includes—semiotic factors which stimulate emotions, *i.e.*, anger, joy, affection, disgust, hate, etc. Offers opportunities for object-ties, transference, identification.	Having one's disc knocked off the court (extension of self) requires affective control to continue game (shuffleboard).
8. *Interaction patterns:*	
(a) Intra-individual—action taking place within the mind of a person or action involving the mind and a part of the body, but requiring no contact with another person or external object.	Pillow puzzles. Finger-flexion tricks.
(b) Extra-individual—action directed by a person toward an object in the environment, requiring no contact with another person.	Jigsaw puzzle. Solitaire.
(c) Aggregate—action directed by a person toward an object in the environment while in the company of other persons who are also directing action toward objects in the environment. Action is not directed toward each other, no inter-action between participants is required or necessary.	Bingo. Roulette.
(d) Inter-individual—action of a competitive nature directed by one person toward another.	Checkers. Tennis.
(e) Unilateral—action of a competitive nature among three or more persons, one of whom is an antagonist or "it." Interaction is in simultaneous competitive dyadic relationships.	Tag. Dodge ball.

Element	Example
(f) Multi-lateral—action of a competitive nature among three or more persons, no one person is an antagonist.	Scrabble. Poker.
(g) Intra-group—action of a co-operative nature by two or more persons intent upon reaching a mutual goal. Action requires positive verbal and non-verbal interaction.	Cat's cradle. Maori sticks.
(h) Inter-group—action of a competitive nature between two or more intra-groups.	Soccer. Basketball.
9. *Physical setting and environmental requirements:*	
(a) Physical setting—man-made or natural facility in which action takes places.	Four-walled court (squash). No special setting (charades).
(b) Environmental requirements —natural circumstances which are indispensable or obligatory.	Pool (water polo).
N.B. This element may not always be present.	No special environment (dominoes).
10. *Required equipment;* man-made or natural artifacts employed in the course of action.	Rackets, bird, net (badminton).
N.B. This element may not always be present.	No equipment necessary (20 questions).

A variety of interesting questions are presented when one examines this list of elements—questions that demand rigorous scholarly inquiry. The most important question to consider is the notion that these elements are present in all games. Subsequent questions might be asked about each of the elements. For example, can the interaction patterns be viewed in a developmental hierarchy? Does one pattern have to be mastered before a participant can function effectively in another pattern, or are the patterns mutually exclusive? Using Guilford's model for *The Structure of Intellect,* can one delimit cognitive process in the same way that we are able to delimit sensory-motor process in a game?[6] Are there other, more effective theoretical models regarding cognition which would lend themselves to this purpose. What of the affective domain—is a psychoanalytic frame of reference the most effective one to use in delimiting ability and skill in this area? Are setting and environment one interrelated element, or are they really two elements? Are there more than eight interaction patterns that can be identified?

Redl, Gump, and Sutton-Smith have indicated that there are a number of behavioral dimensions other than the ones cited which should be considered when examining games. Thus, this exposition must of necessity be considered a preliminary excursion into the structure of games, and until considerable effort has been spent beyond this theoretical attempt, it must remain just that. However, it is hoped that some of these thoughts will stimulate others in this direction.

---

[6] J. P. Guilford, "Intelligence: 1965 Model," *American Psychologist,* **21,** (1), January, 1966, pp. 20–26.

Mathematical Game Theory— Selected References

Bernard, J. "The Theory of Games of Strategy as a Modern Sociology of Conflict," *American Journal of Sociology,* **59,** 1954, pp. 411–424.

Blackwell, D. and Girshick, M. A. *Theory of Games and Statistical Decisions,* New York: John Wiley and Sons, 1954.

Braithwaite, R. B. *Theory of Games As A Tool for the Moral Philosopher,* Cambridge, England: Cambridge University Press, 1955.

Burger, E. *Introduction to the Theory of Games,* Englewood Cliffs: Prentice-Hall, 1963.

Davenport, Wm. "Jamaican Fishing: A Game Theory Analysis," *Yale University Papers in Anthropology,* **59,** 1960, pp. 3–11.

David, F. N. *Games, Gods, and Gambling: The Origins and History of Probability and Statistical Ideas,* New York: Hafner Publishing Co., 1962.

Dresher, M. *Advances in Game Theory,* Princeton, N.J.: Princeton University Press, 1964.

Dresher, M. and Kuhn, H. W. *Contributions to the Theory of Games,* Princeton, N.J.: Princeton University Press, 1950–59. (4 vols. *Annals of Mathematics Studies* Number 24, 25, 39, 40).

Harsanyi, J. C. "On the Rationality Postulates Underlying the Theory of Cooperative Games," *Journal of Conflict Resolution,* **5,** 1961, pp. 179–196.

Harsanyi, J. C. "Rationality Postulates for Bargaining Solutions in Cooperative and Noncooperative Games," *Management Science,* **9,** 1962, pp. 141–153.

Luce, R. D. and Raiffa, H. *Games and Decisions,* New York: John Wiley and Sons, 1957.

McDonald, J. D. *Strategy in Poker, Business, and War*, New York: Norton, 1950.

McKinsey, J. C. *Introduction to the Theory of Games*, New York: McGraw-Hill, 1952.

May, F. B. *Introduction to Games of Strategy*, Boston: Allyn and Bacon, 1964.

Nash, J. F. "Noncooperative Games," *Annals of Mathematics*, 54, 1951, pp. 286–295.

Nash, J. F. "The Bargaining Problem," *Econometrica*, 18, 1950, pp. 155–162.

Nash, J. F. "Two-person Cooperative Games," *Econometrica*, 21, 1953, pp. 128–140.

Rapoport, A. *Fights, Games, and Debates*, Ann Arbor, Michigan; University of Michigan Press, 1960.

Rapoport, A. *Two Person Game Theory*, Ann Arbor, Michigan: University of Michigan Press, 1966.

Rapoport, A. "The Use and Misuse of Game Theory," *Scientific American*, 207(6), 1962, pp. 108–114, 117–118.

Rapoport, A. and Chammah, A. M. *Prisoner's Dilemma: A Study of Conflict and Cooperation*, Ann Arbor, Michigan: University of Michigan Press, 1965.

Shubik, M. *Game Theory and Related Approaches to Social Behavior*, New York: John Wiley and Sons, 1964.

Shubik, M. *Readings in Game Theory and Political Behavior*, New York: Doubleday, 1954.

Ventzel, E. *Lectures on Game Theory*, Delhi: Hindustan Publishing Company, 1961.

Von Neumann, J. and Morgenstein, O. *Theory of Games and Economic Behavior*, New York: John Wiley and Sons, 3rd Ed., 1964; Original edition, 1944.

Williams, J. D. *The complete Strategist, Being A Primer on the Theory of Games*, New York: McGraw Hill, 1954.

CHAPTER 13

THE FUNCTION OF GAMES

By defining games as an exercise of voluntary control systems we have, in effect, decided their function. Still, such a choice has a high recency valence. Social and behavioral science has been accustomed to explaining games in terms of other functional systems, not in terms of voluntary control systems. Any review of historical approaches to explanation must take these other points of view into account. Although these approaches are innumerable and devious, they will be summarized here as consisting of *psychogenic* or *sociogenic* alternatives. The first explains the game in terms of its antecedents, usually psychological, but permitting also physiological and genetic alternatives. The second explains the game in terms of its outcomes, practical usefulness, training and rehearsal values.

The *psychogenic* approach is illustrated in this section with a reading by Reider on the history of chess. In Reider's account we have a characteristic statement that the game gives expression to, and relieves anxieties derived from antecedent psychic states. As he says, "the fascination of the game may very well depend in part on the fact that the devotees experience, sometimes with full measure of affect, the passions and the mysteries of the unconscious."[1]

This point of view, customarily associated with psychoanalysis, has antecedents in the Aristotelian theory of dramatic catharsis, and has entered into common parlance to the point where many persons speak of playing games to relieve their tensions. In psychoanalytic writings one finds a number of different emphases, most of them presaged by Robert Waelder's classic 1933 article "The Psychoanalytic Theory of Play," in

---

[1] Reider, N. "Chess, Oedipus, and the Mater Dolorosa," *International Journal of Psychoanalysis*, **40**, 1959, p. 332.

which he emphasized (summarizing Freud's views on the matter), that play leads not only to tension reduction, but also has values for wish fulfillment, for bringing about a change from the passive to the active, and for giving a temporary leave of absence from reality.

A typical early application to games was Roheim's 1943 article "Children's Games and Rhymes of Duau," where he sought to explain games of the type in which there are good mothers and witches, and in which children entwine each other in arms, clasp each other, divide up into groups, and separate the child players from the mother player, and so forth. Roheim's explanation was that the children in these games were compensating for their separation from the mother. "The loss of the mother . . . is not an irretrievable loss for in the group the playing child finds a substitute for the absent mother."[2] Another, similar psychoanalytic but perhaps more remote interpretation is to be found in Pickford's distinction between Rugby football and association football. In Rugby the ball is handled, whereas in soccer it is propelled with the foot. Pickford presents the opinion:

It might be said that in Association Football the ball is symbolically a dirty and dangerous object, or that it is so powerful in unconscious meaning that it must not be touched with the hand under penalty of foul play. In Rugby Football the ball might be regarded as a loveable object that every player tries to caress and hold as if it were a valued possession. In psychoanalytic terms these attitudes suggest that to Rugby enthusiasts the ball is a symbol of loved maternal images, while to the Association Football enthusiast it is a symbol of paternal potency which is somewhat feared and requires special forms of taboo or control.[3]

Although at present there is little evidence to sustain interpretations of this character, their quite speculative nature should not be taken to suggest that relationships between antecedent states and subsequent play are unworthy of investigation. There is, in fact, a great deal of anecdotal material and a scattering of more systematic studies to suggest that such relationships do exist.[4] The largest number of such studies, however, have to do with play, and derive from work with play diagnosis

[2] Roheim, G. "Children's Games and Rhymes of Duau (Normandy Island, N.G.)," *American Anthropologist*, 45, 1943, p. 110.

[3] Pickford, P. W. "The Psychology of the History and Organization of Association Football," *British Journal of Psychology*, 31, 1940, p. 132.

[4] Beisser, A. *The Madness in Sports*. New York: Appleton-Century-Crofts, 1967; Johnson, W. R. *Science and Medicine of Exercise and Sports*. New York: Harper, 1960; Slovenko, R., and Knight, J. A. *Motivations in Play, Games, and Sports*. Springfield, Ill.: Charles C Thomas, 1967.

and play therapy rather than with games. These studies will be considered in the companion volume on *Childs Play*. In passing, we would mention the names of Erik Erikson and Lilli Peller who have been perhaps the most active interpreters of play and games within the psychoanalytic tradition.

The greatest body of empirical work on games, within this same psychoanalytic tradition derives from the work of Fritz Redl and collaborators. Like Erikson, Redl emphasized the ego supportive character of the games. He says:

Our hyperaggressive and extremely destructive children are in need of a good deal of program activity which involves the happy discharge of surplus aggression, diversion of destructiveness to excited large muscle activity, etc. At the same time, however, these children suffer not only from a surplus of piled-up hatred and aggression, but also from a severe disturbance of the very control machinery which is supposed to cope with it. This means that if we expose them to program opportunities which involve activity and aggression, they can rarely take them without much interference from the adult to "keep things going" and to "avoid the worst." This is, however, where the worst aspect of the problem hits us directly in the face; for remember these are also the "children who hate." This means that adult interference, rather than being considered a welcome help, is rejected or reacted to with fury and counter-attack, and even the helpful attempt at umpiring to make a game possible is usually interpreted simply as hostile meddling of an enemy from above.

It was while in this predicament that we felt the discovery of the wide range of "depersonalized controls" as a special relief. This is what we mean: In almost any neighbourhood there are certain activities, behavioral customs, and games, the "rules" for which, though unwritten, are well known and automatically accepted by everybody. Even our very disturbed youngsters commanded a halt to their total rule rejection when it came to such well-ingrained "neighbourhood codes." In fact, sometimes it seemed to us that those were the only areas where something akin to a conscience or a feeling of decency seemed to be left.

. . . What a wonderful aid in our predicament! If we could only find enough such activity structures with their natural group codes encrusted around them, then we could really "step out for a while" and let the built-in behaviour codes of the game in question do the controlling. . . . We wished there were organized research on this. As it is, we had to worm our way through trial and error and through frantic efforts of "game analysis" in the terms of "native group code relevance." Our findings are still deplorably thin compared with what we think can be found in the uranium mines of psycho-sociological research, were we only given the chance to exploit them.[5]

Some of the thinking that went into efforts to mine this "uranium deposit" is indicated by the game dimensions listed in the previous chapter, and by the article on *It games* in this chapter. Other ideas are included in a chapter by Redl: "The Impact of Game-Ingredients on Children's Play Behavior," in a work *Group Processes*, New York: Josiah Macy, 1959.

The *sociogenic* approach holds by contrast that games are to be understood in terms of what they do for society, rather than in terms of how they meet the needs of the individual. The emphasis is on the preparatory or training value of the games. A primary argument would be, for example, that individuals get into games because they are rewarded for so doing by public applause, honor, group pressure, and so forth. On these grounds the individual's psychology is not important unless it disqualifies him from participation. Within a culture there is usually a sufficient community of motivational structure (for example, to compete and succeed), that idiosyncratic motives need not be taken into account. Given this basic assumption, there follow various types of arguments about the "preparation" that is afforded by the games.

In the nineteenth century two types of rehearsal theory were dominant. Many schoolmen, for example, claimed that games had a character training value. The leadership and teamsmanship learned on the playing field were said to carry over into life. Biologically oriented writers emphasized the more basic exercise of motor and intellectual functions. In this century, emphasis has been on the social and symbolic value of play and game participation. George H. Mead's contention that the player learns to take the role of the other into account through his play and games, is a well-known example. Less well known perhaps are the various suggestions that children acquire moral values through games;[6] develop self-sustaining interests;[7] develop character because the game provides a testing ground for character without too much danger. Goffman[8] says pertinently, that in a game the player can keep his character up and his costs down. Others say that the player can develop various interactional

[5] Redl, F. and Wineman, D. *Children Who Hate*. Glencoe: Free Press, 1951, pp. 110–111.

[6] Piaget, J., op. cit., 1951.

[7] Moore, O. K., and Anderson, A. R. "Some Puzzling Aspects of Interaction," *Review of Metaphysics*, 15 (3), March, 1962, pp. 409–433.

[8] Goffman, E. *Interaction Ritual: Essays on Face to Face Behavior*. New York: Anchor Books, 1967.

strategies of relevance to interpersonal behavior.[9] Many of these writings are individually rich. Unfortunately, they have lead to little systematic research, so that we have many ideas of the ways in which games may prepare persons but little evidence on what they actually do. But to say this is merely to repeat a point already made in the section on usages— that many military men, businessmen, economists, educationists, and others use games to prepare students for various functions, with little evidence that they are particularly successful. Still, unless all these professionals are being misled, games have some sort of preparatory value, and can, therefore, be legitimately explained in that way. We should mention at this point the large-scale but as yet unpublished studies of Rivka Eifermann of Hebrew University, Israel, which are within the sociological framework.

Currently, the largest body of scientific evidence on games has been provided by Roberts & Sutton-Smith, who have claimed that their data may be read to support both the psychogenic and sociogenic viewpoints. Their cross-cultural studies involving 50 to 100 preliterate groups show that games have empirical connections both with antecedent states of anxiety and with general cultural variables for which they might be thought to be a preparation. We include one of the earlier articles by these two investigators. As most of their subsequent work is either unpublished or widely scattered, the following summary will introduce the reader to some of their major findings and explanatory notions.

In their cross-cultural study of games, Roberts and Sutton-Smith found that games were related statistically to innumerable cultural variables.[10] A description of each of their basic game types and the related cultural correlates illustrates the notion that the games are encapsulated within larger controlling cultural configurations. They dealt with three types of games: physical, chance, and strategy. Physical skill games had the widest ethnographic distribution, games of chance next, and games of strategy the smallest.

Cultures with Games of Physical Skill Only

This game category established the minimal level or baseline against which the remaining game categories could be compared. The physical

[9] Szasz, T. S. *The Myth of Mental Illness.* New York: Hoeber Medical Division, Harper and Row, 1961; Berne, E. *Games People Play.* New York: Grove Press, 1964; and Haley, J. *Strategies of Psychotherapy.* Grune and Stratton, 1963.

[10] Roberts, J. M., and Sutton-Smith, B. "Child Training and Game Involvement," *Ethnology,* 1962, pp. 166–185. Reprinted in the *Bobbs-Merrill Series in Social Science,* 1966; and "Cross-Cultural Correlates of Games of Chance," *Behavior Science Notes,* 3, 1966, pp. 131–144.

game cultures were found in tropical regions. Their subsistence economics and technologies were simple. Their communities were small, the level of political integration was low, class stratification was absent, the judicial system was undeveloped, child socialization was easy with low anxieties and conflicts, sexual satisfaction was high, the cultures were not warlike. In general, therefore, these cultures gave the impression of simplicity, particularly when they were contrasted with the cultures with games of chance and strategy. As contrasted with the "no game cultures," which were referred to in the introductory chapter, there seems to have been increased sex segregation and more independent rather than extended families, which, in these physical-game cultures, suggested the possibility of important needs for an emphasis on masculine self-reliance in hunting, fishing, and so forth in these cultures. The ethnographic accounts, for example, contained many records of the elders encouraging the young boys in games of spear-throwing and archery, which had an obvious relationship to the adaptive skills required of males in the adult cultures.

Cultures with Games of Chance

In all probability all cultures possessing games of chance also possess games of physical skill. In addition, however, some of them possess games of strategy. In many ways the chance-game category was the most complex of the three pure types, and it was the least easy to understand theoretically.

In general, chance cultures displayed a wide range of cultural complexity varying from quite simple cultures to the most complex known today. Yet, since these games were fundamentally simpler than games of strategy, and since games of strategy were known to be associated with cultural complexity, it was reasonable to assume that chance playing began in relatively simple settings. The most important conclusion was that games of chance appeared to flourish in the presence of environmental, individual, and social uncertainty regardless of the relative complexity of the cultures in which they occurred. The relationships that were the basis for this conclusion are detailed more fully elsewhere.[11] A game of chance in such cultures appeared to be a way of making up one's mind, with the help of benevolent Fate, when life conditions were sufficiently uncertain that one had no better instrumental procedures for decision making.

---

[11] Roberts and Sutton-Smith, op. cit., 1966.

Cultures with Games of Strategy

Cultures possessing games of strategy were at a higher level of cultural complexity than the cultures in the other game categories. Larger settlements, more complicated subsistence patterns, higher technology, higher levels of political integration, jurisdiction, social stratification, occupational specialization, and many other traits confirmed the fact that these cultures were complex. It is not hard to envisage games of strategy as forms of social-system learning in contexts of this character.

In a parallel study of folktales, furthermore, it was established that folktales with strategic elements flourished in the same cultural environments as games of strategy.[12]

Cultures Possessing Games of Physical Skill, Games of Chance, and Games of Strategy

These were the most complex of all of the cultures discussed. Every modern industrial society was in this group and most, if not all, of the classic cultures known to history. They appeared to be an amalgam of the general physical-skill tradition with an overlay of chance and then, very importantly, an overlay of strategy. The antecedent conditions for involvement in both chance and strategy appeared to be present.

These, then, are a sample of the findings from a number of studies. They challenge the traditional puritanic view that games are of no fundamental significance. This type of data, in fact, makes it difficult to resist the view that the games are embedded in macroscopic control systems; that games of physical skill exist because of the role they play in cultural hunting and warfare, that games of chance exist because of the role they play in cultural divinatory decision-making processes, and games of strategy exist because of the role they play in cultural strategic decision making. The game is an expression of the larger system and perhaps a formative part of it also. Any comprehension of the character of such patterns, however, must take into account both the psychogenic correlates (child training variables) and the sociogenic correlates (political and religious variables that have been referred to above.) In several articles, Roberts and Sutton-Smith have presented a theory to account for the presence of both of these psychogenic and sociogenic correlates.[13] This theory states that the individual and psychological

[12] Roberts, J. M., Sutton-Smith, B., and Kendon, A. "Strategy in Games and Folk Tales," *Journal of Social Psychology*, 61, 1963, pp. 185–199.

[13] Roberts, J. M. and Sutton-Smith, B. op. cit., 1962, and "Rubrics of Competitive Behavior," *Journal of Genetic Psychology*, 105, June, 1964, pp. 13–37.

motivation for game playing is the presence in the player of anxieties and conflicts induced by antecedent child-training processes. The game is enjoyable to the player because it consists in a symbolic statement of these conflicts, and because in the course of the buffered learning that the game provides, the player develops confidence and competence to handle the real life situations toward which the original anxieties point. A brief illustration must suffice. On the basis of an earlier symbolic analysis of children's central-person games (for example, tagging, hide and seek, red rover), these investigators had postulated that these games represent the child's anxieties about exercising independence during the transition from primary to secondary ties. In the course of the game the child can either manifest the endangering independence by running out from safe bases and tackling strange persons (the *It*) or he can retreat to the safety of the home or base.[14] A cross-cultural test for the presence of these types of games demonstrated a significantly greater concern with independence training for females in those cultures where these games were present. In addition, in those same cultures there were marriage customs requiring the girl to go out from her own kin group and marry relative strangers. It was this double relationship of the game both to the inducing child-training procedure and the required adult cultural performance that led Roberts and Sutton-Smith to entitle their theory a *conflict-enculturation* theory of games. Such a theory was, of course, based only on empirically demonstrated correlates. It was not actually demonstrated that the child training did induce these game proclivities or that the games did prepare the children for their role performances, although the great usage of games in social science theorizing, and in war and business simulation does not make it difficult to believe that games actually do influence their players.

If these theses derived from cross-cultural work were true, however, then it would follow that if game players were studied in this culture, there should be systematic connections between their personalities and their game playing (the psychogenesis), and between the game playing and their skills (the sociogenesis). Empirical work that has sought to establish such connections is illustrated by the paper on "Achievement and Strategic Competence," in this chapter.

As a result of this work Roberts and Sutton-Smith have argued that the primary function of games is to act as buffered models of power contests. They suggest that ordinarily activity provides few ready tests of power, but that in games of skill, strategy, and fortune, a player can test out his capacities and fortunes in a buffered fashion or, as Goffman has said more

---

[14] Sutton-Smith, B. "A Formal Analysis of Game Meaning," *Western Folklore Quarterly*, Berkeley, California, **18**, 1959, pp. 13–24.

recently, without having to count up the costs too seriously. For them *games are models of power* into which the players are led by a correspondence between the patterns of play and their own aroused motivational systems. In the above example the girls aroused about independence by child training procedures readily found involvement in a game where alternations between dependence and independence (the bases and the free territory) were a part of the game structure. By playing the game in turn, the girls acquired a confidence in the face of dangerous powers (monsters, bears, *It-figures*), which had preparatory value for their subsequent marriage among strangers.

Obviously other interpretations are possible. This theory has the special virtue that it subsumes without displacing the more classic accounts of games in terms of their psychic or social values. However, it should be made quite clear that this interpretation of games in terms of power functioning, although appropriate to the research introduced in this chapter, is quite at variance with the emphases of the previous section. One would conclude from the military, business, social science, and educational usage of games that any interpretation of games would have to focus on cognitive functioning. Again, from diagnostic and therapeutic usages one would expect a focus on affective or sensory-motor functions. Though, as we have mentioned, the research within education seems to imply that the players are better motivated learners rather than better learners, which perhaps suggests that it is the conations (strivings and determinations) in games that are their most important type of functioning. Whether there is a greater intrinsic connection between such conative functions of games and the power functions presented here, than between cognition and power, or affective states and power, is something for future research to decide.

A major point must remain—despite the presentation of games in terms of power functions, cognitive function and affective functions are also candidates for the theoretical grasp of games. Within the definition of games offered in the introduction and the previous chapter the important issue is not the content of the game (whether about strategic power, business information, or spelling), but the fact that these elements are used as a part of the voluntary opposition between players in order to arrive at a reckoning that gives one of them an advantage.

GAMES AS VOLUNTARY CONTROL SYSTEMS

Having thus surveyed the coventional approaches to game functioning, we wish to conclude with a few further notes on our own preference for the role of explanation.

In the introduction it was suggested that each person defines games in his own way—the anthropologists and folklorists in terms of historical origins; the military men, businessmen, and educators in terms of usages; the social scientists in terms of psychological and social functions. There is overwhelming evidence in all this that the meaning of games is, in part, a function of the ideas of those who think about them.

And yet for as long as we know, men have been playing games with great energy and involvement. So that apart from their own reasons for playing them, or apart from the reasons given by later scholars, the games have always had some compulsive necessity of their own. It is fitting, therefore, to conclude this chapter with further statements on games as exercises of voluntary control systems.

It is possible for all of the things that were said about game function and game structure in the previous chapters to be correct, or if not correct, then incorrect only by omission of more key variables, and yet for games still not to be adequately explained. This occurs because most discussions of games are conducted without adequate attention to the underlying assumptions about adaptation. This omission has usually been disguised by the domination of pragmatic and utilitarian concepts throughout the recent history of the physical and social sciences. That is, behaviors have been judged by their contribution to the organism's survival, tension-reduction, or adjustment. Although the adoption of such utilitarian frameworks appears to have led to considerable insights when dealing with basic adjustive systems, their contribution has been nowhere near as evident when applied to those expressive phenomena that are the subject matter of this work: games.

Indeed, games as behavior systems have had a fluctuating historical and theoretical career. When regarded as utilitarian, they have been conceptualized in one of two ways. Historically, on the one hand, in a work-oriented industrial civilization, they have often been derogated as trivial and unimportant. By contrast, particular sports and physical activities have long been lauded as sources of character training and delinquency reduction. In parallel terms, but on the theoretical level, there have been conceptualizations of play like those of Freud and Piaget in which the play has been said to be only a "projective" or "assimilative" expression of antecedent states and useful mainly as a means of assuaging anxiety or bringing feelings of mastery in relation to those antecedent states. And in contrary fashion, there have been conceptualizations of games, like those of Groos and G. H. Mead, in which play has been said to be a form of serious preparation and role rehearsal. In the first part of this chapter we have presented Roberts and Sutton-Smith's compromise position, which seeks to reconcile both of these classic approaches. Still, neither of these utilitarian theories or that reconciliation pays great attention to the game phenomenon itself except as an epiphenomenon of these other more important ends that are said to control it.

As an alternative to these approaches, some writers have opined that expressive phenomena such as games, play, laughter, babbling, and art are adaptive phenomena whose "utility" lies in their value as terminal representations for the organisms involved. "Symbolic forms are not imitations but organs of reality."[15] If we look only at what is functional in such behavior systems, they say, we are adopting a reductive point of view and neglecting what is important to the player. It is an amusing, if slightly paradoxical, support for this point of view to find that in some recent research with chimpanzees the opportunity to play compares favorably with food as a reinforcer for simple lever-pushing responses. From a reinforcement point of view, this makes play a consummatory or goal response, not merely an instrumental or utilitarian activity.[16] On the phenomenological level, with humans at least, what the player experiences is a sense of being possessed. He is under the control of forces that at rare times he can himself scarcely control, yet as we know the pretense quality of the game means that he can control them. Their vividness is only of the players own making and could only occur because these are, in effect, voluntary control exercises. Whether those who practice such voluntary control exercises also become skilled at other voluntary control procedures we do not as yet know. That is certainly the phylogenetic verdict and the verdict of Section II in this book. In the meantime, this discussion in terms of voluntary control systems provides us with a good explanation for the enjoyment and popularity of games, while we await more fundamental knowledge on their individual implications. The basic structural roles of antithesis, rules, and disequilibrial outcomes appear to provide us with a way of defining the expression of voluntary control through games, and for distinguishing games from other phenomena such as play.

The major purpose of this book has been to introduce an increasing group of practitioners and researchers to the area of game scholarship. This has been our game, and we trust that we have played it well.

We conclude this chapter with three readings regarding the function of games, and a final list of selected references that offer the many points of view about function.

15 Cassirer, E. *Language and Myth*. New York: Dover, 1946, p. 8.

16 Mason, W. A. "Motivational Aspects of Social Responsiveness in Young Chimpanzees," in H. W. Stevenson, E. H. Hess, and H. L. Rheingold (Eds.) *Early Behavior*. New York: John Wiley and Sons, 1967.

21

Chess, Oedipus, and the Mater Dolorosa

NORMAN REIDER

The psycho-analytic study of play and games has been particularly rewarding, but no game is so full of possibilities for such study as that of chess. Chess is the royal game for many reasons. It crystallizes within its elaborate structure the family romance, is replete with symbolism, and has rich potentialities for granting satisfactions and for sublimation of drives. Not without reason is it the one game that, since its invention around A.D. 600, has been played in most of the world, has captivated the imagination and interest of millions, and has been the source of great sorrows and great pleasures.

My introduction has two purposes. First, it indicates the numerous facets inherent in a study of chess: the fascination and the extent of the addiction to the game; the psychological factors involved in its historical development; its social and therapeutic value; its legal involvements; its relation to love and aggression; the problem of genius in chess; the characterological problem of its players and their style of play; and ego functions as manifested in play, especially the distinctions between the psychological meanings of the game, its pieces and rules, and the psychology of the players. My intention is to develop these themes more extensively in later essays and to stimulate the interest of others in these problems. Secondly, this exposition is also meant to convey some of the quality and flavor of the game, especially to non-players, or to those who have never been addicted to or fascinated by chess, so that they may be prepared for the complexities of the legends.

 SOURCE. *International Journal of Psychoanalysis*, **40**, 1959, pp. 320–333.

THE ATTRACTION OF THE GAME

Throughout the ages chess has been praised in poetry, prose, painting, and even music, as witness a few testimonials from devotees. "Chess is the art of the intellect" (42).[1] "Chess is so ancient that by that distinction alone it seems taken beyond the category of games altogether; and it has been said that it probably would have perished long ago, if it had not been destined to live forever" (6, p. 1). "There must have been a time when men were demigods or they could not have invented chess. Could it indeed have been invented? I am almost tempted to believe that chess is a discovered fragment of inexhaustible, ever-creative nature" (69). "Chess is catholic and common to every country. It possesses a history, language, literature, poetry, prose, science and art of its own" (73, p. 5). "I have always had a slight feeling of pity for the man who has no knowledge of chess, just as I would pity the man who has remained ignorant of love. Chess, like love, like music, has the power to make men happy" (74, p. 4).

The universality of chess provides a wide range of satisfactions, from the pragmatic and practical to the aesthetic and poetic. At one extreme is the utilitarian Benjamin Franklin (29), who wrote: "The game of chess is not merely an idle amusement; several very valuable qualities of the mind, useful in the course of human life, are to be acquired and strengthened by it so as to become ready on all occasions; for life is a kind of chess in which we have often points to gain, and competitors or adversaries to contend with, in which there is a vast variety of good and ill events that are, in some degree, the effect of prudence or the want of it." At the other extreme are those who are impressed with its beauty (46, 68). "The chess board is a microcosm; and like Greek drama it fixes our minds on what is high and noble. It deals with the fate of kings and queens, and yet, like the Christian religion, it teaches that the meanest pawn has the stuff of royalty in it and may win its crown. It is a lesson in political science, showing the limited range of royal power and yet insisting on its ultimate importance" (60).

Others, by contrast, are fascinated by the libidinal elements of chess and disturbed by its destructiveness, realizing that aggression is the soul of the game. Burton (10), though acknowledging that chess has been recommended as a cure for depression, had his own opinion of it. "Chess play is a good and witty exercise of the mind for some kind of men . . .

---

[1] I do not know if Jones was aware that Gustavus Selenus made the first description of chess in like terms (*Das Schach oder Koenig Spiel*, Leipzig, 1616). But priorities in such remarks are of no moment. Many others have said the same, all recognizing the synthesis of beauty and reason in chess.

and fit for such melancholy persons that are idle and have impertinent thoughts, or are troubled with cares; nothing better to distract their mind and alter their meditation; invented (some say) by the general of an army in a famine to keep the soldiers from mutiny. But if it proceed from overmuch study in such a case it may do more harm than good; it is a game too troublesome for some men's brain, too full of anxiety, and all out as bad as study; and beside it is a testing cholerick game and very offensive to him that loseth the mate." In a milder yet still disparaging mood, he reported: "In Muscovy, where they live in stoves and hothouses all winter long, come seldom or little abroad, it is a game very necessary and therefore in those parts much used."

Chess has had for many a diabolical attraction, which enchained them, as if its play were an evil habit. "The devil was a great fool to use so many machinations to make poor Job lose his patience. He had only to engage him in a game of chess" (52). This remark, made in 1693, was echoed by H. G. Wells (78) more than 200 years later. "The passion for playing chess is one of the most unaccountable in the world. It slaps the theory of natural selection in the face. It is the most absorbing of occupations. The least satisfying of desires. A nameless excrescence upon life. It annihilates a man. You have, let us say, a promising politician, a rising artist that you wish to destroy. Dagger or bomb are archaic and unreliable—but teach him, inoculate him with chess."

The great damnation of the game has come from those who have been plagued by it. None has expressed so convincingly his sad and resigned self-denial as a minister who in 1680 wrote a letter, giving ten reasons why he refused to play the game (50). Among them is one of the most beautiful lines in English literature: "It hath not done with me when I have done with it." Truly this one sentence could be the motto for all addictions.

THE VICISSITUDES OF CHESS

The early history of chess is filled with developments and episodes which are worthy subjects for psychological study, of which a few will be mentioned: (a) its moral and legal aspects; (b) its historical and cultural aspects; and (c) its libidinal and aggressive elements.

Chess lent itself easily during the Middle Ages as a model for education and morality. Around 1200 Rabbi ben Ezra wrote the first didactic poem in Hebrew on the subject of chess and about the same time Pope Innocent III wrote a morality on chess. The second book, in English, published in 1474 by Caxton, was a morality based on chess.

Chess has been encouraged; it has also been forbidden. In times of stress, when authorities felt people should be punished, the game was forbidden, along with games played with cards and with dice. But some-how its appeal made possible many exceptions. For instance, Jews in the Middle Ages were forbidden to play on the Sabbath all games except chess (40). Pregnant women were allowed to indulge in a game of chess at a time when everyone else was forbidden to do so (25, p. 181).

One practically uncharted field is the derivation of the game from the board games in which magic played a part. Another area of inquiry is the study of the changes that the game, its rules and the power of the pieces underwent in different social and cultural settings—for example, the brilliant research by Colby (16), who turned his attention to the problem of the appearance of the queen on the board and the increase in the strength of the queen in the latter part of the fifteenth century. Originally, the piece now known as the queen was the vizier, a title understandable historically, because in the Arabic world the king was accompanied in battle by his vizier. At one time in the twelfth century the queen began replacing the vizier, and this may very well have cor-responded to the time of the glorification of Mary by the Church. But as yet the queen had only those powers that the king had, or perhaps a few more. Suddenly, about 1485, in Italy, the queen began to be the most powerful piece on the board. Colby presented some historical evidence that this "wild game" may very well have originated in Northern Italy. Studying the prominent women in Italian history of the time, he found that Caterina Sforza was married to a weak prince who did not take care of his duchy. She herself donned armour, led troops into the battle, collected taxes, and protected her partner. Since then the queen has been the most powerful piece on the board.

Future researches into the psychological aspects of chess must of necessity take into consideration historical and cultural factors, as Colby has done. For example, one of the most interesting features is how, in the past, the royal game was definitely restricted to royalty. Commoners were at times even punished for being caught playing the game. In this early era, when chess was a royal game, many a court had its chess master attached to it, just as it had its musician or jester. The chess master taught the young women of the court to become accomplished in chess because in those days much love play took place over the chess board. Some of the tenderest love poems and allegories (46, 68, 56) are in the language of chess. Nowadays the combination of chess and love is ex-tremely rare. The one exception is Gustav Schenk's publication (69) in 1937 of a book of love letters in chess terms, truly an anachronism.

Likewise, in its early days chess was a violent game. In numerous stories (56, pp. 95, 113, 356, 413, 431–432, 436, 443, 501) the chess board was the scene of violence and murder, and in one reference (81) of actual castration. But all this violence and love have slowly dwindled away, as the game has become a democratic one; it has been sublimated into a mathematical science with a somewhat masculine, homosexual flavor. For example, one chess journal in the 1880s was named "Bruderschaft"; alas, it was shortlived.

Chess also had its humor and its insights. In a contest held by a British newspaper on why chess does not appeal to the English, one contributor explained that "Britons never, never shall be Slavs" (59). And as to the proficiency of the Slavs at chess: "In a free government the Russian might appear with equal advantage as in the military department; intelligent, active, reflecting, and endowed with a spirit of calculation. He might succeed in every pursuit; at present he excels only in chess." This was not written by a present-day anti-Soviet writer. It appeared in the *Critical Review* of June 1792 (46, p. 296). How much the world moves can be illustrated by the fact that more than 150 years later Bosshard (9) similarly tried to explain the cause of the Russian superiority in chess by an "ethnopsychological origin." According to his neoracist theory, the specific talent of "Eastern people" for chess is due to innate intellectual powers, slyness, among others, which reveal the qualities that make primitive peoples superior in chess to the "cultured nations."

A SUBJECT FOR PSYCHOLOGICAL INQUIRY

Because of its fascination, chess has lent itself easily to psychological inquiry. I wish now to indicate the areas of some of these efforts, dividing them into three groups. First is the group of speculations and cogitations on the subject, which might well come under the general heading of the "Philosophy of Chess." Writings by Wekerle (79), Junk (44) and Lasker (49) belong to this group. Of these Lasker, once chess champion of the world, styling himself a philosopher, made perhaps the most consistent efforts of anyone not a trained psychological investigator towards understanding the mysteries of the game. He suggested that competition is one of the necessary elements of life and that chess provides artistic, competitive outlets. He also observed that our satisfactions with the game are directly proportional to the kind of obstacles we have to overcome in winning.

A quite insightful remark was that of Reti (66, p. 4) who wrote of the emotional impact made by a successful sacrifice in the game, "since it comes at the risk of material and the victory of the weaker material over the stronger material, it gives the impression of a symbol of the mastery of mind over matter." Reti also tried to understand the psychology of various chess masters, that is, the nature of their particular style of play. The non-psychological literature is full of such common-sense attempts to understand the success and failure of the masters, and some of these works are remarkably good on an intuitive basis, considering the general lack of sound psychological training on the part of the authors. Among these is a study of the psychology of defeat by Vityazev (76). Writers in this first group are also preoccupied with whether chess is a science or an art, and even as late as 1954 Bykov (12) showed concern with this topic.

These writers were struggling with one of the central themes in chess, the problem of man's mastery over a sublimated aggressive situation, although they themselves did not wholly appreciate this aspect of their inquiries. Chess as a military game provides warfare which is organized, controlled, circumscribed, and regulated. These contrasts between magic and reason, chance and planning, and primary and secondary processes, Collins (17) nicely epitomized: "There are two classes of men, those who are content to yield to circumstances, and who play whist; and those who aim to control circumstances, who play chess."

A second group of writers, the academic psychologists, dealt more systematically with some aspects of chess. The earliest classic in the field, Binet's (5), a study of chess players, and especially of those who played chess blindfolded, is interesting even though not particularly productive. Comparable studies were made by Cleveland (14), who studied the learning process and intelligence in relationship to ability to play, and Buttenwieser (11), who compared the relationship of age to skill in chess playing. A more modern attempt to deal with the problem of intelligence and skill in chess was made by H. Davidson (21, pp. 190–196).

The recent increase of interest in chess in the Soviet Union has turned some of its psychologists to formal studies of the psychological processes in chess playing and especially to its psychological effects upon the personality. Diakov, Petrovsky and Rudik (24) gave the participants in the International Chess Tournament in Moscow in 1925 a series of psychometric tests concerning memory, attention, various other intellectual functions, and also the Rorschach Test. These Soviet efforts were not followed up and gave way, obviously under the influence of official attitudes, to a new kind of moralizing and philosophizing about chess, such as appeared in the writings of Vasilevsky (75), who was concerned about the value of chess in the development of intellect and in the maintenance of proper mental hygiene. Likewise, Rochlin (67) discussed creativity in chess, obviously struggling with the problem of whether chess was creative enough to justify continued Soviet governmental sponsorship.

The formal psychological studies that Diakov and his colleagues initiated were not resumed until DeGroot (23) published his thorough study of the thought processes of a number of chess masters during the process of play; this comprehensive work analyzes the structure and dynamics of the planning, formation of alternative planning, the selection of moves, and elimination of moves in chess play. Some of the analysis in a way anticipates the programming of the chess-playing electronic machines, about which a considerable literature now exists (58). A connected problem is that having to do with genius in chess (3) and the general area of ability to conceptualize. Similarities already have been pointed out between the precocious ability to conceptualize in geniuses in chess, music, and mathematics (1, p. 23). I plan in a later work to discuss this topic. (Consider, for example, the fact that the histories of at least three child prodigies in chess are marked by each one beating his father in the first game at chess played between the pair.)

The third group of psychological writings on chess, the psycho-analytic, began a new type of insight into the nature of the game. It is fitting that Freud (31, p. 342) was the first to make mention of the game in the psychoanalytic literature. He likened learning of the game to the learning of psychoanalytic technique: "He who hopes to learn the fine art of the game from books will soon discover that only the opening and closing moves of the game admit of exhaustive systematic description; and that the endless variety of moves which develop from the opening defies description; the gap left in the instructions can only be filled in by the zealous study of games fought out by master hands. The rules which can be laid down for the practical application of psycho-analysis in treatment are subject to similar limitations."

The first paper on chess from the psycho-analytic point of view, presented to the Vienna Psychoanalytic Society on 15 March, 1922 and duly recorded in the minutes, was never published (39, p. 117). Dr. Fokschaner, a dentist, entitled his paper, "Über das Schachspiel." Hoffer (36) recalls that it drew some parallels between chess and obsessional neurosis, with an attempt to interpret symbolically the pieces and their movements on the chessboard. In his discussion Freud was critical of Fokschaner's simplifications, and that ended the topic (15).

The classical psychoanalytic paper on chess is the study by Jones (42) on the famous American prodigy of 100 years ago, Paul Morphy. Jones developed the thesis that chess is a game of father-murder, which became the pattern for most psychoanalytic studies on the subject. Yet the same theme was advanced by an earlier writer, Alexander Herbstman (35), whose work, published in Moscow in 1925, could not have influenced the psychoanalytic literature. Herbstman, a physician, and a chess problemist, made a systematic study of the form and content of chess. He paid tribute to Freud, Sachs, Ferenczi, Rank, Jung, Richlin, Abraham, and Jones for elucidating the unconscious. He began his essay by considering the preoccupation of the game with royal figures, especially the king and queen, and quoted Freud as follows: "In dreams the parents assume a royal or imperial form as a couple. You find a parallel to this in stories. 'There lived once a king and a queen' when obviously the account is about the father and mother." He then developed the thesis that the whole play of the game is an elaboration in numerous varieties and derivatives of the oedipal situation. To him the game consists primarily of the king, queen, and pawn, with the other pieces being displaced images of king or queen. Herbstman also discussed the concept of ambivalence as represented in chess, analyzed some dreams of chess, and attempted to explain certain early legends of chess, on the basis of the oedipal conflict.

PATHOBIOGRAPHY

Jones's study of Morphy set a model for pathobiography in chess. Other studies followed in somewhat different directions. One is the use of clinical studies and psycho-analytic therapy, as in Pfister's (61) work, the first convincing analysis of the chess player by his chess play. Coriat (18) discussed the general problem of the symbolism of the pieces and also the way in which the styles or habits of play revealed the players' motivations. Fleming and Strong (27) reported the first systematic effort to use chess therapeutically in the case of a 16-year-old boy who worked through a problem of inhibition of aggression by mastering the game, thus achieving a sort of belated mastery over his own impulses. In another such study, Slap (72) paid considerably more attention to details of the ego factors involved in a patient's preoccupation with chess. The practising psychoanalyst's interest will often lie in the clinical aspects of the game, and to him it should not be surprising that a player's interest in chess and his style of play reveal dynamics consistent with his character structure; however, consideration must also be given to the fact that the nature of skill in chess does not depend only on derivatives of conflictual forces.

Another trend in pathobiography was taken by Karpman (45) and Fine (26), whose studies are biographical and descriptive rather than clinical. Other psycho-analytic writings on the subject, covering phases in the main described above, are by S. Davidson (22), Menninger (53), and Ibanez (38). Menninger's reflections on the game as a hobby are unique in the sense that its informal therapeutic values are delightfully discussed.

OEDIPUS AND CHESS

At long last I come to the legends of the origin of the game, the study of which may reveal insights into the psychological factors it lets loose. Chess is unique among games in that its origin has been the subject of so much creative imagination, made attractive, I believe, because the family romance of the game in conjunction with its artistic character lends itself as a ready vehicle for displacement on to it of elements of psychic conflicts. Moreover, the mystery of the actual origin of the game adds impetus to its use in myths. Here, as in other phenomena involving historical and psychological factors, the treatment by the created myth may bear little or a most obscure relation to the historical facts. Culin (20) holds that the prehistory of chess is involved in the magical origin of all board games via arrow divination. Murray expatiates on the argument whether chess was a new invention or was a development from a prior game of chance. But these speculations give no basis of actual historical data to tie in with the psychological considerations of its origin.

A total of twenty-four legends have been extracted from the works of Lambe (47), W. Jones (43), Bland (8), Crawley (19), Forbes (28), Raverty (62), Murray (56) and Wilkinson (80). As the legends were copied or retold by one author from another, distortions and elaborations naturally occurred.[2] Therefore, only those myths considered to be the basic ones are cited; almost all of them come from Murray, the most scholarly of the authorities.

The themes of the legends are as follows: (a) father-murder, with chess as the therapeutic agent; (b) chess as a preparation for war; (c) chess as a substitute for war; (d) chess as a diversion; (e) chess as an in-

---

[2] For example, Wilkinson's story of chess as a game invented to divert a mourning Hindu queen from her sorrow is clearly derived from a legend recounted in full detail by Murray. The reader who misses in my list a favorite legend or an elaboration not pertinent to my thesis will therefore understand the reasons.

I have not, however, omitted legends that oppose my thesis, except for the recent flurry of tales that have appeared in popular literature, especially the American men's magazines. These are undocumented, not to be found in the academic literature; for example, the story of a caliph who ordered chess to be invented to relieve the tedium and boredom of his seraglio. This type of legend, however entrancing, reveals, as do all myths, something of the psyche of the author.

tellectual struggle; (*f*) chess as an educative process for morality; and (*g*) the Mater Dolorosa theme.

Several approaches to the study of the myths are possible: from their cultural origin, Moslem, Hindu, or Christian; in their chronological order; or by a consideration of their inherent motivations. I have chosen the last, combining with it the other two. I shall therefore begin with a myth that reflects primitive impulses in their frank crudity, one that represents no displacement of the psychic reality and constitutes no projection.

First to be considered are two European legends, one of them by Jacob de Cessolis (*c.* 1275) (56, p. 541), which contains the naked theme of father-murder. An Eastern philosopher, named Xerses or Hyerses by the Chaldeans and Philometer by the Greeks, invented the game in the reign of Evil-Merodach,[3] who is presented regularly in medieval works as a monster of cruelty. Evil-Merodach chopped up the body of his father Nebuchadnezzar into 300 pieces and threw them to 300 vultures. The sages then invented chess in order to cure him of his madness. In an attenuated version of this story, Galvan de Levanto (*c.* 1291) (56, p. 549) related that a philosopher named Justus invented chess in order to reform a Persian tyrant, Juvenilis.

Here is seen, in all frankness, the son (note that in the second tale the tyrant is called Juvenilis) committing murder of the father and a wise man inventing the game for a therapeutic purpose. (It is of paramount significance that the cure is a disguised version of the crime in these two stories, since it is recognizable that some processes and devices in psychotherapy contain this principle.) The substitute for father-murder that chess represents is seen more clearly here than in any of the other legends, and one can speculate as to why this theme appears so openly in medieval Christian literature, whereas in Hindu and Moslem literature it is extensively masked. Herbstman, not content with a relatively undistorted demonstration of the thesis of the Evil-Merodach legend, felt the need to include the symbolism of the number three and that of the vulture in his explanation, but these are not convincing. He does mention, however, that in chess part of the game is a defence of one's own king, and this affords the "patient-player" a way of redeeming his own guilt. Thus chess can be both patricide and a defence against it.

Now it may be considered presumptuous to take for granted that these two stories are oedipal stories inasmuch as patricide is only one part of the oedipal myth. But, presumptuous though it may be, it has to be acknowledged that omission of some details, often important ones, is a

---

[3] Curious it is indeed that Evil-Merodach (Amel-Marduk) should warrant such a reputation. The only reference to him in the Bible (Jeremiah 52: 31–4) records acts of kindness.

characteristic of myths as it is of dreams. It is justified to accept by implication the omitted portions as part of the work of the unconscious. Moreover, in one of the above stories the omitted element, the taking over of the mother, is present by substitution, i.e., by taking over of the kingdom, an element which will appear later also.

The theme of father-murder is therefore considered central and all other themes are derivatives, displacements, substitutions and taking distance from the central theme. Thus I cannot prove that when chess is clearly intended to be a military substitute the psychological equating of patricide and war is a valid one, but this is my hypothesis. The legends are therefore arranged in increasing distance from the central theme.

The next group are the legends derivative of the aggressive part of the oedipal theme, which portray chess as a preparation for war (56, pp. 211–212). As told by al-Adli, the game was "invented to assist in the military education of a young prince who pleaded that he was incompetent to lead his armies into war owing to his want of experience."

At a greater distance from the original theme is a series of legends in which chess is a substitute for war. The original of this group (56, p. 212) goes as follows: "A certain king of India, who was peaceably inclined, procured the invention of chess in order that his fellow monarchs might settle their disputes over the board without effusion of blood." In tales following this pattern the inference is clear that a philosopher or sage invented the game; but variations occur. In some tales a Chinese king, in another a Buddhist priest, and in still another the queen of the warlord, invents the game.

The next theme, a natural step from the last, has to do with the invention of chess as a distraction or diversion from war. In the earliest legend (56, p. 211) a king, passionately fond of war, had overcome all his enemies and was bored and ill. He instructed a sage to distract him; whereupon chess was invented, and he was shown how to manipulate forces and devise tactics. "The king tried the game, ascertained that the philosopher had spoken truly, and found distraction and health in playing chess." Note here again the therapeutic role of the game. The European versions of this story (56, p. 501) make Ulysses or Palamedes invent the game to relieve boredom during the siege of Troy.

The next step might likewise have been expected. The story is divested of its openly military nature and becomes a preparation for an intellectual struggle, via chance. Some of the Moslem legends of the origin of chess, and these are not the earliest ones, have to do with its development from the dice game, emphasizing consistently the motif of the control of fate. In one of the legends (56, pp. 208–209) an Indian monarch named Hashran appealed to an Indian sage, Qaflan by name, to devise a game that should symbolize man's dependence upon destiny and fate and depict how these forces work. Accordingly, Qaflan invented the game of nard, an elaborate dice game, in which the players move their men in obedience to the throws given by the two dice. Nard thus exemplified man's dependence upon fate for good or evil fortune.

Many of these legends continue with the story of the reward to the philosopher (56, p. 217). When the royal person invited him to choose his own reward he is said to have asked for a quantity of corn, to be placed on the chess board in a particular way: The first square was to hold one grain, the second two, the third four, the fourth eight, and so on. The quantity of corn asked for is of course enormous (enough to cover England to a uniform depth of more than 38 feet), the total being $2^{64} - 1$. The king did not know which to admire most, the invention of nard or the ingenuity of the request.

All the endings of the legends of reward run much the same except for one interesting variation. A sultan who used to challenge all comers in chess, beheading all whom he defeated, after beating ninety-nine opponents, met his superior in a dervish. The latter claimed the usual reward in gold pieces.

The explanation cited by Murray for the recurrent story of the reward seems to be a relic from the invention of chess out of magic and chance: "The Indians describe a mysterious interpretation of the doubling of the squares of the chess board. They establish a connection between the First Cause, which soars above the spheres and on which everything depends, and the sum of the square of its squares. The Indians explain by these calculations the march of time and of the ages, the higher influences which govern the world and the bonds which link them to the human soul" (56, p. 210).

In this ending to many of the legends of the origin of chess we see a return of the repressed, a return of the magical influence. I feel, also, that the story of the reward repeats the theme of the origin of chess, in that the wise man vanquishes the king and proves superior to him, thereby representing the superiority of the intellect over might and force. It is another derivative of the oedipal situation, a derivative of the cultural trends which betray the ambivalence to royalty, the father figure—pleasing him on the one hand and impoverishing him on the other.

The transition from nard as a game of chance to chess as a game of reason is recorded in the following story:

"A little later there arose another king, Balhait, who was advised by a Brahman that this game (nard) was contrary to the precepts of his religion. The king accordingly planned to replace it by a new game which would demonstrate the value of such qualities as prudence, diligence, thrift, knowledge, and in this way oppose the fatalistic teaching of nard. The new game was made on the model of war, because war was the most effective school for teaching the value of administration, decision, prudence, caution, arrangement, strategy, circumspection, vigour, courage, force, endurance, and bravery. Balhait was charmed with the game and did his best to induce his subjects to adopt it in place of nard" (56, p. 210). A Moslem commentary goes to the root idea of the story: One philosopher "maintained that the inventor of chess was a believer in freedom of the will, while the inventor of nard was a fatalist who wished to show by this game that man could do nothing against fate, and that true wisdom is to hold one's life in agreement with the decrees of chance" (56, p. 210).

In the new trend in legends of chess, several points are noteworthy. We see that the cast of characters includes a king, a queen, a priest, a general, a sage, and a philosopher. True, these are all royal personages; but the point is, they are people. The growth of rationality diverts mankind from gods and goddesses and from the sons of gods or prophets, the dramatis personae of so many myths and legends. Indeed, the absence of the divine, the religious, or the magical in chess is striking. It is as if at some time in man's history he set out to devise a game quite devoid of religious or magical elements. In games of dice and cards, factors of luck, chance, and magical propitiation are still important and can still be used for divination. Chess, both in its present form and from the point of its invention, has as an essential element the elimination of the gods of fortune. Skill alone was to determine the outcome. The victory was to be a victory of reason. Only one element of chance remains in chess: the toss for colours. Still, in it are now fused reason and aggression.

Viewed in the terms of psychoanalytic theory, the invention of chess expressed the triumph of secondary process thinking over the primary process. Actual warfare is fluctuating, unpredictable, and chaotic, while the military game of chess, nay, the intellectual game of chess, provides a struggle which is organized, controlled, circumscribed, and regulated. Recall once more the remark by Collins: "There are two classes of men, those who are content to yield to circumstance, and who play whist; and those who aim to control circumstance, who play chess."

Interesting also is another legend of the origin of chess. It contains some premonitions of the rise of the new concept of democracy, of the age of the common man: "A commoner, subject of a Hindu king, annoyed at his monarch's arrogance, violence, and cruelty, invented the game to demonstrate to him that a king unsupported by his subjects, not protected by his pawns, is weak and likely to get into trouble." The king appreciated the moral implied in the invention and changed his ways (47). This story, told by Lambe, I can find in no earlier author. Hence it seems justified to say it is an invention of Lambe's era, by which time royalties were not as absolute as in the times of origin of the other legends.

THE THEME OF THE MATER DOLOROSA

One manuscript (56, p. 219) suggests that chess was invented by Adam to console himself for the death of Abel, and includes Shem, Japhet, and King Solomon among the chess players. From the time of al-Ma'mun onwards, the writings of the famous Greek philosophers became known to the Moslem world in translation. It was, perhaps, inevitable that the scattered allusions to the Greek board games which occur in Plato and other writers should be misapplied to chess, and to this we owe the statements in the manuscript mentioned (56, p. 219) and in later chess books that Hippocrates, Aristotle, and Galen were also chess players. Murray comments that the Moslems, who for some time were involved in an argument as to whether chess was permissible on religious grounds, distorted references about the origins of the game and invented legends about Biblical characters in order to gain religious support that it was indeed permissible. Their reference to Biblical characters is understandable, but why the Greeks were included is not clear, since the one legend needed in this regard they also invented, namely that Mohammed himself played chess.

The legend that Adam invented chess to console himself for the death of Abel, a fifteenth-century story, contains the element of therapy, and is an inversion of the oedipal theme, in that it is the son who dies. This story is a masculinization of the two earliest legends of chess. One (56, pp. 190, 212), recorded in the first century of Islam (c. 875), tells of a queen-prophetess whose favorite son was killed by a rebel. The men of her kingdom tried to prevent her from learning of his sad fate, for they feared her reaction. They went to a philosopher, Qaflan, for counsel on the problem. After three days of thought he summoned a carpenter who fashioned him a chess board according to his direction. Then he invented the game with the remark, "This is war without bloodshed." The news of the invention was permitted to reach the queen, who then asked to see the philosopher and his invention. "He called his disciple and they played before the queen, and the winner said, 'Shah Mat' and she remembered and knew what he wished her to know, and she said, 'My son is dead'."

A slightly later version of the same story, related by Firdawsi (56, pp. 213–215), had the queen's two sons, each by a separate marriage, quarrel and finally resort to war. One died in battle, though not through being slain, and when the news came to the queen, she accused the brother of murder. He could not satisfactorily explain to his mother how the death happened, and so he called together the wise men of his kingdom and laid his case before them. They invented the game of chess and made clear how a king can fall in battle without having been slain. The son then took his game of chess to his mother and thus explained the death of his brother. She continued to study the board all that day and night without desiring food until death released her from her sorrow, "and from that time the chess board has remained in the knowledge of mankind."

The question arises as to why in these two oldest legends the central figure is a queen, and why the queen is so important in the folklore of the game even before it became a piece on the board. Why, indeed, did the early Moslems, whose literature has such sparse mention of women not hesitate to put women into these legends—when they have to do with India?

I would speculate that the importance of the queen-mother in these earliest legends is a relic of the myths of matriarchy. Note the absence of the king in both of these legends and note the sorrowing queen-mother. The stories repeat and strongly remind one of the theme of the Mater Dolorosa. In the first of these legends the theme of father-murder may be the unconscious one, that both mother and son are punished for the death of the father which has been accomplished in the unknown and unmentioned past, and that this is the crime for which the son must die. It is remarkable that Jones (42) anticipated this thesis, without referring to the earliest legends, by considering only the rise in power of the queen on the chessboard, speculations which, coming before Colby's suggestion, rested largely on etymological evidence. He stated, "Whatever may be the truth, therefore, about the linguistic speculations I have just mentioned, it will not surprise the psycho-analyst when he learns of the effect of the change; it is in attacking the father (that) the most potent assistance is afforded by the mother (= queen)."

The Magna Mater

It is logical to explore the earlier legends pertaining to the mother-son relationship, to see what light they may throw on the Mater Dolorosa theme. By far the most widespread of the ancient cults and myths were those of the Magna Mater, the Great Mother. These early legends, that illustrate a particular kind of mother-son relationship, suggest how they may be precursors or masks of the oedipal story. It is not strange that eventually the Magna Mater is considered the source of all things. As MacKenzie (51) pointed out: "As Isis interceded with Osiris, she interceded with Nebo, on behalf of mankind." But this did not signify that she was the least influential of the divine pair. A goddess played many parts: she was at once mother, daughter, and wife of the god; the servant of one god or the "mighty queen of all the gods." The Great Mother was, as has been indicated, regarded as the eternal and undecaying one; the gods passed away, son succeeding father; she alone remained. Thus too, did Semiramis survive in the popular memory, as the queen-goddess of widespread legends, after kings and gods had been forgotten. To her were ascribed all the mighty works of other days in the lands where the indigenous peoples first worshipped the Great Mother as Damkina, Nina, Bau, Ishtar, or Tashmit, because the goddess was anciently believed to be the First Cause, the creatrix, the mighty one who invested the ruling god with the powers he possessed.

How powerful was the force of the queen-mother in the form of Semiramis may be seen in the persistence of the belief in her power, even in regard to chess, where one fantasy, contrary to all historical evidence, attributed to Semiramis a role in the game. Hone, cited by Mitchell (54), suggested that the chess queen was so named in honor of Semiramis because the queen on the board has qualities once ascribed to this ancient queen-goddess. "Strangely inconsistent with our ideas of propriety and probability, the queen is the chief character in the contest. She is not merely the soft excitement of the war who bids her king go forth with her blessing; no, she is the active, undaunted, indefatigable leader of an army, herself a host!"

Let us now examine the general characteristics of these Magna Mater stories. Are they precursors of the oedipal myths? Are they masked or partial oedipal themes? The theme of the Magna Mater and the wish of the son to displace his father, weak or absent as he may appear, has been dealt with in two admirable contributions. Jones (41) showed that the whole system of mother-right may indeed represent one mode of defence among others that have been adopted against oedipal hostility; by way of taming or assimilating the oedipal complex, man instituted the mother-right. In other words, by establishing matriarchal rights and the priority of the mother, it appears as if the conflict with the father is rendered unimportant. This kind of denial can obviously be institutionalized in matriarchies.

Weigert (77) showed even more convincingly that the rites of the Magna Mater contain the oedipal theme, but her thesis is different from that of Jones; to her the rite of sexual union with the mother and the rite of sacrificial castration, as in the Attis myths, serve the dual function of a sacrifice and an approach to the nature of the goddess. The sin, to call it thus, is the wish for sexual union. Weigert explained the rite of castration, of death and of resurrection on the basis of the youth's childish fear of the all-devouring power of the mother. In his craving for union he sacrifices the organ of procreation as if at her command, in order to identify himself with her and to be resurrected—these to be the evidences of not having lost her. In this dyad the primal father can be indeed a shadowy figure. Weigert tends thus to explain the total relationship as being between mother and child alone, an erotic and hostile one. There is no trace of the father figure, no need to call him into the picture.

Let us now argue against this thesis from the point of view which posits or assumes a triangular situation. The sin of the son lover, Atis, in sexual union with its attendant sense of guilt, cannot come simply from the wish for union, the wish for identification with the mother (and the fear of being forsaken), but must contain underneath, hidden as it were, the element of aggression against the father. Her explanation of mother and youth as a sole relationship may indeed be the case in their early infantile relationship. But when genitality is involved, as it is in these rites and myths, Weigert's explanation seems inadequate. For a son to wish to achieve sexual union with his mother need not in itself necessitate castration; guilt must be a necessary component of this complex; even if the wish were for a type of primary identification with the mother, self-castration with all its punitive aspects is indeed not the mode of achievement of this goal. Introjective and incorporating trends are the mode of such an aim. Again, guilt must underlie the castrative aspects, and this guilt must stem from a destructive component. Even if it be granted that guilt can derive from the oral incorporative destruction of the mother in the passionate drive to become one with her, why the self-castration as the way of punishment?

My criticism can be held invalid if one assumes that the rites and castration are explicable from the complexities of the mother-son relation alone. Certainly this is the implication of Graves's (34, pp. 12–18) views from his study of myths, even though the motivation for the castration is not dealt with by Graves. Bettelheim (4) is clear and to the point in giving examples of puberty rites as illustrations of the need for boys to identify with women. I cite this work as a tenable hypothesis for the explanation of self-mutilation in males on other than a self-punitive or guilt-motivated basis.

I am still not content with Weigert's hypothesis, one derivative of which could be the thesis that the classical oedipal situation can be a screen for the more important bipolar mother-son relationship. To such a derivative Jones holds the opposite idea of why the father continues to be shadowy or absent in these legends, and to it Weigert subscribes in part. That is, the father figure is denied in order to avoid the semblance of the son's rivalry with him. Herein also lies, I believe, the fascination that the mother-goddess cults have had throughout the ages—the apparent absence of the murderous intent against the father. His absence or shadowiness has, nevertheless, accomplished the unconscious aim.

Still another approach presents itself. Despite Melanie Klein's conclusions, most of the present work points to a bipolar relationship as preceding the triangular one. Therefore, if one permits a parallelism, it is to be expected that myths of the bipolar relationship should exist and should precede historically the triangular ones. Graves (34) demonstrates this in regard to Greek myths by implication, since he demonstrates the primary role of the mother-goddess in the earliest myths, indicating by what politico-religious factors the father-king is introduced later. Does the Mater Dolorosa myth follow this pattern? Partly; for example, the Demeter-Kore myth wherein Demeter mourns her abducted daughter. Frazer (30) recognizes an important point in myths in picking out the ease of substitution which occurs in them; he stresses that in later versions of this myth a son is substituted for the daughter.

This facile displacement of roles, the condensation in one person of many roles, and the splitting of one role into many are characteristics of myths, as in dreams and other primary process displacements, which I feel are central to the understanding of the development of the form of the triangular oedipal pattern. Let me cite two examples of "transitional" myths: "Adad-nirari desired to be regarded as the legitimate heir to the thrones of Assyria and Babylonia. . . . It is not too much to assume that he was a son of a princess of its ancient royal family. Sammummat (Semiramis) may therefore have been his mother. She could have been called his 'wife' in the mythological sense, the king having become 'husband of his mother'. If such is the case, the royal pair probably posed as the high priest and high priestess of the ancient goddess cult—the incarnations of the Great Mother and the son who displaced his sire" (51, p. 410). This myth has the additional element of the displacement of the father by the son.

The second example goes further: "As the divine sower of seed, Ninip may have developed from Tammuz as Horus did from Osiris. Each was at once the father and the son, different forms of the same deity at various seasons of the year. The elder god was displaced by the son (spring), and when the son grew old his son slew him in turn" (51, p.

302). Isis was an early Mater Dolorosa, since Horus, when he grew up to be Osiris, died for the salvation of his people. The birthplace of Horus was a cave, later to be associated with the birth of Jesus.

These easy changes of identity so characteristic of the most ancient legends remind one of what happens in mental ontogenetic development, when the infant in a non-discriminatory phase can without difficulty exchange one 'object' for another.

As soon as the triangular form of the myth takes on an oedipal nature, interchangeability disappears and a more stable myth pattern is obvious. Perhaps it is from paternalistic cultures alone that these appear, centuries earlier than the Greek bipolar myths. For example, let us proceed to a legend in which the Mater Dolorosa appears more in the setting of the usual family, with the father more obviously present. A Sumerian hymn describes the wailing of the mother of Tammuz, generally represented "to have been a human being, who suffered death at the hands of a king. There is direct evidence that Tammuz, always designated as a god in Sumerian, was originally a defied man. . . . On the whole it is probable that Dumuzi(d) meant originally the 'faithful' son, and that the myth of a beautiful young god arose in prehistoric times when a king sacrificed his son for the welfare of his people. The calamity which instigated this sacrifice may have been some impending national disaster; in Sumerian religion it was the death of a god who perished annually at midsummer with the withering grass and drying soil of the drought-afflicted Mesopotamian valley. One son of a divinely appointed king had died for man, a perpetual atonement and a sacrifice to the merciless powers of the Underworld; a perpetual atonement in that he returned each year with the returning rains and spring sun only to die again in the torrid heat, when the flocks longed for water, and Tammuz their shepherd departed again to the mournful sound of the shepherd's lute and the cries of weeping women . . ." (48).

Note the theme of a son who is killed, not for his sins, but as a sacrifice for mankind. Reik (64, p. 158) believes that the sacrificial aspect masks the sin of incest of all the son gods, Tammuz, Adonis, Attis, and Osiris, who die violent deaths and are mourned for by their lovers and mothers. Once more the question can be raised as to the nature of the sin. We see the main characteristics of the mother-son relationship in these various legends leading to the problem of the death of the son, the reasons for which have been explained as some kind of sacrifice.

I now raise the point whether the guilt of the son (and the mother's role of grief) cannot be better elucidated. Let us use the example of the problem of the death of Jesus, who had but to deny or explain his assumption of the Messianic role in order to avoid death. This he would not do in face of what clearly threatened to be the consequences of his assumption. Schweitzer (71) dealt with this problem extensively and concluded that Jesus accepted death in the expectation that it would result in a "parousia" or manifestation of himself at an appointed time, which would be evidence that he was the "Anointed One." The eschatological and counter-eschatological arguments in Schweitzer's book impress me as ignoring, with understandable reasons, the psychological factor of Jesus's unconscious sense of guilt, for which he had to die, for his aspiration to be the King of Heaven or at least God's equal.

Psychoanalytically, his presumption can be understood to be culpable. This, it may be argued, was Jesus's sin, for which he had to die. Reik (65, pp. 271–273, 278, 301–302) deals extensively with this theme and yet concludes that Jesus was sinless, and took the sins of others and was executed for the crimes of others. But I propose the thesis of emphasizing Jesus's primary guilt as being a personal one, and thus de-emphasizing the secondary guilt, that which he acquired by taking it over from others.

This thesis about Jesus finds some psychological substantiation in two sets of data. The first concerns Talmudic references to Jesus as lame. Goldstein (32, pp. 57–66) reviews these references and concludes that the need to equate Balaam (who is referred to as lame, and in one story as blind in one eye) with Jesus, is historically untenable. Whatever the historical facts are, Graves (33) is closer to the psychological facts when he recognizes the deep unconscious need to equate Jesus with Oedipus.

The other set of data is derived from the Judas legends. Reik (63, pp. 100–120) first emphasized that the need to exculpate, glorify, and eventually deify Jesus led to a concomitant splitting of the image of Jesus into two parts, the evil being posited in Judas, who was made a scapegoat. The crowning artistic and psychological touch, the development of the medieval legend of Judas, the pious intention of which was to further blacken Judas's name, Baum (2) has studied in almost a hundred versions of the Judas legend; they arose in Europe in the latter part of the eleventh century when incest became of great interest because of the controversy over the law of Justinian regarding the marriage of near relatives.

The essential features of the Judas legend are the mother's dream of a son predestined to a wicked career; the setting loose of the infant in a cask on the sea; his rescue and being reared by a king; his banishment because of killing the king's son (in one story the murder occurs over a chess-game!); his return to his native land, the murder of his father and incestuous relation with his mother. Baum is exceptionally skillful in treating the relation of the Judas legend to the oedipal story.

If we now return to Reik's thesis that the evil posited in Judas was what was unconsciously felt as being true of Jesus, the incest motive is thus psychologically valid in these legends of Judas.

In what way Mary was unconsciously an accomplice is not clear. It would be unfair to deprive her in these speculations of the virtue of having maternal ambitions for her son in his quest for the Kingdom of Heaven. At any rate, one possible factor in her glorification may have been an absolution of her guilt in the aspirations of her son. In his psychiatric study of Jesus, Schweitzer (70) does not discuss the possibility of any sin or guilt on the part of Jesus. Nor does he consider the role of Mary, whom he mentions only in a footnote. The theme of the unconscious implication of the mother in the oedipal story, of increasing mention in current psychoanalytic literature, is hardly ever mentioned in belles-lettres. An exception is the famous old ballad, "Edward" (13). Jones mentions this theme in his paper on Morphy.

EPILOGUE

To return to the legends of chess: there exist in them legends of matriarchal and patriarchal settings, of bipolar or oedipal character; there exists also in them a syncretistic tendency to be found in the treatment of all folktales of all times and places. They reveal some part of the family romance, however distorted, condensed, or elaborated.

Since I have been dealing primarily with psychological facts and not historical ones, it should not be surprising if the character of the game itself should include only incompletely and partially its prehistory. Its invention and development, after all, were at a time in the world's history in which paternal figures, especially the royal ones, were ascendant. Its prehistory has the unconscious ingredients of all artistry in which the intellect plays a part. Its character is that of a game of the family romance, for which thesis the works of Herbstman, Jones, Pfister, and Coriat adduce sufficient evidence. The theme of father-murder is not the only one which is enacted, but many derivatives of the family situation, including denials of the general theme of patricide, are also evident. It may even be argued that the fact that women in general find no fascination in chess is explained in the psychological event that they have no need for father-murder.

I wish to conclude by returning to some additional evidence that the game includes not only the theme of patricide but also denials of it. If it can be shown that kings or people of high station approve of the game, it helps a player to be comfortable in his fascination or addiction to it. Therefore these tangential evidences seem in order.

First, there is the general tendency for chess journals, newspaper columns, and anthologies to collect the games of famous people, for the value of the great names and not of the games. Thus, a to-do has been made from time to time about the games reputedly played by Napoleon, J. J. Rousseau, Karl Marx, Tolstoy, Woodrow Wilson, Lenin, and others. Many an American has taken pride in the fact that George Washington and Benjamin Franklin played chess.[4] Participation with the great, via their hobbies, both lessens the sense of guilt over whatever special conscious, personal (and unconscious) meaning the game has—the addiction, the waste of time, masturbation, patricide—and at the same time enhances the pleasure via the indulgence thereby bestowed from on high.

Second, it is noteworthy that many coats-of-arms include chess pieces (56, pp. 772–775). So, likewise, our modern hallmarks of aristocracy, advertising trademarks, have included more and more the royal figures and other chess pieces, notably the knight.

Third, after political revolutions, attempts have occurred to change the names of the chess pieces to conform more with the democratic tradition. One such effort (7), which sought after the American Revolution to replace king, queen, and pawn by governor, general, and pioneer, etc., failed. After the Russian Revolution attempts were made to get rid of the royal family, and one such effort succeeded. The other, on the chess board, failed, and tradition and the strength of the unconscious prevailed; the pieces are still called Korol and Krala (or Ferz).

Fourth, even before Jones's paper, some writers explained that "checkmate" (shah-mat, schach-matt, etc.) which literally means, "The king is dead," indicates something else, e.g., the king is trapped or abandoned or surprised[5] (21, pp. 70–71). After Jones's paper had appeared there was a flurry of writings by modern scholars, especially Moghadam (55), to make further distance from the theme of father-murder. It is asserted that actually in chess the king is not killed; he is indeed simply "forced into helpless immobility" (53). Moreover, after the end of a game another can always be begun.

Ingenious as these proposals are, it seems obvious that the publication of Jones's paper necessitated the marshalling of crudite forces of denial to place the game as far as possible from its unconscious intent; an intent which is supported by considerable etymological evidence ("Mat" means

---

[4] I recall with what interest I spotted a well-played game by one "E. Jones" (57). And I recall my great pleasure when after inquiry, I received from Ernest Jones the message: "Yes, it was I who achieved fame thus."

[5] Murray (56, p. 502) thinks that the story is well founded about Louis VI, who was nearly taken in a chance skirmish near Cisors in 1110. When an English knight laid hands on him and shouted that the king was taken, Louis exclaimed, "Ignorant and insolent knight, not even in chess can a king be taken!"

dead, a finality, Moghadam's niceties notwithstanding). My dismissal of Moghadam's explanations, held by some scholars as far back as Hyde (37), may seem a bit cavalier: All the fuss to prove their point has other motivations in the scholars than that of accurate definition. My point, echoing Jones, is that these extenuations ilustrate to what length some authors will go to attempt to substantiate the denial of the intent of murder. This sort of polemic is an amusing example of how a thesis regarding a historical fact and its significance calls up protagonists and antagonists who have obvious emotional investment in the so-called scientific aspect. In this connection, Jones (42) remarked, ". . . from the point of view of the King, it makes very little difference."

Thus it appears that the fascination of the game may very well depend in part on the fact that its devotees experience, sometimes with full measure of affect, the passions and the mysteries of the unconscious. These break through the defensive intellectual formalism and structure and add to the pleasure of the game. It is as if in the enjoyment of the game one experiences a kind of *unio mystica* with kings and queens, with their family romance, and in participating in its royal richness, a part of lost omnipotence is recaptured.

BIBLIOGRAPHY

1. Abrahams, G. *The Chess Mind.* (London: English Universities Press, 1951.)
2. Baum, P. F. *The Mediaeval Legend of Judas Iscariot.* (Modern Language Association of America Publications (New Series 24), 31 (1916), 481–632, No. 3.)
3. Baumgarten, F. (1930). "Wunderkinder." *Psychologische Untersuchungen,* 8, 184–190.
4. Bettelheim, B. *Symbolic Wounds.* (Glencoe: Free Press, 1954.)
5. Binet, A. *Psychologie des grands calculateurs et des joueurs des échecs.* (Paris: Hachette, 1894.)
6. Bird, H. E. Quoted by Coles, R. N. *The Chess-Players' Week-end Book.* (London: Pitman, 1950.)
7. Blagrove, Wm. *The Elements of Chess.* (Boston, 1805.)
8. Bland, N. (1850). "Persian Chess." *J. Roy. Asiatic Soc.,* 13, 27.
9. Bosshard, K. (1954). "Psychological Causes of the Russian Superiority in Chess." *Caissa,* 1, 12.
10. Burton, Robert (1626). *The Anatomy of Melancholy.*
11. Buttenwieser, P. "The Relation of Age and Skill in Expert Chess Players." (Unpublished Doctoral Dissertation, Stanford University.)
12. Bykov, Y. G. (1954). "What is Chess?" *Shakhmaty,* 31, 359–362.
13. Child, F. J. (ed.). *English and Scottish Popular Ballads.* (Cambridge, Mass.: Houghton Mifflin, 1904.)
14. Cleveland, A. A. (1907). "The Psychology of Chess and of Learning to Play It." *Amer. J. Psychol.,* 18, 269–308.
15. Colby, K. M. Personal communication from S. Bernfeld.
16. ——— (1953). "Gentlemen, The Queen!" *Psychoanal. Rev.,* 10, 144–148.

17. Collins, Mortimer. *Attic Salt*, 1880.
18. Coriat, I. (1941). "Unconscious Motives of Interest in Chess." *Psa. Rev.*, **28**, 30–36.
19. Crawley, C. *Chess Theory and Practice*. (Port Sunlight, 1860.)
20. Culin, S. *Chess and Playing Cards*. (Washington, 1898.)
21. Davidson, H. *A Short History of Chess*. (New York: Greenberg, 1949.)
22. Davidson, S. (1933). "Psychoanalysis of the Chess Game." *Mowiny Psychjat.*, **10**, 249–262.
23. De Groot, A. *Het Denken van den Schaker*. (Amsterdam: Noord-Hollandsche Uitgevers Maatschappij, 1946.)
24. Diakov, J. N., Petrovsky, N. V., and Rudik, P. A. *Psychology of Chess*. (Moscow, 1926.)
25. Feldman, W. M. *The Jewish Child: Its History, Folklore, Biology and Sociology*. (London, 1917.)
26. Fine, R. (1956). "Psychoanalytic Observations on Chess and Chess Masters." *Psychoanalysis*, **4**, 7–77.
27. Fleming, J., and Strong, S. (1943). "Use of Chess in the Therapy of an Adolescent Boy." *Psa. Rev.*, **30**, 399–416.
28. Forms, D. *History of Chess*. (London, 1860.)
29. Franklin, Benjamin (1786). "The Morals of Chess." *Columbian Magazine*, Philadelphia.
30. Frazer, J. G. *The Scapegoat (The Golden Bough)*. (London: Macmillan, 1913.)
31. Freud, S. (1913). "Further Recommendations in the Technique of Psycho-Analysis." *Collected Papers*, Vol. II.
32. Goldstein, M. *Jesus in the Jewish Tradition*. (New York: Macmillan, 1950.)
33. Graves, R. *King Jesus*. (New York: Creative Age Press, 1946.)
34. ——— *The Greek Myths*. (New York: Braziller, 1957.)
35. Herbstman, A. *Psychoanalysis of Chess*. (Moscow: Contemporary Problems Press, 1925.)
36. Hoffer, W. Personal communication.
37. Hyde, T. *Mandragorias seu Historia Shahiludii*. (Oxford, 1694.)
38. Ibañez, F. M. (1944). "Psicoanalisis del Ajedraz." *Rev. Psicoanal.*, **2**, 187–197.
39. *Int. Zeitsch. f. Psa.*, **8**, 1922.
40. *Jewish Encyclopedia*. (New York: Funk and Wagnalls, **4**, 16–21.)
41. Jones, E. (1925). "Mother-right and the Sexual Ignorance of Savages." *Int. J. Psycho-Anal.*, **6**, 109–130.
42. ——— (1931). "The Problem of Paul Morphy." *Int. J. Psycho-Anal.*, **12**, 1–23.
43. Jones, W. (1790). "On the Indian Game of Chess." *Asiatic Researches*, **2**, 159–165.
44. Junk, W. *Philosophie des Schachspiel*. (Leipzig, 1918.)
45. Karpman, B. (1937). "Psychology of Chess." *Psa. Rev.*, **24**, 54–69.
46. Knight, N. *Chess Pieces*. (London: Sampson Low, 1949.)
47. Lambe, R. *History of Chess*. (London, 1765.)
48. Langdon, S. H. *Semitic Mythology* (Vol. V of *Mythology of All Races*). (Boston: Marshall Jones, 1931.)
49. Lasker, E. *Kampf*. (New York, 1907.) (Also unpublished manuscript in my possession.)
50. "Letter from a Minister to his Friend." *Harleian Miscellany*, **8** (London, 1810), pp. 361–363.
51. MacKenzie, D. *Myths of Babylonia and Assyria*. (London: Gresham, n.d.)

52. Menage, Giles. *Menagiana; ou Bon Mot, Recontes agréables, Pensées judicieuses et Observations curieuses,* 1963.
53. Menninger, K. (1942). "Chess." *Bulletin Menn. Clinic,* 6, 80–83.
54. Mitchell, E. *The Art of Chess.* (New York: Burrows-Mussey, 1936.)
55. Moghadam, M. F. (1938). "A Note on the Etymology of the Word Checkmate." *Am. Orient. Soc.* 53, 662–664.
56. Murray, H. J. R. *A History of Chess.* (Oxford: Clarendon Press, 1913.)
57. *The New Statesman and Nation.* (London, 14 February, 1953, p. 188.)
58. Newell, A., Shaw, J. C., and Simon, H. A. (1958). "Chess-Playing Programs and the Problem of Complexity." *I. B. M. Journal of Research and Development,* 2, 320–335.
59. *The Observer.* (London, 22 January, 1939.)
60. Paris, John. *The Island Beyond Japan,* 1929.
61. Pfister, O. (1931). "Ein Hamlet am Schachbrett." *Psa. Beweg.,* 3, 3.
62. Ravirty, H. A. (1902). *J. Asiatic Soc. of Bengal,* 71, 47.
63. Reik, T. *Der eigene und der fremde Gott.* (Leipzig, 1923.)
64. ———— *Ritual: Psychoanalytic Studies of Religion.* (New York: Farrar Straus, 1946.)
65. ———— *Myth and Guilt.* (New York: Braziller, 1957.)
66. Reti, Richard. *Modern Ideas in Chess.* (London: Bell, 1924.)
67. Rochlin, I. G. "To the Question of the Nature of Creativity in Chess." *Shakhmatnoi Listok,* March 10, 1930, pp. 73–74.
68. Salzman, Jerome. *The Chess Reader.* (New York: Greenberg, 1949.)
69. Schink, Gustav. *The Passionate Game.* (London: Routledge, 1937.)
70. Schweitzer, A. *A Psychiatric Study of Jesus.* (Boston: Beacon, 1948.)
71. ———— *The Quest of the Historical Jesus.* (New York: Macmillan, 1950.)
72. Slap, J. W. (1957). "Some Clinical and Theoretical Remarks on Chess." *J. Hillside Hosp.* 6, 150–155.
73. Steele, J. J. Quoted by Coles.
74. Tarrasch, Siegbert. Quoted by Coles.
75. Vasilevski, L. M. *Chess and Health.* (Government Edition.) (Moscow, 1930.)
76. Vityazev, F. I. (1928). "Psychological Types among Chess-players." *Shakhmaty,* 2, 25–29.
77. Weigert, E. (1938). "The Cult and Mythology of the Magna Mater from the Standpoint of Psychoanalysis." *Psychiatry,* 1, 347–378.
78. Wells, H. G. *Certain Personal Matters.* (London, 1898.)
79. Werkele, L. *Die Philosophie des Schach.* (Leipzig, 1879.)
80. Wilkinson, C. K. (1943). *Bull. N.Y. Metropolitan Museum of Art,* 1, 271.
81. Wright, T. *Homes of Other Days.* (New York: Appleton, 1871.)

22

Child Training and
Game Involvement

JOHN M. ROBERTS AND
BRIAN SUTTON-SMITH

Games are systemic culture patterns which are distinctive, ancient, and widespread among the cultures of the world. While games and gamesters have long claimed the scholarly interest of anthropologists and psychologists, no general consideration of the phenomenon of involvement in games has yet been given from both cross-cultural and intra-cultural points of view. The evidence presented herein shows that variations in the distributions of games among cultures throughout the world, and in the game playing of American children and adults, are related to variations in child training. It is held that these relationships can be viewed in terms of psychological conflicts which lead people to become involved in games and other models. In the main, this discussion is limited to game involvement, but it must be recognized that there are other important aspects to game playing. Additional features will be treated in subsequent reports.

In an earlier publication (Roberts, Arth, and Bush 1959: 597), games were defined as recreational activities characterized by organized play, competition, two or more sides, criteria for determining the winner, and agreed-upon rules. Many of the activities described as "games" in the ethnographic literature, however, do not satisfy the above requirements. Instead they are amusements: group pastimes such as the ritual game of

SOURCE. *Ethnology*, 1 (2), April, 1962. Pp. 166–185.

dialogue, "Mother, Mother, the Pot Boils Over"; stunts such as diving and juggling; model play as with dolls, pets, and toy trains; and various other noncompetitive recreational activities. Although this article is focused on games, there is evidence that child-training variables are systematically related to classes of amusements as well.

Games may be grouped into three classes on the basis of outcome attributes: (1) games of *physical skill*, in which the outcome is determined by the players' motor activities; (2) games of *strategy*, in which the outcome is determined by rational choices among possible courses of action; and (3) games of *chance*, in which the outcome is determined by guesses or by some uncontrolled artifact such as a die or a wheel. On the basis of the presence or absence of the attributes of strategy or chance, games of physical skill can be further subdivided into (*a*) games of pure physical skill where only the defining attribute of physical skill is present, as in weight lifting, racing, or bowling; (*b*) games of physical skill and strategy, such as fencing, baseball, or football, where rational decisions also influence outcomes; (*c*) games of physical skill and chance, such as tipcat, musical chairs, or grab, where chance is a factor as well as physical skill; and (*d*) games of physical skill, strategy, and chance, such as Queenie or steal the bacon (Sutton-Smith 1959), where all three defining attributes are present. Games of strategy (which must lack the attribute of physical skill) are subdivided into (*a*) games of pure strategy, such as chess, checkers, or go, where the attribute of chance is absent, and (*b*) games of strategy and chance, such as bridge, poker, or cribbage, where both attributes are present. The category of games of chance is not subdivided, since by definition this class must lack the attributes of physical skill and strategy. It includes such games as roulette, bingo, dice, and coin matching. The fundamental character of a game appears to be related to the principal defining attribute, whether it be physical skill, strategy, or chance; the attribute distributions within the subdivided classes of physical skill and strategy serve only to add secondary characteristics.

While play is a cultural universal, games, as defined above, are not. True, games are found in most tribal and national cultures, but in some interesting cultures they are either absent or very restricted in kind and number. Among the game-playing societies throughout the world the variations in games and game playing are extraordinarily great. All such societies have games of physical skill. Fewer have, in addition, games of strategy, or of chance, or both. Among societies with identical games there can still be variation in gamesters. Although participation in the local array of games can be very broad in some societies, every group restricts the playing of games, in greater or lesser degree, on the basis of age, sex, health, intelligence, social status, and a variety of cultural factors. Finally, within a single society the involvement of individual gamesters is never constant throughout the life cycle, and it can differ greatly from individual to individual. There is even a class of nonplayers—individuals who, though qualified for participation in games, either do not play them at all or play them only involuntarily. These cross-cultural, intra-cultural, and individual differences in game involvement require explanation.

Like other systemic patterns, games are especially amenable to historical and distributional treatment, but the culture history of games must be conjoined with functional analysis if the invention, diffusion, persistence, embellishment, and extinction of games are to be understood. Since games appear to be projective or expressive behaviors, it is reasonable to consider them in relation to learning or, more specifically, to child training. If specific game types can be associated with specific child-training variables, a step toward the functional understanding of game involvement will have been made.

The present inquiry is based on an earlier cross-cultural study of games (Roberts, Arth, and Bush 1959) in which games were viewed as expressive models. Games of strategy were related to cultural complexity; games of chance to the benevolence or coercibility of supernatural beings; and games of physical skill to the environmental setting. These relationships, together with some association with child-training variables, suggested that all games are exercises in mastery, with games of strategy, chance, and physical skill being related, respectively, to the mastery of the social system, the supernatural, and the nexus of the self with the environment. The present study builds on this analysis, but it goes beyond the notion of mastery to offer a conflict interpretation of game involvement.

METHOD

We have utilized a list of child-training ratings for 111 societies prepared by Bacon, Barry, and Child (1952). The authors rated the relative indulgence or severity of child training in the initial infant period, the degree of transition anxiety from infancy to childhood, and the amount of over-all childhood indulgence. Boys and girls were rated separately for child-training procedures with respect to responsibility, obedience, self-reliance, achievement, nurturance, and independence. For each of these latter variables the ratings provide information on the degree of reward received for behaving in a particular way, e.g., being self-reliant, the amount of anxiety about not performing the behavior (punishments inflicted for not showing the behavior), the frequency of the behavior, and the amount of conflict over it. It is thus possible to judge whether a child-training procedure is mainly a positive one involving simply rewards and frequent performance, or mainly a negative one involving anxiety and conflict. Since Bacon, Barry, and Child were unable to provide ratings on all their categories for all of their 111 societies, there are differences in the number of tribes listed in the tables which follow.

A pilot study made use of a more comprehensive set of ratings, including information on such primary socialization variables as weaning and toilet training. While these ratings were not available for the larger sample covered in the present study, results of the pilot study are coordinated with the present findings where they provide amplification and illumination.

In 1959 the Cross-Cultural Survey Files and Human Relations Area Files at Yale University were searched for information on games and game playing for those tribes on which there were child-training ratings. The files on 27 tribes contained moderately complete descriptions of games, and those on an additional 29 societies provided descriptions which were usable though incomplete. Confidence in the descriptions varied with the degree of attention paid to detail and with the presence or absence of explicit statements about the adequacy of coverage. Negative instances presented a problem, since a type of game may have been present but unobserved by the ethnographer, or the ethnographer may not have been interested in the subject of games. The uneven quality of the descriptions resulted in such anomalies as that a particular tribe could sometimes be used for certain comparisons but not for others. It was frequently possible, for example, to ascertain that particular cultures clearly possessed games of chance or of strategy even though little was specifically reported about the games themselves.

Although the importance of acculturation in the study of games was recognized, recently introduced games were excluded from consideration. Games were scored without regard to the age or sex of the players, since the ethnographic evidence did not always provide such information (probably, however, boys and/or men played most of the games noted). For this reason it is uncertain what value should be placed on the distinction between male and female child-training ratings. According to Bacon, Barry, and Child, females tended to receive only positive ratings (reward and frequency), whereas males received both positive and negative ratings; the ratings on infants grouped both sexes together. It was therefore decided to consider the ratings on both boys and girls as presenting a general picture of childhood in a particular society rather than to view them as independent accounts.

Our cross-cultural analysis deals with only four classes of games: (1) those of physical skill, (2) those of physical skill and strategy, (3) those of strategy, and (4) those of chance. No games of physical skill, strategy, and chance were encountered among the tribes used in our survey. The class of physical skill and chance and that of strategy and chance occurred too infrequently in the sample to permit separate discrimination; games of the former class were consequently grouped with those of physical skill, and those of the latter class with games of strategy. The distribution of the four classes of games among the 56 societies of our samples is as follows:

Games of physical skill, of physical skill and strategy, of strategy, and of chance. Complete information: Chagga, Chewa, Hopi, Thonga, Zuni. Incomplete information: Azande, Dahomeans, Papago, Venda. Total: 9 societies.

Games of physical skill, of physical skill and strategy, and of strategy. Complete information: Ganda, Lamba. Incomplete information: Ashanti, Gikuyu, Lakher, Masai, Mbundu, Tanala, Tiv. Total: 9 societies.

Games of physical skill, of physical skill and strategy, and of chance. Complete information: Comanche, Crow, Kwakiutl, Nauruans, Navaho, Muria, Ojibwa, Omaha, Samoans, Trukese. Incomplete information: Aleut, Araucanians, Aymara, Baiga, Chukchee, Kaska, Konde, Mandan, Tallensi. Total: 19 societies.

Games of physical skill and of physical skill and strategy. Complete information: Andamanese, Bena, Koryak, Kurtatchi, Maori, Pukapukans. Incomplete information: Ainu, Alorese, Aranda, Marquesans, Timbira, Trobrianreds, Wogeo, Woleainas. Total: 14 societies.

Games of physical skill only. Complete information: Lepcha, Lesu, Siriono. Incomplete information: Balinese. Total: 4 societies.

No games. Complete information: Murngin. Total: 1 society.

As a world sample of cultural variation the foregoing list of tribes is at best only partially defensible in conventional ethnographic terms. Witness, for example, the preponderance of African tribes among those groups possessing games of strategy. Enlargement of the sample, however, would involve finding additional tribes with adequate data on both child training and games as well as making new ratings with new judges—a procedure which at this state in the general inquiry would be prohibitively expensive. We have therefore sought an alternative means of strengthening confidence in the findings.

Cultural variation occurs within as well as between social groups. Under favorable circumstances, therefore, it is possible to study the relationships among variables at two levels of generality, e.g., in a world sample of societies and in subcultures within a single national culture. If generalizations established on the basis of cross-cultural study are

TABLE 1

Cross-Cultural Relationships Between Games and Child-Training Variables

Game Classes		Child Training Variables	Male Female Infant	Contingency Table Cells				Level of Significance[a]
				a	b	c	d	
Strategy	1	Reward for obedience	M	12	5	7	26	.01
	2	Reward for obedience	F	12	3	9	22	.01
	3	Frequency of obedience	M	10	7	5	25	.01
	4	Frequency of obedience	F	12	3	11	23	.01
	5	Anxiety over nonperformance of obedience	M	11	6	4	25	.01
	6	Amount of childhood indulgence	I	9	6	6	22	.05
	7[b]	Relative importance of love-oriented techniques of punishment by parents	I	5	1	2	8	.05
	8[b]	Defecation permissiveness (less)	I	7	0	3	8	.005
	9[b]	Rank of severity of weaning (higher)	I	6	2	3	9	.05
	10[b]	Rank of severity of independence training (higher)	I	6	2	1	10	.01
Chance	11	Reward for responsibility	M	18	9	8	18	.05
	12	Reward for responsibility	F	16	11	6	17	.10
	13	Anxiety over performance of achievement	M	15	11	6	13	.20
	14[b]	Severity of sex training	I	9	1	4	8	.025
	15[b]	Rank of severity of sex training	I	7	2	3	9	.05
Physical Skill	16	Reward for achievement	M	14	7	4	19	.01
	17	Reward for achievement	F	13	4	4	11	.02
	18	Frequency of achievement	M	15	8	4	17	.01

TABLE 1 (*Continued*)

Game Classes	Child Training Variables	Male Female Infant	Contingency Table Cells				Level of Significance[a]
			a	*b*	*c*	*d*	
	19 Frequency of achievement	F	12	6	4	12	.05
P.S. & Strat.	20 Anxiety over nonperformance of achievement	M	12	6	4	21	.02
All 4 vs. 2	21 Anxiety over performance of achievement	M	8	1	1	11	.005
	22 Conflict over achievement	M	7	2	3	9	.05

[a] Levels of significance were ascertained by chi squares or Fisher's exact probability test, whichever was appropriate according to the size of the N. All game classes were tested against all ratings. All other associations were nonsignificant.

[b] From the smaller Cornell sample.

found to have predictive power within particular cultures, confidence in the cross-cultural generalizations is increased. This technique of validation through subsystem replication is used in the present study.

The United States is one in a set of societies in the world, and is also one in which there is great cultural variation within the national culture. Among such cultural differences are those between sex categories, i.e. between boys and girls, men and women. Since differences also occur in the socialization of males and females, and since the expression of game preferences is relatively free in the United States, the relationships between child training and game preferences by sex categories should be those predicted by the cross-cultural analysis.

Through analysis of children's responses to an 180-item play scale, previously collected for another purpose, Sutton-Smith and Rosenberg (1959) have used the cross-culturally derived generalizations to predict the game preferences of 1,900 children in the third, fourth, fifth, and sixth grades in twelve midwestern American townships. Adult preferences have not been tested in as thorough a fashion, but preliminary work with survey data on file at Williams College supports the general conclusions.

RESULTS

The important findings of the cross-cultural investigation are presented in Table 1. Here ordinary tests of significance are given on the assumption that tribes are defensible as independent cultural units. In a sense, both this assumption and the use of a small, unevenly distributed sample are limitations of the study.

Games of Strategy

Since a relationship has been demonstrated (Roberts, Arth, and Bush 1959) between social complexity (as measured by the degree of political integration and the amount of social stratification) and the presence of games of strategy, it is not surprising that games of strategy are linked either directly with obedience training or with variables which have some bearing on obedience. Indeed, it is virtually certain that every complex social system makes certain demands on obedience (with a corresponding emphasis on commanding or managing). While the present ratings are concerned only with obedience, it is highly probable that obedience training is only one part of a larger system of giving and taking orders which is involved in the functioning of any complex society. Tribes possessing games of strategy were found more likely to have high ratings on child-training procedures which involved rewarding children for being obedient (see Table 2), punishing for being disobedient, anxiety about non-performance of obedience, conflict over obedience, and high frequency of obedient behaviors. In addition, they were, in general, less indulgent in their child-training procedures. The smaller sample showed relationships between games of strategy and higher ratings on love-oriented disciplinary techniques, greater severity of independence training, and less defecation permissiveness. There is in these relationships evidence of a pervasive form of child-training and recreational preferences (cf. Kardiner 1949: 43).

It may be noted that the presence of severity and love-oriented disciplines in association with games of strategy provides a possible parallel to Miller's fining that, in the United States, there is a greater tendency in middle-class (than in lower-class) child training for reasonable requests for obedience to be associated with severe toilet training and severe weaning, together with the use of psychological controls and symbolic rewards. Middle-class families, he found (Miller and Swanson 1959), also show a preference for conceptual rather than physical recreations.

Although nine of the eleven tribes with games of strategy and above median reward for obedience listed in Table 2 are African, it must be remembered that modern nations with their games of strategy were not included in the list of 111 societies for which data were gathered. The geopraphical distribution, though restricted, is compatible with the association between games of strategy and systems of authority.

TABLE 2

Reward for Obedience and Presence of Games of Strategy

	Above Median	Below Median
Strategy present	Ganda (14), Venda (14) Ashanti (13), Chagga (13), Gikuyu (13), Hopi (13), Tanala (13), Azande (12), Lamba (12), Masai (12), Papago (12), Mbundu (11)	Thonga (10), Tiv (10), Zuni (9), Chewa (7), Lakher (7)
Strategy absent	Ainu (13), Aymara (13), Chukchee (12), Tallensi (12), Nauruans (12), Lesu (11), Konde (11)	Crow (10), Kwakiutl (10), Mandan (10), Muria (10), Omaha (10), Navaho (10), Ojibwa (10), Samoans (10), Alorese (9), Balinese (9), Lepcha (9), Pukapukans (9), Murngin (9), Aleut (9), Woleaians (9), Aranda (8), Araucanians (8), Kaska (8), Trukese (8), Wogeo (7), Kurtatchi (6), Comanche (5), Maori (5), Siriono (5), Trobrianders (5), Marquesans (4)

Median = 10

p = .01

Games of Chance

When tribes with games of chance were compared with those lacking such games, relationships were noted with reward for responsibility, frequency of responsibility, and anxiety about the performance of achievement. The smaller sample added several indices of severity of sex training. From Table 3 it will be noted that seven of the nine exceptional societies with games of chance but low scores on reward for responsibility are North American Indian tribes. While this distribution affects the generality of the present thesis, it suggests that the intensity of the game outcome may be important, for in some contexts games of chance are games of courage.

The association between games of chance and training for responsibility is more puzzling than the linkage between games of strategy and obedience. There is, however, an economic theme in these relationships, for many of the responsibilities figuring in the ratings are for the performance

TABLE 3

Reward for Responsibility and Games of Chance

	Above Median	Below Median
Chance present	Araucanians (13), Muria (13), Dahomeans (12), Aymara (11), Baiga (11), Venda (11), Chagga (11), Hopi (11), Konde (11), Navaho (11), Chukchee (11), Ojibwa (11), Papago (11), Tallensi (10), Mandan (10), Chewa (9), Samoans (9), Thonga (9)	Aleut (8), Zuni (8), Kaska (7), Kwakiutl (7), Omaha (7), Comanche (6), Crow (5), Nauruans (5), Trukese (4)
Chance absent	Masai (13), Kurtatchi (11) Ainu (10), Gikuyu (10), Ashanti (9), Ganda (9), Murngin (9), Balinese (9)	Alorese (8), Trobrianders (8) Koryak (8), Lamba (8), Lesu (8), Mbundu (8), Wogeo (8), Woleaians (8), Aranda (7), Bena (7), Lepcha (7), Maori (7), Timbira (7), Tanala (7), Tiv (7), Pukapukans (5), Siriono (4), Marquesans (2)

Median = 8
p = .05

of routine chores of an economic nature, while gambling (which is often associated with chance) is likely to entail the transfer of property. Perhaps the association is that of chance and low-status drudgery.

Games of Physical Skill

Games of physical skill, whether considered separately as pure physical skill or as physical skill and strategy jointly, show significant relationships with reward for achievement and frequency of achievement. In addition, however, the subclass of physical skill and strategy demonstrates a relationship with anxiety about the nonperformance of achievement. These particular games—the most complex of those involving physical skill—are therefore more highly associated with punishment for not achieving. Tables 4 and 5 provide some sample distributions.

Gaming

The foregoing relationships show fairly specifically that strategy is associated with obedience and not with responsibility or achievement, chance with responsibility and not with obedience, and physical skill

TABLE 4

Reward for Achievement and Number of Games of Physical Skill,
Including Games of Physical Skill and Strategy

	Above Median	Below Median
9 or more games	Crow (15), Chagga (14), Comanche (14), Kwakiutl (14), Ojibwa (14), Aranda (13), Maori (13), Papago (13), Aleut (12), Gikuyu (12), Omaha (12), Pukapu-kans (12), Thonga (12), Chukchee (12)	Nauruans (11), Hopi (10), Samoans (10), Koryak (9), Zuni (8), Kaska (6), Trukese (6)
8 or fewer games	Araucanians (13), Mandan (13), Ganda (12), Bena (12)	Venda (11), Konde (11), Masai (11), Muria (11), Navaho (11), Chewa (10), Balinese (10), Siriono (10), Tallensi (10), Tanala (9), Murngin (9), Woleaians (8), Ainu (7), Azande (7), Mbundu (7), Aymara (6), Wogeo (6), Lepcha (5), Lesu (5)

Median number of games = 8
Median rating = 11
p = .01

with achievement and not with obedience and responsibility. There is, however, one additional general finding, namely, that those societies possessing games of strategy, chance, or both, as well as games of physical skill, show anxiety over the performance of achievement (see Table 6). In other words, persons in gaming cultures, particularly those with games of both strategy and chance, are more likely to be directly disapproved, ridiculed, and punished for showing achievement, or to suffer because of the time and effort they must devote to such achievement. Similar relationships emerged between the presence of games of chance and strategy and of conflict over achievement. Since games of chance and strategy are symbolic forms of competition, a relationship is established between anxiety over achievement and symbolic forms of competition.

In sum, three of the six major child-training variables (achievement, obedience, and responsibility) used in this study appear to be associated with ludic expressions in the form of true games. Preliminary work indicates that the remaining three variables (independence, nurturance, and self-reliance) may be associated with ludic expressions other than games.

TABLE 5

Anxiety About Nonperformance of Achievement and Number of
Games of Physical Skill and Strategy

	Above Median	Below Median
4 or more games	Chagga (13), Ojibwa (13), Crow (12), Kwakiutl (12), Aranda (11), Comanche (10), Hopi (10), Maori (10), Thonga (10), Venda (9), Chuckchee (9), Samoans (9)	Araucanians (8), Mandan (8), Omaha (8), Pukapukans (8), Nauruans (6), Timbira (5)
3 or fewer games	Konde (11), Aleut (10), Ganda (9), Bena (9)	Gikuyu (8), Masai (8), Navaho (8), Papago (8), Chewa (7), Balinese (7), Muria (7), Zuni (7), Aymara (6), Koryak (6), Murngin (6), Siriono (6), Ainu (5), Mbundu (5), Tanala (5), Azande (4), Kaska (4), Tallensi (4), Lepcha (3), Wogeo (3), Lesu (2)

Median number of games = 3
Median rating = 8
p = .02

Thus, for example, there seems to be a relationship between independence training and certain group pastimes. Nurturance may be associated with certain types of model play, and stunts with self-reliance. Research in progress is dealing with these forms of ludic expression.

Subsystem Validation

Barry, Bacon, and Child (1957) have shown, in a cross-cultural study based on the same ratings as those used here, that there are consistent differences cross-culturally in the training of boys and girls. Boys, for example, are given higher achievement training, while girls are given more consistent obedience and responsibility training. These differences in socialization correspond to the general differences between adult male and female roles over the world. A number of investigations have indicated that, in the United States, achievement is stressed more often in the child training of boys (see Sears, Maccoby, and Levin 1957: 404). There is support, too, for the view that girls receive higher obedience training. Sears, Maccoby, and Levin (1957: 407) report that those mothers who made the greatest sex-role differentiation imposed higher de-

TABLE 6

Anxiety over the Performance of Achievement and Number
of Game Classes

	Above Median	Below Median
4—PS, PS + S, S, C	Thonga (10), Zuni (10), Azande (9), Papago (9), Chewa (8), Chagga (8), Hopi (8), Venda (7)	Dahomeans (4)
3—PS, PS + S	Mbundu (12), Ganda (9), Tiv (7)	Tanala (6), Ashanti (6), Masai (6), Gikuyu (6)
3—PS, PS + S, C	Ojibwa (11), Samoans (11) Crow (10), Araucanians (9), Kwakiutl (9), Navaho (8), Aleut (8), Mandan (8), Omaha (7)	Aymara (6), Nauruans (6), Konde (6), Trukese (5), Tallensi (5), Comanche (4), Kaska (4)
2—PS, PS + S	Aranda (9)	Maori (6), Bena (6), Koryak (5), Timbira (5), Pukapu- kans (4), Ainu (4), Wogeo (4)
1—PS		Lesu (4), Lepcha (4), Balinese (4)
0—No games		Murngin (5)

mands on girls for instant obedience. With regard to responsibility training, the same investigators (1957: 404) state:

In the overall amount of help and chores assigned, there were no sex differences, but there was clear evidence of sex typing in the nature of the chores assigned.

Doing the dishes, making beds, and setting tables were more often girl's work, while the boys more frequently emptied trash, ash cans, and wastebaskets. It will be noted that the girls' tasks are regular daily chores, whereas those of the boys are more intermittent and nonroutine in nature. Miller and Swanson (1958: 106) mention routine responsibilities only in relation to girls. It would appear, therefore, that American boys receive more achievement training and less obedience and responsibility training than do American girls. In these respects the differences between boys and girls in the United States are analogous to the differences observed in societies throughout the world. If a universal association exists between child-training variables and ludic preferences and expressions, it would be possible to predict the game preferences of American boys and girls.

With such a congruence, the following relationships would be expected to hold:

1. Girls with their higher training in obedience should show a greater preference for games of strategy than boys.
2. Girls with their higher training in responsibility should show a greater preference for games of chance than boys.
3. Boys with their higher training in achievement should show a greater preference for games of physical skill than girls.
4. The difference between boys and girls should be less in regard to games of pure physical skill than in the case of games of physical skill and strategy, since the former are less strongly related to achievement anxiety.

In order to test these hypotheses the responses of 1,900 school children to a list of games were submitted to a chi-square analysis for sex differences. As indicated in Table 7, all the results are in the direction pre-

TABLE 7

Number of Games Differentiating Between the Sexes at p = .05 or Better

Game Classes	Nonsignificant	Favoring Girls	Favoring Boys
Strategy	Beast, Birds & Fish, Dominoes, Chess, Parchesi, Scrabble, Tic Tac Toe, Clue, Monopoly (8)	I've Got a Secret, Name That Tune, Checkers, Twenty Questions, I Spy (5)	(0)
Chance	Coin-Matching, Forfeits, Cards, Seven-Up (4)	Bingo, Spin the Bottle, Post Office, Musical Chairs, Letters, Colors, Initials (7)	Dice (1)
Pure Physical Skill	Quoits (1)	Hopscotch, Jump Rope, Jacks, Tiddleywinks (4)	Bowling, Horseshoes, Racing, Tug of War, Darts, Shuffleboard, Bows & Arrows, Throwing Snowballs, Shooting (9)
Physical Skill and Strategy	Handball, Tennis, Volleyball, Prisoner's Base, Fox & Hounds, Ping Pong (5)	Pick up Sticks (1)	Marbles, Wrestling, Boxing, Basketball, Football, Capture the Flag, Punt Back, Pool, Billiards, Baseball, Soccer (11)

dicted. A difference is assumed when an item differentiates between the sexes at the 5 per cent level of significance or better in at least one of the grades (third to sixth) used in the study.

A full report on adult male and female game preferences will be forthcoming. Preliminary analyses of survey data, however, have confirmed the preference of women for games of strategy and of chance and the preference of men for games of physical skill. Moreover, persons with semi-skilled occupations (emphasizing responsibility) have been found to exhibit a greater preference for games of chance when compared with people in the professions (emphasizing achievement and obedience), who show a greater preference for games of physical skill and games of strategy. These are the findings which would have been expected in the light of the implications of the foregoing cross-cultural and intra-cultural analyses.

Although the above subsystem validation may not be fully convincing, it is promising enough to warrant further inquiry. It certainly suggests that cross-cultural findings may be used to predict intra-cultural variation. At the same time it enhances the confidence with which cross-cultural generalizations may be accepted.

DISCUSSION

The foregoing results detail a relationship between child-training variables and games which must be explained. Although the results permit the formulation of a conflict interpretation of game involvement, it must be recognized that this interpretation is as yet unconfirmed. Studies now in progress are being directed toward this task.

Any theory of free game participation must account for the players' voluntary entry into games. The conflict hypothesis of game involvement holds that players become initially curious about games, learn them, and ultimately acquire high involvement in them because of specific psychological conflicts, and that the eventual decrease in involvement is related, apart from biological changes, to learning or enculturation. Addicted players, it is assumed, remain in a high state of inner psychological conflict, which is not resolved through physical development or learning. But to postulate such a relationship with conflict is to entertain an association which is much more complex than it is novel (cf. Freud 1924). It seems necessary first to assay its credibility.

The research by Child, Storn, and Veroff (1958) on the child-training variables of conflict, reward, frequency, and anxiety suggests that there is substantial correlation among them, so that whenever a rating is received on any one, a certain amount of positive variance in the others can also be assumed. For example, where there is reward there is usually some conflict, and where there is anxiety there is usually some reward. In addition, it is not unusual to regard anxiety as a conflict-producing drive (see Wurtz 1960). When a child is punished for, let us say, achievement, he gradually learns to anticipate punishment whenever he is stimulated to achieve, so that anxiety becomes a drive state in conflict with achievement. The anxiety-instigated responses conflict with those induced by the child's need to achieve. While the present study cannot fully clarify the differential effects of the variety of conflicts noted in the data—those involving anxiety about performance (Table 1, Nos. 13 and 21), anxiety about nonperformance (Table 1, Nos. 5 and 20), and interactions between these two (Table 1, No. 22)—the occurrence of definite associations does suggest the credibility of a conflict formulation of games.

Current play therapy, which sees children's spontaneous play as a projective system (see Erikson 1943), implies that games are symbolic substitutes for responses which are incompatible with the normal behavior of the child. Games of strategy, for example, would reflect an association with anxiety about nonperformance of obedience. Presumably there is here a conflict between being obedient and being anxious about nonperformance of obedience or, to put it more simply, a conflict between obedience and disobedience. When it is remembered that the pattern of child training associated with games of strategy involves much severity (Table 1, Nos. 6, 8, 9, and 10) and therefore much implicit frustration and provocation to aggression, but that it is, at the same time, a pattern in which obedience is strongly rewarded and in which the parents do not practice aggression, the need for a displaced and considerably attenuated form of aggression becomes evident. The players are presumably those who remain obedient to the social system but who relieve their ambivalence about it by displaced attack in the miniature social worlds of the strategy games. Indeed, Menninger (1942: 175) has explicitly taken this last position, saying of a game of strategy: "It enables us to express aggression without reality consequences; we can hurt people without really hurting them; we can even kill them without really killing them." Such a line of argument, however, goes beyond the data provided in the child-training ratings used in this paper.

The explanation of the relationship between conflict and games of chance would also need to invoke variables not provided in the material of this paper. These games are in fact the most enigmatic of all those considered in this research. Yet the cross-cultural relationships between games of chance and responsibility training and the intra-cultural relationship between these phenomena and female preferences, while surprising, do not seem fortuitous. Other papers have also established an overlapping cluster of relationships between chance, the benevolence of divine beings (Roberts, Arth, and Bush 1959), and responsibility (Lambert 1959). Responsibility training is the inculcation of a necessary routine which allows little scope for personal initiative or autonomy. That chores and economics tasks must be done is self-evident, and punishment for not doing them is apparently unnecessary (see Table 1, Nos. 11 and 12), since chance playing is not coupled with anxiety about nonperformance of responsibility (which means punishment for not being responsible) as strategy playing is coupled with punishment for not being obedient (Table 1, No. 5). But although chance players are not punished as part of their responsibility training, they do receive punishment in other elated aspects of training, namely, for showing initiative (Table 1, No. 13) or interest in sex (Table 1, Nos. 14 and 15). It would seem reasonable that punishment for not showing initiative would be likely to force a child into a reliance upon the most elementary of stratagems, a trust in the omnipotence of his own thought processes. And this elementary trust is, according to some (Bergler 1957), the source of all wishful thinking, gambling, and chance-taking activity. According to this interpretation, a game of chance is a response to the passivity of the player's normal life role and an expression of incompatible responses toward irresponsibility which are in conflict with the diligent role of the responsible provider. Benevolent fate, if not fantasy, may lift the routine worker out of his or her present life tasks with magical efficacy.

Games of physical skill appear to be a direct and microcosmic representation of achievement. Indeed they are often used on the tribal level as training procedures for hunting (archery or hoop-and-pole) and in the psychological laboratory, in the form of ring toss and darts, for the measurement of level of aspiration and achievement motivation (McClelland 1955). Nevertheless, although the only obvious relationships we have demonstrated for games of pure physical skill are with reward for achievement and frequency of achievement (Table 1, Nos. 16, 17, 18, and 19), it seems reasonable to assume that there should also be some association with anxiety and conflict. This is definitely the case with games of physical skill and strategy (Table 1, No. 20). Perhaps persons who play these games are in conflict about real achievement and use the simulated achievement of games to assuage their anxiety. It may be concluded for these and other games, as Kagan (1960) has concluded about apperceptive techniques, that they are a better index of preferred modes of defense than they are of motive strength.

It might be noted parenthetically that, if this conception of games of physical skill is correct, it is injudicious to use such games in laboratory experiments as supposedly "neutral" measures of need achievement. The cross-cultural evidence at this point amplifies doubts recently expressed about such usage by Broverman, Jordan, and Phillips (1960).

It is clear from the foregoing formulations that while games of strategy, chance, and physical skill may be played by persons who are in conflict about obedience, responsibility, or achievement, respectively, there are important differences in the relationships between the types of conflict and the nature of the games. Games of strategy and chance express the child-training variables of obedience and responsibility only indirectly, while games of physical skill give direct expression to achievement training. It may be that the differences between the "general expression" theory of fantasy (McClelland 1955) and the "alternative-channels" theory (Lazarus 1957) may be resolved by a theory which postulates that different types of variables lead to different types of expression in fantasy. In any case, there are similarities between these game-type differences and those which have been found in clinical work with children's fantasy within our own culture. It is true that fantasy expression is not the same as game expression, but any formulation that promises an understanding of both is worthy of consideration. It would, in addition, provide a further indication that a relationship which has been found to apply cross-culturally can have value for the understanding of intra-cultural variation.

The present game data permit the formulation of the proposition that there is an inverse relationship between the degree of conflict induced by the learning processes (child-training ratings) and the complexity and symbolism of the games (or, as it will be termed later, their scale of participation). It is noteworthy that games of pure physical skill, which are the least complex and most motor of games, have the fewest obvious associations with indices of conflict; that games of physical skill and strategy, with their higher degree of symbolism and complexity, have an added association with anxiety; and that games of chance and of strategy have many such associations. This statement closely parallels a recent formulation of the relationship between individual conflict and individual fantasy responses to apperceptive stimuli. Kagan (1960) has found that an individual's fantasy is a function of his degree of conflict and of the ambiguity of the stimulus presented to him. In games, the ambiguity of the stimulus and the character of the response are prescribed by the rules. In the clinical situation the investigator manipulates the stimuli and judges from the individual's responses the nature and degree of his conflict. In the game situation, the stimuli and responses are patterned, and individuals who have the necessary conflicts opt their way in. Perhaps even more important than the establishment of this parallel is the fact that it becomes possible to subsume these two quite distinct types of fantasy behavior—cross-cultural ludic models and private individual fantasies—within the confines of Miller's (1959) statement of learning theory, which says, in effect, that the greater the degree of conflict the greater will be the displacement of affect. The existence of such cross-cultural and intra-cultural regularities makes a propitious background for the "scale of participation" to be introduced below.

A question not discussed above is that of the difference between conflict which leads simply to exploratory activity, such as that described by Berlyne (1960) and termed "ludic" by him, and conflict of the sorts which lead to the repetitive substitutive sorts of behaviors with which we are here concerned. It has been customary to reserve the term "ludic" for these latter manifestations alone (Huizinga 1949). The important question, however, is whether the difference between exploratory activity and repetitive ludic behavior is simply one of degree or whether there is some ascertainable hiatus between them. Piaget (1957), who speaks of normal and "distorting" assimilations, apparently assumes the difference to be a matter of degree.

The arguments presented here affirm the credibility of a relationship between psychological conflict and the playing of games, and suggest that the principles governing such a relationship may transcend games and be applicable to intra-cultural variation in fantasy. Thus far, only the motivation which brings the player to the point of game involvement has been discussed. It is suggested that, being in conflict, he becomes interested in the game because it provides a means of assuaging conflict. Attention will now be directed to other features of ludic models yet to be investigated in future papers.

IMPLICATIONS

The joint consideration of anthropological, clinical, and experimental concepts of fantasy adds weight to the view that games are just one part of a cultural participation scale which varies from dreams at one end to full-scale cultural behavior at the other. At the beginning of childhood there are presumably individual dreams and solitary play. As the child develops, these find a matching in such cultural models as songs, dances, folktales, poems, programs, riddles, rhymes, and games. There are arrays of models available at any age level, and within any type a series ranging from lesser to greater complexity. Across all models there is a broader path leading toward greater cultural participation or away from such participation. As models approach full-scale cultural participation they increase in scale, becoming nearer in nature to the reality they copy. As they proceed in the other direction, the scale is reduced and the participation is often vicarious. It is also true that models, regardless of scale of participation, can differ along a scale of similitude, with exact copies marking one end and distorted representations the other.

This discussion can be illustrated by considering specific models. Games, for example, are expressive models of a particular sort. Like the cultural activities which they model, e.g., dueling, war, court trials, or market transactions, they involve behavior in interactive situations, but, unlike their analogies in full-scale cultural life, they involve participation which is usually defined as being recreational or nonsignificant (or, alternatively, smaller in scale). Admittedly, there are times when game activities become salient in a culture, as with professional baseball during a World Series, but even here there is recognition that baseball is recreational and expressive. On the other hand, games also have their analogues in folktales. Cinderella, for example, was clearly a "winner," and the wicked stepsisters were "losers." Many tales, stories, or plays, of course, do not resemble games so much as they resemble other noncompetitive ludic expressions such as pastimes or model play, but many tales can be scored in terms of outcome just as if they were games. In a preliminary study it has been demonstrated that there is a relationship between the presence of games of strategy in a society and the importance of strategic determinations of outcomes in folktales from the same society. Those societies which have an outcome in one ludic model tend to have it in the other. This indicates that games, as part of the participation scale, have their analogues both in full-scale social behaviors and in smaller-scale folktales. A schematic relationship between models and behaviors may be suggested as follows:

Scale of Participation

Outcome Determination	Full-Scale (Activity)	Small-Scale (Models)	
		Behavioral (Games)	Vicarious (Tales)
Physical skill	Herding on foot	Footrace	Tortoise and hare
Strategy	Market activities	Monopoly, poker	The fisherman and his wife
Chance	Striking it rich in a gold field	Roulette	Cinderella

These dimensions of scale and similitude are only two of those involved in the conceptualization of a cultural participation scale. The authors are turning their attention to such dimensions, but as yet the studies have not been completed.

It remains to identify the enculturative effects that games may be supposed to have. The presentation of the participation scale, of course, implies that there is some normal procedure whereby individuals work their way through parts of the scale, presumably as the result of maturation and learning. In general, it is suggested that each game is a microcosmic social structure in which the polarities of winning and losing are variously represented. The individual in conflict is attracted to a model because he can find in it a codification of the emotional and cognitive aspects of his conflict, which is unavailable to him, at his level of maturity, in full-scale cultural participation. In a game of strategy, for example, he can practice deception against his powerful opponent, and can even "kill" him, but in addition he can also command his own forces (as he is commanded by those whom he normally obeys). Because the codification is so adequate to his needs and level of maturity, he is implicitly taught a characteristic success style. Each type of game in unique fashion contributes information as to the relative values and nature of different types of chance, skill, and strategy in assuaging conflict and in learning how to handle social competition. Between the ages of seven and twelve years the child learns, in simple direct form, how to take a chance, how to show skill, and how to deceive. Increasingly, in complex games, he learns the reversibility of these styles—when to rely on one type of success gambit rather than another, how to combine them, etc. What he learns from the games are the cognitive operations involved in competitive success. These cannot be learned by young children in full-scale cultural participation. They can be learned only through models, whether games or models of other types. Unlike the judgments of weight or volume dealt with by Piaget, they are intellectual operations of multi-dimensional complexity, incapable of being represented by simple codifications.

In earlier sections we presented evidence and interpretation in support of the view that psychological conflict leads to game involvement. In considering the implications of our research we have gone further and have advanced (more speculatively) a theory of games which seeks to reconcile the classic theories of play as exercise (Groos 1919) and play as conflict (Freud 1924). This theory asserts that both psychological conflict and cognitive structures must be taken into account in understanding the cultural function of games as part of ludic models in general. The theory implies (1) that there is an over-all process of cultural patterning whereby society induces conflict in children through its child-training processes; (2) that society seeks through appropriate arrays and varieties of ludic models to provide an assuagement of these conflicts by an adequate representation of their emotional and cognitive polarities in ludic structure; and (3) that through these models society tries to provide a form of buffered learning through which the child can make encultura-tive step-by-step progress toward adult behavior.

It must be stressed that the research results presented in this paper do not substantiate a conflict-enculturation interpretation. Rather, the results lead to various tentative formulations which represent the first step in the development of an explicit set of hypotheses to be tested in future re-search. Exploratory research with undergraduate game players at Cornell University, for example, indicates that addicted players of games of strategy are in conflict about their positions in the social system. Earlier studies by Sutton-Smith (1951, 1959) of relationships between Maori and European games suggest that field studies of game acculturation are likely to be illuminating. It is reasonable to presume that culture contact develops both psychological conflicts and needs for cognitive restructuring which lead to a readiness for new games and to the rejection of old ones. In fact, the historical changes in games in the culture of the United States should be symptomatic of changes in basic child-training proce-dures (Sutton-Smith and Rosenberg 1961). Clearly, there is need for additional research in the complex area of games and gamesters.

BIBLIOGRAPHY

Bacon, M., H. Barry III, and I. L. Child. 1952. "Raters' Instructions for Analysis of Socialization Practices with Respect to Dependence and Independence." Mimeographed.

———— 1955. "Cross-Cultural Ratings of Certain Socialization Practices." Mimeographed.

Barry, H., M. K. Bacon, and I. L. Child. 1957. "A Cross-Cultural Survey of Some Sex Differences in Socialization." *Journal of Abnormal and Social Psychology*, **55**: 327–332.

Bergler, E. 1957. The Psychology of Gambling. New York.

Berlyne, D. E. 1960. *Conflict Arousal and Curiosity*. New York.

Broverman, D. M., E. J. Jordan, Jr., and L. Phillips. 1960. "Achievement Motivation in Fantasy Behavior." *Journal of Abnormal and Social Psychology*, **60**: 374–378.

Child, I. L., T. Storn, and J. Veroff. 1958. "Achievement Themes in Folk Tales Related to Socialization Practice." *Motives in Fantasy, Action, and Society*, ed. J. W. Atkinson, pp. 479–492. New York.

Erikson, E. H. 1943. "Clinical Studies in Children's Play." *Child Behavior and Development*, ed. R. G. Barker et al., pp. 411–428. New York.

Freud, S. 1924. *Beyond the Pleasure Principle*. New York.

Groos, K. 1919. *The Play of Man*. New York and London.

Huizinga, J. 1949. *Homo ludens*. London.

Kagan, J. 1960. "Thematic Apperceptive Techniques with Children."

Projective Techniques with Children, ed. A. I. Rabin and M. R. Haworth, pp. 105–129. New York and London.

Kardiner, A. 1939. *The Individual and His Society.* New York.

Lambert, W. W., L. M. Triandis, and M. Wolf. 1959. "Some Correlates of Beliefs in the Malevolence and Benevolence of Supernatural Beings: A Cross-Cultural Study." *Journal of Abnormal and Social Psychology,* **58**: 162–169.

Lazarus, R. S., R. W. Baker, and D. M. Broverman. 1957. "Personality and Psychological Stress." *Journal of Personality,* **25**: 559–577.

Menninger, K. 1942. *Love Against Hate.* New York.

McClelland, D. C. 1955. "Measuring Motivation in Phantasy: The Achievement Motive." *Studies in Motivation,* ed. D. C. McClelland, pp. 401–413. New York.

Miller, D. R., and G. E. Swanson, 1958. *The Changing American Parent.* New York.

———— 1959. *Inner Conflict and Defense.* New York.

Miller, N. E. 1959. "Liberalization of Basic S-R Concepts: Extension to Conflict Behavior, Motivation, and Social Learning." *Psychology: A Study of Science.* ed. S. Koch, **2**: 196–292.

Piaget, J. 1957. *Logic and Psychology.* New York.

Roberts, J. M., M. J. Arth, and R. R. Bush. 1959. "Games in Culture." *American Anthropologist,* **61**: 597–605.

Sears, R. R., E. E. Maccoby, and H. Levin. 1957. *Patterns of Child Rearing.* Evanston.

Sutton-Smith, B. 1951. "The Meeting of Maori and European Cultures and Its Effects upon the Unorganized Games of Maori Children." *Journal of the Polynesian Society,* **60**: 93–107.

———— 1959. *The Games of New Zealand Children.* Berkeley.

Sutton-Smith, B., and B. G. Rosenberg. 1960. "Play and Game List" (I.B.M. Form I.T.S. 100 A 6058). New York.

———— 1961. "Sixty Years of Historical Change in Game Preferences of American Children." *Journal of American Folklore,* **74**: 17–46.

Sutton-Smith, B., B. G. Rosenberg, and E. Morgan, Jr. 1961. "Sex Differences in Role Preferences for Play Activities and Games." Paper Presented to the Society for Research in Child Development.

Wurtz, K. P. 1960. "Some Theory and Data Concerning the Attenuation of Aggression." *Journal of Abnormal and Social Psychology,* **60**: 134–136.

23

Achievement and
Strategic Competence

BRIAN SUTTON-SMITH

This is one of a series of studies on the psychological properties of games. In the main, my collaborator John M. Roberts and I have dealt with games of strategy, games of chance and games of physical skill. We have used cross-cultural techniques, national survey data, studies of groups of skilled players, and intensive studies of individuals whose total absorption in games has led us to speak of them as game addicts. In these studies we have shown that intensive game playing is not a trivial phenomenon either psychologically or socially, but that, on the contrary, involvement in games is systematically related to a variety of personality, cognitive, social and political variables. While the bulk of our evidence to date is of a correlational nature and therefore, open to alternative interpretations, we have tentatively favored the view that games are models of competitive success. To give but one example: games of strategy have been found in cross-cultural studies in association with psychological discipline and cultural complexity; and in studies within this culture, in association with higher status and higher intelligence. One may derive from this the view that persons who are members of the families and the social stratum that is most actively involved in the decision-making processes of the larger society make use of strategy games as a model of such decision making.

SOURCE. A paper presented at the Eastern Psychological Association meeting April 18, 1964. This is an abridged statement of the complete paper: Roberts, J. M., Sutton-Smith, B., and Kozelka, R. M., "Studies in an Elementary Game of Strategy," *Genetic Psychological Monograph*, 1967, **75**, pp. 3–42.

One implication that follows from this theoretical construction, if true, is that individual competence at particular games should systematically parallel other psychological competences in the lives of the players. This is the subject matter of the present study which is concerned with only one class of games, games of strategy and with only one game within that class, the game of ticktacktoe. While ticktacktoe is a trivial game in the mathematical sense it is nevertheless the first game of pure strategy which is widespread amongst children in Western culture. The present study of competence at this game is based on a *Tick Tack Toe Test* which was developed in order to make individual assessment feasible. (The test was developed by Robert Kozelka, Williams College, Massachusetts.) This test is composed of six items chosen to illustrate the standard situations during the game of ticktacktoe. One example has an empty diagram and the testee is asked to make the first move. Two examples have a single move by another player already in place, and the testee is asked to make the next move. Other examples have two and four moves already on the diagram, before the testee makes his next move. Each sample situation is distinct from every other so that there are six parts of six games to which the testee makes a single response. No game is completed. Scores are attached to a testee's responses according to the probabilities that these responses will lead to a win, or a draw. When the item probabilities are summed it is possible to compare players in terms of their tendency to make moves that will lead to a win or that will lead to a draw. That is, each player has a win score and a draw score. We might add that scores on winning and drawing are negatively and significantly correlated for both boys ($-.49$) and girls ($-.53$) at better than the 5% level, in the present study so that players characteristically have a tendency to play *either* for a win or a draw.

In earlier studies using this instrument we have found that there are definite age trends in which the most marked changes in the direction of success occur in the late elementary school years, although at that age period only about 5% of children can be said to really beat the test; the figure rises to 20% in the 8th grade and 30% with college populations. The game may be trivial, but mastering it apparently is not.

The present study of this same instrument was carried out with fifty children (25 girls, 25 boys) from 1st to 6th grade, at Fels Research Institute in the summer of 1962 at Yellow Springs, Ohio, under the direction of the late Vaughn Crandall. In addition to administration of the *Tick Tack Toe Test,* information was available from behavior ratings based on the children's free play activity while at camp. Ratings on achievement behaviors, aggressive behaviors and activity behaviors which seemed potentially relevant to the study were included. (These were

TABLE 1

Variables Associated with Playing for a Win at Ticktacktoe

Variable	Boys (N = 25)	Girls (N = 25)
A. *Status variables*		
Age	.10	.38
Intelligence	.08	−.19
Socioeconomic	.15	−.51[b]
B. *Motivational variable*		
Need achievement	.11	−.17
C. *Behavior variables*		
Achievement		
Concern with fine motor mastery	.20	−.37
Amount of time spent alone on tasks	.18	−.48[a]
Task persistence	.43[a]	−.46[a]
Independent achievement efforts	.34	−.33
Aggression		
Instigation of physical aggression	−.08	.54[b]
Instigation of verbal aggression	−.22	.47[a]
Activity-passivity		
Associative play	−.08	.55[b]
Dominance of same sex peers	−.01	.53[b]
Uncontrolled motoricity	−.05	.50[a]
Concern with mastery of gross motor skills	−.03	−.41[a]
Withdrawal from social environment	−.01	−.64[b]
Withdrawal from aggressive attacks	−.16	−.60[b]

[a] Significant at .05 level (two-tailed tests).
[b] Significant at .01 level (two-tailed tests).

mostly done by Alice Rabson; the techniques and reliabilities are to be found in other publications of the Fels group.) Ratings were available on the children's relationships with parents and adults in terms of the well known *Fels Parent Behavior Rating* variables. In addition there were scores from administration of a McClelland type measure of n Achievement and scores from responses to a self-report inventory of play choices which had been keyed for masculinity or femininity of play preference. (This instrument has been used in a series of studies with B. G. Rosenberg at Bowling Green State University.)

TABLE 2

Variables Associated with Playing for a Draw at Ticktacktoe

Variable	Boys (N = 25)	Girls (N = 25)
A. *Status variables*		
Age	−.03	.05
Intelligence	.37	−.00
Socioeconomic	.07	.51[b]
B. *Motivational variable*		
Need achievement	.40[a]	.41[a]
C. *Behavior variables*		
Achievement		
Concern with fine motor mastery	−.05	.20
Amount of time spent alone on tasks	.14	.23
Task persistence	.05	.08
Independent achievement efforts	.11	.16
Aggression		
Instigation of physical aggression	−.03	−.43[a]
Instigation of verbal aggression	−.18	−.26
Activity-passivity		
Associative play	−.15	.10
Dominance of same sex peers	.13	−.26
Uncontrolled motoricity	.17	−.18
Concern with mastery of gross motor skills	.04	−.42[a]
Withdrawal from social environment	.09	.37
Withdrawal from aggressive attacks	.06	.33

[a] Significant at .05 level (two-tailed tests).
[b] Significant at .01 level (two-tailed tests).

RESULTS

The results in general are that we found many relationships between performance on the *Tick Tack Toe Test* and the other variables for girls, but only a few such relationships for boys. If competence at this test can be considered as a form of achievement, then these results contrast with previous research by Crandall and others which has established many more relationships between achievement measures and the other variables we used, for boys. The difference between Crandall's findings and the present ones may lie in the fact that in the present study results derive

TABLE 3

Relationships with Adults

	Ticktacktoe			
	Wins		Draws	
	Boys	Girls	Boys	Girls
A. Observations free plan at camp				
Recognition: approval seeking from adults	−.05	.38	.46[a]	.06
B. Home observations Accelerational attempts by mother	−.39	−.21	.58[b]	−.29
Severity of actual penalties by mother	.04	.47	−.20	−.23

[a] Significant at .05 level (two-tailed tests).
[b] Significant at .01 level (two-tailed tests).

from what is essentially an interpersonal activity (the game of ticktack-toe—although the test is not), whereas in Crandall's research most of the assessment devices have been individualistic and noncompetitive. It may be that the usual individualistic and impersonal devices evoke a seriousness of response from males that only interpersonal devices will evoke from females. While this is but a speculation, the assertion of such a difference between the sexes in an ego function such as achievement parallels statements about the differences which are said to prevail in a super-ego area such as moral standards.

These sex differences require that the results for winning and drawing for the sexes should be presented separately.

The Winning Girl

The most salient set of correlations in this study were those between winning by girls and the observed free play behaviors. Ten out of the twelve variables were significantly related at the 5% level or better (Range .41 to .64). Winning at ticktacktoe was correlated for girls with associative play rather than withdrawal, with dominance of other girls, with instigating both verbal and physical aggression, with a prefer-ence for gross motor activity with uncontrolled motoricity. This kind of girl does not readily withdraw from aggressive attacks or from her social environment nor does she choose to spend time on her own or show any great persistence at individual tasks. This same girl chooses masculine items on the play preference schedule. In her parent relationships she suffers severe penalties at the hands of her mother.

Here we appear to have a picture of a winning ticktacktoe player who is hyperactive, impulsive, aggressive and a tomboy, and who has a mother who perhaps provides her with a model of physical power assertion. Ticktacktoe can hardly be said to be a very appropriate model of this girl's general style. It is simply one of the ways in which she asserts herself, that is, in her case, it is an epiphenomenon of generalized power, rather than a model of a more specific strategic success style.

The Winning Boy

The results of earlier studies and the present one suggest that winning at ticktacktoe in boys, unlike that for girls, is more nearly *parallel* to other behaviors. In the boy's case the game may indeed be a model of his general approach to success. Thus in the earlier studies it was found that winning on the *Tick Tack Toe Test* was correlated with being perceived as one who gets leadership as a result of ideas, on a sociometric measure. Boys of this sort showed a preference for conceptual reactions, and although popular with other boys, they were not perceived as being good at the most popular physical sports. In two studies of boys at the sixth grade level, winning at ticktacktoe was correlated with scores on arithmetic and intelligence tests. In the present study with the larger age range from first through sixth grade, only the measure of task persistence was found to be related to winning on ticktacktoe. This again, however, is a measure which in other research has been found to be related to intellectual achievement. In sum, it can be argued that winning at ticktacktoe is a model of a more general strategic (or conceptual success or achievement) style in boys, though that does not appear to be the case with the winning girls.

The Drawing Girl

Drawing on this test by girls is correlated with various measures, all of which add up to a picture of sex appropriate orientations and actions. These girls report preferring feminine games, and in their observed behaviors they are neither aggressive nor interested in gross motor (traditionally masculine) activities. Drawing also correlates with the TAT measure of need achievement. In sum, drawing goes with verbally expressed aspirations towards achievement and with ladylike behavior. If drawing on ticktacktoe is indeed a model of this girl's way of life, we might sum it up by saying that the good girl plays it safe.

The Drawing Boy

Boys who play for a draw, like girls who play for a draw, display high need for achievement as reflected in a preoccupation with achievement on responses to TAT stimuli. The present results also indicate that the boys have experienced high accelerational pressures from their mothers and that they seek approval from adults. This is apparently not a chance finding as Winterbottom also found that boys who have high need to achieve were subject to more accelerational pressure by their mothers. It may be a legitimate speculation, although the details are not clear, that we have here a group of boys encouraged by their mothers to show a concern for achievement, but at the same time made unduly dependent on adults to define success for them. In some unascertained way the mother's accelerational attempts appear to have had a constrictive effect upon the boy so that he plays it safe when the situation is not clearly structured for him by adults. Both the boy and girl who display the draw strategy in high degree have in common a greater reliance on adults, the girls show this by being conventional, the boys through making direct bids for adult attention.

Achievement and Playing it Safe

The present association between drawing on the *Tick Tack Toe Test* and high need to achieve is of particular interest in respect to current personality theory concerned with achievement. Many studies have shown that persons of all ages scoring higher on need to achieve tend to have a preference for intermediate level risks in a variety of achievement situations. Playing for a draw on ticktacktoe is not in the probabilistic sense, equivalent to an intermediate level risk except in the sense that the player prefers to play for a draw rather than to risk either losing or winning. One possible explanation for the difference between the present status of the high need achiever and the status ascribed to him in McClelland's work perhaps lies in the differential nature of the situations involved. Most achievement studies have been carried out using games of physical skill in which the goals and probabilities have been clearly structured for the subjects. Even the chance situations which have been used have involved an impersonal setting forth of the probabilities before the subject. But in the present *Tick Tack Toe Test*, which is derived from a game, the situation is considerably less structured. The player who has not contended at length against others in the initially ambiguous and competitive situations of ticktacktoe games is not likely to know what the winning moves are. He may, however, have learned what the draw moves are because it has been established in earlier studies that these come earlier in the normative development of skill at the game. For the present we need only note that high need achievers may play cautiously at this game because in it the situation is interpersonal rather than impersonal, and it involves competition with others, rather than competition with a standard which is clearly defined. In a study of high need achievers in a gambling situation involving competitive bidding and ambiguity as to the competitor's moves, Littig also found that high need achievers played an extremely cautious game. McClelland interpreted this latter finding as due to the dislike of high need achievers for chance situations in which they could not influence the outcome through their own skills and abilities. He says: "In games of pure chance they normally prefer the safest odds they can get." But it has been shown here that these same high need achievers also play it safe when strategic skills are involved. As both chance and strategy have in common a relative lack of structure with respect to outcomes, we might conclude that the critical variables in explaining high need achieving behavior are not alone the influence of the skills and abilities of the players, but also the cognitive structuring of the field in which these skills are to be made manifest. When both paths and outcomes are made clear by adults or authorities, and not made ambiguous by social or chance contingencies and competition, then the high need achiever may be the one who feels safe enough to state a high expectation of success. When these conditions are not guaranteed he pursues more cautious play. This hypothetical sketch of the high need achiever who plays for a draw on ticktacktoe is confirmatory of McClelland's position insofar as it demonstrates that high need achieving does not go with losing. But in terms of ticktacktoe such persons are only intermediately successful; a finding which raises questions about the nature of "achievement" as assessed by McClelland. It is the general position of the present investigators that there are a variety of success styles (or forms of achievement), only two of which, strategic winning and drawing, have been discussed in this paper. It would be our contention that a variety of success styles have played an important role in the development of human culture, and that these are modelled not only in games of strategy, but also in games of strategy and chance (such as poker), games of chance (bingo), games of pure physical skill (ring toss or quoits) and games of physical skill and strategy (football). In general McClelland, Atkinson and others have tended to use only one of these types of games, games of pure physical skill, in correlation with their projective measures of achievement and aspiration level. They have presumed that such games of physical skill are neutral and alternative measures of achievement, whereas the present series of studies suggests that games as such are not any more neutral than the projective measures which they are supposed to validate; that games also are contaminated with the life history of success styles of the individual player.

CONCLUSION

In conclusion, the present study makes it clear that the most trivial game of pure strategy, the game of ticktacktoe is deviously implicated in the lives of its players. In the case of the winning boys, and the drawing boys and girls, the style of play at the game does seem to provide a parallel to other behaviors of these players. In these cases it seems not an unreasonable usage to say that the game models their general style of strategic competence. In the case of the winning girl, however, success at the game is merely a further illustration of her promethean-like tendency to dominate in many social matters. Here the game *illustrates* her power, but does not particularly model it.

While this study supports the view that games as models are an expressive phenomenon, there is a long standing assumption in the larger community that games also have a formative influence on child development, particularly "character" development. The present results suggest that this thesis might be worthy of further study.

REFERENCES

1. Atkinson, J. W. Motivational determinants of risk taking behavior. *Psychol. Rev.,* 1957, **64**, 350–372.
2. Bandura, A., and Walters, R. M. *Social Learning and Personality Development,* New York: Holt, Rinehart and Winston, 1963.
3. Bing, E. Effect of childrearing practices on development of differential cognitive abilities. *Child Develpm.,* 1963, **34**, 631–648.
4. Bing, E. Childrearing antecedents of perceptual cognitive functions. Paper delivered at Soc. Res. Ch. Develpm., Berkeley, April, 1963.
5. Crandall, V. J., Katovsky, W., and Preston, A. A conceptual formulation of some research on children's achievement development. *Child Develpm.,* 1960, **97**, 161–168.
6. Crandall, V. J., Katovsky, W., and Preston, A. Motivational and ability determinants of young children's intellectual achievement behaviors. *Child Develpm.,* 1962, 33, 643–661.
7. Crandall, V. J., Preston, A., and Rabson, A. Maternal reactions and the development of independence and achievement behavior in young children. *Child Develpm.,* 1960, **31**, 243–251.
8. Crandall, V. Achievement. In Stevens, H. (Ed.) *Child Psychology: The sixty-second yearbook of the National Society for the Study of Education.* Chicago: Univ. of Chicago Press, 1963, pp. 416–459.
9. Crandall, V. J., and Sinkeldam, C. Children's dependent and achievement behaviors in social situations and their perceptual field dependence. *J. Pers.,* in press.

10. Roberts, J. M., Hoffman, M., and Sutton-Smith, B. Pattern and competence: a consideration of ticktacktoe, *El Placio,* 1965, 72.
11. Kagan, J., and Moss, H. A. *Birth to maturity.* New York: John Wiley & Sons, 1962.
12. Kohlberg, L. Moral development and identification. In Stevenson, H. (Ed.) *Child Psychology: the Sixty-second yearbook of the National Society for the Study of Education.* Chicago: Univ. of Chicago Press, 1963, pp. 277–332.
13. Lansky, L. M., Crandall, V. J., Kagan, J., and Baker, C. T. Sex differences in aggression and its correlates in middle-class adolescents. *Child Develpm.,* 1961, **32**, 45–58.
14. Levin, H., and Sears, R. R. Identification with parents as a determinant of doll play aggression. *Child Develpm.,* 1956, **27**, 135–153.
15. McClelland, D. C., *The achieving society.* New York: D. Van Nostrand, 1961.
16. McClelland, D. C., Atkinson, J. W., Clark, R. A., and Lowell, E. L. *The achievement motive.* New York: Appleton-Century-Crofts, 1953.
17. Roberts, J. M., Arth, M. J., and Bush, R. R. Games in culture. *Amer. Anthrop.,* 1959, **61**, 597–605.
18. Roberts, J. M., and Sutton-Smith, B. Child training and game involvement. *Ethnology,* 1962, **1**, 166–185.
19. Roberts, J. M., Sutton-Smith, B., and Kendon, A. Strategy in games and folk tales. *J. soc. Psychol.,* **61**, 1963, pp. 185–189.
20. Roberts, J. M., Sutton-Smith, B., and Kozelka, R. M. Studies in an elementary game of strategy, *Genetic Psychological Monograph,* 1967, **75**, 3–42.
21. Roberts, J. M. and Sutton-Smith, B. *Games: models of power.* New York: McGraw-Hill, in process.
22. Rosenberg, B. G., and Sutton-Smith, B. The measurement of masculinity and femininity in children. *Child Develpm.,* 1959, **30**, 373–380.
23. Rosenberg, B. G., Sutton-Smith, B., and Morgan, E. The use of the opposite sex scales as a measure of psychosexual deviancy. *J. consult. Psychol.,* 1961, **25**, 221–225.
24. Sutton-Smith, B. The games of New Zealand children. Berkeley: Univ. of Calif. Press, 1959.
25. Sutton-Smith, B. A formal analysis of game meaning. *Western Folklore,* 1959, **18**, 13–24.
26. Sutton-Smith, B., and Roberts, J. M. Rubrics of competitive behavior, *J. genet. Psychol.,* 1964, **105**, 13–37.
27. Sutton-Smith, B., Roberts, J. M., and Kozelka, R. M. Game involvement in adults. *J. soc. Psychol.,* **60**(1), 1963, pp. 15–30.
28. Sutton-Smith, B., Roberts, J. M., and Rosenberg, B. G. Sibling associations and role involvement. *Merrill-Palmer Quart.,* 1964, **10**, 25–38.
29. Sutton-Smith, B., Rosenberg, B. G., and Morgan, E. Development of sex differences in play choices during preadolescence. *Child Develpm.,* 1963, **34**, 119–126.
30. Sutton-Smith, B., and Rosenberg, B. G. Peer perceptions of impulsive behavior. *Merrill-Palmer Quart.,* 1961, **7**, 233–238.
31. Sutton-Smith, B., and Rosenberg, B. G. Impulsivity and sex preferences. *J. Genet. Psychol.,* 1961, **98**, 187–192.
32. Winterbottom, M. R. The relation of need for achievement to learning experiences in independence and mastery. In J. W. Atkinson (Ed.) *Motives in fantasy, action and Society.* Princeton, N.J.: Van Nostrand, 1958, pp. 453–478.

The Function of Games—
Selected References

Back, K. W. "The Game and Myth As Two Languages of Social Science," *Behavioral Science*, Ann Arbor, Michigan, **8**(1), 1963, pp. 66–71.

Beisser, A. *The Madness in Sports*, New York: Appleton-Century-Crofts, 1967.

Brewster, P. G. "The Earliest Known List of Games: Some Comments," *Acta Orientalia*, Copenhagen, **23**(1–2), 1958, pp. 33–42.

Brewster, P. G. "The Importance of the Collecting and Study of Games," *Eastern Anthropologist*, Lucknow, India, **10**(1), 1956, pp. 5–12.

Caillois, R. *Man, Play, and Games*, New York: The Free Press of Glencoe, 1961.

Caillois, R. "Unity of Play; Diversity of Games," *Diogenes*, **19**, 1957, pp. 92–121.

Culin, S. "The Value of Games in Ethnology," *Proceedings of The American Academy of Arts and Sciences*, **42**, 1890, pp. 355–358.

Dundes, A. "On Game Morphology: A Study of the Structure of Non-Verbal Folklore," *New York Folklore Quarterly*, **20**(4), 1964, pp. 276–288.

Gulick, L. H. "Psychological, Pedagogical, and Religious Aspects of Games," *Pedagogical Seminary*, **6**, 1899, pp. 135–150.

Holland, E. P. "Principles of Simulation," *The American Behavioral Scientist*, **9**(9), 1965, pp. 6–10.

Huizinga, J. *Homo Ludens: A Study of the Play Element in Culture*, Boston: Beacon Press, 1950.

Janus, S. Q., and Britt, S. H. "Toward a Social Psychology of Play," *Journal of Social Psychology*, **13**, 1941, pp. 351–384.

Kerl, H. "Ancient Games and Popular Games: A Psychological Essay," *American Imago*, **15**(1), 1958, pp. 41–89.

Kiesing, F. M. "Recreative Behavior and Culture Change," *Men and Cultures* (Wallace, A. F., ed.), Philadelphia: University of Pennsylvania Press, 1960, pp. 130–133.

Mead, G. H. "Play, The Game, and The Generalized Other," *Mind, Self, and Society* (Morris, C. W., ed.), Chicago: University of Chicago Press, 1934, pp. 152–164.

Mead, M. "The Pattern of Leisure in Contemporary American Culture," *Annals of The American Academy of Political and Social Science,* **313**, 1957, pp. 11–15.

Olmsted, C. *Heads I Win, Tails You Lose: The Psychology and Symbolism of Gambling Games,* New York: Macmillan Co., 1962.

Payne, W. "Acquisition of Strategies in Gaming Situations," *Perceptual and Motor Skills,* **20**, 1965, pp. 473–479.

Phillips, R. H. "The Nature and Function of Children's Formal Games," *Psychoanalytic Quarterly,* **29**, 1960, pp. 200–207.

Potter, S. *The Theory and Practice of Gamesmanship; The Art of Winning Games Without Actually Cheating,* New York: Holt, Rinehart, and Winston, Inc., 1948.

Redl, F. "The Impact of Game Ingredients on Children's Play Behavior," *Group Processes* (Schaffner, B., ed.), New York: Josiah Macy, Jr. Foundation, 1959, pp. 33–81.

Riezler, K. "Play and Seriousness," *Journal of Philosophy,* **38**, 1941, pp. 505–517.

Roberts, J. M., et al. "Games in Culture," *American Anthropologist,* **61** (4), 1959, pp. 597–605.

Roberts, J. M., Sutton-Smith, B., and Kendon, A. "Strategy in Folktales and Games," *Journal of Social Psychology,* **61**, 1963, pp. 185–199.

Slovenko, R., and Knight, J. A. *Motivations in Play, Games, and Sports,* Springfield, Ill.: Charles C Thomas, 1967.

Sutton-Smith, B. "A Formal Analysis of Game Meaning," *Western Folklore Quarterly,* Berkeley, California, **18**, 1959, pp. 13–24.

Bibliography of
Bibliographies

Brody, R. A. "Deterrence Strategies: An Annotated Bibliography," *Conflict Resolution* 4(4), December, 1960, pp. 443–457.

Coffin, T. P. *An Analytical Index to the Journal of American Folklore.* Index to Volumes 1–70. Philadelphia: American Folklore Society, 1958, pp. 140–141 (Folk Games), and p. 252 (Games).

Darken, L. H. "Children's Games: A Bibliography," *Folklore*, **61**, December, 1950, pp. 218–222.

Deacon, A. R. L., Jr. *Selected References on Simulation and Games.* Saranac Lake: American Management Association Academy, April, 1960.

Directory of Organizations and Activities Engaged or Interested in War Gaming. Bethesda, Md.: United States Army Strategy and Tactics Analysis Group, 1962.

Duke, R. De La Barre. *Operational Gaming and Simulation in Urban Research.* Annotated bibliography. Lansing: Michigan State University, 1965.

Herron, R. E., et al. *Children's Play: A Research Bibliography.* Champaign, Ill.: Children's Research Center, University of Illinois, 1967.

"Major Centers Involved in Research and Development of Games with Simulated Environments," *The American Behavioral Scientist*, **10**, November, 1966, pp. 35–36.

Malcolm, D. G. *A Bibliography on the Use of Simulation in Management Analysis.* Santa Monica, Calif.: System Development Corporation, 1959.

Malcolm, D. G. "Bibliography on the Use of Simulation in Management Analysis," *Operations Research*, March–April, 1960, pp. 169–177.

Reiley, V., and J. P. Young. *Bibliography on War Gaming.* Chevy Chase, Md.: Operations Research Office, Johns Hopkins University, April, 1957.

"Selective Bibliography on Simulation Games as Learning Devices," *The American Behavioral Scientist,* **10**, November, 1966, pp. 34–35.

Shubik, M. "Bibliography on Simulation, Gaming, Artificial Intelligence and Allied Topics," *Journal of American Statistical Association,* **55**, December, 1960, pp. 736–751.

"Simulation Games for the Social Studies Classroom: A Resource Guide," *New Dimensions,* 1(1), New York: Foreign Policy Association, 1968.

Stockum, C. M. van. *Sport-Attempt at a Bibliography of Books and Periodicals Published during 1890–1912.* New York: Dodd and Livingston, 1914.

Szukovathy, I. "Some Notes on the History of Sports Bibliographies," *Research Quarterly,* **8**, 1937, pp. 3–14.

Young, J. P. *History and Bibliography of War Gaming.* Arlington, Va.: Armed Services Technical Information Agency, Staff Paper ORO-SP-13, April, 1957.

INDEX OF AUTHORS AND RESEARCHERS

Aberle, D. F., 156, 221
Abrahams, G., 462
Abrahams, R., 164, 168
Abt, C. C., 341
Abu-Bakr....as-Suli, 23
Acer, J. W., 310
Adams, R. H., 301
Addatto, C., 264, 376
Ainsworth, D. S., 259
Amsden, C., 50, 263
Alamayahu, S., 134, 255
Alegria, R. E., 150, 263
Allen, A. B., 52
Altham, H., 135, 264
Anderson, A. J., 52, 149
Anderson, D., 247
Anderson, J. C., 143, 222, 265
Andlinger, G. R., 310
Andrus, A. F., 302, 341
Anna, M., 134, 255
Annaev, K. G., 231
Arbat, J., 233
Archer, J., 376
Armitage, R. J., 52, 135
Armstrong, A., 143
Arnold, E., 266
Arth, M. J., 168
Aspen, J., 24, 48, 136, 260
Atkinson, J. W., 496
Auboyer, J., 16, 145, 266
Aufenanger, H., 140, 219, 266
Austin, R. G., 51, 137, 138, 253
Avedon, E. M., 347, 371, 419

Babcock, W. H., 154, 219
Back, K. W., 497
Backus, E. M., 53, 154
Bacon, M. H., 486
Baggally, W., 217
Bailey, F. L., 156, 260
Baker, G. S., 133, 260
Bancroft, J. H., 207, 213, 392
Bandura, A., 496
Barclay, D., 376
Barlen-Ebert, S., 233
Barry, H., 486
Barton, F. R., 140, 219
Basil, D., 310
Baucomont, J., 169
Bauer, D., 268, 376
Baum, P. F., 462
Baumgarten, F., 462
Bazell, C., 146
Beal, N., 132, 221
Beals, R. L., 149, 263
Beart, C., 17
Beauchamp, W. M., 151, 153
Beckwith, M. W., 150
Beilen, A. H., 343
Beisser, A., 258, 376, 430, 498
Bell, E. T., 383
Bell, F. L., 11, 13, 140
Bell, R. C., 22, 48, 56, 130, 253, 402
Bellman, R., 310
Bennett, G. T., 133, 255
Bennett, H., 52, 143
Beresford, A., 376

Bergler, E., 249, 376, 486
Berlyne, D. E., 486
Bernard, J., 398, 427
Berndt, R. M., 142, 219, 251
Berne, E., 5, 376, 389, 421
Best, E., 60, 143, 144, 219, 260
Bett, H., 48, 217
Bettelheim, B., 462
Bettman, O., 152
Betts, G., 133, 254
Betts, J. R., 53, 151, 260
Binet, A., 462
Bing, E., 496
Bird, H. E., 462
Blackwell, D., 428
Blagrove, W., 462
Blake, T., 141
Bland, E. A., 48
Bland, N., 260, 462
Blasig, R., 151, 260
Blau, L., 350, 376
Bloch, H. A., 249, 398
Blom, F. F., 149, 263
Blomberg, R., 146, 268
Bloomer, R. H., 342
Bloomfield, L. P., 398
Boas, F., 124, 127, 222
Bodmer, E., 169
Boeshart, L. K., 376
Bolton, H. C., 135, 141, 169, 255
Bolton, H. O., 14, 217
Boocock, S. S., 341
Borhegyi, S., 52, 149, 263, 264
Boroff, D., 151, 267
Bosshard, K., 462
Bourne, H., 167
Bowdoen, W. G., 48, 251
Boyd, N., 377
Boyle, R. H., 151, 260
Brachman, D. S., 268, 377
Braithwaite, R. B., 398
Brand, J., 167
Brandes, R. S., 52, 156
Braunholtz, H. J., 255
Breda, E. A., 231
Breen, M. J., 213
Brewster, P. G., 8, 9, 52, 130, 135, 137, 139,
   144, 145, 146, 148, 150, 151, 153, 154,
   155, 161, 192, 217, 219, 221, 222, 223,
   251, 252, 253, 257, 258, 266, 342, 498
Brinton, D. G., 111

Brody, R. A., 398, 500
Bromick, P. K., 145
Brooke, M., 247, 251
Brotman, L., 301
Broverman, D. M., 486
Brown, J. R., 301
Brown, M. E., 377
Brown, O. O., 146
Brown, W. N., 145, 257
Browne, B. W., 221
Browne, R. B., 156, 219
Buchan, J., 310
Buchner, M. J., 151
Buell, C. D., 269
Buell, C. E., 377
Buibat, F., 169
Bunt, C. E., 254
Buranelli, R., 247
Burger, E.,427
Burridge, K. O., 140
Bush, R. R., 168
Butler, B. R., 251
Buttenwieser, P., 462
Bykov, Y. G., 462

Caillois, R., 160, 168, 172, 228, 230, 406, 498
Carabo-Cone, A., 345
Carey, M. A., 145, 257
Carlson, B. W., 247, 350
Carlson, E., 320, 330, 341
Carlson, R. E., 260
Carr, H. H., 9
Carroll, L., 316, 343
Carter, D. S., 140, 268
Carter, W. H., 268
Caso, A., 52, 149
Cassirer, E., 439
Castro, P. R., 233
Casullo, F. H., 233
Cavendish, 24, 252
Cervenak, J., 233
Chakravarti, T. N., 145, 146, 260
Chambers, R., 167
Chaplan, J. H., 134, 255
Chapman, E. C., 247
Chapman, F. M., 269, 377
Chapman, F. R., 14, 144, 251
Chase, J. H., 153, 219
Chateau, J., 10
Cherryholmes, C. H., 321, 337, 341
Cheshire, F., 256

Child, F. J., 462
Child, I. L., 486
Churchill, L. P., 141
Claparede, E., 9
Clark, J. H., 142
Cleveland, A. A., 462
Coffin, T. P.,500
Cohen, B. C., 344
Cohen, K. J., 310
Colby, K. M., 254, 377, 462
Coleman, J. S., 319, 322, 335, 341
Collins, F. D., 48, 258
Collins, G. N., 133, 255
Collins, M., 462
Combrie, J. W., 48
Conn, J. H., 217, 377
Cooper, J. M., 116, 150, 249
Coplin, W. D., 398
Corbin, A., 310
Coriat, I., 463
Cornelius, R., 345
Corrain, C., 233
Cotton, C., 23, 53, 136
Cotton, H. S., 265
Courlander, H., 134, 255
Cozens, F. W., 140, 144, 151, 261
Craft, C. J., 311
Craig, H., 28
Cramer, M. W., 217
Crandall, V. J., 496
Crawley, C., 463
Creamer, M. W., 398
Crespi, I., 252, 398
Crombie, J. W., 217
Cruickshand, J. G., 136
Cruz, E. C., 142, 266
Culick, L. H., 498
Culin, S., 17, 55, 57, 80, 94, 109, 131, 133,
    141, 142, 144, 147, 148, 151, 153, 219,
    249, 251, 254, 255, 256, 264, 401, 463, 498
Curtis, H. S., 340
Cushen, W. E., 302, 311
Cushing, F. H., 56, 111, 151

Dahlerup, B., 17
Daiken, L., 217
Dale, A. G., 311
Danford, H. G., 259
Daniel, Z. T., 155
Danning, E., 37, 77
Darken, L. H., 500

Davenport, W., 268, 427
David, F. N., 48, 427
Davidson, D. S., 139, 222, 266
Davidson, H. A., 463
Davidson, S., 463
Davidson, W. P., 398
Davis, H., 12
Davis, R., 135
Dawson, L., 258
Dawson, R. E., 387
Deacon, A. R., 311, 500
Dean, J. F., 342
Deans, E., 343
Debevec, R. M., 398
De Groot, A., 462
Delany, E., 377
Depew, A. M., 213
Deraniyagela, P., 146, 268
Deschner, R. B., 48, 258
Desmond, G. R., 156, 249
De Sola Pool, I., 387
Deutsch, M., 319, 353, 364, 385
Devereux, G., 249
Diakov, J. N., 463
Diego, A., 52
Dill, W. R., 319, 311
Dodgson, C., 316
Donnelly, R., 247
Dorrer, A., 230
Dorsey, G. A., 156, 249
Dorsey, J. O., 155, 219
Douglas, N., 136, 165, 192, 219
Draper, G., 213
Dresher, M., 301, 427
Duke, R., 398, 500
Dulles, F. R., 48, 213, 261
Dumas, E., 343
Dundes, A., 164, 168, 169, 498
Dunlap, H. L., 141, 261
Dunne, R., 219
Duran, D., 78, 83
Durant, J., 48, 53, 261
Dussek, O. T., 146
Du Vernois, 274

Eifermann, R., 433
Eisenberg, L., 213
Ekholm, G. F., 52, 150, 264
Ellis, J. W., 301
Elo, A. E., 254
Elwin, V., 15

Embree, J., 131, 146, 141, 265
Emerson, J. S., 141, 222
Emory, K. P., 52, 141, 261
Endrei, W., 233
Enriquez, C., 149
Erasmus, C. J., 109, 257
Erikson, E. H., 10, 168, 215, 431, 486
Erman, A., 16, 51, 225
Espinosa, R., 48, 156
Etherton, P. T., 49, 264
Eubank, L., 156
Evans, P. H., 217
Ewers, J. C., 156, 267
Ewing, W. C., 53, 154, 261
Eyler, M. H., 49, 225, 258

Falkener, E., 17, 51
Farran, D. C., 341
Fattu, N. A., 387
Feldman, W. M., 463
Fenstermaker, G. B., 249
Fenton, S., 136, 265
Ferreira, A. J., 364
Ferris, A. L., 242
Fine, R., 254, 347, 377, 463
Fink, R. W., 53, 154
Finney, B. R., 52, 141, 267
Fiske, W., 49, 138, 254
Fitzgerald, R. T., 133
Flackard, G. A., 155
Flannery, R., 155, 250
Fleming, D., 264
Fleming, J., 463
Fletcher, A. C., 152, 221
Fletcher, H., 218, 340
Forbes, D., 75
Ford, R., 218
Forms, D., 463
Fox, J., 156, 265
Fox, T., 247
Fox, S. S., 377
Frankel, L., 247, 377
Frankenberg, R., 136, 265, 399
Franklin, B., 29
Frazer, J. G., 159, 463
Frederickson, F. S., 131
Freud, S., 10, 447, 463, 486
Fritzsch, K. E., 233

Gadd, C. J., 51, 131, 135, 148, 254
Gallop, R., 138, 264

Gamow, G., 343
Gardiner, E. N., 51, 261
Gardner, M., 317, 343
Gearon, J. D., 344
Geisler, M. A., 301
Geister, E., 213
Geithmann, H., 137, 254
Georges, R. A., 168
Gerwig, G. W., 258, 377
Gibson, G. D., 115
Gilmore, M. L., 152
Gilmore, M. R., 155, 263, 219
Ginglend, D. R., 337, 350
Gini, C., 135, 399
Gladston, I., 377
Goddard, H., 27
Godwin, N., 345
Goellner, W. A., 52, 61, 149, 263
Goffman, E., 5, 228, 377, 389, 399, 421, 432
Goggin, J. M., 150, 263
Goldenweiser, A. A., 113
Goldfield, E. D., 242
Goldstein, K. S., 164, 167, 170
Goldstein, M., 463
Golomb, S. W., 343
Gomes De Freitas, L. G., 235
Gomez, A., 233
Gomme, A. B., 31, 32, 38, 45, 49, 136, 160,
    165, 168, 182, 196, 218, 219, 221
Goodman, S., 136, 219
Goodrich, W., 364
Gordon, B. L., 350
Gordon, D., 152, 264
Gordon, H. M., 267
Goren, C. H., 252
Govett, L. A., 261
Graves, R., 463
Greene, J. R., 311
Greenlaw, P. S., 305, 311
Greenson, R. P., 250, 378
Griffin, S. F., 344
Griffith, W. J., 231
Groos, K., 9, 486
Guetzkow, H. S., 319, 332, 344, 399
Guevara, C., 233
Guilford, J. P., 426
Gulick, L. H., 340
Gullen, F. D., 218
Gump, P. V., 218, 365, 378, 390, 399, 408
Gunasekara, W. N., 146
Gupta, H. C., 145

Gusman, P., 51

Haddon, A. C., 11, 13, 131, 140, 142, 152, 220, 222
Haddon, K., 223
Haiding, K., 233
Haile, B., 157, 250
Hall, G. S., 9
Hall, J., 154, 222
Hallett, L. F., 152
Halliwell, J. O., 167
Halpert, H., 164
Hanna, W. A., 258, 399
Hannemann, E., 49, 140
Harbin, E. O., 131, 203, 213, 247
Hargrave, C. P., 49, 252
Harlan, H. V., 49, 261
Harney, W., 142, 261
Harrington, J. P., 157
Harrison, H. S., 134
Harrower, M., 364
Harsanyi, J., 427
Harsha, 254
Hartnoll, M., 134
Hasluck, M., 149
Hass, M. R., 146
Hastofr, A. H., 378
Haun, P., 347
Haywood, O. G., 301
Hazlitt, W. C., 43
Headland, I. T., 148, 220
Hedges, S. G., 247
Heistand, H. O., 271, 302
Helmer, O., 275, 301, 302
Helwig, 24, 271
Hencken, H. O., 52, 138, 257
Henderson, R. W., 54, 152, 261, 265
Herbstman, A., 463
Herder, J. H., 311
Herron, L. W., 305
Herron, R. E., 500
Herskovits, M. J., 126, 131, 170, 255
Hewitt, J. N., 153, 265
Heywood, W., 54, 138, 261
Hildebrand, J., 49, 131, 258
Hill, A. H., 146
Hindman, D., 247
Hrabalova, O., 137, 223
Hobbs, J. F., 142
Hocart, A. M., 140

Hodge, F. W., 157, 267
Hofer, M. R., 218, 222
Hoffer, W., 463
Hoffmann, W. J., 155, 263
Hofsinde, R., 152
Hogben, L., 117
Hohlova, E. N., 234
Holdbrook, E., 136, 218
Hole, C., 49, 136, 261
Holland, E. P., 320, 399, 498
Holliman, J., 54, 152, 261
Holmes, W. H., 57
Holton, G. R., 153
Homer, 21, 22
Hone, W., 24
Hornblower, G. D., 131, 145, 267
Hornell, J., 140
Hornstein, H. A., 386
Howard, D., 142, 143, 160, 165, 166, 179, 220, 251
Howard, G. E., 258, 378, 399
Howell, N., 152
Howson-Wright, A. E., 133
Hoyle, 23, 252
Huggens, S. G., 311
Huizinga, J., 10, 16, 26, 168, 227, 406, 486, 498
Hummel, S., 147, 231
Humphrey, J. H., 342, 343
Humpdige, K., 133
Hunt, S., 131, 247
Hunt, W., 268
Hutton, J. H., 131, 140, 146
Hyde, R. W., 378
Hyde, T., 23, 49, 74, 96, 463
Hye-Kerkdal, K., 139

Ibanez, F. M., 463
Ichikawa, S., 147, 266
Ickis, M., 378
Il'Ina, T., 234
Im Thurn, E. F., 11, 50, 145, 220
Islos, G. L., 149, 220
Israel, H., 236
Ittmann, J., 231

Jacks, L. P., 25
Jackson, E., 150, 220
Jackson, J. R., 311
Janus, S. Q., 498
Jenks, A. E., 142

Jenson, M. B., 348
Jobson, R., 255
Johnson, G. B., 154
Johnson, G. E., 340
Johnson, W. R., 258, 378, 430
Joinville, 67
Jokl, E., 259, 378
Jones, E., 463
Jones, K. G., 139
Jones, W., 463
Junk, W., 463

Kagan, J., 486, 497
Kahler-Meyer, E., 231
Kahn, A. E., 399
Kahn, H., 301, 302
Kaigh, F., 15
Kanai, S., 147, 256
Karasek-Langer, A., 235
Kardiner, A., 487
Karpman, B., 463
Karsten, R., 150
Kauffmann, H. E., 231
Kautz, J., 346
Kay, I. M., 311
Kenn, C. V., 53, 261
Kennedy, J. L., 301
Kennedy, K., 143
Kerl, H., 51, 498
Kerr, B. A., 254
Kibbee, J. M., 312
Kiesing, F. M., 499
King, C. W., 141
Knight, J. A., 379
Knight, N., 463
Kock, V. De., 135
Kohlberg, L., 497
Kolly, I., 157, 263
Kolpakova, N. P., 231
Korbs, W., 235
Kotler, P., 312
Kraft, I., 326, 341
Kraus, R. G., 5, 247, 260
Kretzenbacher, L., 235
Krieger, K., 234
Kroeber, A. L., 113, 115, 157, 224
Krout, J. A., 261
Kuret, N., 231
Kutscher, G., 53, 150, 265

La Cruz, B. A., 142, 220
Lafitau, P., 109
La Hora, S., 13, 145
Lambe, R., 463
Lambert, H. E., 134, 220
Lambert, M. F., 155
Lambert, W., 487
Lanciani, R., 51, 250
Landin, L., 345
Langdon, S. H., 463
Lansky, L. M., 497
La Porte, W. P., 213, 218
La Roux, M., 257
Lasker, E., 147, 256, 463
Laufer, B., 265, 268
Lazarus, R., 487
Leakey, L. S. B., 131, 134, 143, 220
Lear, S., 213
Lebedinskij, L. N., 231
Lee, J., 340
Leeming, J., 223
Leibowitz, M. L., 301
Leites, N., 399
Leont'Ev, V., 231
Lesser, A., 60, 155, 222
Levenson, H. C., 383
Levin, H., 497
Lewin, K., 353
Libkind, E. H., 350
Linder, R. M., 250, 378
Livermore, W. R., 300
Loffer, L. G., 235
Loffler, Lg., 234
Lommatzsch, H., 235
Long, N., 399
Long Sang Ti, 148, 256
Longfellow, 91
Longmore, L., 134, 250
Lopez Ibor, J. J., 230
Loveland, N. T., 364
Lovett, E., 16, 251
Lowie, R. H., 113
Lucas, T., 23
Luce, R. D., 364, 427
Lucile, T., 169

Mac Coby, M., 150
Macfarlan, A., 152
Mac Kenzie, D., 463

Maclagan, R. C., 43, 136
Madelin, S., 213
Mahler, G. H., 302
Maigaard, P., 265
Malan, B. D., 134, 257
Malcolm, D. G., 312, 500
Malinowski, B., 126
Manchester, H., 54, 152, 261
Mann, S., 252
Marshall, H., 378
Martin, E., 312
Martin, G., 134, 255
Martin, R., 51
Martin, R. A., 218
Mason, B. S., 54, 152, 213, 247, 261
Mason, W. A., 439
Masuger, J. B., 231
Matson, A. T., 134, 255
Matthews, D. W., 157, 250
Maude, H. C., 141, 223
May, F. B., 428
May, L. J., 343
McCarthy, F. D., 143, 223
McCaskill, J. C., 152, 261
McClelland, D. C., 487
McClure, S., 342
McGlothlin, W. H., 378
McIntosh, P. C., 259
McKenny, J. C., 345
McKenzie, B., 54, 154, 263
McKindree, O. J., 265, 378
McDonald, J. D., 252, 312, 428
McDonald, T. J., 302
McGlothlin, W. H., 252
McKinsey, J. C., 428
Mead, G. H., 26, 420, 432, 499
Mead, M., 152, 154, 263, 399, 499
Meadows, K., 49, 256
Meggitt, M. J., 143
Mehl, E., 50, 139, 265, 266
Mei, Y., 370
Melchert, S., 234
Melo, V., 231, 232
Menage, G., 464
Mendner, S., 236
Menke, F. G., 260
Menninger, K., 464, 487
Merriam, A. P., 156
Meszaros, I., 234
Meyer, M. W., 348
Micklewaith, J. J., 53, 340

Mignoga, M., 378
Miles, E., 136
Miller, D. R., 487
Milojkovic-Djuric, J., 131, 139, 220
Mishra, D., 145, 220
Mistry, D. K., 145, 220
Mitchell, E., 247, 260, 464
Mitchell, E. D., 213
Moghadam, M. F., 464
Molenaer, J., 17
Molnar, I., 232
Monckton, O. P., 49
Moncreiff, B., 308, 344
Monney, J., 154
Monroe, W. S., 218
Montagu, I., 148, 262
Montell, G., 147
Mook, M. A., 157
Mooney, J., 263
Moore, O, K., 389, 432
Moore, R. D., 156
Moore, R. M., 259, 378
Morgan, L. H., 91
Morgenstein, O., 26
Morley, H. T., 49, 252
Morris, R. P., 250, 378
Morris, S. W., 259, 378
Morris, W., 342
Morris, W. E., 348
Morse, E. S., 147
Morton, H. W., 139, 262
Moses, A. L., 154, 262
Moss, P., 49, 259
Mountford, C. P., 180, 223
Mulac, M. E., 346
Murray, H. J. R., 25, 33, 46, 49, 226, 253, 254,
    272, 402, 464
Myounge, O., 154

Nackebija, K. G., 236
Nally, T. H., 49, 136, 262
Namme, L., 267
Nanus, B., 312
Nash, J. F., 428
Nash, W. I., 51, 257
Nelson, F. E., 157, 262
Nelson, J., 345
Nemeth, J., 232
Nesbitt, W. A., 344
Neumeyer, M. H., 25
Newberry, R. J., 133

Newell, A., 464
Newell, W. W., 135, 145, 152, 159, 165, 167, 202, 220, 222, 253
Newton, M. B., 340
Nolan, J. E., 303
Northall, G. F., 31, 168

Obradovic, M., 232
Ochs, J., 88
Ohara, E., 147, 254
Olmsted, C., 499
Onions, C. T., 3
Opie, P., 136, 161, 164, 180
Opler, M. E., 157, 267
Orgel, M., 135, 251
Oritiz, S. E., 236
Osuilleabhain, S., 136

Padmanabhachari, T. R., 11, 50, 146, 262
Pahaev, E. J., 236
Paris, J., 464
Parker, A. C., 153
Parker, H., 51, 146
Parsons, E. W., 53, 133, 157, 264
Pascal, B., 79, 383
Patel, J. S., 146
Patterson, T., 153, 223
Paxson, E. W., 278
Payne, L. W., 155, 222
Payne, W., 499
Pecorini, D., 256
Pennington, A. W., 303
Perez De Castro, J. L., 234
Perry, R. E., 253
Pescereva, E. M., 234
Pessemier, E. A., 312
Petraschk, M., 232
Petrie, F., 135, 255
Pfister, O., 464
Phelps, H. R., 211
Phillips, R. H., 218, 378, 499
Piaget, J., 5, 10, 168, 218, 432, 487
Picaud, A., 230
Pick, J. B., 248
Pickford, P. W., 430
Pinon, R., 169
Piper, E. F., 198, 211
Plath, D., 147
Platts, M. E., 342, 343, 345
Poliscuk, N. S., 232
Pollock, H. J., 139

Pomeroy, J., 269
Pool, L., 262
Pope, C. H., 155
Portmann, P., 54, 138, 218
Potter, S., 499
Powell, R. B., 218, 248
Powell-Cotton, P. H., 133, 255
Proudfoot, B. F., 220
Pukui, M. K., 142, 220

Raghamen, M., 146
Ragimov, E. T., 232
Rainwater, C. E., 152
Ramson, J. E., 156, 220
Randle, M. C., 156, 250
Randolph, V., 154, 222
Rapoport, A., 384, 403, 428
Raum, O. F., 12, 266
Raverty, H., 254, 256
Ravich, R. A., 352, 364
Ravirty, H. A., 464
Rawdon, R. H., 305
Read, D. H., 136, 262
Reagan, A. B., 155, 262
Reaney, M. J., 340, 346
Redl, F., 218, 379, 408, 431, 499
Redstone, V. B., 53, 137, 257
Reed, A. W., 144
Regan, A. B., 157
Reider, N., 254, 379, 429, 440
Reik, T., 464
Reiley, V., 500
Reynolds, M. G., 150
Rice, G. E., 379
Richard, W. L., 256
Richardson, U., 379
Rider, C., 54, 152, 262
Ridgeway, W., 51, 257
Riedl, A., 234
Riemschneider, M., 236
Riezler, K., 499
Rinaldo, J. B., 152, 264
Riti, F., 464
Roberts, J. M., 61, 132, 168, 218, 250, 257, 379, 404, 433, 465, 487, 497, 499
Robins, F. G., 399
Rochford, D., 153, 267
Rochlin, I. G., 464
Roderman, C. R., 264, 379
Roeder, A. E., 138, 222
Rogers, G., 370
Roheim, G., 140, 220, 430

Rohlfs, G., 236
Rohrbough, R., 255
Rolland, E., 168
Romero, E., 234
Rose, A. W., 341
Rosenberg, B. G., 153, 497
Rosenfeld, H., 231
Ross, A., 341
Roth, W. E., 143, 262
Rowe, A. J., 312
Rowell, M. K., 154
Roy, M. M., 344
Rudolph, R., 148

Sabbatucci, D., 232
Salt, L. E., 50
Salter, M. A., 143
Salzman, J., 464
Salzman, L. F., 29
Sander, B., 268
Sanderson, M. G., 134
Sandin, B., 140
Sando, J. S., 152, 262
Sapora, A. V., 260, 269
Sayne, C. F., 223
Schaaf, W. I., 343
Schelling, T. G., 399
Schleichkorn, J. S., 370
Schoolcraft, 91
Schroeder, A. H., 132, 149, 157, 265
Schwab, G., 13
Schwander, N., 346
Schweitzer, A., 464
Scot, R., 35
Scotch, N., 134, 266
Scott, G. R., 268
Scott, H. A., 260
Scott, M. G., 259, 379
Sears, R., 487
Seboek, T. A., 139
Seeberger, M., 232
Sellin, T., 250
Serkele, L., 464
Serrano, C., 142, 250
Seymour, R., 343
Shackell, R., 134, 255
Sharp, F., 140, 262
Shaw, C., 269, 379
Shea, J. J., 248
Shipley, J. T., 342

Shubik, M., 312, 385, 399, 428, 507
Sieber, S., 232
Siegel, M., 133, 251
Simmerman, R. E., 303
Simms, S. S., 142
Simpson, G. G., 114
Siska, C. P., 301
Sjovold, T., 53, 138, 257
Skeat, W. W., 3
Skinner, H. D., 144
Slap, J. W., 464
Slaugh, S. F., 156
Slawik, A., 232
Slovenko, R., 259, 379, 430
Slusher, H. S., 259
Smith, A., 148, 256
Smith, A. L., 53, 150, 265
Smith, H., 50, 267
Smith, H. W., 54, 154, 262
Smith, L. R., 218
Smith, S. L., 318, 345
Soupault, P., 169
Southworth, P. D., 155
Sparkes, B. A., 137, 251
Sparkman, C. F., 248
Specht, R. D., 275, 303
Speck, F. G., 153, 154, 155
Spence, L., 53
Spencer, H., 10
Spolin, V., 342
Sprague, H. T., 342, 344
Stafford, G. T., 269, 379
Staley, S. C., 259
Stearns, R. E., 153, 221
Steele, J. D., 312
Steele, J. J., 464
Stern, T., 132, 149, 264
Sterns, R. E., 132
Stevenson, M. C., 157
Stockum, C. M., 269, 501
Stokes, A., 265, 379
Stone, G., 153, 262
Stratmann, F. H., 3
Strauser, K., 148, 256
Strutt, J., 24, 31, 34, 38, 137, 167, 190, 262
Stumpf, F., 140, 144, 262
Sullivan, M. W., 254
Surant, J., 152
Sutton-Smith, B., 4, 6, 132, 144, 153, 155, 166,
   168, 182, 192, 194, 218, 221, 242, 250, 379,
   390, 399, 408, 433, 465, 487, 488, 497, 499

Svobodova-Goldmannova, F., 234
Sweet, H., 3
Szasz, T. S., 380, 421, 433
Szukovathy, I., 50, 269, 500, 501

Tarrasch, S., 464
Taylor, J. L., 300
Taylor, L. E., 342
Thomas, C. J., 300, 303
Thompson, D. W., 51
Thrall, R. M., 303
Tiedt, S. W., 346
Tinsdale, N. B., 143
Tod, M. N., 138, 264
Toor, F., 150
Torquemada, J. De., 82
Towry-White, E., 257
Trevelyan, G. O., 34
Tugutov, I. E., 232
Tunis, J. R., 259, 266
Turner, E. J., 317
Turner, F. M., 141
Tylor, E. B., 50, 53, 55, 63, 110, 150, 251, 256, 257, 401

Uspenskaja, S., 234

Valnickja, S., 235
Vance, S., 312
Van Der Goltz, 273
Van Der Smissen, B., 253
Van Rensselear, J. K., 148, 252
Van Zyl, H. J., 134
Vasilevski, L. M., 464
Veiga De Oliveira, E., 232
Venturini, 24, 273
Ventzel, E., 428
Verco, J., 179
Verghese, M., 380
Vityazev, F. I., 464
Vivian, C., 344
Volpicelli, Z., 148, 256
Von Neumann, J., 26, 383, 420
Von Reisswitz, 273
Vysotskaja, O., 235

Waelder, R., 429
Wagner, G., 317, 318, 342, 343, 344, 346
Walker, J. R., 156

Wanchope, R., 54, 149, 264
Watkins, F. E., 153
Watkins, H. R., 312
Watson, W., 137, 221, 235
Watt, W., 141, 221
Wayland, V., 157, 252
Weaver, R. B., 54, 153, 262
Webster, D., 137, 262
Weigert, E., 464
Weinberg, S. K., 267
Weiss, H. B., 54, 153, 263
Welker, W., 6
Wells, H. G., 218, 248, 442
Wenkart, S., 259, 380
Werner, G. L., 260, 346
Westevelt, W. D., 142
Whitaker, I., 137
Whitehouse, F. R., 54, 137
Whyte, W. H., 207
Wichmann, H., 254
Wilkinson, C. K., 464
Wilkinson, R. J., 147
Wilkinson, W. H., 148, 252
Willems, E., 151
Willett, F., 156, 251
Williams, E., 268
Williams, J. D., 428
Williams, M. O., 137, 263
Wilson, J. A., 52
Wilson, P., 259
Witaker, I., 268
Witerbottom, M. R., 497
Withers, C., 164, 165
Wohl, A., 259
Wolcolcott, T. H., 213
Wolf, G., 269, 380
Wolfe, K. E., 264
Wolff, P., 344
Wolford, L. J., 155, 222
Wood, A., 380
Woods, C., 153, 267
Woolley, L., 52
Worchester, D. C., 142, 263
Wright, R. H., 133
Wright, T., 53, 464
Wrightson, H. A., 380
Wurts, K. P., 487
Wykes, A., 226, 241, 250
Wymer, N., 29

Yankovic, L., 17
Yoshino, N., 148, 252
Youd, J., 141, 266
Young, J. P., 50, 275, 300, 303, 500, 501

Young, N. D., 266

Zazoff, P., 232
Zengeni, S., 134
Zwinge, H., 235

INDEX OF HISTORIC PERSONAGES

Achilles, 21
Adam, 453
Adonis, 458
Ajax, 21
Alexander, 67, 73, 240
Aristophanes, 22, 65
Aristotle, 22, 453
Artaxerxes, 82
Arthur, King, 241
Athenaeus, 22
Augustine, Saint, 419

Bathsheba, 240
Brueghel, the Elder, 17, 22

Charlemagne, 240
Charles the First, 29, 240
Charles the Second, 29
Charles the Seventh, 241
Chevalier De Mere, 71, 383
Christ, 65, 458
Confucius, 78
Constantine the Great, 240

Darius, 67
David, 240
Dido, 240
Duke of Brunswick, 271
Duke of Wellington, 240

Edward the Second, 36
Edward the Seventh, 44
Elizabeth I, 28, 29, 31, 33, 34, 36, 37, 40, 240

Etienne De Vignoles, 241

Flavius Arrianus, 22
Franklin, Benjamin, 441
Frederick the Great, 271

Hector De Maris, 241
Hecuba, 241
Helen of Troy, 240
Henry the Seventh, 28, 45
Henry the Eighth, 28, 29, 31, 33, 36, 37, 38, 44, 46
Herodotus, 22
Hiawatha, 91
Hippocrates, 453
Homer, 21, 23
Hugo, V., 240

Joan of Arc, 240
Judas, 459
Judith, 240
Julius Caesar, 240
Juno, 240

Kama, 160
Krishna, 160

Lenin, 461
Louis the Fifteenth, 273
Lucretia, 241
Luke, 65

Mark, 65
Mary, 460
Matthew, 65

Montezuma, 72, 82
Morgan Le Fay, 241

Napoleon, 240, 461

Oedipus, 448
Ogier the Dane, 241
Osiris, 458
Ovid, 22, 73

Pallas Athena, 240
Pausanias, 22
Penelope, 73
Penthisilea, 240
Philostratus, 22
Plato, 22
Pliny, 22
Plutarch, 22
Publius Papinus Statius, 22

Rachel, 240, 241
Ramses I, 39

Robin Hood, 241
Roland, 241
Roxane, 240

Seneca, 22
Shakespere, 27, 37, 67
Sir Lancelot, 241
Socrates, 22
Sophocles, 73

Tacitus, 22, 51
Thucydides, 22

Victoria, 31

Washington, George, 460

Xenophon, 22

Yamamoto, Admiral, 298

Zeno, 72

CULTURAL INDEX

Abyssinia, 16
Africa, games, diffusion of, 61
  to West Indies, 90
  distribution of Mancala, 97
  tribal variations, 16
  Liberia, Sasswood ordeal in, 13
  Nigeria, 11, 12
  references to, 132
  rolling target, 12
  tribes playing, 469
American Indians, Apache, game counter, 118
  game of Tze-Tiehl, 89
  Arapaho, game rings as ornament, 106
    dice, 117
    game counter, 120
  Blackfeet, game counter, 120
  California, Patolli, 88
  Cheyenne, game rings as ornament, 106
    game counter, 120
  Dakota, game counter, 120
    game rings as ornament, 106
    lot games, 91
  general, borrowed games, 105
    child training, 469
    classification of games, 103, 401
    diffusion of games, 61
    European analogies, 57
  Hano, game counters, 118
  Hopi, fertility game, 107
    game counters, 118
    hoop and pole game, 106
  Hupa, dart as ornament, 106
  Huron, gambling, 90

    game counter, 120
  Iroquois, ball game, 68
    festival games, 90
  Keres, game counter, 118
  Kiowa, game counter, 118
  Navaho, game counter, 118
    marriage basket, 108
  Ojibways, lot games, 91
  Onondaga, game counter, 120
  Paiute, game counter, 117
  Pawnee, buffalo game, 107
    hand game, 60
  Seminoles, ball players, 54
  Seneca, game counter, 120
  Tewa, game counters, 118
  Walapai, game counters, 118
  Wasco, fertility game, 107
  Yokuts, game counter, 117
  Zuni, dice game, 108
    game counter, 228
    games and religion, 105
Anglo-Saxon, dictionary of, 3
Annamite, game, board, 17
  language, 41
Arabic, documents about games in, 23
Asia, South East, game diffusion, 55
  kites, origin of, 64
Australia, children's games, study of, 166
  marble games, 179
  Tanga, play life of, 11
    puberty rite, 13

Babylonia, chess, 51

Baghdad, chess master, employed by
    Caliph of, 23
  boxing and wrestling near, 51
Bali, Mancala board game in, 16
Basque, ball play of, 69
Bering Strait, game diffusion, 55
Borneo, Dayak, Cat's Cradle, 64
Burma, 59

Celebes, 59
Ceylon, Mancala board game in, 16, 59
Chile, Araucanians, ball game, 68
China, games, diffusion, 61
    guessing, 65
  field expeditions, 56
  Honan, Wei-Chi, early reference to, 22
  kites, 64
  lot casting, 70

Egypt, ancient, draughts, 51
    games in the Fifth Dynasty, 16
    recreation in, 51
  Cairo, mancala, 96
    game played by donkey boys, 73
  Games, ceremonial, 52
    diffusion, 61
    rolling target, 12
  tomb mural, game of "Odds & Evens," 21
  tomb of Ank-Hor, mural of Game, 17
    Beni Hassan, 65
    Hatasu, Game Board from, 21
England, British Museum, sculpture of girls
    playing Astragals, 16
  game board cut into cathedral seats,
    Canterbury, 21
    Gloucester, 21
    Norwich, 21
    Salisbury, 21
    Westminster Abby, 21
  kites, 64
  London, fencing instruction in, 36
  Norman, archery, 28
  traditional games of, 49
  Whitehall Palace, cock-fighting at, 33
Eskimo, 59
  dice, 117, 124
  games of, 104
Europe, American Indian games, analogies, 57
  game dissusion, 61, 62

Far East, Mancala variations played in, 16

Germany, Hanover, war school, 274
  Nuremberg, legislation limiting marble games,
    22
  popularity of chess, 272
Greece, Ancient, foot races, 21
    wrestling, 22
    board games, 51
    football, 52
    game diffusion, 61
Guatemala, ball courts, 53
    Kekchi, game counter, 118

Hawaii, ancient games, 52
    sports, 53
    ancient surfing, 52
    games, 59
Hungary, Budapest, Fine Arts Museum, 17

Iceland, chess, 49
India, Bombay, language game, 41
    dice, nuts used as, 70
    games, diffusion, 61
    Hindu Harvest Festival, 15
    Mancala, 16
    monopoly, comparisons with, 128
    prehistoric, 11, 50
    sedentary, 13
    invention of chess, 272
    liturgical swing, 160
Indo-European, "Game" (origin of word), 3
Iran, Teheran, gambling game in, 35
Ireland, Tailteann games, 49
Israel, Hebrew University, 433
Italy, guessing games, 65
    Sicily, marionettes, 58
    sports, history of, 54

Japan, field expeditions of Culin, 56
    war college, 274

Kalmuks, chess playing, 63
Korea, field expeditions, 56

Latin, counting-out rhymes, prayers in, 14
    documents about games in, 23

Malaysia, games, hypnotic, 15
    Mancala, 16

Masonic, counting-out rhymes, ritual found
    in, 14
Mesopotamia, dice, 50
Mexico, Aztecs, board games, 72
    diversions, 52
    games compared with monopoly, 128
    Mayas, court ball games, 52
    Spanish invaders, 82
    Tula, ceremonial ball courts at, 21
    Yucatan, court ball game, 61
Middle East, game diffusion, 62
    reference to chess, 23

New Guinea, children's games in, 13
New Zealand, games, diffusion, 55
    Maori, 52
      knuckle-bone, 14
      pastimes, 60
      study of children's, 166
    kites, 64
North America, gambling games, 110
    game diffusion, 61

Persia, game of Chugan, 67
Peru, ancient, ceremonial badminton, 53
Philippines, Mancala board game in, 16
Polynesians, connection with Asiatic culture,
    76
Puerto Rico, ancient, ball games, 52

Romany, counting-out rhymes, slang in, 14
Rome, ancient, game diffusion, 59
   antigambling laws, 61
   gambling, 22
    ancient, 51
   games and playthings, 51
   board games, 51

   football, 52
Sandwich Islands, draught playing, 64
Sanskrit, records of chess anticedents, 23
Saracen, in sport of Quintain, 42
Saxons, archery developed by, 28
  game, 52
Scandinavia, Viking Age, game board, 52
Scotland, legislation prohibiting golf, 22
  traditional games of, 49
Siam, 59
Siberia, nonexistent gambling games, 122
South Africa, changed playing card symbols, 241
Sumer, Cemetery at Ur, game board from, 21
Sweden, bowling, twelfth century, 31

Tibet, 59
Turkey, Mancala, 59

United States, academic olympics, 324, 330
  colonial, 53
  Johns Hopkins University, 336
  New Jersey, early sports in, 54
  North Carolina, children's games, 161
  Ohio, adolescent kissing games, 194
  Philadelphia, field study of "counting-out,"
    170
  Smithsonian Institution, 57
U.S.S.R., chess playing, 442

Vietnam, Mancala type game, 244

West Indies, game from Africa, 90
  Mancala, 100

Yugoslavia, Belgrade, Folkdance center for
   study of, 17

SUBJECT INDEX

Abacus, relationship to, 72
Adolescents, kissing games, 194
American Management Association, 305
Anthropologists, importance to, 11, 12, 13
Antigambling Laws, 22
Antiquarianism, definition, 161
Artists, importance to, 16
Aspects of games, abilities and skills required for action, 423
  body contact, 408
  bodily activity, 408
  challenges, 418
  chance determination, 410
  competition factors, 410
  institutionalized cheating, 415
  interaction patterns, 424
  interdependence of players, 412
  introduction of ritual, 416
  invariant elements, 422
  marginal impulse expression, 413
  mirroring of life, 416
  obstacles in, 415
  outcome clarity, 418
  permanence of alliances, 415
  personalization of props, 416
  physical setting and environmental requirements, 425
  pleasure-pain content, 414
  potential humor-producing range, 417
  potential sexualization range, 416
  procedure for action, 422
  prop usage, 411
  purpose of game, 422

  required equipment, 425
  required participants, 423
  results, pay-off, rewards, penalties, 423
  role taking factors, 411
  roles of participants, 423
  rule complexity, 412
  rules governing action, 422
  skill requirements, 409
  spread of winnership, 414
  suspense emphasis, 413
  switches between opposites, 414
  time considerations, 411
  trust dependence, 415
  use of space, 410
  volume and distributions of participation, 413

Ball (dance), etomology of, 66
Ballad, etomology of, 66
Bandy, etomology of, 68
Brewster, P. G., bibliography, 162

Catholic Church, satirized by Tudor play, 33
Chicanery, etomology of, 68
Child training variables, 479
Choreographers, importance to, 17
Christ, Roman soldiers, buffet game, 65
Classification, problems, 406
Computer assisted war games, 276
Counting devices, 118
Cross-cultural transmission, 92
Crusaders, and diffusion, 62
Cultural domains, play and work, 229
Cultures, chance games, 434

519

child training, 465
physical skill games only, 433
strategy games, 435
with aspects of, 169
Customs, rise and fall of, 161

Decision making, essence of a game, 385
Developmental change, represented by games, 213
Diffusion, patterns of, 61
Diffusionists, theories under attack, 60

Education, study relating to game participation, 242
tampering with traditional play, 180
Educational device, war games, 272
Educators, importance to, 16
Elements of games, mathematically invariant, 384
Enculturative effects of games, 485
Equipment, modified as treatment device, 350
more accessible today, 242
Evolution of survival activities, 225
Evolutionary parallelism, 126

Folklore, antiquarianism, linkage with, 159
field methods, 164
first published classic, 159
games, uncertain domain of, 56
major motif, 159
Functions, games, models of power, 436
psychogenic approaches, 429
sociogenic approaches, 432

Gambling casino, society as, 34
Game, common meaning of word, 5
etymologic rationale, 3
etymology, 2
common uses of word, 2
definition, 7, 401, 405
older concepts, 9, 10
differentiated from play, 7
example of, 7
related words in other languages, 3
taxonomy, 401
Games, classification of, 466
copyright law, 128
European & American Indians, analogies between, 57
geography of, 49

historical evolution of, 76
learning through, 324, 332
modern compared with ancient, 128
origins of, 226
survival activity, 225
role of, in human development, 213
rules, psychological aspects, 328
study of, folklore contributions, 168
Fulbright, 166
importance, 161
stated rules and operant rules, 169
types, relationship of, 322
Game Theory, matiematical, origins of, 384
Gregariousness, and game playing, 227

Handicapped, see Physical disability
Health related services, games in, diagnostic, 347, 352
origins of, 350
treatment, 348
affective disorders, 373
cognitive disorders, 372
physical disorders, 371
High Schools, games and academic activity, 323
Historical information, source of, archaeological, 21
dice, 123
artifacts, 21
Bayeux Tapestry, 28
graphics, 21
legislation, 22
literature, 22, 23
paintings, 21
unintentional writings, 22
Homologies, distinguished from analogies, 113
Hospitals, games in, 351
Human sacrifices, in gambling, 84

Interaction patterns, in games, 355
It role, effect upon game participants, 397

Jesuit missionaries, lacrosse, 69
wrote of Indian gambling, 88

Kibitzing, attitude toward, Tudor period, 30

Literature, English, allusions to games, 28

Logistical gaming, 276

Magic, American Indians relation to games, 105
Marionettes, Italian New York City, 56
Mathematics, dangerous use, 124
Mental retardation, early publication on, 25
  games and, 350
Military decisions, diagram of, 27
Monte Carlo, *see* Simulations
Multi-analysis, susceptibility to, 4
Musicologists, importance to, 17

Nongame cultures, 4

Philogists, importance to, 14
Physical disability, game playing, 244, 350, 365
  references, 268
Physicians, importance to, 15
Piers Plowman, guessing game mentioned in, 36
Play, definition, 6, 227
  older concepts, 9, 10
  differentiated from game, 7
  example of, 5
  relation to culture, 227
  therapy, 480
  traditional, educational tampering, 180
Play and work, dualism of, 228
Prayer, related to game playing, 85
Preadolescent, and kissing games, 213
Probability Theory, origins of, 383
Professional groups concerned with game
  playing, 245
Psychiatrists, importance to, 15
Psychogenic approaches to functions, 429
Psychologists, importance to, 15
Psychotherapy, games in, 347, 352

Publications, types during the nineteenth
  century, 24

Reality Simulations, essence of, 329
Recreation, contribution to therapeutic
    process, 375
  definition, 239
  games for, 239
  history of, Ancient Egyptian, 51
    British, 49
    United States, 50
  therapeutic, games for, 347, 371
  traditional taxonomies, 419
Religious beliefs and practices, games con-
    nected with, 57
Rules, study of, 169

Sculptors, importance to, 16
Shakespeare, interest in games, 27
  hunting, 37
Simulations, administrative structures, 288
  Monte Carlo, 282
Social science, games in, contrasted with
    other uses, 388
Sociogenic Approaches to functions, 432
Strategic Gaming, 275

Tactical Gaming, 275
Testing Devices, games as, 351
Therapists, mental and physical, importance
    to, 17

Trivial concerns, games regarded as, 26

Universality of, 3

Writing, influence on, 128

INDEX OF GAMES

Academic games, range of topics, 22
  see also Educational games
Acme-Bolt game, 319
  application of Game Theory, 385
Active games, motor analysis of, 367
  physical disability and, 366
Alquerque, Parker, 51
Animal-baiting, during Tudor period, 29
Archery, American and Oriental variants, 57
  American Indians, 104
  adult activity, former, 160
  advocated by B. Franklin, 29
  golf distracting from, 22
  military value to state, 4
  restrictive Tudor laws, 31
  status of during Tudor period, 28
Ashtapada, chess anticedent, 23
Astragals, girls playing, sculpture of, 16
  see also Dice; Knucklebones
Athletics, ancient, 51

Backgammon, 45, 51
  class of ancient games, 71
  Illiad, allusion to, 21
  old world type, 79
  references to, 256
  simulating racing, 226
Badminton, ceremonial, Peru, 53
      Kutscher, 53
Ball courts, Mexico, 21
  Guatemala, 53
Ball games, ancient Greece, 66
  Borhegyi, 52

ceremonial significance, 107
  sculpture depicting, 16
Balls, during Tudor times, 46
Baseball computerized, 387
  Mehl, 50
Base kiss, kissing game, 196
Battledore, relationship to Japanese festival, 60
Billiards, during Tudor Period, 30
Biting the apple, kissing game, 196
Blindman's Buff, during Tudor Period, 30
Blowpoint, bowling game, 42
Board games, children playing, painting of, 17
  contemporary versus Aztec and Hindu, 128
  Murray, 49
  of the sixteenth century, 33
  origin of, 71
  references, 253
  wall paintings of, 16
  see also Tables
Boss and span, see Span counter
Bowling, in psychotherapy, 374
  restrictive Tudor laws, 31
Boxing, ancient, 51
Boys catch girls, kissing game, 197
Brag, card game rarely played, 23
Bridge, kissing game, 197
  reality of, 329
  in Psychotherapy, 374
Buffet-Game, see Kollabismos
Business games, description of, 332
  origins of, 305
  values of, 307

522

Candy, cigarettes, kissing game, 197
Canuet, American Indian game, 48
Catch-dolt, sixteenth century board game, 33
Cat's cradle, Borneo, 64
    Oceania, 59
Chance games, cross cultural investigation, 473
Chase and kiss, kissing game, 198
Chasing games, rhymes used to determine "it," 14
Chaturanga, chess forebear, 272
    sanskrit word, 74
Chess, argument for diffusion, 92
    Babylonian, 51
    during Tudor Period, 32
    early Middle Eastern reference to, 23
    history of, 442
    legends concerning, 460
    Mater Dolorosa, 453
    nineteenth century articles on, 24
    Oedipus, 448
    origins of, 74, 75, 272
    playing out conflict, 374
    popularity, 441
    psychoanalytic aspects, 440
    psychological study of, 444
    reality of, 329
    references to, 254
    relationship to draughts, 74
    war-game, 73
Checkers, Ancient Egyptian, 51
    modified as treatment device, 350
    see also Draughts
Cherry pit, children's games, 32
Chew the string, kissing game, 198
Children's games, Brueghel painting, 17
    diffusion of, 64
    hide and seek, 37
    "It" role, 390
    leapfrog, 38
    more sacks to the mill, 38
    muss, 39
    origins, Gomme's theory, 160
    prison base, 41
    psychiatric use, redlight, 348
    psycholanalytic interpretation, 430
    references, 217
    rule rejection, 431
    shoeing the wild mare, 43

Choo choo, kissing game, 198
Christmas Games, dun's in the Mire, 34
    mistletoe kissing, 202
    snapdragon, 44
Club fist, 165
Cock-fighting, during Tudor Period, 33
    references to, 268
Counting-out rhymes, ancient practices, survivals of, 159
    ethnographic study, 169
    field study, 167
    function of, 170
    procedures for, 171
    to determine "it," 14
    strategy of, 172
    see also Rhymes
Court ball game, Mayas, 52, 61
Courtship games, see Kissing games
Cribbage card game, 40
Cricket, origin of, 69
Croquet, origin of, 67, 69

Dancing games, musicologists, value to, 17
Dart games, example of evolved activity, 225
    in training young warriors, 14
    treatment device, 350
Dice, archaeological evidence in the Americas, 123
    Chinese American, 56
    discussed by Tacitus, 22
    during Tudor Period, 33
    early Chinese references, 22
    flat, 116
    invocation to God of, 85
    origin of, 70
    recovered from Egyptian tomb, 21
    see also Astragals; Knucklebones
Dice games, novum, 40
    one and thirty, 40
    Probability Theory origins in, 383
    references, 250
    traytrip, 47
    trick-tack, 46
Doll play, structure of reality, 160
Dominoes, Chinese, 56
Doublets, sixteenth century board game, 33
Drag-strip racing, example of evolved activity, 225
Draughts, relationship to chess, 74

Sandwich Islands, 64
see also Checkers
Draw and kiss, kissing game, 199
Dun's in the mire, Christmas game, 34
Dynamite, kissing game, 199

Educational games, accepted hypothesis for, 321
  arithmetic games, 316
  critique of, 315, 316
  documented value of, 318, 337
  early publications on, 25
  reading games, 316
  schools using, 331
  social studies games, 317, 327
  values of, 320, 338
  writing games, 316
  see also academic games

Falconry, Elizabethan sport, 34
Fan T'An, Chinese gambling game, 58
Fast and loose, Tudor gambling game, 35
Fencing, allusions to, 35
Fiddle diddle, kissing game, 200
Finger Games, Morra, 65
  "odds and evens," 7
  voluntary control system exercise of, 7
  see also "Odds and evens"
Five minute date, kissing game, 200
Flashlight, kissing game, 200
Football, ancient, 51
  evolution of, 66
  Greeks and Romans, 52
  kissing game, 201
  Middle Ages, prohibitions against, 36
  psychoanalytic interpretation, 430
Foot races, Greece, ancient, 21
Follow-me-taw, marble chasing game, 182
Forfeits, *see* Kissing games
Fox and geese, relationship to war games, 74
Freeze tag, kissing game, 201

Gambling games, Apache, diagram of, 89
  casinos, 246
  Chinese, 56
  hazard, 37
  human sacrifices, 84
  North America, 110
  past and present, 241
  references to, 249

shovegroat, 44
  see also Dice; Playing cards
Go, in psychotherapy, 374
  reference to, 256
Golf, formal education and, 242
  legislation prohibiting, 22
  origin of, 69
Guessing games, American Indians, 105
  handy dandy, 36
  played with fingers, 65

Hazard, gambling game, 37
  old technical term in tennis, 37
Hand clapping games, wall painting of, 17
Handball, origin of, 69
Handy dandy, guessing game, 36
Hayride kissing, 201
Hearts, kissing game, 201
Heavy, heavy, hang over the head, kissing gam
  201
Hide and seek, children's game, 37
  psychological factors, 349
Hit or span, *see* Span counter
Hockey, children at, 64
  origin of, 67
Hoop and pole game, American Indians, 106
Hopscotch, *see* Traytrip
Horseshoes, in psychotherapy, 374
Hot cockles, English game, 65
Hunting, Tudor sport, 37
Hurling, origin of, 67
Hypnotic games, Hantu Musang, 15

Indoor games, Middle Ages, 53
Intop, international trade game, 3

Jacks, ancient Greek game, 241
Jumping games, wall paintings of, 16
Jumping ropes, 165

Kings and queens, kissing game, 202
Kissing games, adolescents, 194
  origins, 211
  types, couple, 210
    chasing, 209
    mixing, 209
Kiss under water, kissing game, 202
Kites, children at, 64
  origin of, 64
Knucklebones, girls playing, sculpture of, 16

Kollabismos, Greek game, 65
  wall painting of, 16
Kriegspiel, rigid and free, explanation of, 274
  see also War games

Lacrosse, origin of, 68
Language games, lotto, 316
Latrunculi, Roman game, 73
Leapfrog, children's game, 38
Legislative game, description of, 323
Loggats, Tudor bowling game, 38
London bridge, burying a child alive, vestige
  of, 159

Mah Jong, origin of, 60
  references to, 256
Mancala, definition, 95
  diagram of, 95
  distribution of, 96
  peculiar distribution, 94
  primitive children's proficiency at, 16
  reference to, 255
  see also O–lan
Marble games, anthropoligical reporting, 12
  at a rural school, 165
  Australian, 179
  categorized, 182
  description of game of poo, 16
  legislation limiting, 22
  span counter, 44
  types, chasing, 181, 182
    circle, 182
    half-circle, 184
    hole, 185
Marriage Games, *see* Kissing games
Minx, kissing game, 202
Monopologs, first business game, 305
Monopoly, compaired with Aztec and Hindu
    games, 128
  in psychotherapy, 374
  reproduces function of capitalism, 160
More sacks to the mill, children's game, 38
Morris boards, cut into cathedral cloister
    seats, 21
Morris games, dance, 39
  distribution of, 74
  history of, 39
  nine men, 53
Mulberry bush, opposition in, 7
Murderer and detective, kissing game, 203

Musicle circle, kissing game, 203
Muss, children's game, 39

Namo, bingo variation, 315
Necking, 203
Ninepins, bowling game, 38
Noddy, card game, 40
Novum, dice game, 40
Number games, educator, value to, 16
Numbers, kissing game, 203
Nuts and may, marriage by capture, relic of, 159
Nyoot, in psychotherapy, 374
Nyoot (Nyut), diagram of, 80

Odds and evens, China to Italy, 65
  Egyptian tomb mural, 21
O–Lan, Vietnamese mancala, 244
Olympic games, academic, 324, 330
  in ancient writtings, 22
One and thirty, dice game, 40

Pachisi, argument for diffusion, 93
  diagram of, 121
  group of games, 72
  in relation to patolli, 77
Pak Kop Piu, Chinese lottery, 58
Pallmall, origin of, 67
Patolli, American in origin, 111
  Aztec game, 72
  diagram of, 121
  in relation to Pachisi, 77
Pass the kiss, kissing game, 204
Pass the lifesaver, kissing game, 204
Pass the orange, kissing game, 204
Peashooters, prehistoric children's use, 160
Perdiddle, kissing game, 204
Photography, kissing game, 205
Physical skill games, cross cultural investiga-
    tion, 474
Ping-pong, treatment device, 350
Piquet, card game rarely played, 23
Playing cards, Bowdoin, 48
  the card game, 197
  cribbage, 40
  England, eighteenth century, 34
  hearts, 201
  history of, 240
  nineteenth century articles on, 24
  noddy, 40
  poker, mathematical game theory origins in,
    384

praying for good cards, 85
primero, 40
references, 251
Play-party, bibliography (Note #32), 213
  see also Kissing games
Plumbstones, game of, American Indian, 72 ·
Pollax, *see* Jacks
Polo, origin of, 67
Pony express, kissing game, 205
Popeye, *see* Perdiddle
Post Office, kissing game, 205
Pretty please, kissing game, 206
Pricking at the belt, Tudor gambling game, 35
Primero, card game, 40
Prison base, children's game, 41
Professor, kissing game, 206
Proverb-capping, riddle contest, 41
Pushpin, bowling game, 42
Puzzles, opposition in, 7

Quail-fighting, compared to cock-fighting, 42
Quintain, military sport, 42
Quoits, 43
  score nullification, 229

Racing games, American Indians, 104
Racket games, American Indian, 107
Reality Game, experimental game, 386
Rhymes, modernization altering, 161
  see also Counting-out rhymes
Ring-toss, modified for physical limitations,
  368
Rinky dink, *see* Perdiddle
Rugby, psychoanalytic interpretation, 430
  supposed character training value of, 4

Sardines, kissing game, 206
Serve it in the dark, kissing game, 207
Shaturanga, chess anticedent, 23
Shoeing the wild mare, children's game, 43
Shove-groat, gambling game, 44
Shovelboard, Shuffleboard, 44
Shuffleboard, in psychotherapy, 374
  modified for physical limitations, 368
Shuttlecock, relationship to Japanese festival
  60
Simulations, assets of, 324
  in the classroom, 319
  inter-nation, description of, 332
  world series, 387
Simuload, General Electric educational game,
  306

Singing games, musicologist, value to, 17
Slingshots, prehistoric children's use, 160
Snake, sixteenth century board game, 33
Snapdragon, Christmas games, 44
Span counter, marble game, 44
Spear-throwing games, in training young
  hunters, 14
Spelling bee, not a good game, 315
Spin the bottle, kissing game, 207
Sports, artificial, 63
  origins of, 225
  reference to, 258
  see also Specific game by name
Spotlight, kissing game, 207
Stilts, children at, 64
Strategic games, cross cultural investigation, 472
Street games, Brooklyn, New York, 56
String games, bibliography, 222
  see also Cat's cradle
Sugoroku, Japanese game, 60
Sumerian game, economics simulation, 308
Surfing, ancient, 52

Tables, generic term applied to board games, 45
Tag, American Indian, 103
Tag Games, attitudes in, 394
  black tom, 392
  dodge the skunk, 392
  freeze tag, 201
  kissing tag, 202
  pom-pom pullaway, 392
  responses in, 391
  swat, in psychotherapy, 374
Tailtean Games, 49
Tennis, diffusion of, during Tudor period, 45,
  63
  origin of, 70
  in psychotherapy, 374
  relating to education, 242
Tether ball, modified for physical limitations,
  369
The card game, kissing game, 197
This or that, kissing game, 207
Tick-Tack, race-game, 46
Tick tack toe, subject of game study, 489
Tinker-toy objects game, A.T.&T. business
  game, 306
Tops, children at, 64
  during Tudor period, 46
  painting and sculpture depicting, 17

use as a speech metaphor, 28
Toys, babies rattles, ancient, 51
    games as in education, 334
Traytrip, dice game, 47
Trictrac, dice game, 71
Troll-my-dame, board game, 47
Truth or consequences, kissing game, 208
Tug-of-war, miracle play, degraded, 159
Turtle climb, kissing game, 208

War games, computer assisted, 276
    contemporary definition, 278
    content of early, 273
    critique of, 297
    educational device, 272
    first publications concerning, 24
    free games, 291
    origins, 271

purpose of, 279
    rigid games, 289
Wei-Chi, discussed in book by T. Hyde, 23
    early reference, 22
    relationship to draughts, 74
    see also "Go"
Wif'N Proff, educational game, 244
Whist, according to Hoyle, 23
Who struck, see Kollabismos
William William tremble toe, 165
Willpower, kissing game, 208
Windshield wiper, kissing game, 209
Winks, kissing game, 209
Wrestling, ancient, 51
    during Tudor period, 47
    Greece, ancient, 22
    natural activity, 63

REFERENCES TO GAMES IN ENGLISH LITERATURE

(TUDOR-STUART PERIOD)—CITED IN CHAPTER II

Ascham, Roger (1515–1568)
  Toxophilus 1545, 43

Beaumont, Francis (1548–1616) and
    Fletcher, John (1579–1625)
  Knight of the Burning Pestle 1607, 43, 45
  Monsieur Thomas, 40, 44
  Night Walker, 46
  Philaster 1609, 34
  Scornful Lady 1614, 31, 45, 46
  Woman Hater 1606, 34
Brand
  Dutchesse of Suffolke, 34
Breton, Nicholas (1545?–1626)
  Fantastics, 43
Brome, Richard D. (1652)
  Antipodes, 41
Browne, William (1591–1643)
  Britannia's Pastorals 1613, 36

Caxton, William (1422–1491)
  Game and Play of Chess 1475, 0
  Reynard the Fox, 33
Chamberlayne, William (?1619–1689)
  Angliae Notitia, 31, 44, 45, 47
Chapman, George (1559?–1634)
  All Fooles 1599, 31, 45
  Eastward Hoe 1605, 37, 40, 45
  Gentleman Usher 1602, 34
Chaucer, Geoffrey (1343–1400)
  Death of Blanche, 32
  Franklin's Tale, 32
  Harrowing of Hell, 33

Manciple's Tale, 34
Monk's Tale, 33
Pardoner's Tale, 33
Chettle, Henry (1560–1607)
  Hoffman, the Tragedy of 1602, 41
Child, Francis James (1825–1896)
  English and Scotish Popular Ballads 1857–1858,
    42
Congreve, William (1670–1729)
  Double-Dealer 1693, 31
  Old Bachlor 1693, 31

Dekker, Thomas (1572?–1632)
  Bellman of London, 31
  Gull's Hornbook 1609, 37, 40, 45
  Honest Whore 1604, 31, 34, 38
  Northward Ho 1607 (with J. Webster), 42, 45,
    46
  Satiromastix 1602, 37
  Shirburn Ballads (with J. Webster), 42
  Westward Ho 1607 (with J. Webster), 34
  Witch of Edmonton, the, 1621, 32
Dodsley, Robert (1703–1746)
  Old Plays 1744, 37
Donne, John (1572?–1631)
  Satire Four, 44
Drayton, Michael (1563–1631)
  Ballad of Agincourt 1605, 45
  Poly-Olbion 1612, 41

Elyot, Thomas (1499?–1546)
  Instruction of a Gentleman, 32

Farquhar, George (1678–1707)

Beaux Stratagem 1706, 31
Field, Nathan (1587–?)
  Woman in a Weathercock 1609, 31, 40, 42
Fletcher, John (1579–1625)
  Two Noble Kinsmen 1634 (with Shakespeare),
    46
  Wild Goose Chase 1614, 34, 35
Ford, John (1586–1640)
  Fancies, Chaste and Noble 1635, 45
  Lover's Melancholy 1628, 32
  Tis Pity She's a Whore, 40
  Witch of Edmonton 1623, 45

Gascoigne, George (1527–1577)
  Supposes 1566, 40, 45
Grevill, Fulke (1554–1628)
  Coelica, 46

Herrick, Robert (1591–1674)
  Hesperides 1648, 32
  Poor Robin's Almanac 1622, 40, 44, 45
Heywood, Thomas (1570–1641)
  Woman Killed with Kindness, 34, 40
  Wise Woman of Hogsden, 1604, 31

John of Salisbury (1110–1180)
  Polycraticus, 45
Johnson, Ben (1573–1637)
  Alchemist 1610, 40, 47
  Bartholomew Fair 1614, 33, 36, 38
  Cynthia Revels 1600, 40, 45
  Everyman in His Humour 1598, 34, 35,
    40, 44
  Gipsies Metamorphosed, 35
  Love Restored, 43
  Magnetic Lady 1632, 39
  New Inn, 46
  Sad Shepherd 1641, 41
  Silent Woman 1609, 45
  Staple of News 1625, 45
  Tale of a Tub 1633, 38
  Volpone 1605–1606, 40

Kyd, Thomas (1557?–1594)
  Arden of Faversham, 45

Layamon, (Father) (1189–1207)
  Brut 1205, 45
Lee, Nathaniel (1653–1692)
  Princess of Cleve, 46

Mannyng, Robert (1264–1340)
  Handlyng Synne (Handling Sin) 1303, 32
Marlowe, Christopher (1564–1593)
  Edward the Second 1593, 41
Marston, John (1575–1634)
  Malcontent 1604, 42
Massinger, Philip (1583–1640)
  City Madam 1632, 31
  Guardian, 30, 43
  New Way to Pay Old Debts 1633, 36, 42, 43
Middleton, Thomas (1580–1627)
  Blurt, Master Constable, 40, 45
  Changeling 1623 (with W. Rowley), 42
  Family of Love 1606, 42
  Game at Chess 1624, 33
  Mad World, My Masters 1606, 31, 39
  No Wit, No Help Like a Woman's 1613, 31
  Phoenix, 45
  Roaring Girl 1610 (with T. Dekker), 44
  Spanish Gypsy 1623, 40
  Trick to Catch the Old One 1606, 46
  World Toast at Tennis 1618, 46
  Your Five Gallants, 40

Nash, Thomas (1567–1601)
  Apologie, the First Part of Pasquil's 1590,
    42

Pepys, Samuel (1633–1703)
  Diary, 44
Porter, Henry
  Two Angry Women of Abington 1599, 31,
    37, 45

Rollins, Hyden E. (Ed.)
  Pepys Ballads, 31, 38, 40, 45
Rowland, (?)
  Humors Ordinaire, 34
  Letting of Humors Blood, 31, 38, 40, 41, 44
  Return from Parnassus, 31, 40, 42
Rowley, William (1585–1637)
  All's Lost by Lust 1622, 36
  Changeling 1623 (with T. Middleton), 42
  New Wonder, 47

Scot, Reginald
  Discoverie of Witchcraft, 35
Shakespeare, William (1564–1616)
  All's Well That Ends Well 1602, 30, 34, 39,
    41, 46

Antony and Cleopatra 1607–1608, 30, 33, 34, 39, 42
As You Like It 1599–1600, 33, 37, 42, 46, 47
Comedy of Errors 1590–1592, 36, 38
Coriolanus, Tragedy of 1608–1609, 32, 47
Cymbeline 1609–1610, 31, 34, 41
Hamlet, Prince of Denmark; Tragedy of, 29, 30, 32, 35, 36, 37, 38, 46
Julius Caesar 1599–1600, 30, 35
King Henry Fourth, Part One 1597–1598, 34
King Henry Fourth, Part Two 1597–1598, 29, 35, 38, 43, 44, 46
King Henry Fifth 1598–1599, 30, 32, 34, 35, 37, 38, 39, 40, 41, 46
King Henry Sixth, Part One 1590–1592, 35
King Henry Sixth, Part Two 1590–1592, 30, 35, 39, 45
King Henry Sixth, Part Three 1590–1592, 29, 35, 37
King Henry Eight 1623, 40, 46
King John, Life and Death of 1596–1597, 46
King Lear, Tragedy of 1605–1606, 29, 32, 36, 40, 46
King Richard Second 1592, 32
King Richard Third 1594, 34
Love's Labour's Lost 1593–1594, 29, 31, 34, 35, 36, 37, 38, 40, 42, 44, 45, 46, 47
Macbeth, Tragedy of 1606, 30
Measure for Measure 1604–1605, 46
Merchant of Venice 1596, 34, 37, 41, 47
Merry Wives of Windsor 1597–1600, 29, 34, 40, 44, 46
Midsummer-Night's Dream 1595–1596, 37, 39, 40
Much Ado About Nothing 1598–1599, 29, 38, 46, 47
Othello, Moor of Venice 1604, 34, 35, 47

Pericles, Prince of Tyre 1608–1609, 46
Romeo and Juliet, Tragedy of 1596, 29, 34, 35, 41
Taming of the Shrew 1594, 29, 32, 35, 38, 40, 42
Tempest 1611–1612, 33, 35, 37
Titus Andronicus 1590–1592, 35, 37
Troilus and Cressida 1600–1602, 32, 40
Twelfth Night; or, What You Will 1599, 29, 30, 32, 35, 47
Two Gentlemen of Verona 1592, 41
Venus and Adonis 1593, 41
Winter's Tale 1610–1611, 29, 34, 44, 47
Shirley, James (1596–1666)
Famous Victories of Henry the Fifth, 33
Grateful Servant, 42
Hyde Park 1632, 40
Lady of Pleasure, 33
Love's Cruelty, 40
St. Patrick for Ireland, 34
Spenser, Edmund (1552?–1599)
Faerie Queene 1590–1596, 41

Tailor, Robert
Hog Hath Lost His Pearl, 37
Tourneur, Cyril (1557–1626)
Revenger's Tragedy, 37

Webster, John (1580?–1625?)
Duchess of Malfi 1623, 42, 43, 46
Northward Ho 1607 (with T. Dekker), 42, 44, 46
Shirburn Ballads (with T. Dekker), 42
Weakest Goeth to the Wall, 31
Westward Ho 1607 (with T. Dekker), 34
White Devil 1612, 31, 36, 37, 45
Whitestone, George (1551–1587)
Promos and Cassandra 1578, 35
Wilson, (?)
Three Ladies of London, 31